P9-CCl-411

The Editor

BRYAN WATERMAN is Associate Professor of English at New York University. He is the author of *The Friendly Club of New York City and the Making of American Literature* and several essays on American literature and culture published in *American Literary History, Early American Literature, The William and Mary Quarterly,* and elsewhere. He is the co-editor, with Cyrus R. K. Patell, of *The Cambridge Companion to the Literature of New York*.

W. W. NORTON & COMPANY, INC.
Also Publishes

ENGLISH RENAISSANCE DRAMA: A NORTON ANTHOLOGY
edited by David Bevington et al.

THE NORTON ANTHOLOGY OF AFRICAN AMERICAN LITERATURE
edited by Henry Louis Gates Jr. and Nellie Y. McKay et al.

THE NORTON ANTHOLOGY OF AMERICAN LITERATURE
edited by Nina Baym et al.

THE NORTON ANTHOLOGY OF CHILDREN'S LITERATURE
edited by Jack Zipes et al.

THE NORTON ANTHOLOGY OF DRAMA
edited by J. Ellen Gainor, Stanton B. Garner Jr., and Martin Puchner

THE NORTON ANTHOLOGY OF ENGLISH LITERATURE
edited by M. H. Abrams and Stephen Greenblatt et al.

THE NORTON ANTHOLOGY OF LITERATURE BY WOMEN
edited by Sandra M. Gilbert and Susan Gubar

THE NORTON ANTHOLOGY OF MODERN AND CONTEMPORARY POETRY
edited by Jahan Ramazani, Richard Ellmann, and Robert O'Clair

THE NORTON ANTHOLOGY OF POETRY
edited by Margaret Ferguson, Mary Jo Salter, and Jon Stallworthy

THE NORTON ANTHOLOGY OF SHORT FICTION
edited by R. V. Cassill and Richard Bausch

THE NORTON ANTHOLOGY OF THEORY AND CRITICISM
edited by Vincent B. Leitch et al.

THE NORTON ANTHOLOGY OF WORLD LITERATURE
edited by Sarah Lawall et al.

THE NORTON FACSIMILE OF THE FIRST FOLIO OF SHAKESPEARE
prepared by Charlton Hinman

THE NORTON INTRODUCTION TO LITERATURE
edited by Alison Booth and Kelly J. Mays

THE NORTON READER
edited by Linda H. Peterson and John C. Brereton

THE NORTON SAMPLER
edited by Thomas Cooley

THE NORTON SHAKESPEARE, BASED ON THE OXFORD EDITION
edited by Stephen Greenblatt et al.

For a complete list of Norton Critical Editions, visit
www.wwnorton.com/college/English/nce_home.htm

A NORTON CRITICAL EDITION

Charles Brockden Brown
WIELAND
and
MEMOIRS OF CARWIN
THE BILOQUIST

AUTHORITATIVE TEXTS
SOURCES AND CONTEXTS
CRITICISM

Edited by

BRYAN WATERMAN
NEW YORK UNIVERSITY

W · W · NORTON & COMPANY · *New York* · *London*

W. W. Norton & Company has been independent since its founding in 1923, when William Warder Norton and Mary D. Herter Norton first published lectures delivered at the People's Institute, the adult education division of New York City's Cooper Union. The firm soon expanded its program beyond the Institute, publishing books by celebrated academics from America and abroad. By mid-century, the two major pillars of Norton's publishing program—trade books and college text—were firmly established. In the 1950s, the Norton family transferred control of the company to its employees, and today—with a staff of four hundred and a comparable number of trade, college, and professional titles published each year—W. W. Norton & Company stands as the largest and oldest publishing house owned wholly by its employees.

Copyright © 2011 by W. W. Norton & Company, Inc.

All rights reserved.
Printed in the United States of America.
First Edition.

Publication of this book has been aided by a grant from the Abraham and Rebecca Stein Faculty Publication Fund of New York University, Department of English.

Book design by Antonina Krass
Production manager: Eric Pier-Hocking

Library of Congress Cataloging-in-Publication Data
Brown, Charles Brockden, 1771–1810.
   Wieland ; and Memoirs of Carwin the biloquist : authoritative texts, sources and contexts, criticism / Charles Brockden Brown ; edited by Bryan Waterman.—1st ed.
         p.   cm. — (A Norton critical edition)
   Includes bibliographical references.
   ISBN 978-0-393-93253-9 (pbk.)
      1. Gentry—Pennsylvania—Fiction.   2. Ventriloquists—Fiction.
   3. Pennsylvania—History—Colonial period, ca. 1600–1775—Fiction.
   4. Brown, Charles Brockden, 1771–1810. Wieland.   5. Brown, Charles Brockden, 1771–1810. Memoirs of Carwin the biloquist.   I. Waterman, Bryan, 1970–   II. Brown, Charles Brockden, 1771–1810. Memoirs of Carwin the biloquist.   III. Title.
   PS11354. W5 2010a
   813' .2—dc22

                                                          2010041085

W. W. Norton & Company, Inc., 500 Fifth Avenue, New York, N.Y. 10110
wwnorton.com
W. W. Norton & Company Ltd., Castle House, 75/76 Wells Street,
London W1T 3QT

1   2   3   4   5   6   7   8   9   0

Contents

Preface

On July 4, 1798, Charles Brockden Brown, a twenty-seven-year-old law-school dropout and prodigal son of a family of Philadelphia Quaker merchants, arrived in New York City and presented his circle of friends there with a partially completed novel: *Wieland, or the Transformation.* Over the summer they helped him compose a "suitable catastrophe" for it, as one friend, Elihu Hubbard Smith, wrote in his diary. When the novel was published in September, readers discovered the bizarre tale of an itinerant ventriloquist who visits a country estate outside Philadelphia, impersonates the voice of God, and may or may not be responsible for inspiring a young father (whose own father had died by spontaneously combusting, apparently while in prayer) to take a hatchet to his wife and children, murdering them all. It was, as critics have often pointed out, the birth of the American Gothic novel.

Wieland was the third long work Brown had completed in two years' time. The first was a pamphlet-length dialogue on women's rights, serialized and abbreviated in early 1798 in the Philadelphia *Weekly Magazine*, to which Brown was a regular contributor, and published in long form in New York as *Alcuin; A Dialogue.* The second was a novel, *Sky-Walk; or, Man Unknown to Himself,* an exploration of the morally ambiguous disorder of somnambulism, set to be printed in Philadelphia by the *Weekly Magazine*'s editor, James Watters. It went missing later that summer when Watters died in the city's perennial yellow fever outbreak; in New York, Brown himself fell sick during a fever epidemic there, and his roommate Elihu Smith succumbed to it, just as *Wieland* was coming off the press. Published by the French emigrant bookseller Hoquet Caritat and printed by T. & J. Swords, whose regular clients included the faculty of Columbia College, the novel met with enough success that Brown worked on a sequel, *Memoirs of Carwin the Biloquist,* and undertook several more novels, five of which were published over the next three years. In February 1799, less than half a year after *Wieland*'s publication, he wrote to a brother that "to be the writer of *Wieland* and *Ormond* is a greater recommendation than ever I imagined it would be." Brown and his surviving New York friends established a periodical, the *Monthly Magazine and American Review*, which Brown edited until returning to Philadelphia at the end of 1800. Writing would not pay a living wage, it turned out, but Brown had laid much of the groundwork that would secure him a transatlantic reputation as America's first major writer of fiction.

Readers from Brown's time to our own have debated the meaning of the strange events recounted in *Wieland*. Contemporaries would have understood its references to recent events, from the French and Indian War and the American Revolution to a set of sensational family murders that resembled the domestic violence depicted in the novel. Disregarding the characters' suggestion that it would be absurd to "make the picture of a single family a model from which to sketch the condition of a nation," many of Brown's critics view the story as an allegory of post-revolutionary American society; others as commenting on the limits of Enlightenment rationalism or sensory experience in general; and still others as being self-referentially concerned with the status of fiction, the profession of authorship, and the politics of reading in the early republic. Brown's gift copy to Thomas Jefferson (see the accompanying letter in this volume, p. 312) has been understood both as signaling Brown's Jeffersonian sympathies and as a cheeky nod to what some critics argue is actually his anti-Jeffersonianism. Part of the reason for such contradictory interpretations rests with Brown himself: questions of agency and meaning remain notoriously open-ended at the novel's conclusion, almost as if Brown wanted his readers to engage in debate over his book's intentions, and his novels all maintain something of the form of his first long publication, a philosophical dialogue. If Brown wanted his readers to work out their own conclusions, perhaps by arguing with one another, such an end would be consistent with the principles of the writer Brown admired above all others in the 1790s: the radical British philosopher William Godwin, whose enormous work of moral philosophy, *An Enquiry Concerning Political Justice* (1793), Brown considered his "oracle" and whose novel *Things as They Are, or the Adventures of Caleb Williams* (1794) was a model for Brown and other young novelists on both sides of the Atlantic. Even so, and in spite of Brown's long-standing reputation as "the American Godwin," critics have treated *Wieland* variously as upholding or critiquing the thought of Brown's favorite writer.

Wieland was something of a cult novel in the nineteenth century, read and admired by writers such as Percy and Mary Shelley (the latter of whom was William Godwin's daughter), Godwin himself, John Keats, William Hazlitt, Nathaniel Hawthorne, Margaret Fuller, Edgar Allan Poe, John Greenleaf Whittier, and a later Philadelphia gothic novelist, George Lippard. American literary critics rescued and reprinted the novel periodically throughout the twentieth century, though always with a small measure of dissatisfaction, either with its perceived aesthetic limitations or what some saw as a servile indebtedness to British and German novelistic conventions. In the late twentieth century, however, *Wieland* and its author rose dramatically in critical estimation as new literary historicists began to recognize its nuanced engagements not only with literary precursors and contemporaries but with the historical pressures of the period, from women's rights to class and party politics to the place of religion in American life and the formation of the new nation's public sphere. Brown's obsessive attention to the mechanics of cognition and questions of motivation spoke to psychoanalytic critics, and his attention to processes of representation, signification, narratology, and appearances appealed to poststructuralists. It is now commonplace for critics to view Brown as among the shrewd moral and philosophical observers of his generation. "Unlike the oppressive didactic fiction of his American contemporaries," the eminent historian Gordon Wood wrote almost thirty years ago, in advance of Brown's full revival among literary scholars, "Brown's novels are intellectual explorations into causality, deception, and the moral complexity of life."

Brown's critics and biographers disagree about the reasons he stopped publishing novels from 1801 until his death in 1810. He seemed aware that many readers, especially but not only women, were put off by what he called the "doleful tone" of his early works. One Philadelphia magazine insinuated during his lifetime that he had few female readers, but within ten years of Brown's death *Wieland* was being serialized in the *Ladies' Literary Cabinet* in New York. Brown's turn from novel writing may have been related to his protracted courtship, in the early 1800s, of Elizabeth Linn, the daughter and sister of Dutch Reformed ministers, who likely did not approve of Brown's literary activities or his Godwinian cast of mind. (In Brown's final novel, *Jane Talbot*, the protagonist's lover undergoes a reconversion to Christianity and renounces Godwin in an attempt to appease her guardian.) Instead of writing novels, after 1801 Brown turned to geography and statistics, publishing literary and scientific miscellanies and a handful of anonymous political pamphlets. He and Elizabeth Linn finally married and had four children; Brown was turned out of Quaker fellowship for marrying outside the faith and for having a "hireling minister"—his new father-in-law—perform the ceremony, contrary to Quaker practice. He edited his magazines in relative obscurity, living on supplemental income derived from the estates of his Philadelphia progenitors. He died at age thirty-nine of pulmonary consumption.

This Norton Critical Edition of Brown's first published novel works from the assumption that Brown was, in fact, a careful diagnostician of his culture—both of the new American nation and of the transatlantic world of late-Enlightenment philosophical culture and revolution. The "Sources and Contexts" section includes material directly related to the novel's concerns, including news accounts of the murders that provided Brown with a template for his story, discussion of the Illuminati crisis that swept the United States at century's end (alluded to in *Memoirs of Carwin*), and selections from writings important to Brown's development as a novelist and thinker, including work by William Godwin and Erasmus Darwin, the latter of whom Brown cites in a footnote in the novel. The "Criticism" section includes some material from Brown's nineteenth-century readers in Great Britain and America but focuses mostly on the novel's critical reception over the last three decades. (The oldest of these "modern" critical works contain in their footnotes several inroads into Brown criticism from the 1970s and earlier.) These essays suggest a variety of reasons Brown has become, two centuries after his death, a cornerstone of the early American literary canon and an important figure in understanding American engagements with European philosophical traditions in the Age of Revolutions.

In preparing the notes for this volume, I have been aided by the invaluable efforts and insights of several predecessors, some of whom are friends and colleagues. I am especially grateful for what I have learned about Brown and his works, including *Wieland*, from the editorial efforts of Philip Barnard and Stephen Shapiro, Caleb Crain, the late Jay Fliegelman and Emory Elliott, and the editors of the Kent State Bicentennial Edition of *Wieland*, especially Sydney J. Krause, S. W. Reid, and Alexander Cowie. Several additional members of the Charles Brockden Brown Society have taught me much over the years and I value our ongoing exchange of ideas. Thanks to Carol Bemis at Norton for the invitation to edit this volume and Nancy Ruttenburg for pushing me to accept. Many thanks also to Rivka Genesen at Norton for help at every stage. My research assistant, Matt Bruen, provided advice about the critical and contextual material and managed the process of securing texts and permissions. Blevin Shelnutt helped with proofing. My daughter, Molly Waterman, helped me with photocopying and other office work. She and her sister, Anna, and my wife, Stephanie, let me go to work on Saturdays and spend late nights at the computer when under deadline, time much appreciated. Special thanks for Stephanie's patience and support. My son, Charlie, came too late in the game to have much to say about it, but he's been a good sport nonetheless, and so I dedicate this volume to him, bearing in mind the multiple warnings Brown intended it to offer.

A Note on the Texts

Only one edition of *Wieland* appeared in Charles Brockden Brown's lifetime. It was printed in New York City in 1798 by Thomas and James Swords for Brown's publisher, Hoquet Caritat. The Swords brothers were also printers for the faculty of Columbia College, including several of Brown's close associates in the Friendly Club. From the diaries of Brown's fellow club members Elihu Hubbard Smith and William Dunlap, we know that the printers were setting type beginning in July and that Brown and his friends were proofing early sheets before the novel was completed in August. The novel was published September 14, 1798, in the midst of a yellow fever epidemic; five days later, the fever would claim Elihu Smith's life. Brown fell sick himself but had managed to read proof for the novel before it made its way from the press.

Brown had begun work on the sequel (actually a prequel), *Memoirs of Carwin the Biloquist*, before *Wieland* was published, and though he mentions it in *Wieland*'s preface, it remained unpublished until its serialization between 1803 and 1805 in his *Literary Magazine and American Register*, published in Philadelphia. Most if not all of the uncompleted work was composed in 1798.

The Norton Critical Edition uses the 1798 printing of *Wieland* and the original serialization of *Memoirs of Carwin* as copy texts. In addition to shortening the long *s* (ſ) used in typesetting the original, I have sought to simplify Brown's use of quotation marks, which threaten to become quite convoluted when one narrative is embedded within another narrator's voice. I have also silently corrected obvious printer's errors and have made a limited number of more substantive emendations based on a consultation with the Bicentennial Edition of Brown's novels, edited by Sydney J. Krause and S. W. Reid and published by Kent State University Press. As that edition does, I have standardized the use of the name "Ludloe," where Brown alternates between that spelling and "Ludlow." Unlike that edition, I have also chosen to standardize the surname "Benington," which Brown in places rendered as "Bennington." Otherwise I have sought to retain idiosyncratic or period usage and spelling. For an exhaustive discussion of textual matters, see S. W. Reid, "Textual Notes," in *Wieland*:

or, The Transformation, an American Tale; Memoirs of Carwin, the Biloquist; The Novels and Related Works of Charles Brockden Brown, vol. 1 (Kent, OH: Kent State University Press, 1977), 372–93.

The Texts of
WIELAND
and
MEMOIRS OF CARWIN
THE BILOQUIST

WIELAND;

or
THE TRANSFORMATION
An American Tale

From Virtue's blissful paths away
The double-tongued are sure to stray;
Good is a forth-right journey still,
And mazy paths but lead to ill.[1]

---

1. The verse is Brown's. "Double-tongued": appears in contemporary translations of 1 Timothy 3:8, in which the apostle admonishes deacons. In Brown's lifetime Quaker writers used this verse and phrase to enjoin plain speech. See *The Book of Discipline, Agreed on by the Yearly-Meeting of Friends for New-England* (1785). The warning is also consistent with the British philosopher William Godwin's principle of sincerity or frankness, in *Enquiry Concerning Political Justice* (1793), esp. bk. 4, ch. 6.

Advertisement

The following Work is delivered to the world as the first of a series of performances, which the favorable reception of this will induce the Writer to publish. His purpose is neither selfish nor temporary, but aims at the illustration of some important branches of the moral constitution of man. Whether this tale will be classed with the ordinary or frivolous sources of amusement, or be ranked with the few productions whose usefulness secures to them a lasting reputation, the reader must be permitted to decide.

The incidents related are extraordinary and rare. Some of them, perhaps, approach as nearly to the nature of miracles as can be done by that which is not truly miraculous. It is hoped that intelligent readers will not disapprove of the manner in which appearances are solved, but that the solution will be found to correspond with the known principles of human nature. The power which the principal person is said to possess can scarcely be denied to be real. It must be acknowledged to be extremely rare; but no fact, equally uncommon, is supported by the same strength of historical evidence.

Some readers may think the conduct of the younger Wieland impossible. In support of its possibility the Writer must appeal to Physicians and to men conversant with the latent springs and occasional perversions of the human mind. It will not be objected that the instances of similar delusion are rare, because it is the business of moral painters to exhibit their subject in its most instructive and memorable forms. If history furnishes one parallel fact, it is a sufficient vindication of the Writer; but most readers will probably recollect an authentic case, remarkably similar to that of Wieland.[2]

It will be necessary to add, that this narrative is addressed, in an epistolary form, by the Lady[3] whose story it contains, to a small number of friends, whose curiosity, with regard to it, had been greatly awakened. It may likewise be mentioned, that these events took place between the conclusion of the French and the beginning

---

2. In 1781 James Yates, a farmer in rural Tomhanick, New York, near Albany, murdered his wife and children. The story appeared much later in the *New-York Weekly Magazine* and the Philadelphia *Minerva*, in July and August 1796, respectively (see p. 266 in this vol.). Recent scholars have recognized a second familicide case, that of William Beadle of Wethersfield, Connecticut, in 1782, as another possible "authentic case" behind Brown's plot.

3. Clara Wieland. The correspondent to whom she directs the narrative remains unidentified throughout.

of the revolutionary war.[4] The memoirs of Carwin,[5] alluded to at the conclusion of the work, will be published or suppressed according to the reception which is given to the present attempt.

C.B.B.

September 3, 1798.

4. The French and Indian War (1756–63), an imperial contest between France and England in North America, sparked the Seven Years' War in Europe. Both conflicts concluded with the Treaties of Hubertusburg and Paris. The American Revolution commenced in 1775. Brown was born in 1771, in the interim between these conflicts.
5. Brown commenced the sequel in August 1798, before *Wieland* was completed or published; it was serialized, but never completed, in his Philadelphia-based *Literary Magazine* between 1803 and 1805 (see p. 183 in this vol.).

Wieland; or, The Transformation

Chapter I

I feel little reluctance in complying with your request. You know not fully the cause of my sorrows. You are a stranger to the depth of my distresses. Hence your efforts at consolation must necessarily fail. Yet the tale that I am going to tell is not intended as a claim upon your sympathy. In the midst of my despair, I do not disdain to contribute what little I can to the benefit of mankind. I acknowledge your right to be informed of the events that have lately happened in my family. Make what use of the tale you shall think proper. If it be communicated to the world, it will inculcate the duty of avoiding deceit. It will exemplify the force of early impressions,[1] and show the immeasurable evils that flow from an erroneous or imperfect discipline.

My state is not destitute of tranquillity. The sentiment that dictates my feelings is not hope. Futurity has no power over my thoughts. To all that is to come I am perfectly indifferent. With regard to myself, I have nothing more to fear. Fate has done its worst. Henceforth, I am callous to misfortune.

I address no supplication to the Deity. The power that governs the course of human affairs has chosen his path. The decree that ascertained the condition of my life, admits of no recal. No doubt it squares with the maxims of eternal equity. That is neither to be questioned nor denied by me. It suffices that the past is exempt from mutation. The storm that tore up our happiness, and changed into dreariness and desert the blooming scene of our existence, is lulled into grim repose; but not until the victim was transfixed and mangled; till every obstacle was dissipated by its rage; till every remnant of good was wrested from our grasp and exterminated.

How will your wonder, and that of your companions, be excited by my story! Every sentiment will yield to your amazement. If my testimony were without corroborations, you would reject it as incredible.

---

1. John Locke (1632–1704) famously argued for the significance of associations formed in early childhood, especially by traumatic events. See *An Essay Concerning Human Understanding* (1690), ch. 33, "Of the Association of Ideas."

The experience of no human being can furnish a parallel: That I, beyond the rest of mankind, should be reserved for a destiny without alleviation, and without example! Listen to my narrative, and then say what it is that has made me deserve to be placed on this dreadful eminence, if, indeed, every faculty be not suspended in wonder that I am still alive, and am able to relate it.

My father's ancestry was noble on the paternal side; but his mother was the daughter of a merchant. My grand-father was a younger brother, and a native of Saxony.[2] He was placed, when he had reached the suitable age, at a German college. During the vacations, he employed himself in traversing the neighbouring territory. On one occasion it was his fortune to visit Hamburg. He formed an acquaintance with Leonard Weise, a merchant of that city, and was a frequent guest at his house. The merchant had an only daughter, for whom his guest speedily contracted an affection; and, in spite of parental menaces and prohibitions, he, in due season, became her husband.

By this act he mortally offended his relations. Thenceforward he was entirely disowned and rejected by them. They refused to contribute any thing to his support. All intercourse ceased, and he received from them merely that treatment to which an absolute stranger, or detested enemy, would be entitled.

He found an asylum in the house of his new father, whose temper was kind, and whose pride was flattered by this alliance. The nobility of his birth was put in the balance against his poverty. Weise conceived himself, on the whole, to have acted with the highest discretion, in thus disposing of his child. My grand-father found it incumbent on him to search out some mode of independent subsistence. His youth had been eagerly devoted to literature and music. These had hitherto been cultivated merely as sources of amusement. They were now converted into the means of gain. At this period there were few works of taste in the Saxon dialect. My ancestor may be considered as the founder of the German Theatre. The modern poet of the same name[3] is sprung from the same family, and, perhaps, surpasses but little, in the fruitfulness of his invention, or the sound-

2. Presently southeastern Germany. Until 1806, when it became a kingdom during the Napoleonic Wars, Saxony was an hereditary electorate of the Holy Roman Empire. Located along the Elbe River and including the cities of Leipzig and Dresden, it was from the sixteenth to the eighteenth centuries a site of German artistic and intellectual culture as well as of political strife surrounding the Protestant Reformation.
3. Christoph Martin Wieland (1733–1813), a forerunner of other German writers whose work Brown knew and admired, including Goethe and Schiller. Wieland wrote in several genres, edited periodicals, and translated English literature, including Shakespeare, into German. His works translated into English and available in eighteenth-century America include his early Pietistic poem *Der geprüfte Abraham* (1753), translated into prose in English as *The Trial of Abraham* ([Boston?], 1764; Norwich, Conn., 1777; see p. 237 in this vol.). Wieland's later works moved from Pietism toward a more skeptical stance toward religious claims. The common ancestor of Brown's char-

ness of his taste, the elder Wieland. His life was spent in the composition of sonatas and dramatic pieces. They were not unpopular, but merely afforded him a scanty subsistence. He died in the bloom of his life, and was quickly followed to the grave by his wife. Their only child was taken under the protection of the merchant. At an early age he was apprenticed to a London trader, and passed seven years of mercantile servitude.

My father was not fortunate in the character of him under whose care he was now placed. He was treated with rigor, and full employment was provided for every hour of his time. His duties were laborious and mechanical. He had been educated with a view to this profession, and, therefore, was not tormented with unsatisfied desires. He did not hold his present occupations in abhorrence, because they withheld him from paths more flowery and more smooth, but he found in unintermitted labour, and in the sternness of his master, sufficient occasions for discontent. No opportunities of recreation were allowed him. He spent all his time pent up in a gloomy apartment, or traversing narrow and crowded streets. His food was coarse, and his lodging humble.

His heart gradually contracted a habit of morose and gloomy reflection. He could not accurately define what was wanting to his happiness. He was not tortured by comparisons drawn between his own situation and that of others. His state was such as suited his age and his views as to fortune. He did not imagine himself treated with extraordinary or unjustifiable rigor. In this respect he supposed the condition of others, bound like himself to mercantile service, to resemble his own; yet every engagement was irksome, and every hour tedious in its lapse.

In this state of mind he chanced to light upon a book written by one of the teachers of the Albigenses, or French Protestants.[4] He entertained no relish for books, and was wholly unconscious of any power they possessed to delight or instruct. This volume had lain for years in a corner of his garret, half buried in dust and rubbish. He had marked it as it lay; had thrown it, as his occasions required, from one spot to another; but had felt no inclination to examine its contents, or even to inquire what was the subject of which it treated.

One Sunday afternoon, being induced to retire for a few minutes to his garret, his eye was attracted by a page of this book, which, by some accident, had been opened and placed full in his view. He was

acters and C. M. Wieland is fictional, though Brown's description of him bears some resemblance to the German dramatist Gotthold Ephraim Lessing (1729–1781).
4. A heretical Christian sect in medieval France whose beliefs centered on a radical dualism that saw the world as evil; only adherents to their doctrines, also known as Cathars, could attain godly perfection. The Roman Catholic Church sought to suppress the heresy through violence in the early thirteenth century, with political as well as religious ramifications for the Languedoc region.

seated on the edge of his bed, and was employed in repairing a rent
in some part of his clothes. His eyes were not confined to his work,
but occasionally wandering, lighted at length upon the page. The
words "Seek and ye shall find,"[5] were those that first offered themselves to his notice. His curiosity was roused by these so far as to
prompt him to proceed. As soon as he finished his work, he took up
the book and turned to the first page. The further he read, the more
inducement he found to continue, and he regretted the decline of
the light which obliged him for the present to close it.

The book contained an exposition of the doctrine of the sect of
Camissards,[6] and an historical account of its origin. His mind was
in a state peculiarly fitted for the reception of devotional sentiments. The craving which had haunted him was now supplied with
an object. His mind was at no loss for a theme of meditation. On
days of business, he rose at the dawn, and retired to his chamber
not till late at night. He now supplied himself with candles, and
employed his nocturnal and Sunday hours in studying this book. It,
of course, abounded with allusions to the Bible. All its conclusions
were deduced from the sacred text. This was the fountain, beyond
which it was unnecessary to trace the stream of religious truth; but
it was his duty to trace it thus far.

A Bible was easily procured, and he ardently entered on the study
of it. His understanding had received a particular direction. All his
reveries were fashioned in the same mould. His progress towards
the formation of his creed was rapid. Every fact and sentiment in
this book were viewed through a medium which the writings of the
Camissard apostle had suggested. His constructions of the text
were hasty, and formed on a narrow scale. Every thing was viewed
in a disconnected position. One action and one precept were not
employed to illustrate and restrict the meaning of another. Hence
arose a thousand scruples to which he had hitherto been a stranger.
He was alternately agitated by fear and by ecstacy. He imagined himself beset by the snares of a spiritual foe, and that his security lay in
ceaseless watchfulness and prayer.

His morals, which had never been loose, were now modelled by a
stricter standard. The empire of religious duty extended itself to his
looks, gestures, and phrases. All levities of speech, and negligences
of behaviour, were proscribed. His air was mournful and contem-

5. See Matthew 7:7 and Luke 11:9.
6. Or Camisards. An apocalyptic Protestant sect that arose in the Languedoc region 500
   years after the Albigensian heresy. In the early eighteenth century, they revolted
   against the French monarch after decades of anti-Protestant persecution. Some leaders fled to London in 1706, where they became known as "the French prophets" and
   sought converts by preaching while in ecstatic trances. Camisard publications in
   English include François Mission's *A Cry from the Desart* and Elias Marion's *Propheti-
   cal Warnings of Elias Marion*, both published in London in 1707.

plative. He laboured to keep alive a sentiment of fear, and a belief of the awe-creating presence of the Deity. Ideas foreign to this were sedulously excluded. To suffer their intrusion was a crime against the Divine Majesty inexpiable but by days and weeks of the keenest agonies.

No material variation had occurred in the lapse of two years. Every day confirmed him in his present modes of thinking and acting. It was to be expected that the tide of his emotions would sometimes recede, that intervals of despondency and doubt would occur; but these gradually were more rare, and of shorter duration; and he, at last, arrived at a state considerably uniform in this respect.

His apprenticeship was now almost expired. On his arrival of age he became entitled, by the will of my grandfather, to a small sum. This sum would hardly suffice to set him afloat as a trader in his present situation, and he had nothing to expect from the generosity of his master. Residence in England had, besides, become almost impossible, on account of his religious tenets. In addition to these motives for seeking a new habitation, there was another of the most imperious and irresistable necessity. He had imbibed an opinion that it was his duty to disseminate the truths of the gospel among the unbelieving nations. He was terrified at first by the perils and hardships to which the life of a missionary is exposed. This cowardice made him diligent in the invention of objections and excuses; but he found it impossible wholly to shake off the belief that such was the injunction of his duty. The belief, after every new conflict with his passions, acquired new strength; and, at length, he formed a resolution of complying with what he deemed the will of heaven.

The North-American Indians naturally presented themselves as the first objects for this species of benevolence. As soon as his servitude expired, he converted his little fortune into money, and embarked for Philadelphia. Here his fears were revived, and a nearer survey of savage manners once more shook his resolution. For a while he relinquished his purpose, and purchasing a farm on Schuylkill,[7] within a few miles of the city, set himself down to the cultivation of it. The cheapness of land, and the service of African slaves, which were then in general use, gave him who was poor in Europe all the advantages of wealth. He passed fourteen years in a thrifty and laborious manner. In this time new objects, new employments, and new associates appeared to have nearly obliterated the devout impressions of his youth. He now became acquainted with a woman of a meek and quiet disposition, and of slender acquirements like himself. He proffered his hand and was accepted.

7. The Schuylkill River, Philadelphia's western boundary at the time.

His previous industry had now enabled him to dispense with personal labour, and direct attention to his own concerns. He enjoyed leisure, and was visited afresh by devotional contemplation. The reading of the scriptures, and other religious books, became once more his favorite employment. His ancient belief relative to the conversion of the savage tribes, was revived with uncommon energy. To the former obstacles were now added the pleadings of parental and conjugal love. The struggle was long and vehement; but his sense of duty would not be stifled or enfeebled, and finally triumphed over every impediment.

His efforts were attended with no permanent success. His exhortations had sometimes a temporary power, but more frequently were repelled with insult and derision. In pursuit of this object he encountered the most imminent perils, and underwent incredible fatigues, hunger, sickness, and solitude. The licence of savage passion, and the artifices of his depraved countrymen, all opposed themselves to his progress. His courage did not forsake him till there appeared no reasonable ground to hope for success. He desisted not till his heart was relieved from the supposed obligation to persevere. With a constitution somewhat decayed, he at length returned to his family. An interval of tranquillity succeeded. He was frugal, regular, and strict in the performance of domestic duties. He allied himself with no sect, because he perfectly agreed with none. Social worship is that by which they are all distinguished; but this article found no place in his creed. He rigidly interpreted that precept which enjoins us, when we worship, to retire into solitude, and shut out every species of society.[8] According to him devotion was not only a silent office, but must be performed alone. An hour at noon, and an hour at midnight were thus appropriated.

At the distance of three hundred yards from his house, on the top of a rock whose sides were steep, rugged, and encumbered with dwarf cedars and stony asperities, he built what to a common eye would have seemed a summerhouse. The eastern verge of this precipice was sixty feet above the river which flowed at its foot. The view before it consisted of a transparent current, fluctuating and rippling in a rocky channel, and bounded by a rising scene of cornfields and orchards. The edifice was slight and airy. It was no more than a circular area, twelve feet in diameter, whose flooring was the rock, cleared of moss and shrubs, and exactly levelled, edged by twelve Tuscan columns, and covered by an undulating dome.[9] My father furnished the dimensions and outlines, but allowed the artist whom

8. See Matthew 6:6.
9. Features of classical Roman architecture.

he employed to complete the structure on his own plan. It was without seat, table, or ornament of any kind.

This was the temple of his Deity. Twice in twenty-four hours he repaired hither, unaccompanied by any human being. Nothing but physical inability to move was allowed to obstruct or postpone this visit. He did not exact from his family compliance with his example. Few men, equally sincere in their faith, were as sparing in their censures and restrictions, with respect to the conduct of others, as my father. The character of my mother was no less devout; but her education had habituated her to a different mode of worship. The loneliness of their dwelling prevented her from joining any established congregation; but she was punctual in the offices of prayer, and in the performance of hymns to her Saviour, after the manner of the disciples of Zinzendorf.[1] My father refused to interfere in her arrangements. His own system was embraced not, accurately speaking, because it was the best, but because it had been expressly prescribed to him. Other modes, if practised by other persons, might be equally acceptable.

His deportment to others was full of charity and mildness. A sadness perpetually overspread his features, but was unmingled with sternness or discontent. The tones of his voice, his gestures, his steps were all in tranquil unison. His conduct was characterised by a certain forbearance and humility, which secured the esteem of those to whom his tenets were most obnoxious. They might call him a fanatic and a dreamer, but they could not deny their veneration to his invincible candour and invariable integrity. His own belief of rectitude was the foundation of his happiness. This, however, was destined to find an end.

Suddenly the sadness that constantly attended him was deepened. Sighs, and even tears, sometimes escaped him. To the expostulations of his wife he seldom answered any thing. When he deigned to be communicative, he hinted that his peace of mind was flown, in consequence of deviation from his duty. A command had been laid upon him, which he had delayed to perform. He felt as if a certain period of hesitation and reluctance had been allowed him, but that this period was passed. He was no longer permitted to obey. The duty assigned to him was transferred, in consequence of his disobedience, to another, and all that remained was to endure the penalty.

---

1. Count Nikolaus Zinzendorf (1700–1760), a native of Saxony and patron to Moravian Christians, an early Protestant sect, within which he was ordained a bishop. Zinzendorf sheltered Moravians who fled persecution elsewhere and funded missionary expeditions to the West Indies, Greenland, and North America (among Native Americans in Pennsylvania and Ohio). He visited Pennsylvania in 1741–42 and established Moravian communities in the towns of Nazareth and Bethlehem.

He did not describe this penalty. It appeared to be nothing more
for some time than a sense of wrong. This was sufficiently acute, and
was aggravated by the belief that his offence was incapable of expia-
tion. No one could contemplate the agonies which he seemed to
suffer without the deepest compassion. Time, instead of lightening
the burthen, appeared to add to it. At length he hinted to his wife,
that his end was near. His imagination did not prefigure the mode
or the time of his decease, but was fraught with an incurable persuasion that his death was at hand. He was likewise haunted by the
belief that the kind of death that awaited him was strange and terrible. His anticipations were thus far vague and indefinite; but they
sufficed to poison every moment of his being, and devote him to
ceaseless anguish.

Chapter II

Early in the morning of a sultry day in August, he left Mettingen,[1]
to go to the city. He had seldom passed a day from home since his
return from the shores of the Ohio. Some urgent engagements at
this time existed, which would not admit of further delay. He
returned in the evening, but appeared to be greatly oppressed with
fatigue. His silence and dejection were likewise in a more than ordinary degree conspicuous. My mother's brother, whose profession was
that of a surgeon, chanced to spend this night at our house. It was
from him that I have frequently received an exact account of the
mournful catastrophe that followed.

As the evening advanced, my father's inquietudes increased. He sat
with his family as usual, but took no part in their conversation. He
appeared fully engrossed by his own reflections. Occasionally his
countenance exhibited tokens of alarm; he gazed stedfastly and wildly
at the ceiling; and the exertions of his companions were scarcely sufficient to interrupt his reverie. On recovering from these fits, he
expressed no surprize; but pressing his hand to his head, complained,
in a tremulous and terrified tone, that his brain was scorched to cinders. He would then betray marks of insupportable anxiety.

My uncle perceived, by his pulse, that he was indisposed, but in
no alarming degree, and ascribed appearances chiefly to the workings of his mind. He exhorted him to recollection and composure,
but in vain. At the hour of repose he readily retired to his chamber.
At the persuasion of my mother he even undressed and went to bed.
Nothing could abate his restlessness. He checked her tender expos-

---

1. The name of the Wieland family estate outside Philadelphia, after its first owner. Also
   a town in northwestern Germany.

tulations with some sternness. "Be silent," said he, "for that which
I feel there is but one cure, and that will shortly come. You can
help me nothing. Look to your own condition, and pray to God to
strengthen you under the calamities that await you." "What am I to
fear?" she answered. "What terrible disaster is it that you think of?"
"Peace—as yet I know it not myself, but come it will, and shortly."
She repeated her inquiries and doubts; but he suddenly put an end
to the discourse, by a stern command to be silent.

   She had never before known him in this mood. Hitherto all was
benign in his deportment. Her heart was pierced with sorrow at the
contemplation of this change. She was utterly unable to account for
it, or to figure to herself the species of disaster that was menaced.

   Contrary to custom, the lamp, instead of being placed on the
hearth, was left upon the table. Over it against the wall there hung
a small clock, so contrived as to strike a very hard stroke at the end
of every sixth hour. That which was now approaching was the signal
for retiring to the fane[2] at which he addressed his devotions. Long
habit had occasioned him to be always awake at this hour, and the
toll was instantly obeyed.

   Now frequent and anxious glances were cast at the clock. Not a
single movement of the index appeared to escape his notice. As the
hour verged towards twelve his anxiety visibly augmented. The trepidations of my mother kept pace with those of her husband; but she
was intimidated into silence. All that was left to her was to watch
every change of his features, and give vent to her sympathy in tears.

   At length the hour was spent, and the clock tolled. The sound
appeared to communicate a shock to every part of my father's frame.
He rose immediately, and threw over himself a loose gown. Even
this office was performed with difficulty, for his joints trembled, and
his teeth chattered with dismay. At this hour his duty called him to
the rock, and my mother naturally concluded that it was thither he
intended to repair. Yet these incidents were so uncommon, as to fill
her with astonishment and foreboding. She saw him leave the room,
and heard his steps as they hastily descended the stairs. She half
resolved to rise and pursue him, but the wildness of the scheme
quickly suggested itself. He was going to a place whither no power
on earth could induce him to suffer an attendant.

   The window of her chamber looked toward the rock. The atmosphere was clear and calm, but the edifice could not be discovered at
that distance through the dusk. My mother's anxiety would not allow
her to remain where she was. She rose, and seated herself at the window. She strained her sight to get a view of the dome, and of the path
that led to it. The first painted itself with sufficient distinctness on

2. Temple.

her fancy, but was undistinguishable by the eye from the rocky mass on which it was erected. The second could be imperfectly seen; but her husband had already passed, or had taken a different direction.

What was it that she feared? Some disaster impended over her husband or herself. He had predicted evils, but professed himself ignorant of what nature they were. When were they to come? Was this night, or this hour to witness the accomplishment? She was tortured with impatience, and uncertainty. All her fears were at present linked to his person, and she gazed at the clock, with nearly as much eagerness as my father had done, in expectation of the next hour.

An half hour passed away in this state of suspence. Her eyes were fixed upon the rock; suddenly it was illuminated. A light proceeding from the edifice, made every part of the scene visible. A gleam diffused itself over the intermediate space, and instantly a loud report, like the explosion of a mine, followed. She uttered an involuntary shriek, but the new sounds that greeted her ear, quickly conquered her surprise. They were piercing shrieks, and uttered without intermission. The gleams which had diffused themselves far and wide were in a moment withdrawn, but the interior of the edifice was filled with rays.

The first suggestion was that a pistol was discharged, and that the structure was on fire. She did not allow herself time to meditate a second thought, but rushed into the entry and knocked loudly at the door of her brother's chamber. My uncle had been previously roused by the noise, and instantly flew to the window. He also imagined what he saw to be fire. The loud and vehement shrieks which succeeded the first explosion, seemed to be an invocation of succour. The incident was inexplicable; but he could not fail to perceive the propriety of hastening to the spot. He was unbolting the door, when his sister's voice was heard on the outside conjuring him to come forth.

He obeyed the summons with all the speed in his power. He stopped not to question her, but hurried down stairs and across the meadow which lay between the house and the rock. The shrieks were no longer to be heard; but a blazing light was clearly discernible between the columns of the temple. Irregular steps, hewn in the stone, led him to the summit. On three sides, this edifice touched the very verge of the cliff. On the fourth side, which might be regarded as the front, there was an area of small extent, to which the rude staircase conducted you. My uncle speedily gained this spot. His strength was for a moment exhausted by his haste. He paused to rest himself. Meanwhile he bent the most vigilant attention towards the object before him.

Within the columns he beheld what he could no better describe, than by saying that it resembled a cloud impregnated with light. It had the brightness of flame, but was without its upward motion. It did not occupy the whole area, and rose but a few feet above the floor. No part of the building was on fire. This appearance was astonishing. He approached the temple. As he went forward the light retired, and, when he put his feet within the apartment, utterly vanished. The suddenness of this transition increased the darkness that succeeded in a tenfold degree. Fear and wonder rendered him powerless. An occurrence like this, in a place assigned to devotion, was adapted to intimidate the stoutest heart.

His wandering thoughts were recalled by the groans of one near him. His sight gradually recovered its power, and he was able to discern my father stretched on the floor. At that moment, my mother and servants arrived with a lanthorn,[3] and enabled my uncle to examine more closely this scene. My father, when he left the house, besides a loose upper vest and slippers, wore a shirt and drawers. Now he was naked, his skin throughout the greater part of his body was scorched and bruised. His right arm exhibited marks as of having been struck by some heavy body. His clothes had been removed, and it was not immediately perceived that they were reduced to ashes. His slippers and his hair were untouched.

He was removed to his chamber, and the requisite attention paid to his wounds, which gradually became more painful. A mortification speedily shewed itself in the arm, which had been most hurt. Soon after, the other wounded parts exhibited the like appearance.

Immediately subsequent to this disaster, my father seemed nearly in a state of insensibility. He was passive under every operation. He scarcely opened his eyes, and was with difficulty prevailed upon to answer the questions that were put to him. By his imperfect account, it appeared, that while engaged in silent orisons,[4] with thoughts full of confusion and anxiety, a faint gleam suddenly shot athwart the apartment. His fancy immediately pictured to itself, a person bearing a lamp. It seemed to come from behind. He was in the act of turning to examine the visitant, when his right arm received a blow from a heavy club. At the same instant, a very bright spark was seen to light upon his clothes. In a moment, the whole was reduced to ashes. This was the sum of the information which he chose to give. There was somewhat in his manner that indicated an imperfect tale. My uncle was inclined to believe that half the truth had been suppressed.

Meanwhile, the disease thus wonderfully generated, betrayed more terrible symptoms. Fever and delirium terminated in lethargic slumber, which, in the course of two hours, gave place to death. Yet

3. Lantern.
4. Prayers.

not till insupportable exhalations and crawling putrefaction had driven from his chamber and the house every one whom their duty did not detain.

Such was the end of my father. None surely was ever more mysterious. When we recollect his gloomy anticipations and unconquerable anxiety; the security from human malice which his character, the place, and the condition of the times, might be supposed to confer; the purity and cloudlessness of the atmosphere, which rendered it impossible that lightning was the cause; what are the conclusions that we must form?

The prelusive[5] gleam, the blow upon his arm, the fatal spark, the explosion heard so far, the fiery cloud that environed him, without detriment to the structure, though composed of combustible materials, the sudden vanishing of this cloud at my uncle's approach—what is the inference to be drawn from these facts? Their truth cannot be doubted. My uncle's testimony is peculiarly worthy of credit, because no man's temper is more sceptical, and his belief is unalterably attached to natural causes.

I was at this time a child of six years of age. The impressions that were then made upon me, can never be effaced. I was ill qualified to judge respecting what was then passing; but as I advanced in age, and became more fully acquainted with these facts, they oftener became the subject of my thoughts. Their resemblance to recent events revived them with new force in my memory, and made me more anxious to explain them. Was this the penalty of disobedience? this the stroke of a vindictive and invisible hand? Is it a fresh proof that the Divine Ruler interferes in human affairs, meditates an end, selects and commissions his agents, and enforces, by unequivocal sanctions, submission to his will? Or, was it merely the irregular expansion of the fluid that imparts warmth to our heart and our blood caused by the fatigue of the preceding day, or flowing, by established laws, from the condition of his thoughts?[6]

---

5. Serving as a prelude.

6. "A case, in its symptoms exactly parallel to this, is published in one of the Journals of Florence. See, likewise, similar cases reported by Messrs. Merille and Muraire, in the 'Journal de Medicine,' for February and May, 1783. The researches of Maffei and Fontana have thrown some light upon this subject" [Brown's note]. In October 1776, an Italian surgeon named Joseph Battaglia published an account of a priest named Bertholi who burst into flames while praying. The anecdote was widely referenced throughout the nineteenth century in Europe and America. Brown refers specifically to the article by Merille and Muraire, "Sur un effet singulier de la combustion," which appeared in the Paris Journal de Medicine in February and May 1783 and contains Battaglia's story. Like the elder Wieland's, Bertholi's arm was injured, as if by a blow from a cudgel. His body began to decompose and stink before his death. The account appeared in English, attributed to "one of the journals of Florence," in the London Literary Magazine and British Review (May 1790) and the Philadelphia American Museum, or, Universal Magazine (April 1792). (See p. 282 in this vol.)

Chapter III

The shock which this disastrous occurrence occasioned to my mother, was the foundation of a disease which carried her, in a few months, to the grave. My brother and myself were children at this time, and were now reduced to the condition of orphans. The property which our parents left was by no means inconsiderable. It was entrusted to faithful hands, till we should arrive at a suitable age. Meanwhile, our education was assigned to a maiden aunt who resided in the city, and whose tenderness made us in a short time cease to regret that we had lost a mother.

The years that succeeded were tranquil and happy. Our lives were molested by few of those cares that are incident to childhood. By accident more than design, the indulgence and yielding temper of our aunt was mingled with resolution and stedfastness. She seldom deviated into either extreme of rigour or lenity. Our social pleasures were subject to no unreasonable restraints. We were instructed in most branches of useful knowledge, and were saved from the corruption and tyranny of colleges and boarding-schools.

Our companions were chiefly selected from the children of our neighbours. Between one of these and my brother, there quickly grew the most affectionate intimacy. Her name was Catharine Pleyel.[1] She was rich, beautiful, and contrived to blend the most bewitching softness with the most exuberant vivacity. The tie by which my brother and she were united, seemed to add force to the love which I bore her, and which was amply returned. Between her and myself there was every circumstance tending to produce and foster friendship. Our sex and age were the same. We lived within sight of each other's abode. Our tempers were remarkably congenial, and the superintendants of our education not only prescribed to us the same pursuits, but allowed us to cultivate them together.

Every day added strength to the triple bonds that united us. We gradually withdrew ourselves from the society of others, and found every moment irksome that was not devoted to each other. My brother's advance in age made no change in our situation. It was determined that his profession should be agriculture. His fortune exempted him from the necessity of personal labour. The task to be performed by him was nothing more than superintendance. The skill that was demanded by this was merely theoretical, and was furnished by casual inspection, or by closet study. The attention that was paid to this subject did not seclude him for any long time from us, on whom

1. Also the surname of the well-known Austrian-born composer Ignaz Joseph Pleyel (1757–1831), a pupil of Haydn.

time had no other effect than to augment our impatience in the absence of each other and of him. Our tasks, our walks, our music, were seldom performed but in each other's company.

It was easy to see that Catharine and my brother were born for each other. The passion which they mutually entertained quickly broke those bounds which extreme youth had set to it; confessions were made or extorted, and their union was postponed only till my brother had passed his minority. The previous lapse of two years was constantly and usefully employed.

O my brother! But the task I have set myself let me perform with steadiness. The felicity of that period was marred by no gloomy anticipations. The future, like the present, was serene. Time was supposed to have only new delights in store. I mean not to dwell on previous incidents longer than is necessary to illustrate or explain the great events that have since happened. The nuptial day at length arrived. My brother took possession of the house in which he was born, and here the long protracted marriage was solemnized.

My father's property was equally divided between us. A neat dwelling, situated on the bank of the river, three quarters of a mile from my brother's, was now occupied by me. These domains were called, from the name of the first possessor, Mettingen. I can scarcely account for my refusing to take up my abode with him, unless it were from a disposition to be an economist of pleasure. Self-denial, seasonably exercised, is one means of enhancing our gratifications. I was, beside, desirous of administering a fund, and regulating an household, of my own. The short distance allowed us to exchange visits as often as we pleased. The walk from one mansion to the other was no undelightful prelude to our interviews. I was sometimes their visitant, and they, as frequently, were my guests.

Our education had been modelled by no religious standard. We were left to the guidance of our own understanding, and the casual impressions which society might make upon us. My friend's temper, as well as my own, exempted us from much anxiety on this account. It must not be supposed that we were without religion, but with us it was the product of lively feelings, excited by reflection on our own happiness, and by the grandeur of external nature. We sought not a basis for our faith, in the weighing of proofs, and the dissection of creeds. Our devotion was a mixed and casual sentiment, seldom verbally expressed, or solicitously sought, or carefully retained. In the midst of present enjoyment, no thought was bestowed on the future. As a consolation in calamity religion is dear. But calamity was yet at a distance, and its only tendency was to heighten enjoyments which needed not this addition to satisfy every craving.

My brother's situation was somewhat different. His deportment was grave, considerate, and thoughtful. I will not say whether he was indebted to sublimer views for this disposition. Human life, in his opinion, was made up of changeable elements, and the principles of duty were not easily unfolded. The future, either as anterior, or subsequent to death, was a scene that required some preparation and provision to be made for it. These positions we could not deny, but what distinguished him was a propensity to ruminate on these truths. The images that visited us were blithsome and gay, but those with which he was most familiar were of an opposite hue. They did not generate affliction and fear, but they diffused over his behaviour a certain air of forethought and sobriety. The principal effect of this temper was visible in his features and tones. These, in general, bespoke a sort of thrilling melancholy. I scarcely ever knew him to laugh. He never accompanied the lawless mirth of his companions with more than a smile, but his conduct was the same as ours.

He partook of our occupations and amusements with a zeal not less than ours, but of a different kind. The diversity in our temper was never the parent of discord, and was scarcely a topic of regret. The scene was variegated, but not tarnished or disordered by it. It hindered the element in which we moved from stagnating. Some agitation and concussion is requisite to the due exercise of human understanding. In his studies, he pursued an austerer and more arduous path. He was much conversant with the history of religious opinions, and took pains to ascertain their validity. He deemed it indispensable to examine the ground of his belief, to settle the relation between motives and actions, the criterion of merit, and the kinds and properties of evidence.

There was an obvious resemblance between him and my father, in their conceptions of the importance of certain topics, and in the light in which the vicissitudes of human life were accustomed to be viewed. Their characters were similar, but the mind of the son was enriched by science, and embellished with literature.

The temple was no longer assigned to its ancient use. From an Italian adventurer, who erroneously imagined that he could find employment for his skill, and sale for his sculptures in America, my brother had purchased a bust of Cicero.[2] He professed to have copied this piece from an antique dug up with his own hands in the environs of Modena.[3] Of the truth of his assertions we were not qualified to judge; but the marble was pure and polished, and we were contented to admire the performance, without waiting for the sanction of connoisseurs. We hired the same artist to hew a suitable pedestal from a neighbouring quarry. This was placed in the temple,

2. Roman statesman and orator Marcus Tullius Cicero (104–43 B.C.E.), defender of the Roman republic who was executed by Octavius Caeser at Marc Antony's bidding.
3. A town in northern Italy.

and the bust rested upon it. Opposite to this was a harpsichord, sheltered by a temporary roof from the weather. This was the place of resort in the evenings of summer. Here we sung, and talked, and read, and occasionally banqueted. Every joyous and tender scene most dear to my memory, is connected with this edifice. Here the performances of our musical and poetical ancestor were rehearsed. Here my brother's children received the rudiments of their education; here a thousand conversations, pregnant with delight and improvement, took place; and here the social affections were accustomed to expand, and the tear of delicious sympathy to be shed.

My brother was an indefatigable student. The authors whom he read were numerous, but the chief object of his veneration was Cicero. He was never tired of conning[4] and rehearsing his productions. To understand them was not sufficient. He was anxious to discover the gestures and cadences with which they ought to be delivered. He was very scrupulous in selecting a true scheme of pronunciation for the Latin tongue, and in adapting it to the words of his darling writer. His favorite occupation consisted in embellishing his rhetoric with all the proprieties of gesticulation and utterance.

Not contented with this, he was diligent in settling and restoring the purity of the text. For this end, he collected all the editions and commentaries that could be procured, and employed months of severe study in exploring and comparing them. He never betrayed more satisfaction than when he made a discovery of this kind.

It was not till the addition of Henry Pleyel, my friend's only brother, to our society, that his passion for Roman eloquence was countenanced and fostered by a sympathy of tastes. This young man had been some years in Europe. We had separated at a very early age, and he was now returned to spend the remainder of his days among us.

Our circle was greatly enlivened by the accession of a new member. His conversation abounded with novelty. His gaiety was almost boisterous, but was capable of yielding to a grave deportment, when the occasion required it. His discernment was acute, but he was prone to view every object merely as supplying materials for mirth. His conceptions were ardent but ludicrous,[5] and his memory, aided, as he honestly acknowledged, by his invention, was an inexhaustible fund of entertainment.

His residence was at the same distance below the city as ours was above, but there seldom passed a day without our being favoured with a visit. My brother and he were endowed with the same attachment to the Latin writers; and Pleyel was not behind his friend in his knowledge of the history and metaphysics of religion. Their

4. Studying carefully or committing to memory.
5. Humorous or playful.

creeds, however, were in many respects opposite. Where one discovered only confirmations of his faith, the other could find nothing
but reasons for doubt. Moral necessity, and calvinistic inspiration,
were the props on which my brother thought proper to repose. Pleyel
was the champion of intellectual liberty, and rejected all guidance
but that of his reason. Their discussions were frequent, but, being
managed with candour as well as with skill, they were always listened to by us with avidity and benefit.

Pleyel, like his new friends, was fond of music and poetry. Henceforth our concerts consisted of two violins, an harpsichord, and
three voices. We were frequently reminded how much happiness
depends upon society. This new friend, though, before his arrival,
we were sensible of no vacuity, could not now be spared. His departure would occasion a void which nothing could fill, and which
would produce insupportable regret. Even my brother, though his
opinions were hourly assailed, and even the divinity of Cicero contested, was captivated with his friend, and laid aside some part of
his ancient gravity at Pleyel's approach.

Chapter IV

Six years of uninterrupted happiness had rolled away, since my
brother's marriage. The sound of war had been heard,[1] but it was at
such a distance as to enhance our enjoyment by affording objects of
comparison. The Indians were repulsed on the one side, and Canada
was conquered on the other. Revolutions and battles, however calamitous to those who occupied the scene, contributed in some sort to
our happiness, by agitating our minds with curiosity, and furnishing
causes of patriotic exultation. Four children, three of whom were of
an age to compensate, by their personal and mental progress, the
cares of which they had been, at a more helpless age, the objects,
exercised my brother's tenderness. The fourth was a charming babe
that promised to display the image of her mother, and enjoyed perfect health. To these were added a sweet girl fourteen years old, who
was loved by all of us, with an affection more than parental.

Her mother's story was a mournful one. She had come hither
from England when this child was an infant, alone, without friends,
and without money. She appeared to have embarked in a hasty and
clandestine manner. She passed three years of solitude and anguish
under my aunt's protection, and died a martyr to woe; the source of
which she could, by no importunities, be prevailed upon to unfold.
Her education and manners bespoke her to be of no mean birth.

1. The French and Indian War.

Her last moments were rendered serene, by the assurances she received from my aunt, that her daughter should experience the same protection that had been extended to herself.

On my brother's marriage, it was agreed that she should make a part of his family. I cannot do justice to the attractions of this girl. Perhaps the tenderness she excited might partly originate in her personal resemblance to her mother, whose character and misfortunes were still fresh in our remembrance. She was habitually pensive, and this circumstance tended to remind the spectator of her friendless condition; and yet that epithet was surely misapplied in this case. This being was cherished by those with whom she now resided, with unspeakable fondness. Every exertion was made to enlarge and improve her mind. Her safety was the object of a solicitude that almost exceeded the bounds of discretion. Our affection indeed could scarcely transcend her merits. She never met my eye, or occurred to my reflections, without exciting a kind of enthusiasm. Her softness, her intelligence, her equanimity, never shall I see surpassed. I have often shed tears of pleasure at her approach, and pressed her to my bosom in an agony of fondness.

While every day was adding to the charms of her person, and the stores of her mind, there occurred an event which threatened to deprive us of her. An officer of some rank, who had been disabled by a wound at Quebec, had employed himself, since the ratification of peace, in travelling through the colonies. He remained a considerable period at Philadelphia, but was at last preparing for his departure. No one had been more frequently honoured with his visits than Mrs. Baynton, a worthy lady with whom our family were intimate. He went to her house with a view to perform a farewell visit, and was on the point of taking his leave, when I and my young friend entered the apartment. It is impossible to describe the emotions of the stranger, when he fixed his eyes upon my companion. He was motionless with surprise. He was unable to conceal his feelings, but sat silently gazing at the spectacle before him. At length he turned to Mrs. Baynton, and more by his looks and gestures than by words, besought her for an explanation of the scene. He seized the hand of the girl, who, in her turn, was surprised by his behaviour, and drawing her forward, said in an eager and faultering tone, "Who is she? whence does she come? what is her name?"

The answers that were given only increased the confusion of his thoughts. He was successively told, that she was the daughter of one whose name was Louisa Conway, who arrived among us at such a time, who sedulously concealed her parentage, and the motives of her flight, whose incurable griefs had finally destroyed her, and who had left this child under the protection of her friends. Having heard the tale, he melted into tears, eagerly clasped the young lady in his arms, and called himself her father. When the tumults excited in his breast by this unlooked-for meeting were somewhat subsided, he gratified our curiosity by relating the following incidents.

Miss Conway was the only daughter of a banker in London, who discharged towards her every duty of an affectionate father. He had chanced to fall into her company, had been subdued by her attractions, had tendered her his hand, and been joyfully accepted both by parent and child. His wife had given him every proof of the fondest attachment. Her father, who possessed immense wealth, treated him with distinguished respect, liberally supplied his wants, and had made one condition of his consent to their union, a resolution to take up their abode with him.

They had passed three years of conjugal felicity, which had been augmented by the birth of this child, when his professional duty called him into Germany.[2] It was not without an arduous struggle, that she was persuaded to relinquish the design of accompanying him through all the toils and perils of war. No parting was ever more distressful. They strove to alleviate, by frequent letters, the evils of their lot. Those of his wife, breathed nothing but anxiety for his safety, and impatience of his absence. At length, a new arrangement was made, and he was obliged to repair from Westphalia to Canada.[3] One advantage attended this change. It afforded him an opportunity of meeting his family. His wife anticipated this interview, with no less rapture than himself. He hurried to London, and the moment he alighted from the stage-coach, ran with all speed to Mr. Conway's house.

It was an house of mourning. His father was overwhelmed with grief, and incapable of answering his inquiries. The servants, sorrowful and mute, were equally refractory. He explored the house, and called on the names of his wife and daughter, but his summons was fruitless. At length, this new disaster was explained. Two days before his arrival, his wife's chamber was found empty. No search, however diligent and anxious, could trace her steps. No cause could be assigned for her disappearance. The mother and child had fled away together.

New exertions were made, her chamber and cabinets were ransacked, but no vestige was found serving to inform them as to the motives of her flight, whether it had been voluntary or otherwise, and in what corner of the kingdom or of the world she was concealed. Who shall describe the sorrow and amazement of the husband? His restlessness, his vicissitudes of hope and fear, and his ultimate

2. I.e., to participate in the Seven Years' War, the European conflict sparked by the French and Indian War in North America.
3. I.e., transferred from Westphalia, a northern German region, the site of military conflict during the Seven Years' War, to Canada, the site of the French and Indian War.

despair? His duty called him to America. He had been in this city,
and had frequently passed the door of the house in which his wife, at
that moment, resided. Her father had not remitted his exertions to
elucidate this painful mystery, but they had failed. This disappointment hastened his death; in consequence of which, Louisa's father
became possessor of his immense property.

This tale was a copious theme of speculation. A thousand questions were started and discussed in our domestic circle, respecting
the motives that influenced Mrs. Stuart to abandon her country. It
did not appear that her proceeding was involuntary. We recalled and
reviewed every particular that had fallen under our own observation.
By none of these were we furnished with a clue. Her conduct, after
the most rigorous scrutiny, still remained an impenetrable secret. On
a nearer view, Major Stuart proved himself a man of most amiable
character. His attachment to Louisa appeared hourly to increase.
She was no stranger to the sentiments suitable to her new character.
She could not but readily embrace the scheme which was proposed
to her, to return with her father to England. This scheme his regard
for her induced him, however, to postpone. Some time was necessary
to prepare her for so great a change and enable her to think without
agony of her separation from us.

I was not without hopes of prevailing on her father entirely to
relinquish this unwelcome design. Meanwhile, he pursued his travels through the southern colonies, and his daughter continued with
us. Louisa and my brother frequently received letters from him,
which indicated a mind of no common order. They were filled with
amusing details, and profound reflections. While here, he often partook of our evening conversations at the temple; and since his departure, his correspondence had frequently supplied us with topics of
discourse.

One afternoon in May, the blandness of the air, and brightness of
the verdure, induced us to assemble, earlier than usual, in the temple. We females were busy at the needle, while my brother and Pleyel
were bandying quotations and syllogisms. The point discussed was
the merit of the oration for Cluentius,[4] as descriptive, first, of the
genius of the speaker; and, secondly, of the manners of the times.
Pleyel laboured to extenuate both these species of merit, and tasked
his ingenuity, to shew that the orator had embraced a bad cause; or,
at least, a doubtful one. He urged, that to rely on the exaggerations of

4. In *Pro Cluentius* (66 B.C.E.), Cicero defends Cluentius against charges that he had poi-
   soned his stepfather, who had earlier been convicted of trying to poison Cluentius. The
   oration was both celebrated and condemned by writers on law and rhetoric. Cicero characterized his own defense as "throwing dust in the jury's eyes." Cicero was well known to
   classically educated eighteenth-century Americans and was a republican hero for many
   of the American revolutionary generation, though his character—and the character of
   the legal profession—was a point of debate among Brown's contemporaries.

an advocate, or to make the picture of a single family a model from which to sketch the condition of a nation, was absurd. The controversy was suddenly diverted into a new channel, by a misquotation. Pleyel accused his companion of saying *"polliceatur"* when he should have said *"polliceretur."*[5] Nothing would decide the contest, but an appeal to the volume. My brother was returning to the house for this purpose, when a servant met him with a letter from Major Stuart. He immediately returned to read it in our company.

Besides affectionate compliments to us, and paternal benedictions on Louisa, his letter contained a description of a waterfall on the Monongahela.[6] A sudden gust of rain falling, we were compelled to remove to the house. The storm passed away, and a radiant moonlight succeeded. There was no motion to resume our seats in the temple. We therefore remained where we were, and engaged in sprightly conversation. The letter lately received naturally suggested the topic. A parallel was drawn between the cataract there described, and one which Pleyel had discovered among the Alps of Glarus.[7] In the state of the former, some particular was mentioned, the truth of which was questionable. To settle the dispute which thence arose, it was proposed to have recourse to the letter. My brother searched for it in his pocket. It was no where to be found. At length, he remembered to have left it in the temple, and he determined to go in search of it. His wife, Pleyel, Louisa, and myself, remained where we were.

In a few minutes he returned. I was somewhat interested in the dispute, and was therefore impatient for his return; yet, as I heard him ascending the stairs, I could not but remark, that he had executed his intention with remarkable dispatch. My eyes were fixed upon him on his entrance. Methought he brought with him looks considerably different from those with which he departed. Wonder, and a slight portion of anxiety were mingled in them. His eyes seemed to be in search of some object. They passed quickly from one person to another, till they rested on his wife. She was seated in a careless attitude on the sofa, in the same spot as before. She had the same muslin in her hand, by which her attention was chiefly engrossed.

The moment he saw her, his perplexity visibly increased. He quietly seated himself, and fixing his eyes on the floor, appeared to be absorbed in meditation. These singularities suspended the inquiry which I was preparing to make respecting the letter. In a short time, the company relinquished the subject which engaged them,

5. Two forms of the verb *polliceor,* meaning "to promise" or "to make an offer." Pleyel is mistaken in this dispute.
6. A river in southwestern Pennsylvania.
7. In central Switzerland, a German-speaking Protestant region.

and directed their attention to Wieland. They thought that he only waited for a pause in the discourse, to produce the letter. The pause was uninterrupted by him. At length Pleyel said, "Well, I suppose you have found the letter."

"No," said he, without any abatement of his gravity, and looking stedfastly at his wife, "I did not mount the hill."—"Why not?"—"Catharine, have you not moved from that spot since I left the room?"—She was affected with the solemnity of his manner, and laying down her work, answered in a tone of surprise, "No; Why do you ask that question?"—His eyes were again fixed upon the floor, and he did not immediately answer. At length, he said, looking round upon us, "Is it true that Catharine did not follow me to the hill? That she did not just now enter the room?"—We assured him, with one voice, that she had not been absent for a moment, and inquired into the motive of his questions.

"Your assurances," said he, "are solemn and unanimous; and yet I must deny credit to your assertions, or disbelieve the testimony of my senses, which informed me, when I was half way up the hill, that Catharine was at the bottom."

We were confounded at this declaration. Pleyel rallied[8] him with great levity on his behaviour. He listened to his friend with calmness, but without any relaxation of features.

"One thing," said he with emphasis, "is true; either I heard my wife's voice at the bottom of the hill, or I do not hear your voice at present."

"Truly," returned Pleyel, "it is a sad dilemma to which you have reduced yourself. Certain it is, if our eyes can give us certainty, that your wife has been sitting in that spot during every moment of your absence. You have heard her voice, you say, upon the hill. In general, her voice, like her temper, is all softness. To be heard across the room, she is obliged to exert herself. While you were gone, if I mistake not, she did not utter a word. Clara and I had all the talk to ourselves. Still it may be that she held a whispering conference with you on the hill; but tell us the particulars."

"The conference," said he, "was short; and far from being carried on in a whisper. You know with what intention I left the house. Half way to the rock, the moon was for a moment hidden from us by a cloud. I never knew the air to be more bland and more calm. In this interval I glanced at the temple, and thought I saw a glimmering between the columns. It was so faint, that it would not perhaps have been visible, if the moon had not been shrouded. I looked again, but saw nothing. I never visit this building alone, or at night, without being reminded of the fate of my father. There was nothing wonder-

8. Teased.

ful in this appearance; yet it suggested something more than mere solitude and darkness in the same place would have done.

"I kept on my way. The images that haunted me were solemn; and I entertained an imperfect curiosity, but no fear, as to the nature of this object. I had ascended the hill little more than half way, when a voice called me from behind. The accents were clear, distinct, powerful, and were uttered, as I fully believed, by my wife. Her voice is not commonly so loud. She has seldom occasion to exert it, but, nevertheless, I have sometimes heard her call with force and eagerness. If my ear was not deceived, it was her voice which I heard.

"'Stop, go no further. There is danger in your path.' The suddenness and unexpectedness of this warning, the tone of alarm with which it was given, and, above all, the persuasion that it was my wife who spoke, were enough to disconcert and make me pause. I turned and listened to assure myself that I was not mistaken. The deepest silence succeeded. At length, I spoke in my turn. 'Who calls? is it you, Catharine?' I stopped and presently received an answer. 'Yes, it is I; go not up; return instantly; you are wanted at the house.' Still the voice was Catharine's, and still it proceeded from the foot of the stairs.

"What could I do? The warning was mysterious. To be uttered by Catharine at a place, and on an occasion like these, enhanced the mystery. I could do nothing but obey. Accordingly, I trod back my steps, expecting that she waited for me at the bottom of the hill. When I reached the bottom, no one was visible. The moon-light was once more universal and brilliant, and yet, as far as I could see no human or moving figure was discernable. If she had returned to the house, she must have used wonderous expedition to have passed already beyond the reach of my eye. I exerted my voice, but in vain. To my repeated exclamations, no answer was returned.

"Ruminating on these incidents, I returned hither. There was no room to doubt that I had heard my wife's voice; attending incidents were not easily explained; but you now assure me that nothing extraordinary has happened to urge my return, and that my wife has not moved from her seat."

Such was my brother's narrative. It was heard by us with different emotions. Pleyel did not scruple to regard the whole as a deception of the senses. Perhaps a voice had been heard; but Wieland's imagination had misled him in supposing a resemblance to that of his wife, and giving such a signification to the sounds. According to his custom he spoke what he thought. Sometimes, he made it the theme of grave discussion, but more frequently treated it with ridicule. He did not believe that sober reasoning would convince his friend, and gaiety, he thought, was useful to take away the solemnities which, in a mind like Wieland's, an accident of this kind was calculated to produce.

Pleyel proposed to go in search of the letter. He went and speedily
returned, bearing it in his hand. He had found it open on the pedestal; and neither voice nor visage had risen to impede his design.

Catharine was endowed with an uncommon portion of good
sense; but her mind was accessible, on this quarter, to wonder and
panic. That her voice should be thus inexplicably and unwarrant-
ably assumed, was a source of no small disquietude. She admitted
the plausibility of the arguments by which Pleyel endeavoured to
prove, that this was no more than an auricular deception; but this
conviction was sure to be shaken, when she turned her eyes upon
her husband, and perceived that Pleyel's logic was far from having
produced the same effect upon him.

As to myself, my attention was engaged by this occurrence. I could
not fail to perceive a shadowy resemblance between it and my father's
death. On the latter event, I had frequently reflected; my reflections
never conducted me to certainty, but the doubts that existed were
not of a tormenting kind. I could not deny that the event was miraculous, and yet I was invincibly averse to that method of solution. My
wonder was excited by the inscrutableness of the cause, but my wonder was unmixed with sorrow or fear. It begat in me a thrilling, and
not unpleasing solemnity. Similar to these were the sensations produced by the recent adventure.

But its effect upon my brother's imagination was of chief moment.
All that was desirable was, that it should be regarded by him with
indifference. The worst effect that could flow, was not indeed very
formidable. Yet I could not bear to think that his senses should be
the victims of such delusion. It argued a diseased condition of his
frame, which might show itself hereafter in more dangerous symptoms. The will is the tool of the understanding, which must fashion
its conclusions on the notices of sense. If the senses be depraved, it
is impossible to calculate the evils that may flow from the consequent deductions of the understanding.

I said, this man is of an ardent and melancholy character. Those
ideas which, in others, are casual or obscure, which are entertained
in moments of abstraction and solitude, and easily escape when
the scene is changed, have obtained an immoveable hold upon his
mind. The conclusions which long habit has rendered familiar, and,
in some sort, palpable to his intellect, are drawn from the deepest
sources. All his actions and practical sentiments are linked with
long and abstruse deductions from the system of divine government
and the laws of our intellectual constitution. He is, in some respects,
an enthusiast, but is fortified in his belief by innumerable arguments
and subtilties.

His father's death was always regarded by him as flowing from a
direct and supernatural decree. It visited his meditations oftener

than it did mine. The traces which it left were more gloomy and permanent. This new incident had a visible effect in augmenting his gravity. He was less disposed than formerly to converse and reading. When we sifted his thoughts, they were generally found to have a relation, more or less direct, with this incident. It was difficult to ascertain the exact species of impression which it made upon him. He never introduced the subject into conversation, and listened with a silent and half-serious smile to the satirical effusions of Pleyel.

One evening we chanced to be alone together in the temple. I seized that opportunity of investigating the state of his thoughts. After a pause, which he seemed in no wise inclined to interrupt, I spoke to him—"How almost palpable is this dark; yet a ray from above would dispel it." "Ay," said Wieland, with fervor, "not only the physical, but moral night would be dispelled." "But why," said I, "must the Divine Will address its precepts to the eye?" He smiled significantly. "True," said he, "the understanding[9] has other avenues." "You have never," said I, approaching nearer to the point—"you have never told me in what way you considered the late extraordinary incident." "There is no determinate way in which the subject can be viewed. Here is an effect, but the cause is utterly inscrutable.[1] To suppose a deception will not do. Such is possible, but there are twenty other suppositions more probable. They must all be set aside before we reach that point." "What are these twenty suppositions?" "It is needless to mention them. They are only less improbable than Pleyel's. Time may convert one of them into certainty. Till then it is useless to expatiate on them."

Chapter V

Some time had elapsed when there happened another occurrence, still more remarkable. Pleyel, on his return from Europe, brought information of considerable importance to my brother. My ancestors were noble Saxons, and possessed large domains in Lusatia.[1] The Prussian wars had destroyed those persons whose right to these estates precluded my brother's. Pleyel had been exact in his

9. Eighteenth-century faculty psychology posited a central opposition between "the understanding" and "the will." The former encompassed powers of awareness and sensory experience; the latter involved a hierarchy of motivations or actions, from moral or rational motives, down to animal or emotional motives, and finally to mechanical or reflexive motives.
1. Theories of causation formed an important part of Enlightenment discussions of agency and epistemology. David Hume (1711–1776), for instance, argued that the connection between cause and effect is subject not to observation but to inference.
1. A part of Saxony, the site of religious and political conflict from the seventeenth to the nineteenth centuries.

inquiries, and had discovered that, by the law of male-primogeniture,[2] my brother's claims were superior to those of any other person now living. Nothing was wanting but his presence in that country, and a legal application to establish this claim.

Pleyel strenuously recommended this measure. The advantages he thought attending it were numerous, and it would argue the utmost folly to neglect them. Contrary to his expectation he found my brother averse to the scheme. Slight efforts, he, at first, thought would subdue his reluctance; but he found this aversion by no means slight. The interest that he took in the happiness of his friend and his sister, and his own partiality to the Saxon soil, from which he had likewise sprung, and where he had spent several years of his youth, made him redouble his exertions to win Wieland's consent. For this end he employed every argument that his invention could suggest. He painted, in attractive colours, the state of manners and government in that country, the security of civil rights, and the freedom of religious sentiments. He dwelt on the privileges of wealth and rank, and drew from the servile condition of one class, an argument in favor of his scheme, since the revenue and power annexed to a German principality afford so large a field for benevolence. The evil flowing from this power, in malignant hands, was proportioned to the good that would arise from the virtuous use of it. Hence, Wieland, in forbearing to claim his own, withheld all the positive felicity that would accrue to his vassals from his success, and hazarded all the misery that would redound from a less enlightened proprietor.

It was easy for my brother to repel these arguments, and to shew that no spot on the globe enjoyed equal security and liberty to that which he at present inhabited. That if the Saxons had nothing to fear from mis-government, the external causes of havoc and alarm were numerous and manifest. The recent devastations committed by the Prussians furnished a specimen of these. The horrors of war would always impend over them, till Germany were seized and divided by Austrian and Prussian tyrants; an event which he strongly suspected was at no great distance. But setting these considerations aside, was it laudable to grasp at wealth and power even when they were within our reach? Were not these the two great sources of depravity? What security had he, that in this change of place and condition, he should not degenerate into a tyrant and voluptuary? Power and riches were chiefly to be dreaded on account of their tendency to deprave the possessor. He held them in abhorrence, not only as instruments of misery to others, but to him on whom they were conferred. Besides, riches were comparative, and was he not

---

2. The law of inheritance by which property passes to the oldest son or male heir.

rich already? He lived at present in the bosom of security and luxury. All the instruments of pleasure, on which his reason or imagination set any value, were within his reach. But these he must forego, for the sake of advantages which, whatever were their value, were as yet uncertain. In pursuit of an imaginary addition to his wealth, he must reduce himself to poverty, he must exchange present certainties for what was distant and contingent; for who knows not that the law is a system of expence, delay and uncertainty? If he should embrace this scheme, it would lay him under the necessity of making a voyage to Europe, and remaining for a certain period, separate from his family. He must undergo the perils and discomforts of the ocean; he must divest himself of all domestic pleasures; he must deprive his wife of her companion, and his children of a father and instructor, and all for what? For the ambiguous advantages which overgrown wealth and flagitious[3] tyranny have to bestow? For a precarious possession in a land of turbulence and war? Advantages, which will not certainly be gained, and of which the acquisition, if it were sure, is necessarily distant.

Pleyel was enamoured of his scheme on account of its instrinsic benefits, but, likewise, for other reasons. His abode at Leipsig made that country appear to him like home. He was connected with this place by many social ties. While there he had not escaped the amorous contagion.[4] But the lady, though her heart was impressed in his favor, was compelled to bestow her hand upon another. Death had removed this impediment, and he was now invited by the lady herself to return. This he was of course determined to do, but was anxious to obtain the company of Wieland; he could not bear to think of an eternal separation from his present associates. Their interest, he thought, would be no less promoted by the change than his own. Hence he was importunate[5] and indefatigable in his arguments and solicitations.

He knew that he could not hope for mine or his sister's ready concurrence in this scheme. Should the subject be mentioned to us, we should league our efforts against him, and strengthen that reluctance in Wieland which already was sufficiently difficult to conquer. He, therefore, anxiously concealed from us his purpose. If Wieland were previously enlisted in his cause, he would find it a less difficult task to overcome our aversion. My brother was silent on this subject, because he believed himself in no danger of changing his opinion, and he was willing to save us from any uneasiness.

3. Criminal or villainous.
4. I.e., love.
5. Persistent.

The mere mention of such a scheme, and the possibility of his embracing it, he knew, would considerably impair our tranquillity.

One day, about three weeks subsequent to the mysterious call, it was agreed that the family should be my guests. Seldom had a day been passed by us, of more serene enjoyment. Pleyel had promised us his company, but we did not see him till the sun had nearly declined. He brought with him a countenance that betokened disappointment and vexation. He did not wait for our inquiries, but immediately explained the cause. Two days before a packet had arrived from Hamburgh, by which he had flattered himself with the expectation of receiving letters, but no letters had arrived. I never saw him so much subdued by an untoward event. His thoughts were employed in accounting for the silence of his friends. He was seized with the torments of jealousy, and suspected nothing less than the infidelity of her to whom he had devoted his heart. The silence must have been concerted. Her sickness, or absence, or death, would have increased the certainty of some one's having written. No supposition could be formed but that his mistress had grown indifferent, or that she had transferred her affections to another. The miscarriage of a letter was hardly within the reach of possibility. From Leipsig to Hamburgh,[6] and from Hamburgh hither, the conveyance was exposed to no hazard.

He had been so long detained in America chiefly in consequence of Wieland's aversion to the scheme which he proposed. He now became more impatient than ever to return to Europe. When he reflected that, by his delays, he had probably forfeited the affections of his mistress, his sensations amounted to agony. It only remained, by his speedy departure, to repair, if possible, or prevent so intolerable an evil. Already he had half resolved to embark in this very ship which, he was informed, would set out in a few weeks on her return.

Meanwhile he determined to make a new attempt to shake the resolution of Wieland. The evening was somewhat advanced when he invited the latter to walk abroad with him. The invitation was accepted, and they left Catharine, Louisa and me, to amuse ourselves by the best means in our power. During this walk, Pleyel renewed the subject that was nearest his heart. He re-urged all his former arguments, and placed them in more forcible lights.

They promised to return shortly; but hour after hour passed, and they made not their appearance. Engaged in sprightly conversation, it was not till the clock struck twelve that we were reminded of the lapse of time. The absence of our friends excited some uneasy apprehensions. We were expressing our fears, and comparing our conjectures as to what might be the cause, when they entered together.

6. Hamburg was a significant European port at the time.

There were indications in their countenances that struck me mute. These were unnoticed by Catharine, who was eager to express her surprize and curiosity at the length of their walk. As they listened to her, I remarked that their surprize was not less than ours. They gazed in silence on each other, and on her. I watched their looks, but could not understand the emotions that were written in them.

These appearances diverted Catharine's inquiries into a new channel. What did they mean, she asked, by their silence, and by their thus gazing wildly at each other, and at her? Pleyel profited by this hint, and assuming an air of indifference, framed some trifling excuse, at the same time darting significant glances at Wieland, as if to caution him against disclosing the truth. My brother said nothing, but delivered himself up to meditation. I likewise was silent, but burned with impatience to fathom this mystery. Presently my brother and his wife, and Louisa, returned home. Pleyel proposed, of his own accord, to be my guest for the night. This circumstance, in addition to those which preceded, gave new edge to my wonder.

As soon as we were left alone, Pleyel's countenance assumed an air of seriousness, and even consternation, which I had never before beheld in him. The steps with which he measured the floor betokened the trouble of his thoughts. My inquiries were suspended by the hope that he would give me the information that I wanted without the importunity of questions. I waited some time, but the confusion of his thoughts appeared in no degree to abate. At length I mentioned the apprehensions which their unusual absence had occasioned, and which were increased by their behaviour since their return, and solicited an explanation. He stopped when I began to speak, and looked stedfastly at me. When I had done, he said, to me, in a tone which faultered through the vehemence of his emotions, "How were you employed during our absence?" "In turning over the Della Crusca dictionary,[7] and talking on different subjects; but just before your entrance, we were tormenting ourselves with omens and prognosticks relative to your absence." "Catharine was with you the whole time?" "Yes." "But are you sure?" "Most sure. She was not absent a moment." He stood, for a time, as if to assure himself of my sincerity. Then, clenching his hands, and wildly lifting them above his head, "Lo," cried he, "I have news to tell you. The Baroness de Stolberg[8] is dead!"

---

7. The *Vocabulario della Crusca* (1612), published in Florence by the Accademia della Crusca in an attempt to purify the Italian language.
8. Pleyel's intended belongs to the Saxon nobility. Her surname is shared by the German travel writer Friederich von Stolberg, whose *Travels through Germany, Switzerland, Italy, and Sicily* was well known to English readers and excerpted in Brown's later literary magazines.

This was her whom he loved. I was not surprised at the agitations which he betrayed. But how was the information procured? How was the truth of this news connected with the circumstance of Catharine's remaining in our company? He was for some time inattentive to my questions. When he spoke, it seemed merely a continuation of the reverie into which he had been plunged.

"And yet it might be a mere deception. But could both of us in that case have been deceived? A rare and prodigious coincidence! Barely not impossible. And yet, if the accent be oracular—Theresa is dead. No, no," continued he, covering his face with his hands, and in a tone half broken into sobs, "I cannot believe it. She has not written, but if she were dead, the faithful Bertrand would have given me the earliest information. And yet if he knew his master, he must have easily guessed at the effect of such tidings. In pity to me he was silent.

"Clara, forgive me; to you, this behaviour is mysterious. I will explain as well as I am able. But say not a word to Catharine. Her strength of mind is inferior to your's. She will, besides, have more reason to be startled. She is Wieland's angel."

Pleyel proceeded to inform me, for the first time, of the scheme which he had pressed, with so much earnestness, on my brother. He enumerated the objections which had been made, and the industry with which he had endeavoured to confute them. He mentioned the effect upon his resolutions produced by the failure of a letter. "During our late walk," continued he, "I introduced the subject that was nearest my heart. I re-urged all my former arguments, and placed them in more forcible lights. Wieland was still refractory.[9] He expatiated on the perils of wealth and power, on the sacredness of conjugal and parental duties, and the happiness of mediocrity.[1]

"No wonder that the time passed, unperceived, away. Our whole souls were engaged in this cause. Several times we came to the foot of the rock; as soon as we perceived it, we changed our course, but never failed to terminate our circuitous and devious ramble at this spot. At length your brother observed, 'We seem to be led hither by a kind of fatality. Since we are so near, let us ascend and rest ourselves a while. If you are not weary of this argument we will resume it there.'

"I tacitly consented. We mounted the stairs, and drawing the sofa in front of the river, we seated ourselves upon it. I took up the thread of our discourse where we had dropped it. I ridiculed his dread of the sea, and his attachment to home. I kept on in this strain, so congenial with my disposition, for some time, uninterrupted by him. At length,

9. Stubborn.
1. The connotation here is positive: contentment with a moderate station in life.

he said to me, 'Suppose now that I, whom argument has not convinced, should yield to ridicule, and should agree that your scheme is eligible; what will you have gained? Nothing. You have other enemies beside myself to encounter. When you have vanquished me, your toil has scarcely begun. There are my sister and wife, with whom it will remain for you to maintain the contest. And trust me, they are adversaries whom all your force and stratagem will never subdue.' I insinuated that they would model themselves by his will: that Catharine would think obedience her duty. He answered, with some quickness, 'You mistake. Their concurrence is indispensable. It is not my custom to exact sacrifices of this kind. I live to be their protector and friend, and not their tyrant and foe. If my wife shall deem her happiness, and that of her children, most consulted by remaining where she is, here she shall remain.' 'But,' said I, 'when she knows your pleasure, will she not conform to it?' Before my friend had time to answer this question, a negative was clearly and distinctly uttered from another quarter. It did not come from one side or the other, from before us or behind. Whence then did it come? By whose organs was it fashioned?

"If any uncertainty had existed with regard to these particulars, it would have been removed by a deliberate and equally distinct repetition of the same monosyllable, 'No.' The voice was my sister's. It appeared to come from the roof. I started from my seat. 'Catharine,' exclaimed I, 'where are you?' No answer was returned. I searched the room, and the area before it, but in vain. Your brother was motionless in his seat. I returned to him, and placed myself again by his side. My astonishment was not less than his.

"'Well,' said he, at length, 'What think you of this? This is the self-same voice which I formerly heard; you are now convinced that my ears were well informed.'

"'Yes,' said I, 'this, it is plain, is no fiction of the fancy.' We again sunk into mutual and thoughtful silence. A recollection of the hour, and of the length of our absence, made me at last propose to return. We rose up for this purpose. In doing this, my mind reverted to the contemplation of my own condition. 'Yes,' said I aloud, but without particularly addressing myself to Wieland, 'my resolution is taken. I cannot hope to prevail with my friends to accompany me. They may doze away their days on the banks of Schuylkill, but as to me, I go in the next vessel; I will fly to her presence, and demand the reason of this extraordinary silence.'

"I had scarcely finished the sentence, when the same mysterious voice exclaimed, 'You shall not go. The seal of death is on her lips. Her silence is the silence of the tomb.' Think of the effects which accents like these must have had upon me. I shuddered as I listened. As soon as I recovered from my first amazement, 'Who is it

that speaks?' said I, 'whence did you procure these dismal tidings?'
I did not wait long for an answer. 'From a source that cannot fail.
Be satisfied. She is dead.' You may justly be surprised, that, in the
circumstances in which I heard the tidings, and notwithstanding
the mystery which environed him by whom they were imparted, I
could give an undivided attention to the facts, which were the subject of our dialogue. I eagerly inquired, when and where did she
die? What was the cause of her death? Was her death absolutely
certain? An answer was returned only to the last of these questions.
'Yes,' was pronounced by the same voice; but it now sounded from a
greater distance, and the deepest silence was all the return made to
my subsequent interrogatories.

"It was my sister's voice; but it could not be uttered by her; and
yet, if not by her, by whom was it uttered? When we returned
hither, and discovered you together, the doubt that had previously
existed was removed. It was manifest that the intimation came not
from her. Yet if not from her, from whom could it come? Are the
circumstances attending the imparting of this news proof that the
tidings are true? God forbid that they should be true."

Here Pleyel sunk into anxious silence, and gave me leisure to
ruminate on this inexplicable event. I am at a loss to describe the
sensations that affected me. I am not fearful of shadows. The tales
of apparitions and enchantments did not possess that power over
my belief which could even render them interesting. I saw nothing
in them but ignorance and folly, and was a stranger even to that terror which is pleasing. But this incident was different from any that
I had ever before known. Here were proofs of a sensible and intelligent existence, which could not be denied. Here was information
obtained and imparted by means unquestionably super-human.

That there are conscious beings, beside ourselves, in existence,
whose modes of activity and information surpass our own, can
scarcely be denied. Is there a glimpse afforded us into a world of
these superior beings? My heart was scarcely large enough to give
admittance to so swelling a thought. An awe, the sweetest and most
solemn that imagination can conceive, pervaded my whole frame. It
forsook me not when I parted from Pleyel and retired to my chamber. An impulse was given to my spirits utterly incompatible with
sleep. I passed the night wakeful and full of meditation. I was
impressed with the belief of mysterious, but not of malignant agency.
Hitherto nothing had occurred to persuade me that this airy minister was busy to evil rather than to good purposes. On the contrary,
the idea of superior virtue had always been associated in my mind
with that of superior power. The warnings that had thus been heard
appeared to have been prompted by beneficent intentions. My
brother had been hindered by this voice from ascending the hill. He

was told that danger lurked in his path, and his obedience to the intimation had perhaps saved him from a destiny similar to that of my father.

Pleyel had been rescued from tormenting uncertainty, and from the hazards and fatigues of a fruitless voyage, by the same interposition. It had assured him of the death of his Theresa.

This woman was then dead. A confirmation of the tidings, if true, would speedily arrive. Was this confirmation to be deprecated or desired? By her death, the tie that attached him to Europe, was taken away. Henceforward every motive would combine to retain him in his native country, and we were rescued from the deep regrets that would accompany his hopeless absence from us. Propitious was the spirit that imparted these tidings. Propitious he would perhaps have been, if he had been instrumental in producing, as well as in communicating the tidings of her death. Propitious to us, the friends of Pleyel, to whom has thereby been secured the enjoyment of his society; and not unpropitious to himself; for though this object of his love be snatched away, is there not another who is able and willing to console him for her loss?

Twenty days after this, another vessel arrived from the same port. In this interval, Pleyel, for the most part, estranged himself from his old companions. He was become the prey of a gloomy and unsociable grief. His walks were limited to the bank of the Delaware. This bank is an artificial one. Reeds and the river are on one side, and a watery marsh on the other, in that part which bounded his lands, and which extended from the mouth of Hollander's creek[2] to that of Schuylkill. No scene can be imagined less enticing to a lover of the picturesque than this. The shore is deformed with mud, and incumbered with a forest of reeds. The fields, in most seasons, are mire; but when they afford a firm footing, the ditches by which they are bounded and intersected, are mantled with stagnating green, and emit the most noxious exhalations. Health is no less a stranger to those seats than pleasure. Spring and autumn are sure to be accompanied with agues and bilious remittents.[3]

The scenes which environed our dwellings at Mettingen constituted the reverse of this. Schuylkill was here a pure and translucid current, broken into wild and ceaseless music by rocky points, murmuring on a sandy margin, and reflecting on its surface, banks of all varieties of height and degrees of declivity. These banks were chequered by patches of dark verdure and shapeless masses of white marble, and crowned by copses of cedar, or by the regular magnificence of orchards, which, at this season, were in blossom, and were

2. Between two and three miles south of Philadelphia.
3. Fevers.

prodigal of odours. The ground which receded from the river was scooped into valleys and dales. Its beauties were enhanced by the horticultural skill of my brother, who bedecked this exquisite assemblage of slopes and risings with every species of vegetable ornament, from the giant arms of the oak to the clustering tendrils of the honey-suckle.

To screen him from the unwholesome airs of his own residence, it had been proposed to Pleyel to spend the months of spring with us. He had apparently acquiesced in this proposal; but the late event induced him to change his purpose. He was only to be seen by visiting him in his retirements. His gaiety had flown, and every passion was absorbed in eagerness to procure tidings from Saxony. I have mentioned the arrival of another vessel from the Elbe.[4] He descried her early one morning as he was passing along the skirt of the river. She was easily recognized, being the ship in which he had performed his first voyage to Germany. He immediately went on board, but found no letters directed to him. This omission was, in some degree, compensated by meeting with an old acquaintance among the passengers, who had till lately been a resident in Leipsig. This person put an end to all suspense respecting the fate of Theresa, by relating the particulars of her death and funeral.

Thus was the truth of the former intimation attested. No longer devoured by suspense, the grief of Pleyel was not long in yielding to the influence of society. He gave himself up once more to our company. His vivacity had indeed been damped; but even in this respect he was a more acceptable companion than formerly, since his seriousness was neither incommunicative nor sullen.

These incidents, for a time, occupied all our thoughts. In me they produced a sentiment not unallied to pleasure, and more speedily than in the case of my friends were intermixed with other topics. My brother was particularly affected by them. It was easy to perceive that most of his meditations were tinctured from this source. To this was to be ascribed a design in which his pen was, at this period, engaged, of collecting and investigating the facts which relate to that mysterious personage, the Dæmon of Socrates.[5]

My brother's skill in Greek and Roman learning was exceeded by that of few, and no doubt the world would have accepted a treatise upon this subject from his hand with avidity; but alas! this and

4. River in Saxony that would connect Leipzig to Hamburg and the port of Hamburg to the North Sea.
5. In Plato's *Symposium*, Socrates is instructed by the priestess Diotima that love is a "dæmon" mediating between divine and human concerns. In the *Apology*, Socrates describes his dæmon as a spirit whose voice protects him from missteps. In part for these claims, Socrates was tried for heresy and condemned to death in 399 B.C.E. Whether this dæmon was supernatural or a function of Socrates's own rational behavior was a matter of dispute from antiquity to Brown's time.

every other scheme of felicity and honor, were doomed to sudden blast and hopeless extermination.

Chapter VI

I now come to the mention of a person with whose name the most turbulent sensations are connected. It is with a shuddering reluctance that I enter on the province of describing him. Now it is that I begin to perceive the difficulty of the task which I have undertaken; but it would be weakness to shrink from it. My blood is congealed: and my fingers are palsied when I call up his image. Shame upon my cowardly and infirm heart! Hitherto I have proceeded with some degree of composure, but now I must pause. I mean not that dire remembrance shall subdue my courage or baffle my design, but this weakness cannot be immediately conquered. I must desist for a little while.

I have taken a few turns in my chamber, and have gathered strength enough to proceed. Yet have I not projected a task beyond my power to execute? If thus, on the very threshold of the scene, my knees faulter and I sink, how shall I support myself, when I rush into the midst of horrors such as no heart has hitherto conceived, nor tongue related? I sicken and recoil at the prospect, and yet my irresolution is momentary. I have not formed this design upon slight grounds, and though I may at times pause and hesitate, I will not be finally diverted from it.

And thou, O most fatal and potent of mankind, in what terms shall I describe thee? What words are adequate to the just delineation of thy character? How shall I detail the means which rendered the secrecy of thy purposes unfathomable? But I will not anticipate. Let me recover if possible, a sober strain. Let me keep down the flood of passion that would render me precipitate or powerless. Let me stifle the agonies that are awakened by thy name. Let me, for a time, regard thee as a being of no terrible attributes. Let me tear myself from contemplation of the evils of which it is but too certain that thou wast the author, and limit my view to those harmless appearances which attended thy entrance on the stage.

One sunny afternoon, I was standing in the door of my house, when I marked a person passing close to the edge of the bank that was in front. His pace was a careless and lingering one, and had none of that gracefulness and ease which distinguish a person with certain advantages of education from a clown.[1] His gait was rustic and aukward. His form was ungainly and disproportioned. Shoulders

1. A rustic.

broad and square, breast sunken, his head drooping, his body of uniform breadth, supported by long and lank legs, were the ingredients of his frame. His garb was not ill adapted to such a figure. A slouched hat, tarnished by the weather, a coat of thick grey cloth, cut and wrought, as it seemed, by a country tailor, blue worsted[2] stockings, and shoes fastened by thongs, and deeply discoloured by dust, which brush had never disturbed, constituted his dress.

There was nothing remarkable in these appearances; they were frequently to be met with on the road, and in the harvest field. I cannot tell why I gazed upon them, on this occasion, with more than ordinary attention, unless it were that such figures were seldom seen by me, except on the road or field. This lawn was only traversed by men whose views were directed to the pleasures of the walk, or the grandeur of the scenery.

He passed slowly along, frequently pausing, as if to examine the prospect more deliberately, but never turning his eye towards the house, so as to allow me a view of his countenance. Presently, he entered a copse at a small distance, and disappeared. My eye followed him while he remained in sight. If his image remained for any duration in my fancy after his departure, it was because no other object occurred sufficient to expel it.

I continued in the same spot for half an hour, vaguely, and by fits, contemplating the image of this wanderer, and drawing, from outward appearances, those inferences with respect to the intellectual history of this person, which experience affords us. I reflected on the alliance which commonly subsists between ignorance and the practice of agriculture, and indulged myself in airy speculations as to the influence of progressive knowledge in dissolving this alliance, and embodying the dreams of the poets.[3] I asked why the plough and the hoe might not become the trade of every human being, and how this trade might be made conducive to, or, at least, consistent with the acquisition of wisdom and eloquence.

Weary with these reflections, I returned to the kitchen to perform some household office. I had usually but one servant, and she was a girl about my own age. I was busy near the chimney, and she was employed near the door of the apartment, when some one knocked. The door was opened by her, and she was immediately addressed with "Pry'thee, good girl, canst thou supply a thirsty man with a glass of buttermilk?" She answered that there was none in the house. "Aye, but there is some in the dairy yonder. Thou knowest as well as I, though Hermes[4] never taught thee, that though every dairy be an

2. Woolen.
3. I.e., the pastoral reverence for rural landscape and agriculture.
4. In Greek mythology, the messenger of the gods and the mediator between divine and human realms (as in his delivery of Pandora to the mortal world). Also the god of

house, every house is not a dairy." To this speech, though she understood only a part of it, she replied by repeating her assurances, that
she had none to give. "Well then," rejoined the stranger, "for charity's
sweet sake, hand me forth a cup of cold water." The girl said she
would go to the spring and fetch it. "Nay, give me the cup, and suffer
me to help myself. Neither manacled nor lame, I should merit burial
in the maw of carrion crows, if I laid this task upon thee." She gave
him the cup, and he turned to go to the spring.

I listened to this dialogue in silence. The words uttered by the
person without, affected me as somewhat singular, but what chiefly
rendered them remarkable, was the tone that accompanied them. It
was wholly new. My brother's voice and Pleyel's were musical and
energetic. I had fondly imagined, that, in this respect, they were
surpassed by none. Now my mistake was detected. I cannot pretend
to communicate the impression that was made upon me by these
accents, or to depict the degree in which force and sweetness were
blended in them. They were articulated with a distinctness that was
unexampled in my experience. But this was not all. The voice was
not only mellifluent[5] and clear, but the emphasis was so just, and
the modulation so impassioned, that it seemed as if an heart of
stone could not fail of being moved by it. It imparted to me an emotion altogether involuntary and incontroulable. When he uttered
the words "for charity's sweet sake," I dropped the cloth that I held
in my hand, my heart overflowed with sympathy, and my eyes with
unbidden tears.

This description will appear to you trifling or incredible. The
importance of these circumstances will be manifested in the
sequel. The manner in which I was affected on this occasion, was,
to my own apprehension, a subject of astonishment. The tones were
indeed such as I never heard before; but that they should, in an
instant, as it were, dissolve me in tears, will not easily be believed
by others, and can scarcely be comprehended by myself.

It will be readily supposed that I was somewhat inquisitive as to
the person and demeanour of our visitant. After a moment's pause,
I stepped to the door and looked after him. Judge my surprize,
when I beheld the self-same figure that had appeared an half hour
before upon the bank. My fancy had conjured up a very different
image. A form, and attitude, and garb, were instantly created worthy to accompany such elocution; but this person was, in all visible
respects, the reverse of this phantom. Strange as it may seem, I
could not speedily reconcile myself to this disappointment. Instead

---

communication, commerce, travel, and thievery. Many legends associate Hermes with
stolen cattle; his first act after birth was the theft of Apollo's cattle.
5. Flowing sweetly.

of returning to my employment, I threw myself in a chair that was placed opposite the door, and sunk into a fit of musing.

My attention was, in a few minutes, recalled by the stranger, who returned with the empty cup in his hand. I had not thought of the circumstance, or should certainly have chosen a different seat. He no sooner shewed himself, than a confused sense of impropriety, added to the suddenness of the interview, for which, not having foreseen it, I had made no preparation, threw me into a state of the most painful embarrassment. He brought with him a placid brow; but no sooner had he cast his eyes upon me, than his face was as glowingly suffused as my own. He placed the cup upon the bench, stammered out thanks, and retired.

It was some time before I could recover my wonted composure. I had snatched a view of the stranger's countenance. The impression that it made was vivid and indelible. His cheeks were pallid and lank, his eyes sunken, his forehead overshadowed by coarse straggling hairs, his teeth large and irregular, though sound and brilliantly white, and his chin discoloured by a tetter.[6] His skin was of coarse grain, and sallow hue. Every feature was wide of beauty, and the outline of his face reminded you of an inverted cone.

And yet his forehead, so far as shaggy locks would allow it to be seen, his eyes lustrously black, and possessing, in the midst of haggardness, a radiance inexpressibly serene and potent, and something in the rest of his features, which it would be in vain to describe, but which served to betoken a mind of the highest order, were essential ingredients in the portrait. This, in the effects which immediately flowed from it, I count among the most extraordinary incidents of my life. This face, seen for a moment, continued for hours to occupy my fancy, to the exclusion of almost every other image. I had purposed to spend the evening with my brother, but I could not resist the inclination of forming a sketch upon paper of this memorable visage. Whether my hand was aided by any peculiar inspiration, or I was deceived by my own fond conceptions, this portrait, though hastily executed, appeared unexceptionable to my own taste.

I placed it at all distances, and in all lights; my eyes were rivetted upon it. Half the night passed away in wakefulness and in contemplation of this picture. So flexible, and yet so stubborn, is the human mind. So obedient to impulses the most transient and brief, and yet so unalterably observant of the direction which is given to it! How little did I then foresee the termination of that chain, of which this may be regarded as the first link?

Next day arose in darkness and storm. Torrents of rain fell during the whole day, attended with incessant thunder, which reverberated

6. A skin irritation, possibly ringworm or herpes.

in stunning echoes from the opposite declivity. The inclemency of the air would not allow me to walk out. I had, indeed, no inclination to leave my apartment. I betook myself to the contemplation of this portrait, whose attractions time had rather enhanced than diminished. I laid aside my usual occupations, and seating myself at a window, consumed the day in alternately looking out upon the storm, and gazing at the picture which lay upon a table before me. You will, perhaps, deem this conduct somewhat singular, and ascribe it to certain peculiarities of temper. I am not aware of any such peculiarities. I can account for my devotion to this image no otherwise, than by supposing that its properties were rare and prodigious. Perhaps you will suspect that such were the first inroads of a passion incident to every female heart, and which frequently gains a footing by means even more slight, and more improbable than these. I shall not controvert the reasonableness of the suspicion, but leave you at liberty to draw, from my narrative, what conclusions you please.

Night at length returned, and the storm ceased. The air was once more clear and calm, and bore an affecting contrast to that uproar of the elements by which it had been preceded. I spent the darksome hours, as I spent the day, contemplative and seated at the window. Why was my mind absorbed in thoughts ominous and dreary? Why did my bosom heave with sighs, and my eyes overflow with tears? Was the tempest that had just past a signal of the ruin which impended over me? My soul fondly dwelt upon the images of my brother and his children, yet they only increased the mournfulness of my contemplations. The smiles of the charming babes were as bland as formerly. The same dignity sat on the brow of their father, and yet I thought of them with anguish. Something whispered that the happiness we at present enjoyed was set on mutable foundations. Death must happen to all. Whether our felicity was to be subverted by it to-morrow, or whether it was ordained that we should lay down our heads full of years and of honor, was a question that no human being could solve. At other times, these ideas seldom intruded. I either forbore to reflect upon the destiny that is reserved for all men, or the reflection was mixed up with images that disrobed it of terror; but now the uncertainty of life occurred to me without any of its usual and alleviating accompaniments. I said to myself, we must die. Sooner or later, we must disappear for ever from the face of the earth. Whatever be the links that hold us to life, they must be broken. This scene of existence is, in all its parts, calamitous. The greater number is oppressed with immediate evils, and those, the tide of whose fortunes is full, how small is their portion of enjoyment, since they know that it will terminate.

For some time I indulged myself, without reluctance, in these gloomy thoughts; but at length, the dejection which they produced

became insupportably painful. I endeavoured to dissipate it with
music. I had all my grand-father's melody as well as poetry by rote.
I now lighted by chance on a ballad, which commemorated the fate
of a German Cavalier, who fell at the siege of Nice under Godfrey
of Bouillon.[7] My choice was unfortunate, for the scenes of violence
and carnage which were here wildly but forcibly pourtrayed, only
suggested to my thoughts a new topic in the horrors of war.

I sought refuge, but ineffectually, in sleep. My mind was thronged
by vivid, but confused images, and no effort that I made was sufficient to drive them away. In this situation I heard the clock, which
hung in the room, give the signal for twelve. It was the same instrument which formerly hung in my father's chamber, and which, on
account of its being his workmanship, was regarded, by every one
of our family, with veneration. It had fallen to me, in the division of
his property, and was placed in this asylum. The sound awakened a
series of reflections, respecting his death. I was not allowed to pursue them; for scarcely had the vibrations ceased, when my attention
was attracted by a whisper, which, at first, appeared to proceed from
lips that were laid close to my ear.

No wonder that a circumstance like this startled me. In the first
impulse of my terror, I uttered a slight scream, and shrunk to the
opposite side of the bed. In a moment, however, I recovered from my
trepidation. I was habitually indifferent to all the causes of fear, by
which the majority are afflicted. I entertained no apprehension of
either ghosts or robbers. Our security had never been molested by
either, and I made use of no means to prevent or counterwork their
machinations. My tranquillity, on this occasion, was quickly retrieved.
The whisper evidently proceeded from one who was posted at my
bed-side. The first idea that suggested itself was, that it was uttered
by the girl who lived with me as a servant. Perhaps, somewhat had
alarmed her, or she was sick, and had come to request my assistance. By whispering in my ear, she intended to rouse without
alarming me.

Full of this persuasion, I called; "Judith," said I, "is it you? What
do you want? Is there any thing the matter with you?" No answer
was returned. I repeated my inquiry, but equally in vain. Cloudy as
was the atmosphere, and curtained as my bed was, nothing was visible. I withdrew the curtain, and leaning my head on my elbow,
I listened with the deepest attention to catch some new sound.

---

7. A Frankish leader of the First Crusade who helped take Nicaea (in modern-day Turkey)
in 1097. The First Crusade saw the capture of Jerusalem and much of Palestine. Godfrey
established himself as a ruler in Jerusalem. "Ballad": resembles Gottfried Bürger's
Lenore (1773), translated from German into several English versions in the 1790s.
Bürger (1747–1794) set his version of this gothic ballad during the Seven Years' War, but
some English translations, including one published in the Philadelphia *Weekly Magazine*
in March 1798, changed the setting to the Crusades (in this case, the Third Crusade).

Meanwhile, I ran over in my thoughts, every circumstance that could assist my conjectures.

My habitation was a wooden edifice, consisting of two stories. In each story were two rooms, separated by an entry, or middle passage, with which they communicated by opposite doors. The passage, on the lower story, had doors at the two ends, and a stair-case. Windows answered to the doors on the upper story. Annexed to this, on the eastern side, were wings, divided, in like manner, into an upper and lower room; one of them comprized a kitchen, and chamber above it for the servant, and communicated, on both stories, with the parlour adjoining it below, and the chamber adjoining it above. The opposite wing is of smaller dimensions, the rooms not being above eight feet square. The lower of these was used as a depository of household implements, the upper was a closet in which I deposited my books and papers. They had but one inlet, which was from the room adjoining. There was no window in the lower one, and in the upper, a small aperture which communicated light and air, but would scarcely admit the body. The door which led into this, was close to my bed-head, and was always locked, but when I myself was within. The avenues below were accustomed to be closed and bolted at nights.

The maid was my only companion, and she could not reach my chamber without previously passing through the opposite chamber, and the middle passage, of which, however, the doors were usually unfastened. If she had occasioned this noise, she would have answered my repeated calls. No other conclusion, therefore, was left me, but that I had mistaken the sounds, and that my imagination had transformed some casual noise into the voice of a human creature. Satisfied with this solution, I was preparing to relinquish my listening attitude, when my ear was again saluted with a new and yet louder whispering. It appeared, as before, to issue from lips that touched my pillow. A second effort of attention, however, clearly shewed me, that the sounds issued from within the closet, the door of which was not more than eight inches from my pillow.

This second interruption occasioned a shock less vehement than the former. I started, but gave no audible token of alarm. I was so much mistress of my feelings, as to continue listening to what should be said. The whisper was distinct, hoarse, and uttered so as to shew that the speaker was desirous of being heard by some one near, but, at the same time, studious to avoid being overheard by any other.

"Stop, stop, I say; madman as you are! there are better means than that. Curse upon your rashness! There is no need to shoot."

Such were the words uttered in a tone of eagerness and anger, within so small a distance of my pillow. What construction could I put upon them? My heart began to palpitate with dread of some unknown danger. Presently, another voice, but equally near me, was heard whispering in answer. "Why not? I will draw a trigger in this business, but perdition be my lot if I do more." To this, the first voice returned, in a tone which rage had heightened in a small degree above a whisper, "Coward! stand aside, and see me do it. I will grasp her throat; I will do her business in an instant; she shall not have time so much as to groan." What wonder that I was petrified by sounds so dreadful! Murderers lurked in my closet. They were planning the means of my destruction. One resolved to shoot, and the other menaced suffocation. Their means being chosen, they would forthwith break the door. Flight instantly suggested itself as most eligible in circumstances so perilous. I deliberated not a moment; but, fear adding wings to my speed, I leaped out of bed, and scantily robed as I was, rushed out of the chamber, down stairs, and into the open air. I can hardly recollect the process of turning keys, and withdrawing bolts. My terrors urged me forward with almost a mechanical impulse. I stopped not till I reached my brother's door. I had not gained the threshold, when, exhausted by the violence of my emotions, and by my speed, I sunk down in a fit.

How long I remained in this situation I know not. When I recovered, I found myself stretched on a bed, surrounded by my sister and her female servants. I was astonished at the scene before me, but gradually recovered the recollection of what had happened. I answered their importunate inquiries as well as I was able. My brother and Pleyel, whom the storm of the preceding day chanced to detain here, informing themselves of every particular, proceeded with lights and weapons to my deserted habitation. They entered my chamber and my closet, and found every thing in its proper place and customary order. The door of the closet was locked, and appeared not to have been opened in my absence. They went to Judith's apartment. They found her asleep and in safety. Pleyel's caution induced him to forbear alarming the girl; and finding her wholly ignorant of what had passed, they directed her to return to her chamber. They then fastened the doors, and returned.

My friends were disposed to regard this transaction as a dream. That persons should be actually immured in this closet, to which, in the circumstances of the time, access from without or within was apparently impossible, they could not seriously believe. That any human beings had intended murder, unless it were to cover a scheme of pillage, was incredible; but that no such design had been formed, was evident from the security in which the furniture of the house and the closet remained.

I revolved every incident and expression that had occurred. My senses assured me of the truth of them, and yet their abruptness and improbability made me, in my turn, somewhat incredulous.

The adventure had made a deep impression on my fancy, and it was not till after a week's abode at my brother's, that I resolved to resume the possession of my own dwelling.

There was another circumstance that enhanced the mysteriousness of this event. After my recovery it was obvious to inquire by what means the attention of the family had been drawn to my situation. I had fallen before I had reached the threshold, or was able to give any signal. My brother related, that while this was transacting in my chamber, he himself was awake, in consequence of some slight indisposition, and lay, according to his custom, musing on some favorite topic. Suddenly the silence, which was remarkably profound, was broken by a voice of most piercing shrillness, that seemed to be uttered by one in the hall below his chamber. "Awake! arise!" it exclaimed: "hasten to succour one that is dying at your door."

This summons was effectual. There was no one in the house who was not roused by it. Pleyel was the first to obey, and my brother overtook him before he reached the hall. What was the general astonishment when your friend was discovered stretched upon the grass before the door, pale, ghastly, and with every mark of death!

This was the third instance of a voice, exerted for the benefit of this little community. The agent was no less inscrutable in this, than in the former case. When I ruminated upon these events, my soul was suspended in wonder and awe. Was I really deceived in imagining that I heard the closet conversation? I was no longer at liberty to question the reality of those accents which had formerly recalled my brother from the hill; which had imparted tidings of the death of the German lady to Pleyel; and which had lately summoned them to my assistance.

But how was I to regard this midnight conversation? Hoarse and manlike voices conferring on the means of death, so near my bed, and at such an hour! How had my ancient security vanished! That dwelling, which had hitherto been an inviolate asylum, was now beset with danger to my life. That solitude, formerly so dear to me, could no longer be endured. Pleyel, who had consented to reside with us during the months of spring, lodged in the vacant chamber, in order to quiet my alarms. He treated my fears with ridicule, and in a short time very slight traces of them remained: but as it was wholly indifferent to him whether his nights were passed at my house or at my brother's, this arrangement gave general satisfaction.

Chapter VII

I will not enumerate the various inquiries and conjectures which these incidents occasioned. After all our efforts, we came no nearer to dispelling the mist in which they were involved; and time, instead of facilitating a solution, only accumulated our doubts.

In the midst of thoughts excited by these events, I was not unmindful of my interview with the stranger. I related the particulars, and shewed the portrait to my friends. Pleyel recollected to have met with a figure resembling my description in the city; but neither his face or garb made the same impression upon him that it made upon me. It was a hint to rally me upon my prepossessions, and to amuse us with a thousand ludicrous anecdotes which he had collected in his travels. He made no scruple to charge me with being in love; and threatened to inform the swain, when he met him, of his good fortune.

Pleyel's temper made him susceptible of no durable impressions. His conversation was occasionally visited by gleams of his ancient vivacity; but, though his impetuosity was sometimes inconvenient, there was nothing to dread from his malice. I had no fear that my character or dignity would suffer in his hands, and was not heartily displeased when he declared his intention of profiting by his first meeting with the stranger to introduce him to our acquaintance.

Some weeks after this I had spent a toilsome day, and, as the sun declined, found myself disposed to seek relief in a walk. The river bank is, at this part of it, and for some considerable space upward, so rugged and steep as not to be easily descended. In a recess of this declivity, near the southern verge of my little demesne,[1] was placed a slight building, with seats and lattices. From a crevice of the rock, to which this edifice was attached, there burst forth a stream of the purest water, which, leaping from ledge to ledge, for the space of sixty feet, produced a freshness in the air, and a murmur, the most delicious and soothing imaginable. These, added to the odours of the cedars which embowered it, and of the honeysuckle which clustered among the lattices, rendered this my favorite retreat in summer.

On this occasion I repaired hither. My spirits drooped through the fatigue of long attention, and I threw myself upon a bench, in a state, both mentally and personally, of the utmost supineness. The lulling sounds of the waterfall, the fragrance and the dusk combined to becalm my spirits, and, in a short time, to sink me into sleep. Either the uneasiness of my posture, or some slight indisposition molested my repose with dreams of no cheerful hue. After various incoherences had taken their turn to occupy my fancy, I at length imagined myself walking, in the evening twilight, to my brother's habitation. A pit, methought, had been dug in the path I had taken, of which I was not aware. As I carelessly pursued my

---

1. Or domain, with special reference to land.

walk, I thought I saw my brother, standing at some distance before me, beckoning and calling me to make haste. He stood on the opposite edge of the gulph. I mended my pace, and one step more would have plunged me into this abyss, had not some one from behind caught suddenly my arm, and exclaimed, in a voice of eagerness and terror, "Hold! hold!"

The sound broke my sleep, and I found myself, at the next moment, standing on my feet, and surrounded by the deepest darkness. Images so terrific and forcible disabled me, for a time, from distinguishing between sleep and wakefulness, and withheld from me the knowledge of my actual condition. My first panics were succeeded by the perturbations of surprize, to find myself alone in the open air, and immersed in so deep a gloom. I slowly recollected the incidents of the afternoon, and how I came hither. I could not estimate the time, but saw the propriety of returning with speed to the house. My faculties were still too confused, and the darkness too intense, to allow me immediately to find my way up the steep. I sat down, therefore, to recover myself, and to reflect upon my situation.

This was no sooner done, than a low voice was heard from behind the lattice, on the side where I sat. Between the rock and the lattice was a chasm not wide enough to admit a human body; yet, in this chasm he that spoke appeared to be stationed. "Attend! attend! but be not terrified."

I started and exclaimed, "Good heavens! what is that? Who are you?"

"A friend; one come, not to injure, but to save you; fear nothing."

This voice was immediately recognized to be the same with one of those which I had heard in the closet; it was the voice of him who had proposed to shoot, rather than to strangle, his victim. My terror made me, at once, mute and motionless. He continued, "I leagued to murder you. I repent. Mark my bidding, and be safe. Avoid this spot. The snares of death encompass it. Elsewhere danger will be distant; but this spot, shun it as you value your life. Mark me further; profit by this warning, but divulge it not. If a syllable of what has passed escape you, your doom is sealed. Remember your father, and be faithful."

Here the accents ceased, and left me overwhelmed with dismay. I was fraught with the persuasion, that during every moment I remained here, my life was endangered; but I could not take a step without hazard of falling to the bottom of the precipice. The path, leading to the summit, was short, but rugged and intricate. Even star-light was excluded by the umbrage, and not the faintest gleam was afforded to guide my steps. What should I do? To depart or remain was equally and eminently perilous.

In this state of uncertainty, I perceived a ray flit across the gloom and disappear. Another succeeded, which was stronger, and remained for a passing moment. It glittered on the shrubs that were scattered at the entrance, and gleam continued to succeed gleam for a few seconds, till they, finally, gave place to unintermitted darkness.

The first visitings of this light called up a train of horrors in my mind; destruction impended over this spot; the voice which I had lately heard had warned me to retire, and had menaced me with the fate of my father if I refused. I was desirous, but unable, to obey; these gleams were such as preluded the stroke by which he fell; the hour, perhaps, was the same—I shuddered as if I had beheld, suspended over me, the exterminating sword.

Presently a new and stronger illumination burst through the lattice on the right hand, and a voice, from the edge of the precipice above, called out my name. It was Pleyel. Joyfully did I recognize his accents; but such was the tumult of my thoughts that I had not power to answer him till he had frequently repeated his summons. I hurried, at length, from the fatal spot, and, directed by the lanthorn which he bore, ascended the hill.

Pale and breathless, it was with difficulty I could support myself. He anxiously inquired into the cause of my affright, and the motive of my unusual absence. He had returned from my brother's at a late hour, and was informed by Judith, that I had walked out before sunset, and had not yet returned. This intelligence was somewhat alarming. He waited some time; but, my absence continuing, he had set out in search of me. He had explored the neighbourhood with the utmost care, but, receiving no tidings of me, he was preparing to acquaint my brother with this circumstance, when he recollected the summer-house on the bank, and conceived it possible that some accident had detained me there. He again inquired into the cause of this detention, and of that confusion and dismay which my looks testified.

I told him that I had strolled hither in the afternoon, that sleep had overtaken me as I sat, and that I had awakened a few minutes before his arrival. I could tell him no more. In the present impetuosity of my thoughts, I was almost dubious, whether the pit, into which my brother had endeavoured to entice me, and the voice that talked through the lattice, were not parts of the same dream. I remembered, likewise, the charge of secrecy, and the penalty denounced, if I should rashly divulge what I had heard. For these reasons, I was silent on that subject, and shutting myself in my chamber, delivered myself up to contemplation.

What I have related will, no doubt, appear to you a fable. You will believe that calamity has subverted my reason, and that I am amusing you with the chimeras of my brain,[2] instead of facts that have really happened. I shall not be surprized or offended, if these be your suspicions. I know not, indeed, how you can deny them admission. For, if to me, the immediate witness, they were fertile of perplexity and doubt, how must they affect another to whom they are recommended only by my testimony? It was only by subsequent events, that I was fully and incontestibly assured of the veracity of my senses.

Meanwhile what was I to think? I had been assured that a design had been formed against my life. The ruffians had leagued to murder me. Whom had I offended? Who was there with whom I had ever maintained intercourse, who was capable of harbouring such atrocious purposes?

My temper was the reverse of cruel and imperious. My heart was touched with sympathy for the children of misfortune. But this sympathy was not a barren sentiment. My purse, scanty as it was, was ever open, and my hands ever active, to relieve distress. Many were the wretches whom my personal exertions had extricated from want and disease, and who rewarded me with their gratitude. There was no face which lowered at my approach, and no lips which uttered imprecations in my hearing. On the contrary, there was none, over whose fate I had exerted any influence, or to whom I was known by reputation, who did not greet me with smiles, and dismiss me with proofs of veneration; yet did not my senses assure me that a plot was laid against my life?

I am not destitute of courage. I have shewn myself deliberative and calm in the midst of peril. I have hazarded my own life, for the preservation of another, but now was I confused and panic-struck. I have not lived so as to fear death, yet to perish by an unseen and secret stroke, to be mangled by the knife of an assassin, was a thought at which I shuddered; what had I done to deserve to be made the victim of malignant passions?

But soft! was I not assured, that my life was safe in all places but one? And why was the treason limited to take effect in this spot? I was every where equally defenceless. My house and chamber were, at all times, accessible. Danger still impended over me; the bloody purpose was still entertained, but the hand that was to execute it, was powerless in all places but one!

Here I had remained for the last four or five hours, without the means of resistance or defence, yet I had not been attacked. A human being was at hand, who was conscious of my presence, and warned me hereafter to avoid this retreat. His voice was not absolutely new, but had I never heard it but once before? But why did he

2. Figments of the imagination.

prohibit me from relating this incident to others, and what species of death will be awarded if I disobey?

He talked of my father. He intimated, that disclosure would pull upon my head, the same destruction. Was then the death of my father, portentous and inexplicable as it was, the consequence of human machinations? It should seem, that this being is apprised of the true nature of this event, and is conscious of the means that led to it. Whether it shall likewise fall upon me, depends upon the observance of silence. Was it the infraction of a similar command, that brought so horrible a penalty upon my father?

Such were the reflections that haunted me during the night, and which effectually deprived me of sleep. Next morning, at breakfast, Pleyel related an event which my disappearance had hindered him from mentioning the night before. Early the preceding morning, his occasions called him to the city; he had stepped into a coffee-house to while away an hour; here he had met a person whose appearance instantly bespoke him to be the same whose hasty visit I have mentioned, and whose extraordinary visage and tones had so powerfully affected me. On an attentive survey, however, he proved, likewise, to be one with whom my friend had had some intercourse in Europe. This authorised the liberty of accosting him, and after some conversation, mindful, as Pleyel said, of the footing which this stranger had gained in my heart, he had ventured to invite him to Mettingen. The invitation had been cheerfully accepted, and a visit promised on the afternoon of the next day.

This information excited no sober emotions in my breast. I was, of course, eager to be informed as to the circumstances of their ancient intercourse. When, and where had they met? What knew he of the life and character of this man?

In answer to my inquiries, he informed me that, three years before, he was a traveller in Spain. He had made an excursion from Valencia to Murviedro[3] with a view to inspect the remains of Roman magnificence, scattered in the environs of that town. While traversing the scite of the theatre of old Saguntum he lighted upon this man, seated on a stone, and deeply engaged in perusing the work of the deacon Marti.[4] A short conversation ensued, which proved the stranger to be English. They returned to Valencia together.

His garb, aspect, and deportment, were wholly Spanish. A residence of three years in the country, indefatigable attention to the language, and a studious conformity with the customs of the people,

---

3. Cities in the Valencia province, on the eastern coast of Spain.
4. Manuel Martí y Zaragoza, *Descripción del Teatro de Sagunto* (1705). "Saguntum": Roman name for Murviedo, present-day Sagunto. The Roman theater there seated thousands; its ruins were an important tourist destination in the eighteenth century and were destroyed by Napoleon's army in 1812.

had made him indistinguishable from a native, when he chose to assume that character. Pleyel found him to be connected, on the footing of friendship and respect, with many eminent merchants in that city. He had embraced the catholic religion, and adopted a Spanish name instead of his own, which was CARWIN, and devoted himself to the literature and religion of his new country. He pursued no profession, but subsisted on remittances from England.

While Pleyel remained in Valencia, Carwin betrayed no aversion to intercourse, and the former found no small attractions in the society of this new acquaintance. On general topics he was highly intelligent and communicative. He had visited every corner of Spain, and could furnish the most accurate details respecting its ancient and present state. On topics of religion and of his own history, previous to his *transformation*[5] into a Spaniard, he was invariably silent. You could merely gather from his discourse that he was English, and that he was well acquainted with the neighbouring countries.

His character excited considerable curiosity in this observer. It was not easy to reconcile his conversion to the Romish faith, with those proofs of knowledge and capacity that were exhibited by him on different occasions. A suspicion was, sometimes, admitted, that his belief was counterfeited for some political purpose. The most careful observation, however, produced no discovery. His manners were, at all times, harmless and inartificial, and his habits those of a lover of contemplation and seclusion. He appeared to have contracted an affection for Pleyel, who was not slow to return it.

My friend, after a month's residence in this city, returned into France, and, since that period, had heard nothing concerning Carwin till his appearance at Mettingen.

On this occasion Carwin had received Pleyel's greeting with a certain distance and solemnity to which the latter had not been accustomed. He had waved noticing the inquiries of Pleyel respecting his desertion of Spain, in which he had formerly declared that it was his purpose to spend his life. He had assiduously diverted the attention of the latter to indifferent topics, but was still, on every theme, as eloquent and judicious as formerly. Why he had assumed the garb of a rustic, Pleyel was unable to conjecture. Perhaps it might be poverty, perhaps he was swayed by motives which it was his interest to conceal, but which were connected with consequences of the utmost moment.

Such was the sum of my friend's information. I was not sorry to be left alone during the greater part of this day. Every employment was irksome which did not leave me at liberty to meditate. I had now a new subject on which to exercise my thoughts. Before evening I

---

5. Brown's italics here obviously aim to recall the novel's subtitle.

should be ushered into his presence, and listen to those tones whose magical and thrilling power I had already experienced. But with what new images would he then be accompanied?

Carwin was an adherent to the Romish faith, yet was an Englishman by birth, and, perhaps, a protestant by education. He had adopted Spain for his country, and had intimated a design to spend his days there, yet now was an inhabitant of this district, and disguised by the habiliments of a clown! What could have obliterated the impressions of his youth, and made him abjure his religion and his country? What subsequent events had introduced so total a change in his plans? In withdrawing from Spain, had he reverted to the religion of his ancestors; or was it true, that his former conversion was deceitful, and that his conduct had been swayed by motives which it was prudent to conceal?

Hours were consumed in revolving these ideas. My meditations were intense; and, when the series was broken, I began to reflect with astonishment on my situation. From the death of my parents, till the commencement of this year, my life had been serene and blissful, beyond the ordinary portion of humanity; but, now, my bosom was corroded by anxiety. I was visited by dread of unknown dangers, and the future was a scene over which clouds rolled, and thunders muttered. I compared the cause with the effect, and they seemed disproportioned to each other. All unaware, and in a manner which I had no power to explain, I was pushed from my immoveable and lofty station, and cast upon a sea of troubles.

I determined to be my brother's visitant on this evening, yet my resolves were not unattended with wavering and reluctance. Pleyel's insinuations that I was in love, affected, in no degree, my belief, yet the consciousness that this was the opinion of one who would, probably, be present at our introduction to each other, would excite all that confusion which the passion itself is apt to produce. This would confirm him in his error, and call forth new railleries. His mirth, when exerted upon this topic, was the source of the bitterest vexation. Had he been aware of its influence upon my happiness, his temper would not have allowed him to persist; but this influence, it was my chief endeavour to conceal. That the belief of my having bestowed my heart upon another, produced in my friend none but ludicrous sensations, was the true cause of my distress; but if this had been discovered by him, my distress would have been unspeakably aggravated.

Chapter VIII

As soon as evening arrived, I performed my visit. Carwin made one of the company, into which I was ushered. Appearances were the same as when I before beheld him. His garb was equally negligent and rustic. I gazed upon his countenance with new curiosity. My situation was such as to enable me to bestow upon it a deliberate examination. Viewed at more leisure, it lost none of its wonderful properties. I could not deny my homage to the intelligence expressed in it, but was wholly uncertain, whether he were an object to be dreaded or adored, and whether his powers had been exerted to evil or to good.

He was sparing in discourse; but whatever he said was pregnant with meaning, and uttered with rectitude of articulation, and force of emphasis, of which I had entertained no conception previously to my knowledge of him. Notwithstanding the uncouthness of his garb, his manners were not unpolished. All topics were handled by him with skill, and without pedantry or affectation. He uttered no sentiment calculated to produce a disadvantageous impression: on the contrary, his observations denoted a mind alive to every generous and heroic feeling. They were introduced without parade, and accompanied with that degree of earnestness which indicates sincerity.

He parted from us not till late, refusing an invitation to spend the night here, but readily consented to repeat his visit. His visits were frequently repeated. Each day introduced us to a more intimate acquaintance with his sentiments, but left us wholly in the dark, concerning that about which we were most inquisitive. He studiously avoided all mention of his past or present situation. Even the place of his abode in the city he concealed from us.

Our sphere, in this respect, being somewhat limited, and the intellectual endowments of this man being indisputably great, his deportment was more diligently marked, and copiously commented on by us, than you, perhaps, will think the circumstances warranted. Not a gesture, or glance, or accent, that was not, in our private assemblies, discussed, and inferences deduced from it. It may well be thought that he modelled his behaviour by an uncommon standard, when, with all our opportunities and accuracy of observation, we were able, for a long time, to gather no satisfactory information. He afforded us no ground on which to build even a plausible conjecture.

There is a degree of familiarity which takes place between constant associates, that justifies the negligence of many rules of which, in an earlier period of their intercourse, politeness requires the exact observance. Inquiries into our condition are allowable when they are prompted by a disinterested concern for our welfare; and this solicitude is not only pardonable, but may justly be demanded from those who chuse us for their companions. This state of things was more slow to arrive on this occasion than on most others, on account of the gravity and loftiness of this man's behaviour.

Pleyel, however, began, at length, to employ regular means for this end. He occasionally alluded to the circumstances in which they had formerly met, and remarked the incongruousness between the religion and habits of a Spaniard, with those of a native of Britain. He expressed his astonishment at meeting our guest in this corner of the globe, especially as, when they parted in Spain, he was taught to believe that Carwin should never leave that country. He insinuated, that a change so great must have been prompted by motives of a singular and momentous kind.

No answer, or an answer wide of the purpose, was generally made to these insinuations. Britons and Spaniards, he said, are votaries of the same Deity, and square their faith by the same precepts; their ideas are drawn from the same fountains of literature, and they speak dialects of the same tongue; their government and laws have more resemblances than differences; they were formerly provinces of the same civil, and till lately, of the same religious, Empire.[1]

As to the motives which induce men to change the place of their abode, these must unavoidably be fleeting and mutable. If not bound to one spot by conjugal or parental ties, or by the nature of that employment to which we are indebted for subsistence, the inducements to change are far more numerous and powerful, than opposite inducements.

He spoke as if desirous of shewing that he was not aware of the tendency of Pleyel's remarks; yet, certain tokens were apparent, that proved him by no means wanting in penetration. These tokens were to be read in his countenance, and not in his words. When any thing was said, indicating curiosity in us, the gloom of his countenance was deepened, his eyes sunk to the ground, and his wonted air was not resumed without visible struggle. Hence, it was obvious to infer, that some incidents of his life were reflected on by him with regret; and that, since these incidents were carefully concealed, and even that regret which flowed from them laboriously stifled, they had not been merely disastrous. The secrecy that was observed appeared not designed to provoke or baffle the inquisitive, but was prompted by the shame, or by the prudence of guilt.

---

1. I.e., the Roman Empire. Carwin overstates the case. Britain was no longer a Catholic nation in the late eighteenth century. Moreover, English is a Germanic language, whereas Spanish is a Romance language, though Carwin may be suggesting a common origin for both; Indo-European linguistics was the subject of much academic discussion in the eighteenth century but would not be named as such until 1813.

These ideas, which were adopted by Pleyel and my brother, as well as myself, hindered us from employing more direct means for accomplishing our wishes. Questions might have been put in such terms, that no room should be left for the pretence of misapprehension, and if modesty merely had been the obstacle, such questions would not have been wanting; but we considered, that, if the disclosure were productive of pain or disgrace, it was inhuman to extort it.

Amidst the various topics that were discussed in his presence, allusions were, of course, made to the inexplicable events that had lately happened. At those times, the words and looks of this man were objects of my particular attention. The subject was extraordinary; and any one whose experience or reflections could throw any light upon it, was entitled to my gratitude. As this man was enlightened by reading and travel, I listened with eagerness to the remarks which he should make.

At first, I entertained a kind of apprehension, that the tale would be heard by him with incredulity and secret ridicule. I had formerly heard stories that resembled this in some of their mysterious circumstances, but they were, commonly, heard by me with contempt. I was doubtful, whether the same impression would not now be made on the mind of our guest; but I was mistaken in my fears.

He heard them with seriousness, and without any marks either of surprize or incredulity. He pursued, with visible pleasure, that kind of disquisition which was naturally suggested by them. His fancy was eminently vigorous and prolific, and if he did not persuade us, that human beings are, sometimes, admitted to a sensible intercourse with the author of nature, he, at least, won over our inclination to the cause. He merely deduced, from his own reasonings, that such intercourse was probable; but confessed that, though he was acquainted with many instances somewhat similar to those which had been related by us, none of them were perfectly exempted from the suspicion of human agency.

On being requested to relate these instances, he amused us with many curious details. His narratives were constructed with so much skill, and rehearsed with so much energy, that all the effects of a dramatic exhibition were frequently produced by them. Those that were most coherent and most minute, and, of consequence, least entitled to credit, were yet rendered probable by the exquisite art of this rhetorician. For every difficulty that was suggested, a ready and plausible solution was furnished. Mysterious voices had always a share in producing the catastrophe, but they were always to be explained on some known principles, either as reflected into a focus, or communicated through a tube. I could not but remark that his narratives, however complex or marvellous, contained no instance sufficiently parallel to those that had befallen ourselves, and in which the solution was applicable to our own case.

My brother was a much more sanguine[2] reasoner than our guest. Even in some of the facts which were related by Carwin, he maintained the probability of celestial interference, when the latter was disposed to deny it, and had found, as he imagined, footsteps of an human agent. Pleyel was by no means equally credulous. He scrupled not to deny faith to any testimony but that of his senses, and allowed the facts which had lately been supported by this testimony, not to mould his belief, but merely to give birth to doubts.

It was soon observed that Carwin adopted, in some degree, a similar distinction. A tale of this kind, related by others, he would believe, provided it was explicable upon known principles; but that such notices were actually communicated by beings of an higher order, he would believe only when his own ears were assailed in a manner which could not be otherwise accounted for. Civility forbad him to contradict my brother or myself, but his understanding refused to acquiesce in our testimony. Besides, he was disposed to question whether the voices heard in the temple, at the foot of the hill, and in my closet, were not really uttered by human organs. On this supposition he was desired to explain how the effect was produced.

He answered, that the power of mimickry was very common. Catharine's voice might easily be imitated by one at the foot of the hill, who would find no difficulty in eluding, by flight, the search of Wieland. The tidings of the death of the Saxon lady were uttered by one near at hand, who overheard the conversation, who conjectured her death, and whose conjecture happened to accord with the truth. That the voice appeared to come from the ceiling was to be considered as an illusion of the fancy. The cry for help, heard in the hall on the night of my adventure, was to be ascribed to an human creature, who actually stood in the hall when he uttered it. It was of no moment, he said, that we could not explain by what motives he that made the signal was led hither. How imperfectly acquainted were we with the condition and designs of the beings that surrounded us? The city was near at hand, and thousands might there exist whose powers and purposes might easily explain whatever was mysterious in this transaction. As to the closet dialogue, he was obliged to adopt one of two suppositions, and affirm either that it was fashioned in my own fancy, or that it actually took place between two persons in the closet.

Such was Carwin's mode of explaining these appearances. It is such, perhaps, as would commend itself as most plausible to the most sagacious minds, but it was insufficient to impart conviction to us.

2. Hopeful.

As to the treason that was meditated against me, it was doubtless just to conclude that it was either real or imaginary; but that it was real was attested by the mysterious warning in the summer-house, the secret of which I had hitherto locked up in my own breast.

A month passed away in this kind of intercourse. As to Carwin, our ignorance was in no degree enlightened respecting his genuine character and views. Appearances were uniform. No man possessed a larger store of knowledge, or a greater degree of skill in the communication of it to others: Hence he was regarded as an inestimable addition to our society. Considering the distance of my brother's house from the city, he was frequently prevailed upon to pass the night where he spent the evening. Two days seldom elapsed without a visit from him; hence he was regarded as a kind of inmate of the house. He entered and departed without ceremony. When he arrived he received an unaffected welcome, and when he chose to retire, no importunities were used to induce him to remain.

The temple was the principal scene of our social enjoyments; yet the felicity that we tasted when assembled in this asylum, was but the gleam of a former sun-shine. Carwin never parted with his gravity. The inscrutableness of his character, and the uncertainty whether his fellowship tended to good or to evil, were seldom absent from our minds. This circumstance powerfully contributed to sadden us.

My heart was the seat of growing disquietudes. This change in one who had formerly been characterized by all the exuberances of soul, could not fail to be remarked by my friends. My brother was always a pattern of solemnity. My sister was clay, moulded by the circumstances in which she happened to be placed. There was but one whose deportment remains to be described as being of importance to our happiness. Had Pleyel likewise dismissed his vivacity?

He was as whimsical and jestful as ever, but he was not happy. The truth, in this respect, was of too much importance to me not to make me a vigilant observer. His mirth was easily perceived to be the fruit of exertion. When his thoughts wandered from the company, an air of dissatisfaction and impatience stole across his features. Even the punctuality and frequency of his visits were somewhat lessened. It may be supposed that my own uneasiness was heightened by these tokens; but, strange as it may seem, I found, in the present state of my mind, no relief but in the persuasion that Pleyel was unhappy.

That unhappiness, indeed, depended, for its value in my eyes, on the cause that produced it. It did not arise from the death of the Saxon lady: it was not a contagious emanation from the countenances of Wieland or Carwin. There was but one other source whence it could flow. A nameless ecstacy thrilled through my frame when any new proof occurred that the ambiguousness of my behaviour was the cause.

Chapter IX

My brother had received a new book from Germany. It was a tragedy, and the first attempt of a Saxon poet, of whom my brother had been taught to entertain the highest expectations. The exploits of Zisca,[1] the Bohemian hero, were woven into a dramatic series and connection. According to German custom, it was minute and diffuse, and dictated by an adventurous and lawless fancy. It was a chain of audacious acts, and unheard-of disasters. The moated fortress, and the thicket; the ambush and the battle; and the conflict of headlong passions, were pourtrayed in wild numbers, and with terrific energy. An afternoon was set apart to rehearse this performance. The language was familiar to all of us but Carwin, whose company, therefore, was tacitly dispensed with.

The morning previous to this intended rehearsal, I spent at home. My mind was occupied with reflections relative to my own situation. The sentiment which lived with chief energy in my heart, was connected with the image of Pleyel. In the midst of my anguish, I had not been destitute of consolation. His late deportment had given spring to my hopes. Was not the hour at hand, which should render me the happiest of human creatures? He suspected that I looked with favorable eyes upon Carwin. Hence arose disquietudes, which he struggled in vain to conceal. He loved me, but was hopeless that his love would be compensated. Is it not time, said I, to rectify this error? But by what means is this to be effected? It can only be done by a change of deportment in me; but how must I demean myself for this purpose?

I must not speak. Neither eyes, nor lips, must impart the information. He must not be assured that my heart is his, previous to the tender of his own; but he must be convinced that it has not been given to another; he must be supplied with space whereon to build a doubt as to the true state of my affections; he must be prompted to avow himself. The line of delicate propriety; how hard it is, not to fall short, and not to overleap it!

This afternoon we shall meet at the temple. We shall not separate till late. It will be his province to accompany me home. The airy

---

1. Jan Ziska (1360–1424), a follower of the Moravian founder, Jan Hus. The name *Ziska* in Czech means "one-eyed." Ziska led early Moravians in a military resistance to the reinstatement of Roman Catholicism in Bohemia. He was noted for his fierceness in battle and his merciless treatment of those he considered blasphemers. The play the Wieland-Pleyel circle rehearses is apparently Brown's invention.

expanse is without a speck. This breeze is usually stedfast, and its promise of a bland and cloudless evening, may be trusted. The moon will rise at eleven, and at that hour, we shall wind along this bank. Possibly that hour may decide my fate. If suitable encouragement be given, Pleyel will reveal his soul to me; and I, ere I reach this threshold, will be made the happiest of beings. And is this good to be mine? Add wings to thy speed, sweet evening; and thou, moon, I charge thee, shroud thy beams at the moment when my Pleyel whispers love. I would not for the world, that the burning blushes, and the mounting raptures of that moment, should be visible.

But what encouragement is wanting? I must be regardful of insurmountable limits. Yet when minds are imbued with a genuine sympathy, are not words and looks superfluous? Are not motion and touch sufficient to impart feelings such as mine? Has he not eyed me at moments, when the pressure of his hand has thrown me into tumults, and was it possible that he mistook the impetuosities of love, for the eloquence of indignation?

But the hastening evening will decide. Would it were come! And yet I shudder at its near approach. An interview that must thus terminate, is surely to be wished for by me; and yet it is not without its terrors. Would to heaven it were come and gone!

I feel no reluctance, my friends to be thus explicit. Time was, when these emotions would be hidden with immeasurable solicitude, from every human eye. Alas! these airy and fleeting impulses of shame are gone. My scruples were preposterous and criminal. They are bred in all hearts, by a perverse and vicious education, and they would still have maintained their place in my heart, had not my portion been set in misery. My errors have taught me thus much wisdom; that those sentiments which we ought not to disclose, it is criminal to harbour.

It was proposed to begin the rehearsal at four o'clock; I counted the minutes as they passed; their flight was at once too rapid and too slow; my sensations were of an excruciating kind; I could taste no food, nor apply to any task, nor enjoy a moment's repose: when the hour arrived, I hastened to my brother's.

Pleyel was not there. He had not yet come. On ordinary occasions, he was eminent for punctuality. He had testified great eagerness to share in the pleasures of this rehearsal. He was to divide the task with my brother, and, in tasks like these, he always engaged with peculiar zeal. His elocution was less sweet than sonorous; and, therefore, better adapted than the mellifluences of his friend, to the outrageous vehemence of this drama.

What could detain him? Perhaps he lingered through forgetfulness. Yet this was incredible. Never had his memory been known to fail upon even more trivial occasions. Not less impossible was it, that the scheme had lost its attractions, and that he staid, because his coming would afford him no gratification. But why should we expect him to adhere to the minute?

An half hour elapsed, but Pleyel was still at a distance. Perhaps he had misunderstood the hour which had been proposed. Perhaps he had conceived that to-morrow, and not to-day, had been selected for this purpose: but no. A review of preceding circumstances demonstrated that such misapprehension was impossible; for he had himself proposed this day, and this hour. This day, his attention would not otherwise be occupied; but to-morrow, an indispensible engagement was foreseen, by which all his time would be engrossed: his detention, therefore, must be owing to some unforeseen and extraordinary event. Our conjectures were vague, tumultuous, and sometimes fearful. His sickness and his death might possibly have detained him.

Tortured with suspense, we sat gazing at each other, and at the path which led from the road. Every horseman that passed was, for a moment, imagined to be him. Hour succeeded hour, and the sun, gradually declining, at length, disappeared. Every signal of his coming proved fallacious, and our hopes were at length dismissed. His absence affected my friends in no insupportable degree. They should be obliged, they said, to defer this undertaking till the morrow; and, perhaps, their impatient curiosity would compel them to dispense entirely with his presence. No doubt, some harmless occurrence had diverted him from his purpose; and they trusted that they should receive a satisfactory account of him in the morning.

It may be supposed that this disappointment affected me in a very different manner. I turned aside my head to conceal my tears. I fled into solitude, to give vent to my reproaches, without interruption or restraint. My heart was ready to burst with indignation and grief. Pleyel was not the only object of my keen but unjust upbraiding. Deeply did I execrate my own folly. Thus fallen into ruins was the gay fabric which I had reared! Thus had my golden vision melted into air!

How fondly did I dream that Pleyel was a lover! If he were, would he have suffered any obstacle to hinder his coming? Blind and infatuated man! I exclaimed. Thou sportest with happiness. The good that is offered thee, thou hast the insolence and folly to refuse. Well, I will henceforth intrust my felicity to no one's keeping but my own.

The first agonies of this disappointment would not allow me to be reasonable or just. Every ground on which I had built the persuasion that Pleyel was not unimpressed in my favor, appeared to vanish. It seemed as if I had been misled into this opinion, by the most palpable illusions.

I made some trifling excuse, and returned, much earlier than I expected, to my own house. I retired early to my chamber, without designing to sleep. I placed myself at a window, and gave the reins to reflection.

The hateful and degrading impulses which had lately controuled me were, in some degree, removed. New dejection succeeded, but was now produced by contemplating my late behaviour. Surely that passion is worthy to be abhorred which obscures our understanding, and urges us to the commission of injustice. What right had I to expect his attendance? Had I not demeaned myself like one indifferent to his happiness, and as having bestowed my regards upon another? His absence might be prompted by the love which I considered his absence as a proof that he wanted. He came not because the sight of me, the spectacle of my coldness or aversion, contributed to his despair. Why should I prolong, by hypocrisy or silence, his misery as well as my own? Why not deal with him explicitly, and assure him of the truth?

You will hardly believe that, in obedience to this suggestion, I rose for the purpose of ordering a light, that I might instantly make this confession in a letter. A second thought shewed me the rashness of this scheme, and I wondered by what infirmity of mind I could be betrayed into a momentary approbation of it. I saw with the utmost clearness that a confession like that would be the most remediless and unpardonable outrage upon the dignity of my sex, and utterly unworthy of that passion which controuled me.

I resumed my seat and my musing. To account for the absence of Pleyel became once more the scope of my conjectures. How many incidents might occur to raise an insuperable impediment in his way? When I was a child, a scheme of pleasure, in which he and his sister were parties, had been, in like manner, frustrated by his absence; but his absence, in that instance, had been occasioned by his falling from a boat into the river, in consequence of which he had run the most imminent hazard of being drowned. Here was a second disappointment endured by the same persons, and produced by his failure. Might it not originate in the same cause? Had he not designed to cross the river that morning to make some necessary purchases in Jersey? He had preconcerted to return to his own house to dinner; but, perhaps, some disaster had befallen him. Experience had taught me the insecurity of a canoe, and that was the only kind of boat which Pleyel used: I was, likewise, actuated by an hereditary dread of water. These circumstances combined to bestow considerable plausibility on this conjecture; but the consternation with which I began to be seized was allayed by reflecting, that if this disaster had happened my brother would have received the speediest information of it. The consolation which this idea imparted was ravished from me by a new thought. This disaster might have happened, and his family not be apprized of it. The first intelligence of his fate may be communicated by the livid corpse which the tide may cast, many days hence, upon the shore.

Thus was I distressed by opposite conjectures: thus was I tormented by phantoms of my own creation. It was not always thus. I cannot ascertain the date when my mind became the victim of this imbecility; perhaps it was coeval with the inroad of a fatal passion; a passion that will never rank me in the number of its eulogists; it was alone sufficient to the extermination of my peace: it was itself a plenteous source of calamity, and needed not the concurrence of other evils to take away the attractions of existence, and dig for me an untimely grave.

The state of my mind naturally introduced a train of reflections upon the dangers and cares which inevitably beset an human being. By no violent transition was I led to ponder on the turbulent life and mysterious end of my father. I cherished, with the utmost veneration, the memory of this man, and every relique connected with his fate was preserved with the most scrupulous care. Among these was to be numbered a manuscript, containing memoirs of his own life. The narrative was by no means recommended by its eloquence; but neither did all its value flow from my relationship to the author. Its stile had an unaffected and picturesque simplicity. The great variety and circumstantial display of the incidents, together with their intrinsic importance, as descriptive of human manners and passions, made it the most useful book in my collection. It was late; but being sensible of no inclination to sleep, I resolved to betake myself to the perusal of it.

To do this it was requisite to procure a light. The girl[2] had long since retired to her chamber: it was therefore proper to wait upon myself. A lamp, and the means of lighting it, were only to be found in the kitchen. Thither I resolved forthwith to repair; but the light was of use merely to enable me to read the book. I knew the shelf and the spot where it stood. Whether I took down the book, or prepared the lamp in the first place, appeared to be a matter of no moment. The latter was preferred, and, leaving my seat, I approached the closet in which, as I mentioned formerly, my books and papers were deposited.

Suddenly the remembrance of what had lately passed in this closet occurred. Whether midnight was approaching, or had passed, I knew not. I was, as then, alone, and defenceless. The wind was in that direction in which, aided by the deathlike repose of nature, it brought to me the murmur of the water-fall. This was mingled with

2. Judith, Clara's servant.

that solemn and enchanting sound, which a breeze produces among the leaves of pines. The words of that mysterious dialogue, their fearful import, and the wild excess to which I was transported by my terrors, filled my imagination anew. My steps faultered, and I stood a moment to recover myself.

I prevailed on myself at length to move towards the closet. I touched the lock, but my fingers were powerless; I was visited afresh by unconquerable apprehensions. A sort of belief darted into my mind, that some being was concealed within, whose purposes were evil. I began to contend with these fears, when it occurred to me that I might, without impropriety, go for a lamp previously to opening the closet. I receded a few steps; but before I reached my chamber door my thoughts took a new direction. Motion seemed to produce a mechanical influence upon me. I was ashamed of my weakness. Besides, what aid could be afforded me by a lamp?

My fears had pictured to themselves no precise object. It would be difficult to depict, in words, the ingredients and hues of that phantom which haunted me. An hand invisible and of preternatural strength, lifted by human passions, and selecting my life for its aim, were parts of this terrific image. All places were alike accessible to this foe, or if his empire were restricted by local bounds, those bounds were utterly inscrutable by me. But had I not been told by some one in league with this enemy, that every place but the recess in the bank was exempt from danger?

I returned to the closet, and once more put my hand upon the lock. O! may my ears lose their sensibility, ere they be again assailed by a shriek so terrible! Not merely my understanding was subdued by the sound: it acted on my nerves like an edge of steel. It appeared to cut asunder the fibres of my brain, and rack every joint with agony.

The cry, loud and piercing as it was, was nevertheless human. No articulation was ever more distinct. The breath which accompanied it did not fan my hair, yet did every circumstance combine to persuade me that the lips which uttered it touched my very shoulder.

"Hold! Hold!" were the words of this tremendous prohibition, in whose tone the whole soul seemed to be rapt up, and every energy converted into eagerness and terror.

Shuddering, I dashed myself against the wall, and by the same involuntary impulse, turned my face backward to examine the mysterious monitor. The moon-light streamed into each window, and every corner of the room was conspicuous, and yet I beheld nothing!

The interval was too brief to be artificially measured, between the utterance of these words, and my scrutiny directed to the quarter whence they came. Yet if a human being had been there, could he fail to have been visible? Which of my senses was the prey of a fatal illusion? The shock which the sound produced was still felt in

every part of my frame. The sound, therefore, could not but be a
genuine commotion. But that I had heard it, was not more true
than that the being who uttered it was stationed at my right ear; yet
my attendant was invisible.

I cannot describe the state of my thoughts at that moment. Surprize had mastered my faculties. My frame shook, and the vital current was congealed. I was conscious only to the vehemence of my
sensations. This condition could not be lasting. Like a tide, which
suddenly mounts to an overwhelming height, and then gradually
subsides, my confusion slowly gave place to order, and my tumults to
a calm. I was able to deliberate and move. I resumed my feet, and
advanced into the midst of the room. Upward, and behind, and on
each side, I threw penetrating glances. I was not satisfied with one
examination. He that hitherto refused to be seen, might change his
purpose, and on the next survey be clearly distinguishable.

Solitude imposes least restraint upon the fancy. Dark is less fertile
of images than the feeble lustre of the moon. I was alone, and the
walls were chequered by shadowy forms. As the moon passed behind
a cloud and emerged, these shadows seemed to be endowed with life,
and to move. The apartment was open to the breeze, and the curtain
was occasionally blown from its ordinary position. This motion was
not unaccompanied with sound. I failed not to snatch a look, and to
listen when this motion and this sound occurred. My belief that my
monitor was posted near, was strong, and instantly converted these
appearances to tokens of his presence, and yet I could discern
nothing.

When my thoughts were at length permitted to revert to the past,
the first idea that occurred was the resemblance between the words
of the voice which I had just heard, and those which had terminated my dream in the summerhouse. There are means by which
we are able to distinguish a substance from a shadow, a reality from
the phantom of a dream. The pit, my brother beckoning me forward,
the seizure of my arm, and the voice behind, were surely imaginary.
That these incidents were fashioned in my sleep, is supported by the
same indubitable evidence that compels me to believe myself awake
at present; yet the words and the voice were the same. Then, by some
inexplicable contrivance, I was aware of the danger, while my actions
and sensations were those of one wholly unacquainted with it. Now,
was it not equally true that my actions and persuasions were at
war? Had not the belief, that evil lurked in the closet, gained admittance, and had not my actions betokened an unwarrantable security? To obviate the effects of my infatuation, the same means had
been used.

In my dream, he that tempted me to my destruction, was my
brother. Death was ambushed in my path. From what evil was I

now rescued? What minister or implement of ill was shut up in this recess? Who was it whose suffocating grasp I was to feel, should I dare to enter it? What monstrous conception is this? my brother!

No; protection, and not injury is his province. Strange and terrible chimera![3] Yet it would not be suddenly dismissed. It was surely no vulgar agency that gave this form to my fears. He to whom all parts of time are equally present, whom no contingency approaches, was the author of that spell which now seized upon me. Life was dear to me. No consideration was present that enjoined me to relinquish it. Sacred duty combined with every spontaneous sentiment to endear to me my being. Should I not shudder when my being was endangered? But what emotion should possess me when the arm lifted against me was Wieland's?

Ideas exist in our minds that can be accounted for by no established laws. Why did I dream that my brother was my foe? Why but because an omen of my fate was ordained to be communicated? Yet what salutary end did it serve? Did it arm me with caution to elude, or fortitude to bear the evils to which I was reserved? My present thoughts were, no doubt, indebted for their hue to the similitude existing between these incidents and those of my dream. Surely it was phrenzy that dictated my deed. That a ruffian was hidden in the closet, was an idea, the genuine tendency of which was to urge me to flight. Such had been the effect formerly produced. Had my mind been simply occupied with this thought at present, no doubt, the same impulse would have been experienced; but now it was my brother whom I was irresistably persuaded to regard as the contriver of that ill of which I had been forewarned. This persuasion did not extenuate my fears or my danger. Why then did I again approach the closet and withdraw the bolt? My resolution was instantly conceived, and executed without faultering.

The door was formed of light materials. The lock, of simple structure, easily forewent its hold. It opened into the room, and commonly moved upon its hinges, after being unfastened, without any effort of mine. This effort, however, was bestowed upon the present occasion. It was my purpose to open it with quickness, but the exertion which I made was ineffectual. It refused to open.

At another time, this circumstance would not have looked with a face of mystery. I should have supposed some casual obstruction, and repeated my efforts to surmount it. But now my mind was accessible to no conjecture but one. The door was hindered from opening by human force. Surely, here was new cause for affright. This was confirmation proper to decide my conduct. Now was all ground of hesitation taken away. What could be supposed but that I deserted

3. A phantom or figment of the imagination.

the chamber and the house? that I at least endeavoured no longer to withdraw the door?

Have I not said that my actions were dictated by phrenzy? My reason had forborne, for a time, to suggest or to sway my resolves. I reiterated my endeavours. I exerted all my force to overcome the obstacle, but in vain. The strength that was exerted to keep it shut, was superior to mine.

A casual observer might, perhaps, applaud the audaciousness of this conduct. Whence, but from an habitual defiance of danger, could my perseverance arise? I have already assigned, as distinctly as I am able, the cause of it. The frantic conception that my brother was within, that the resistance made to my design was exerted by him, had rooted itself in my mind. You will comprehend the height of this infatuation, when I tell you, that, finding all my exertions vain, I betook myself to exclamations. Surely I was utterly bereft of understanding.

Now had I arrived at the crisis of my fate. "O! hinder not the door to open," I exclaimed, in a tone that had less of fear than of grief in it. "I know you well. Come forth, but harm me not. I beseech you come forth."

I had taken my hand from the lock, and removed to a small distance from the door. I had scarcely uttered these words, when the door swung upon its hinges, and displayed to my view the interior of the closet. Whoever was within, was shrouded in darkness. A few seconds passed without interruption of the silence. I knew not what to expect or to fear. My eyes would not stray from the recess. Presently, a deep sigh was heard. The quarter from which it came heightened the eagerness of my gaze. Some one approached from the farther end. I quickly perceived the outlines of a human figure. Its steps were irresolute and slow. I recoiled as it advanced.

By coming at length within the verge of the room, his form was clearly distinguishable. I had prefigured to myself a very different personage. The face that presented itself was the last that I should desire to meet at an hour, and in a place like this. My wonder was stifled by my fears. Assassins had lurked in this recess. Some divine voice warned me of danger, that at this moment awaited me. I had spurned the intimation, and challenged my adversary.

I recalled the mysterious countenance and dubious character of Carwin. What motive but atrocious ones could guide his steps hither? I was alone. My habit[4] suited the hour, and the place, and the warmth of the season. All succour was remote. He had placed himself between me and the door. My frame shook with the vehemence of my apprehensions.

---

4. Clothing.

Yet I was not wholly lost to myself: I vigilantly marked his demeanour. His looks were grave, but not without perturbation. What species of inquietude it betrayed, the light was not strong enough to enable me to discover. He stood still; but his eyes wandered from one object to another. When these powerful organs were fixed upon me, I shrunk into myself. At length, he broke silence. Earnestness, and not embarrassment, was in his tone. He advanced close to me while he spoke.

"What voice was that which lately addressed you?"

He paused for an answer; but observing my trepidation, he resumed, with undiminished solemnity: "Be not terrified. Whoever he was, he hast done you an important service. I need not ask you if it were the voice of a companion. That sound was beyond the compass of human organs. The knowledge that enabled him to tell you who was in the closet, was obtained by incomprehensible means.

"You knew that Carwin was there. Were you not apprized of his intents? The same power could impart the one as well as the other. Yet, knowing these, you persisted. Audacious girl! but, perhaps, you confided in his guardianship. Your confidence was just. With succour like this at hand you may safely defy me.

"He is my eternal foe; the baffler of my best concerted schemes. Twice have you been saved by his accursed interposition. But for him I should long ere now have borne away the spoils of your honor."

He looked at me with greater stedfastness than before. I became every moment more anxious for my safety. It was with difficulty I stammered out an entreaty that he would instantly depart, or suffer me to do so. He paid no regard to my request, but proceeded in a more impassioned manner.

"What is it you fear? Have I not told you, you are safe? Has not one in whom you more reasonably place trust assured you of it? Even if I execute my purpose, what injury is done? Your prejudices will call it by that name, but it merits it not.

"I was impelled by a sentiment that does you honor; a sentiment, that would sanctify my deed; but, whatever it be, you are safe. Be this chimera[5] still worshipped; I will do nothing to pollute it." Here he stopped.

The accents and gestures of this man left me drained of all courage. Surely, on no other occasion should I have been thus pusillanimous.[6] My state I regarded as a hopeless one. I was wholly at the mercy of this being. Whichever way I turned my eyes, I saw no avenue by which I might escape. The resources of my personal strength, my ingenuity, and my eloquence, I estimated at nothing. The dignity

5. Here, her virtue or virginity.
6. Lacking courage.

of virtue, and the force of truth, I had been accustomed to celebrate; and had frequently vaunted of the conquests which I should make with their assistance.

I used to suppose that certain evils could never befall a being in possession of a sound mind; that true virtue supplies us with energy which vice can never resist; that it was always in our power to obstruct, by his own death, the designs of an enemy who aimed at less than our life. How was it that a sentiment like despair had now invaded me, and that I trusted to the protection of chance, or to the pity of my persecutor?

His words imparted some notion of the injury which he had meditated. He talked of obstacles that had risen in his way. He had relinquished his design. These sources supplied me with slender consolation. There was no security but in his absence. When I looked at myself, when I reflected on the hour and the place, I was overpowered by horror and dejection.

He was silent, museful, and inattentive to my situation, yet made no motion to depart. I was silent in my turn. What could I say? I was confident that reason in this contest would be impotent. I must owe my safety to his own suggestions. Whatever purpose brought him hither, he had changed it. Why then did he remain? His resolutions might fluctuate, and the pause of a few minutes restore to him his first resolutions.

Yet was not this the man whom we had treated with unwearied kindness? Whose society was endeared to us by his intellectual elevation and accomplishments? Who had a thousand times expatiated on the usefulness and beauty of virtue? Why should such a one be dreaded? If I could have forgotten the circumstances in which our interview had taken place, I might have treated his words as jests. Presently, he resumed:

"Fear me not: the space that severs us is small, and all visible succour is distant. You believe yourself completely in my power; that you stand upon the brink of ruin. Such are your groundless fears. I cannot lift a finger to hurt you. Easier it would be to stop the moon in her course than to injure you. The power that protects you would crumble my sinews, and reduce me to a heap of ashes in a moment, if I were to harbour a thought hostile to your safety.

"Thus are appearances at length solved. Little did I expect that they originated hence. What a portion is assigned to you? Scanned by the eyes of this intelligence, your path will be without pits to swallow, or snares to entangle you. Environed by the arms of this protection, all artifices will be frustrated, and all malice repelled."

Here succeeded a new pause. I was still observant of every gesture and look. The tranquil solemnity that had lately possessed his countenance gave way to a new expression. All now was trepidation and anxiety.

"I must be gone," said he in a faltering accent. "Why do I linger here? I will not ask your forgiveness. I see that your terrors are invincible. Your pardon will be extorted by fear, and not dictated by compassion. I must fly from you forever. He that could plot against your honor, must expect from you and your friends persecution and death. I must doom myself to endless exile."

Saying this, he hastily left the room. I listened while he descended the stairs, and, unbolting the outer door, went forth. I did not follow him with my eyes, as the moon-light would have enabled me to do. Relieved by his absence, and exhausted by the conflict of my fears, I threw myself on a chair, and resigned myself to those bewildering ideas which incidents like these could not fail to produce.

Chapter X

Order could not readily be introduced into my thoughts. The voice still rung in my ears. Every accent that was uttered by Carwin was fresh in my remembrance. His unwelcome approach, the recognition of his person, his hasty departure, produced a complex impression on my mind which no words can delineate. I strove to give a slower motion to my thoughts, and to regulate a confusion which became painful; but my efforts were nugatory. I covered my eyes with my hand, and sat, I know not how long, without power to arrange or utter my conceptions.

I had remained for hours, as I believed, in absolute solitude. No thought of personal danger had molested my tranquillity. I had made no preparation for defence. What was it that suggested the design of perusing my father's manuscript? If, instead of this, I had retired to bed, and to sleep, to what fate might I not have been reserved? The ruffian, who must almost have suppressed his breathings to screen himself from discovery, would have noticed this signal, and I should have awakened only to perish with affright, and to abhor myself. Could I have remained unconscious of my danger? Could I have tranquilly slept in the midst of so deadly a snare?

And who was he that threatened to destroy me? By what means could he hide himself in this closet? Surely he is gifted with supernatural power. Such is the enemy of whose attempts I was forewarned. Daily I had seen him and conversed with him. Nothing could be discerned through the impenetrable veil of his duplicity. When busied in conjectures, as to the author of the evil that was threatened, my mind did not light, for a moment, upon his image.

Yet has he not avowed himself my enemy? Why should he be here if
he had not meditated evil?

He confesses that this has been his second attempt. What was
the scene of his former conspiracy? Was it not he whose whispers
betrayed him? Am I deceived; or was there not a faint resemblance
between the voice of this man and that which talked of grasping my
throat, and extinguishing my life in a moment? Then he had a colleague in his crime; now he is alone. Then death was the scope of
his thoughts; now an injury unspeakably more dreadful. How
thankful should I be to the power that has interposed to save me!

That power is invisible. It is subject to the cognizance of one of
my senses. What are the means that will inform me of what nature
it is? He has set himself to counterwork the machinations of this
man, who had menaced destruction to all that is dear to me, and
whose cunning had surmounted every human impediment. There
was none to rescue me from his grasp. My rashness even hastened
the completion of his scheme, and precluded him from the benefits
of deliberation. I had robbed him of the power to repent and forbear.
Had I been apprized of the danger, I should have regarded my conduct as the means of rendering my escape from it impossible. Such,
likewise, seem to have been the fears of my invisible protector. Else
why that startling intreaty to refrain from opening the closet? By
what inexplicable infatuation was I compelled to proceed?

Yet my conduct was wise. Carwin, unable to comprehend my
folly, ascribed my behaviour to my knowledge. He conceived himself previously detected, and such detection being possible to flow
only from *my* heavenly friend, and *his* enemy, his fears acquired
additional strength.

He is apprized of the nature and intentions of this being. Perhaps
he is a human agent. Yet, on that supposition his atchievements are
incredible. Why should I be selected as the object of his care; or, if a
mere mortal, should I not recognize some one, whom, benefits
imparted and received had prompted to love me? What were the limits and duration of his guardianship? Was the genius[1] of my birth
entrusted by divine benignity with this province? Are human faculties adequate to receive stronger proofs of the existence of unfettered
and beneficent intelligences than I have received?

But who was this man's coadjutor?[2] The voice that acknowledged an alliance in treachery with Carwin warned me to avoid the
summer-house. He assured me that there only my safety was endangered. His assurance, as it now appears, was fallacious. Was there

1. Protective spirit; dæmon.
2. Accomplice.

not deceit in his admonition? Was his compact really annulled? Some purpose was, perhaps, to be accomplished by preventing my future visits to that spot. Why was I enjoined silence to others, on the subject of this admonition, unless it were for some unauthorized and guilty purpose?

No one but myself was accustomed to visit it. Backward, it was hidden from distant view by the rock, and in front, it was screened from all examination, by creeping plants, and the branches of cedars. What recess could be more propitious to secrecy? The spirit which haunted it formerly was pure and rapturous. It was a fane sacred to the memory of infantile days, and to blissful imaginations of the future! What a gloomy reverse had succeeded since the ominous arrival of this stranger! Now, perhaps, it is the scene of his meditations. Purposes fraught with horror, that shun the light, and contemplate the pollution of innocence, are here engendered, and fostered, and reared to maturity.

Such were the ideas that, during the night, were tumultuously revolved by me. I reviewed every conversation in which Carwin had borne a part. I studied to discover the true inferences deducible from his deportment and words with regard to his former adventures and actual views. I pondered on the comments which he made on the relation which I had given of the closet dialogue. No new ideas suggested themselves in the course of this review. My expectation had, from the first, been disappointed on the small degree of surprize which this narrative excited in him. He never explicitly declared his opinion as to the nature of those voices, or decided whether they were real or visionary. He recommended no measures of caution or prevention.

But what measures were now to be taken? Was the danger which threatened me at an end? Had I nothing more to fear? I was lonely, and without means of defence. I could not calculate the motives and regulate the footsteps of this person. What certainty was there, that he would not re-assume his purposes, and swiftly return to the execution of them?

This idea covered me once more with dismay. How deeply did I regret the solitude in which I was placed, and how ardently did I desire the return of day! But neither of these inconveniencies were susceptible of remedy. At first, it occurred to me to summon my servant, and make her spend the night in my chamber; but the inefficacy of this expedient to enhance my safety was easily seen. Once I resolved to leave the house, and retire to my brother's, but was deterred by reflecting on the unseasonableness of the hour, on the alarm which my arrival, and the account which I should be obliged to give, might occasion, and on the danger to which I might expose myself in the way thither. I began, likewise, to consider Carwin's return to molest me as exceedingly improbable. He had relinquished, of his own accord, his design, and departed without compulsion.

Surely, said I, there is omnipotence in the cause that changed the views of a man like Carwin. The divinity that shielded me from his attempts will take suitable care of my future safety. Thus to yield to my fears is to deserve that they should be realized.

Scarcely had I uttered these words, when my attention was startled by the sound of footsteps. They denoted some one stepping into the piazza in front of my house. My new-born confidence was extinguished in a moment. Carwin, I thought, had repented his departure, and was hastily returning. The possibility that his return was prompted by intentions consistent with my safety, found no place in my mind. Images of violation and murder assailed me anew, and the terrors which succeeded almost incapacitated me from taking any measures for my defence. It was an impulse of which I was scarcely conscious, that made me fasten the lock and draw the bolts of my chamber door. Having done this, I threw myself on a seat; for I trembled to a degree which disabled me from standing, and my soul was so perfectly absorbed in the act of listening, that almost the vital motions were stopped.

The door below creaked on its hinges. It was not again thrust to, but appeared to remain open. Footsteps entered, traversed the entry, and began to mount the stairs. How I detested the folly of not pursuing the man when he withdrew, and bolting after him the outer door! Might he not conceive this omission to be a proof that my angel had deserted me, and be thereby fortified in guilt?

Every step on the stairs, which brought him nearer to my chamber, added vigor to my desperation. The evil with which I was menaced was to be at any rate eluded. How little did I preconceive the conduct which, in an exigence[3] like this, I should be prone to adopt. You will suppose that deliberation and despair would have suggested the same course of action, and that I should have, unhesitatingly, resorted to the best means of personal defence within my power. A penknife lay open upon my table. I remembered that it was there, and seized it. For what purpose you will scarcely inquire. It will be immediately supposed that I meant it for my last refuge, and that if all other means should fail, I should plunge it into the heart of my ravisher.

I have lost all faith in the stedfastness of human resolves. It was thus that in periods of calm I had determined to act. No cowardice had been held by me in greater abhorrence than that which prompted an injured female to destroy, not her injurer ere the

---

3. Emergency.

injury was perpetrated, but herself when it was without remedy. Yet now this penknife appeared to me of no other use than to baffle my assailant, and prevent the crime by destroying myself. To deliberate at such a time was impossible; but among the tumultuous suggestions of the moment, I do not recollect that it once occurred to me to use it as an instrument of direct defence.

The steps had now reached the second floor. Every footfall accelerated the completion, without augmenting the certainty of evil. The consciousness that the door was fast, now that nothing but that was interposed between me and danger, was a source of some consolation. I cast my eye towards the window. This, likewise, was a new suggestion. If the door should give way, it was my sudden resolution to throw myself from the window. Its height from the ground, which was covered beneath by a brick pavement, would insure my destruction; but I thought not of that.

When opposite to my door the footsteps ceased. Was he listening whether my fears were allayed, and my caution were asleep? Did he hope to take me by surprise? Yet, if so, why did he allow so many noisy signals to betray his approach? Presently the steps were again heard to approach the door. An hand was laid upon the lock, and the latch pulled back. Did he imagine it possible that I should fail to secure the door? A slight effort was made to push it open, as if all bolts being withdrawn, a slight effort only was required.

I no sooner perceived this, than I moved swiftly towards the window. Carwin's frame might be said to be all muscle. His strength and activity had appeared, in various instances, to be prodigious. A slight exertion of his force would demolish the door. Would not that exertion be made? Too surely it would; but, at the same moment that this obstacle should yield, and he should enter the apartment, my determination was formed to leap from the window. My senses were still bound to this object. I gazed at the door in momentary expectation that the assault would be made. The pause continued. The person without was irresolute and motionless.

Suddenly, it occurred to me that Carwin might conceive me to have fled. That I had not betaken myself to flight was, indeed, the least probable of all conclusions. In this persuasion he must have been confirmed on finding the lower door unfastened, and the chamber door locked. Was it not wise to foster this persuasion? Should I maintain deep silence, this, in addition to other circumstances, might encourage the belief, and he would once more depart. Every new reflection added plausibility to this reasoning. It was presently more strongly enforced, when I noticed footsteps withdrawing from the door. The blood once more flowed back to my heart, and a dawn of exultation began to rise: but my joy was short lived. Instead of descending the stairs, he passed to the door of the opposite chamber, opened it, and having entered, shut it after him with a violence that shook the house.

How was I to interpret this circumstance? For what end could he have entered this chamber? Did the violence with which he closed the door testify the depth of his vexation? This room was usually occupied by Pleyel. Was Carwin aware of his absence on this night? Could he be suspected of a design so sordid as pillage? If this were his view there were no means in my power to frustrate it. It behoved me to seize the first opportunity to escape; but if my escape were supposed by my enemy to have been already effected, no asylum was more secure than the present. How could my passage from the house be accomplished without noises that might incite him to pursue me?

Utterly at a loss to account for his going into Pleyel's chamber, I waited in instant expectation of hearing him come forth. All, however, was profoundly still. I listened in vain for a considerable period, to catch the sound of the door when it should again be opened. There was no other avenue by which he could escape, but a door which led into the girl's chamber. Would any evil from this quarter befall the girl?

Hence arose a new train of apprehensions. They merely added to the turbulence and agony of my reflections. Whatever evil impended over her, I had no power to avert it. Seclusion and silence were the only means of saving myself from the perils of this fatal night. What solemn vows did I put up, that if I should once more behold the light of day, I would never trust myself again within the threshold of this dwelling!

Minute lingered after minute, but no token was given that Carwin had returned to the passage. What, I again asked, could detain him in this room? Was it possible that he had returned, and glided, unperceived, away? I was speedily aware of the difficulty that attended an enterprize like this; and yet, as if by that means I were capable of gaining any information on that head, I cast anxious looks from the window.

The object that first attracted my attention was an human figure standing on the edge of the bank. Perhaps my penetration was assisted by my hopes. Be that as it will, the figure of Carwin was clearly distinguishable. From the obscurity of my station, it was impossible that I should be discerned by him, and yet he scarcely suffered me to catch a glimpse of him. He turned and went down the steep, which, in this part, was not difficult to be scaled.

My conjecture then had been right. Carwin has softly opened the door, descended the stairs, and issued forth. That I should not have overheard his steps, was only less incredible than that my eyes had deceived me. But what was now to be done? The house was at length delivered from this detested inmate. By one avenue might he again re-enter. Was it not wise to bar the lower door? Perhaps he had gone out by the kitchen door. For this end, he must have passed through Judith's chamber. These entrances being closed and bolted, as great security was gained as was compatible with my lonely condition.

The propriety of these measures was too manifest not to make me struggle successfully with my fears. Yet I opened my own door with the utmost caution, and descended as if I were afraid that Carwin had been still immured in Pleyel's chamber. The outer door was a-jar. I shut, with trembling eagerness, and drew every bolt that appended to it. I then passed with light and less cautious steps through the parlour, but was surprized to discover that the kitchen door was secure. I was compelled to acquiesce in the first conjecture that Carwin had escaped through the entry.

My heart was now somewhat eased of the load of apprehension. I returned once more to my chamber, the door of which I was careful to lock. It was no time to think of repose. The moon-light began already to fade before the light of the day. The approach of morning was betokened by the usual signals. I mused upon the events of this night, and determined to take up my abode henceforth at my brother's. Whether I should inform him of what had happened was a question which seemed to demand some consideration. My safety unquestionably required that I should abandon my present habitation.

As my thoughts began to flow with fewer impediments, the image of Pleyel, and the dubiousness of his condition, again recurred to me. I again ran over the possible causes of his absence on the preceding day. My mind was attuned to melancholy. I dwelt, with an obstinacy for which I could not account, on the idea of his death. I painted to myself his struggles with the billows, and his last appearance. I imagined myself a midnight wanderer on the shore, and to have stumbled on his corpse, which the tide had cast up. These dreary images affected me even to tears. I endeavoured not to restrain them. They imparted a relief which I had not anticipated. The more copiously they flowed, the more did my general sensations appear to subside into calm, and a certain restlessness give way to repose.

Perhaps, relieved by this effusion, the slumber so much wanted might have stolen on my senses, had there been no new cause of alarm.

Chapter XI

I was aroused from this stupor by sounds that evidently arose in the next chamber. Was it possible that I had been mistaken in the figure which I had seen on the bank? or had Carwin, by some inscrutable means, penetrated once more into this chamber? The opposite door opened; footsteps came forth, and the person, advancing to mine, knocked.

So unexpected an incident robbed me of all presence of mind, and, starting up, I involuntarily exclaimed, "Who is there?" An answer was immediately given. The voice, to my inexpressible astonishment, was Pleyel's.

"It is I. Have you risen? If you have not, make haste; I want three minutes conversation with you in the parlour—I will wait for you there." Saying this he retired from the door.

Should I confide in the testimony of my ears? If that were true, it was Pleyel that had been hitherto immured in the opposite chamber: he whom my rueful fancy had depicted in so many ruinous and ghastly shapes: he whose footsteps had been listened to with such inquietude! What is man, that knowledge is so sparingly conferred upon him! that his heart should be wrung with distress, and his frame be exanimated with fear, though his safety be encompassed with impregnable walls! What are the bounds of human imbecility! He that warned me of the presence of my foe refused the intimation by which so many racking fears would have been precluded.

Yet who would have imagined the arrival of Pleyel at such an hour? His tone was desponding and anxious. Why this unseasonable summons? and why this hasty departure? Some tidings he, perhaps, bears of mysterious and unwelcome import.

My impatience would not allow me to consume much time in deliberation: I hastened down. Pleyel I found standing at a window, with eyes cast down as in meditation, and arms folded on his breast. Every line in his countenance was pregnant with sorrow. To this was added a certain wanness and air of fatigue. The last time I had seen him appearances had been the reverse of these. I was startled at the change. The first impulse was to question him as to the cause. This impulse was supplanted by some degree of confusion, flowing from a consciousness that love had too large, and, as it might prove, a perceptible share in creating this impulse. I was silent.

Presently he raised his eyes and fixed them upon me. I read in them an anguish altogether ineffable. Never had I witnessed a like demeanour in Pleyel. Never, indeed, had I observed an human countenance in which grief was more legibly inscribed. He seemed struggling for utterance; but his struggles being fruitless, he shook his head and turned away from me.

My impatience would not allow me to be longer silent: "What," said I, "for heaven's sake, my friend, what is the matter?"

He started at the sound of my voice. His looks, for a moment, became convulsed with an emotion very different from grief. His accents were broken with rage.

"The matter—O wretch!—thus exquisitely fashioned—on whom nature seemed to have exhausted all her graces; with charms so awful and so pure! how art thou fallen! From what height fallen! A ruin so complete—so unheard of!"

His words were again choked by emotion. Grief and pity were again mingled in his features. He resumed, in a tone half suffocated by sobs:

"But why should I upbraid thee? Could I restore to thee what thou has lost; efface this cursed stain; snatch thee from the jaws of this fiend; I would do it. Yet what will avail my efforts? I have not arms with which to contend with so consummate, so frightful a depravity.

"Evidence less than this would only have excited resentment and scorn. The wretch who should have breathed a suspicion injurious to thy honor, would have been regarded without anger; not hatred or envy could have prompted him; it would merely be an argument of madness. That my eyes, that my ears, should bear witness to thy fall! By no other way could detestible conviction be imparted.

"Why do I summon thee to this conference? Why expose myself to thy derision? Here admonition and entreaty are vain. Thou knowest him already, for a murderer and thief. I had thought to have been the first to disclose to thee his infamy; to have warned thee of the pit to which thou art hastening; but thy eyes are open in vain. O foul and insupportable disgrace!

"There is but one path. I know you will disappear together. In thy ruin, how will the felicity and honor of multitudes be involved! But it must come. This scene shall not be blotted by his presence. No doubt thou wilt shortly see thy detested paramour. This scene will be again polluted by a midnight assignation.[1] Inform him of his danger; tell him that his crimes are known; let him fly far and instantly from this spot, if he desires to avoid the fate which menaced him in Ireland.

"And wilt thou not stay behind?—But shame upon my weakness. I know not what I would say.—I have done what I purposed. To stay longer, to expostulate, to beseech, to enumerate the consequences of thy act—what end can it serve but to blazon thy infamy and embitter our woes? And yet, O think, think ere it be too late, on the distresses which thy flight will entail upon us; on the base, grovelling, and atrocious character of the wretch to whom thou hast sold thy honor. But what is this? Is not thy effrontery impenetrable, and thy heart thoroughly cankered? O most specious, and most profligate of women!"

Saying this, he rushed out of the house. I saw him in a few moments hurrying along the path which led to my brother's. I had no power to prevent his going, or to recall, or to follow him. The accents I had heard were calculated to confound and bewilder. I

---

1. Meeting between lovers; rendezvous.

looked around me to assure myself that the scene was real. I moved that I might banish the doubt that I was awake. Such enormous imputations from the mouth of Pleyel! To be stigmatized with the names of wanton and profligate! To be charged with the sacrifice of honor! with midnight meetings with a wretch known to be a murderer and thief! with an intention to fly in his company!

What I had heard was surely the dictate of phrenzy, or it was built upon some fatal, some incomprehensible mistake. After the horrors of the night, after undergoing perils so imminent from this man, to be summoned to an interview like this; to find Pleyel fraught with a belief that, instead of having chosen death as a refuge from the violence of this man, I had hugged his baseness to my heart, had sacrificed for him my purity, my spotless name, my friendships, and my fortune! that even madness could engender accusations like these was not to be believed.

What evidence could possibly suggest conceptions so wild? After the unlooked-for interview with Carwin in my chamber, he retired. Could Pleyel have observed his exit? It was not long after that Pleyel himself entered. Did he build on this incident, his odious conclusions? Could the long series of my actions and sentiments grant me no exemption from suspicions so foul? Was it not more rational to infer that Carwin's designs had been illicit; that my life had been endangered by the fury of one whom, by some means, he had discovered to be an assassin and robber; that my honor had been assailed, not by blandishments, but by violence?

He has judged me without hearing. He has drawn from dubious appearances, conclusions the most improbable and unjust. He has loaded me with all outrageous epithets. He has ranked me with prostitutes and thieves. I cannot pardon thee, Pleyel, for this injustice. Thy understanding must be hurt. If it be not, if thy conduct was sober and deliberate, I can never forgive an outrage so unmanly, and so gross.

These thoughts gradually gave place to others. Pleyel was possessed by some momentary phrenzy: appearances had led him into palpable errors. Whence could his sagacity have contracted this blindness? Was it not love? Previously assured of my affection for Carwin, distracted with grief and jealousy, and impelled hither at that late hour by some unknown instigation, his imagination transformed shadows into monsters, and plunged him into these deplorable errors.

This idea was not unattended with consolation. My soul was divided between indignation at his injustice, and delight on account of the source from which I conceived it to spring. For a long time they would allow admission to no other thoughts. Surprize is an emotion that enfeebles, not invigorates. All my meditations were accompanied with wonder. I rambled with vagueness, or clung to one image with an obstinacy which sufficiently testified the maddening influence of late transactions.

Gradually I proceeded to reflect upon the consequences of Pleyel's mistake, and on the measures I should take to guard myself against future injury from Carwin. Should I suffer this mistake to be detected by time? When his passion should subside, would he not perceive the flagrancy of his injustice, and hasten to atone for it? Did it not become my character to testify resentment for language and treatment so opprobrious?[2] Wrapt up in the consciousness of innocence, and confiding in the influence of time and reflection to confute so groundless a charge, it was my province to be passive and silent.

As to the violences meditated by Carwin, and the means of eluding them, the path to be taken by me was obvious. I resolved to tell the tale to my brother, and regulate myself by his advice. For this end, when the morning was somewhat advanced, I took the way to his house. My sister was engaged in her customary occupations. As soon as I appeared, she remarked a change in my looks. I was not willing to alarm her by the information which I had to communicate. Her health was in that condition[3] which rendered a disastrous tale particularly unsuitable. I forbore a direct answer to her inquiries, and inquired, in my turn, for Wieland.

"Why," said she, "I suspect something mysterious and unpleasant has happened this morning. Scarcely had we risen when Pleyel dropped among us. What could have prompted him to make us so early and so unseasonable a visit I cannot tell. To judge from the disorder of his dress, and his countenance, something of an extraordinary nature has occurred. He permitted me merely to know that he had slept none, nor even undressed, during the past night. He took your brother to walk with him. Some topic must have deeply engaged them, for Wieland did not return till the breakfast hour was passed, and returned alone. His disturbance was excessive; but he would not listen to my importunities, or tell me what had happened. I gathered from hints which he let fall, that your situation was, in some way, the cause: yet he assured me that you were at your own house, alive, in good health, and in perfect safety. He scarcely ate a morsel, and immediately after breakfast went out again. He would not inform me whither he was going, but mentioned that he probably might not return before night."

I was equally astonished and alarmed by this information. Pleyel had told his tale to my brother, and had, by a plausible and exaggerated picture, instilled into him unfavorable thoughts of me. Yet would not the more correct judgment of Wieland perceive and expose

2. Abusive or scornful.
3. I.e., she is pregnant.

the fallacy of his conclusions? Perhaps his uneasiness might arise from some insight into the character of Carwin, and from apprehensions for my safety. The appearances by which Pleyel had been misled, might induce him likewise to believe that I entertained an indiscreet, though not dishonorable affection for Carwin. Such were the conjectures rapidly formed. I was inexpressibly anxious to change them into certainty. For this end an interview with my brother was desirable. He was gone, no one knew whither, and was not expected speedily to return. I had no clue by which to trace his footsteps.

My anxieties could not be concealed from my sister. They heightened her solicitude to be acquainted with the cause. There were many reasons persuading me to silence: at least, till I had seen my brother, it would be an act of inexcusable temerity to unfold what had lately passed. No other expedient for eluding her importunities occurred to me, but that of returning to my own house. I recollected my determination to become a tenant of this roof. I mentioned it to her. She joyfully acceded to this proposal, and suffered me, with less reluctance, to depart, when I told her that it was with a view to collect and send to my new dwelling what articles would be immediately useful to me.

Once more I returned to the house which had been the scene of so much turbulence and danger. I was at no great distance from it when I observed my brother coming out. On seeing me he stopped, and after ascertaining, as it seemed, which way I was going, he returned into the house before me. I sincerely rejoiced at this event, and I hastened to set things, if possible, on their right footing.

His brow was by no means expressive of those vehement emotions with which Pleyel had been agitated. I drew a favorable omen from this circumstance. Without delay I began the conversation.

"I have been to look for you," said I, "but was told by Catharine that Pleyel had engaged you on some important and disagreeable affair. Before his interview with you he spent a few minutes with me. These minutes he employed in upbraiding me for crimes and intentions with which I am by no means chargeable. I believe him to have taken up his opinions on very insufficient grounds. His behaviour was in the highest degree precipitate and unjust, and, until I receive some atonement, I shall treat him, in my turn, with that contempt which he justly merits: meanwhile I am fearful that he has prejudiced my brother against me. That is an evil which I most anxiously deprecate, and which I shall indeed exert myself to remove. Has he made me the subject of this morning's conversation?"

My brother's countenance testified no surprize at my address. The benignity of his looks were no wise diminished.

"It is true," said he, "your conduct was the subject of our discourse. I am your friend, as well as your brother. There is no human being whom I love with more tenderness, and whose welfare is nearer my heart. Judge then with what emotions I listened to Pleyel's story. I expect and desire you to vindicate yourself from aspersions so foul, if vindication be possible."

The tone with which he uttered the last words affected me deeply. "If vindication be possible!" repeated I. "From what you know, do you deem a formal vindication necessary? Can you harbour for a moment the belief of my guilt?"

He shook his head with an air of acute anguish. "I have struggled," said he, "to dismiss that belief. You speak before a judge who will profit by any pretence to acquit you: who is ready to question his own senses when they plead against you."

These words incited a new set of thoughts in my mind. I began to suspect that Pleyel had built his accusations on some foundation unknown to me. "I may be a stranger to the grounds of your belief. Pleyel loaded me with indecent and virulent invectives, but he withheld from me the facts that generated his suspicions. Events took place last night of which some of the circumstances were of an ambiguous nature. I conceived that these might possibly have fallen under his cognizance, and that, viewed through the mists of prejudice and passion, they supplied a pretence for his conduct, but believed that your more unbiassed judgment would estimate them at their just value. Perhaps his tale has been different from what I suspect it to be. Listen then to my narrative. If there be any thing in his story inconsistent with mine, his story is false."

I then proceeded to a circumstantial relation of the incidents of the last night. Wieland listened with deep attention. Having finished, "This," continued I, "is the truth; you see in what circumstances an interview took place between Carwin and me. He remained for hours in my closet, and for some minutes in my chamber. He departed without haste or interruption. If Pleyel marked him as he left the house, and it is not impossible that he did, inferences injurious to my character might suggest themselves to him. In admitting them, he gave proofs of less discernment and less candor than I once ascribed to him."

"His proofs," said Wieland, after a considerable pause, "are different. That he should be deceived, is not possible. That he himself is not the deceiver, could not be believed, if his testimony were not inconsistent with yours; but the doubts which I entertained are now removed. Your tale, some parts of it, is marvellous; the voice which exclaimed against your rashness in approaching the closet, your persisting notwithstanding that prohibition, your belief that I was the ruffian, and your subsequent conduct, are believed by me, because I have known you from childhood, because a thousand instances have attested your veracity, and because nothing less than my own hearing and vision would convince me, in opposition to her own assertions, that my sister had fallen into wickedness like this."

I threw my arms around him, and bathed his cheek with my tears. "That," said I, "is spoken like my brother. But what are the proofs?"

He replied—"Pleyel informed me that, in going to your house, his attention was attracted by two voices. The persons speaking sat beneath the bank out of sight. These persons, judging by their voices, were Carwin and you. I will not repeat the dialogue. If my sister was the female, Pleyel was justified in concluding you to be, indeed, one of the most profligate of women. Hence, his accusations of you, and his efforts to obtain my concurrence to a plan by which an eternal separation should be brought about between my sister and this man."

I made Wieland repeat this recital. Here, indeed, was a tale to fill me with terrible foreboding. I had vainly thought that my safety could be sufficiently secured by doors and bars, but this is a foe from whose grasp no power of divinity can save me! His artifices will ever lay my fame and happiness at his mercy. How shall I counterwork his plots, or detect his coadjutor? He has taught some vile and abandoned female to mimic my voice. Pleyel's ears were the witnesses of my dishonor. This is the midnight assignation to which he alluded. Thus is the silence he maintained when attempting to open the door of my chamber, accounted for. He supposed me absent, and meant, perhaps, had my apartment been accessible, to leave in it some accusing memorial.

Pleyel was no longer equally culpable. The sincerity of his anguish, the depth of his despair, I remembered with some tendencies to gratitude. Yet was he not precipitate? Was the conjecture that my part was played by some mimic so utterly untenable? Instances of this faculty are common. The wickedness of Carwin must, in his opinion, have been adequate to such contrivances, and yet the supposition of my guilt was adopted in preference to that.

But how was this error to be unveiled? What but my own assertion had I to throw in the balance against it? Would this be permitted to outweigh the testimony of his senses? I had no witnesses to prove my existence in another place. The real events of that night are marvellous. Few, to whom they should be related, would scruple to discredit them. Pleyel is sceptical in a transcendant degree. I cannot summon Carwin to my bar, and make him the attestor of my innocence, and the accuser of himself.

My brother saw and comprehended my distress. He was unacquainted, however, with the full extent of it. He knew not by how many motives I was incited to retrieve the good opinion of Pleyel. He endeavored to console me. Some new event, he said, would occur to disentangle the maze. He did not question the influence of my eloquence, if I thought proper to exert it. Why not seek an interview with

Pleyel, and exact from him a minute relation, in which something may be met with serving to destroy the probability of the whole?

I caught, with eagerness, at this hope; but my alacrity was damped by new reflections. Should I, perfect in this respect, and unblemished as I was, thrust myself, uncalled, into his presence, and make my felicity depend upon his arbitrary verdict?

"If you chuse to seek an interview," continued Wieland, "you must make haste, for Pleyel informed me of his intention to set out this evening or to-morrow on a long journey."

No intelligence was less expected or less welcome than this. I had thrown myself in a window seat; but now, starting on my feet, I exclaimed, "Good heavens! what is it you say? a journey? whither? when?"

"I cannot say whither. It is a sudden resolution I believe. I did not hear of it till this morning. He promises to write to me as soon as he is settled."

I needed no further information as to the cause and issue of this journey. The scheme of happiness to which he had devoted his thoughts was blasted by the discovery of last night. My preference of another, and my unworthiness to be any longer the object of his adoration, were evinced by the same act and in the same moment. The thought of utter desertion, a desertion originating in such a cause, was the prelude to distraction. That Pleyel should abandon me forever, because I was blind to his excellence, because I coveted pollution, and wedded infamy, when, on the contrary, my heart was the shrine of all purity, and beat only for his sake, was a destiny which, as long as my life was in my own hands, I would by no means consent to endure.

I remembered that this evil was still preventable; that this fatal journey it was still in my power to procrastinate, or, perhaps, to occasion it to be laid aside. There were no impediments to a visit: I only dreaded lest the interview should be too long delayed. My brother befriended my impatience, and readily consented to furnish me with a chaise and servant to attend me. My purpose was to go immediately to Pleyel's farm, where his engagements usually detained him during the day.

Chapter XII

My way lay through the city.[1] I had scarcely entered it when I was seized with a general sensation of sickness. Every object grew dim and swam before my sight. It was with difficulty I prevented myself

1. Philadelphia.

from sinking to the bottom of the carriage. I ordered myself to be carried to Mrs. Baynton's,[2] in hope that an interval of repose would invigorate and refresh me. My distracted thoughts would allow me but little rest. Growing somewhat better in the afternoon, I resumed my journey.

My contemplations were limited to a few objects. I regarded my success, in the purpose which I had in view, as considerably doubtful. I depended, in some degree, on the suggestions of the moment, and on the materials which Pleyel himself should furnish me. When I reflected on the nature of the accusation, I burned with disdain. Would not truth, and the consciousness of innocence, render me triumphant? Should I not cast from me, with irresistible force, such atrocious imputations?

What an entire and mournful change has been effected in a few hours! The gulf that separates man from insects is not wider than that which severs the polluted from the chaste among women. Yesterday and to-day I am the same. There is a degree of depravity to which it is impossible for me to sink; yet, in the apprehension of another, my ancient and intimate associate, the perpetual witness of my actions, and partaker of my thoughts, I had ceased to be the same. My integrity was tarnished and withered in his eyes. I was the colleague of a murderer, and the paramour of a thief!

His opinion was not destitute of evidence: yet what proofs could reasonably avail to establish an opinion like this? If the sentiments corresponded not with the voice that was heard, the evidence was deficient; but this want of correspondence would have been supposed by me if I had been the auditor and Pleyel the criminal. But mimicry might still more plausibly have been employed to explain the scene. Alas! it is the fate of Clara Wieland to fall into the hands of a precipitate and inexorable judge.

But what, O man of mischief! is the tendency of thy thoughts? Frustrated in thy first design, thou wilt not forego the immolation of thy victim. To exterminate my reputation was all that remained to thee, and this my guardian has permitted. To dispossess Pleyel of this prejudice may be impossible; but if that be effected, it cannot be supposed that thy wiles are exhausted; thy cunning will discover innumerable avenues to the accomplishment of thy malignant purpose.

Why should I enter the lists against thee? Would to heaven I could disarm thy vengeance by my deprecations! When I think of all the resources with which nature and education have supplied thee; that thy form is a combination of steely fibres and organs of exquisite ductility[3] and boundless compass, actuated by an intelli-

---

2. The family friend mentioned in Chapter 4.
3. Malleability.

gence gifted with infinite endowments, and comprehending all knowledge, I perceive that my doom is fixed. What obstacle will be able to divert thy zeal or repel thy efforts? That being who has hitherto protected me has borne testimony to the formidableness of thy attempts, since nothing less than supernatural interference could check thy career.

Musing on these thoughts, I arrived, towards the close of the day, at Pleyel's house. A month before, I had traversed the same path; but how different were my sensations! Now I was seeking the presence of one who regarded me as the most degenerate of human kind. I was to plead the cause of my innocence, against witnesses the most explicit and unerring, of those which support the fabric of human knowledge. The nearer I approached the crisis, the more did my confidence decay. When the chaise stopped at the door, my strength refused to support me, and I threw myself into the arms of an ancient female domestic. I had not courage to inquire whether her master was at home. I was tormented with fears that the projected journey was already undertaken. These fears were removed, by her asking me whether she should call her young master, who had just gone into his own room. I was somewhat revived by this intelligence, and resolved immediately to seek him there.

In my confusion of mind, I neglected to knock at the door, but entered his apartment without previous notice. This abruptness was altogether involuntary. Absorbed in reflections of such unspeakable moment, I had no leisure to heed the niceties of punctilio.[4] I discovered him standing with his back towards the entrance. A small trunk, with its lid raised, was before him, in which it seemed as if he had been busy in packing his clothes. The moment of my entrance, he was employed in gazing at something which he held in his hand.

I imagined that I fully comprehended this scene. The image which he held before him, and by which his attention was so deeply engaged, I doubted not to be my own. These preparations for his journey, the cause to which it was to be imputed, the hopelessness of success in the undertaking on which I had entered, rushed at once upon my feelings, and dissolved me into a flood of tears.

Startled by this sound, he dropped the lid of the trunk and turned. The solemn sadness that previously overspread his countenance, gave sudden way to an attitude and look of the most vehement astonishment. Perceiving me unable to uphold myself, he stepped towards me without speaking, and supported me by his arm. The kindness of this action called forth a new effusion from my eyes. Weeping was a solace to which, at that time, I had not grown familiar, and which, therefore, was peculiarly delicious. Indignation was no longer to be

4. Etiquette.

read in the features of my friend. They were pregnant with a mixture of wonder and pity. Their expression was easily interpreted. This visit, and these tears, were tokens of my penitence. The wretch whom he had stigmatized as incurably and obdurately wicked, now shewed herself susceptible of remorse, and had come to confess her guilt.

This persuasion had no tendency to comfort me. It only shewed me, with new evidence, the difficulty of the task which I had assigned myself. We were mutually silent. I had less power and less inclination than ever to speak. I extricated myself from his hold, and threw myself on a sofa. He placed himself by my side, and appeared to wait with impatience and anxiety for some beginning of the conversation. What could I say? If my mind had suggested any thing suitable to the occasion, my utterance was suffocated by tears.

Frequently he attempted to speak, but seemed deterred by some degree of uncertainty as to the true nature of the scene. At length, in faltering accents he spoke:

"My friend! would to heaven I were still permitted to call you by that name. The image that I once adored existed only in my fancy; but though I cannot hope to see it realized, you may not be totally insensible to the horrors of that gulf into which you are about to plunge. What heart is forever exempt from the goadings of compunction and the influx of laudable propensities?

"I thought you accomplished and wise beyond the rest of women. Not a sentiment you uttered, not a look you assumed, that were not, in my apprehension, fraught with the sublimities of rectitude and the illuminations of genius. Deceit has some bounds. Your education could not be without influence. A vigorous understanding cannot be utterly devoid of virtue; but you could not counterfeit the powers of invention and reasoning. I was rash in my invectives. I will not, but with life, relinquish all hopes of you. I will shut out every proof that would tell me that your heart is incurably diseased.

"You come to restore me once more to happiness; to convince me that you have torn her mask from vice, and feel nothing but abhorrence for the part you have hitherto acted."

At these words my equanimity[5] forsook me. For a moment I forgot the evidence from which Pleyel's opinions were derived, the benevolence of his remonstrances, and the grief which his accents bespoke; I was filled with indignation and horror at charges so black; I shrunk back and darted at him a look of disdain and anger. My passion supplied me with words.

"What detestable infatuation was it that led me hither! Why do I patiently endure these horrible insults! My offences exist only in your own distempered imagination: you are leagued with the traitor

5. Balance or poise, especially under pressure.

who assailed my life: you have vowed the destruction of my peace and honor. I deserve infamy for listening to calumnies so base!"

These words were heard by Pleyel without visible resentment. His countenance relapsed into its former gloom; but he did not even look at me. The ideas which had given place to my angry emotions returned, and once more melted me into tears. "O!" I exclaimed, in a voice broken by sobs, "what a task is mine! Compelled to hearken to charges which I feel to be false, but which I know to be believed by him that utters them; believed too not without evidence, which, though fallacious, is not unplausible.

"I came hither not to confess, but to vindicate. I know the source of your opinions. Wieland has informed me on what your suspicions are built. These suspicions are fostered by you as certainties; the tenor of my life, of all my conversations and letters, affords me no security; every sentiment that my tongue and my pen have uttered, bear testimony to the rectitude of my mind; but this testimony is rejected. I am condemned as brutally profligate: I am classed with the stupidly and sordidly wicked.

"And where are the proofs that must justify so foul and so improbable an accusation? You have overheard a midnight conference. Voices have saluted your ear, in which you imagine yourself to have recognized mine, and that of a detected villain. The sentiments expressed were not allowed to outweigh the casual or concerted resemblance of voice. Sentiments the reverse of all those whose influence my former life had attested, denoting a mind polluted by grovelling vices, and entering into compact with that of a thief and a murderer. The nature of these sentiments did not enable you to detect the cheat, did not suggest to you the possibility that my voice had been counterfeited by another.

"You were precipitate and prone to condemn. Instead of rushing on the impostors, and comparing the evidence of sight with that of hearing, you stood aloof, or you fled. My innocence would not now have stood in need of vindication, if this conduct had been pursued. That you did not pursue it, your present thoughts incontestibly prove. Yet this conduct might surely have been expected from Pleyel. That he would not hastily impute the blackest of crimes, that he would not couple my name with infamy, and cover me with ruin for inadequate or slight reasons, might reasonably have been expected." The sobs which convulsed my bosom would not suffer me to proceed.

Pleyel was for a moment affected. He looked at me with some expression of doubt; but this quickly gave place to a mournful solemnity. He fixed his eyes on the floor as in reverie, and spoke:

"Two hours hence I am gone. Shall I carry away with me the sorrow that is now my guest? or shall that sorrow be accumulated tenfold? What is she that is now before me? Shall every hour supply me

with new proofs of a wickedness beyond example? Already I deem
her the most abandoned and detestable of human creatures. Her
coming and her tears imparted a gleam of hope, but that gleam has
vanished."

He now fixed his eyes upon me, and every muscle in his face
trembled. His tone was hollow and terrible—"Thou knowest that I
was a witness of your interview, yet thou comest hither to upbraid
me for injustice! Thou canst look me in the face and say that I am
deceived!—An inscrutable providence has fashioned thee for some
end. Thou wilt live, no doubt, to fulfil the purposes of thy maker, if
he repent not of his workmanship, and send not his vengeance to
exterminate thee, ere the measure of thy days be full. Surely nothing in the shape of man can vie with thee!

"But I thought I had stifled this fury. I am not constituted thy
judge. My office is to pity and amend, and not to punish and revile.
I deemed myself exempt from all tempestuous passions. I had almost
persuaded myself to weep over thy fall; but I am frail as dust, and
mutable as water; I am calm, I am compassionate only in thy absence.—
Make this house, this room, thy abode as long as thou wilt, but
forgive me if I prefer solitude for the short time during which I shall
stay." Saying this, he motioned as if to leave the apartment.

The stormy passions of this man affected me by sympathy. I
ceased to weep. I was motionless and speechless with agony. I sat
with my hands clasped, mutely gazing after him as he withdrew. I
desired to detain him, but was unable to make any effort for that
purpose, till he had passed out of the room. I then uttered an involuntary and piercing cry—"Pleyel! Art thou gone? Gone forever?"

At this summons he hastily returned. He beheld me wild, pale,
gasping for breath, and my head already sinking on my bosom. A
painful dizziness seized me, and I fainted away.

When I recovered, I found myself stretched on a bed in the outer
apartment, and Pleyel, with two female servants, standing beside it.
All the fury and scorn which the countenance of the former lately
expressed, had now disappeared, and was succeeded by the most tender anxiety. As soon as he perceived that my senses were returned
to me, he clasped his hands, and exclaimed, "God be thanked! you
are once more alive. I had almost despaired of your recovery. I fear
I have been precipitate and unjust. My senses must have been the
victims of some inexplicable and momentary phrenzy. Forgive me, I
beseech you, forgive my reproaches. I would purchase conviction of
your purity, at the price of my existence here and hereafter."

He once more, in a tone of the most fervent tenderness, besought
me to be composed, and then left me to the care of the women.

Chapter XIII

Here was wrought a surprizing change in my friend. What was it that had shaken conviction so firm? Had any thing occurred during my fit, adequate to produce so total an alteration? My attendants informed me that he had not left my apartment; that the unusual duration of my fit, and the failure, for a time, of all the means used for my recovery, had filled him with grief and dismay. Did he regard the effect which his reproaches had produced as a proof of my sincerity?

In this state of mind, I little regarded my languors of body. I rose and requested an interview with him before my departure, on which I was resolved, notwithstanding his earnest solicitation to spend the night at his house. He complied with my request. The tenderness which he had lately betrayed, had now disappeared, and he once more relapsed into a chilling solemnity.

I told him that I was preparing to return to my brother's; that I had come hither to vindicate my innocence from the foul aspersions which he had cast upon it. My pride had not taken refuge in silence or distance. I had not relied upon time, or the suggestions of his cooler thoughts, to confute his charges. Conscious as I was that I was perfectly guiltless, and entertaining some value for his good opinion, I could not prevail upon myself to believe that my efforts to make my innocence manifest, would be fruitless. Adverse appearances might be numerous and specious, but they were unquestionably false. I was willing to believe him sincere, that he made no charges which he himself did not believe; but these charges were destitute of truth. The grounds of his opinion were fallacious; and I desired an opportunity of detecting their fallacy. I entreated him to be explicit, and to give me a detail of what he had heard, and what he had seen.

At these words, my companion's countenance grew darker. He appeared to be struggling with his rage. He opened his lips to speak, but his accents died away ere they were formed. This conflict lasted for some minutes, but his fortitude was finally successful. He spoke as follows:

"I would fain put an end to this hateful scene: what I shall say, will be breath idly and unprofitably consumed. The clearest narrative will add nothing to your present knowledge. You are acquainted with the grounds of my opinion, and yet you avow yourself innocent: Why then should I rehearse these grounds? You are apprized of the character of Carwin: Why then should I enumerate the discoveries which I have made respecting him? Yet, since it is your request; since, considering the limitedness of human faculties, some

error may possibly lurk in those appearances which I have witnessed, I will briefly relate what I know.

"Need I dwell upon the impressions which your conversation and
deportment originally made upon me? We parted in childhood; but
our intercourse, by letter, was copious and uninterrupted. How fondly
did I anticipate a meeting with one whom her letters had previously
taught me to consider as the first of women, and how fully realized
were the expectations that I had formed!

"Here, said I, is a being, after whom sages may model their transcendent intelligence, and painters, their ideal beauty. Here is exemplified, that union between intellect and form, which has hitherto
existed only in the conceptions of the poet. I have watched your eyes;
my attention has hung upon your lips. I have questioned whether the
enchantments of your voice were more conspicuous in the intricacies
of melody, or the emphasis of rhetoric. I have marked the transitions
of your discourse, the felicities of your expression, your refined argumentation, and glowing imagery; and been forced to acknowledge,
that all delights were meagre and contemptible, compared with those
connected with the audience and sight of you. I have contemplated
your principles, and been astonished at the solidity of their foundation, and the perfection of their structure. I have traced you to your
home. I have viewed you in relation to your servants, to your family,
to your neighbours, and to the world. I have seen by what skilful
arrangements you facilitate the performance of the most arduous
and complicated duties; what daily accessions of strength your judicious discipline bestowed upon your memory; what correctness and
abundance of knowledge was daily experienced by your unwearied
application to books, and to writing. If she that possesses so much
in the bloom of youth, will go on accumulating her stores, what,
said I, is the picture she will display at a mature age?

"You know not the accuracy of my observation. I was desirous that
others should profit by an example so rare. I therefore noted down, in
writing, every particular of your conduct. I was anxious to benefit by
an opportunity so seldom afforded us. I laboured not to omit the
slightest shade, or the most petty line in your portrait. Here there
was no other task incumbent on me but to copy; there was no need to
exaggerate or overlook, in order to produce a more unexceptionable
pattern. Here was a combination of harmonies and graces, incapable
of diminution or accession without injury to its completeness.

"I found no end and no bounds to my task. No display of a scene
like this could be chargeable with redundancy or superfluity. Even
the colour of a shoe, the knot of a ribband, or your attitude in
plucking a rose, were of moment to be recorded. Even the arrangements of your breakfast-table and your toilet have been amply
displayed.

"I know that mankind are more easily enticed to virtue by example than by precept. I know that the absoluteness of a model, when supplied by invention, diminishes its salutary influence, since it is useless, we think, to strive after that which we know to be beyond our reach. But the picture which I drew was not a phantom; as a model, it was devoid of imperfection; and to aspire to that height which had been really attained, was by no means unreasonable. I had another and more interesting object in view. One existed who claimed all my tenderness. Here, in all its parts, was a model worthy of assiduous study, and indefatigable imitation. I called upon her, as she wished to secure and enhance my esteem, to mould her thoughts, her words, her countenance, her actions, by this pattern.

"The task was exuberant of pleasure, and I was deeply engaged in it, when an imp of mischief was let loose in the form of Carwin. I admired his powers and accomplishments. I did not wonder that they were admired by you. On the rectitude of your judgment, however, I relied to keep this admiration within discreet and scrupulous bounds. I assured myself, that the strangeness of his deportment, and the obscurity of his life, would teach you caution. Of all errors, my knowledge of your character informed me that this was least likely to befall you.

"You were powerfully affected by his first appearance; you were bewitched by his countenance and his tones; your description was ardent and pathetic: I listened to you with some emotions of surprize. The portrait you drew in his absence, and the intensity with which you mused upon it, were new and unexpected incidents. They bespoke a sensibility somewhat too vivid; but from which, while subjected to the guidance of an understanding like yours, there was nothing to dread.

"A more direct intercourse took place between you. I need not apologize for the solicitude which I entertained for your safety. He that gifted me with perception of excellence, compelled me to love it. In the midst of danger and pain, my contemplations have ever been cheered by your image. Every object in competition with you, was worthless and trivial. No price was too great by which your safety could be purchased. For that end, the sacrifice of ease, of health, and even of life, would cheerfully have been made by me. What wonder then, that I scrutinized the sentiments and deportment of this man with ceaseless vigilance; that I watched your words and your looks when he was present; and that I extracted cause for the deepest inquietudes, from every token which you gave of having put your happiness into this man's keeping?

"I was cautious in deciding. I recalled the various conversations in which the topics of love and marriage had been discussed. As a woman, young, beautiful, and independent, it behoved you to have

fortified your mind with just principles on this subject. Your principles were eminently just. Had not their rectitude and their firmness
been attested by your treatment of that specious seducer Dashwood?[1]
These principles, I was prone to believe, exempted you from danger
in this new state of things. I was not the last to pay my homage to
the unrivalled capacity, insinuation, and eloquence of this man. I
have disguised, but could never stifle the conviction, that his eyes
and voice had a witchcraft in them, which rendered him truly formidable: but I reflected on the ambiguous expression of his countenance—an ambiguity which you were the first to remark; on the
cloud which obscured his character; and on the suspicious nature
of that concealment which he studied; and concluded you to be
safe. I denied the obvious construction to appearances. I referred
your conduct to some principle which had not been hitherto disclosed, but which was reconcileable with those already known.

"I was not suffered to remain long in this suspense. One evening,
you may recollect, I came to your house, where it was my purpose,
as usual, to lodge, somewhat earlier than ordinary. I spied a light in
your chamber as I approached from the outside, and on inquiring
of Judith, was informed that you were writing. As your kinsman
and friend, and fellow-lodger, I thought I had a right to be familiar.
You were in your chamber, but your employment and the time were
such as to make it no infraction of decorum to follow you thither.
The spirit of mischievous gaiety possessed me. I proceeded on tip-
toe. You did not perceive my entrance; and I advanced softly till I
was able to overlook your shoulder.

"I had gone thus far in error, and had no power to recede. How
cautiously should we guard against the first inroads of temptation! I
knew that to pry into your papers was criminal; but I reflected that
no sentiment of yours was of a nature which made it your interest to
conceal it. You wrote much more than you permitted your friends to
peruse. My curiosity was strong, and I had only to throw a glance
upon the paper, to secure its gratification. I should never have deliberately committed an act like this. The slightest obstacle would
have repelled me; but my eye glanced almost spontaneously upon
the paper. I caught only parts of sentences; but my eyes comprehended more at a glance, because the characters were short-hand. I
lighted on the words *summer-house, midnight*, and made out a passage which spoke of the propriety and of the effects to be expected
from *another* interview. All this passed in less than a moment. I then
checked myself, and made myself known to you, by a tap upon your
shoulder.

"I could pardon and account for some trifling alarm; but your
trepidation and blushes were excessive. You hurried the paper out of

---

1. Francis Dashwood (1708–1781), an English politician and notorious rake.

sight, and seemed too anxious to discover whether I knew the contents to allow yourself to make any inquiries. I wondered at these appearances of consternation, but did not reason on them until I had retired. When alone, these incidents suggested themselves to my reflections anew.

"To what scene, or what interview, I asked, did you allude? Your disappearance on a former evening, my tracing you to the recess in the bank, your silence on my first and second call, your vague answers and invincible embarrassment, when you, at length, ascended the hill, I recollected with new surprize. Could this be the summer-house alluded to? A certain timidity and consciousness had generally attended you, when this incident and this recess had been the subjects of conversation. Nay, I imagined that the last time that adventure was mentioned, which happened in the presence of Carwin, the countenance of the latter betrayed some emotion. Could the interview have been with him?

"This was an idea calculated to rouse every faculty to contemplation. An interview at that hour, in this darksome retreat, with a man of this mysterious but formidable character; a clandestine interview, and one which you afterwards endeavoured with so much solicitude to conceal! It was a fearful and portentous occurrence. I could not measure his power, or fathom his designs. Had he rifled from you the secret of your love, and reconciled you to concealment and nocturnal meetings? I scarcely ever spent a night of more inquietude.

"I knew not how to act. The ascertainment of this man's character and views seemed to be, in the first place, necessary. Had he openly preferred his suit to you, we should have been impowered to make direct inquiries; but since he had chosen this obscure path, it seemed reasonable to infer that his character was exceptionable. It, at least, subjected us to the necessity of resorting to other means of information. Yet the improbability that you should commit a deed of such rashness, made me reflect anew upon the insufficiency of those grounds on which my suspicions had been built, and almost to condemn myself for harbouring them.

"Though it was mere conjecture that the interview spoken of had taken place with Carwin, yet two ideas occurred to involve me in the most painful doubts. This man's reasonings might be so specious, and his artifices so profound, that, aided by the passion which you had conceived for him, he had finally succeeded; or his situation might be such as to justify the secrecy which you maintained. In neither case did my wildest reveries suggest to me, that your honor had been forfeited.

"I could not talk with you on this subject. If the imputation was false, its atrociousness would have justly drawn upon me your resentment, and I must have explained by what facts it had been suggested.

If it were true, no benefit would follow from the mention of it. You had chosen to conceal it for some reasons, and whether these reasons were true or false, it was proper to discover and remove them in the first place. Finally, I acquiesced in the least painful supposition, trammelled as it was with perplexities, that Carwin was upright, and that, if the reasons of your silence were known, they would be found to be just.

Chapter XIV

"Three days have elapsed since this occurrence. I have been haunted by perpetual inquietude. To bring myself to regard Carwin without terror, and to acquiesce in the belief of your safety, was impossible. Yet to put an end to my doubts, seemed to be impracticable. If some light could be reflected on the actual situation of this man, a direct path would present itself. If he were, contrary to the tenor of his conversation, cunning and malignant, to apprize you of this, would be to place you in security. If he were merely unfortunate and innocent, most readily would I espouse his cause; and if his intentions were upright with regard to you, most eagerly would I sanctify your choice by my approbation.

"It would be vain to call upon Carwin for an avowal of his deeds. It was better to know nothing, than to be deceived by an artful tale. What he was unwilling to communicate, and this unwillingness had been repeatedly manifested, could never be extorted from him. Importunity might be appeased, or imposture effected by fallacious representations. To the rest of the world he was unknown. I had often made him the subject of discourse; but a glimpse of his figure in the street was the sum of their knowledge who knew most. None had ever seen him before, and received as new, the information which my intercourse with him in Valencia,[1] and my present intercourse, enabled me to give.

"Wieland was your brother. If he had really made you the object of his courtship, was not a brother authorized to interfere and demand from him the confession of his views? Yet what were the grounds on which I had reared this supposition? Would they justify a measure like this? Surely not.

"In the course of my restless meditations, it occurred to me, at length, that my duty required me to speak to you, to confess the indecorum of which I had been guilty, and to state the reflections to which it had led me. I was prompted by no mean or selfish views. The heart within my breast was not more precious than your safety: most

1. In Spain, see p. 54, n. 3.

cheerfully would I have interposed my life between you and danger. Would you cherish resentment at my conduct? When acquainted with the motive which produced it, it would not only exempt me from censure, but entitle me to gratitude.

"Yesterday had been selected for the rehearsal of the newly-imported tragedy. I promised to be present. The state of my thoughts but little qualified me for a performer or auditor in such a scene; but I reflected that, after it was finished, I should return home with you, and should then enjoy an opportunity of discoursing with you fully on this topic. My resolution was not formed without a remnant of doubt, as to its propriety. When I left this house to perform the visit I had promised, my mind was full of apprehension and despondency. The dubiousness of the event of our conversation, fear that my interference was too late to secure your peace, and the uncertainty, to which hope gave birth, whether I had not erred in believing you devoted to this man, or, at least, in imagining that he had obtained your consent to midnight conferences, distracted me with contradictory opinions, and repugnant emotions.

"I can assign no reason for calling at Mrs. Baynton's. I had seen her in the morning, and knew her to be well. The concerted hour had nearly arrived, and yet I turned up the street which leads to her house, and dismounted at her door. I entered the parlour and threw myself in a chair. I saw and inquired for no one. My whole frame was overpowered by dreary and comfortless sensations. One idea possessed me wholly; the inexpressible importance of unveiling the designs and character of Carwin, and the utter improbability that this ever would be effected. Some instinct induced me to lay my hand upon a newspaper. I had perused all the general intelligence it contained in the morning, and at the same spot. The act was rather mechanical than voluntary.

"I threw a languid glance at the first column that presented itself. The first words which I read, began with the offer of a reward of three hundred guineas for the apprehension of a convict under sentence of death, who had escaped from Newgate prison in Dublin. Good heaven! how every fibre of my frame tingled when I proceeded to read that the name of the criminal was Francis Carwin!

"The descriptions of his person and address were minute. His stature, hair, complexion, the extraordinary position and arrangement of his features, his aukward and disproportionate form, his gesture and gait, corresponded perfectly with those of our mysterious visitant. He had been found guilty in two indictments. One for the murder of the Lady Jane Conway, and the other for a robbery committed on the person of the honorable Mr. Ludloe.

"I repeatedly perused this passage. The ideas which flowed in upon my mind, affected me like an instant transition from death to life. The purpose dearest to my heart was thus effected, at a time and by means the least of all others within the scope of my foresight. But what purpose? Carwin was detected. Acts of the blackest and most sordid guilt had been committed by him. Here was evidence which imparted to my understanding the most luminous certainty. The name, visage, and deportment, were the same. Between the time of his escape, and his appearance among us, there was a sufficient agreement. Such was the man with whom I suspected you to maintain a clandestine correspondence. Should I not haste to snatch you from the talons of this vulture? Should I see you rushing to the verge of a dizzy precipice, and not stretch forth a hand to pull you back? I had no need to deliberate. I thrust the paper in my pocket, and resolved to obtain an immediate conference with you. For a time, no other image made its way to my understanding. At length, it occurred to me, that though the information I possessed was, in one sense, sufficient, yet if more could be obtained, more was desirable. This passage was copied from a British paper; part of it only, perhaps, was transcribed. The printer was in possession of the original.

"Towards his house I immediately turned my horse's head. He produced the paper, but I found nothing more than had already been seen. While busy in perusing it, the printer stood by my side. He noticed the object of which I was in search. 'Aye,' said he, 'that is a strange affair. I should never have met with it, had not Mr. Hallet sent to me the paper, with a particular request to republish that advertisement.'

"Mr. Hallet! What reasons could he have for making this request? Had the paper sent to him been accompanied by any information respecting the convict? Had he personal or extraordinary reasons for desiring its republication? This was to be known only in one way. I speeded to his house. In answer to my interrogations, he told me that Ludloe had formerly been in America, and that during his residence in this city, considerable intercourse had taken place between them. Hence a confidence arose, which has since been kept alive by occasional letters. He had lately received a letter from him, enclosing the newspaper from which this extract had been made. He put it into my hands, and pointed out the passages which related to Carwin.

"Ludloe confirms the facts of his conviction and escape; and adds, that he had reason to believe him to have embarked for America. He describes him in general terms, as the most incomprehensible and formidable among men; as engaged in schemes, reasonably suspected to be, in the highest degree, criminal, but such as no human intelligence is able to unravel: that his ends are pursued by means which leave it in doubt whether he be not in league with some infernal spirit: that his crimes have hitherto been perpetrated with the aid of some unknown but desperate accomplices: that he wages a perpetual war against the happiness of mankind, and sets his engines of destruction at work against every object that presents itself.

"This is the substance of the letter. Hallet expressed some surprize at the curiosity which was manifested by me on this occasion. I was too much absorbed by the ideas suggested by this letter, to pay attention to his remarks. I shuddered with the apprehension of the evil to which our indiscreet familiarity with this man had probably exposed us. I burnt with impatience to see you, and to do what in me lay to avert the calamity which threatened us. It was already five o'clock. Night was hastening, and there was no time to be lost. On leaving Mr. Hallet's house, who should meet me in the street, but Bertrand, the servant whom I left in Germany. His appearance and accoutrements bespoke him to have just alighted from a toilsome and long journey. I was not wholly without expectation of seeing him about this time, but no one was then more distant from my thoughts. You know what reasons I have for anxiety respecting scenes with which this man was conversant. Carwin was for a moment forgotten. In answer to my vehement inquiries, Bertrand produced a copious packet.[2] I shall not at present mention its contents, nor the measures which they obliged me to adopt. I bestowed a brief perusal on these papers, and having given some directions to Bertrand, resumed my purpose with regard to you. My horse I was obliged to resign to my servant, he being charged with a commission that required speed. The clock had struck ten, and Mettingen was five miles distant. I was to journey thither on foot. These circumstances only added to my expedition.

"As I passed swiftly along, I reviewed all the incidents accompanying the appearance and deportment of that man among us. Late events have been inexplicable and mysterious beyond any of which I have either read or heard. These events were coeval[3] with Carwin's introduction. I am unable to explain their origin and mutual dependance; but I do not, on that account, believe them to have a supernatural original. Is not this man the agent? Some of them seem to be propitious; but what should I think of those threats of assassination with which you were lately alarmed? Bloodshed is the trade, and horror is the element of this man. The process by which the sympathies of nature are extinguished in our hearts, by which evil is made our good, and by which we are made susceptible of no activity but in the infliction, and no joy but in the spectacle of woes, is an obvious process. As to an alliance with evil geniuses, the power and the malice of dæmons have been a thousand times exemplified in human beings.

---

2. A bundle of letters.
3. Occurring simultaneously with.

There are no devils but those which are begotten upon selfishness, and reared by cunning.

"Now, indeed, the scene was changed. It was not his secret poniard[4] that I dreaded. It was only the success of his efforts to make you a confederate in your own destruction, to make your will the instrument by which he might bereave you of liberty and honor.

"I took, as usual, the path through your brother's ground. I ranged with celerity and silence along the bank. I approached the fence, which divides Wieland's estate from yours. The recess in the bank being near this line, it being necessary for me to pass near it, my mind being tainted with inveterate suspicions concerning you; suspicions which were indebted for their strength to incidents connected with this spot; what wonder that it seized upon my thoughts!

"I leaped on the fence; but before I descended on the opposite side, I paused to survey the scene. Leaves dropping with dew, and glistening in the moon's rays, with no moving object to molest the deep repose, filled me with security and hope. I left the station at length, and tended forward. You were probably at rest. How should I communicate without alarming you, the intelligence of my arrival? An immediate interview was to be procured. I could not bear to think that a minute should be lost by remissness or hesitation. Should I knock at the door? or should I stand under your chamber windows, which I perceived to be open, and awaken you by my calls?

"These reflections employed me, as I passed opposite to the summer-house. I had scarcely gone by, when my ear caught a sound unusual at this time and place. It was almost too faint and too transient to allow me a distinct perception of it. I stopped to listen; presently it was heard again, and now it was somewhat in a louder key. It was laughter; and unquestionably produced by a female voice. That voice was familiar to my senses. It was yours.

"Whence it came, I was at first at a loss to conjecture; but this uncertainty vanished when it was heard the third time. I threw back my eyes towards the recess. Every other organ and limb was useless to me. I did not reason on the subject. I did not, in a direct manner, draw my conclusions from the hour, the place, the hilarity which this sound betokened, and the circumstance of having a companion, which it no less incontestably proved. In an instant, as it were, my heart was invaded with cold, and the pulses of life at a stand.

"Why should I go further? Why should I return? Should I not hurry to a distance from a sound, which, though formerly so sweet and delectable, was now more hideous than the shrieks of owls?

"I had no time to yield to this impulse. The thought of approaching and listening occurred to me. I had no doubt of which I was

4. Dagger.

conscious. Yet my certainty was capable of increase. I was likewise stimulated by a sentiment that partook of rage. I was governed by an half-formed and tempestuous resolution to break in upon your interview, and strike you dead with my upbraiding.

"I approached with the utmost caution. When I reached the edge of the bank immediately above the summer-house, I thought I heard voices from below, as busy in conversation. The steps in the rock are clear of bushy impediments. They allowed me to descend into a cavity beside the building without being detected. Thus to lie in wait could only be justified by the momentousness of the occasion."

Here Pleyel paused in his narrative, and fixed his eyes upon me. Situated as I was, my horror and astonishment at this tale gave way to compassion for the anguish which the countenance of my friend betrayed. I reflected on his force of understanding. I reflected on the powers of my enemy. I could easily divine the substance of the conversation that was overheard. Carwin had constructed his plot in a manner suited to the characters of those whom he had selected for his victims. I saw that the convictions of Pleyel were immutable. I forbore to struggle against the storm, because I saw that all struggles would be fruitless. I was calm; but my calmness was the torpor of despair, and not the tranquillity of fortitude. It was calmness invincible by any thing that his grief and his fury could suggest to Pleyel. He resumed—

"Woman! wilt thou hear me further? Shall I go on to repeat the conversation? Is it shame that makes thee tongue-tied? Shall I go on? or art thou satisfied with what has been already said?"

I bowed my head. "Go on," said I. "I make not this request in the hope of undeceiving you. I shall no longer contend with my own weakness. The storm is let loose, and I shall peaceably submit to be driven by its fury. But go on. This conference will end only with affording me a clearer foresight of my destiny; but that will be some satisfaction, and I will not part without it."

Why, on hearing these words, did Pleyel hesitate? Did some unlooked-for doubt insinuate itself into his mind? Was his belief suddenly shaken by my looks, or my words, or by some newly recollected circumstance? Whencesoever it arose, it could not endure the test of deliberation. In a few minutes the flame of resentment was again lighted up in his bosom. He proceeded with his accustomed vehemence—

"I hate myself for this folly. I can find no apology for this tale. Yet I am irresistibly impelled to relate it. She that hears me is apprized of every particular. I have only to repeat to her her own words. She will listen with a tranquil air, and the spectacle of her obduracy will drive me to some desperate act. Why then should I persist! yet persist I must."

Again he paused. "No," said he, "it is impossible to repeat your avowals of love, your appeals to former confessions of your tenderness, to former deeds of dishonor, to the circumstances of the first interview that took place between you. It was on that night when I traced you to this recess. Thither had he enticed you, and there had you ratified an unhallowed compact by admitting him—

"Great God! Thou witnessedst the agonies that tore my bosom at that moment! Thou witnessedst my efforts to repel the testimony of my ears! It was in vain that you dwelt upon the confusion which my unlooked-for summons excited in you; the tardiness with which a suitable excuse occurred to you; your resentment that my impertinent intrusion had put an end to that charming interview: A disappointment for which you endeavoured to compensate yourself, by the frequency and duration of subsequent meetings.

"In vain you dwelt upon incidents of which you only could be conscious; incidents that occurred on occasions on which none beside your own family were witnesses. In vain was your discourse characterized by peculiarities inimitable of sentiment and language. My conviction was effected only by an accumulation of the same tokens. I yielded not but to evidence which took away the power to withhold my faith.

"My sight was of no use to me. Beneath so thick an umbrage, the darkness was intense. Hearing was the only avenue to information, which the circumstances allowed to be open. I was couched within three feet of you. Why should I approach nearer? I could not contend with your betrayer. What could be the purpose of a contest? You stood in no need of a protector. What could I do, but retire from the spot overwhelmed with confusion and dismay? I sought my chamber, and endeavoured to regain my composure. The door of the house, which I found open, your subsequent entrance, closing, and fastening it, and going into your chamber, which had been thus long deserted, were only confirmations of the truth.

"Why should I paint the tempestuous fluctuation of my thoughts between grief and revenge, between rage and despair? Why should I repeat my vows of eternal implacability and persecution, and the speedy recantation of these vows?

"I have said enough. You have dismissed me from a place in your esteem. What I think, and what I feel, is of no importance in your eyes. May the duty which I owe myself enable me to forget your existence. In a few minutes I go hence. Be the maker of your fortune, and may adversity instruct you in that wisdom, which education was unable to impart to you."

These were the last words which Pleyel uttered. He left the room, and my new emotions enabled me to witness his departure without any apparent loss of composure. As I sat alone, I ruminated on these incidents. Nothing was more evident than that I had taken an eternal leave of happiness. Life was a worthless thing, separate from that good which had now been wrested from me; yet the sentiment that now possessed me had no tendency to palsy my exertions, and overbear my strength. I noticed that the light was declining, and perceived the propriety of leaving this house. I placed myself again in the chaise, and returned slowly towards the city.

Chapter XV

Before I reached the city it was dusk. It was my purpose to spend the night at Mettingen. I was not solicitous, as long as I was attended by a faithful servant, to be there at an early hour. My exhausted strength required me to take some refreshment. With this view, and in order to pay respect to one whose affection for me was truly maternal, I stopped at Mrs. Baynton's. She was absent from home; but I had scarcely entered the house when one of her domestics presented me a letter. I opened and read as follows:

> "To Clara Wieland,
>
> "What shall I say to extenuate the misconduct of last night? It is my duty to repair it to the utmost of my power, but the only way in which it can be repaired, you will not, I fear, be prevailed on to adopt. It is by granting me an interview, at your own house, at eleven o'clock this night. I have no means of removing any fears that you may entertain of my designs, but my simple and solemn declarations. These, after what has passed between us, you may deem unworthy of confidence. I cannot help it. My folly and rashness has left me no other resource. I will be at your door by that hour. If you chuse to admit me to a conference, provided that conference has no witnesses, I will disclose to you particulars, the knowledge of which is of the utmost importance to your happiness. Farewell.
>
> CARWIN."

What a letter was this! A man known to be an assassin and robber; one capable of plotting against my life and my fame; detected lurking in my chamber, and avowing designs the most flagitious[1] and dreadful, now solicits me to grant him a midnight interview! To admit him alone into my presence! Could he make this request with the expectation of my compliance? What had he seen in me, that could justify him in admitting so wild a belief? Yet this request is preferred with the utmost gravity. It is not unaccompanied by an

---

1. Wicked.

appearance of uncommon earnestness. Had the misconduct to which he alludes been a slight incivility, and the interview requested to take place in the midst of my friends, there would have been no extravagance in the tenor of this letter; but, as it was, the writer had surely been bereft of his reason.

I perused this epistle frequently. The request it contained might be called audacious or stupid, if it had been made by a different person; but from Carwin, who could not be unaware of the effect which it must naturally produce, and of the manner in which it would unavoidably be treated, it was perfectly inexplicable. He must have counted on the success of some plot, in order to extort my assent. None of those motives by which I am usually governed would ever have persuaded me to meet any one of his sex, at the time and place which he had prescribed. Much less would I consent to a meeting with a man, tainted with the most detestable crimes, and by whose arts my own safety had been so imminently endangered, and my happiness irretrievably destroyed. I shuddered at the idea that such a meeting was possible. I felt some reluctance to approach a spot which he still visited and haunted.

Such were the ideas which first suggested themselves on the perusal of the letter. Meanwhile, I resumed my journey. My thoughts still dwelt upon the same topic. Gradually from ruminating on this epistle, I reverted to my interview with Pleyel. I recalled the particulars of the dialogue to which he had been an auditor. My heart sunk anew on viewing the inextricable complexity of this deception, and the inauspicious concurrence of events, which tended to confirm him in his error. When he approached my chamber door, my terror kept me mute. He put his ear, perhaps, to the crevice, but it caught the sound of nothing human. Had I called, or made any token that denoted some one to be within, words would have ensued; and as omnipresence was impossible, this discovery, and the artless narrative of what had just passed, would have saved me from his murderous invectives. He went into his chamber, and after some interval, I stole across the entry and down the stairs, with inaudible steps. Having secured the outer doors, I returned with less circumspection. He heard me not when I descended; but my returning steps were easily distinguished. Now, he thought, was the guilty interview at an end. In what other way was it possible for him to construe these signals?

How fallacious and precipitate[2] was my decision! Carwin's plot owed its success to a coincidence of events scarcely credible. The balance was swayed from its equipoise by a hair. Had I even begun the conversation with an account of what befel me in my chamber, my

2. Headlong, without deliberation.

previous interview with Wieland would have taught him to suspect me of imposture; yet, if I were discoursing with this ruffian, when Pleyel touched the lock of my chamber door, and when he shut his own door with so much violence, how, he might ask, should I be able to relate these incidents? Perhaps he had withheld the knowledge of these circumstances from my brother, from whom, therefore, I could not obtain it, so that my innocence would have thus been irresistibly demonstrated.

The first impulse which flowed from these ideas was to return upon my steps, and demand once more an interview; but he was gone: his parting declarations were remembered.

Pleyel, I exclaimed, thou art gone for ever! Are thy mistakes beyond the reach of detection? Am I helpless in the midst of this snare? The plotter is at hand. He even speaks in the style of penitence. He solicits an interview which he promises shall end in the disclosure of something momentous to my happiness. What can he say which will avail to turn aside this evil? But why should his remorse be feigned? I have done him no injury. His wickedness is fertile only of despair; and the billows of remorse will some time overbear him. Why may not this event have already taken place? Why should I refuse to see him?

This idea was present, as it were, for a moment. I suddenly recoiled from it, confounded at that frenzy which could give even momentary harbour to such a scheme; yet presently it returned. At length I even conceived it to deserve deliberation. I questioned whether it was not proper to admit, at a lonely spot, in a sacred hour, this man of tremendous and inscrutable attributes, this performer of horrid deeds, and whose presence was predicted to call down unheard-of and unutterable horrors.

What was it that swayed me? I felt myself divested of the power to will contrary to the motives that determined me to seek his presence. My mind seemed to be split into separate parts, and these parts to have entered into furious and implacable contention. These tumults gradually subsided. The reasons why I should confide in that interposition which had hitherto defended me; in those tokens of compunction which this letter contained; in the efficacy of this interview to restore its spotlessness to my character, and banish all illusions from the mind of my friend, continually acquired new evidence and new strength.

What should I fear in his presence? This was unlike an artifice intended to betray me into his hands. If it were an artifice, what purpose would it serve? The freedom of my mind was untouched, and that freedom would defy the assaults of blandishments or magic. Force was I not able to repel. On the former occasion my courage, it is true, had failed at the imminent approach of danger; but then I had not enjoyed opportunities of deliberation; I had foreseen nothing; I was sunk into imbecility by my previous thoughts; I had been the victim of recent disappointments and anticipated ills: Witness my infatuation in opening the closet in opposition to divine injunctions.

Now, perhaps, my courage was the offspring of a no less erring principle. Pleyel was for ever lost to me. I strove in vain to assume his person, and suppress my resentment; I strove in vain to believe in the assuaging influence of time, to look forward to the birth-day of new hopes, and the re-exaltation of that luminary, of whose effulgencies I had so long and so liberally partaken.

What had I to suffer worse than was already inflicted?

Was not Carwin my foe? I owed my untimely fate to his treason. Instead of flying from his presence, ought I not to devote all my faculties to the gaining of an interview, and compel him to repair the ills of which he has been the author? Why should I suppose him impregnable to argument? Have I not reason on my side, and the power of imparting conviction? Cannot he be made to see the justice of unravelling the maze in which Pleyel is bewildered?

He may, at least, be accessible to fear. Has he nothing to fear from the rage of an injured woman? But suppose him inaccessible to such inducements; suppose him to persist in all his flagitious purposes; are not the means of defence and resistance in my power?

In the progress of such thoughts, was the resolution at last formed. I hoped that the interview was sought by him for a laudable end; but, be that as it would, I trusted that, by energy of reasoning or of action, I should render it auspicious, or, at least, harmless.

Such a determination must unavoidably fluctuate. The poet's chaos[3] was no unapt emblem of the state of my mind. A torment was awakened in my bosom, which I foresaw would end only when this interview was past, and its consequences fully experienced. Hence my impatience for the arrival of the hour which had been prescribed by Carwin.

Meanwhile, my meditations were tumultuously active. New impediments to the execution of the scheme were speedily suggested. I had apprized Catharine of my intention to spend this and many future nights with her. Her husband was informed of this arrangement, and had zealously approved it. Eleven o'clock exceeded their hour of retiring. What excuse should I form for changing my plan? Should I shew this letter to Wieland, and submit myself to his direction? But I knew in what way he would decide. He would fervently dissuade me from going. Nay, would he not do more? He was apprized of the offences

---

3. See Ovid, *Metamorphoses*, bk. I, on the chaos that predated creation. Ovid (43 B.C.E.–17 or 18 C.E.) was the last Roman poet of the Augustan age, born in the year of Cicero's death.

of Carwin, and of the reward offered for his apprehension. Would he not seize this opportunity of executing justice on a criminal?

This idea was new. I was plunged once more into doubt. Did not equity enjoin me thus to facilitate his arrest? No. I disdained the office of betrayer. Carwin was unapprized of his danger, and his intentions were possibly beneficent. Should I station guards about the house, and make an act, intended perhaps for my benefit, instrumental to his own destruction? Wieland might be justified in thus employing the knowledge which I should impart, but I, by imparting it, should pollute myself with more hateful crimes than those undeservedly imputed to me. This scheme, therefore, I unhesitatingly rejected. The views with which I should return to my own house, it would therefore be necessary to conceal. Yet some pretext must be invented. I had never been initiated into the trade of lying. Yet what but falsehood was a deliberate suppression of the truth? To deceive by silence or by words is the same.

Yet what would a lie avail me? What pretext would justify this change in my plan? Would it not tend to confirm the imputations of Pleyel? That I should voluntarily return to an house in which honor and life had so lately been endangered, could be explained in no way favorable to my integrity.

These reflections, if they did not change, at least suspended my decision. In this state of uncertainty I alighted at the hut. We gave this name to the house tenanted by the farmer and his servants, and which was situated on the verge of my brother's ground, and at a considerable distance from the mansion. The path to the mansion was planted by a double row of walnuts. Along this path I proceeded alone. I entered the parlour, in which was a light just expiring in the socket. There was no one in the room. I perceived by the clock that stood against the wall, that it was near eleven. The lateness of the hour startled me. What had become of the family? They were usually retired an hour before this; but the unextinguished taper, and the unbarred door were indications that they had not retired. I again returned to the hall, and passed from one room to another, but still encountered not a human being.

I imagined that, perhaps, the lapse of a few minutes would explain these appearances. Meanwhile I reflected that the preconcerted hour had arrived. Carwin was perhaps waiting my approach. Should I immediately retire to my own house, no one would be apprized of my proceeding. Nay, the interview might pass, and I be enabled to return in half an hour. Hence no necessity would arise for dissimulation.

I was so far influenced by these views that I rose to execute this design; but again the unusual condition of the house occurred to me, and some vague solicitude as to the condition of the family. I was nearly certain that my brother had not retired; but by what motives he could be induced to desert his house thus unseasonably, I could by no means divine. Louisa Conway, at least, was at home, and had, probably, retired to her chamber; perhaps she was able to impart the information I wanted.

I went to her chamber, and found her asleep. She was delighted and surprized at my arrival, and told me with how much impatience and anxiety my brother and his wife had waited my coming. They were fearful that some mishap had befallen me, and had remained up longer than the usual period. Notwithstanding the lateness of the hour, Catharine would not resign the hope of seeing me. Louisa said she had left them both in the parlour, and she knew of no cause for their absence.

As yet I was not without solicitude on account of their personal safety. I was far from being perfectly at ease on that head, but entertained no distinct conception of the danger that impended over them. Perhaps to beguile the moments of my long protracted stay, they had gone to walk upon the bank. The atmosphere, though illuminated only by the star-light, was remarkably serene. Meanwhile the desireableness of an interview with Carwin again returned, and I finally resolved to seek it.

I passed with doubting and hasty steps along the path. My dwelling, seen at a distance, was gloomy and desolate. It had no inhabitant, for my servant, in consequence of my new arrangement, had gone to Mettingen. The temerity of this attempt began to shew itself in more vivid colours to my understanding. Whoever has pointed steel is not without arms; yet what must have been the state of my mind when I could meditate, without shuddering, on the use of a murderous weapon, and believe myself secure merely because I was capable of being made so by the death of another? Yet this was not my state. I felt as if I was rushing into deadly toils, without the power of pausing or receding.

Chapter XVI

As soon as I arrived in sight of the front of the house, my attention was excited by a light from the window of my own chamber. No appearance could be less explicable. A meeting was expected with Carwin, but that he pre-occupied my chamber, and had supplied himself with light, was not to be believed. What motive could influence him to adopt this conduct? Could I proceed until this was explained? Perhaps, if I should proceed to a distance in front, some one would be visible. A sidelong but feeble beam from the window, fell upon the piny copse[1] which skirted the bank. As I eyed it, it sud-

1. A thicket of trees, in this case pines.

denly became mutable, and after flitting to and fro, for a short time, it vanished. I turned my eye again toward the window, and perceived that the light was still there; but the change which I had noticed was occasioned by a change in the position of the lamp or candle within. Hence, that some person was there was an unavoidable inference.

I paused to deliberate on the propriety of advancing. Might I not advance cautiously, and, therefore, without danger? Might I not knock at the door, or call, and be apprized of the nature of my visitant before I entered? I approached and listened at the door, but could hear nothing. I knocked at first timidly, but afterwards with loudness. My signals were unnoticed. I stepped back and looked, but the light was no longer discernible. Was it suddenly extinguished by a human agent? What purpose but concealment was intended? Why was the illumination produced, to be thus suddenly brought to an end? And why, since some one was there, had silence been observed?

These were questions, the solution of which may be readily supposed to be entangled with danger. Would not this danger, when measured by a woman's fears, expand into gigantic dimensions? Menaces of death; the stunning exertions of a warning voice; the known and unknown attributes of Carwin; our recent interview in this chamber; the pre-appointment of a meeting at this place and hour, all thronged into my memory. What was to be done?

Courage is no definite or stedfast principle. Let that man who shall purpose to assign motives to the actions of another, blush at his folly and forbear. Not more presumptuous would it be to attempt the classification of all nature, and the scanning of supreme intelligence. I gazed for a minute at the window, and fixed my eyes, for a second minute, on the ground. I drew forth from my pocket, and opened, a penknife. This, said I, be my safe-guard and avenger. The assailant shall perish, or myself shall fall.

I had locked up the house in the morning, but had the key of the kitchen door in my pocket. I, therefore, determined to gain access behind. Thither I hastened, unlocked and entered. All was lonely, darksome, and waste. Familiar as I was with every part of my dwelling, I easily found my way to a closet, drew forth a taper, a flint, tinder, and steel, and, in a moment, as it were, gave myself the guidance and protection of light.

What purpose did I meditate? Should I explore my way to my chamber, and confront the being who had dared to intrude into this recess, and had laboured for concealment? By putting out the light did he seek to hide himself, or mean only to circumvent my incautious steps? Yet was it not more probable that he desired my absence by thus encouraging the supposition that the house was unoccupied? I would see this man in spite of all impediments; ere I died, I would see his face, and summon him to penitence and retribution;

no matter at what cost an interview was purchased. Reputation and life might be wrested from me by another, but my rectitude and honor were in my own keeping, and were safe.

I proceeded to the foot of the stairs. At such a crisis my thoughts may be supposed at no liberty to range; yet vague images rushed into my mind, of the mysterious interposition which had been experienced on the last night. My case, at present, was not dissimilar; and, if my angel were not weary of fruitless exertions to save, might not a new warning be expected? Who could say whether his silence were ascribable to the absence of danger, or to his own absence?

In this state of mind, no wonder that a shivering cold crept through my veins; that my pause was prolonged; and, that a fearful glance was thrown backward.

Alas! my heart droops, and my fingers are enervated; my ideas are vivid, but my language is faint; now know I what it is to entertain incommunicable sentiments. The chain of subsequent incidents is drawn through my mind, and being linked with those which forewent, by turns rouse up agonies and sink me into hopelessness.

Yet I will persist to the end. My narrative may be invaded by inaccuracy and confusion; but if I live no longer, I will, at least, live to complete it. What but ambiguities, abruptnesses, and dark transitions, can be expected from the historian who is, at the same time, the sufferer of these disasters?

I have said that I cast a look behind. Some object was expected to be seen, or why should I have gazed in that direction? Two senses were at once assailed. The same piercing exclamation of *hold! hold!* was uttered within the same distance of my ear. This it was that I heard. The airy undulation, and the shock given to my nerves, were real. Whether the spectacle which I beheld existed in my fancy or without, might be doubted.

I had not closed the door of the apartment I had just left. The staircase, at the foot of which I stood, was eight or ten feet from the door, and attached to the wall through which the door led. My view, therefore, was sidelong, and took in no part of the room.

Through this aperture was an head thrust and drawn back with so much swiftness, that the immediate conviction was, that thus much of a form, ordinarily invisible, had been unshrouded. The face was turned towards me. Every muscle was tense; the forehead and brows were drawn into vehement expression; the lips were stretched as in the act of shrieking; and the eyes emitted sparks, which, no doubt, if I had been unattended by a light, would have illuminated like the corruscations of a meteor. The sound and the vision were present, and departed together at the same instant; but the cry was blown into my ear, while the face was many paces distant.

This face was well suited to a being whose performances exceeded the standard of humanity, and yet its features were akin to those I had before seen. The image of Carwin was blended in a thousand ways with the stream of my thoughts. This visage was, perhaps, pourtrayed by my fancy. If so, it will excite no surprize that some of his lineaments were now discovered. Yet affinities were few and unconspicuous, and were lost amidst the blaze of opposite qualities.

What conclusion could I form? Be the face human or not, the intimation was imparted from above. Experience had evinced the benignity of that being who gave it. Once he had interposed to shield me from harm, and subsequent events demonstrated the usefulness of that interposition. Now was I again warned to forbear. I was hurrying to the verge of the same gulf, and the same power was exerted to recall my steps. Was it possible for me not to obey? Was I capable of holding on in the same perilous career? Yes. Even of this I was capable!

The intimation was imperfect: it gave no form to my danger, and prescribed no limits to my caution. I had formerly neglected it, and yet escaped. Might I not trust to the same issue? This idea might possess, though imperceptibly, some influence. I persisted; but it was not merely on this account. I cannot delineate the motives that led me on. I now speak as if no remnant of doubt existed in my mind as to the supernal origin of these sounds; but this is owing to the imperfection of my language, for I only mean that the belief was more permanent, and visited more frequently my sober meditations than its opposite. The immediate effects served only to undermine the foundations of my judgment and precipitate my resolutions.

I must either advance or return. I chose the former, and began to ascend the stairs. The silence underwent no second interruption. My chamber door was closed, but unlocked, and, aided by vehement efforts of my courage, I opened and looked in.

No hideous or uncommon object was discernible. The danger, indeed, might easily have lurked out of sight, have sprung upon me as I entered, and have rent me with his iron talons; but I was blind to this fate, and advanced, though cautiously, into the room.

Still every thing wore its accustomed aspect. Neither lamp nor candle was to be found. Now, for the first time, suspicions were suggested as to the nature of the light which I had seen. Was it possible to have been the companion of that supernatural visage; a meteorous refulgence producible at the will of him to whom that visage belonged, and partaking of the nature of that which accompanied my father's death?

The closet was near, and I remembered the complicated horrors of which it had been productive. Here, perhaps, was inclosed the source of my peril, and the gratification of my curiosity. Should I adventure once more to explore its recesses? This was a resolution not easily formed. I was suspended in thought: when glancing my eye on a table, I perceived a written paper. Carwin's hand was instantly recognized, and snatching up the paper, I read as follows:—

"There was folly in expecting your compliance with my invitation. Judge how I was disappointed in finding another in your place. I have waited, but to wait any longer would be perilous. I shall still seek an interview, but it must be at a different time and place: meanwhile, I will write this—How will you bear—How inexplicable will be this transaction!—An event so unexpected—a sight so horrible!"

Such was this abrupt and unsatisfactory script. The ink was yet moist, the hand was that of Carwin. Hence it was to be inferred that he had this moment left the apartment, or was still in it. I looked back, on the sudden expectation of seeing him behind me.

What other did he mean? What transaction had taken place adverse to my expectations? What sight was about to be exhibited? I looked around me once more, but saw nothing which indicated strangeness. Again I remembered the closet, and was resolved to seek in that the solution of these mysteries. Here, perhaps, was inclosed the scene destined to awaken my horrors and baffle my foresight.

I have already said, that the entrance into this closet was beside my bed, which, on two sides, was closely shrouded by curtains. On that side nearest the closet, the curtain was raised. As I passed along I cast my eye thither. I started, and looked again. I bore a light in my hand, and brought it nearer my eyes, in order to dispel any illusive mists that might have hovered before them. Once more I fixed my eyes upon the bed, in hope that this more stedfast scrutiny would annihilate the object which before seemed to be there.

This then was the sight which Carwin had predicted! This was the event which my understanding was to find inexplicable! This was the fate which had been reserved for me, but which, by some untoward chance, had befallen on another!

I had not been terrified by empty menaces. Violation and death awaited my entrance into this chamber. Some inscrutable chance had led *her* hither before me, and the merciless fangs of which I was designed to be the prey, had mistaken their victim, and had fixed themselves in *her* heart. But where was my safety? Was the mischief exhausted or flown? The steps of the assassin had just been here; they could not be far off; in a moment he would rush into my presence, and I should perish under the same polluting and suffocating grasp!

My frame shook, and my knees were unable to support me. I gazed alternately at the closet door and at the door of my room. At one of these avenues would enter the exterminator of my honor and my life. I was prepared for defence; but now that danger was imminent, my means of defence, and my power to use them were gone. I was not qualified, by education and experience, to encounter perils like these: or, perhaps, I was powerless because I was again assaulted by surprize, and had not fortified my mind by foresight and previous reflection against a scene like this.

Fears for my own safety again yielded place to reflections on the scene before me. I fixed my eyes upon her countenance. My sister's well-known and beloved features could not be concealed by convulsion or lividness. What direful illusion led thee hither? Bereft of thee, what hold on happiness remains to thy offspring and thy spouse? To lose thee by a common fate would have been sufficiently hard; but thus suddenly to perish—to become the prey of this ghastly death! How will a spectacle like this be endured by Wieland? To die beneath his grasp would not satisfy thy enemy. This was mercy to the evils which he previously made thee suffer! After these evils death was a boon which thou besoughtest him to grant. He entertained no enmity against thee: I was the object of his treason; but by some tremendous mistake his fury was misplaced. But how earnest thou hither? and where was Wieland in thy hour of distress?

I approached the corpse: I lifted the still flexible hand, and kissed the lips which were breathless. Her flowing drapery was discomposed. I restored it to order, and seating myself on the bed, again fixed stedfast eyes upon her countenance. I cannot distinctly recollect the ruminations of that moment. I saw confusedly, but forcibly, that every hope was extinguished with the life of *Catharine*. All happiness and dignity must henceforth be banished from the house and name of Wieland: all that remained was to linger out in agonies a short existence; and leave to the world a monument of blasted hopes and changeable fortune. Pleyel was already lost to me; yet, while Catharine lived life was not a detestable possession: but now, severed from the companion of my infancy, the partaker of all my thoughts, my cares, and my wishes, I was like one set afloat upon a stormy sea, and hanging his safety upon a plank; night was closing upon him, and an unexpected surge had torn him from his hold and overwhelmed him forever.

Chapter XVII

I had no inclination nor power to move from this spot. For more than an hour, my faculties and limbs seemed to be deprived of all activity. The door below creaked on its hinges, and steps ascended the stairs. My wandering and confused thoughts were instantly recalled by these sounds, and dropping the curtain of the bed, I moved to a part of the room where any one who entered should be visible; such are

the vibrations of sentiment, that notwithstanding the seeming fulfilment of my fears, and increase of my danger, I was conscious, on this
occasion, to no turbulence but that of curiosity.

At length he entered the apartment, and I recognized my brother.
It was the same Wieland whom I had ever seen. Yet his features were
pervaded by a new expression. I supposed him unacquainted with
the fate of his wife, and his appearance confirmed this persuasion.
A brow expanding into exultation I had hitherto never seen in him,
yet such a brow did he now wear. Not only was he unapprized of the
disaster that had happened, but some joyous occurrence had betided.
What a reverse was preparing to annihilate his transitory bliss! No
husband ever doated more fondly, for no wife ever claimed so boundless a devotion. I was not uncertain as to the effects to flow from the
discovery of her fate. I confided not at all in the efforts of his reason
or his piety. There were few evils which his modes of thinking would
not disarm of their sting; but here, all opiates to grief, and all com-
pellers of patience were vain. This spectacle would be unavoidably
followed by the outrages of desperation, and a rushing to death.

For the present, I neglected to ask myself what motive brought him
hither. I was only fearful of the effects to flow from the sight of the
dead. Yet could it be long concealed from him? Some time and
speedily he would obtain this knowledge. No stratagems could considerably or usefully prolong his ignorance. All that could be sought
was to take away the abruptness of the change, and shut out the confusion of despair, and the inroads of madness: but I knew my brother,
and knew that all exertions to console him would be fruitless.

What could I say? I was mute, and poured forth those tears on his
account, which my own unhappiness had been unable to extort. In
the midst of my tears, I was not unobservant of his motions. These
were of a nature to rouse some other sentiment than grief, or, at
least, to mix with it a portion of astonishment.

His countenance suddenly became troubled. His hands were
clasped with a force that left the print of his nails in his flesh. His
eyes were fixed on my feet. His brain seemed to swell beyond its continent. He did not cease to breathe, but his breath was stifled into
groans. I had never witnessed the hurricane of human passions. My
element had, till lately, been all sunshine and calm. I was unconver-
sant with the altitudes and energies of sentiment, and was transfixed
with inexplicable horror by the symptoms which I now beheld.

After a silence and a conflict which I could not interpret, he
lifted his eyes to heaven, and in broken accents exclaimed, "This is
too much! Any victim but this, and thy will be done. Have I not sufficiently attested my faith and my obedience? She that is gone, they
that have perished, were linked with my soul by ties which only thy
command would have broken; but here is sanctity and excellence

surpassing human. This workmanship is thine, and it cannot be thy will to heap it into ruins."

Here suddenly unclasping his hands, he struck one of them against his forehead, and continued—"Wretch! who made thee quicksighted in the councils of thy Maker? Deliverance from mortal fetters is awarded to this being, and thou art the minister of this decree."

So saying, Wieland advanced towards me. His words and his motions were without meaning, except on one supposition. The death of Catharine was already known to him, and that knowledge, as might have been suspected, had destroyed his reason. I had feared nothing less; but how that I beheld the extinction of a mind the most luminous and penetrating that ever dignified the human form, my sensations were fraught with new and insupportable anguish.

I had not time to reflect in what way my own safety would be affected by this revolution, or what I had to dread from the wild conceptions of a mad-man. He advanced towards me. Some hollow noises were wafted by the breeze. Confused clamours were succeeded by many feet traversing the grass, and then crowding into the piazza.

These sounds suspended my brother's purpose, and he stood to listen. The signals multiplied and grew louder; perceiving this, he turned from me, and hurried out of my sight. All about me was pregnant with motives to astonishment. My sister's corpse, Wieland's frantic demeanour, and, at length, this crowd of visitants so little accorded with my foresight, that my mental progress was stopped. The impulse had ceased which was accustomed to give motion and order to my thoughts.

Footsteps thronged upon the stairs, and presently many faces shewed themselves within the door of my apartment. These looks were full of alarm and watchfulness. They pryed into corners as if in search of some fugitive; next their gaze was fixed upon me, and betokened all the vehemence of terror and pity. For a time I questioned whether these were not shapes and faces like that which I had seen at the bottom of the stairs, creatures of my fancy or airy existences.

My eye wandered from one to another, till at length it fell on a countenance which I well knew. It was that of Mr. Hallet. This man was a distant kinsman of my mother, venerable for his age, his uprightness, and sagacity. He had long discharged the functions of a magistrate and good citizen. If any terrors remained, his presence was sufficient to dispel them.

He approached, took my hand with a compassionate air, and said in a low voice, "Where, my dear Clara, are your brother and sister?" I made no answer, but pointed to the bed. His attendants drew aside the curtain, and while their eyes glared with horror at the spectacle which they beheld, those of Mr. Hallet overflowed with tears.

After considerable pause, he once more turned to me. "My dear girl, this sight is not for you. Can you confide in my care, and that of Mrs. Baynton's? We will see performed all that circumstances require."

I made strenuous opposition to this request. I insisted on remaining near her till she were interred. His remonstrances, however, and my own feelings, shewed me the propriety of a temporary dereliction. Louisa stood in need of a comforter, and my brother's children of a nurse. My unhappy brother was himself an object of solicitude and care. At length, I consented to relinquish the corpse, and go to my brother's, whose house, I said, would need a mistress, and his children a parent.

During this discourse, my venerable friend struggled with his tears, but my last intimation called them forth with fresh violence. Meanwhile, his attendants stood round in mournful silence, gazing on me and at each other. I repeated my resolution, and rose to execute it; but he took my hand to detain me. His countenance betrayed irresolution and reluctance. I requested him to state the reason of his opposition to this measure. I entreated him to be explicit. I told him that my brother had just been there, and that I knew his condition. This misfortune had driven him to madness, and his offspring must not want a protector. If he chose, I would resign Wieland to his care; but his innocent and helpless babes stood in instant need of nurse and mother, and these offices I would by no means allow another to perform while I had life.

Every word that I uttered seemed to augment his perplexity and distress. At last he said, "I think, Clara, I have entitled myself to some regard from you. You have professed your willingness to oblige me. Now I call upon you to confer upon me the highest obligation in your power. Permit Mrs. Baynton to have the management of your brother's house for two or three days; then it shall be yours to act in it as you please. No matter what are my motives in making this request: perhaps I think your age, your sex, or the distress which this disaster must occasion, incapacitates you for the office. Surely you have no doubt of Mrs. Baynton's tenderness or discretion."

New ideas now rushed into my mind. I fixed my eyes stedfastly on Mr. Hallet. "Are they well?" said I. "Is Louisa well? Are Benjamin, and William, and Constantine, and Little Clara, are they safe? Tell me truly, I beseech you!"

"They are well," he replied; "they are perfectly safe."

"Fear no effeminate weakness in me: I can bear to hear the truth. Tell me truly, are they well?"

He again assured me that they were well.[1]

---

1. Cf. Ross to MacDuff in *Macbeth* 4.3.176 ff.

"What then," resumed I, "do you fear? Is it possible for any calamity to disqualify me for performing my duty to these helpless innocents? I am willing to divide the care of them with Mrs. Baynton; I shall be grateful for her sympathy and aid; but what should I be to desert them at an hour like this!"

I will cut short this distressful dialogue. I still persisted in my purpose, and he still persisted in his opposition. This excited my suspicions anew; but these were removed by solemn declarations of their safety. I could not explain this conduct in my friend; but at length consented to go to the city, provided I should see them for a few minutes at present, and should return on the morrow.

Even this arrangement was objected to. At length he told me they were removed to the city. Why were they removed, I asked, and whither? My importunities would not now be eluded. My suspicions were roused, and no evasion or artifice was sufficient to allay them. Many of the audience began to give vent to their emotions in tears. Mr. Hallet himself seemed as if the conflict were too hard to be longer sustained. Something whispered to my heart that havoc had been wider than I now witnessed. I suspected this concealment to arise from apprehensions of the effects which a knowledge of the truth would produce in me. I once more entreated him to inform me truly of their state. To enforce my entreaties, I put on an air of insensibility. "I can guess," said I, "what has happened—They are indeed beyond the reach of injury, for they are dead! Is it not so?" My voice faltered in spite of my courageous efforts.

"Yes," said he, "they are dead! Dead by the same fate, and by the same hand, with their mother!"

"Dead!" replied I; "what, all?"

"All!" replied he: "he spared *not one!*"

Allow me, my friends, to close my eyes upon the after-scene. Why should I protract a tale which I already begin to feel is too long? Over this scene at least let me pass lightly. Here, indeed, my narrative would be imperfect. All was tempestuous commotion in my heart and in my brain. I have no memory for ought but unconscious transitions and rueful sights. I was ingenious and indefatigable in the invention of torments. I would not dispense with any spectacle adapted to exasperate my grief. Each pale and mangled form I crushed to my bosom. Louisa, whom I loved with so ineffable a passion, was denied to me at first, but my obstinacy conquered their reluctance.

They led the way into a darkened hall. A lamp pendant from the ceiling was uncovered, and they pointed to a table. The assassin had defrauded me of my last and miserable consolation. I sought not in her visage, for the tinge of the morning, and the lustre of heaven. These had vanished with life; but I hoped for liberty to print a last kiss upon her lips. This was denied me; for such had been the merciless blow that destroyed her, that not a *lineament remained*!

I was carried hence to the city. Mrs. Hallet was my companion and my nurse. Why should I dwell upon the rage of fever, and the effusions of delirium? Carwin was the phantom that pursued my dreams, the giant oppressor under whose arm I was for ever on the point of being crushed. Strenuous muscles were required to hinder my flight, and hearts of steel to withstand the eloquence of my fears. In vain I called upon them to look upward, to mark his sparkling rage and scowling contempt. All I sought was to fly from the stroke that was lifted. Then I heaped upon my guards the most vehement reproaches, or betook myself to wailings on the haplessness of my condition.

This malady, at length, declined, and my weeping friends began to look for my restoration. Slowly, and with intermitted beams, memory revisited me. The scenes that I had witnessed were revived, became the theme of deliberation and deduction, and called forth the effusions of more rational sorrow.

Chapter XVIII

I had imperfectly recovered my strength, when I was informed of the arrival of my mother's brother, Thomas Cambridge. Ten years since, he went to Europe, and was a surgeon in the British forces in Germany, during the whole of the late war.[1] After its conclusion, some connection that he had formed with an Irish officer, made him retire into Ireland. Intercourse had been punctually maintained by letters with his sister's children, and hopes were given that he would shortly return to his native country, and pass his old age in our society. He was now in an evil hour arrived.

I desired an interview with him for numerous and urgent reasons. With the first returns of my understanding I had anxiously sought information of the fate of my brother. During the course of my disease I had never seen him; and vague and unsatisfactory answers were returned to all my inquiries. I had vehemently interrogated Mrs. Hallet and her husband, and solicited an interview with this unfortunate man; but they mysteriously insinuated that his reason was still unsettled, and that his circumstances rendered an interview impossible. Their reserve on the particulars of this destruction, and the author of it, was equally invincible.

For some time, finding all my efforts fruitless, I had desisted from direct inquiries and solicitations, determined, as soon as my strength was sufficiently renewed, to pursue other means of dispelling my

1. The Seven Years' War.

uncertainty. In this state of things my uncle's arrival and intention to visit me were announced. I almost shuddered to behold the face of this man. When I reflected on the disasters that had befallen us, I was half unwilling to witness that dejection and grief which would be disclosed in his countenance. But I believed that all transactions had been thoroughly disclosed to him, and confided in my importunity to extort from him the knowledge that I sought.

I had no doubt as to the person of our enemy; but the motives that urged him to perpetrate these horrors, the means that he used, and his present condition, were totally unknown. It was reasonable to expect some information on this head, from my uncle. I therefore waited his coming with impatience. At length, in the dusk of the evening, and in my solitary chamber, this meeting took place.

This man was our nearest relation, and had ever treated us with the affection of a parent. Our meeting, therefore, could not be without overflowing tenderness and gloomy joy. He rather encouraged than restrained the tears that I poured out in his arms, and took upon himself the task of comforter. Allusions to recent disasters could not be long omitted. One topic facilitated the admission of another. At length, I mentioned and deplored the ignorance in which I had been kept respecting my brother's destiny, and the circumstances of our misfortunes. I entreated him to tell me what was Wieland's condition, and what progress had been made in detecting or punishing the author of this unheard-of devastation.

"The author!" said he; "Do you know the author?"

"Alas!" I answered, "I am too well acquainted with him. The story of the grounds of my suspicions would be painful and too long. I am not apprized of the extent of your present knowledge. There are none but Wieland, Pleyel, and myself, who are able to relate certain facts."

"Spare yourself the pain," said he. "All that Wieland and Pleyel can communicate, I know already. If any thing of moment has fallen within your own exclusive knowledge, and the relation be not too arduous for your present strength, I confess I am desirous of hearing it. Perhaps you allude to one by the name of Carwin. I will anticipate your curiosity by saying, that since these disasters, no one has seen or heard of him. His agency is, therefore, a mystery still unsolved."

I readily complied with his request, and related as distinctly as I could, though in general terms, the events transacted in the summer-house and my chamber. He listened without apparent surprize to the tale of Pleyel's errors and suspicions, and with augmented seriousness, to my narrative of the warnings and inexplicable vision, and the letter found upon the table. I waited for his comments.

"You gather from this," said he, "that Carwin is the author of all this misery."

"Is it not," answered I, "an unavoidable inference? But what know you respecting it? Was it possible to execute this mischief without witness or coadjutor? I beseech you to relate to me, when and why Mr. Hallet was summoned to the scene, and by whom this disaster was first suspected or discovered. Surely, suspicion must have fallen upon some one, and pursuit was made."

My uncle rose from his seat, and traversed the floor with hasty steps. His eyes were fixed upon the ground, and he seemed buried in perplexity. At length he paused, and said with an emphatic tone, "It is true; the instrument is known. Carwin may have plotted, but the execution was another's. That other is found, and his deed is ascertained."

"Good heaven!" I exclaimed, "what say you? Was not Carwin the assassin? Could any hand but his have carried into act this dreadful purpose?"

"Have I not said," returned he, "that the performance was another's? Carwin, perhaps, or heaven, or insanity, prompted the murderer; but Carwin is unknown. The actual performer has, long since, been called to judgment and convicted, and is, at this moment, at the bottom of a dungeon loaded with chains."

I lifted my hands and eyes. "Who then is this assassin? By what means, and whither was he traced? What is the testimony of his guilt?"

"His own, corroborated with that of a servant-maid who spied the murder of the children from a closet where she was concealed. The magistrate returned from your dwelling to your brother's. He was employed in hearing and recording the testimony of the only witness, when the criminal himself, unexpected, unsolicited, unsought, entered the hall, acknowledged his guilt, and rendered himself up to justice.

"He has since been summoned to the bar. The audience was composed of thousands whom rumours of this wonderful event had attracted from the greatest distance. A long and impartial examination was made, and the prisoner was called upon for his defence. In compliance with this call he delivered an ample relation of his motives and actions." There he stopped.

I besought him to say who this criminal was, and what the instigations that compelled him. My uncle was silent. I urged this inquiry with new force. I reverted to my own knowledge, and sought in this some basis to conjecture. I ran over the scanty catalogue of the men whom I knew; I lighted on no one who was qualified for ministering to malice like this. Again I resorted to importunity. Had I ever seen the criminal? Was it sheer cruelty, or diabolical revenge that produced this overthrow?

He surveyed me, for a considerable time, and listened to my interrogations in silence. At length he spoke: "Clara, I have known thee by report, and in some degree by observation. Thou art a being of no vulgar sort. Thy friends have hitherto treated thee as a child. They meant well, but, perhaps, they were unacquainted with thy strength. I assure myself that nothing will surpass thy fortitude.

"Thou art anxious to know the destroyer of thy family, his actions, and his motives. Shall I call him to thy presence, and permit him to confess before thee? Shall I make him the narrator of his own tale?"

I started on my feet, and looked round me with fearful glances, as if the murderer was close at hand. "What do you mean?" said I; "put an end, I beseech you, to this suspence."

"Be not alarmed; you will never more behold the face of this criminal, unless he be gifted with supernatural strength, and sever like threads the constraint of links and bolts. I have said that the assassin was arraigned at the bar, and that the trial ended with a summons from the judge to confess or to vindicate his actions. A reply was immediately made with significance of gesture, and a tranquil majesty, which denoted less of humanity than god-head. Judges, advocates and auditors were panic-struck and breathless with attention. One of the hearers faithfully recorded the speech. There it is," continued he, putting a roll of papers in my hand, "you may read it at your leisure."

With these words my uncle left me alone. My curiosity refused me a moment's delay. I opened the papers, and read as follows.

Chapter XIX

Theodore Wieland, the prisoner at the bar, was now called upon for his defence. He looked around him for some time in silence, and with a mild countenance. At length he spoke:

"It is strange; I am known to my judges and my auditors. Who is there present a stranger to the character of Wieland? who knows him not as an husband—as a father—as a friend? yet here am I arraigned as a criminal. I am charged with diabolical malice; I am accused of the murder of my wife and my children!

"It is true, they were slain by me; they all perished by my hand. The task of vindication is ignoble. What is it that I am called to vindicate? and before whom?

"You know that they are dead, and that they were killed by me. What more would you have? Would you extort from me a statement of my motives? Have you failed to discover them already? You charge me with malice; but your eyes are not shut; your reason is still vigorous; your memory has not forsaken you. You know whom it is that you thus charge. The habits of his life are known to you; his treatment of his wife and his offspring is known to you; the soundness of his integrity, and the unchangeableness of his principles, are familiar to your apprehension; yet you persist in this charge! You lead me hither manacled as a felon; you deem me worthy of a vile and tormenting death!

"Who are they whom I have devoted to death? My wife—the little ones, that drew their being from me—that creature who, as she surpassed them in excellence, claimed a larger affection than those whom natural affinities bound to my heart. Think ye that malice could have urged me to this deed? Hide your audacious fronts from the scrutiny of heaven. Take refuge in some cavern unvisited by human eyes. Ye may deplore your wickedness or folly, but ye cannot expiate it.

"Think not that I speak for your sakes. Hug to your hearts this detestable infatuation. Deem me still a murderer, and drag me to untimely death. I make not an effort to dispel your illusion: I utter not a word to cure you of your sanguinary[1] folly: but there are probably some in this assembly who have come from far: for their sakes, whose distance has disabled them from knowing me, I will tell what I have done, and why.

"It is needless to say that God is the object of my supreme passion. I have cherished, in his presence, a single and upright heart. I have thirsted for the knowledge of his will. I have burnt with ardour to approve my faith and my obedience.

"My days have been spent in searching for the revelation of that will; but my days have been mournful, because my search failed. I solicited direction: I turned on every side where glimmerings of light could be discovered. I have not been wholly uninformed; but my knowledge has always stopped short of certainty. Dissatisfaction has insinuated itself into all my thoughts. My purposes have been pure; my wishes indefatigable; but not till lately were these purposes thoroughly accomplished, and these wishes fully gratified.

"I thank thee, my father, for thy bounty; that thou didst not ask a less sacrifice than this;[2] that thou placedst me in a condition to testify my submission to thy will! What have I withheld which it was thy pleasure to exact? Now may I, with dauntless and erect eye, claim my reward, since I have given thee the treasure of my soul.

"I was at my own house: it was late in the evening: my sister had gone to the city, but proposed to return. It was in expectation of her

1. Overconfident.
2. Cf. the story of Abraham and Isaac in Genesis 22. Abraham's willingness to obey a divine command to sacrifice his son was the subject of Christoph Martin Wieland's *The Trial of Abraham* (1753) (see p. 237 in this vol.).

return that my wife and I delayed going to bed beyond the usual hour; the rest of the family, however, were retired.

"My mind was contemplative and calm; not wholly devoid of apprehension on account of my sister's safety. Recent events, not easily explained, had suggested the existence of some danger; but this danger was without a distinct form in our imagination, and scarcely ruffled our tranquillity.

"Time passed, and my sister did not arrive; her house is at some distance from mine, and though her arrangements had been made with a view to residing with us, it was possible that, through forgetfulness, or the occurrence of unforeseen emergencies, she had returned to her own dwelling.

"Hence it was conceived proper that I should ascertain the truth by going thither. I went. On my way my mind was full of those ideas which related to my intellectual condition. In the torrent of fervid conceptions, I lost sight of my purpose. Some times I stood still; some times I wandered from my path, and experienced some difficulty, on recovering from my fit of musing, to regain it.

"The series of my thoughts is easily traced. At first every vein beat with raptures known only to the man whose parental and conjugal love is without limits, and the cup of whose desires, immense as it is, overflows with gratification. I know not why emotions that were perpetual visitants should now have recurred with unusual energy. The transition was not new from sensations of joy to a consciousness of gratitude. The author of my being was likewise the dispenser of every gift with which that being was embellished. The service to which a benefactor like this was entitled, could not be circumscribed. My social sentiments were indebted to their alliance with devotion for all their value. All passions are base, all joys feeble, all energies malignant, which are not drawn from this source.

"For a time, my contemplations soared above earth and its inhabitants. I stretched forth my hands; I lifted my eyes, and exclaimed, O! that I might be admitted to thy presence; that mine were the supreme delight of knowing thy will, and of performing it! The blissful privilege of direct communication with thee, and of listening to the audible enunciation of thy pleasure!

"What task would I not undertake, what privation would I not cheerfully endure, to testify my love of thee? Alas! thou hidest thyself from my view: glimpses only of thy excellence and beauty are afforded me. Would that a momentary emanation from thy glory would visit me! that some unambiguous token of thy presence would salute my senses!

"In this mood, I entered the house of my sister. It was vacant. Scarcely had I regained recollection of the purpose that brought me hither. Thoughts of a different tendency had such absolute possession of my mind, that the relations of time and space were almost obliterated from my understanding. These wanderings, however, were restrained, and I ascended to her chamber.

"I had no light, and might have known by external observation, that the house was without any inhabitant. With this, however, I was not satisfied. I entered the room, and the object of my search not appearing, I prepared to return.

"The darkness required some caution in descending the stair. I stretched my hand to seize the balustrade by which I might regulate my steps. How shall I describe the lustre, which, at that moment, burst upon my vision!

"I was dazzled. My organs were bereaved of their activity. My eye-lids were half-closed, and my hands withdrawn from the balustrade. A nameless fear chilled my veins, and I stood motionless. This irradiation did not retire or lessen. It seemed as if some powerful effulgence covered me like a mantle.

"I opened my eyes and found all about me luminous and glowing. It was the element of heaven that flowed around. Nothing but a fiery stream was at first visible; but, anon, a shrill voice from behind called upon me to attend.

"I turned: It is forbidden to describe what I saw: Words, indeed, would be wanting to the task. The lineaments of that being, whose veil was now lifted, and whose visage beamed upon my sight, no hues of pencil or of language can pourtray.

"As it spoke, the accents thrilled to my heart. 'Thy prayers are heard. In proof of thy faith, render me thy wife. This is the victim I chuse. Call her hither, and here let her fall.'—The sound, and visage, and light vanished at once.

"What demand was this? The blood of Catharine was to be shed! My wife was to perish by my hand! I sought opportunity to attest my virtue. Little did I expect that a proof like this would have been demanded.

"'My wife!' I exclaimed: 'O God! substitute some other victim. Make me not the butcher of my wife. My own blood is cheap. This will I pour out before thee with a willing heart; but spare, I beseech thee, this precious life, or commission some other than her husband to perform the bloody deed.'

"In vain. The conditions were prescribed; the decree had gone forth, and nothing remained but to execute it. I rushed out of the house and across the intermediate fields, and stopped not till I entered my own parlour.

"My wife had remained here during my absence, in anxious expectation of my return with some tidings of her sister. I had none to communicate. For a time, I was breathless with my speed: This, and the tremors that shook my frame, and the wildness of my looks, alarmed her. She immediately suspected some disaster to have happened to her friend, and her own speech was as much overpowered by emotion as mine.

"She was silent, but her looks manifested her impatience to hear what I had to communicate. I spoke, but with so much precipitation as scarcely to be understood; catching her, at the same time, by the arm, and forcibly pulling her from her seat.

"'Come along with me: fly: waste not a moment: time will be lost, and the deed will be omitted. Tarry not; question not; but fly with me!'

"This deportment added afresh to her alarms. Her eyes pursued mine, and she said, 'What is the matter? For God's sake what is the matter? Where would you have me go?'

"My eyes were fixed upon her countenance while she spoke. I thought upon her virtues; I viewed her as the mother of my babes; as my wife: I recalled the purpose for which I thus urged her attendance. My heart faltered, and I saw that I must rouse to this work all my faculties. The danger of the least delay was imminent.

"I looked away from her, and again exerting my force, drew her towards the door—'You must go with me—indeed you must.'

"In her fright she half-resisted my efforts, and again exclaimed, 'Good heaven! what is it you mean? Where go? What has happened? Have you found Clara?'

"'Follow me, and you will see,' I answered, still urging her reluctant steps forward.

"'What phrenzy has seized you? Something must needs have happened. Is she sick? Have you found her?'

"'Come and see. Follow me, and know for yourself.'

"Still she expostulated and besought me to explain this mysterious behaviour. I could not trust myself to answer her; to look at her; but grasping her arm, I drew her after me. She hesitated, rather through confusion of mind than from unwillingness to accompany me. This confusion gradually abated, and she moved forward, but with irresolute footsteps, and continual exclamations of wonder and terror. Her interrogations of what was the matter? and whither was I going? were ceaseless and vehement.

"It was the scope of my efforts not to think; to keep up a conflict and uproar in my mind in which all order and distinctness should be lost; to escape from the sensations produced by her voice. I was, therefore, silent. I strove to abridge this interval by my haste, and to waste all my attention in furious gesticulations.

"In this state of mind we reached my sister's door. She looked at the windows and saw that all was desolate—'Why come we here? There is no body here. I will not go in.'

"Still I was dumb; but opening the door, I drew her into the entry. This was the allotted scene: here she was to fall. I let go her hand,

and pressing my palms against my forehead, made one mighty effort to work up my soul to the deed.

"In vain; it would not be; my courage was appalled; my arms nerveless: I muttered prayers that my strength might be aided from above. They availed nothing.

"Horror diffused itself over me. This conviction of my cowardice, my rebellion, fastened upon me, and I stood rigid and cold as marble. From this state I was somewhat relieved by my wife's voice, who renewed her supplications to be told why we came hither, and what was the fate of my sister.

"What could I answer? My words were broken and inarticulate. Her fears naturally acquired force from the observation of these symptoms; but these fears were misplaced. The only inference she deduced from my conduct was, that some terrible mishap had befallen Clara.

"She wrung her hands, and exclaimed in an agony, 'O tell me, where is she? What has become of her? Is she sick? Dead? Is she in her chamber? O let me go thither and know the worst!'

"This proposal set my thoughts once more in motion. Perhaps what my rebellious heart refused to perform here, I might obtain strength enough to execute elsewhere.

"'Come then,' said I, 'let us go.'

"'I will, but not in the dark. We must first procure a light.'

"'Fly then and procure it; but I charge you, linger not. I will await for your return.'

"While she was gone, I strode along the entry. The fellness of a gloomy hurricane but faintly resembled the discord that reigned in my mind. To omit this sacrifice must not be; yet my sinews had refused to perform it. No alternative was offered. To rebel against the mandate was impossible; but obedience would render me the executioner of my wife. My will was strong, but my limbs refused their office.

"She returned with a light; I led the way to the chamber; she looked round her; she lifted the curtain of the bed; she saw nothing.

"At length, she fixed inquiring eyes upon me. The light now enabled her to discover in my visage what darkness had hitherto concealed. Her cares were now transferred from my sister to myself, and she said in a tremulous voice, 'Wieland! you are not well: What ails you? Can I do nothing for you?'

"That accents and looks so winning should disarm me of my resolution, was to be expected. My thoughts were thrown anew into anarchy. I spread my hand before my eyes that I might not see her, and answered only by groans. She took my other hand between her's, and pressing it to her heart, spoke with that voice which had ever swayed my will, and wafted away sorrow.

"'My friend! my soul's friend! tell me thy cause of grief. Do I not merit to partake with thee in thy cares? Am I not thy wife?'

"This was too much. I broke from her embrace, and retired to a corner of the room. In this pause, courage was once more infused into me. I resolved to execute my duty. She followed me, and renewed her passionate entreaties to know the cause of my distress.

"I raised my head and regarded her with stedfast looks. I muttered something about death, and the injunctions of my duty. At these words she shrunk back, and looked at me with a new expression of anguish. After a pause, she clasped her hands, and exclaimed—

"'O Wieland! Wieland! God grant that I am mistaken; but surely something is wrong. I see it: it is too plain: thou art undone—lost to me and to thyself.' At the same time she gazed on my features with intensest anxiety, in hope that different symptoms would take place. I replied to her with vehemence—

"'Undone! No; my duty is known, and I thank my God that my cowardice is now vanquished, and I have power to fulfil it. Catharine! I pity the weakness of thy nature: I pity thee, but must not spare. Thy life is claimed from my hands: thou must die!'

"Fear was now added to her grief. 'What mean you? Why talk you of death? Bethink yourself, Wieland: bethink yourself, and this fit will pass. O why came I hither! Why did you drag me hither?'

"'I brought thee hither to fulfil a divine command. I am appointed thy destroyer, and destroy thee I must.' Saying this I seized her wrists. She shrieked aloud, and endeavoured to free herself from my grasp; but her efforts were vain.

"'Surely, surely Wieland, thou dost not mean it. Am I not thy wife? and wouldst thou kill me? Thou wilt not; and yet—I see—thou art Wieland no longer! A fury resistless and horrible possesses thee—Spare me—spare—help—help——'

"Till her breath was stopped she shrieked for help—for mercy. When she could speak no longer, her gestures, her looks appealed to my compassion. My accursed hand was irresolute and tremulous. I meant thy death to be sudden, thy struggles to be brief. Alas! my heart was infirm; my resolves mutable. Thrice I slackened my grasp, and life kept its hold, though in the midst of pangs. Her eye-balls started from their sockets. Grimness and distortion took place of all that used to bewitch me into transport, and subdue me into reverence.

"I was commissioned to kill thee, but not to torment thee with the foresight of thy death; not to multiply thy fears, and prolong thy agonies. Haggard, and pale, and lifeless, at length thou ceasedst to contend with thy destiny.

"This was a moment of triumph. Thus had I successfully subdued the stubbornness of human passions: the victim which had been demanded was given: the deed was done past recal.

"I lifted the corpse in my arms and laid it on the bed. I gazed upon it with delight. Such was the elation of my thoughts, that I even broke into laughter. I clapped my hands and exclaimed, 'It is done!³ My sacred duty is fulfilled! To that I have sacrificed, O my God! thy last and best gift, my wife!'

"For a while I thus soared above frailty. I imagined I had set myself forever beyond the reach of selfishness; but my imaginations were false. This rapture quickly subsided. I looked again at my wife. My joyous ebullitions vanished, and I asked myself who it was whom I saw? Methought it could not be Catharine. It could not be the woman who had lodged for years in my heart; who had slept, nightly, in my bosom; who had borne in her womb, who had fostered at her breast, the beings who called me father; whom I had watched with delight, and cherished with a fondness ever new and perpetually growing: it could not be the same.

"Where was her bloom! These deadly and blood-suffused orbs but ill resemble the azure and exstatic tenderness of her eyes. The lucid stream that meandered over that bosom, the glow of love that was wont to sit upon that cheek, are much unlike these livid stains and this hideous deformity. Alas! these were the traces of agony; the gripe of the assassin had been here!

"I will not dwell upon my lapse into desperate and outrageous sorrow. The breath of heaven that sustained me was withdrawn, and I sunk into *mere man*. I leaped from the floor: I dashed my head against the wall: I uttered screams of horror: I panted after torment and pain. Eternal fire, and the bickerings of hell, compared with what I felt, were music and a bed of roses.

"I thank my God that this degeneracy was transient, that he deigned once more to raise me aloft. I thought upon what I had done as a sacrifice to duty, and *was calm*. My wife was dead; but I reflected, that though this source of human consolation was closed, yet others were still open. If the transports of an husband were no more, the feelings of a father had still scope for exercise. When remembrance of their mother should excite too keen a pang, I would look upon them, and *be comforted*.

"While I revolved these ideas, new warmth flowed in upon my heart—I was wrong. These feelings were the growth of selfishness. Of this I was not aware, and to dispel the mist that obscured my perceptions, a new effulgence and a new mandate were necessary.

"From these thoughts I was recalled by a ray that was shot into the room. A voice spake like that which I had before heard—'Thou hast done well; but all is not done—the sacrifice is incomplete—thy children must be offered—they must perish with their mother!—'"

3. Cf. Jesus in John 19:30: "It is finished."

Chapter XX

Will you wonder that I read no farther? Will you not rather be astonished that I read thus far? What power supported me through such a
task I know not. Perhaps the doubt from which I could not disengage
my mind, that the scene here depicted was a dream, contributed to
my perseverance. In vain the solemn introduction of my uncle, his
appeals to my fortitude, and allusions to something monstrous in the
events he was about to disclose; in vain the distressful perplexity, the
mysterious silence and ambiguous answers of my attendants, especially when the condition of my brother was the theme of my inquiries, were remembered. I recalled the interview with Wieland in my
chamber, his preternatural tranquillity succeeded by bursts of passion and menacing actions. All these coincided with the tenor of this
paper.

Catharine and her children, and Louisa were dead. The act that
destroyed them was, in the highest degree, inhuman. It was worthy
of savages trained to murder, and exulting in agonies.

Who was the performer of the deed? Wieland! My brother! The
husband and the father! That man of gentle virtues and invincible
benignity! placable and mild—an idolater of peace! Surely, said I, it
is a dream. For many days have I been vexed with frenzy. Its dominion is still felt; but new forms are called up to diversify and augment my torments.

The paper dropped from my hand, and my eyes followed it. I
shrunk back, as if to avoid some petrifying influence that approached
me. My tongue was mute; all the functions of nature were at a stand,
and I sunk upon the floor lifeless.

The noise of my fall, as I afterwards heard, alarmed my uncle, who
was in a lower apartment, and whose apprehensions had detained
him. He hastened to my chamber, and administered the assistance
which my condition required. When I opened my eyes I beheld him
before me. His skill as a reasoner as well as a physician, was exerted
to obviate the injurious effects of this disclosure; but he had wrongly
estimated the strength of my body or of my mind. This new shock
brought me once more to the brink of the grave, and my malady was
much more difficult to subdue than at first.

I will not dwell upon the long train of dreary sensations, and the
hideous confusion of my understanding. Time slowly restored its customary firmness to my frame, and order to my thoughts. The images
impressed upon my mind by this fatal paper were somewhat effaced
by my malady. They were obscure and disjointed like the parts of a
dream. I was desirous of freeing my imagination from this chaos. For
this end I questioned my uncle, who was my constant companion.

He was intimidated by the issue of his first experiment, and took pains to elude or discourage my inquiry. My impetuosity some times compelled him to have resort to misrepresentations and untruths.

Time effected that end, perhaps, in a more beneficial manner. In the course of my meditations the recollections of the past gradually became more distinct. I revolved them, however, in silence, and being no longer accompanied with surprize, they did not exercise a death-dealing power. I had discontinued the perusal of the paper in the midst of the narrative; but what I read, combined with information elsewhere obtained, threw, perhaps, a sufficient light upon these detestable transactions; yet my curiosity was not inactive. I desired to peruse the remainder.

My eagerness to know the particulars of this tale was mingled and abated by my antipathy to the scene which would be disclosed. Hence I employed no means to effect my purpose. I desired knowledge, and, at the same time, shrunk back from receiving the boon.

One morning, being left alone, I rose from my bed, and went to a drawer where my finer clothing used to be kept. I opened it, and this fatal paper saluted my sight. I snatched it involuntarily, and withdrew to a chair. I debated, for a few minutes, whether I should open and read. Now that my fortitude was put to trial, it failed. I felt myself incapable of deliberately surveying a scene of so much horror. I was prompted to return it to its place, but this resolution gave way, and I determined to peruse some part of it. I turned over the leaves till I came near the conclusion. The narrative of the criminal was finished. The verdict of *guilty* reluctantly pronounced by the jury, and the accused interrogated why sentence of death should not pass. The answer was brief, solemn, and emphatical.

"No. I have nothing to say. My tale has been told. My motives have been truly stated. If my judges are unable to discern the purity of my intentions, or to credit the statement of them, which I have just made; if they see not that my deed was enjoined by heaven; that obedience was the test of perfect virtue, and the extinction of selfishness and error, they must pronounce me a murderer.

"They refuse to credit my tale; they impute my acts to the influence of dæmons; they account me an example of the highest wickedness of which human nature is capable; they doom me to death and infamy. Have I power to escape this evil? If I have, be sure I will exert it. I will not accept evil at their hand, when I am entitled to good; I will suffer only when I cannot elude suffering.

"You say that I am guilty. Impious and rash! thus to usurp the prerogatives of your Maker! to set up your bounded views and halting reason, as the measure of truth!

"Thou, Omnipotent and Holy! Thou knowest that my actions were conformable to thy will. I know not what is crime; what actions are evil in their ultimate and comprehensive tendency or what are good. Thy knowledge, as thy power, is unlimited. I have taken thee for my guide, and cannot err. To the arms of thy protection, I entrust my safety. In the awards of thy justice, I confide for my recompense.

"Come death when it will, I am safe. Let calumny and abhorrence pursue me among men; I shall not be defrauded of my dues. The peace of virtue, and the glory of obedience, will be my portion hereafter."

Here ended the speaker. I withdrew my eyes from the page; but before I had time to reflect on what I had read, Mr. Cambridge entered the room. He quickly perceived how I had been employed, and betrayed some solicitude respecting the condition of my mind.

His fears, however, were superfluous. What I had read, threw me into a state not easily described. Anguish and fury, however, had no part in it. My faculties were chained up in wonder and awe. Just then, I was unable to speak. I looked at my friend with an air of inquisitiveness, and pointed at the roll. He comprehended my inquiry, and answered me with looks of gloomy acquiescence. After some time, my thoughts found their way to my lips.

"Such then were the acts of my brother. Such were his words. For this he was condemned to die: To die upon the gallows! A fate, cruel and unmerited! And is it so?" continued I, struggling for utterance, which this new idea made difficult; "is he—dead!"

"No. He is alive. There could be no doubt as to the cause of these excesses. They originated in sudden madness; but that madness continues, and he is condemned to perpetual imprisonment."

"Madness, say you? Are you sure? Were not these sights, and these sounds, really seen and heard?"

My uncle was surprized at my question. He looked at me with apparent inquietude. "Can you doubt," said he, "that these were illusions? Does heaven, think you, interfere for such ends?"

"O no; I think it not. Heaven cannot stimulate to such unheard-of outrage. The agent was not good, but evil."

"Nay, my dear girl," said my friend, "lay aside these fancies. Neither angel nor devil had any part in this affair."

"You misunderstand me," I answered; "I believe the agency to be external and real, but not supernatural."

"Indeed!" said he, in an accent of surprize. "Whom do you then suppose to be the agent?"

"I know not. All is wildering conjecture. I cannot forget Carwin. I cannot banish the suspicion that he was the setter of these snares. But how can we suppose it to be madness? Did insanity ever before assume this form?"

"Frequently. The illusion, in this case, was more dreadful in its consequences, than any that has come to my knowledge; but, I repeat that similar illusions are not rare. Did you never hear of an instance which occurred in your mother's family?"

"No. I beseech you relate it. My grandfather's death I have understood to have been extraordinary, but I know not in what respect. A brother, to whom he was much attached, died in his youth, and this, as I have heard, influenced, in some remarkable way, the fate of my grandfather; but I am unacquainted with particulars."

"On the death of that brother," resumed my friend, "my father was seized with dejection, which was found to flow from two sources. He not only grieved for the loss of a friend, but entertained the belief that his own death would be inevitably consequent on that of his brother. He waited from day to day in expectation of the stroke which he predicted was speedily to fall upon him. Gradually, however, he recovered his cheerfulness and confidence. He married, and performed his part in the world with spirit and activity. At the end of twenty-one years it happened that he spent the summer with his family at an house which he possessed on the sea coast in Cornwall.[1] It was at no great distance from a cliff which overhung the ocean, and rose into the air to a great height. The summit was level and secure, and easily ascended on the land side. The company frequently repaired hither in clear weather, invited by its pure airs and extensive prospects. One evening in June my father, with his wife and some friends, chanced to be on this spot. Every one was happy, and my father's imagination seemed particularly alive to the grandeur of the scenery.

"Suddenly, however, his limbs trembled and his features betrayed alarm. He threw himself into the attitude of one listening. He gazed earnestly in a direction in which nothing was visible to his friends. This lasted for a minute; then turning to his companions, he told them that his brother had just delivered to him a summons, which must be instantly obeyed. He then took an hasty and solemn leave of each person, and, before their surprize would allow them to understand the scene, he rushed to the edge of the cliff, threw himself headlong, and was seen no more.

"In the course of my practice in the German army, many cases, equally remarkable, have occurred. Unquestionably the illusions were maniacal, though the vulgar thought otherwise. They are all reducible to one class,[2] and are not more difficult of explication and cure than most affections of our frame."

---

1. A seaside county in southwestern England.
2. "Mania Mutabilis. See Darwin's Zoonomia, vol. ii. Class III. 1. 2. where similar cases are stated" [Brown's note]. Erasmus Darwin (1731–1802), grandfather of Charles Darwin, a scientist and poet. Brown's friends had published an American edition of the first volume of Darwin's 1794 treatise *Zoonomia; or, the Laws of Organic Life* in New York in 1796 (see p. 270 in this vol.).

This opinion my uncle endeavoured, by various means, to impress upon me. I listened to his reasonings and illustrations with silent respect. My astonishment was great on finding proofs of an influence of which I had supposed there were no examples; but I was far from accounting for appearances in my uncle's manner. Ideas thronged into my mind which I was unable to disjoin or to regulate. I reflected that this madness, if madness it were, had affected Pleyel and myself as well as Wieland. Pleyel had heard a mysterious voice. I had seen and heard. A form had showed itself to me as well as to Wieland. The disclosure had been made in the same spot. The appearance was equally complete and equally prodigious in both instances. Whatever supposition I should adopt, had I not equal reason to tremble? What was my security against influences equally terrific and equally irresistable?

It would be vain to attempt to describe the state of mind which this idea produced. I wondered at the change which a moment had effected in my brother's condition. Now was I stupified with tenfold wonder in contemplating myself. Was I not likewise transformed from rational and human into a creature of nameless and fearful attributes? Was I not transported to the brink of the same abyss? Ere a new day should come, my hands might be embrued in blood, and my remaining life be consigned to a dungeon and chains.

With moral sensibility like mine, no wonder that this new dread was more insupportable than the anguish I had lately endured. Grief carries its own antidote along with it. When thought becomes merely a vehicle of pain, its progress must be stopped. Death is a cure which nature or ourselves must administer: To this cure I now looked forward with gloomy satisfaction.

My silence could not conceal from my uncle the state of my thoughts. He made unwearied efforts to divert my attention from views so pregnant with danger. His efforts, aided by time, were in some measure successful. Confidence in the strength of my resolution, and in the healthful state of my faculties, was once more revived. I was able to devote my thoughts to my brother's state, and the causes of this disasterous proceeding.

My opinions were the sport of eternal change. Some times I conceived the apparition to be more than human. I had no grounds on which to build a disbelief. I could not deny faith to the evidence of my religion; the testimony of men was loud and unanimous: both these concurred to persuade me that evil spirits existed, and that their energy was frequently exerted in the system of the world.

These ideas connected themselves with the image of Carwin. Where is the proof, said I, that dæmons may not be subjected to the controul of men? This truth may be distorted and debased in the minds of the ignorant. The dogmas of the vulgar, with regard to this subject, are glaringly absurd; but though these may justly be neglected by the wise, we are scarcely justified in totally rejecting the possibility that men may obtain supernatural aid.

The dreams of superstition are worthy of contempt. Witchcraft, its instruments and miracles, the compact ratified by a bloody signature, the apparatus of sulpherous smells and thundering explosions, are monstrous and chimerical. These have no part in the scene over which the genius of Carwin presides. That conscious beings, dissimilar from human, but moral and voluntary agents as we are, some where exist, can scarcely be denied. That their aid may be employed to benign or malignant purposes, cannot be disproved.

Darkness rests upon the designs of this man. The extent of his power is unknown; but is there not evidence that it has been now exerted?

I recurred to my own experience. Here Carwin had actually appeared upon the stage; but this was in a human character. A voice and a form were discovered; but one was apparently exerted, and the other disclosed, not to befriend, but to counteract Carwin's designs. There were tokens of hostility, and not of alliance, between them. Carwin was the miscreant whose projects were resisted by a minister of heaven. How can this be reconciled to the stratagem which ruined my brother? There the agency was at once preternatural and malignant.

The recollection of this fact led my thoughts into a new channel. The malignity of that influence which governed my brother had hitherto been no subject of doubt. His wife and children were destroyed; they had expired in agony and fear; yet was it indisputably certain that their murderer was criminal? He was acquitted at the tribunal of his own conscience; his behaviour at his trial and since, was faithfully reported to me; appearances were uniform; not for a moment did he lay aside the majesty of virtue; he repelled all invectives by appealing to the deity, and to the tenor of his past life; surely there was truth in this appeal: none but a command from heaven could have swayed his will; and nothing but unerring proof of divine approbation could sustain his mind in its present elevation.

Chapter XXI

Such, for some time, was the course of my meditations. My weakness, and my aversion to be pointed at as an object of surprise or compassion, prevented me from going into public. I studiously avoided the visits of those who came to express their sympathy, or gratify their curiosity. My uncle was my principal companion. Nothing more powerfully tended to console me than his conversation.

With regard to Pleyel, my feelings seemed to have undergone a total revolution. It often happens that one passion supplants another. Late disasters had rent my heart, and now that the wound was in some degree closed, the love which I had cherished for this man seemed likewise to have vanished.

Hitherto, indeed, I had had no cause for despair. I was innocent of that offence which had estranged him from my presence. I might reasonably expect that my innocence would at some time be irresistably demonstrated, and his affection for me be revived with his esteem. Now my aversion to be thought culpable by him continued, but was unattended with the same impatience. I desired the removal of his suspicions, not for the sake of regaining his love, but because I delighted in the veneration of so excellent a man, and because he himself would derive pleasure from conviction of my integrity.

My uncle had early informed me that Pleyel and he had seen each other, since the return of the latter from Europe. Amidst the topics of their conversation, I discovered that Pleyel had carefully omitted the mention of those events which had drawn upon me so much abhorrence. I could not account for his silence on this subject. Perhaps time or some new discovery had altered or shaken his opinion. Perhaps he was unwilling, though I were guilty, to injure me in the opinion of my venerable kinsman. I understood that he had frequently visited me during my disease, had watched many successive nights by my bedside, and manifested the utmost anxiety on my account.

The journey which he was preparing to take, at the termination of our last interview, the catastrophe of the ensuing night induced him to delay. The motives of this journey I had, till now, totally mistaken. They were explained to me by my uncle, whose tale excited my astonishment without awakening my regret. In a different state of mind, it would have added unspeakably to my distress, but now it was more a source of pleasure than pain. This, perhaps, is not the least extraordinary of the facts contained in this narrative. It will excite less wonder when I add, that my indifference was temporary, and that the lapse of a few days shewed me that my feelings were deadened for a time, rather than finally extinguished.

Theresa de Stolberg was alive. She had conceived the resolution of seeking her lover in America. To conceal her flight, she had caused the report of her death to be propagated. She put herself under the conduct of Bertrand, the faithful servant of Pleyel. The pacquet which the latter received from the hands of his servant, contained the tidings of her safe arrival at Boston, and to meet her there was the purpose of his journey.

This discovery had set this man's character in a new light. I had mistaken the heroism of friendship for the phrenzy of love. He who had gained my affections, may be supposed to have previously entitled himself to my reverence; but the levity which had formerly characterized the behaviour of this man, tended to obscure the greatness of his sentiments. I did not fail to remark, that since this lady was still alive, the voice in the temple which asserted her death, must either have been intended to deceive, or have been itself deceived. The latter supposition was inconsistent with the notion of a spiritual, and the former with that of a benevolent being.

When my disease abated, Pleyel had forborne his visits, and had lately set out upon this journey. This amounted to a proof that my guilt was still believed by him. I was grieved for his errors, but trusted that my vindication would, sooner or later, be made.

Meanwhile, tumultuous thoughts were again set afloat by a proposal made to me by my uncle. He imagined that new airs would restore my languishing constitution, and a varied succession of objects tend to repair the shock which my mind had received. For this end, he proposed to me to take up my abode with him in France or Italy.

At a more prosperous period, this scheme would have pleased for its own sake. Now my heart sickened at the prospect of nature. The world of man was shrouded in misery and blood, and constituted a loathsome spectacle. I willingly closed my eyes in sleep, and regretted that the respite it afforded me was so short. I marked with satisfaction the progress of decay in my frame, and consented to live, merely in the hope that the course of nature would speedily relieve me from the burthen. Nevertheless, as he persisted in his scheme, I concurred in it merely because he was entitled to my gratitude, and because my refusal gave him pain.

No sooner was he informed of my consent, than he told me I must make immediate preparation to embark, as the ship in which he had engaged a passage would be ready to depart in three days. This expedition was unexpected. There was an impatience in his manner when he urged the necessity of dispatch that excited my surprize. When I questioned him as to the cause of this haste, he generally stated reasons which, at that time, I could not deny to be plausible; but which, on the review, appeared insufficient. I suspected that the true motives were concealed, and believed that these motives had some connection with my brother's destiny.

I now recollected that the information respecting Wieland which had, from time to time, been imparted to me, was always accompanied with airs of reserve and mysteriousness. What had appeared sufficiently explicit at the time it was uttered, I now remembered to have been faltering and ambiguous. I was resolved to remove my doubts, by visiting the unfortunate man in his dungeon.

Heretofore the idea of this visit had occurred to me; but the horrors of his dwelling-place, his wild yet placid physiognomy, his

neglected locks, the fetters which constrained his limbs, terrible as
they were in description, how could I endure to behold!

Now, however, that I was preparing to take an everlasting farewell of my country, now that an ocean was henceforth to separate
me from him, how could I part without an interview? I would examine his situation with my own eyes. I would know whether the representations which had been made to me were true. Perhaps the sight
of the sister whom he was wont to love with a passion more than
fraternal, might have an auspicious influence on his malady.

Having formed this resolution, I waited to communicate it to Mr.
Cambridge. I was aware that, without his concurrence, I could not
hope to carry it into execution, and could discover no objection to
which it was liable. If I had not been deceived as to his condition,
no inconvenience could arise from this proceeding. His consent,
therefore, would be the test of his sincerity.

I seized this opportunity to state my wishes on this head. My
suspicions were confirmed by the manner in which my request
affected him. After some pause, in which his countenance betrayed
every mark of perplexity, he said to me, "Why would you pay this
visit? What useful purpose can it serve?"

"We are preparing," said I, "to leave the country forever: What
kind of being should I be to leave behind me a brother in calamity
without even a parting interview? Indulge me for three minutes in
the sight of him. My heart will be much easier after I have looked
at him, and shed a few tears in his presence."

"I believe otherwise. The sight of him would only augment your
distress, without contributing, in any degree, to his benefit."

"I know not that," returned I. "Surely the sympathy of his sister,
proofs that her tenderness is as lively as ever, must be a source of
satisfaction to him. At present he must regard all mankind as his
enemies and calumniators.[1] His sister he, probably, conceives to partake in the general infatuation, and to join in the cry of abhorrence
that is raised against him. To be undeceived in this respect, to be
assured that, however I may impute his conduct to delusion, I still
retain all my former affection for his person, and veneration for the
purity of his motives, cannot but afford him pleasure. When he
hears that I have left the country, without even the ceremonious
attention of a visit, what will he think of me? His magnanimity may
hinder him from repining, but he will surely consider my behaviour
as savage and unfeeling. Indeed, dear Sir, I must pay this visit. To
embark with you without paying it, will be impossible. It may be of
no service to him, but will enable me to acquit myself of what I cannot but esteem a duty. Besides," continued I, "if it be a mere fit of

1. Bearers of false witness; liars.

insanity that has seized him, may not my presence chance to have a salutary influence? The mere sight of me, it is not impossible, may rectify his perceptions."

"Ay," said my uncle, with some eagerness; "it is by no means impossible that your interview may have that effect; and for that reason, beyond all others, would I dissuade you from it."

I expressed my surprize at this declaration. "Is it not to be desired that an error so fatal as this should be rectified?"

"I wonder at your question. Reflect on the consequences of this error. Has he not destroyed the wife whom he loved, the children whom he idolized? What is it that enables him to bear the remembrance, but the belief that he acted as his duty enjoined? Would you rashly bereave him of this belief? Would you restore him to himself, and convince him that he was instigated to this dreadful outrage by a perversion of his organs, or a delusion from hell?

"Now his visions are joyous and elate.[2] He conceives himself to have reached a loftier degree of virtue, than any other human being. The merit of his sacrifice is only enhanced in the eyes of superior beings, by the detestation that pursues him here, and the sufferings to which he is condemned. The belief that even his sister has deserted him, and gone over to his enemies, adds to his sublimity of feelings, and his confidence in divine approbation and future recompense.

"Let him be undeceived in this respect, and what floods of despair and of horror will overwhelm him! Instead of glowing approbation and serene hope, will he not hate and torture himself? Self-violence, or a phrenzy far more savage and destructive than this, may be expected to succeed. I beseech you, therefore, to relinquish this scheme. If you calmly reflect upon it, you will discover that your duty lies in carefully shunning him."

Mr. Cambridge's reasonings suggested views to my understanding, that had not hitherto occurred. I could not but admit their validity, but they shewed, in a new light, the depth of that misfortune in which my brother was plunged. I was silent and irresolute.

Presently, I considered, that whether Wieland was a maniac, a faithful servant of his God, the victim of hellish illusions, or the dupe of human imposture, was by no means certain. In this state of my mind it became me to be silent during the visit that I projected. This visit should be brief: I should be satisfied merely to snatch a look at him. Admitting that a change in his opinions were not to be desired, there was no danger, from the conduct which I should pursue, that this change should be wrought.

But I could not conquer my uncle's aversion to this scheme. Yet I persisted, and he found that to make me voluntarily relinquish it, it

2. Elated.

was necessary to be more explicit than he had hitherto been. He took both my hands, and anxiously examining my countenance as he spoke, "Clara," said he, "this visit must not be paid. We must hasten with the utmost expedition from this shore. It is folly to conceal the truth from you, and, since it is only by disclosing the truth that you can be prevailed upon to lay aside this project, the truth shall be told.

"O my dear girl!" continued he with increasing energy in his accent, "your brother's phrenzy is, indeed, stupendous and frightful. The soul that formerly actuated his frame has disappeared. The same form remains; but the wise and benevolent Wieland is no more. A fury that is rapacious of blood, that lifts his strength almost above that of mortals, that bends all his energies to the destruction of whatever was once dear to him, possesses him wholly.

"You must not enter his dungeon; his eyes will no sooner be fixed upon you, than an exertion of his force will be made. He will shake off his fetters in a moment, and rush upon you. No interposition will then be strong or quick enough to save you.

"The phantom that has urged him to the murder of Catharine and her children is not yet appeased. Your life, and that of Pleyel, are exacted from him by this imaginary being. He is eager to comply with this demand. Twice he has escaped from his prison. The first time, he no sooner found himself at liberty, than he hasted to Pleyel's house. It being midnight, the latter was in bed. Wieland penetrated unobserved to his chamber, and opened his curtain. Happily, Pleyel awoke at the critical moment, and escaped the fury of his kinsman, by leaping from his chamber-window into the court. Happily, he reached the ground without injury. Alarms were given, and after diligent search, your brother was found in a chamber of your house, whither, no doubt, he had sought you.

"His chains, and the watchfulness of his guards, were redoubled; but again, by some miracle, he restored himself to liberty. He was now incautiously apprized of the place of your abode: and had not information of his escape been instantly given, your death would have been added to the number of his atrocious acts.

"You now see the danger of your project. You must not only forbear to visit him, but if you would save him from the crime of embruing his hands in your blood, you must leave the country. There is no hope that his malady will end but with his life, and no precaution will ensure your safety, but that of placing the ocean between you.

"I confess I came over with an intention to reside among you, but these disasters have changed my views. Your own safety and my happiness require that you should accompany me in my return, and I entreat you to give your cheerful concurrence to this measure."

After these representations from my uncle, it was impossible to retain my purpose. I readily consented to seclude myself from

Wieland's presence. I likewise acquiesced in the proposal to go to
Europe; not that I ever expected to arrive there, but because, since
my principles forbad me to assail my own life, change had some tendency to make supportable the few days which disease should spare
to me.

What a tale had thus been unfolded! I was hunted to death, not
by one whom my misconduct had exasperated, who was conscious
of illicit motives, and who sought his end by circumvention and
surprize; but by one who deemed himself commissioned for this act
by heaven, who regarded this career of horror as the last refinement
of virtue, whose implacability was proportioned to the reverence
and love which he felt for me, and who was inaccessible to the fear
of punishment and ignominy!

In vain should I endeavour to stay his hand by urging the claims
of a sister or friend: these were his only reasons for pursuing my
destruction. Had I been a stranger to his blood; had I been the most
worthless of human kind; my safety had not been endangered.

Surely, said I, my fate is without example. The phrenzy which is
charged upon my brother, must belong to myself. My foe is manacled
and guarded; but I derive no security from these restraints. I live not
in a community of savages; yet, whether I sit or walk, go into crouds,
or hide myself in solitude, my life is marked for a prey to inhuman
violence; I am in perpetual danger of perishing; of perishing under
the grasp of a brother!

I recollected the omens of this destiny; I remembered the gulf to
which my brother's invitation had conducted me; I remembered that,
when on the brink of danger, the author of my peril was depicted by
my fears in his form: Thus realized, were the creatures of prophetic
sleep, and of wakeful terror!

These images were unavoidably connected with that of Carwin.
In this paroxysm of distress, my attention fastened on him as the
grand deceiver; the author of this black conspiracy; the intelligence
that governed in this storm.

Some relief is afforded in the midst of suffering, when its author
is discovered or imagined; and an object found on which we may
pour out our indignation and our vengeance. I ran over the events
that had taken place since the origin of our intercourse with him,
and reflected on the tenor of that description which was received
from Ludloe. Mixed up with notions of supernatural agency, were
the vehement suspicions which I entertained, that Carwin was the
enemy whose machinations had destroyed us.

I thirsted for knowledge and for vengeance. I regarded my hasty
departure with reluctance, since it would remove me from the means
by which this knowledge might be obtained, and this vengeance
gratified. This departure was to take place in two days. At the end of

two days I was to bid an eternal adieu to my native country. Should I
not pay a parting visit to the scene of these disasters? Should I not
bedew with my tears the graves of my sister and her children? Should
I not explore their desolate habitation, and gather from the sight of
its walls and furniture food for my eternal melancholy?

This suggestion was succeeded by a secret shuddering. Some
disastrous influence appeared to overhang the scene. How many
memorials should I meet with serving to recall the images of those
I had lost!

I was tempted to relinquish my design, when it occurred to me that
I had left among my papers a journal of transactions in short-hand. I
was employed in this manuscript on that night when Pleyel's incautious curiosity tempted him to look over my shoulder. I was then
recording my adventure in *the recess*, an imperfect sight of which led
him into such fatal errors.

I had regulated the disposition of all my property. This manuscript, however, which contained the most secret transactions of my
life, I was desirous of destroying. For this end I must return to my
house, and this I immediately determined to do.

I was not willing to expose myself to opposition from my friends,
by mentioning my design; I therefore bespoke the use of Mr. Hallet's
chaise, under pretence of enjoying an airing, as the day was remarkably bright.

This request was gladly complied with, and I directed the servant
to conduct me to Mettingen. I dismissed him at the gate, intending
to use, in returning, a carriage belonging to my brother.

Chapter XXII

The inhabitants of the *Hut* received me with a mixture of joy and
surprize. Their homely welcome, and their artless sympathy, were
grateful to my feelings. In the midst of their inquiries, as to my
health, they avoided all allusions to the source of my malady. They
were honest creatures, and I loved them well. I participated in the
tears which they shed when I mentioned to them my speedy departure for Europe, and promised to acquaint them with my welfare
during my long absence.

They expressed great surprize when I informed them of my intention to visit my cottage. Alarm and foreboding overspread their
features, and they attempted to dissuade me from visiting an house
which they firmly believed to be haunted by a thousand ghastly
apparitions.

These apprehensions, however, had no power over my conduct. I
took an irregular path which led me to my own house. All was

vacant and forlorn. A small enclosure, near which the path led, was the burying-ground belonging to the family. This I was obliged to pass. Once I had intended to enter it, and ponder on the emblems and inscriptions which my uncle had caused to be made on the tombs of Catharine and her children; but now my heart faltered as I approached, and I hastened forward, that distance might conceal it from my view.

When I approached the recess, my heart again sunk. I averted my eyes, and left it behind me as quickly as possible. Silence reigned through my habitation, and a darkness, which closed doors and shutters produced. Every object was connected with mine or my brother's history. I passed the entry, mounted the stair, and unlocked the door of my chamber. It was with difficulty that I curbed my fancy and smothered my fears. Slight movements and casual sounds were transformed into beckoning shadows and calling shapes.

I proceeded to the closet. I opened and looked round it with fearfulness. All things were in their accustomed order. I sought and found the manuscript where I was used to deposit it. This being secured, there was nothing to detain me; yet I stood and contemplated awhile the furniture and walls of my chamber. I remembered how long this apartment had been a sweet and tranquil asylum; I compared its former state with its present dreariness, and reflected that I now beheld it for the last time.

Here it was that the incomprehensible behaviour of Carwin was witnessed: this the stage on which that enemy of man shewed himself for a moment unmasked. Here the menaces of murder were wafted to my ear; and here these menaces were executed.

These thoughts had a tendency to take from me my self-command. My feeble limbs refused to support me, and I sunk upon a chair. Incoherent and half-articulate exclamations escaped my lips. The name of Carwin was uttered, and eternal woes, woes like that which his malice had entailed upon us, were heaped upon him. I invoked all-seeing heaven to drag to light and to punish this betrayer, and accused its providence for having thus long delayed the retribution that was due to so enormous a guilt.

I have said that the window shutters were closed. A feeble light, however, found entrance through the crevices. A small window illuminated the closet, and the door being closed, a dim ray streamed through the key-hole. A kind of twilight was thus created, sufficient for the purposes of vision; but, at the same time, involving all minuter objects in obscurity.

This darkness suited the colour of my thoughts. I sickened at the remembrance of the past. The prospect of the future excited my loathing. I muttered in a low voice, Why should I live longer? Why should I drag on a miserable being? All, for whom I ought to live, have perished. Am I not myself hunted to death?

At that moment, my despair suddenly became vigorous. My nerves were no longer unstrung. My powers, that had long been deadened, were revived. My bosom swelled with a sudden energy, and the conviction darted through my mind, that to end my torments was, at once, practicable and wise.

I knew how to find way to the recesses of life. I could use a lancet with some skill, and could distinguish between vein and artery. By piercing deep into the latter, I should shun the evils which the future had in store for me, and take refuge from my woes in quiet death.

I started on my feet, for my feebleness was gone, and hasted to the closet. A lancet and other small instruments were preserved in a case which I had deposited here. Inattentive as I was to foreign considerations, my ears were still open to any sound of mysterious import that should occur. I thought I heard a step in the entry. My purpose was suspended, and I cast an eager glance at my chamber door, which was open. No one appeared, unless the shadow which I discerned upon the floor, was the outline of a man. If it were, I was authorized to suspect that some one was posted close to the entrance, who possibly had overheard my exclamations.

My teeth chattered, and a wild confusion took place of my momentary calm. Thus it was when a terrific visage had disclosed itself on a former night. Thus it was when the evil destiny of Wieland assumed the lineaments of something human. What horrid apparition was preparing to blast my sight?

Still I listened and gazed. Not long, for the shadow moved; a foot, unshapely and huge, was thrust forward; a form advanced from its concealment, and stalked into the room. It was Carwin!

While I had breath I shrieked. While I had power over my muscles, I motioned with my hand that he should vanish. My exertions could not last long; I sunk into a fit.

O that this grateful oblivion had lasted for ever! Too quickly I recovered my senses. The power of distinct vision was no sooner restored to me, than this hateful form again presented itself, and I once more relapsed.

A second time, untoward nature recalled me from the sleep of death. I found myself stretched upon the bed. When I had power to look up, I remembered only that I had cause to fear. My distempered fancy fashioned to itself no distinguishable image. I threw a languid glance round me; once more my eyes lighted upon Carwin.

He was seated on the floor, his back rested against the wall, his knees were drawn up, and his face was buried in his hands. That his station was at some distance, that his attitude was not menacing, that his ominous visage was concealed, may account for my now escaping a shock, violent as those which were past. I withdrew my eyes, but was not again deserted by my senses.

On perceiving that I had recovered my sensibility, he lifted his head. This motion attracted my attention. His countenance was mild, but sorrow and astonishment sat upon his features. I averted my eyes and feebly exclaimed—"O! fly—fly far and for ever!—I cannot behold you and live!"

He did not rise upon his feet, but clasped his hands, and said in a tone of deprecation—"I will fly. I am become a fiend, the sight of whom destroys. Yet tell me my offence! You have linked curses with my name; you ascribe to me a malice monstrous and infernal. I look around; all is loneliness and desert! This house and your brother's are solitary and dismantled! You die away at the sight of me! My fear whispers that some deed of horror has been perpetrated; that I am the undesigning cause."

What language was this? Had he not avowed himself a ravisher? Had not this chamber witnessed his atrocious purposes? I besought him with new vehemence to go.

He lifted his eyes—"Great heaven! what have I done? I think I know the extent of my offences. I have acted, but my actions have possibly effected more than I designed. This fear has brought me back from my retreat. I come to repair the evil of which my rashness was the cause, and to prevent more evil. I come to confess my errors."

"Wretch!" I cried when my suffocating emotions would permit me to speak, "the ghosts of my sister and her children, do they not rise to accuse thee? Who was it that blasted the intellects of Wieland? Who was it that urged him to fury, and guided him to murder? Who, but thou and the devil, with whom thou art confederated?"

At these words a new spirit pervaded his countenance. His eyes once more appealed to heaven. "If I have memory, if I have being, I am innocent. I intended no ill; but my folly, indirectly and remotely, may have caused it; but what words are these! Your brother lunatic! His children dead!"

What should I infer from this deportment? Was the ignorance which these words implied real or pretended?—Yet how could I imagine a mere human agency in these events? But if the influence was preternatural or maniacal in my brother's case, they must be equally so in my own. Then I remembered that the voice exerted, was to save me from Carwin's attempts. These ideas tended to abate my abhorrence of this man, and to detect the absurdity of my accusations.

"Alas!" said I, "I have no one to accuse. Leave me to my fate. Fly from a scene stained with cruelty; devoted to despair."

Carwin stood for a time musing and mournful. At length he said, "What has happened? I came to expiate my crimes: let me know them in their full extent. I have horrible forebodings! What has happened?"

I was silent; but recollecting the intimation given by this man when he was detected in my closet, which implied some knowledge of that power which interfered in my favor, I eagerly inquired, "What was that voice which called upon me to hold when I attempted to open the closet? What face was that which I saw at the bottom of the stairs? Answer me truly."

"I came to confess the truth. Your allusions are horrible and strange. Perhaps I have but faint conceptions of the evils which my infatuation has produced; but what remains I will perform. It was *my voice* that you heard! It was *my face* that you saw!"

For a moment I doubted whether my remembrance of events were not confused. How could he be at once stationed at my shoulder and shut up in my closet? How could he stand near me and yet be invisible? But if Carwin's were the thrilling voice and the fiery visage which I had heard and seen, then was he the prompter of my brother, and the author of these dismal outrages.

Once more I averted my eyes and struggled for speech. "Begone! thou man of mischief! Remorseless and implacable miscreant! begone!"

"I will obey," said he in a disconsolate voice; "yet, wretch as I am, am I unworthy to repair the evils that I have committed? I came as a repentant criminal. It is you whom I have injured, and at your bar am I willing to appear, and confess and expiate my crimes. I have deceived you: I have sported with your terrors: I have plotted to destroy your reputation. I come now to remove your errors; to set you beyond the reach of similar fears; to rebuild your fame as far as I am able.

"This is the amount of my guilt, and this the fruit of my remorse. Will you not hear me? Listen to my confession, and then denounce punishment. All I ask is a patient audience."

"What!" I replied, "was not thine the voice that commanded my brother to imbrue his hands in the blood of his children—to strangle that angel of sweetness his wife? Has he not vowed my death, and the death of Pleyel, at thy bidding? Hast thou not made him the butcher of his family; changed him who was the glory of his species into worse than brute; robbed him of reason; and consigned the rest of his days to fetters and stripes?"

Carwin's eyes glared, and his limbs were petrified at this intelligence. No words were requisite to prove him guiltless of these enormities: at the time, however, I was nearly insensible to these exculpatory tokens. He walked to the farther end of the room, and having recovered some degree of composure, he spoke—

"I am not this villain; I have slain no one; I have prompted none to slay; I have handled a tool of wonderful efficacy without malignant intentions, but without caution; ample will be the punishment of my temerity, if my conduct has contributed to this evil." He paused.—

I likewise was silent. I struggled to command myself so far as to listen to the tale which he should tell. Observing this, he continued—

"You are not apprized of the existence of a power which I possess. I know not by what name to call it.[1] It enables me to mimic exactly the voice of another, and to modify the sound so that it shall appear to come from what quarter, and be uttered at what distance I please.

"I know not that every one possesses this power. Perhaps, though a casual position of my organs in my youth shewed me that I possessed it, it is an art which may be taught to all. Would to God I had died unknowing of the secret! It has produced nothing but degradation and calamity.

"For a time the possession of so potent and stupendous an endowment elated me with pride. Unfortified by principle, subjected to poverty, stimulated by headlong passions, I made this powerful engine subservient to the supply of my wants, and the gratification of my vanity. I shall not mention how diligently I cultivated this gift, which seemed capable of unlimited improvement; nor detail the various occasions on which it was successfully exerted to lead superstition, conquer avarice, or excite awe.

"I left America, which is my native soil, in my youth. I have been engaged in various scenes of life, in which my peculiar talent has been exercised with more or less success. I was finally betrayed by one who called himself my friend, into acts which cannot be justified, though they are susceptible of apology.

---

1. "*Biloquium*, or vetrilocution. Sound is varied according to the variations of direction and distance. The art of the ventriloquist consists in modifying his voice according to all these variations, without changing his place. See the work of the Abbe de la Chappelle, in which are accurately recorded the performances of one of these artists, and some ingenious, though unsatisfactory speculations are given on the means by which the effects are produced. This power is, perhaps, given by nature, but is doubtless improvable, if not acquirable, by art. It may, possibly, consist in an unusual flexibility or exertion of the bottom of the tongue and the uvula. That speech is producible by these alone must be granted, since anatomists mention two instances of persons speaking without a tongue. In one case, the organ was originally wanting, but its place was supplied by a small tubercle, and the uvula was perfect. In the other, the tongue was destroyed by disease, but probably a small part of it remained.

"This power is difficult to explain, but the fact is undeniable. Experience shews that the human voice can imitate the voice of all men and of all inferior animals. The sound of musical instruments, and even noises from the contact of inanimate substances, have been accurately imitated. The mimicry of animals is notorious; and Dr. Burney (Musical Travels) mentions one who imitated a flute and violin, so as to deceive even his ears" [Brown's note]. "*Biloquium*": Brown's neologism. It and "ventrilocution" are both synonyms for *ventriloquism*. Jean Baptiste de la Chapelle (1710–1792) wrote his treatise *Le ventriloque* (1772), on ventriloquism, to expose frauds claiming supernatural ability. His work was summarized in the *Encylopaedia Britannica*, 3rd ed., reprinted and emended in Philadelphia in 1798 by Thomas Dobson (see p. 286 in this vol.). "Uvula": the fleshy, conical projection hanging down at the rear of the soft palate. Charles Burney (1726–1814) was the father of the British novelist Fanny Burney (1752–1840). This reference is to his *The Present State of Music in France and Italy* (1771) and *The Present State of Music in Germany, The Netherlands, and United Provinces* (1773).

"The perfidy of this man compelled me to withdraw from Europe. I returned to my native country, uncertain whether silence and obscurity would save me from his malice. I resided in the purlieus[2] of the city. I put on the garb and assumed the manners of a clown.

"My chief recreation was walking. My principal haunts were the lawns and gardens of Mettingen. In this delightful region the luxuriances of nature had been chastened by judicious art, and each successive contemplation unfolded new enchantments.

"I was studious of seclusion: I was satiated with the intercourse of mankind, and discretion required me to shun their intercourse. For these reasons I long avoided the observation of your family, and chiefly visited these precincts at night.

"I was never weary of admiring the position and ornaments of *the temple*. Many a night have I passed under its roof, revolving no pleasing meditations. When, in my frequent rambles, I perceived this apartment was occupied, I gave a different direction to my steps. One evening, when a shower had just passed, judging by the silence that no one was within, I ascended to this building. Glancing carelessly round, I perceived an open letter on the pedestal. To read it was doubtless an offence against politeness. Of this offence, however, I was guilty.

"Scarcely had I gone half through when I was alarmed by the approach of your brother. To scramble down the cliff on the opposite side was impracticable. I was unprepared to meet a stranger. Besides the aukwardness attending such an interview in these circumstances, concealment was necessary to my safety. A thousand times had I vowed never again to employ the dangerous talent which I possessed; but such was the force of habit and the influence of present convenience, that I used this method of arresting his progress and leading him back to the house, with his errand, whatever it was, unperformed. I had often caught parts, from my station below, of your conversation in this place, and was well acquainted with the voice of your sister.

"Some weeks after this I was again quietly seated in this recess. The lateness of the hour secured me, as I thought, from all interruption. In this, however, I was mistaken, for Wieland and Pleyel, as I judged by their voices, earnest in dispute, ascended the hill.

"I was not sensible that any inconvenience could possibly have flowed from my former exertion; yet it was followed with compunction, because it was a deviation from a path which I had assigned to myself. Now my aversion to this means of escape was enforced by an unauthorized curiosity, and by the knowledge of a bushy hollow

2. Suburb or outer edge; often a slum.

on the edge of the hill, where I should be safe from discovery. Into this hollow I thrust myself.

"The propriety of removal to Europe was the question eagerly discussed. Pleyel intimated that his anxiety to go was augmented by the silence of Theresa de Stolberg. The temptation to interfere in this dispute was irresistible. In vain I contended with inveterate habits. I disguised to myself the impropriety of my conduct, by recollecting the benefits which it might produce. Pleyel's proposal was unwise, yet it was enforced with plausible arguments and indefatigable zeal. Your brother might be puzzled and wearied, but could not be convinced. I conceived that to terminate the controversy in favor of the latter was conferring a benefit on all parties. For this end I profited by an opening in the conversation, and assured them of Catharine's irreconcilable aversion to the scheme, and of the death of the Saxon baroness. The latter event was merely a conjecture, but rendered extremely probable by Pleyel's representations. My purpose, you need not be told, was effected.

"My passion for mystery, and a species of imposture, which I deemed harmless, was thus awakened afresh. This second lapse into error made my recovery more difficult. I cannot convey to you an adequate idea of the kind of gratification which I derived from these exploits; yet I meditated nothing. My views were bounded to the passing moment, and commonly suggested by the momentary exigence.

"I must not conceal any thing. Your principles teach you to abhor a voluptuous temper; but, with whatever reluctance, I acknowledge this temper to be mine. You imagine your servant Judith to be innocent as well as beautiful; but you took her from a family where hypocrisy, as well as licentiousness, was wrought into a system. My attention was captivated by her charms, and her principles were easily seen to be flexible.

"Deem me not capable of the iniquity of seduction. Your servant is not destitute of feminine and virtuous qualities; but she was taught that the best use of her charms consists in the sale of them. My nocturnal visits to Mettingen were now prompted by a double view, and my correspondence with your servant gave me, at all times, access to your house.

"The second night after our interview, so brief and so little foreseen by either of us, some dæmon of mischief seized me. According to my companion's report, your perfections were little less than divine. Her uncouth but copious narratives converted you into an object of worship. She chiefly dwelt upon your courage, because she herself was deficient in that quality. You held apparitions and goblins in contempt. You took no precautions against robbers. You were just as tranquil and secure in this lonely dwelling, as if you were in the midst of a crowd.

"Hence a vague project occurred to me, to put this courage to the test. A woman capable of recollection in danger, of warding off groundless panics, of discerning the true mode of proceeding, and profiting by her best resources, is a prodigy. I was desirous of ascertaining whether you were such an one.

"My expedient was obvious and simple: I was to counterfeit a murderous dialogue; but this was to be so conducted that another, and not yourself, should appear to be the object. I was not aware of the possibility that you should appropriate these menaces to yourself. Had you been still and listened, you would have heard the struggles and prayers of the victim, who would likewise have appeared to be shut up in the closet, and whose voice would have been Judith's. This scene would have been an appeal to your compassion; and the proof of cowardice or courage which I expected from you, would have been your remaining inactive in your bed, or your entering the closet with a view to assist the sufferer. Some instances which Judith related of your fearlessness and promptitude made me adopt the latter supposition with some degree of confidence.

"By the girl's direction I found a ladder, and mounted to your closet window. This is scarcely large enough to admit the head, but it answered my purpose too well.

"I cannot express my confusion and surprize at your abrupt and precipitate flight. I hastily removed the ladder; and, after some pause, curiosity and doubts of your safety induced me to follow you. I found you stretched on the turf before your brother's door, without sense or motion. I felt the deepest regret at this unlooked-for consequence of my scheme. I knew not what to do to procure you relief. The idea of awakening the family naturally presented itself. This emergency was critical, and there was no time to deliberate. It was a sudden thought that occurred. I put my lips to the key-hole, and sounded an alarm which effectually roused the sleepers. My organs were naturally forcible, and had been improved by long and assiduous exercise.

"Long and bitterly did I repent of my scheme. I was somewhat consoled by reflecting that my purpose had not been evil, and renewed my fruitless vows never to attempt such dangerous experiments. For some time I adhered, with laudable forbearance, to this resolution.

"My life has been a life of hardship and exposure. In the summer I prefer to make my bed of the smooth turf, or, at most, the shelter of a summer-house suffices. In all my rambles I never found a spot in which so many picturesque beauties and rural delights were assembled as at Mettingen. No corner of your little domain unites fragrance and secrecy in so perfect a degree as the recess in the bank. The odour of its leaves, the coolness of its shade, and the music of its water-fall, had early attracted my attention. Here my sadness was converted into peaceful melancholy—here my slumbers were sound, and my pleasures enhanced.

"As most free from interruption, I chose this as the scene of my midnight interviews with Judith. One evening, as the sun declined, I was seated here, when I was alarmed by your approach. It was with difficulty that I effected my escape unnoticed by you.

"At the customary hour, I returned to your habitation, and was made acquainted by Judith, with your unusual absence. I half suspected the true cause, and felt uneasiness at the danger there was that I should be deprived of my retreat; or, at least, interrupted in the possession of it. The girl, likewise, informed me, that among your other singularities, it was not uncommon for you to leave your bed, and walk forth for the sake of night-airs and starlight contemplations.

"I desired to prevent this inconvenience. I found you easily swayed by fear. I was influenced, in my choice of means, by the facility and certainty of that to which I had been accustomed. All that I foresaw was, that, in future, this spot would be cautiously shunned by you.

"I entered the recess with the utmost caution, and discovered, by your breathings, in what condition you were. The unexpected interpretation which you placed upon my former proceeding, suggested my conduct on the present occasion. The mode in which heaven is said by the poet, to interfere for the prevention of crimes,[3] was somewhat analogous to my province, and never failed to occur to me at seasons like this. It was requisite to break your slumbers, and for this end I uttered the powerful monosyllable, 'hold! hold!' My purpose was not prescribed by duty, yet surely it was far from being atrocious and inexpiable. To effect it, I uttered what was false, but it was well suited to my purpose. Nothing less was intended than to injure you. Nay, the evil resulting from my former act, was partly removed by assuring you that in all places but this you were safe.

Chapter XXIII

"My morals will appear to you far from rigid, yet my conduct will fall short of your suspicions. I am now to confess actions less excusable, and yet surely they will not entitle me to the name of a desperate or sordid criminal.

"Your house was rendered, by your frequent and long absences, easily accessible to my curiosity. My meeting with Pleyel was the

3. "—Peeps through the blanket of the dark, and cries Hold! Hold!—SHAKESPEARE" [Brown's note]. Cf. *Macbeth* 1.5.50–54. Lady Macbeth fears heaven will confound her plot to murder Duncan, though in the end it does not: "Come, thick night / And pall thee in dunnest smoke of hell, / That my keen knife see not the wound it makes, / Nor heaven peep through the blanket of the dark, / To cry, 'Hold, hold!'"

prelude to direct intercourse with you. I had seen much of the world, but your character exhibited a specimen of human powers that was wholly new to me. My intercourse with your servant furnished me with curious details of your domestic management. I was of a different sex: I was not your husband; I was not even your friend; yet my knowledge of you was of that kind, which conjugal intimacies can give, and, in some respects, more accurate. The observation of your domestic was guided by me.

"You will not be surprised that I should sometimes profit by your absence, and adventure to examine with my own eyes, the interior of your chamber. Upright and sincere, you used no watchfulness, and practised no precautions. I scrutinized every thing, and pried every where. Your closet was usually locked, but it was once my fortune to find the key on a bureau. I opened and found new scope for my curiosity in your books. One of these was manuscript, and written in characters which essentially agreed with a shorthand system which I had learned from a Jesuit[1] missionary.

"I cannot justify my conduct, yet my only crime was curiosity. I perused this volume with eagerness. The intellect which it unveiled, was brighter than my limited and feeble organs could bear. I was naturally inquisitive as to your ideas respecting my deportment, and the mysteries that had lately occurred.

"You know what you have written. You know that in this volume the key to your inmost soul was contained. If I had been a profound and malignant impostor, what plenteous materials were thus furnished me of stratagems and plots!

"The coincidence of your dream in the summer-house with my exclamation, was truly wonderful. The voice which warned you to forbear was, doubtless, mine; but mixed by a common process of the fancy, with the train of visionary incidents.

"I saw in a stronger light than ever, the dangerousness of that instrument which I employed, and renewed my resolutions to abstain from the use of it in future; but I was destined perpetually to violate my resolutions. By some perverse fate, I was led into circumstances in which the exertion of my powers was the sole or the best means of escape.

"On that memorable night on which our last interview took place, I came as usual to Mettingen. I was apprized of your engagement at your brother's, from which you did not expect to return till late. Some incident suggested the design of visiting your chamber. Among your books which I had not examined, might be something tending to illustrate your character, or the history of your family. Some intimation had been dropped by you in discourse, respecting a

1. A member of the Society of Jesus, a Roman Catholic order founded by the Spanish Basque priest Ignatius of Loyola and others in sixteenth-century Paris.

performance of your father, in which some important transaction in his life was recorded.

"I was desirous of seeing this book; and such was my habitual attachment to mystery, that I preferred the clandestine perusal of it. Such were the motives that induced me to make this attempt. Judith had disappeared, and finding the house unoccupied, I supplied myself with a light, and proceeded to your chamber.

"I found it easy, on experiment, to lock and unlock your closet door without the aid of a key. I shut myself in this recess, and was busily exploring your shelves, when I heard some one enter the room below. I was at a loss who it could be, whether you or your servant. Doubtful, however, as I was, I conceived it prudent to extinguish the light. Scarcely was this done, when some one entered the chamber. The footsteps were easily distinguished to be yours.

"My situation was now full of danger and perplexity. For some time, I cherished the hope that you would leave the room so long as to afford me an opportunity of escaping. As the hours passed, this hope gradually deserted me. It was plain that you had retired for the night.

"I knew not how soon you might find occasion to enter the closet. I was alive to all the horrors of detection, and ruminated without ceasing, on the behaviour which it would be proper, in case of detection, to adopt. I was unable to discover any consistent method of accounting for my being thus immured.

"It occurred to me that I might withdraw you from your chamber for a few minutes, by counterfeiting a voice from without. Some message from your brother might be delivered, requiring your presence at his house. I was deterred from this scheme by reflecting on the resolution I had formed, and on the possible evils that might result from it. Besides, it was not improbable that you would speedily retire to bed, and then, by the exercise of sufficient caution, I might hope to escape unobserved.

"Meanwhile I listened with the deepest anxiety to every motion from without. I discovered nothing which betokened preparation for sleep. Instead of this I heard deep-drawn sighs, and occasionally an half-expressed and mournful ejaculation. Hence I inferred that you were unhappy. The true state of your mind with regard to Pleyel your own pen had disclosed; but I supposed you to be framed of such materials, that, though a momentary sadness might affect you, you were impregnable to any permanent and heartfelt grief. Inquietude for my own safety was, for a moment, suspended by sympathy with your distress.

"To the former consideration I was quickly recalled by a motion of yours which indicated I knew not what. I fostered the persuasion that you would now retire to bed; but presently you approached the closet, and detection seemed to be inevitable. You put your hand upon the lock. I had formed no plan to extricate myself from the dilemma in which the opening of the door would involve me. I felt an irreconcilable aversion to detection. Thus situated, I involuntarily seized the door with a resolution to resist your efforts to open it.

"Suddenly you receded from the door. This deportment was inexplicable, but the relief it afforded me was quickly gone. You returned, and I once more was thrown into perplexity. The expedient that suggested itself was precipitate and inartificial. I exerted my organs and called upon you *to hold*.

"That you should persist in spite of this admonition, was a subject of astonishment. I again resisted your efforts; for the first expedient having failed, I knew not what other to resort to. In this state, how was my astonishment increased when I heard your exclamations!

"It was now plain that you knew me to be within. Further resistance was unavailing and useless. The door opened, and I shrunk backward. Seldom have I felt deeper mortification, and more painful perplexity. I did not consider that the truth would be less injurious than any lie which I could hastily frame. Conscious as I was of a certain degree of guilt, I conceived that you would form the most odious suspicions. The truth would be imperfect, unless I were likewise to explain the mysterious admonition which had been given; but that explanation was of too great moment, and involved too extensive consequences to make me suddenly resolve to give it.

"I was aware that this discovery would associate itself in your mind, with the dialogue formerly heard in this closet. Thence would your suspicions be aggravated, and to escape from these suspicions would be impossible. But the mere truth would be sufficiently opprobrious, and deprive me for ever of your good opinion.

"Thus was I rendered desperate, and my mind rapidly passed to the contemplation of the use that might be made of previous events. Some good genius would appear to you to have interposed to save you from injury intended by me. Why, I said, since I must sink in her opinion, should I not cherish this belief? Why not personate an enemy, and pretend that celestial interference has frustrated my schemes? I must fly, but let me leave wonder and fear behind me. Elucidation of the mystery will always be practicable. I shall do no injury, but merely talk of evil that was designed, but is now past.

"Thus I extenuated my conduct to myself, but I scarcely expect that this will be to you a sufficient explication of the scene that followed. Those habits which I have imbibed, the rooted passion which possesses me for scattering around me amazement and fear, you enjoy no opportunities of knowing. That a man should wantonly impute to himself the most flagitious designs, will hardly be credited, even though you reflect that my reputation was already, by my own folly, irretrievably ruined; and that it was always in my power to communicate the truth, and rectify the mistake.

"I left you to ponder on this scene. My mind was full of rapid and incongruous ideas. Compunction,[2] self-upbraiding, hopelessness, satisfaction at the view of those effects likely to flow from my new scheme, misgivings as to the beneficial result of this scheme, took possession of my mind, and seemed to struggle for the mastery.

"I had gone too far to recede. I had painted myself to you as an assassin and ravisher, withheld from guilt only by a voice from heaven. I had thus reverted into the path of error, and now, having gone thus far, my progress seemed to be irrevocable. I said to myself, I must leave these precincts for ever. My acts have blasted my fame in the eyes of the Wielands. For the sake of creating a mysterious dread, I have made myself a villain. I may complete this mysterious plan by some new imposture, but I cannot aggravate my supposed guilt.

"My resolution was formed, and I was swiftly ruminating on the means for executing it, when Pleyel appeared in sight. This incident decided my conduct. It was plain that Pleyel was a devoted lover, but he was, at the same time, a man of cold resolves and exquisite sagacity. To deceive him would be the sweetest triumph I had ever enjoyed. The deception would be momentary, but it would likewise be complete. That his delusion would so soon be rectified, was a recommendation to my scheme, for I esteemed him too much to desire to entail upon him lasting agonies.

"I had no time to reflect further, for he proceeded, with a quick step, towards the house. I was hurried onward involuntarily and by a mechanical impulse. I followed him as he passed the recess in the bank, and shrowding myself in that spot, I counterfeited sounds which I knew would arrest his steps.

"He stopped, turned, listened, approached, and overheard a dialogue whose purpose was to vanquish his belief in a point where his belief was most difficult to vanquish. I exerted all my powers to imitate your voice, your general sentiments, and your language. Being master, by means of your journal, of your personal history and most secret thoughts, my efforts were the more successful. When I reviewed the tenor of this dialogue, I cannot believe but that Pleyel was deluded. When I think of your character, and of the inferences which this dialogue was intended to suggest, it seems incredible that this delusion should be produced.

"I spared not myself. I called myself murderer, thief, guilty of innumerable perjuries and misdeeds: that you had debased yourself to the level of such an one, no evidence, methought, would suffice to convince him who knew you so thoroughly as Pleyel; and yet the

2. A guiltiness of conscience.

imposture amounted to proof which the most jealous scrutiny would find to be unexceptionable.

"He left his station precipitately and resumed his way to the house. I saw that the detection of his error would be instantaneous, since, not having gone to bed, an immediate interview would take place between you. At first this circumstance was considered with regret; but as time opened my eyes to the possible consequences of this scene, I regarded it with pleasure.

"In a short time the infatuation which had led me thus far began to subside. The remembrance of former reasonings and transactions was renewed. How often I had repented this kind of exertion; how many evils were produced by it which I had not foreseen; what occasions for the bitterest remorse it had administered, now passed through my mind. The black catalogue of stratagems was now increased. I had inspired you with the most vehement terrors: I had filled your mind with faith in shadows and confidence in dreams: I had depraved the imagination of Pleyel: I had exhibited you to his understanding as devoted to brutal gratifications and consummate in hypocrisy. The evidence which accompanied this delusion would be irresistible to one whose passion had perverted his judgment, whose jealousy with regard to me had already been excited, and who, therefore, would not fail to overrate the force of this evidence. What fatal act of despair or of vengeance might not this error produce?

"With regard to myself, I had acted with a phrenzy that surpassed belief. I had warred against my peace and my fame: I had banished myself from the fellowship of vigorous and pure minds: I was self-expelled from a scene which the munificence of nature had adorned with unrivalled beauties, and from haunts in which all the muses and humanities had taken refuge.

"I was thus torn by conflicting fears and tumultuous regrets. The night passed away in this state of confusion; and next morning in the gazette left at my obscure lodging, I read a description and an offer of reward for the apprehension of my person. I was said to have escaped from an Irish prison, in which I was confined as an offender convicted of enormous and complicated crimes.

"This was the work of an enemy, who, by falsehood and stratagem, had procured my condemnation. I was, indeed, a prisoner, but escaped, by the exertion of my powers, the fate to which I was doomed, but which I did not deserve. I had hoped that the malice of my foe was exhausted; but I now perceived that my precautions had been wise, for that the intervention of an ocean was insufficient for my security.

"Let me not dwell on the sensations which this discovery produced. I need not tell by what steps I was induced to seek an interview with you, for the purpose of disclosing the truth, and repairing, as far as possible, the effects of my misconduct. It was unavoidable that this gazette would fall into your hands, and that it would tend to confirm every erroneous impression.

"Having gained this interview, I purposed to seek some retreat in the wilderness, inaccessible to your inquiry and to the malice of my foe, where I might henceforth employ myself in composing a faithful narrative of my actions. I designed it as my vindication from the aspersions that had rested on my character, and as a lesson to mankind on the evils of credulity on the one hand, and of imposture on the other.

"I wrote you a billet,[3] which was left at the house of your friend, and which I knew would, by some means, speedily come to your hands. I entertained a faint hope that my invitation would be complied with. I knew not what use you would make of the opportunity which this proposal afforded you of procuring the seizure of my person; but this fate I was determined to avoid, and I had no doubt but due circumspection, and the exercise of the faculty which I possessed, would enable me to avoid it.

"I lurked, through the day, in the neighbourhood of Mettingen: I approached your habitation at the appointed hour: I entered it in silence, by a trap-door which led into the cellar. This had formerly been bolted on the inside, but Judith had, at an early period in our intercourse, removed this impediment. I ascended to the first floor, but met with no one, nor any thing that indicated the presence of an human being.

"I crept softly up stairs, and at length perceived your chamber door to be opened, and a light to be within. It was of moment to discover by whom this light was accompanied. I was sensible of the inconveniencies to which my being discovered at your chamber door by any one within would subject me; I therefore called out in my own voice, but so modified that it should appear to ascend from the court below, 'Who is in the chamber? Is it Miss Wieland?'

"No answer was returned to this summons. I listened, but no motion could be heard. After a pause I repeated my call, but no less ineffectually.

"I now approached nearer the door, and adventured to look in. A light stood on the table, but nothing human was discernible. I entered cautiously, but all was solitude and stillness.

"I knew not what to conclude. If the house were inhabited, my call would have been noticed; yet some suspicion insinuated itself that silence was studiously kept by persons who intended to surprize me. My approach had been wary, and the silence that ensued

3. A note.

my call had likewise preceded it; a circumstance that tended to dissipate my fears.

"At length it occurred to me that Judith might possibly be in her own room. I turned my steps thither; but she was not to be found. I passed into other rooms, and was soon convinced that the house was totally deserted. I returned to your chamber, agitated by vain surmises and opposite conjectures. The appointed hour had passed, and I dismissed the hope of an interview.

"In this state of things I determined to leave a few lines on your toilet, and prosecute my journey to the mountains. Scarcely had I taken the pen when I laid it aside, uncertain in what manner to address you. I rose from the table and walked across the floor. A glance thrown upon the bed acquainted me with a spectacle to which my conceptions of horror had not yet reached.

"In the midst of shuddering and trepidation, the signal of your presence in the court below recalled me to myself. The deed was newly done: I only was in the house: what had lately happened justified any suspicions, however enormous. It was plain that this catastrophe was unknown to you: I thought upon the wild commotion which the discovery would awaken in your breast: I found the confusion of my own thoughts unconquerable, and perceived that the end for which I sought an interview was not now to be accomplished.

"In this state of things it was likewise expedient to conceal my being within. I put out the light and hurried down stairs. To my unspeakable surprize, notwithstanding every motive to fear, you lighted a candle and proceeded to your chamber.

"I retired to that room below from which a door leads into the cellar. This door concealed me from your view as you passed. I thought upon the spectacle which was about to present itself. In an exigence so abrupt and so little foreseen, I was again subjected to the empire of mechanical and habitual impulses. I dreaded the effects which this shocking exhibition, bursting on your unprepared senses, might produce.

"Thus actuated, I stept swiftly to the door, and thrusting my head forward, once more pronounced the mysterious interdiction. At that moment, by some untoward fate, your eyes were cast back, and you saw me in the very act of utterance. I fled through the darksome avenue at which I entered, covered with the shame of this detection.

"With diligence, stimulated by a thousand ineffable emotions, I pursued my intended journey. I have a brother whose farm is situated in the bosom of a fertile desert, near the sources of the Leheigh,[4] and thither I now repaired.

4. The Lehigh, a river beginning in the mountains north of Philadelphia.

Chapter XXIV

"Deeply did I ruminate on the occurrences that had just passed. Nothing excited my wonder so much as the means by which you discovered my being in the closet. This discovery appeared to be made at the moment when you attempted to open it. How could you have otherwise remained so long in the chamber apparently fearless and tranquil? And yet, having made this discovery, how could you persist in dragging me forth: persist in defiance of an interdiction so emphatical and solemn?

"But your sister's death was an event detestable and ominous. She had been the victim of the most dreadful species of assassination. How, in a state like yours, the murderous intention could be generated, was wholly inconceivable.

"I did not relinquish my design of confessing to you the part which I had sustained in your family, but I was willing to defer it till the task which I had set myself was finished. That being done, I resumed the resolution. The motives to incite me to this continually acquired force. The more I revolved the events happening at Mettingen, the more insupportable and ominous my terrors became. My waking hours and my sleep were vexed by dismal presages and frightful intimations.

"Catharine was dead by violence. Surely my malignant stars had not made me the cause of her death; yet had I not rashly set in motion a machine, over whose progress I had no controul, and which experience had shewn me was infinite in power? Every day might add to the catalogue of horrors of which this was the source, and a seasonable disclosure of the truth might prevent numberless ills.

"Fraught with this conception, I have turned my steps hither. I find your brother's house desolate: the furniture removed, and the walls stained with damps. Your own is in the same situation. Your chamber is dismantled and dark, and you exhibit an image of incurable grief, and of rapid decay.

"I have uttered the truth. This is the extent of my offences. You tell me an horrid tale of Wieland being led to the destruction of his wife and children, by some mysterious agent. You charge me with the guilt of this agency; but I repeat that the amount of my guilt has been truly stated. The perpetrator of Catharine's death was unknown to me till now; nay, it is still unknown to me."

At that moment, the closing of a door in the kitchen was distinctly heard by us. Carwin started and paused. "There is some one coming. I must not be found here by my enemies, and need not, since my purpose is answered."

I had drunk in, with the most vehement attention, every word that he had uttered. I had no breath to interrupt his tale by interrogations or comments. The power that he spoke of was hitherto unknown to me: its existence was incredible; it was susceptible of no direct proof.

He owns that his were the voice and face which I heard and saw. He attempts to give an human explanation of these phantasms; but it is enough that he owns himself to be the agent; his tale is a lie, and his nature devilish. As he deceived me, he likewise deceived my brother, and now do I behold the author of all our calamities!

Such were my thoughts when his pause allowed me to think. I should have bad him begone if the silence had not been interrupted; but now I feared no more for myself; and the milkiness of my nature was curdled into hatred and rancour. Some one was near, and this enemy of God and man might possibly be brought to justice. I reflected not that the preternatural power which he had hitherto exerted, would avail to rescue him from any toils in which his feet might be entangled. Meanwhile, looks, and not words of menace and abhorrence, were all that I could bestow.

He did not depart. He seemed dubious, whether, by passing out of the house, or by remaining somewhat longer where he was, he should most endanger his safety. His confusion increased when steps of one barefoot were heard upon the stairs. He threw anxious glances sometimes at the closet, sometimes at the window, and sometimes at the chamber door, yet he was detained by some inexplicable fascination. He stood as if rooted to the spot.

As to me, my soul was bursting with detestation and revenge. I had no room for surmises and fears respecting him that approached. It was doubtless a human being, and would befriend me so far as to aid me in arresting this offender.

The stranger quickly entered the room. My eyes and the eyes of Carwin were, at the same moment, darted upon him. A second glance was not needed to inform us who he was. His locks were tangled, and fell confusedly over his forehead and ears. His shirt was of coarse stuff, and open at the neck and breast. His coat was once of bright and fine texture, but now torn and tarnished with dust. His feet, his legs, and his arms were bare. His features were the seat of a wild and tranquil solemnity, but his eyes bespoke inquietude and curiosity.

He advanced with firm step, and looking as in search of some one. He saw me and stopped. He bent his sight on the floor, and clenching his hands, appeared suddenly absorbed in meditation. Such were the figure and deportment of Wieland! Such, in his fallen state, were the aspect and guise of my brother!

Carwin did not fail to recognize the visitant. Care for his own safety was apparently swallowed up in the amazement which this spectacle produced. His station was conspicuous, and he could not have escaped the roving glances of Wieland; yet the latter seemed totally unconscious of his presence.

Grief at this scene of ruin and blast was at first the only sentiment of which I was conscious. A fearful stillness ensued. At length Wieland, lifting his hands, which were locked in each other, to his breast, exclaimed, "Father! I thank thee. This is thy guidance. Hither thou hast led me, that I might perform thy will: yet let me not err: let me hear again thy messenger!"

He stood for a minute as if listening; but recovering from his attitude, he continued—"It is not needed. Dastardly wretch! thus eternally questioning the behests of thy Maker! weak in resolution! wayward in faith!"

He advanced to me, and, after another pause, resumed: "Poor girl! a dismal fate has set its mark upon thee. Thy life is demanded as a sacrifice. Prepare thee to die. Make not my office difficult by fruitless opposition. Thy prayers might subdue stones; but none but he who enjoined my purpose can shake it."

These words were a sufficient explication of the scene. The nature of his phrenzy, as described by my uncle, was remembered. I who had sought death, was now thrilled with horror because it was near. Death in this form, death from the hand of a brother, was thought upon with undescribable repugnance.

In a state thus verging upon madness, my eye glanced upon Carwin. His astonishment appeared to have struck him motionless and dumb. My life was in danger, and my brother's hand was about to be embrued in my blood. I firmly believed that Carwin's was the instigation. I could rescue me from this abhorred fate; I could dissipate this tremendous illusion; I could save my brother from the perpetration of new horrors, by pointing out the devil who seduced him; to hesitate a moment was to perish. These thoughts gave strength to my limbs, and energy to my accents: I started on my feet.

"O brother! spare me, spare thyself: There is thy betrayer. He counterfeited the voice and face of an angel, for the purpose of destroying thee and me. He has this moment confessed it. He is able to speak where he is not. He is leagued with hell, but will not avow it; yet he confesses that the agency was his."

My brother turned slowly his eyes, and fixed them upon Carwin. Every joint in the frame of the latter trembled. His complexion was paler than a ghost's. His eye dared not meet that of Wieland, but wandered with an air of distraction from one space to another.

"Man," said my brother, in a voice totally unlike that which he had used to me, "what art thou? The charge has been made. Answer it. The visage—the voice—at the bottom of these stairs—at the hour of eleven—To whom did they belong? To thee?"

Twice did Carwin attempt to speak, but his words died away upon his lips. My brother resumed in a tone of greater vehemence—

"Thou falterest; faltering is ominous; say yes or no: one word will suffice; but beware of falsehood. Was it a stratagem of hell to overthrow my family? Wast thou the agent?"

I now saw that the wrath which had been prepared for me was to be heaped upon another. The tale that I heard from him, and his present trepidations, were abundant testimonies of his guilt. But what if Wieland should be undeceived! What if he shall find his acts to have proceeded not from an heavenly prompter, but from human treachery! Will not his rage mount into whirlwind? Will not he tear limb from limb this devoted wretch?

Instinctively I recoiled from this image, but it gave place to another. Carwin may be innocent, but the impetuosity of his judge may misconstrue his answers into a confession of guilt. Wieland knows not that mysterious voices and appearances were likewise witnessed by me. Carwin may be ignorant of those which misled my brother. Thus may his answers unwarily betray himself to ruin.

Such might be the consequences of my frantic precipitation, and these, it was necessary, if possible, to prevent. I attempted to speak, but Wieland, turning suddenly upon me, commanded silence, in a tone furious and terrible. My lips closed, and my tongue refused its office.

"What art thou?" he resumed, addressing himself to Carwin. "Answer me; whose form—whose voice—was it thy contrivance? Answer me."

The answer was now given, but confusedly and scarcely articulated. "I meant nothing—I intended no ill—if I understand—if I do not mistake you—it is too true—I did appear—in the entry—did speak. The contrivance was mine, but—"

These words were no sooner uttered, than my brother ceased to wear the same aspect. His eyes were downcast: he was motionless: his respiration became hoarse, like that of a man in the agonies of death. Carwin seemed unable to say more. He might have easily escaped, but the thought which occupied him related to what was horrid and unintelligible in this scene, and not to his own danger.

Presently the faculties of Wieland, which, for a time, were chained up, were seized with restlessness and trembling. He broke silence. The stoutest heart would have been appalled by the tone in which he spoke. He addressed himself to Carwin.

"Why art thou here? Who detains thee? Go and learn better. I will meet thee, but it must be at the bar of thy Maker. There shall I bear witness against thee."

Perceiving that Carwin did not obey, he continued; "Dost thou wish me to complete the catalogue by thy death? Thy life is a worthless thing. Tempt me no more. I am but a man, and thy presence may awaken a fury which may spurn my controul. Begone!"

Carwin, irresolute, striving in vain for utterance, his complexion pallid as death, his knees beating one against another, slowly obeyed the mandate and withdrew.

Chapter XXV

A few words more and I lay aside the pen for ever. Yet why should I not relinquish it now? All that I have said is preparatory to this scene, and my fingers, tremulous and cold as my heart, refuse any further exertion. This must not be. Let my last energies support me in the finishing of this task. Then will I lay down my head in the lap of death. Hushed will be all my murmurs in the sleep of the grave.

Every sentiment has perished in my bosom. Even friendship is extinct. Your love for me has prompted me to this task; but I would not have complied if it had not been a luxury thus to feast upon my woes. I have justly calculated upon my remnant of strength. When I lay down the pen the taper of life will expire: my existence will terminate with my tale.

Now that I was left alone with Wieland, the perils of my situation presented themselves to my mind. That this paroxysm should terminate in havock and rage it was reasonable to predict. The first suggestion of my fears had been disproved by my experience. Carwin had acknowledged his offences, and yet had escaped. The vengeance which I had harboured had not been admitted by Wieland, and yet the evils which I had endured, compared with those inflicted on my brother, were as nothing. I thirsted for his blood, and was tormented with an insatiable appetite for his destruction; yet my brother was unmoved, and had dismissed him in safety. Surely thou wast more than man, while I am sunk below the beasts.

Did I place a right construction on the conduct of Wieland? Was the error that misled him so easily rectified? Were views so vivid and faith so strenuous thus liable to fading and to change? Was there not reason to doubt the accuracy of my perceptions? With images like these was my mind thronged, till the deportment of my brother called away my attention.

I saw his lips move and his eyes cast up to heaven. Then would he listen and look back, as if in expectation of some one's appearance. Thrice he repeated these gesticulations and this inaudible prayer. Each time the mist of confusion and doubt seemed to grow darker and to settle on his understanding. I guessed at the meaning of these tokens. The words of Carwin had shaken his belief, and he was employed in summoning the messenger who had formerly communed with him, to attest the value of these new doubts. In vain the summons was repeated, for his eye met nothing but vacancy, and not a sound saluted his ear.

He walked to the bed, gazed with eagerness at the pillow which had sustained the head of the breathless Catharine, and then returned to the place where I sat. I had no power to lift my eyes to his face: I was dubious of his purpose: this purpose might aim at my life.

Alas! nothing but subjection to danger, and exposure to temptation, can show us what we are. By this test was I now tried, and found to be cowardly and rash. Men can deliberately untie the thread of life, and of this I had deemed myself capable; yet now that I stood upon the brink of fate, that the knife of the sacrificer was aimed at my heart, I shuddered and betook myself to any means of escape, however monstrous.

Can I bear to think—can I endure to relate the outrage which my heart meditated? Where were my means of safety? Resistance was vain. Not even the energy of despair could set me on a level with that strength which his terrific prompter had bestowed upon Wieland. Terror enables us to perform incredible feats; but terror was not then the state of my mind: where then were my hopes of rescue?

Methinks it is too much. I stand aside, as it were, from myself; I estimate my own deservings; a hatred, immortal and inexorable, is my due. I listen to my own pleas, and find them empty and false: yes, I acknowledge that my guilt surpasses that of all mankind: I confess that the curses of a world, and the frowns of a deity, are inadequate to my demerits. Is there a thing in the world worthy of infinite abhorrence? It is I.

What shall I say! I was menaced, as I thought, with death, and, to elude this evil, my hand was ready to inflict death upon the menacer. In visiting my house, I had made provision against the machinations of Carwin. In a fold of my dress an open penknife was concealed. This I now seized and drew forth. It lurked out of view; but I now see that my state of mind would have rendered the deed inevitable if my brother had lifted his hand. This instrument of my preservation would have been plunged into his heart.

O, insupportable remembrance! hide thee from my view for a time; hide it from me that my heart was black enough to meditate the stabbing of a brother! a brother thus supreme in misery; thus towering in virtue!

He was probably unconscious of my design, but presently drew back. This interval was sufficient to restore me to myself. The madness, the iniquity of that act which I had purposed rushed upon my apprehension. For a moment I was breathless with agony. At the next moment I recovered my strength, and threw the knife with violence on the floor.

The sound awoke my brother from his reverie. He gazed alternately at me and at the weapon. With a movement equally solemn he stooped and took it up. He placed the blade in different positions, scrutinizing it accurately, and maintaining, at the same time, a profound silence.

Again he looked at me, but all that vehemence and loftiness of spirit which had so lately characterized his features, were flown. Fallen muscles, a forehead contracted into folds, eyes dim with unbidden drops, and a ruefulness of aspect which no words can describe, were now visible.

His looks touched into energy the same sympathies in me, and I poured forth a flood of tears. This passion was quickly checked by fear, which had now, no longer my own, but his safety for their object. I watched his deportment in silence. At length he spoke:

"Sister," said he, in an accent mournful and mild, "I have acted poorly my part in this world. What thinkest thou? Shall I not do better in the next?"

I could make no answer. The mildness of his tone astonished and encouraged me. I continued to regard him with wistful and anxious looks.

"I think," resumed he, "I will try. My wife and my babes have gone before. Happy wretches! I have sent you to repose, and ought not to linger behind."

These words had a meaning sufficiently intelligible. I looked at the open knife in his hand and shuddered, but knew not how to prevent the deed which I dreaded. He quickly noticed my fears, and comprehended them. Stretching towards me his hand, with an air of increasing mildness: "Take it," said he: "Fear not for thy own sake, nor for mine. The cup is gone by, and its transient inebriation is succeeded by the soberness of truth.

"Thou angel whom I was wont to worship! fearest thou, my sister, for thy life? Once it was the scope of my labours to destroy thee, but I was prompted to the deed by heaven; such, at least, was my belief. Thinkest thou that thy death was sought to gratify malevolence? No. I am pure from all stain. I believed that my God was my mover!

"Neither thee nor myself have I cause to injure. I have done my duty, and surely there is merit in having sacrificed to that, all that is dear to the heart of man. If a devil has deceived me, he came in the habit of an angel. If I erred, it was not my judgment that deceived me, but my senses. In thy sight, being of beings! I am still pure. Still will I look for my reward in thy justice!"

Did my ears truly report these sounds? If I did not err, my brother was restored to just perceptions. He knew himself to have been betrayed to the murder of his wife and children, to have been the victim of infernal artifice; yet he found consolation in the rectitude of his motives. He was not devoid of sorrow, for this was written on his countenance; but his soul was tranquil and sublime.

Perhaps this was merely a transition of his former madness into a new shape. Perhaps he had not yet awakened to the memory of the horrors which he had perpetrated. Infatuated wretch that I was! To set myself up as a model by which to judge of my heroic brother! My reason taught me that his conclusions were right; but conscious of the impotence of reason over my own conduct; conscious of my cowardly, rashness and my criminal despair, I doubted whether any one could be stedfast and wise.

Such was my weakness, that even in the midst of these thoughts, my mind glided into abhorrence of Carwin, and I uttered in a low voice, "O! Carwin! Carwin! What hast thou to answer for?"

My brother immediately noticed the involuntary exclamation: "Clara!" said he, "be thyself. Equity used to be a theme for thy eloquence. Reduce its lessons to practice, and be just to that unfortunate man. The instrument has done its work, and I am satisfied.

"I thank thee, my God, for this last illumination! My enemy is thine also. I deemed him to be man, the man with whom I have often communed; but now thy goodness has unveiled to me his true nature. As the performer of thy behests, he is my friend."

My heart began now to misgive me. His mournful aspect had gradually yielded place to a serene brow. A new soul appeared to actuate his frame, and his eyes to beam with preternatural lustre. These symptoms did not abate, and he continued:

"Clara! I must not leave thee in doubt. I know not what brought about thy interview with the being whom thou callest Carwin. For a time, I was guilty of thy error, and deduced from his incoherent confessions that I had been made the victim of human malice. He left us at my bidding, and I put up a prayer that my doubts should be removed. Thy eyes were shut, and thy ears sealed to the vision that answered my prayer.

"I was indeed deceived. The form thou hast seen was the incarnation of a dæmon. The visage and voice which urged me to the sacrifice of my family, were his. Now he personates a human form: then he was invironed with the lustre of heaven.—

"Clara," he continued, advancing closer to me, "thy death must come. This minister is evil, but he from whom his commission was received is God. Submit then with all thy wonted resignation to a decree that cannot be reversed or resisted. Mark the clock. Three minutes are allowed to thee in which to call up thy fortitude, and prepare thee for thy doom." There he stopped.

Even now, when this scene exists only in memory, when life and all its functions have sunk into torpor, my pulse throbs, and my hairs uprise: my brows are knit, as then; and I gaze around me in distraction. I was unconquerably averse to death; but death, imminent and full of agony as that which was threatened, was nothing. This was not the only or chief inspirer of my fears.

For him, not for myself, was my soul tormented. I might die, and no crime, surpassing the reach of mercy, would pursue me to the presence of my Judge; but my assassin would survive to contemplate his deed, and that assassin was Wieland!

Wings to bear me beyond his reach I had not. I could not vanish with a thought. The door was open, but my murderer was interposed between that and me. Of self-defence I was incapable. The phrenzy that lately prompted me to blood was gone; my state was desperate; my rescue was impossible.

The weight of these accumulated thoughts could not be borne. My sight became confused; my limbs were seized with convulsion; I spoke, but my words were half-formed:—

"Spare me, my brother! Look down, righteous Judge! snatch me from this fate! take away this fury from him, or turn it elsewhere!"

Such was the agony of my thoughts, that I noticed not steps entering my apartment. Supplicating eyes were cast upward, but when my prayer was breathed, I once more wildly gazed at the door. A form met my sight: I shuddered as if the God whom I invoked were present. It was Carwin that again intruded, and who stood before me, erect in attitude, and stedfast in look!

The sight of him awakened new and rapid thoughts. His recent tale was remembered: his magical transitions and mysterious energy of voice: Whether he were infernal, or miraculous, or human, there was no power and no need to decide. Whether the contriver or not of this spell, he was able to unbind it, and to check the fury of my brother. He had ascribed to himself intentions not malignant. Here now was afforded a test of his truth. Let him interpose, as from above; revoke the savage decree which the madness of Wieland has assigned to heaven; and extinguish for ever this passion for blood!

My mind detected at a glance this avenue to safety. The recommendations it possessed thronged as it were together, and made but one impression on my intellect. Remoter effects and collateral dangers I saw not. Perhaps the pause of an instant had sufficed to call them up. The improbability that the influence which governed Wieland was external or human; the tendency of this stratagem to sanction so fatal an error, or substitute a more destructive rage in place of this; the sufficiency of Carwin's mere muscular forces to counteract the efforts, and restrain the fury of Wieland, might, at a second glance, have been discovered; but no second glance was allowed. My first thought hurried me to action, and, fixing my eyes upon Carwin I exclaimed—

"O wretch! once more hast thou come? Let it be to abjure thy malice; to counterwork this hellish stratagem; to turn from me and from my brother, this desolating rage!

"Testify thy innocence or thy remorse: exert the powers which pertain to thee, whatever they be, to turn aside this ruin. Thou art the author of these horrors! What have I done to deserve thus to die? How have I merited this unrelenting persecution? I adjure thee, by that God whose voice thou hast dared to counterfeit, to save my life!

"Wilt thou then go? leave me! Succourless!"

Carwin listened to my intreaties unmoved, and turned from me. He seemed to hesitate a moment: then glided through the door. Rage and despair stifled my utterance. The interval of respite was passed; the pangs reserved for me by Wieland, were not to be endured; my thoughts rushed again into anarchy. Having received the knife from his hand, I held it loosely and without regard; but now it seized again my attention, and I grasped it with force.

He seemed to notice not the entrance or exit of Carwin. My gesture and the murderous weapon appeared to have escaped his notice. His silence was unbroken; his eye, fixed upon the clock for a time, was now withdrawn; fury kindled in every feature; all that was human in his face gave way to an expression supernatural and tremendous. I felt my left arm within his grasp.—

Even now I hesitated to strike. I shrunk from his assault, but in vain.—

Here let me desist. Why should I rescue this event from oblivion? Why should I paint this detestable conflict? Why not terminate at once this series of horrors?—Hurry to the verge of the precipice, and cast myself for ever beyond remembrance and beyond hope?

Still I live: with this load upon my breast; with this phantom to pursue my steps; with adders lodged in my bosom, and stinging me to madness: still I consent to live!

Yes, I will rise above the sphere of mortal passions: I will spurn at the cowardly remorse that bids me seek impunity in silence, or comfort in forgetfulness. My nerves shall be new strung to the task. Have I not resolved? I will die. The gulph before me is inevitable and near. I will die, but then only when my tale is at an end.

Chapter XXVI

My right hand, grasping the unseen knife, was still disengaged. It was lifted to strike. All my strength was exhausted, but what was sufficient to the performance of this deed. Already was the energy awakened, and the impulse given, that should bear the fatal steel to his heart, when—Wieland shrunk back: his hand was withdrawn. Breathless with affright and desperation, I stood, freed from his grasp; unassailed; untouched.

Thus long had the power which controuled the scene forborne to interfere; but now his might was irresistible, and Wieland in a moment was disarmed of all his purposes. A voice, louder than human organs could produce, shriller than language can depict, burst from the ceiling, and commanded him—*to hold!*

Trouble and dismay succeeded to the stedfastness that had lately been displayed in the looks of Wieland. His eyes roved from one quarter to another, with an expression of doubt. He seemed to wait for a further intimation.

Carwin's agency was here easily recognized. I had besought him to interpose in my defence. He had flown. I had imagined him deaf to my prayer, and resolute to see me perish: yet he disappeared merely to devise and execute the means of my relief.

Why did he not forbear when this end was accomplished? Why did his misjudging zeal and accursed precipitation overpass that limit? Or meant he thus to crown the scene, and conduct his inscrutable plots to this consummation?

Such ideas were the fruit of subsequent contemplation. This moment was pregnant with fate. I had no power to reason. In the career of my tempestuous thoughts, rent into pieces, as my mind was, by accumulating horrors, Carwin was unseen and unsuspected. I partook of Wieland's credulity, shook with his amazement, and panted with his awe.

Silence took place for a moment; so much as allowed the attention to recover its post. Then new sounds were uttered from above.

"Man of errors! cease to cherish thy delusion: not heaven or hell, but thy senses have misled thee to commit these acts. Shake off thy phrenzy, and ascend into rational and human. Be lunatic no longer."

My brother opened his lips to speak. His tone was terrific and faint. He muttered an appeal to heaven. It was not difficult to comprehend the theme of his inquiries. They implied doubt as to the nature of the impulse that hitherto had guided him, and questioned whether he had acted in consequence of insane perceptions.

To these interrogatories the voice, which now seemed to hover at his shoulder, loudly answered in the affirmative. Then uninterrupted silence ensued.

Fallen from his lofty and heroic station; now finally restored to the perception of truth; weighed to earth by the recollection of his own deeds; consoled no longer by a consciousness of rectitude, for the loss of offspring and wife—a loss for which he was indebted to his own misguided hand; Wieland was transformed at once into the *man of sorrows*![1]

He reflected not that credit should be as reasonably denied to the last, as to any former intimation; that one might as justly be ascribed to erring or diseased senses as the other. He saw not that this dis-

---

1. Isaiah 53:3: "He is despised and rejected of men; a man of sorrows, and acquainted with grief." In Christian tradition, the verse applies to the resurrected Christ.

covery in no degree affected the integrity of his conduct; that his motives had lost none of their claims to the homage of mankind; that the preference of supreme good, and the boundless energy of duty, were undiminished in his bosom.

It is not for me to pursue him through the ghastly changes of his countenance. Words he had none. Now he sat upon the floor, motionless in all his limbs, with his eyes glazed and fixed; a monument of woe.

Anon a spirit of tempestuous but undesigning activity seized him. He rose from his place and strode across the floor, tottering and at random. His eyes were without moisture, and gleamed with the fire that consumed his vitals. The muscles of his face were agitated by convulsion. His lips moved, but no sound escaped him.

That nature should long sustain this conflict was not to be believed. My state was little different from that of my brother. I entered, as it were, into his thought. My heart was visited and rent by his pangs—Oh that thy phrenzy had never been cured! that thy madness, with its blissful visions, would return! or, if that must not be, that thy scene would hasten to a close! that death would cover thee with his oblivion!

What can I wish for thee? Thou who hast vied with the great preacher of thy faith in sanctity of motives, and in elevation above sensual and selfish! Thou whom thy fate has changed into paricide and savage! Can I wish for the continuance of thy being? No.

For a time his movements seemed destitute of purpose. If he walked; if he turned; if his fingers were entwined with each other; if his hands were pressed against opposite sides of his head with a force sufficient to crush it into pieces; it was to tear his mind from self-contemplation; to waste his thoughts on external objects.

Speedily this train was broken. A beam appeared to be darted into his mind, which gave a purpose to his efforts. An avenue to escape presented itself; and now he eagerly gazed about him: when my thoughts became engaged by his demeanour, my fingers were stretched as by a mechanical force, and the knife, no longer heeded or of use, escaped from my grasp, and fell unperceived on the floor. His eye now lighted upon it; he seized it with the quickness of thought.

I shrieked aloud, but it was too late. He plunged it to the hilt in his neck; and his life instantly escaped with the stream that gushed from the wound. He was stretched at my feet; and my hands were sprinkled with his blood as he fell.

Such was thy last deed, my brother! For a spectacle like this was it my fate to be reserved! Thy eyes were closed—thy face ghastly with death—thy arms, and the spot where thou liedest, floated in thy life's blood! These images have not, for a moment, forsaken me. Till I am breathless and cold, they must continue to hover in my sight.

Carwin, as I said, had left the room, but he still lingered in the house. My voice summoned him to my aid; but I scarcely noticed his re-entrance, and now faintly recollect his terrified looks, his broken exclamations, his vehement avowals of innocence, the effusions of his pity for me, and his offers of assistance.

I did not listen—I answered him not—I ceased to upbraid or accuse. His guilt was a point to which I was indifferent. Ruffian or devil, black as hell or bright as angels, thenceforth he was nothing to me. I was incapable of sparing a look or a thought from the ruin that was spread at my feet.

When he left me, I was scarcely conscious of any variation in the scene. He informed the inhabitants of the hut of what had passed, and they flew to the spot. Careless of his own safety, he hasted to the city to inform my friends of my condition.

My uncle speedily arrived at the house. The body of Wieland was removed from my presence, and they supposed that I would follow it; but no, my home is ascertained; here I have taken up my rest, and never will I go hence, till, like Wieland, I am borne to my grave.

Importunity was tried in vain: they threatened to remove me by violence—nay, violence was used; but my soul prizes too dearly this little roof to endure to be bereaved of it. Force should not prevail when the hoary locks and supplicating tears of my uncle were ineffectual. My repugnance to move gave birth to ferociousness and phrenzy when force was employed, and they were obliged to consent to my return.

They besought me—they remonstrated—they appealed to every duty that connected me with him that made me, and with my fellow-men—in vain. While I live I will not go hence. Have I not fulfilled my destiny?

Why will ye torment me with your reasonings and reproofs? Can ye restore to me the hope of my better days? Can ye give me back Catharine and her babes? Can ye recall to life him who died at my feet?

I will eat—I will drink—I will lie down and rise up at your bidding—all I ask is the choice of my abode. What is there unreasonable in this demand? Shortly will I be at peace. This is the spot which I have chosen in which to breathe my last sigh. Deny me not, I beseech you, so slight a boon.

Talk not to me, O my revered friend! of Carwin. He has told thee his tale, and thou exculpatest him from all direct concern in the fate of Wieland. This scene of havock was produced by an illusion of the senses. Be it so: I care not from what source these disasters have flowed; it suffices that they have swallowed up our hopes and our existence.

What his agency began, his agency conducted to a close. He intended, by the final effort of his power, to rescue me and to banish his illusions from my brother. Such is his tale, concerning the truth of which I care not. Henceforth I foster but one wish—I ask only quick deliverance from life and all the ills that attend it.—

Go wretch! torment me not with thy presence and thy prayers.— Forgive thee? Will that avail thee when thy fateful hour shall arrive? Be thou acquitted at thy own tribunal, and thou needest not fear the verdict of others. If thy guilt be capable of blacker hues, if hitherto thy conscience be without stain, thy crime will be made more flagrant by thus violating my retreat. Take thyself away from my sight if thou wouldest not behold my death!

Thou art gone! murmuring and reluctant! And now my repose is coming—my work is done!

Chapter XXVII

[Written three years after the foregoing, and dated at Montpellier.][1]

I imagined that I had forever laid aside the pen; and that I should take up my abode in this part of the world, was of all events the least probable. My destiny I believed to be accomplished, and I looked forward to a speedy termination of my life with the fullest confidence.

Surely I had reason to be weary of existence, to be impatient of every tie which held me from the grave. I experienced this impatience in its fullest extent. I was not only enamoured of death, but conceived, from the condition of my frame, that to shun it was impossible, even though I had ardently desired it; yet here am I, a thousand leagues from my native soil, in full possession of life and of health, and not destitute of happiness.

Such is man. Time will obliterate the deepest impressions. Grief the most vehement and hopeless, will gradually decay and wear itself out. Arguments may be employed in vain: every moral prescription may be ineffectually tried: remonstrances, however cogent or pathetic, shall have no power over the attention, or shall be repelled with disdain; yet, as day follows day, the turbulence of our emotions shall subside, and our fluctuations be finally succeeded by a calm.

Perhaps, however, the conquest of despair was chiefly owing to an accident which rendered my continuance in my own house impossible. At the conclusion of my long, and, as I then supposed, my last letter to you, I mentioned my resolution to wait for death in the very spot which had been the principal scene of my misfortunes. From this resolution my friends exerted themselves with the utmost zeal

1. A city in the Languedoc region of southern France, where the Albigensian heresy and the Camisard Prophets originated (see p. 10, n. 6).

and perseverance to make me depart. They justly imagined that to be thus surrounded by memorials of the fate of my family, would tend to foster my disease. A swift succession of new objects, and the exclusion of every thing calculated to remind me of my loss, was the only method of cure.

I refused to listen to their exhortations. Great as my calamity was, to be torn from this asylum was regarded by me as an aggravation of it. By a perverse constitution of mind, he was considered as my greatest enemy who sought to withdraw me from a scene which supplied eternal food to my melancholy, and kept my despair from languishing.

In relating the history of these disasters I derived a similar species of gratification. My uncle earnestly dissuaded me from this task; but his remonstrances were as fruitless on this head as they had been on others. They would have withheld from me the implements of writing; but they quickly perceived that to withstand would be more injurious than to comply with my wishes. Having finished my tale, it seemed as if the scene were closing. A fever lurked in my veins, and my strength was gone. Any exertion, however slight, was attended with difficulty, and, at length, I refused to rise from my bed.

I now see the infatuation and injustice of my conduct in its true colours. I reflect upon the sensations and reasonings of that period with wonder and humiliation. That I should be insensible to the claims and tears of my friends; that I should overlook the suggestions of duty, and fly from that post in which only I could be instrumental to the benefit of others; that the exercise of the social and beneficent affections, the contemplation of nature and the acquisition of wisdom should not be seen to be means of happiness still within my reach, is, at this time, scarcely credible.

It is true that I am now changed; but I have not the consolation to reflect that my change was owing to my fortitude or to my capacity for instruction. Better thoughts grew up in my mind imperceptibly. I cannot but congratulate myself on the change, though, perhaps, it merely argues a fickleness of temper, and a defect of sensibility.

After my narrative was ended I betook myself to my bed, in the full belief that my career in this world was on the point of finishing. My uncle took up his abode with me, and performed for me every office of nurse, physician and friend. One night, after some hours of restlessness and pain, I sunk into deep sleep. Its tranquillity, however, was of no long duration. My fancy became suddenly distempered, and my brain was turned into a theatre of uproar and confusion. It would not be easy to describe the wild and phantastical incongruities that pestered me. My uncle, Wieland, Pleyel and Carwin were successively and momently discerned amidst the storm. Sometimes I was swallowed up by whirlpools, or caught up in the air by half-seen and gigantic forms, and thrown upon pointed rocks, or cast among the billows. Sometimes gleams of light were shot into a dark abyss, on the verge of which I was standing, and enabled me to discover, for a moment, its enormous depth and hideous precipices. Anon, I was transported to some ridge of Ætna,[2] and made a terrified spectator of its fiery torrents and its pillars of smoke.

However strange it may seem, I was conscious, even during my dream, of my real situation. I knew myself to be asleep, and struggled to break the spell, by muscular exertions. These did not avail, and I continued to suffer these abortive creations till a loud voice, at my bed side, and some one shaking me with violence, put an end to my reverie. My eyes were unsealed, and I started from my pillow.

My chamber was filled with smoke, which, though in some degree luminous, would permit me to see nothing, and by which I was nearly suffocated. The crackling of flames, and the deafening clamour of voices without, burst upon my ears. Stunned as I was by this hubbub, scorched with heat, and nearly choaked by the accumulating vapours, I was unable to think or act for my own preservation; I was incapable, indeed, of comprehending my danger.

I was caught up, in an instant, by a pair of sinewy arms, borne to the window, and carried down a ladder which had been placed there. My uncle stood at the bottom and received me. I was not fully aware of my situation till I found myself sheltered in the *Hut*, and surrounded by its inhabitants.

By neglect of the servant, some unextinguished embers had been placed in a barrel in the cellar of the building. The barrel had caught fire; this was communicated to the beams of the lower floor, and thence to the upper part of the structure. It was first discovered by some persons at a distance, who hastened to the spot and alarmed my uncle and the servants. The flames had already made considerable progress, and my condition was overlooked till my escape was rendered nearly impossible.

My danger being known, and a ladder quickly procured, one of the spectators ascended to my chamber, and effected my deliverance in the manner before related.

This incident, disastrous as it may at first seem, had, in reality, a beneficial effect upon my feelings. I was, in some degree, roused from the stupor which had seized my faculties. The monotonous and gloomy series of my thoughts was broken. My habitation was levelled with the ground, and I was obliged to seek a new one. A new train of images, disconnected with the fate of my family, forced itself on my attention, and a belief insensibly sprung up, that tranquillity, if not happiness, was still within my reach. Notwithstanding the shocks

2. A volcanic mountain in Sicily.

which my frame had endured, the anguish of my thoughts no sooner abated than I recovered my health.

I now willingly listened to my uncle's solicitations to be the companion of his voyage. Preparations were easily made, and after a tedious passage, we set our feet on the shore of the ancient world. The memory of the past did not forsake me; but the melancholy which it generated, and the tears with which it filled my eyes, were not unprofitable. My curiosity was revived, and I contemplated, with ardour, the spectacle of living manners and the monuments of past ages.

In proportion as my heart was reinstated in the possession of its ancient tranquillity, the sentiment which I had cherished with regard to Pleyel returned. In a short time he was united to the Saxon woman, and made his residence in the neighbourhood of Boston. I was glad that circumstances would not permit an interview to take place between us. I could not desire their misery; but I reaped no pleasure from reflecting on their happiness. Time, and the exertions of my fortitude, cured me, in some degree, of this folly. I continued to love him, but my passion was disguised to myself; I considered it merely as a more tender species of friendship, and cherished it without compunction.

Through my uncle's exertions a meeting was brought about between Carwin and Pleyel, and explanations took place which restored me at once to the good opinion of the latter. Though separated so widely our correspondence was punctual and frequent, and paved the way for that union which can only end with the death of one of us.

In my letters to him I made no secret of my former sentiments. This was a theme on which I could talk without painful, though not without delicate emotions. That knowledge which I should never have imparted to a lover, I felt little scruple to communicate to a friend.

A year and an half elapsed when Theresa was snatched from him by death, in the hour in which she gave him the first pledge of their mutual affection.[3] This event was borne by him with his customary fortitude. It induced him, however, to make a change in his plans. He disposed of his property in America, and joined my uncle and me, who had terminated the wanderings of two years at Montpellier, which will henceforth, I believe, be our permanent abode.

If you reflect upon that entire confidence which had subsisted from our infancy between Pleyel and myself; on the passion that I had contracted, and which was merely smothered for a time; and on the esteem which was mutual, you will not, perhaps, be surprized that the renovation of our intercourse should give birth to that

3. I.e., their first child.

union which at present subsists. When the period had elapsed necessary to weaken the remembrance of Theresa, to whom he had been bound by ties more of honor than of love, he tendered his affections to me. I need not add that the tender was eagerly accepted.

Perhaps you are somewhat interested in the fate of Carwin. He saw, when too late, the danger of imposture. So much affected was he by the catastrophe to which he was a witness, that he laid aside all regard to his own safety. He sought my uncle, and confided to him the tale which he had just related to me. He found a more impartial and indulgent auditor in Mr. Cambridge, who imputed to maniacal illusion the conduct of Wieland, though he conceived the previous and unseen agency of Carwin, to have indirectly but powerfully predisposed him to this deplorable perversion of mind.

It was easy for Carwin to elude the persecutions of Ludloe. It was merely requisite to hide himself in a remote district of Pennsylvania. This, when he parted from us, he determined to do. He is now probably engaged in the harmless pursuits of agriculture, and may come to think, without insupportable remorse, on the evils to which his fatal talents have given birth. The innocence and usefulness of his future life may, in some degree, atone for the miseries so rashly or so thoughtlessly inflicted.

More urgent considerations hindered me from mentioning, in the course of my former mournful recital, any particulars respecting the unfortunate father of Louisa Conway.[4] That man surely was reserved to be a monument of capricious fortune. His southern journies being finished, he returned to Philadelphia. Before he reached the city he left the highway, and alighted at my brother's door. Contrary to his expectation, no one came forth to welcome him, or hail his approach. He attempted to enter the house, but bolted doors, barred windows, and a silence broken only by unanswered calls, shewed him that the mansion was deserted.

He proceeded thence to my habitation, which he found, in like manner, gloomy and tenantless. His surprize may be easily conceived. The rustics who occupied the hut told him an imperfect and incredible tale. He hasted to the city, and extorted from Mrs. Baynton a full disclosure of late disasters.

He was inured to adversity, and recovered, after no long time, from the shocks produced by this disappointment of his darling scheme. Our intercourse did not terminate with his departure from America. We have since met with him in France, and light has at length been thrown upon the motives which occasioned the disappearance of his wife, in the manner which I formerly related to you.

---

4. See Chapter 4. Brown appears to be tying up loose ends in conclusion; early chapters had already gone to press before the novel was completed.

I have dwelt upon the ardour of their conjugal attachment, and mentioned that no suspicion had ever glanced upon her purity. This, though the belief was long cherished, recent discoveries have shewn to be questionable. No doubt her integrity would have survived to the present moment, if an extraordinary fate had not befallen her.

Major Stuart had been engaged, while in Germany, in a contest of honor with an Aid de Camp of the Marquis of Granby.[5] His adversary had propagated a rumour injurious to his character. A challenge was sent; a meeting ensued; and Stuart wounded and disarmed the calumniator. The offence was atoned for, and his life secured by suitable concessions.[6]

Maxwell, that was his name, shortly after, in consequence of succeeding to a rich inheritance, sold his commission and returned to London. His fortune was speedily augmented by an opulent marriage. Interest was his sole inducement to this marriage, though the lady had been swayed by a credulous affection. The true state of his heart was quickly discovered, and a separation, by mutual consent, took place. The lady withdrew to an estate in a distant county, and Maxwell continued to consume his time and fortune in the dissipation of the capital.

Maxwell, though deceitful and sensual, possessed great force of mind and specious accomplishments. He contrived to mislead the generous mind of Stuart, and to regain the esteem which his misconduct, for a time, had forfeited. He was recommended by her husband to the confidence of Mrs. Stuart. Maxwell was stimulated by revenge, and by a lawless passion, to convert this confidence into a source of guilt.

The education and capacity of this woman, the worth of her husband, the pledge of their alliance which time had produced, her maturity in age and knowledge of the world—all combined to render this attempt hopeless. Maxwell, however, was not easily discouraged. The most perfect being, he believed, must owe his exemption from vice to the absence of temptation. The impulses of love are so subtile, and the influence of false reasoning, when enforced by eloquence and passion, so unbounded, that no human virtue is secure from degeneracy. All arts being tried, every temptation being summoned to his aid, dissimulation being carried to its utmost bound, Maxwell, at length, nearly accomplished his purpose. The lady's affections were withdrawn from her husband and transferred to him. She could not, as yet, be reconciled to dishonor. All efforts to induce her to elope with him were ineffectual. She permitted herself to love, and to avow her love; but at this limit she stopped, and was immoveable.

5. An officer who serves as assistant to John Manners, marquess of Granby (1721–1770), the commander of British forces in Germany during the Seven Years' War.
6. Details related to dueling.

Hence this revolution in her sentiments was productive only of despair. Her rectitude of principle preserved her from actual guilt, but could not restore to her her ancient affection, or save her from being the prey of remorseful and impracticable wishes. Her husband's absence produced a state of suspense. This, however, approached to a period, and she received tidings of his intended return. Maxwell, being likewise apprized of this event, and having made a last and unsuccessful effort to conquer her reluctance to accompany him in a journey to Italy, whither he pretended an invincible necessity of going, left her to pursue the measures which despair might suggest. At the same time she received a letter from the wife of Maxwell, unveiling the true character of this man, and revealing facts which the artifices of her seducer had hitherto concealed from her. Mrs. Maxwell had been prompted to this disclosure by a knowledge of her husband's practices, with which his own impetuosity had made her acquainted.

This discovery, joined to the delicacy of her scruples and the anguish of remorse, induced her to abscond. This scheme was adopted in haste, but effected with consummate prudence. She fled, on the eve of her husband's arrival, in the disguise of a boy, and embarked at Falmouth in a packet[7] bound for America.

The history of her disastrous intercourse with Maxwell, the motives inducing her to forsake her country, and the measures she had taken to effect her design, were related to Mrs. Maxwell, in reply to her communication. Between these women an ancient intimacy and considerable similitude of character subsisted. This disclosure was accompanied with solemn injunctions of secrecy, and these injunctions were, for a long time, faithfully observed.

Mrs. Maxwell's abode was situated on the banks of the Wey.[8] Stuart was her kinsman; their youth had been spent together; and Maxwell was in some degree indebted to the man whom he betrayed, for his alliance with this unfortunate lady. Her esteem for the character of Stuart had never been diminished. A meeting between them was occasioned by a tour which the latter had undertaken, in the year after his return from America, to Wales and the western counties. This interview produced pleasure and regret in each. Their own transactions naturally became the topics of their conversation; and the untimely fate of his wife and daughter were related by the guest.

Mrs. Maxwell's regard for her friend, as well as for the safety of her husband, persuaded her to concealment; but the former being dead, and the latter being out of the kingdom, she ventured to produce Mrs. Stuart's letter, and to communicate her own knowledge

7. A postal vessel. Falmouth is a port town in Cornwall, England.
8. A tributary of the Thames.

of the treachery of Maxwell. She had previously extorted from her guest a promise[9] not to pursue any scheme of vengeance; but this promise was made while ignorant of the full extent of Maxwell's depravity, and his passion refused to adhere to it.

At this time my uncle and I resided at Avignon.[1] Among the English resident there, and with whom we maintained a social intercourse, was Maxwell. This man's talents and address rendered him a favorite both with my uncle and myself. He had even tendered me his hand in marriage; but this being refused, he had sought and obtained permission to continue with us the intercourse of friendship. Since a legal marriage was impossible, no doubt, his views were flagitious. Whether he had relinquished these views I was unable to judge.

He was one in a large circle at a villa in the environs, to which I had likewise been invited, when Stuart abruptly entered the apartment. He was recognized with genuine satisfaction by me, and with seeming pleasure by Maxwell. In a short time, some affair of moment being pleaded, which required an immediate and exclusive interview, Maxwell and he withdrew together. Stuart and my uncle had been known to each other in the German army; and the purpose contemplated by the former in this long and hasty journey, was confided to his old friend.

A defiance was given and received, and the banks of a rivulet, about a league from the city, was selected as the scene of this contest. My uncle, having exerted himself in vain to prevent an hostile meeting, consented to attend them as a surgeon.—Next morning, at sun-rise, was the time chosen.

I returned early in the evening to my lodgings. Preliminaries being settled between the combatants, Stuart had consented to spend the evening with us, and did not retire till late. On the way to his hotel he was exposed to no molestation, but just as he stepped within the portico, a swarthy and malignant figure started from behind a column, and plunged a stiletto into his body.

The author of this treason could not certainly be discovered; but the details communicated by Stuart, respecting the history of Maxwell, naturally pointed him out as an object of suspicion. No one expressed more concern, on account of this disaster, than he; and he pretended an ardent zeal to vindicate his character from the aspersions that were cast upon it. Thenceforth, however, I denied myself to his visits; and shortly after he disappeared from this scene.

Few possessed more estimable qualities, and a better title to happiness and the tranquil honors of long life, than the mother and father

9. Cf. William Godwin's arguments against promise-making in *Enquiry Concerning Political Justice* (1793), bk. 3, ch. 3.
1. A city in southern France, under papal control before the French Revolution.

of Louisa Conway: yet they were cut off in the bloom of their days; and their destiny was thus accomplished by the same hand. Maxwell was the instrument of their destruction, though the instrument was applied to this end in so different a manner.

I leave you to moralize on this tale. That virtue should become the victim of treachery is, no doubt, a mournful consideration; but it will not escape your notice, that the evils of which Carwin and Maxwell were the authors, owed their existence to the errors of the sufferers. All efforts would have been ineffectual to subvert the happiness or shorten the existence of the Stuarts, if their own frailty had not seconded these efforts. If the lady had crushed her disastrous passion in the bud, and driven the seducer from her presence, when the tendency of his artifices was seen; if Stuart had not admitted the spirit of absurd revenge, we should not have had to deplore this catastrophe. If Wieland had framed juster notions of moral duty, and of the divine attributes; or if I had been gifted with ordinary equanimity or foresight, the double-tongued deceiver would have been baffled and repelled.

Memoirs of Carwin the Biloquist

I was the second son of a farmer, whose place of residence was a western district of Pennsylvania. My eldest brother seemed fitted by nature for the employment to which he was destined. His wishes never led him astray from the hay-stack and the furrow. His ideas never ranged beyond the sphere of his vision, or suggested the possibility that to-morrow could differ from to-day. He could read and write, because he had no alternative between learning the lesson prescribed to him, and punishment. He was diligent, as long as fear urged him forward, but his exertions ceased with the cessation of this motive. The limits of his acquirements consisted in signing his name, and spelling out a chapter in the bible.

My character was the reverse of his. My thirst of knowledge was augmented in proportion as it was supplied with gratification. The more I heard or read, the more restless and unconquerable my curiosity became. My senses were perpetually alive to novelty, my fancy teemed with visions of the future, and my attention fastened upon every thing mysterious or unknown.

My father intended that my knowledge should keep pace with that of my brother, but conceived that all beyond the mere capacity to write and read was useless or pernicious. He took as much pains to keep me within these limits, as to make the acquisitions of my brother come up to them, but his efforts were not equally successful in both cases. The most vigilant and jealous scrutiny was exerted in vain: Reproaches and blows, painful privations and ignominious penances had no power to slacken my zeal and abate my perseverance. He might enjoin upon me the most laborious tasks, set the envy of my brother to watch me during the performance, make the most diligent search after my books, and destroy them without mercy, when they were found; but he could not outroot my darling propensity. I exerted all my powers to elude his watchfulness. Censures and stripes were sufficiently unpleasing to make me strive to avoid them. To effect this desirable end, I was incessantly employed in the invention of stratagems and the execution of expedients.

My passion was surely not deserving of blame, and I have frequently lamented the hardships to which it subjected me; yet,

perhaps, the claims which were made upon my ingenuity and fortitude were not without beneficial effects upon my character.

This contention lasted from the sixth to the fourteenth year of
my age. My father's opposition to my schemes was incited by a sincere though unenlightened desire for my happiness. That all his
efforts were secretly eluded or obstinately repelled, was a source of
the bitterest regret. He has often lamented, with tears, what he
called my incorrigible depravity, and encouraged himself to perseverance by the notion of the ruin that would inevitably overtake me if I
were allowed to persist in my present career. Perhaps the sufferings
which arose to him from the disappointment, were equal to those
which he inflicted on me.

In my fourteenth year, events happened which ascertained my
future destiny. One evening I had been sent to bring cows from a
meadow, some miles distant from my father's mansion. My time was
limited, and I was menaced with severe chastisement if, according to
my custom, I should stay beyond the period assigned.

For some time these menaces rung in my ears, and I went on my
way with speed. I arrived at the meadow, but the cattle had broken
the fence and escaped. It was my duty to carry home the earliest tidings of this accident, but the first suggestion was to examine the
cause and manner of this escape. The field was bounded by cedar rail-
ing. Five of these rails were laid horizontally from post to post. The
upper one had been broken in the middle, but the rest had merely
been drawn out of the holes on one side, and rested with their ends on
the ground. The means which had been used for this end, the reason
why one only was broken, and that one the uppermost, how a pair of
horns could be so managed as to effect that which the hands of man
would have found difficult, supplied a theme of meditation.

Some accident recalled me from this reverie, and reminded me
how much time had thus been consumed. I was terrified at the consequences of my delay, and sought with eagerness how they might be
obviated. I asked myself if there were not a way back shorter than
that by which I had come. The beaten road was rendered circuitous
by a precipice that projected into a neighbouring stream, and closed
up a passage by which the length of the way would have been diminished one half: at the foot of the cliff the water was of considerable
depth, and agitated by an eddy. I could not estimate the danger which
I should incur by plunging into it, but I was resolved to make the
attempt. I have reason to think, that this experiment, if it had been
tried, would have proved fatal, and my father, while he lamented my
untimely fate, would have been wholly unconscious that his own
unreasonable demands had occasioned it.

I turned my steps towards the spot. To reach the edge of the stream
was by no means an easy undertaking, so many abrupt points and

gloomy hollows were interposed. I had frequently skirted and penetrated this tract, but had never been so completely entangled in the
maze as now: hence I had remained unacquainted with a narrow
pass, which, at the distance of an hundred yards from the river, would
conduct me, though not without danger and toil, to the opposite side
of the ridge.

This glen was now discovered, and this discovery induced me to
change my plan. If a passage could be here effected, it would be
shorter and safer than that which led through the stream, and its
practicability was to be known only by experiment. The path was narrow, steep, and overshadowed by rocks. The sun was nearly set, and
the shadow of the cliff above, obscured the passage almost as much
as midnight would have done: I was accustomed to despise danger
when it presented itself in a sensible form, but, by a defect common
in every one's education, goblins and spectres were to me the objects
of the most violent apprehensions. These were unavoidably connected
with solitude and darkness, and were present to my fears when I
entered this gloomy recess.

These terrors are always lessened by calling the attention away to
some indifferent object. I now made use of this expedient, and began
to amuse myself by hallowing as loud as organs of unusual compass
and vigour would enable me. I uttered the words which chanced to
occur to me, and repeated in the shrill tones of a Mohock savage[1] . . .
"Cow! cow! come home! home!" . . . These notes were of course
reverberated from the rocks which on either side towered aloft, but
the echo was confused and indistinct.

I continued, for some time, thus to beguile the way, till I reached a
space more than commonly abrupt, and which required all my attention. My rude ditty was suspended till I had surmounted this impediment. In a few minutes I was at leisure to renew it. After finishing
the strain, I paused. In a few seconds a voice, as I then imagined,
uttered the same cry from the point of a rock some hundred feet
behind me; the same words, with equal distinctness and deliberation, and in the same tone, appeared to be spoken. I was startled by
this incident, and cast a fearful glance behind, to discover by whom
it was uttered. The spot where I stood was buried in dusk, but the
eminences were still invested with a luminous and vivid twilight.
The speaker, however, was concealed from my view.

I had scarcely begun to wonder at this occurrence, when a new
occasion for wonder, was afforded me. A few seconds, in like manner,
elapsed, when my ditty was again rehearsed, with a no less perfect
imitation, in a different quarter. . . . To this quarter I eagerly turned

---

1. Native American tribe dwelling in Mohawk Valley in upstate New York, original members of the Iroquois Confederacy.

my eyes, but no one was visible. . . . The station, indeed, which this new speaker seemed to occupy, was inaccessible to man or beast.

If I were surprized at this second repetition of my words, judge how much my surprise must have been augmented, when the same calls were a third time repeated, and coming still in a new direction. Five times was this ditty successively resounded, at intervals nearly equal, always from a new quarter, and with little abatement of its original distinctness and force.

A little reflection was sufficient to shew that this was no more than an echo of an extraordinary kind. My terrors were quickly supplanted by delight. The motives to dispatch were forgotten, and I amused myself for an hour, with talking to these cliffs: I placed myself in new positions, and exhausted my lungs and my invention in new clamours.

The pleasures of this new discovery were an ample compensation for the ill treatment which I expected on my return. By some caprice in my father I escaped merely with a few reproaches. I seized the first opportunity of again visiting this recess, and repeating my amusement; time, and incessant repetition, could scarcely lessen its charms or exhaust the variety produced by new tones and new positions.

The hours in which I was most free from interruption and restraint were those of moonlight. My brother and I occupied a small room above the kitchen, disconnected, in some degree, with the rest of the house. It was the rural custom to retire early to bed and to anticipate the rising of the sun. When the moonlight was strong enough to permit me to read, it was my custom to escape from bed, and hie with my book to some neighbouring eminence, where I would remain stretched on the mossy rock, till the sinking or beclouded moon, forbade me to continue my employment. I was indebted for books to a friendly person in the neighbourhood, whose compliance with my solicitations was prompted partly by benevolence and partly by enmity to my father, whom he could not more egregiously offend than by gratifying my perverse and pernicious curiosity.

In leaving my chamber I was obliged to use the utmost caution to avoid rousing my brother, whose temper disposed him to thwart me in the least of my gratifications. My purpose was surely laudable, and yet on leaving the house and returning to it, I was obliged to use the vigilance and circumspection of a thief.

One night I left my bed with this view. I posted first to my vocal glen, and thence scrambling up a neighbouring steep, which overlooked a wide extent of this romantic country, gave myself up to contemplation, and the perusal of Milton's Comus.[2]

---

2. John Milton's *A Mask Presented at Ludlow Castle, 1634,* first printed in 1637 and known colloquially as *Comus.* In the masque an unnamed lady is subject to the seductive ploys of a licentious deity; she is aided by an "attendant spirit." Eighteenth-century

My reflections were naturally suggested by the singularity of this echo. To hear my own voice speak at a distance would have been formerly regarded as prodigious.[3] To hear too, that voice, not uttered by another, by whom it might easily be mimicked, but by myself! I cannot now recollect the transition which led me to the notion of sounds, similar to these, but produced by other means than reverberation. Could I not so dispose my organs as to make my voice appear at a distance?

From speculation I proceeded to experiment. The idea of a distant voice, like my own, was intimately present to my fancy. I exerted myself with a most ardent desire, and with something like a persuasion that I should succeed. I started with surprise, for it seemed as if success had crowned my attempts. I repeated the effort, but failed. A certain position of the organs took place on the first attempt, altogether new, unexampled and, as it were, by accident, for I could not attain it on the second experiment.

You[4] will not wonder that I exerted myself with indefatigable zeal to regain what had once, though for so short a space, been in my power. Your own ears have witnessed the success of these efforts. By perpetual exertion I gained it a second time, and now was a diligent observer of the circumstances attending it. Gradually I subjected these finer and more subtle motions to the command of my will. What was at first difficult, by exercise and habit was rendered easy. I learned to accommodate my voice to all the varieties of distance and direction.

It cannot be denied that this faculty is wonderful and rare, but when we consider the possible modifications of muscular motion, how few of these are usually exerted, how imperfectly they are subjected to the will,[5] and yet that the will is capable of being rendered unlimited and absolute, will not our wonder cease?

We have seen men who could hide their tongues so perfectly that even an Anatomist, after the most accurate inspection that a living subject could admit, has affirmed the organ to be wanting, but this was effected by the exertion of muscles unknown and incredible to the greater part of mankind.

The concurrence of teeth, palate and tongue, in the formation of speech should seem to be indispensable, and yet men have spoken distinctly though wanting a tongue, and to whom, therefore, teeth and palate were superfluous. The tribe of motions requisite to this end, are wholly latent and unknown, to those who possess that organ.

editions of Milton's works note that one manuscript for *Comus* refers to this spirit as "Dæmon" (c. p. 40, n. 5).
3. Miraculous.
4. Carwin's addressee is not named, but may be a member of the Wieland family (see p. 205, n. 9).
5. See p. 31, n. 9, on the notion of "the will" in faculty psychology.

I mean not to be more explicit. I have no reason to suppose a peculiar conformation or activity in my own organs, or that the power which I possess may not, with suitable directions and by steady efforts, be obtained by others, but I will do nothing to facilitate the acquisition. It is by far, too liable to perversion for a good man to desire to possess it, or to teach it to another.

There remained but one thing to render this instrument as powerful in my hands as it was capable of being. From my childhood, I was remarkably skilful at imitation. There were few voices whether of men or birds or beasts which I could not imitate with success. To add my ancient, to my newly acquired skill, to talk from a distance, and at the same time, in the accents of another, was the object of my endeavours, and this object, after a certain number of trials, I finally obtained.

In my present situation every thing that denoted intellectual exertion was a crime, and exposed me to invectives if not to stripes. This circumstance induced me to be silent to all others, on the subject of my discovery. But, added to this, was a confused belief, that it might be made, in some way instrumental to my relief from the hardships and restraints of my present condition. For some time I was not aware of the mode in which it might be rendered subservient to this end.

My father's sister was an ancient lady, resident in Philadelphia, the relict[6] of a merchant, whose decease left her the enjoyment of a frugal competence. She was without children, and had often expressed her desire that her nephew Frank, whom she always considered as a sprightly and promising lad, should be put under her care. She offered to be at the expense of my education, and to bequeath to me at her death her slender patrimony.

This arrangement was obstinately rejected by my father, because it was merely fostering and giving scope to propensities, which he considered as hurtful, and because his avarice desired that this inheritance should fall to no one but himself. To me, it was a scheme of ravishing felicity, and to be debarred from it was a source of anguish known to few. I had too much experience of my father's pertinaciousness ever to hope for a change in his views; yet the bliss of living with my aunt, in a new and busy scene, and in the unbounded indulgence of my literary passion, continually occupied my thoughts: for a long time these thoughts were productive only of despondency and tears.

Time only enhanced the desirableness of this scheme; my new faculty would naturally connect itself with these wishes, and the question could not fail to occur whether it might not aid me in the execution of my favourite plan.

6. Widow.

A thousand superstitious tales were current in the family. Apparitions had been seen, and voices had been heard, on a multitude of
occasions. My father was a confident believer in supernatural tokens.
The voice of his wife, who had been many years dead, had been
twice heard at midnight whispering at his pillow. I frequently asked
myself whether a scheme favourable to my views might not be built
upon these foundations. Suppose (thought I) my mother should be
made to enjoin upon him compliance with my wishes?

This idea bred in me a temporary consternation. To imitate the
voice of the dead, to counterfeit a commission from heaven, bore the
aspect of presumption and impiety. It seemed an offence which could
not fail to draw after it the vengeance of the deity. My wishes for a
time yielded to my fears, but this scheme in proportion as I meditated
on it, became more plausible; no other occurred to me so easy and
so efficacious. I endeavoured to persuade myself that the end proposed, was, in the highest degree praiseworthy, and that the excellence of my purpose would justify the means employed to attain it.

My resolutions were, for a time, attended with fluctuations and
misgivings. These gradually disappeared, and my purpose became
firm; I was next to devise the means of effecting my views; this did
not demand any tedious deliberation. It was easy to gain access to my
father's chamber without notice or detection; cautious footsteps and
the suppression of breath would place me, unsuspected and un-
thought of, by his bed side. The words I should use, and the mode of
utterance were not easily settled, but having at length selected these,
I made myself by much previous repetition, perfectly familiar with
the use of them.

I selected a blustering and inclement night, in which the darkness was augmented by a veil of the blackest clouds. The building
we inhabited was slight in its structure, and full of crevices through
which the gale found easy way, and whistled in a thousand caden-
cies. On this night the elemental music was remarkably sonorous,
and was mingled not unfrequently with *thunder heard remote.*[7]

I could not divest myself of secret dread. My heart faultered with
a consciousness of wrong. Heaven seemed to be present and to disapprove my work; I listened to the thunder and the wind, as to the
stern voice of this disapprobation. Big drops stood on my forehead,
and my tremors almost incapacitated me from proceeding.

These impediments however I surmounted; I crept up stairs at midnight, and entered my father's chamber. The darkness was intense,
and I sought with outstretched hands for his bed. The darkness,
added to the trepidation of my thoughts, disabled me from making a

7. See John Milton, *Paradise Lost* (1667), 2.477.

right estimate of distances: I was conscious of this, and when I advanced within the room, paused.

I endeavoured to compare the progress I had made with my knowledge of the room, and governed by the result of this comparison, proceeded cautiously and with hands still outstretched in search of the foot of the bed. At this moment lightning flashed into the room: the brightness of the gleam was dazzling, yet it afforded me an exact knowledge of my situation. I had mistaken my way, and discovered that my knees nearly touched the bedstead, and that my hands at the next step, would have touched my father's cheek. His closed eyes and every line in his countenance, were painted, as it were, for an instant on my sight.

The flash was accompanied with a burst of thunder, whose vehemence was stunning. I always entertained a dread of thunder, and now recoiled, overborne with terror. Never had I witnessed so luminous a gleam and so tremendous a shock, yet my father's slumber appeared not to be disturbed by it.

I stood irresolute and trembling; to prosecute my purpose in this state of mind was impossible. I resolved for the present to relinquish it, and turned with a view of exploring my way out of the chamber. Just then a light seen through the window, caught my eye. It was at first weak but speedily increased; no second thought was necessary to inform me that the barn, situated at a small distance from the house, and newly stored with hay, was in flames, in consequence of being struck by the lightning.

My terror at this spectacle made me careless of all consequences relative to myself. I rushed to the bed and throwing myself on my father, awakened him by loud cries. The family were speedily roused, and were compelled to remain impotent spectators of the devastation. Fortunately the wind blew in a contrary direction, so that our habitation was not injured.

The impression that was made upon me by the incidents of that night is indelible. The wind gradually rose into an hurricane; the largest branches were torn from the trees, and whirled aloft into the air; others were uprooted and laid prostrate on the ground. The barn was a spacious edifice, consisting wholly of wood, and filled with a plenteous harvest. Thus supplied with fuel, and fanned by the wind, the fire raged with incredible fury; meanwhile clouds rolled above, whose blackness was rendered more conspicuous by reflection from the flames; the vast volumes of smoke were dissipated in a moment by the storm, while glowing fragments and cinders were borne to an immense hight, and tossed everywhere in wild confusion. Ever and anon the sable canopy that hung around us was streaked with lightning, and the peals, by which it was accompanied, were deafning, and with scarcely any intermission.

It was, doubtless, absurd to imagine any connexion between this portentous scene and the purpose that I had meditated, yet a belief of this connexion, though wavering and obscure, lurked in my mind; something more than a coincidence merely casual, appeared to have subsisted between my situation, at my father's bed side, and the flash that darted through the window, and diverted me from my design. It palsied my courage, and strengthened my conviction, that my scheme was criminal.

After some time had elapsed, and tranquility was, in some degree, restored in the family, my father reverted to the circumstances in which I had been discovered on the first alarm of this event. The truth was impossible to be told. I felt the utmost reluctance to be guilty of a falsehood, but by falsehood only could I elude detection. That my guilt was the offspring of a fatal necessity,[8] that the injustice of others gave it birth and made it unavoidable, afforded me slight consolation. Nothing can be more injurous than a lie, but its evil tendency chiefly respects our future conduct. Its direct consequences may be transient and few, but it facilitates a repetition, strengthens temptation, and grows into habit. I pretended some necessity had drawn me from my bed, and that discovering the condition of the barn, I hastened to inform my father.

Some time after this, my father summoned me to his presence. I had been previously guilty of disobedience to his commands, in a matter about which he was usually very scrupulous. My brother had been privy to my offence, and had threatened to be my accuser. On this occasion I expected nothing but arraignment and punishment. Weary of oppression, and hopeless of any change in my father's temper and views, I had formed the resolution of eloping from his house, and of trusting, young as I was, to the caprice of fortune. I was hesitating whether to abscond without the knowledge of the family, or to make my resolutions known to them, and while I avowed my resolution, to adhere to it in spite of opposition and remonstrances, when I received this summons.

I was employed at this time in the field; night was approaching, and I had made no preparation for departure; all the preparation in my power to make, was indeed small; a few clothes made into a bundle, was the sum of my possessions. Time would have little influence in improving my prospects, and I resolved to execute my scheme immediately.

I left my work intending to seek my chamber, and taking what was my own, to disappear forever. I turned a stile that led out of the

---

8. In *Enquiry Concerning Political Justice* (1793), esp. bks. 4 and 6, William Godwin argued for the ideal of absolute sincerity or frankness but acknowledged that political and social institutions conspire to make falsehood almost inevitable.

field into a bye path, when my father appeared before me, advancing in an opposite direction; to avoid him was impossible, and I summoned my fortitude to a conflict with his passion.

As soon as we met, instead of anger and upbraiding, he told me, that he had been reflecting on my aunt's proposal, to take me under her protection, and had concluded that the plan was proper; if I still retained my wishes on that head, he would readily comply with them; and that, if I chose, I might set off for the city next morning, as a neighbour's waggon was preparing to go.

I shall not dwell on the rapture with which this proposal was listened to: it was with difficulty that I persuaded myself that he was in earnest in making it, nor could I divine the reasons, for so sudden and unexpected a change in his maxims. . . . These I afterwards discovered. Some one had instilled into him fears, that my aunt exasperated at his opposition to her request, respecting the unfortunate Frank, would bequeath her property to strangers; to obviate this evil, which his avarice prompted him to regard as much greater than any mischief, that would accrue to me, from the change of my abode, he embraced her proposal.

I entered with exultation and triumph on this new scene; my hopes were by no means disappointed. Detested labour was exchanged for luxurious idleness. I was master of my time, and the chuser of my occupations. My kinswoman on discovering that I entertained no relish for the drudgery of colleges, and was contented with the means of intellectual gratification, which I could obtain under her roof, allowed me to pursue my own choice.

Three tranquil years passed away, during which, each day added to my happiness, by adding to my knowledge. My biloquial faculty was not neglected. I improved it by assiduous exercise; I deeply reflected on the use to which it might be applied. I was not destitute of pure intentions; I delighted not in evil; I was incapable of knowingly contributing to another's misery, but the sole or principal end of my endeavours was not the happiness of others.

I was actuated by ambition. I was delighted to possess superior power; I was prone to manifest that superiority, and was satisfied if this were done, without much solicitude concerning consequences. I sported frequently with the apprehensions of my associates, and threw out a bait for their wonder, and supplied them with occasions for the structure of theories. It may not be amiss to enumerate one or two adventures in which I was engaged.

I had taken much pains to improve the sagacity of a favourite Spaniel. It was my purpose, indeed, to ascertain to what degree of improvement the principles of reasoning and imitation could be carried in a dog. There is no doubt that the animal affixes distinct ideas to sounds. What are the possible limits of his vocabulary no one can tell. In conversing with my dog I did not use English words, but selected simple monosyllables. Habit likewise enabled him to comprehend my gestures. If I crossed my hands on my breast he understood the signal and laid down behind me. If I joined my hands and lifted them to my breast, he returned home. If I grasped one arm above the elbow he ran before me. If I lifted my hand to my forehead he trotted composedly behind. By one motion I could make him bark; by another I could reduce him to silence. He would howl in twenty different strains of mournfulness, at my bidding. He would fetch and carry with undeviating faithfulness.

His actions being thus chiefly regulated by gestures, that to a stranger would appear indifferent or casual, it was easy to produce a belief that the animal's knowledge was much greater than in truth, it was.

One day, in a mixed company, the discourse turned upon the unrivaled abilities of *Damon*.[9] Damon had, indeed, acquired in all the circles which I frequented, an extraordinary reputation. Numerous instances of his sagacity were quoted and some of them exhibited on the spot. Much surprise was excited by the readiness with which he appeared to comprehend sentences of considerable abstraction and complexity, though, he in reality, attended to nothing but the movements of hand or fingers with which I accompanied my words. I enhanced the astonishment of some and excited the ridicule of others, by observing that my dog not only understood English when spoken by others, but actually spoke the language himself, with no small degree of precision.

This assertion could not be admitted without proof; proof, therefore, was readily produced. At a known signal, Damon began a low interrupted noise, in which the astonished hearers clearly distinguished English words. A dialogue began between the animal and his master, which was maintained, on the part of the former, with great vivacity and spirit. In this dialogue the dog asserted the dignity of his species and capacity of intellectual improvement. The company separated lost in wonder, but perfectly convinced by the evidence that had been produced.

On a subsequent occasion a select company was assembled at a garden, at a small distance from the city. Discourse glided through a variety of topics, till it lighted at length on the subject of invisible beings. From the speculations of philosophers we proceeded to the

9. In Greek mythology, Damon and Pythias, friends willing to give their lives for one another, were held up as ideal companions. The name *Damon* may also pun on "dæmon" as used throughout *Wieland* (see p. 40, n. 5).

creations of the poet. Some maintained the justness of Shakspear's delineations of aerial beings, while others denied it. By no violent transition, Ariel[1] and his songs were introduced, and a lady, celebrated for her musical skill, was solicited to accompany her pedal harp with the song of "Five fathom deep thy father lies."[2] . . . She was known to have set, for her favourite instrument, all the songs of Shakspeare.

My youth made me little more than an auditor on this occasion. I sat apart from the rest of the company, and carefully noted every thing. The track which the conversation had taken, suggested a scheme which was not thoroughly digested when the lady began her enchanting strain.

She ended and the audience were mute with rapture. The pause continued, when a strain was wafted to our ears from another quarter. The spot where we sat was embowered by a vine. The verdant arch was lofty and the area beneath was spacious.

The sound proceeded from above. At first it was faint and scarcely audible; presently it reached a louder key, and every eye was cast up in expectation of beholding a face among the pendant clusters. The strain was easily recognized, for it was no other than that which Ariel is made to sing when finally absolved from the service of the wizard.

> In the Cowslip's bell I lie,
> On the Bat's back I do fly . . .
> After summer merrily, &c.[3]

Their hearts palpitated as they listened: they gazed at each other for a solution of the mystery. At length the strain died away at distance, and an interval of silence was succeeded by an earnest discussion of the cause of this prodigy. One supposition only could be adopted, which was, that the strain was not uttered by human organs. That the songster was stationed on the roof of the arbour, and having finished his melody had risen into the viewless fields of air.

I had been invited to spend a week at this house: this period was nearly expired when I received information that my aunt was suddenly taken sick, and that her life was in imminent danger. I immediately set out on my return to the city, but before my arrival she was dead.

This lady was entitled to my gratitude and esteem; I had received the most essential benefits at her hand. I was not destitute of sensibility, and was deeply affected by this event: I will own, however, that my grief was lessened by reflecting on the consequences of her death,

1. In Shakespeare's *The Tempest* (1611), the spirit who serves the magician Prospero.
2. *The Tempest*, 1.2.399, part of Ariel's attempt, on Prospero's orders, to deceive Ferdinand. The line ("full fathom five thy father lies") is slightly misquoted.
3. Cf. *The Tempest* 5.1.89–94, also slightly misquoted.

with regard to my own condition. I had been ever taught to consider myself as her heir, and her death, therefore, would free me from certain restraints.

My aunt had a female servant, who had lived with her for twenty years: she was married, but her husband, who was an artizan, lived apart from her: I had no reason to suspect the woman's sincerity and disinterestedness; but my aunt was no sooner consigned to the grave than a will was produced, in which Dorothy was named her sole and universal heir.

It was in vain to urge my expectations and my claims . . . the instrument was legibly and legally drawn up. . . . Dorothy was exasperated by my opposition and surmises, and vigorously enforced her title. In a week after the decease of my kinswoman, I was obliged to seek a new dwelling. As all my property consisted in my clothes and my papers, this was easily done.

My condition was now calamitous and forlorn. Confiding in the acquisition of my aunt's patrimony, I had made no other provision for the future; I hated manual labour, or any task of which the object was gain. To be guided in my choice of occupations by any motive but the pleasure which the occupation was qualified to produce, was intolerable to my proud, indolent, and restive temper.

This resource was now cut off; the means of immediate subsistence were denied me: If I had determined to acquire the knowledge of some lucrative art, the acquisition would demand time, and, meanwhile, I was absolutely destitute of support. My father's house was, indeed, open to me, but I preferred to stifle myself with the filth of the kennel, rather than to return to it.

Some plan it was immediately necessary to adopt. The exigence of my affairs, and this reverse of fortune, continually occupied my thoughts; I estranged myself from society and from books, and devoted myself to lonely walks and mournful meditation.

One morning as I ranged along the bank of Schuylkill, I encountered a person, by name Ludloe,[4] of whom I had some previous knowledge. He was from Ireland; was a man of some rank and apparently rich: I had met with him before, but in mixed companies, where little direct intercourse had taken place between us. Our last meeting was in the arbour where Ariel was so unexpectedly introduced.

Our acquaintance merely justified a transient salutation;[5] but he did not content himself with noticing me as I passed, but joined me in my walk and entered into conversation. It was easy to advert to the occasion on which we had last met, and to the mysterious incident which then occurred. I was solicitous to dive into his thoughts

4. See *Wieland*, p. 99 in this vol.
5. I.e., a passive wave or gesture.

upon this head and put some questions which tended to the point that I wished.

I was somewhat startled when he expressed his belief, that the performer of this mystic strain was one of the company then present, who exerted, for this end, a faculty not commonly possessed. Who this person was he did not venture to guess, and I could not discover, by the tokens which he suffered to appear, that his suspicions glanced at me. He expatiated with great profoundness and fertility of ideas, on the uses to which a faculty like this might be employed. No more powerful engine, he said, could be conceived, by which the ignorant and credulous might be moulded to our purposes; managed by a man of ordinary talents, it would open for him the straightest and surest avenues to wealth and power.

His remarks excited in my mind a new strain of thoughts. I had not hitherto considered the subject in this light, though vague ideas of the importance of this art could not fail to be occasionally suggested: I ventured to inquire into his ideas of the mode, in which an art like this could be employed, so as to effect the purposes he mentioned.

He dealt chiefly in general representations.[6] Men, he said, believed in the existence and energy of invisible powers, and in the duty of discovering and conforming to their will. This will was supposed to be sometimes made known to them through the medium of their senses. A voice coming from a quarter where no attendant form could be seen would, in most cases, be ascribed to supernal agency, and a command imposed on them, in this manner, would be obeyed with religious scrupulousness.[7] Thus men might be imperiously directed in the disposal of their industry, their property, and even of their lives. Men, actuated by a mistaken sense of duty, might, under this influence, be led to the commission of the most flagitious, as well as the most heroic acts: If it were his desire to accumulate wealth, or institute a new sect, he should need no other instrument.

I listened to this kind of discourse with great avidity, and regretted when he thought proper to introduce new topics. He ended by requesting me to visit him, which I eagerly consented to do. When left alone, my imagination was filled with the images suggested by this conversation. The hopelessness of better fortune, which I had lately harboured, now gave place to cheering confidence. Those motives of rectitude which should deter me from this species of imposture, had never been vivid or stable, and were still more weakened by the artifices of which I had already been guilty. The utility or harmlessness of the end, justified, in my eyes, the means.

6. Generalizations.
7. Cf. the basic premise for *Wieland*'s plot.

No event had been more unexpected, by me, than the bequest of my aunt to her servant. The will, under which the latter claimed, was dated prior to my coming to the city. I was not surprised, therefore, that it had once been made, but merely that it had never been cancelled or superseded by a later instrument. My wishes inclined me to suspect the existence of a later will, but I had conceived that, to ascertain its existence, was beyond my power.

Now, however, a different opinion began to be entertained. This woman like those of her sex and class was unlettered and superstitious.[8] Her faith in spells and apparitions, was of the most lively kind. Could not her conscience be awakened by a voice from the grave! Lonely and at midnight, my aunt might be introduced, upbraiding her for her injustice, and commanding her to attone for it by acknowledging the claim of the rightful proprietor.

True it was, that no subsequent will might exist, but this was the fruit of mistake, or of negligence. She probably intended to cancel the old one, but this act might, by her own weakness, or by the artifices of her servant, be delayed till death had put it out of her power. In either case a mandate from the dead could scarcely fail of being obeyed.

I considered this woman as the usurper of my property. Her husband as well as herself, were laborious and covetous; their good fortune had made no change in their mode of living, but they were as frugal and as eager to accumulate as ever. In their hands, money was inert and sterile, or it served to foster their vices. To take it from them would, therefore, be a benefit both to them and to myself; not even an imaginary injury would be inflicted. Restitution, if legally compelled to it, would be reluctant and painful, but if enjoined by Heaven would be voluntary, and the performance of a seeming duty would carry with it, its own reward.

These reasonings, aided by inclination, were sufficient to determine me. I have no doubt but their fallacy would have been detected in the sequel, and my scheme have been productive of nothing but confusion and remorse. From these consequences, however, my fate interposed, as in the former instance, to save me.

Having formed my resolution, many preliminaries to its execution were necessary to be settled. These demanded deliberation and delay; meanwhile I recollected my promise to Ludloe, and paid him a visit. I met a frank and affectionate reception. It would not be easy to paint the delight which I experienced in this man's society. I was at first oppressed with the sense of my own inferiority in age, knowledge and rank. Hence arose numberless reserves and incapacitating diffidences; but these were speedily dissipated by the fascinations

8. I.e., she suffers from educational disadvantage for reasons of gender and class.

of this man's address. His superiority was only rendered, by time, more conspicuous, but this superiority, by appearing never to be present to his own mind, ceased to be uneasy to me. My questions required to be frequently answered, and my mistakes to be rectified; but my keenest scrutiny, could detect in his manner, neither arrogance nor contempt. He seemed to talk merely from the overflow of his ideas, or a benevolent desire of imparting information.

My visits gradually became more frequent. Meanwhile my wants increased, and the necessity of some change in my condition became daily more urgent. This incited my reflections on the scheme which I had formed. The time and place suitable to my design, were not selected without much anxious inquiry and frequent waverings of purpose. These being at length fixed, the interval to elapse, before the carrying of my design into effect, was not without perturbation and suspense. These could not be concealed from my new friend and at length prompted him to inquire into the cause.

It was not possible to communicate the whole truth; but the warmth of his manner inspired me with some degree of ingenuousness. I did not hide from him my former hopes and my present destitute condition. He listened to my tale with no expressions of sympathy, and when I had finished, abruptly inquired whether I had any objection to a voyage to Europe? I answered in the negative. He then said that he was preparing to depart in a fortnight and advised me to make up my mind to accompany him.

This unexpected proposal gave me pleasure and surprize, but the want of money occurred to me as an insuperable objection. On this being mentioned, Oho! said he, carelessly, that objection is easily removed; I will bear all expenses of your passage myself.

The extraordinary beneficence of this act as well as the air of uncautiousness attending it, made me doubt the sincerity of his offer, and when new declarations removed this doubt, I could not forbear expressing at once my sense of his generosity and of my own unworthiness.

He replied that generosity had been expunged from his catalogue as having no meaning or a vicious one.[9] It was the scope of his exertions to be just. This was the sum of human duty, and he that fell short, ran beside, or outstripped justice was a criminal. What he gave me was my due or not my due. If it were my due, I might reasonably demand it from him and it was wicked to withhold it. Merit on one side or gratitude on the other, were contradictory and unintelligible.

If I were fully convinced that this benefit was not my due and yet received it, he should hold me in contempt. The rectitude of my prin-

9. In this and other maxims, Ludloe seems to echo Godwin's *Political Justice*, though he in some cases blatantly undermines Godwin's intent.

ciples and conduct would be the measure of his approbation, and
no benefit should he ever bestow which the receiver was not entitled to claim, and which it would not be criminal in him to refuse.

These principles were not new from the mouth of Ludloe, but
they had, hitherto, been regarded as the fruits of a venturous speculation in my mind. I had never traced them into their practical
consequences, and if his conduct on this occasion had not squared
with his maxims, I should not have imputed to him inconsistency. I
did not ponder on these reasonings at this time: objects of immediate importance engrossed my thoughts.

One obstacle to this measure was removed. When my voyage was
performed how should I subsist in my new abode? I concealed not
my perplexity and he commented on it in his usual manner. How
did I mean to subsist, he asked, in my own country? The means of
living would be, at least, as much within my reach there as here. As
to the pressure of immediate and absolute want, he believed I should
be exposed to little hazard. With talents such as mine, I must be
hunted by a destiny peculiarly malignant, if I could not provide
myself with necessaries wherever my lot were cast.

He would make allowances, however, for my diffidence and self-
distrust, and would obviate my fears by expressing his own intentions
with regard to me. I must be apprized, however, of his true meaning.
He laboured to shun all hurtful and vitious things, and therefore
carefully abstained from making or confiding *in promises*.[1] It was
just to assist, me in this voyage, and it would probably be equally
just to continue to me similar assistance when it was finished. That
indeed was a subject, in a great degree, within my own cognizance.
His aid would be proportioned to my wants and to my merits, and
I had only to take care that my claims were just, for them to be
admitted.

This scheme could not but appear to me eligible. I thirsted after an
acquaintance with new scenes; my present situation could not be
changed for a worse; I trusted to the constancy of Ludloe's friendship; to this at least it was better to trust than to the success of my
imposture on Dorothy, which was adopted merely as a desperate
expedient: finally I determined to embark with him.

In the course of this voyage my mind was busily employed. There
were no other passengers beside ourselves, so that my own condition
and the character of Ludloe, continually presented themselves to my
reflections. It will be supposed that I was not a vague or indifferent
observer.

1. Cf. Godwin, *Political Justice*, bk. 3, ch. 3, which argues that promises often bind their
   makers to unjust or inconsistent behavior; a promise to keep a secret, for instance, is
   antithetical to Godwin's ideal of complete sincerity.

There were no vicissitudes in the deportment or lapses in the discourse of my friend. His feelings appeared to preserve an unchangeable tenor, and his thoughts and words always to flow with the same rapidity. His slumber was profound and his wakeful hours serene. He was regular and temperate in all his exercises and gratifications. Hence were derived his clear perceptions and exuberant health.

This treatment of me, like all his other mental and corporal operations, was modelled by one inflexible standard. Certain scruples and delicacies were incident to my situation. Of the existence of these he seemed to be unconscious, and yet nothing escaped him inconsistent with a state of absolute equality.

I was naturally inquisitive as to his fortune and the collateral circumstances of his condition. My notions of politeness hindered me from making direct inquiries.[2] By indirect means I could gather nothing but that his state was opulent and independent, and that he had two sisters whose situation resembled his own.

Though, in conversation, he appeared to be governed by the utmost candour; no light was let in upon the former transactions of his life. The purpose of his visit to America I could merely guess to be the gratification of curiosity.

My future pursuits must be supposed chiefly to occupy my attention. On this head I was destitute of all stedfast views. Without profession or habits of industry or sources of permanent revenue, the world appeared to me an ocean on which my bark was set afloat, without compass or sail. The world into which I was about to enter, was untried and unknown, and though I could consent to profit by the guidance, I was unwilling to rely on the support of others.

This topic, being nearest my heart, I frequently introduced into conversation with my friend; but on this subject he always allowed himself to be led by me, while on all others, he was zealous to point the way. To every scheme that I proposed he was sure to cause objections. All the liberal professions were censured as perverting the understanding, by giving scope to the sordid motive of gain, or embuing the mind with erroneous principles. Skill was slowly obtained, and success, though integrity and independence must be given for it, dubious and instable. The mechanical trades were equally obnoxious; they were vitious by contributing to the spurious gratifications of the rich and multiplying the objects of luxury; they were destruction to the intellect and vigour of the artizan; they enervated his frame and brutalized his mind.

---

2. In the moral philosophy of William Godwin (as well as that of Mary Wollstonecraft, Godwin's wife), "politeness" implied an indirection and restraint in conversation that were antithetical to sincerity and especially worked to the disadvantage of subordinates or the socially marginal.

When I pointed out to him the necessity of some species of labour, he tacitly admitted that necessity, but refused to direct me in the choice of a pursuit, which though not free from defect should yet have the fewest inconveniences. He dwelt on the fewness of our actual wants, the temptations which attend the possession of wealth, the benefits of seclusion and privacy, and the duty of unfettering our minds from the prejudices which govern the world.

His discourse tended merely to unsettle my views and increase my perplexity. This effect was so uniform that I at length desisted from all allusions to this theme and endeavoured to divert my own reflections from it. When our voyage should be finished, and I should actually tread this new stage, I believed that I should be better qualified to judge of the measures to be taken by me.

At length we reached Belfast. From thence we immediately repaired to Dublin. I was admitted as a member of his family. When I expressed my uncertainty as to the place to which it would be proper for me to repair, he gave me a blunt but cordial invitation to this house. My circumstances allowed me no option and I readily complied. My attention was for a time engrossed by a diversified succession of new objects. Their novelty, however, disappearing left me at liberty to turn my eyes upon myself and my companion, and here my reflections were supplied with abundant food.

His house was spacious and commodious, and furnished with profusion and elegance. A suit of apartments was assigned to me, in which I was permitted to reign uncontrouled, and access was permitted to a well furnished library. My food was furnished in my own room, prepared in the manner which I had previously directed. Occasionally Ludloe would request my company to breakfast, when an hour was usually consumed in earnest or sprightly conversation. At all other times he was invisible, and his apartments being wholly separate from mine, I had no opportunity of discovering in what way his hours were employed.

He defended this mode of living as being most compatible with liberty. He delighted to expatiate on the evils of cohabitation.[3] Men, subjected to the same regimen, compelled to eat and sleep and associate at certain hours, were strangers to all rational independence and liberty. Society would never be exempt from servitude and misery, till those artificial ties which held human beings together under the same roof were dissolved. He endeavoured to regulate his own conduct in pursuance of these principles, and to secure to himself as much freedom as the present regulations of society would permit.

---

3. Part of Godwin's rationale for opposing marriage. "Cohabitation" here refers to any joint living arrangement. See the appendix to *Political Justice*, bk. 8, ch. 8.

The same independence which he claimed for himself he likewise extended to me. The distribution of my own time, the selection of my own occupations and companions should belong to myself.

But these privileges, though while listening to his arguments I could not deny them to be valuable, I would have willingly dispensed with. The solitude in which I lived became daily more painful. I ate and drank, enjoyed clothing and shelter, without the exercise of fore-thought or industry; I walked and sat, went out and returned for as long and at what seasons I thought proper, yet my condition was a fertile source of discontent.

I felt myself removed to a comfortless and chilling distance from Ludloe. I wanted to share in his occupations and views. With all his ingenuousness of aspect and overflow of thoughts, when he allowed me his company, I felt myself painfully bewildered with regard to his genuine condition and sentiments.

He had it in his power to introduce me to society, and without an introduction, it was scarcely possible to gain access to any social cir-cle or domestic fireside. Add to this, my own obscure prospects and dubious situation. Some regular intellectual pursuit would render my state less irksome, but I had hitherto adopted no scheme of this kind.

Time tended, in no degree, to alleviate my dissatisfaction. It increased till the determination became at length formed of opening my thoughts to Ludloe. At the next breakfast interview which took place, I introduced the subject, and expatiated without reserve, on the state of my feelings. I concluded with intreating him to point out some path in which my talents might be rendered useful to himself or to mankind.

After a pause of some minutes, he said, What would you do? You forget the immaturity of your age. If you are qualified to act a part in the theatre of life, step forth; but you are not qualified. You want knowledge, and with this you ought previously to endow yourself. . . . Means, for this end, are within your reach. Why should you waste your time in idleness, and torment yourself with unprofitable wishes? Books are at hand . . . books from which most sciences and languages can be learned. Read, analise, digest; collect facts, and investigate theories: ascertain the dictates of reason, and supply yourself with the inclination and the power to adhere to them. You will not, legally speaking, be a man in less than three years. Let this period be devoted to the acquisition of wisdom. Either stay here, or retire to an house I have on the banks of Killarney,[4] where you will find all the conveniences of study.

I could not but reflect with wonder at this man's treatment of me. I could plead none of the rights of relationship; yet I enjoyed the

---

4. In County Kerry, Ireland.

privileges of a son. He had not imparted to me any scheme, by pursuit of which I might finally compensate him for the expense to which my maintainance and education would subject him. He gave me reason to hope for the continuance of his bounty. He talked and acted as if my fortune were totally disjoined from his; yet was I indebted to him for the morsel which sustained my life. Now it was proposed to withdraw myself to studious leisure, and romantic solitude. All my wants, personal and intellectual, were to be supplied gratuitously and copiously. No means were prescribed by which I might make compensation for all these benefits. In conferring them he seemed to be actuated by no view to his own ultimate advantage. He took no measures to secure my future services.

I suffered these thoughts to escape me, on this occasion, and observed that to make my application successful, or useful, it was necessary to pursue some end. I must look forward to some post which I might hereafter occupy beneficially to myself or others; and for which all the efforts of my mind should be bent to qualify myself.

These hints gave him visible pleasure; and now, for the first time, he deigned to advise me on this head. His scheme, however, was not suddenly produced. The way to it was circuitous and long. It was his business to make every new step appear to be suggested by my own reflections. His own ideas were the seeming result of the moment, and sprung out of the last idea that was uttered. Being hastily taken up, they were, of course, liable to objection. These objections, sometimes occurring to me and sometimes to him, were admitted or contested with the utmost candour. One scheme went through numerous modifications before it was proved to be ineligible, or before it yielded place to a better. It was easy to perceive, that books alone were insufficient to impart knowledge: that man must be examined with our own eyes to make us acquainted with their nature: that ideas collected from observation and reading, must correct and illustrate each other: that the value of all principles, and their truth, lie in their practical effects. Hence, gradually arose, the usefulness of travelling, of inspecting the habits and manners of a nation, and investigating, on the spot, the causes of their happiness and misery. Finally, it was determined that Spain was more suitable than any other, to the views of a judicious traveller.

My language, habits, and religion were mentioned as obstacles to close and extensive views; but these difficulties successively and slowly vanished. Converse with books, and natives of Spain, a steadfast purpose and unwearied diligence would efface all differences between me and a Castilian[5] with respect to speech. Personal habits,

5. A native of Castile, the north-central region of Spain, which has strong dialect variations in its spoken Spanish.

were changeable, by the same means. The bars to unbounded intercourse, rising from the religion of Spain being irreconcilably opposite to mine, cost us no little trouble to surmount, and here the skill
of Ludloe was eminently displayed.

I had been accustomed to regard as unquestionable, the fallacy
of the Romish faith.[6] This persuasion was habitual and the child of
prejudice, and was easily shaken by the artifices of this logician. I
was first led to bestow a kind of assent on the doctrines of the Roman
church; but my convictions were easily subdued by a new species of
argumentation, and, in a short time, I reverted to my ancient disbelief, so that if an exterior conformity to the rites of Spain were requisite to the attainment of my purpose, that conformity must be
dissembled.

My moral principles had hitherto been vague and unsettled. My
circumstances had led me to the frequent practice of insincerity; but
my transgressions, as they were slight and transient, did not much
excite my previous reflections, or subsequent remorse. My deviations, however, though rendered easy by habit, were by no means
sanctioned by my principles. Now an imposture, more profound and
deliberate, was projected; and I could not hope to perform well my
part, unless steadfastly and thoroughly persuaded of its rectitude.

My friend was the eulogist of sincerity.[7] He delighted to trace its
influence on the happiness of mankind; and proved that nothing but
the universal practice of this virtue was necessary to the perfection
of human society. His doctrine was splendid and beautiful. To detect
its imperfections was no easy task; to lay the foundations of virtue
in utility, and to limit, by that scale, the operation of general principles; to see that the value of sincerity, like that of every other mode
of action, consisted in its tendency to good, and that, therefore the
obligation to speak truth was not paramount or intrinsical; that my
duty is modelled on a knowledge and foresight of the conduct of others; and that, since men in their actual state, are infirm and deceitful,
a just estimate of consequences may sometimes make dissimulation
my duty, were truths that did not speedily occur. The discovery,
when made, appeared to be a joint work. I saw nothing in Ludloe
but proofs of candour, and a judgment incapable of bias.

The means which this man employed to fit me for his purpose,
perhaps owed their success to my youth and ignorance. I may have
given you exaggerated ideas of his dexterity and address. Of that I am
unable to judge. Certain it is, that no time or reflection has abated
my astonishment at the profoundness of his schemes, and the perseverance with which they were pursued by him. To detail their

6. I.e., Roman Catholicism.
7. Cf. Godwin, *Political Justice*, bk. 4.

progress would expose me to the risk of being tedious, yet none but minute details would sufficiently display his patience and subtlety.

It will suffice to relate, that after a sufficient period of preparation and arrangements being made for maintaining a copious intercourse with Ludloe, I embarked for Barcelona. A restless curiosity and vigorous application have distinguished my character in every scene. Here was spacious field for the exercise of all my energies. I sought out a preceptor in my new religion. I entered into the hearts of priests and confessors; the *hidalgo* and the peasant, the monk and the prelate, the austere and voluptuous devotee[8] were scrutinized in all their forms.

Man was the chief subject of my study, and the social sphere that in which I principally moved; but I was not inattentive to inanimate nature, nor unmindful of the past. If the scope of virtue were to maintain the body in health, and to furnish its highest enjoyments to every sense, to increase the number, and accuracy, and order of our intellectual stores, no virtue was ever more unblemished than mine. If to act upon our conceptions of right, and to acquit ourselves of all prejudice and selfishness in the formation of our principles, entitle us to the testimony of a good conscience, I might justly claim it.

I shall not pretend to ascertain my rank in the moral scale. Your notions of duty differ widely from mine. If a system of deceit, pursued merely from the love of truth; if voluptuousness, never gratified at the expense of health, may incur censure, I am censurable. This, indeed, was not the limit of my deviations. Deception was often unnecessarily practised, and my biloquial faculty did not lie unemployed. What has happened to yourselves[9] may enable you, in some degree, to judge of the scenes in which my mystical exploits engaged me. In none of them, indeed, were the effects equally disastrous, and they were, for the most part, the result of well digested projects.

To recount these would be an endless task. They were designed as mere specimens of power, to illustrate the influence of superstition: to give sceptics the consolation of certainty: to annihilate the scruples of a tender female, or facilitate my access to the bosoms of courtiers and monks.

The first achievement of this kind took place in the convent of the Escurial.[1] For some time the hospitality of this brotherhood allowed me a cell in that magnificent and gloomy fabric. I was drawn

---

8. Female adherents, perhaps nuns, either chaste or licentious. *"Hidalgo"*: a Spanish gentleman. "Prelate": a high-ranking member of the priesthood.
9. The clearest indication that Carwin addresses his memoirs to members of the Wieland family.
1. San Lorenzo de Escorial, a palace and monastery outside Madrid, dating to the late sixteenth century.

hither chiefly by the treasures of Arabian literature, which are preserved here in the keeping of a learned Maronite,[2] from Lebanon.
Standing one evening on the steps of the great altar, this devout friar
expatiated on the miraculous evidences of his religion; and, in a
moment of enthusiasm, appealed to San Lorenzo, whose martyrdom
was displayed before us.[3] No sooner was the appeal made than the
saint, obsequious to the summons, whispered his responses from
the shrine, and commanded the heretic to tremble and believe. This
event was reported to the convent. With whatever reluctance, I could
not refuse my testimony to its truth, and its influence on my faith
was clearly shewn in my subsequent conduct.

A lady of rank, in Seville, who had been guilty of many unauthorized indulgences, was, at last, awakened to remorse, by a voice from
Heaven, which she imagined had commanded her to expiate her
sins by an abstinence from all food for thirty days.[4] Her friends
found it impossible to outroot this persuasion, or to overcome her
resolution even by force. I chanced to be one in a numerous company
where she was present. This fatal illusion was mentioned, and an
opportunity afforded to the lady of defending her scheme. At a pause
in the discourse, a voice was heard from the ceiling, which confirmed the truth of her tale; but, at the same time revoked the command, and, in consideration of her faith, pronounced her absolution.
Satisfied with this proof, the auditors dismissed their unbelief, and
the lady consented to eat.

In the course of a copious correspondence with Ludloe, the observations I had collected were given. A sentiment, which I can hardly
describe, induced me to be silent on all adventures connected with
my bivocal projects. On other topics, I wrote fully, and without
restraint. I painted, in vivid hues, the scenes with which I was daily
conversant, and pursued, fearlessly, every speculation on religion
and government that occurred. This spirit was encouraged by Ludloe, who failed not to comment on my narrative, and multiply deductions from my principles.

He taught me to ascribe the evils that infest society to the errors of
opinion. The absurd and unequal distribution of power and property
gave birth to poverty and riches, and these were the sources of luxury and crimes.[5] These positions were readily admitted; but the
remedy for these ills, the means of rectifying these errors were not
easily discovered. We have been inclined to impute them to inher-

2. A member of the Lebanese or Syriac Eastern Catholic Church. The name *Maronite*
derives from a fifth-century Syriac monk.
3. The Escorial's architecture was intended to suggest the pyre on which San Lorenzo
was martyred.
4. Cf. Erasmus Darwin, *Zoonomia; or, The Laws of Organic Life* (1794) 3 on p. 270 in this
vol. See also p. 134 n. 2.
5. Cf. Godwin, *Political Justice*, bk. 8.

ent defects in the moral constitution of men: that oppression and tyranny grow up by a sort of natural necessity, and that they will perish only when the human species is extinct. Ludloe laboured to prove that this was, by no means, the case: that man is the creature of circumstances: that he is capable of endless improvement: that his progress has been stopped by the artificial impediment of government: that by the removal of this, the fondest dreams of imagination will be realized.

From detailing and accounting for the evils which exist under our present institutions, he usually proceeded to delineate some scheme of Utopian felicity, where the empire of reason should supplant that of force; where justice should be universally understood and practised; where the interest of the whole and of the individual should be seen by all to be the same; where the public good should be the scope of all activity; where the tasks of all should be the same, and the means of subsistence equally distributed.[6]

No one could contemplate his pictures without rapture. By their comprehensiveness and amplitude they filled the imagination. I was unwilling to believe that in no region of the world, or at no period could these ideas be realized. It was plain that the nations of Europe were tending to greater depravity, and would be the prey of perpetual vicissitude. All individual attempts at their reformation would be fruitless. He therefore who desired the diffusion of right principles, to make a just system be adopted by a whole community, must pursue some extraordinary method.

In this state of mind I recollected my native country,[7] where a few colonists from Britain had sown the germe of populous and mighty empires. Attended, as they were, into their new abode, by all their prejudices, yet such had been the influence of new circumstances, of consulting for their own happiness, of adopting simple forms of government, and excluding nobles and kings from their system, that they enjoyed a degree of happiness far superior to their parent state.

To conquer the prejudices and change the habits of millions, are impossible. The human mind, exposed to social influences, inflexibly adheres to the direction that is given to it; but for the same reason why men who begin in error will continue, those who commence in truth, may be expected to persist. Habit and example will operate with equal force in both instances.

Let a few, sufficiently enlightened and disinterested, take up their abode in some unvisited region. Let their social scheme be founded in equity, and how small soever their original number may be, their growth into a nation is inevitable. Among other effects of national

6. Ibid.
7. I.e., the British colonies in North America.

justice, was to be ranked the swift increase of numbers. Exempt from servile obligations and perverse habits, endowed with property, wisdom, and health, hundreds will expand, with inconceivable rapidity into thousands, and thousands into millions; and a new race, tutored in truth, may, in a few centuries, overflow the habitable world.

Such were the visions of youth! I could not banish them from my mind. I knew them to be crude; but believed that deliberation would bestow upon them solidity and shape. Meanwhile I imparted them to Ludloe.

In answer to the reveries and speculations which I sent to him respecting this subject, Ludloe informed me, that they had led his mind into a new sphere of meditation. He had long and deeply considered in what way he might essentially promote my happiness. He had entertained a faint hope that I would one day be qualified for a station like that to which he himself had been advanced. This post required an elevation and stability of views which human beings seldom reach, and which could be attained by me only by a long series of heroic labours. Hitherto every new stage in my intellectual progress had added vigour to his hopes, and he cherished a stronger belief than formerly that my career would terminate auspiciously. This, however, was necessarily distant. Many preliminaries must first be settled; many arduous accomplishments be first obtained; and my virtue be subjected to severe trials. At present it was not in his power to be more explicit; but if my reflections suggested no better plan, he advised me to settle my affairs in Spain, and return to him immediately. My knowledge of this country would be of the highest use, on the supposition of my ultimately arriving at the honours to which he had alluded; and some of these preparatory measures could be taken only with his assistance, and in his company.

This intimation was eagerly obeyed, and, in a short time, I arrived at Dublin. Meanwhile my mind had copious occupation in commenting on my friend's letter. This scheme, whatever it was, seemed to be suggested by my mention of a plan of colonization, and my preference of that mode of producing extensive and permanent effects on the condition of mankind. It was easy therefore to conjecture that this mode had been pursued under some mysterious modifications and conditions.

It had always excited my wonder that so obvious an expedient had been overlooked. The globe which we inhabit was very imperfectly known. The regions and nations unexplored, it was reasonable to believe, surpassed in extent, and perhaps in populousness, those with which we were familiar. The order of Jesuits had furnished an example of all the errors and excellencies of such a scheme. Their plan was founded on erroneous notions of religion and policy, and they had absurdly chosen a scene[8] within reach of the injustice and ambition of an European tyrant.

It was wise and easy to profit by their example. Resting on the two props of fidelity and zeal, an association might exist for ages in the heart of Europe, whose influence might be felt, and might be boundless, in some region of the southern hemisphere; and by whom a moral and political structure might be raised, the growth of pure wisdom, and totally unlike those fragments of Roman and Gothic barbarism, which cover the face of what are called the civilized nations. The belief now rose in my mind that some such scheme had actually been prosecuted, and that Ludloe was a coadjutor. On this supposition, the caution with which he approached to his point, the arduous probation which a candidate for a part on this stage must undergo, and the rigours of that test by which his fortitude and virtue must be tried, were easily explained. I was too deeply imbued with veneration for the effects of such schemes, and too sanguine in my confidence in the rectitude of Ludloe, to refuse my concurrence in any scheme by which my qualifications might at length be raised to a due point.

Our interview was frank and affectionate. I found him situated just as formerly. His aspect, manners, and deportment were the same. I entered once more on my former mode of life, but our intercourse became more frequent. We constantly breakfasted together, and our conversation was usually prolonged through half the morning.

For a time our topics were general. I thought proper to leave to him the introduction of more interesting themes: this, however, he betrayed no inclination to do. His reserve excited some surprise, and I began to suspect that whatever design he had formed with regard to me, had been laid aside. To ascertain this question, I ventured, at length, to recall his attention to the subject of his last letter, and to enquire whether subsequent reflection had made any change in his views.

He said that his views were too momentous to be hastily taken up, or hastily dismissed; the station, my attainment of which depended wholly on myself, was high above vulgar heads, and was to be gained by years of solicitude and labour. This, at least, was true with regard to minds ordinarily constituted; I, perhaps, deserved to be regarded as an exception, and might be able to accomplish in a few months that for which others were obliged to toil during half their lives.

---

8. "Paraguay" [Brown's note]. In seventeenth- and eighteenth-century Paraguay, Jesuit missionaries sought to create model communities among native populations. Their efforts were hampered by tensions with Spanish and Portuguese colonial officials, resulting in the expulsion of the Jesuits from Portugal in 1766.

Man, continued he, is the slave of habit. Convince him to-day that his duty leads straight forward: he shall advance, but at every step his belief shall fade; habit will resume its empire, and to-morrow he shall turn back, or betake himself to oblique paths.

We know not our strength till it be tried. Virtue, till confirmed by habit, is a dream. You are a man imbued by errors, and vincible by slight temptations. Deep enquiries must bestow light on your opinions, and the habit of encountering and vanquishing temptation must inspire you with fortitude. Till this be done, you are unqualified for that post, in which you will be invested with divine attributes, and prescribe the condition of a large portion of mankind.

Confide not in the firmness of your principles, or the stedfastness of your integrity. Be always vigilant and fearful. Never think you have enough of knowledge, and let not your caution slumber for a moment, for you know not when danger is near.

I acknowledged the justice of his admonitions, and professed myself willing to undergo any ordeal which reason should prescribe. What, I asked, were the conditions, on the fulfilment of which depended my advancement to the station he alluded to? Was it necessary to conceal from me the nature and obligations of this rank?

These enquiries sunk him more profoundly into meditation than I had ever before witnessed. After a pause, in which some perplexity was visible, he answered:

I scarcely know what to say. As to promises, I claim them not from you. We are now arrived at a point, in which it is necessary to look around with caution, and that consequences should be fully known. A number of persons are leagued together for an end of some moment. To make yourself one of these is submitted to your choice. Among the conditions of their alliance are mutual fidelity and secrecy.[9]

Their existence depends upon this: their existence is known only to themselves. This secrecy must be obtained by all the means which are possible. When I have said thus much, I have informed you, in some degree, of their existence, but you are still ignorant of the purpose contemplated by this association, and of all the members, except myself. So far no dangerous disclosure is yet made: but this degree of concealment is not sufficient. Thus much is made known to you, because it is unavoidable. The individuals which compose this fraternity are not immortal, and the vacancies occasioned by death must be supplied from among the living. The candidate must be instructed and prepared, and they are always at liberty to recede. Their reason must approve the obligations and duties of their station,

---

9. A possible reference to the Illuminati conspiracy, discussion of which reached a high point in the United States at the end of the 1790s. See Robison (p. 291 in this vol.) and Dwight (p. 302 in this vol.). Godwin argues against secrecy in his discussion of sincerity, *Political Justice*, bk. 4, ch. 4.

or they are unfit for it. If they recede, one duty is still incumbent upon them: they must observe an inviolable silence. To this they are not held by any promise. They must weigh consequences, and freely decide; but they must not fail to number among these consequences their own death.

Their death will not be prompted by vengeance. The executioner will say, he that has once revealed the tale is likely to reveal it a second time; and, to prevent this, the betrayer must die. Nor is this the only consequence: to prevent the further revelation, he, to whom the secret was imparted, must likewise perish. He must not console himself with the belief that his trespass will be unknown. The knowledge cannot, by human means, be withheld from this fraternity. Rare, indeed, will it be that his purpose to disclose is not discovered before it can be effected, and the disclosure prevented by his death.

Be well aware of your condition. What I now, or may hereafter mention, mention not again. Admit not even a doubt as to the propriety of hiding it from all the world. There are eyes who will discern this doubt amidst the closest folds of your heart, and your life will instantly be sacrificed.

At present be the subject dismissed. Reflect deeply on the duty which you have already incurred. Think upon your strength of mind, and be careful not to lay yourself under impracticable obligations. It will always be in your power to recede. Even after you are solemnly enrolled a member, you may consult the dictates of your own understanding, and relinquish your post; but while you live, the obligation to be silent will perpetually attend you.

We seek not the misery or death of any one, but we are swayed by an immutable calculation. Death is to be abhorred, but the life of the betrayer is productive of more evil than his death: his death, therefore, we chuse, and our means are instantaneous and unerring.

I love you. The first impulse of my love is to dissuade you from seeking to know more. Your mind will be full of ideas; your hands will be perpetually busy to a purpose into which no human creature, beyond the verge of your brotherhood, must pry. Believe me, who have made the experiment, that compared with this task, the task of inviolable secrecy, all others are easy. To be dumb will not suffice; never to know any remission in your zeal or your watchfulness will not suffice. If the sagacity of others detect your occupations, however strenuously you may labour for concealment, your doom is ratified, as well as that of the wretch whose evil destiny led him to pursue you.

Yet if your fidelity fail not, great will be your recompence. For all your toils and self-devotion, ample will be the retribution. Hitherto you have been wrapt in darkness and storm; then will you be exalted to a pure and unruffled element. It is only for a time that temptation will environ you, and your path will be toilsome. In a few

years you will be permitted to withdraw to a land of sages, and the
remainder of your life will glide away in the enjoyments of beneficence and wisdom.

Think deeply on what I have said. Investigate your own motives
and opinions, and prepare to submit them to the test of numerous
hazards and experiments.

Here my friend passed to a new topic. I was desirous of reverting to
this subject, and obtaining further information concerning it, but he
assiduously repelled all my attempts, and insisted on my bestowing
deep and impartial attention on what had already been disclosed. I
was not slow to comply with his directions. My mind refused to
admit any other theme of contemplation than this.

As yet I had no glimpse of the nature of this fraternity. I was permitted to form conjectures, and previous incidents bestowed but one
form upon my thoughts. In reviewing the sentiments and deportment of Ludloe, my belief continually acquired new strength. I even
recollected hints and ambiguous allusions in his discourse, which
were easily solved, on the supposition of the existence of a new model
of society, in some unsuspected corner of the world.

I did not fully perceive the necessity of secrecy; but this necessity
perhaps would be rendered apparent, when I should come to know
the connection that subsisted between Europe and this imaginary
colony. But what was to be done? I was willing to abide by these conditions. My understanding might not approve of all the ends proposed by this fraternity, and I had liberty to withdraw from it, or to
refuse to ally myself with them. That the obligation of secrecy should
still remain, was unquestionably reasonable.

It appeared to be the plan of Ludloe rather to damp than to stimulate my zeal. He discouraged all attempts to renew the subject in
conversation. He dwelt upon the arduousness of the office to which
I aspired, the temptations to violate my duty with which I should
be continually beset, the inevitable death with which the slightest
breach of my engagements would be followed, and the long apprenticeship which it would be necessary for me to serve, before I should
be fitted to enter into this conclave.

Sometimes my courage was depressed by these representations. . . .
My zeal, however, was sure to revive; and at length Ludloe declared
himself willing to assist me in the accomplishment of my wishes. For
this end, it was necessary, he said, that I should be informed of a
second obligation, which every candidate must assume. Before any
one could be deemed qualified, he must be thoroughly known to his
associates. For this end, he must determine to disclose every fact in
his history, and every secret of his heart. I must begin with making
these confessions, with regard to my past life, to Ludloe, and must
continue to communicate, at stated seasons, every new thought, and

every new occurrence, to him. This confidence was to be absolutely limitless: no exceptions were to be admitted, and no reserves to be practised; and the same penalty attended the infraction of this rule as of the former. Means would be employed, by which the slightest deviation, in either case, would be detected, and the deathful consequence would follow with instant and inevitable expedition. If secrecy were difficult to practise, sincerity, in that degree in which it was here demanded, was a task infinitely more arduous, and a period of new deliberation was necessary before I should decide. I was at liberty to pause: nay, the longer was the period of deliberation which I took, the better; but, when I had once entered this path, it was not in my power to recede. After having solemnly avowed my resolution to be thus sincere in my confession, any particle of reserve or duplicity would cost me my life.

This indeed was a subject to be deeply thought upon. Hitherto I had been guilty of concealment with regard to my friend. I had entered into no formal compact, but had been conscious to a kind of tacit obligation to hide no important transaction of my life from him. This consciousness was the source of continual anxiety. I had exerted, on numerous occasions, my bivocal faculty, but, in my intercourse with Ludloe, had suffered not the slightest intimation to escape me with regard to it. This reserve was not easily explained. It was, in a great degree, the product of habit; but I likewise considered that the efficacy of this instrument depended upon its existence being unknown. To confide the secret to one, was to put an end to my privilege: how widely the knowledge would thenceforth be diffused, I had no power to foresee.

Each day multiplied the impediments to confidence. Shame hindered me from acknowledging my past reserves. Ludloe, from the nature of our intercourse, would certainly account my reserve, in this respect, unjustifiable, and to excite his indignation or contempt was an unpleasing undertaking. Now, if I should resolve to persist in my new path, this reserve must be dismissed: I must make him master of a secret which was precious to me beyond all others; by acquainting him with past concealments, I must risk incurring his suspicion and his anger. These reflections were productive of considerable embarrassment.

There was, indeed, an avenue by which to escape these difficulties, if it did not, at the same time, plunge me into greater. My confessions might, in other respects, be unbounded, but my reserves, in this particular, might be continued. Yet should I not expose myself to formidable perils? Would my secret be for ever unsuspected and undiscovered?

When I considered the nature of this faculty, the impossibility of going farther than suspicion, since the agent could be known only by his own confession, and even this confession would not be believed by the greater part of mankind, I was tempted to conceal it.

In most cases, if I had asserted the possession of this power, I should be treated as a liar; it would be considered as an absurd and audacious expedient to free myself from the suspicion of having entered into compact with a dæmon, or of being myself an emissary of the grand foe. Here, however, there was no reason to dread a similar imputation, since Ludloe had denied the preternatural pretensions of these airy sounds.

My conduct on this occasion was nowise influenced by the belief of any inherent sanctity in truth. Ludloe had taught me to model myself in this respect entirely with a view to immediate consequences. If my genuine interest, on the whole, was promoted by veracity, it was proper to adhere to it; but, if the result of my investigation were opposite, truth was to be sacrificed without scruple.

Meanwhile, in a point of so much moment, I was not hasty to determine. My delay seemed to be, by no means, unacceptable to Ludloe, who applauded my discretion, and warned me to be circumspect. My attention was chiefly absorbed by considerations connected with this subject, and little regard was paid to any foreign occupation or amusement.

One evening, after a day spent in my closet, I sought recreation by walking forth. My mind was chiefly occupied by the review of incidents which happened in Spain. I turned my face towards the fields, and recovered not from my reverie, till I had proceeded some miles on the road to Meath.[1] The night had considerably advanced, and the darkness was rendered intense, by the setting of the moon. Being somewhat weary, as well as undetermined in what manner next to proceed, I seated myself on a grassy bank beside the road. The spot which I had chosen was aloof from passengers, and shrowded in the deepest obscurity.

Some time elapsed, when my attention was excited by the slow approach of an equipage.[2] I presently discovered a coach and six horses, but unattended, except by coachman and postillion, and with no light to guide them on their way. Scarcely had they passed the spot where I rested, when some one leaped from beneath the hedge, and seized the head of the fore-horses. Another called upon the coachman to stop, and threatened him with instant death if he disobeyed. A third drew open the coach-door, and ordered those within to deliver their purses. A shriek of terror showed me that a lady was within, who eagerly consented to preserve her life by the loss of her money.

To walk unarmed in the neighbourhood of Dublin, especially at night, has always been accounted dangerous. I had about me the

1. Situated to the northwest of Dublin, Meath is an eastern county in Ireland.
2. A carriage with attendants.

usual instruments of defence. I was desirous of rescuing this person from the danger which surrounded her, but was somewhat at a loss how to effect my purpose. My single strength was insufficient to contend with three ruffians. After a moment's debate, an expedient was suggested, which I hastened to execute.

Time had not been allowed for the ruffian who stood beside the carriage to receive the plunder, when several voices, loud, clamorous, and eager, were heard in the quarter whence the traveller had come. By trampling with quickness, it was easy to imitate the sound of many feet. The robbers were alarmed, and one called upon another to attend. The sounds increased, and, at the next moment, they betook themselves to flight, but not till a pistol was discharged. Whether it was aimed at the lady in the carriage, or at the coachman, I was not permitted to discover, for the report affrighted the horses, and they set off at full speed.

I could not hope to overtake them: I knew not whither the robbers had fled, and whether, by proceeding, I might not fall into their hands. . . . These considerations induced me to resume my feet, and retire from the scene as expeditiously as possible. I regained my own habitation without injury.

I have said that I occupied separate apartments from those of Ludloe. To these there were means of access without disturbing the family. I hasted to my chamber, but was considerably surprized to find, on entering my apartment, Ludloe seated at a table, with a lamp before him.

My momentary confusion was greater than his. On discovering who it was, he assumed his accustomed looks, and explained appearances, by saying, that he wished to converse with me on a subject of importance, and had therefore sought me at this secret hour, in my own chamber. Contrary to his expectation, I was absent. Conceiving it possible that I might shortly return, he had waited till now. He took no further notice of my absence, nor manifested any desire to know the cause of it, but proceeded to mention the subject which had brought him hither. These were his words.

You have nothing which the laws permit you to call your own. Justice entitles you to the supply of your physical wants, from those who are able to supply them; but there are few who will acknowledge your claim, or spare an atom of their superfluity to appease your cravings. That which they will not spontaneously give, it is not right to wrest from them by violence. What then is to be done?

Property is necessary to your own subsistence. It is useful, by enabling you to supply the wants of others. To give food, and clothing, and shelter, is to give life, to annihilate temptation, to unshackle virtue, and propagate felicity. How shall property be gained?

You may set your understanding or your hands at work. You may weave stockings, or write poems, and exchange them for money;

but these are tardy and meagre schemes. The means are disproportioned to the end, and I will not suffer you to pursue them. My justice will supply your wants.

But dependance on the justice of others is a precarious condition.
To be the object is a less ennobling state than to be the bestower of
benefit. Doubtless you desire to be vested with competence and
riches, and to hold them by virtue of the law, and not at the will of
a benefactor. . . . He paused as if waiting for my assent to his positions. I readily expressed my concurrence, and my desire to pursue
any means compatible with honesty. He resumed.

There are various means, besides labour, violence, or fraud. It is
right to select the easiest within your reach. It happens that the easiest is at hand. A revenue of some thousands a year, a stately mansion
in the city, and another in Kildare,[3] old and faithful domestics, and
magnificent furniture, are good things. Will you have them?

A gift like that, replied I, will be attended by momentous conditions. I cannot decide upon its value, until I know these conditions.

The sole condition is your consent to receive them. Not even the
airy obligation of gratitude will be created by acceptance. On the
contrary, by accepting them, you will confer the highest benefit upon
another.

I do not comprehend you. Something surely must be given in
return.

Nothing. It may seem strange that, in accepting the absolute
controul of so much property, you subject yourself to no conditions;
that no claims of gratitude or service will accrue; but the wonder
is greater still. The law equitably enough fetters the gift with no
restraints, with respect to you that receive it; but not so with regard
to the unhappy being who bestows it. That being must part, not only
with property but liberty. In accepting the property, you must consent to enjoy the services of the present possessor. They cannot be
disjoined.

Of the true nature and extent of the gift, you should be fully
apprized. Be aware, therefore, that, together with this property, you
will receive absolute power over the liberty and person of the being
who now possesses it. That being must become your domestic slave;
be governed, in every particular, by your caprice.

Happily for you, though fully invested with this power, the degree
and mode in which it will be exercised will depend upon yourself. . . .
You may either totally forbear the exercise, or employ it only for the
benefit of your slave. However injurious, therefore, this authority
may be to the subject of it, it will, in some sense, only enhance the
value of the gift to you.

---

3. County Kildare, southeast of Dublin.

The attachment and obedience of this being will be chiefly evident in one thing. Its duty will consist in conforming, in every instance, to your will. All the powers of this being are to be devoted to your happiness; but there is one relation between you, which enables you to confer, while exacting, pleasure. . . . This relation is *sexual*. Your slave is a woman; and the bond, which transfers her property and person to you, is . . . *marriage*.[4]

My knowledge of Ludloe, his principles, and reasonings, ought to have precluded that surprise which I experienced at the conclusion of his discourse. I knew that he regarded the present institution of marriage as a contract of servitude, and the terms of it unequal and unjust. When my surprise had subsided, my thoughts turned upon the nature of his scheme. After a pause of reflection, I answered:

Both law and custom have connected obligations with marriage, which, though heaviest on the female, are not light upon the male. Their weight and extent are not immutable and uniform; they are modified by various incidents, and especially by the mental and personal qualities of the lady.

I am not sure that I should willingly accept the property and person of a woman decrepid with age, and enslaved by perverse habits and evil passions: whereas youth, beauty, and tenderness would be worth accepting, even for their own sake, and disconnected with fortune.

As to altar vows, I believe they will not make me swerve from equity. I shall exact neither service nor affection from my spouse. The value of these, and, indeed, not only the value, but the very existence of the latter depends upon its spontaneity. A promise to love tends rather to loosen than strengthen the tie.

As to myself, the age of illusion is past. I shall not wed, till I find one whose moral and physical constitution will make personal fidelity easy. I shall judge without mistiness or passion, and habit will come in aid of an enlightened and deliberate choice.

I shall not be fastidious in my choice. I do not expect, and scarcely desire, much intellectual similitude between me and my wife. Our opinions and pursuits cannot be in common. While women are formed by their education, and their education continues in its present state, tender hearts and misguided understandings are all that we can hope to meet with.[5]

What are the character, age, and person of the woman to whom you allude? and what prospect of success would attend my exertions to obtain her favour?

4. Cf. Godwin's opposition to marriage in the appendix to bk. 8 of *Political Justice*. Here as elsewhere Ludloe both echoes Godwin and contradicts Godwin's highest ideal of sincerity.
5. Cf. Wollstonecraft's criticism of female education in *A Vindication of the Rights of Woman* (1792), esp. ch. 8.

I have told you she is rich. She is a widow, and owes her riches to the liberality of her husband, who was a trader of great opulence, and who died while on a mercantile adventure to Spain. He was not unknown to you. Your letters from Spain often spoke of him. In short, she is the widow of Benington, whom you met at Barcelona. She is still in the prime of life; is not without many feminine attractions; has an ardent and credulent temper; and is particularly given to devotion.[6] This temper it would be easy to regulate according to your pleasure and your interest, and I now submit to you the expediency of an alliance with her.

I am a kinsman, and regarded by her with uncommon deference; and my commendations, therefore, will be of great service to you, and shall be given.

I will deal ingenuously with you. It is proper you should be fully acquainted with the grounds of this proposal. The benefits of rank, and property, and independence, which I have already mentioned as likely to accrue to you from this marriage, are solid and valuable benefits; but these are not the sole advantages, and to benefit you, in these respects, is not my whole view.

No. My treatment of you henceforth will be regulated by one principle. I regard you only as one undergoing a probation or apprenticeship; as subjected to trials of your sincerity and fortitude. The marriage I now propose to you is desirable, because it will make you independent of me. Your poverty might create an unsuitable bias in favour of proposals, one of whose effects would be to set you beyond fortune's reach. That bias will cease, when you cease to be poor and dependent.

Love is the strongest of all human delusions. That fortitude, which is not subdued by the tenderness and blandishments of woman, may be trusted; but no fortitude, which has not undergone that test, will be trusted by us.

This woman is a charming enthusiast.[7] She will never marry but him whom she passionately loves. Her power over the heart that loves her will scarcely have limits. The means of prying into your transactions, of suspecting and sifting your thoughts, which her constant society with you, while sleeping and waking, her zeal and watchfulness for your welfare, and her curiosity, adroitness, and penetration will afford her, are evident. Your danger, therefore, will be imminent. Your fortitude will be obliged to have recourse, not to flight, but to vigilance. Your eye must never close.

Alas! what human magnanimity can stand this test! How can I persuade myself that you will not fail? I waver between hope and

6. I.e., she is gullible and pious.
7. A Romantic.

fear. Many, it is true, have fallen, and dragged with them the author of their ruin, but some have soared above even these perils and temptations, with their fiery energies unimpaired, and great has been, as great ought to be, their recompence.

But you are doubtless aware of your danger. I need not repeat the consequences of betraying your trust, the rigour of those who will judge your fault, the unerring and unbounded scrutiny to which your actions, the most secret and indifferent, will be subjected.

Your conduct, however, will be voluntary. At your own option be it, to see or not to see this woman. Circumspection, deliberation, forethought, are your sacred duties and highest interest.

Ludloe's remarks on the seductive and bewitching powers of women, on the difficulty of keeping a secret which they wish to know, and to gain which they employ the soft artillery of tears and prayers, and blandishments and menaces, are familiar to all men, but they had little weight with me, because they were unsupported by my own experience. I had never had any intellectual or sentimental connection with the sex. My meditations and pursuits had all led a different way, and a bias had gradually been given to my feelings, very unfavourable to the refinements of love. I acknowledge, with shame and regret, that I was accustomed to regard the physical and sensual consequences of the sexual relation as realities, and every thing intellectual, disinterested, and heroic, which enthusiasts connect with it, as idle dreams. Besides, said I, I am yet a stranger to the secret, on the preservation of which so much stress is laid, and it will be optional with me to receive it or not. If, in the progress of my acquaintance with Mrs. Benington, I should perceive any extraordinary danger in the gift, cannot I refuse, or at least delay to comply with any new conditions from Ludloe? Will not his candour and his affection for me rather commend than disapprove my diffidence? In fine, I resolved to see this lady.

She was, it seems, the widow of Benington, whom I knew in Spain. This man was an English merchant settled at Barcelona, to whom I had been commended by Ludloe's letters, and through whom my pecuniary supplies were furnished. . . . Much intercourse and some degree of intimacy had taken place between us, and I had gained a pretty accurate knowledge of his character. I had been informed, through different channels, that his wife was much his superior in rank, that she possessed great wealth in her own right, and that some disagreement of temper or views occasioned their separation. She had married him for love, and still doated on him: the occasions for separation having arisen, it seems, not on her side but on his. As his habits of reflection were nowise friendly to religion, and as hers, according to Ludloe, were of the opposite kind, it is possible that some jarring had arisen between them from this source. Indeed, from some casual and broken hints of Benington, especially in the latter part of his life, I had long since gathered this conjecture. . . . Something, thought I, may be derived from my acquaintance with her husband favourable to my views.

I anxiously waited for an opportunity of acquainting Ludloe with my resolution. On the day of our last conversation, he had made a short excursion from town, intending to return the same evening, but had continued absent for several days. As soon as he came back, I hastened to acquaint him with my wishes.

Have you well considered this matter, said he. Be assured it is of no trivial import. The moment at which you enter the presence of this woman will decide your future destiny. Even putting out of view the subject of our late conversations, the light in which you shall appear to her will greatly influence your happiness, since, though you cannot fail to love her, it is quite uncertain what return she may think proper to make. Much, doubtless, will depend on your own perseverance and address, but you will have many, perhaps insuperable, obstacles to encounter on several accounts, and especially in her attachment to the memory of her late husband. As to her devout temper, this is nearly allied to a warm imagination in some other respects, and will operate much more in favour of an ardent and artful lover, than against him.

I still expressed my willingness to try my fortune with her.

Well, said he, I anticipated your consent to my proposal, and the visit I have just made was to her. I thought it best to pave the way, by informing her that I had met with one for whom she had desired me to look out. You must know that her father was one of these singular men who set a value upon things exactly in proportion to the difficulty of obtaining or comprehending them. His passion was for antiques, and his favourite pursuit during a long life was monuments in brass, marble, and parchment, of the remotest antiquity. He was wholly indifferent to the character or conduct of our present sovereign and his ministers, but was extremely solicitous about the name and exploits of a king of Ireland that lived two or three centuries before the flood. He felt no curiosity to know who was the father of his wife's child, but would travel a thousand miles, and consume months, in investigating which son of Noah it was that first landed on the coast of Munster.[8] He would give a hundred guineas from the mint for a piece of old decayed copper no bigger than his nail, provided it had aukward characters upon it, too much defaced to be read. The whole stock of a great bookseller was, in his eyes, a cheap

8. A province taking up most of southwestern Ireland; in the eighteenth century, it was one of four provinces into which Ireland was divided. In Irish folklore, the Gaels are descended from Noah's son Japeth or Japhet. Other legends trace Ireland's settlement back to an extra-biblical son of Noah named Bith.

exchange for a shred of parchment, containing half a homily written by St. Patrick.[9] He would have gratefully given all his patrimo-
nial domains to one who should inform him what pendragon or
druid it was who set up the first stone on Salisbury plain.[1]

This spirit, as you may readily suppose, being seconded by great
wealth and long life, contributed to form a very large collection of
venerable lumber,[2] which, though beyond all price to the collector
himself, is of no value to his heiress but so far as it is marketable. She
designs to bring the whole to auction, but for this purpose a catalogue and description are necessary. Her father trusted to a faithful
memory, and to vague and scarcely legible memorandums, and has
left a very arduous task to any one who shall be named to the office.
It occurred to me, that the best means of promoting your views was
to recommend you to this office.

You are not entirely without the antiquarian frenzy yourself. The
employment, therefore, will be somewhat agreeable to you for its
own sake. It will entitle you to become an inmate of the same house,
and thus establish an incessant intercourse between you, and the
nature of the business is such, that you may perform it in what time,
and with what degree of diligence and accuracy you please.

I ventured to insinuate that, to a woman of rank and family, the
character of a hireling was by no means a favourable recommendation.

He answered, that he proposed, by the account he should give of
me, to obviate every scruple of that nature. Though my father was no
better than a farmer, it is not absolutely certain but that my remoter
ancestors had princely blood in their veins: but as long as proofs
of my low extraction did not impertinently intrude themselves, my
silence, or, at most, equivocal surmises, seasonably made use of,
might secure me from all inconveniences on the score of birth. He
should represent me, and I was such, as his friend, favourite, and
equal, and my passion for antiquities should be my principal inducement to undertake this office, though my poverty would make no
objection to a reasonable pecuniary recompense.

Having expressed my acquiescence in his measures, he thus proceeded: My visit was made to my kinswoman, for the purpose, as
I just now told you, of paving your way into her family; but, on my
arrival at her house, I found nothing but disorder and alarm. Mrs.
Benington, it seems, on returning from a longer ride than customary,
last Thursday evening, was attacked by robbers. Her attendants

9. A fifth-century Christian missionary to Ireland, generally considered Ireland's patron
saint.
1. The site of Stonehenge, located outside the English town of Salisbury. "Pendragon": an
ancient British chieftain or king.
2. Something cumbersome or useless.

related an imperfect tale of somebody advancing at the critical moment to her rescue. It seems, however, they did more harm than good; for the horses took to flight and overturned the carriage, in consequence of which Mrs. Benington was severely bruised. She has kept her bed ever since, and a fever was likely to ensue, which has only left her out of danger to-day.

As the adventure before related, in which I had so much concern, occurred at the time mentioned by Ludloe, and as all other circumstances were alike, I could not doubt that the person whom the exertion of my mysterious powers had relieved was Mrs. Benington: but what an ill-omened interference was mine! The robbers would probably have been satisfied with the few guineas in her purse, and, on receiving these, would have left her to prosecute her journey in peace and security, but, by absurdly offering a succour, which could only operate upon the fears of her assailants, I endangered her life, first by the desperate discharge of a pistol, and next by the fright of the horses. . . . My anxiety, which would have been less if I had not been, in some degree, myself the author of the evil, was nearly removed by Ludloe's proceeding to assure me that all danger was at an end, and that he left the lady in the road to perfect health. He had seized the earliest opportunity of acquainting her with the purpose of his visit, and had brought back with him her cheerful acceptance of my services. The next week was appointed for my introduction.

With such an object in view, I had little leisure to attend to any indifferent object. My thoughts were continually bent upon the expected introduction, and my impatience and curiosity drew strength, not merely from the character of Mrs. Benington, but from the nature of my new employment. Ludloe had truly observed, that I was infected with somewhat of this antiquarian mania myself, and I now remembered that Benington had frequently alluded to this collection in possession of his wife. My curiosity had then been more than once excited by his representations, and I had formed a vague resolution of making myself acquainted with this lady and her learned treasure, should I ever return to Ireland. . . . Other incidents had driven this matter from my mind.

Meanwhile, affairs between Ludloe and myself remained stationary. Our conferences, which were regular and daily, related to general topics, and though his instructions were adapted to promote my improvement in the most useful branches of knowledge, they never afforded a glimpse towards that quarter where my curiosity was most active.

The next week now arrived, but Ludloe informed me that the state of Mrs. Benington's health required a short excursion into the country, and that he himself proposed to bear her company. The journey was to last about a fortnight, after which I might prepare myself for an introduction to her.

This was a very unexpected and disagreeable trial to my patience. The interval of solitude that now succeeded would have passed rapidly and pleasantly enough, if an event of so much moment were not in suspense. Books, of which I was passionately fond, would have afforded me delightful and incessant occupation, and Ludloe, by way of reconciling me to unavoidable delays, had given me access to a little closet, in which his rarer and more valuable books were kept.

All my amusements, both by inclination and necessity, were centered in myself and at home. Ludloe appeared to have no visitants, and though frequently abroad, or at least secluded from me, had never proposed my introduction to any of his friends, except Mrs. Benington. My obligations to him were already too great to allow me to lay claim to new favours and indulgences, nor, indeed, was my disposition such as to make society needful to my happiness. My character had been, in some degree, modelled by the faculty which I possessed. This deriving all its supposed value from impenetrable secrecy, and Ludloe's admonitions tending powerfully to impress me with the necessity of wariness and circumspection in my general intercourse with mankind, I had gradually fallen into sedate, reserved, mysterious, and unsociable habits. My heart wanted not a friend.

In this temper of mind, I set myself to examine the novelties which Ludloe's private book-cases contained. 'Twill be strange, thought I, if his favourite volumes do not show some marks of my friend's character. To know a man's favourite or most constant studies cannot fail of letting in some little light upon his secret thoughts, and though he would not have given me the reading of these books, if he had thought them capable of unveiling more of his concerns than he wished, yet possibly my ingenuity may go one step farther than he dreams of. You shall judge whether I was right in my conjectures.

The books which composed this little library were chiefly the voyages and travels of the missionaries of the sixteenth and seventeenth centuries. Added to these were some works upon political economy and legislation. Those writers who have amused themselves with reducing their ideas to practice, and drawing imaginary pictures of nations or republics, whose manners or government came up to their standard of excellence, were, all of whom I had ever heard, and some I had never heard of before, to be found in this collection. A translation of Aristotle's republic, the political romances of sir Thomas Moore, Harrington, and Hume,[3] appeared to have been much read, and Ludloe had not been sparing of his marginal comments. In

---

3. David Hume (1711–1776) published "Idea of a Perfect Commonwealth" in 1754; in it he comments on Harrington, Moore, and Plato before positing his own model government. "Republic": Brown mistakes Aristotle for Plato as author of *The Republic*. Thomas Moore (1478–1535) published his *Utopia* in 1516. James Harrington (1611–1677) published *The Commonwealth of Oceana* in 1656.

these writers he appeared to find nothing but error and absurdity;
and his notes were introduced for no other end than to point out
groundless principles and false conclusions. . . . The style of these
remarks was already familiar to me. I saw nothing new in them, or
different from the strain of those speculations with which Ludloe
was accustomed to indulge himself in conversation with me.

After having turned over the leaves of the printed volumes, I at
length lighted on a small book of maps, from which, of course, I
could reasonably expect no information, on that point about which I
was most curious. It was an atlas, in which the maps had been drawn
by the pen. None of them contained any thing remarkable, so far as
I, who was indeed a smatterer in geography, was able to perceive, till
I came to the end, when I noticed a map, whose prototype I was
wholly unacquainted with. It was drawn on a pretty large scale, representing two islands, which bore some faint resemblance, in their
relative proportions, at least, to Great Britain and Ireland. In shape
they were widely different, but as to size there was no scale by which
to measure them. From the great number of subdivisions, and from
signs, which apparently represented towns and cities, I was allowed
to infer, that the country was at least as extensive as the British isles.
This map was apparently unfinished, for it had no names inscribed
upon it.

I have just said, my geographical knowledge was imperfect.
Though I had not enough to draw the outlines of any country by
memory, I had still sufficient to recognize what I had before seen,
and to discover that none of the larger islands in our globe resembled the one before me. Having such and so strong motives to curiosity, you may easily imagine my sensations on surveying this map.
Suspecting, as I did, that many of Ludloe's intimations alluded to
a country well known to him, though unknown to others, I was, of
course, inclined to suppose that this country was now before me.

In search of some clue to this mystery, I carefully inspected the
other maps in this collection. In a map of the eastern hemisphere I
soon observed the outlines of islands, which, though on a scale
greatly diminished, were plainly similar to that of the land above
described.

It is well known that the people of Europe are strangers to very
nearly one half of the surface of the globe.[4] From the south pole up
to the equator, it is only the small space occupied by southern Africa

4. "The reader must be reminded that the incidents of this narrative are supposed to have
taken place before the voyages of Bougainville and Cook—EDITOR" [Brown's note].
I.e., the events Carwin recounts predate 1766, when Louis Antoine de Bougainville,
who had defended Quebec for the French during the Seven Years' War, undertook his
Pacific voyage. James Cook (1728–1779) served in the British Navy during the Seven
Years' War and began his exploration of the Pacific in 1768.

and by South America with which we are acquainted. There is a vast extent, sufficient to receive a continent as large as North America, which our ignorance has filled only with water. In Ludloe's maps nothing was still to be seen, in these regions, but water, except in that spot where the transverse parallels of the southern tropic and the 150th degree east longitude intersect each other.[5] On this spot were Ludloe's islands placed, though without any name or inscription whatever.

I needed not to be told that this spot had never been explored by any European voyager, who had published his adventures. What authority had Ludloe for fixing a habitable land in this spot? and why did he give us nothing but the courses of shores and rivers, and the scite of towns and villages, without a name?

As soon as Ludloe had set out upon his proposed journey of a fortnight, I unlocked his closet, and continued rummaging among these books and maps till night. By that time I had turned over every book and almost every leaf in this small collection, and did not open the closet again till near the end of that period. Meanwhile I had many reflections upon this remarkable circumstance. Could Ludloe have intended that I should see this atlas? It was the only book that could be styled a manuscript on these shelves, and it was placed beneath several others, in a situation far from being obvious and forward to the eye or the hand. Was it an oversight in him to leave it in my way, or could he have intended to lead my curiosity and knowledge a little farther onward by this accidental disclosure? In either case how was I to regulate my future deportment toward him? Was I to speak and act as if this atlas had escaped my attention or not? I had already, after my first examination of it, placed the volume exactly where I found it. On every supposition I thought this was the safest way, and unlocked the closet a second time, to see that all was precisely in the original order. . . . How was I dismayed and confounded on inspecting the shelves to perceive that the atlas was gone. This was a theft, which, from the closet being under lock and key, and the key always in my own pocket, and which, from the very nature of the thing stolen, could not be imputed to any of the domestics. After a few moments a suspicion occurred, which was soon changed into certainty by applying to the housekeeper, who told me that Ludloe had returned, apparently in much haste, the evening of the day on which he had set out upon his journey, and just after I had left the house, that he had gone into the room where this closet of books was, and, after a few minutes' stay, came out again and went away.

5. The Southern Tropic, or Tropic of Capricorn, intersects 150 degrees east longitude in northeast Australia. Although Ludloe positions his islands there, Bougainville's and Cook's voyages would have remapped the region.

She told me also, that he had made general enquiries after me, to which she had answered, that she had not seen me during the day, and supposed that I had spent the whole of it abroad. From this account it was plain, that Ludloe had returned for no other purpose but to remove this book out of my reach. But if he had a double key to this door, what should hinder his having access, by the same means, to every other locked up place in the house?

This suggestion made me start with terror. Of so obvious a means for possessing a knowledge of every thing under his roof, I had never been till this moment aware. Such is the infatuation which lays our most secret thoughts open to the world's scrutiny. We are frequently in most danger when we deem ourselves most safe, and our fortress is taken sometimes through a point, whose weakness nothing, it should seem, but the blindest stupidity could overlook.

My terrors, indeed, quickly subsided when I came to recollect that there was nothing in any closet or cabinet of mine which could possibly throw light upon subjects which I desired to keep in the dark. The more carefully I inspected my own drawers, and the more I reflected on the character of Ludloe, as I had known it, the less reason did there appear in my suspicions; but I drew a lesson of caution from this circumstance, which contributed to my future safety.

From this incident I could not but infer Ludloe's unwillingness to let me so far into his geographical secret, as well as the certainty of that suspicion, which had very early been suggested to my thoughts, that Ludloe's plans of civilization had been carried into practice in some unvisited corner of the world. It was strange, however, that he should betray himself by such an inadvertency. One who talked so confidently of his own powers, to unveil any secret of mine, and, at the same time, to conceal his own transactions, had surely committed an unpardonable error in leaving this important document in my way. My reverence, indeed, for Ludloe was such, that I sometimes entertained the notion that this seeming oversight was, in truth, a regular contrivance to supply me with a knowledge, of which, when I came maturely to reflect, it was impossible for me to make any ill use. There is no use in relating what would not be believed; and should I publish to the world the existence of islands in the space allotted by Ludloe's maps to these *incognitæ*,[6] what would the world answer? That whether the space described was sea or land was of no importance. That the moral and political condition of its inhabitants was the only topic worthy of rational curiosity. Since I had gained no information upon this point; since I had nothing to disclose but vain and fantastic surmises; I might as well be ignorant of every thing. Thus, from secretly condemning Ludloe's imprudence, I gradually

6. Unknown or unmapped territory.

passed to admiration of his policy. This discovery had no other effect than to stimulate my curiosity;[7] to keep up my zeal to prosecute the journey I had commenced under his auspices.

I had hitherto formed a resolution to stop where I was in Ludloe's confidence: to wait till the success should be ascertained of my projects with respect to Mrs. Benington, before I made any new advance in the perilous and mysterious road into which he had led my steps. But, before this tedious fortnight had elapsed, I was grown extremely impatient for an interview, and had nearly resolved to undertake whatever obligation he should lay upon me.

This obligation was indeed a heavy one, since it included the confession of my vocal powers. In itself the confession was little. To possess this faculty was neither laudable nor culpable, nor had it been exercised in a way which I should be very much ashamed to acknowledge. It had led me into many insincerities and artifices, which, though not justifiable by any creed, was entitled to some excuse, on the score of youthful ardour and temerity. The true difficulty in the way of these confessions was the not having made them already. Ludloe had long been entitled to this confidence, and, though the existence of this power was venial or wholly innocent, the obstinate concealment of it was a different matter, and would certainly expose me to suspicion and rebuke. But what was the alternative? To conceal it. To incur those dreadful punishments awarded against treason in this particular. Ludloe's menaces still rung in my ears, and appalled my heart. How should I be able to shun them? By concealing from every one what I concealed from him? How was my concealment of such a faculty to be suspected or proved? Unless I betrayed myself, who could betray me?

In this state of mind, I resolved to confess myself to Ludloe in the way that he required, reserving only the secret of this faculty. Awful, indeed, said I, is the crisis of my fate. If Ludloe's declarations are true, a horrid catastrophe awaits me: but as fast as my resolutions were shaken, they were confirmed anew by the recollection—Who can betray me but myself? If I deny, who is there can prove? Suspicion can never light upon the truth. If it does, it can never be converted into certainty. Even my own lips cannot confirm it, since who will believe my testimony?

By such illusions was I fortified in my desperate resolution. Ludloe returned at the time appointed. He informed me that Mrs. Benington expected me next morning. She was ready to depart for her country residence, where she proposed to spend the ensuing summer,

---

7. In citing his "curiosity," Carwin invokes the defining characteristic of William Godwin's protagonist in *Caleb Williams* (1794) and suggests a parallel between Carwin, discoverer of Ludloe's secrets, and Caleb, discoverer of his master Falkland's guilt.

and would carry me along with her. In consequence of this arrangement, he said, many months would elapse before he should see me
again. You will indeed, continued he, be pretty much shut up from
all society. Your books and your new friend will be your chief, if not
only companions. Her life is not a social one, because she has formed
extravagant notions of the importance of lonely worship and devout
solitude. Much of her time will be spent in meditation upon pious
books in her closet. Some of it in long solitary rides in her coach,
for the sake of exercise. Little will remain for eating and sleeping,
so that unless you can prevail upon her to violate her ordinary rules
for your sake, you will be left pretty much to yourself. You will have
the more time to reflect upon what has hitherto been the theme of
our conversations. You can come to town when you want to see me.
I shall generally be found in these apartments.

In the present state of my mind, though impatient to see Mrs. Benington, I was still more impatient to remove the veil between Ludloe
and myself. After some pause, I ventured to enquire if there was any
impediment to my advancement in the road he had already pointed
out to my curiosity and ambition.

He replied, with great solemnity, that I was already acquainted
with the next step to be taken in this road. If I was prepared to make
him my confessor, as to the past, the present, and the future, *without
exception or condition*, but what arose from defect of memory, he
was willing to receive my confession.

I declared myself ready to do so.

I need not, he returned, remind you of the consequences of concealment or deceit. I have already dwelt upon these consequences.
As to the past, you have already told me, perhaps, all that is of any
moment to know. It is in relation to the future that caution will be
chiefly necessary. Hitherto your actions have been nearly indifferent
to the ends of your future existence. Confessions of the past are
required, because they are an earnest of the future character and
conduct. Have you then—but this is too abrupt. Take an hour to
reflect and deliberate. Go by yourself; take yourself to severe task,
and make up your mind with a full, entire, and unfailing resolution;
for the moment in which you assume this new obligation will make
you a new being. Perdition or felicity will hang upon that moment.

This conversation was late in the evening. After I had consented to
postpone this subject, we parted, he telling me that he would leave
his chamber door open, and as soon as my mind was made up I might
come to him.

I retired accordingly to my apartment, and spent the prescribed
hour in anxious and irresolute reflections. They were no other than
had hitherto occurred, but they occurred with more force than
ever. Some fatal obstinacy, however, got possession of me, and I

persisted in the resolution of concealing *one thing*. We become fondly attached to objects and pursuits, frequently for no conceivable reason but the pain and trouble they cost us. In proportion to the danger in which they involve us do we cherish them. Our darling potion is the poison that scorches our vitals.

After some time, I went to Ludloe's apartment. I found him solemn, and yet benign, at my entrance. After intimating my compliance with the terms prescribed, which I did, in spite of all my labour for composure, with accents half faultering, he proceeded to put various questions to me, relative to my early history.

I knew there was no other mode of accomplishing the end in view, but by putting all that was related in the form of answers to questions; and when meditating on the character of Ludloe, I experienced excessive uneasiness as to the consummate art and penetration which his questions would manifest. Conscious of a purpose to conceal, my fancy invested my friend with the robe of a judicial inquisitor, all whose questions should aim at extracting the truth, and entrapping the liar.

In this respect, however, I was wholly disappointed. All his inquiries were general and obvious.—They betokened curiosity, but not suspicion; yet there were moments when I saw, or fancied I saw, some dissatisfaction betrayed in his features; and when I arrived at that period of my story which terminated with my departure, as his companion, for Europe, his pauses were, I thought, a little longer and more museful than I liked. At this period, our first conference ended. After a talk, which had commenced at a late hour, and had continued many hours, it was time to sleep, and it was agreed that next morning the conference should be renewed.

On retiring to my pillow, and reviewing all the circumstances of this interview, my mind was filled with apprehension and disquiet. I seemed to recollect a thousand things, which showed that Ludloe was not fully satisfied with my part in this interview. A strange and nameless mixture of wrath and of pity appeared, on recollection, in the glances which, from time to time, he cast upon me. Some emotion played upon his features, in which, as my fears conceived, there was a tincture of resentment and ferocity. In vain I called my usual sophistries to my aid. In vain I pondered on the inscrutable nature of my peculiar faculty. In vain I endeavoured to persuade myself, that, by telling the truth, instead of entitling myself to Ludloe's approbation, I should only excite his anger, by what he could not but deem an attempt to impose upon his belief an incredible tale of impossible events. I had never heard or read of any instance of this faculty. I supposed the case to be absolutely singular, and I should be no more entitled to credit in proclaiming it, than if I should maintain that a certain billet of wood possessed the faculty

of articulate speech. It was now, however, too late to retract. I had
been guilty of a solemn and deliberate concealment. I was now in the
path in which there was no turning back, and I must go forward.

The return of day's encouraging beams in some degree quieted
my nocturnal terrors, and I went, at the appointed hour, to Ludloe's
presence. I found him with a much more cheerful aspect than I
expected, and began to chide myself, in secret, for the folly of my late
apprehensions.

After a little pause, he reminded me, that he was only one among
many, engaged in a great and arduous design. As each of us, continued he, is mortal, each of us must, in time, yield his post to another.—
Each of us is ambitious to provide himself a successor, to have his
place filled by one selected and instructed by himself. All our personal feelings and affections are by no means intended to be swallowed up by a passion for the general interest; when they can be kept
alive and be brought into play, in subordination and subservience to
the *great end*, they are cherished as useful, and revered as laudable;
and whatever austerity and rigour you may impute to my character,
there are few more susceptible of personal regards than I am.

You cannot know, till *you* are what *I* am, what deep, what all-
absorbing interest I have in the success of my tutorship on this occasion. Most joyfully would I embrace a thousand deaths, rather than
that you should prove a recreant.[8] The consequences of any failure in
your integrity will, it is true, be fatal to yourself: but there are some
minds, of a generous texture, who are more impatient under ills they
have inflicted upon others, than of those they have brought upon
themselves; who had rather perish, themselves, in infamy, than bring
infamy or death upon a benefactor.

Perhaps of such noble materials is your mind composed. If I had
not thought so, you would never have been an object of my regard,
and therefore, in the motives that shall impel you to fidelity, sincerity, and perseverance, some regard to my happiness and welfare will,
no doubt, have place.

And yet I exact nothing from you on this score. If your own safety
be insufficient to controul you, you are not fit for us. There is, indeed,
abundant need of all possible inducements to make you faithful. The
task of concealing nothing from me must be easy. That of concealing
every thing from others must be the only arduous one. The *first* you
can hardly fail of performing, when the exigence requires it, for what
motive can you possibly have to practice evasion or disguise with
me? You have surely committed no crime; you have neither robbed,
nor murdered, nor betrayed. If you have, there is no room for the

8. Coward or apostate.

fear of punishment or the terror of disgrace to step in, and make you hide your guilt from me. You cannot dread any further disclosure, because I can have no interest in your ruin or your shame: and what evil could ensue the confession of the foulest murder, even before a bench of magistrates, more dreadful than that which will inevitably follow the practice of the least concealment to me, or the least undue disclosure to others?

You cannot easily conceive the emphatical solemnity with which this was spoken. Had he fixed piercing eyes on me while he spoke; had I perceived him watching my looks, and labouring to penetrate my secret thoughts, I should doubtless have been ruined: but he fixed his eyes upon the floor, and no gesture or look indicated the smallest suspicion of my conduct. After some pause, he continued, in a more pathetic tone, while his whole frame seemed to partake of his mental agitation.

I am greatly at a loss by what means to impress you with a full conviction of the truth of what I have just said. Endless are the sophistries by which we seduce ourselves into perilous and doubtful paths. What we do not see, we disbelieve, or we heed not. The sword may descend upon our infatuated head from above, but we who are, meanwhile, busily inspecting the ground at our feet, or gazing at the scene around us, are not aware or apprehensive of its irresistible coming. In this case, it must not be seen before it is felt, or before that time comes when the danger of incurring it is over. I cannot withdraw the veil, and disclose to your view the exterminating angel. All must be vacant and blank, and the danger that stands armed with death at your elbow must continue to be totally invisible, till that moment when its vengeance is provoked or unprovokable. I will do my part to encourage you in good, or intimidate you from evil. I am anxious to set before you all the motives which are fitted to influence your conduct; but how shall I work on your convictions?

Here another pause ensued, which I had not courage enough to interrupt. He presently resumed.

Perhaps you recollect a visit which you paid, on Christmas day, in the year——, to the cathedral church at Toledo.[9] Do you remember?

A moment's reflection recalled to my mind all the incidents of that day. I had good reason to remember them. I felt no small trepidation when Ludloe referred me to that day, for, at the moment, I was doubtful whether there had not been some bivocal[1] agency exerted on that occasion. Luckily, however, it was almost the only similar occasion in which it had been wholly silent.

9. City in central Spain, in New Castile, near Madrid.
1. Ventriloquial.

I answered in the affirmative: I remember them perfectly.

And yet, said Ludloe, with a smile that seemed intended to disarm this declaration of some of its terrors, I suspect your recollection is not as exact as mine, nor, indeed, your knowledge as extensive. You met there, for the first time, a female, whose nominal uncle, but real father, a dean of that ancient church, resided in a blue stone house, the third from the west angle of the square of St. Jago.

All this was exactly true.

This female, continued he, fell in love with you. Her passion made her deaf to all the dictates of modesty and duty, and she gave you sufficient intimations, in subsequent interviews at the same place, of this passion; which, she being fair and enticing, you were not slow in comprehending and returning. As not only the safety of your intercourse, but even of both your lives, depended on being shielded even from suspicion, the utmost wariness and caution was observed in all your proceedings. Tell me whether you succeeded in your efforts to this end.

I replied, that, at the time, I had no doubt but I had.

And yet, said he, drawing something from his pocket, and putting it into my hand, there is the slip of paper, with the preconcerted emblem inscribed upon it, which the infatuated girl dropped in your sight, one evening, in the left aisle of that church. That paper you imagined you afterwards burnt in your chamber lamp. In pursuance of this token, you deferred your intended visit, and next day the lady was accidentally drowned, in passing a river. Here ended your connexion with her, and with her was buried, as you thought, all memory of this transaction.

I leave you to draw your own inference from this disclosure. Meditate upon it when alone. Recal all the incidents of that drama, and labour to conceive the means by which my sagacity has been able to reach events that took place so far off, and under so deep a covering. If you cannot penetrate these means, learn to reverence my assertions, that I cannot be deceived; and let sincerity be henceforth the rule of your conduct towards me, not merely because it is right, but because concealment is impossible.

We will stop here. There is no haste required of us. Yesterday's discourse will suffice for to-day, and for many days to come. Let what has already taken place be the subject of profound and mature reflection. Review, once more, the incidents of your early life, previous to your introduction to me, and, at our next conference, prepare to supply all those deficiencies occasioned by negligence, forgetfulness, or design on our first. There must be some. There must be many. The whole truth can only be disclosed after numerous and repeated conversations. These must take place at considerable intervals, and when *all* is told, then shall you be ready to encounter the final ordeal, and load yourself with heavy and terrific sanctions.

I shall be the proper judge of the completeness of your confession.—Knowing previously, and by unerring means, your whole history, I shall be able to detect all that is deficient, as well as all that is redundant. Your confessions have hitherto adhered to the truth, but deficient they are, and they must be, for who, at a single trial, can detail the secrets of his life? whose recollection can fully serve him at an instant's notice? who can free himself, by a single effort, from the dominion of fear and shame? We expect no miracles of fortitude and purity from our disciples. It is our discipline, our wariness, our laborious preparation that creates the excellence we have among us. We find it not ready made.

I counsel you to join Mrs. Benington without delay. You may see me when and as often as you please. When it is proper to renew the present topic, it shall be renewed. Till then we will be silent.—Here Ludloe left me alone, but not to indifference or vacuity. Indeed I was overwhelmed with the reflections that arose from this conversation. So, said I, I am still saved, if I have wisdom enough to use the opportunity, from the consequences of past concealments. By a distinction which I had wholly overlooked, but which could not be missed by the sagacity and equity of Ludloe, I have praise for telling the truth, and an excuse, for withholding some of the truth. It was, indeed, a praise to which I was entitled, for I have made no *additions* to the tale of my early adventures. I had no motive to exaggerate or dress out in false colours. What I sought to conceal, I was careful to exclude entirely, that a lame or defective narrative might awaken no suspicions.

The allusion to incidents at Toledo confounded and bewildered all my thoughts. I still held the paper he had given me. So far as memory could be trusted, it was the same which, an hour after I had received it, I burnt, as I conceived, with my own hands. How Ludloe came into possession of this paper; how he was apprised of incidents, to which only the female mentioned and myself were privy; which she had too good reason to hide from all the world, and which I had taken infinite pains to bury in oblivion, I vainly endeavoured to conjecture.

SOURCES AND CONTEXTS

SOURCES AND CONTEXTS

CHRISTOPH MARTIN WIELAND

From The Trial of Abraham[†]

Canto I

Daughter of Heaven![1] nursed among Eden's blooming hills, in more than golden times, who did converse with Sipha's daughters[2] in the fragrant shades of paradise, their associate most endearing, thou goddess of song, parent of virtue, aid me to sing the triumph of obedient faith, the trial of resigned Abraham, who, at the divine command, subduing natural affection, led his son, a blooming youth, up Moriah as a destined victim;[3] O teach me to celebrate heavenly virtue in heavenly lays! From past scenes withdraw the shrouding night, open to me a smiling prospect of that delicious spot, where Sarah,[4] instilling into the youth early sanctity, fitted him for future converse with God and angels. Well were known to thee the transactions of that blessed family; thou wert present at the birth of ancient events; oft amidst Mamre's oaks dist thou walk, often in Haran didst thou visit the sweet-featured Ribkah[5] whose wifely embraces were one day to reward Isaac's virtue. Indulge my request, O sacred muse! Consecrate me thy priest; emulous am I of Bodmer's[6] fame, taught by thee how nobly he strikes the lyre in wisdom's praise; with what a nervous flow he sings the ways of providence, the charms of virtue, and the sublimites of religion! By thee, Saint-like muse, were the bands of our amity tied; thee shall my advanced years thank. Serena[7] thanks thee that one shining year of my happy youth, interwoven with the days of a sage, has crowned my life: On that model form my heart; form is to the noble simplicity, to the wisdom of the early world, which our times know not; so shall I with more impassioned numbers display the full beauty of ancient manners, of the patriarchal

---

[†] From Christoph Martin Wieland, *The Trial of Abraham* (Norwich, Conn.: Trumbull, 1777), pp. 1–5, 34–46. This English prose translation of Wieland's 1753 poem *Der geprüfte Abraham*, first published in London in 1764, saw multiple North American printings.

1. Urania, muse of astrology, invoked by Milton in *Paradise Lost* and often understood as a figure for the Holy Spirit.

2. Traditionally, Sipha's daughters marry the sons of Noah before the flood. Sipha is Noah's brother-in-law.

3. Abraham was asked by God to sacrifice his son Isaac on Mount Moriah. See Genesis 22.

4. Abraham's wife and Isaac's mother.

5. Or Rebekah, named in Genesis as Isaac's wife. Mamre was the site of Abraham's camp. Haran was Abraham's former home, a city in northwestern Mesopotamia.

6. Johann Jakob Bodmer (1698–1783), a Swiss poet and translator of Milton whose epic *Noah* (1751) Wieland both admired and imitated. Wieland lived and trained with Bodmer in Zurich from 1752 to 1754.

7. Sophie Gutermann, Wieland's distant cousin and love interest. The nickname Serena had been given by the British writer John Toland to Sophia Charlotte, the first queen of Prussia, in his *Letters to Serena* (1704).

virtues, and of incorrupt nature. From the grove where I sing, avaunt, ye who languid trill in praise of simpering Venus, or revelling roar to bloated Bacchus;[8] in the squalid cellars of the licentious town, hold your brutal orgies. It is to you, ye well principled fair, I consecrate my lays; to you, who superior to a delusory education, would blush to unhallow virtue's name, giving it to ostentation or inane politeness: To you also I devote my lays, ye youths enamoured with wisdom's permanent charms; but chiefly thee have I in view beloved Serena, excellent maid! unknown ornament of thy sex, of human nature, to angels more known than to low-thoughted man. May the hymeneal union be the rich recompence of my pious song; else, fame, spurn me from thy wings.

Now from the eastern hills advanced, serene the gladsome morn, which, from Haran, where in Nahor's house he had dwelt a year with the affectionate Milca,[9] was to bring back lovely Isaac, the son of the promise; with expanded wings it skimmed lucid over the plains along which lay Isaac's way: Abraham was already risen, and with smiling looks fixed on the eastern hills, he often fancied that through the impurpled glimmer he discerned the long-necked camels, and his paternal heart rejoiced in the deception of his eyes. Now, at the call of morning, and a holy impulse excited in him by the approach of God, he went up to a grove of ceders which crowned the summit of an adjacent hill; here he had erected an altar for more solemn worship: here with pure hands he burned to the Lord myrrh and cassia; his orisons ascended with the grateful odours, and more grateful and higher their ascent, through all the heavens, even to the empyreal throne: Eternal goodness! thus spoke the patriarch's heart and awed countenance, though silent his lips, thou who didst make choice of Abraham to declare thine infinite power to his kindred, author of that blessing which now rests on Isaac, thy best gift, the heir of thy promise, be thy servant permitted to praise thee, prostrate in the dust: Grant that we, whom on earth thou deignest to favour with a sight of thee, may perform all thy will, even as the celestial essences perform it; for thine awful word governs seraphs and cherubs. O may Isaac walk with thee! O thou father of angels and men, indulge the affectionate supplication of a father's solicitous heart! O grant me to see the dear youth endued with heavenly sanctity, and worthy that the world's Saviour should arise from his offspring! O may this day, so serene and fair, restore him to thy suppliant! Thus prayed he with visage fixed on the ground.

And now a sudden effulgence diffuses itself over the hill, and with increasing radiancy, like a cloud of light, moved through the azure

---

8. Or Dionysus, the Greek god of wine. Venus was the Roman goddess of love.
9. Abraham's brother and sister-in-law.

sky: Abraham lifted up his eyes, felt the presence of the Deity; an angel, by God's intuitive command, descended invisible, to strengthen the patriarch's eyes: At one look, for only of one is the human soul capable, he saw the divine glory through inconceivable ranks of adoring angels, between them Jehovah inthroned on cherubs; celestial scene, which verbal description would obscure! Under the divine aspect the son of earth sunk down trembling, but not without delight, pervades his whole frame, and he worshipped, falling on his face. Never had the Deity shewed himself to him with such pomp of majesty: Strange anxieties stir within his breast, but, strengthened by the ambrosial light, he again raised himself; when, from the deep silence of shaken heaven, issued Jehovah's tremendous voice: Abraham, take Isaac thine only son, with him go into the land of Moriah, and there on a mountain, which I shall shew thee, sacrifice him to me.

Abraham again fell on his face, and without communication of strength from the divine glory, lifeless had he fallen, struck with the thunder of the severe command; yet pierced it to the marrow of his bones: Sharp as the pangs were which rent his heart, he received the stroke submissively, not a single thought rose in opposition to the divine word; he worshipped, weeping in the dust, stretched out before the Lord, and his determined soul was now filled with more profound veneration and resigned obedience. The omniscient eye of God, to which futurity is present, and man's most hidden thoughts lie open, saw into Abraham's heart, saw the resigned obedience in which his soul with silent composure acquiesced; he saw also the act and triumph of devoted faith, and tacitly blessing his servant returned to heaven. In solemn silence cherubim and seraphim attended his way, and the æthereal effulgence mingled with the golden morn.

Now the patriarch rose to come down from the sacred hill: West of his mansion stood a grove of lofty oaks, forming a crescent around the peaceful cot; never had noon entered within its covert; and when the sun shot its hottest beams through the sultry atmosphere, here twilight breathed the refreshing cool; fit place for secret intercourse, or inviting to mediation! Hither Abraham withdrew, labouring under terrific sensations; scarce more terrific sensations agitated Adam's fond heart, when expelled from paradise with his weeping Eve, her tears brightning her charms, he saw behind him the happy fields, flowery vales, and trees with golden fruit; the festal bower, once gay witness of their connubial endearments, now withering; yet with mute sorrow he eyed it whilst in sight, then turned his dejected looks towards his future abode, which lay before him dreary; desolate, and dark; sad image of his changed life! Thus lonely, and oppressed with thought, Abraham retired amidst the solemn oaks; but soon his conflicted mind powerfully shook off the load of gloomy thoughts, and his sensations, gradually cleared from perplexity, thus severally rented themselves.

When the Infinite speaks, when he who makes the earth his foot-stool enjoins, when God deigns to talk with angels or men, reverential silence and immediate obedience becomes them. He, source of wisdom, planner of sacred destiny, alone knows the divine decrees; what is proper for him to do is well known to him; but the knowledge of cherubs it passeth; with him the heavenly host, were he to annihilate them with a blast of that breath which gave them being, could not contend. Angels expiring with their last sentiments must praise Jehovah the Lord of power, should it be his pleasure to silence their hymning voices by irretrievable death; and shall not I, of a nature so much more subject to death, so much beneath the angels, bow submissive to his behest? But forgive, O Lord, that a father's sighs break in on my resigned silence! O my Creator and Father, be not angry, that powerful nature still conflicts with thy will! O permit me to bestow a few tears on a son, so deserving a son! not so many tears as when in my arms, elate with joy, I first received the smiling babe. Thou knowest, as to thee all spirits are known, with what inward fervour I thanked thy loving-kindness for that best gift; thou sawest the devout complacency I felt at the virtuous turn of his young soul, and my sedulity in the cultivation of it; how amiable he grew, confirming the hopes from thyself derived; O the exalted hopes, which now are utterly vanished! But my fondness launches out into presumption. I obey, and with cheerful resignation adore thine unsearchable command. O strengthen me, strengthen me, Father, that not a single movement of my heart may rise up against the divine disposal! thy will be done.

Thus cried he with raised eyes, and restrained the suffusing tears. From an argent cloud, Elhanan,[1] a celestial essence, Isaac's angel, saw in the patriarch's placid aspect his pious resignation, and in his eyes, directed towards heaven, adoring homage, veneration unfeigned; though a gentle grief had bereft his eyes and lips of their smiles: that scene drew tears even from the angel[.] * * *

* * *

Canto III

* * *

With the travellers Elhanan winged his way, invisible, as the appointed witness of this singular transaction, and attentively observed the patriarch's looks.

Thou, under whose auspices I have attempted the pious song, O sacred muse, to whom the thoughts of men and angels are revealed, who hearest the softest stirrings within the concealing breast, incline

---

1. The name Wieland gives the guardian angel of Isaac, a figure of his own invention.

thy ear to me! propitious impart what Elhanan read in Abraham's visage, what his sensations, what thoughts agitated his soul, when in abstractive pensiveness, he regarded neither the chearing progress of the sunny day, the varying richness of the extensive prospects, nor even his beloved Isaac, who in rapturous hymns adored the creator of all he saw.

I am then a going to thee, thou land of vision; it is to Moriah I am thus hastening, and to distain it with the innocent blood of my only son, and by this hand he is to bleed! Ye hills, and ye surmounting ceders, an only and beloved son shall ye see fall under a father's hands. Such is Shaddai's command. He has selected him for a sacrifice! Will then the dear child's harmless blood delight him! Oh my withered glory! Sad extinction of such heavenly hopes! Alas! sweet lamb, thou singest blyth, thou knowest not thy fate. Thy blooming face still smiles like this valley; still in thee circulate the springs of life, like flowing breaks, like streams in the garden of the Lord. But how soon is all this to pass away! Soon will thy beautiful face be disfigured by the agonies of death, thy body lie shivering, pale, and bloody. Methinks the dreadful spot is before me; my dear Isaac bleeds; I see the last throb of his convulsed breast. Oh his languid eyes still show affectionate resignation! on thou fairest flower! Nature appalled, is every-where silent. Moriah, thou quakest under me; Zion, the deed affrights thee, to more pleasing sights accustomed; for amidst thine umbrageous cedars Noah oft poured forth his fervent oraisons, oft have Deborah's hymns consecrated thy summits; and thy rosy Sharon[2] is the cheerful resort of the neighbouring youth. But now the lugubrious moans of death will be heard, and the blood of an only son shed by his own father will defile thy sides. Ah how my blood chills! how my heart recoils! Silence, nature. My will is dedicated to God. Withold me not from swift obedience to his command. A dark veil indeed is drawn over my fate; a thicker gloom encompasses me, than when, in obscure imagery, terrified I saw the remote transactions of my progeny; when in the night the terrors of the Lord came on me, and he uttered his voice in thunder. Lord, unfathomable art thou in thy judgments! lofty and dark are thy ways! a sacred obscurity, to human eye impervious, covers thy decrees. But oh! a beam suddenly breaks in on my distressed soul, and disperses the gloom. Is it illusion! or is the thought which now rises in me from God! is it not to threw a light on my dark destiny? Why, visit totally unexpected, comes my first son, by unhappy Hagar,[3] on the very day when God demands Isaac of me! By what mazy ways has the Lord

2. A coastal plain along the Mediterranean Sea. In Bodmer's *Noah*, Deborah was the wife of Noah's son, Shem. She sings praises to God on being delivered safely from the flood and shown a vision of the coming Christ.
3. The mother of Abraham's son Ishmael. Hagar was Sarah's handmaid and bore Abraham's child when it seemed Sarah would be unable to produce an heir.

242 CHRISTOPH MARTIN WIELAND

brought him hither, as for some mysterious view! Can it be Nabajoth[4]
to whom the promise is assigned! Was it only to try my faith, that for
a few years he bestowed on me such a child as Isaac, in every excellence so complete! Is it in Ishmael's seed that the nations are to be
blessed! God of my fathers, thy will be done. Welcome, thou blessed
of the Lord; as he is pleased to take Isaac to himself, thou shalt be
my Isaac. Yet this may be but a vain imagination. Forgive, O Lord,
forgive the presumptuous conjecture which approaches thy secret;
trembling it recedes. Let not man with bold enquiry profane thy
counsels! there let cherubs veil! Whatever be the divine decree, the
promise thou didst deign to give me standeth sure. The heavens
may pass away, but the word of the Lord abideth. Sooner shall the
ashes of my son's consumed corse, impregnated by thy breath, bring
forth a youth; sooner shall the animated stones become men, than
the word of thy glorious promise fail.

Such were the patriarch's thoughts; and now he turned his pitying
looks to Isaac, who answering them with a smile, said: Father, the
country now before us brings to my mind a beautiful spot, where Ribkah taught me a hymn; if you please, you shall hear it. This fine
weather and pleasant country, with the singing of the birds, reminds
me of many delightful hours I passed in the fields, with that beautiful damsel, and my dear Abiasaph.

Abraham smiled assent; and thus the pleased youth began.

Joy, delight of God and man, associate of innocence, from yonder sunny hill, or from this flowery vale, where enamoured spring
embraces thee, come and aid my song; quit the field of lillies and the
spicy grove. Who is this issuing from the spicy grove, fair as the
silver moon, stately as the cedar? Is she a seraph, one of the celestial
youth, of fresh creation? Her eye gently darts love into the charmed
breast! She can be no other than a seraph! Or is thy name Joy? O
happy, beyond all words happy they who bask in thy beams! Yes, it is
she; at my request she comes. See how ambrosial flowers shoot thick
up under her steps, and with fragrance and varied lustre announce
her coming oh. Hail, sister of the spring! the smiling hours with rosy
chaplets attend thee, all beautiful, and of the same birth all! O Joy,
spread thy enrapturing wings, and bear me to the empyreal regions!
I lose sight of terrestrial scenes. O Creator, elevated by sacred joy, I
approach thy throne, to sing thy praise. Nature joins in my hymns to
thee, from the waving grove melody ascends, and to thee the odor-
ous vales breathe incense. Second my song, ye offspring of creation,
chaunt Almighty Love, the source of our being. Ye seraphs, ye hosts
of heaven, resound his praise; and ye limpid streams, which mean-
dering wind along roseate margins, warble his praise through all

4. Ishmael's son; Abraham's grandson.

your course, carry it to the mighty waves; let every thing that lives in air, sea, and land, praise the Lord, and rejoice in his goodness.

Thus sang he; and to the lay succeeded discourse of high concernment, shortening the way. Two days and nights had passed, and the third morning was now advancing from the chambers of the east, when the divine Abraham, lifting up his eyes, in the grey distance perceived a mountain supereminent in height; this was Moriah. The patriarch knew the country. The preceding night he had a vision of celestial essence, saying to him: In token of the hill where God requires thy sacrifice, a dove shall meet thee from Sharon; follow it till thou seest it alight on one of the hills; there is Isaac to be offered. The shining guide now appears in view, its flight directed towards them. The youth first descried it, and rejoiced, immediately concluding it to be of the breed of that auspicious dove, which, as antient song records, met Shem at Sion.[5] The patriarch saw it, and the sight pierced his heart; but, as enjoined, he followed it towards Moriah. The patriarch halting at the foot of the hill, ordered his servants there to wait his return. Then laying the wood for the burnt-offering on Isaac's shoulders, and taking the knife and fire, he ascended the hill, his son alone accompanying him, and the dove leading the way. The youth's heart dilates with heavenly ideas, a silent awe impresses him, a devout blush overspreads his fixed countenance, as if under a sense of the near approach of God.

Having reached the summit, he said to Abraham: Father, we are on the mount where God has appointed the sacrifice, yonder I see the dove alighted; but where is the lamb we are to offer?

These innocent words were another poiniard in the father's heart; and, with looks of sore conflict, he thus answered: The God Shaddai,[6] my dear, will provide a lamb. Here grief stopped his speech. The youth also forbore farther enquiry; both silent ascend the long acclivity of the sacred hill; to this summit of it latter ages have given the name of Golgotha.[7] Here, thou Messiah; incarnate God, be astonished ye heavens, and humble thyself, O earth! didst bleed for mankind. Both having reverentially prostrated themselves, Abraham raised an alter of the verdant sod, and having placed the wood on it, thus spoke to his wondering son.

Now, son, hear what lamb God hath chosen: tremble not, my dear—Jehovah[8] has ordered, and he is Lord over all, he has ordered me, to sacrifice—thee—thee—to him—thee, mine only son, by thy

5. In Bodmer's *Noah*, Shem, the son of Noah, encounters the dove sent forth from the ark at Mount Sion. He is told that the dove signifies the Holy Spirit.
6. The name by which God reveals himself to Abraham in Genesis 17:1, typically translated as "Almighty."
7. The mount on which Jesus would be crucified, making Isaac's sacrifice a type of Jesus'.
8. English rendering of the Hebrew name for the God of Israel.

mother—there is no gainsaying his command, though with a bleeding heart I execute it.—God gave thee to me; to him thou belongst, he now takes thee away—but it is for thy happiness.—Weep not, my child; rather rejoice that the most High chases thy blood preferable to that of the lambs in the vale, to be a type of the Redeemer. Look up, behold the gates of heaven open to receive thee; seraphs wreath chaplets for thee; there shalt thou see God, and live. This thou didst ardently wish; and in much greater glory shalt thou see him, that mortal eye can bear, even face to face! Surely such hopes, so superior to whatever the earth displays, should suppress all tears.— With becoming willingness resign thy life to the Creator—he removes thee to one infinitely better, to the state of his elect.

Whilst Abraham was thus speaking, the youth, with child-like warmth, threw his arms about him, and a few tears dropped on his father's pallid cheeks, as stooping he held him in his embraces. This sight affected Elhanan, his emotions dimmed his celestial mein. As a soft damsel, on a visit to a favourite companion, a thousand pleasing ideas dancing in her gay imagination, with step alert enters the room, when, instead of being met with open arms, she sees the worthy object of her tenderness languishing under sickness, and faintly hold out to her a withered hand, at once the sympathizing maid stands bereft of every charm, deadened is the sparkle of her eye, the bloom of her cheek suddenly fades; nor less was the seraph's beauty overcast. And now he hears Isaac thus sedately address the admonishing patriarch: The tears, my father, which thou sawest me shed, are not involuntary tears; and much less proceed they from fear. The eye shews the heart: view me, and be that the token of my obedience. I did, indeed, hope for a longer life on this earth, to be the support and joy of your declining years, and to sooth the last hours of the best of mothers. Hopes of great delight presented themselves to me, so that, at the very thought of them, tears have burst forth— yet willingly, O father, forego I every joy for that which God has appointed for me: but my mother—that thought harrows my soul—I weep for her—how will her tenderness bear my unexpected death? O divine Messiah, through whom my blood will be a grateful offering to the Deity, strengthen her; assuage her distress with heavenly solacements. I trust he will comfort her, and you also, my father. And now away all sorrow, tears, and sighs; no earthly regret swells my heart; it is devoted to God. Here I am father; the offering is willing to bleed; do unto me as God has ordered—O elevating thought! O thought of sweetness inexpressible! to behold the Deity, to contemplate him, in adoring prostrations before his throne, and live! What a tranquility dost thou impart! My soul is now all light and triumph!—No hopes, no lamenting friends, nor dearest Ribkah, nor thy tears or wringing hands, thou best of mothers, could disturb this heavenly calm, could draw from me one wish of continuing in an earthly life, the least inclination to turn my back on those glorious views opening before me. Father and mother, relations and associates, lament not for me; or if natural love forces your tears for my untimely death, rejoice also at my felicity.

The raptured seraph, at these words, recovered all his native beauty, and moved forward in wide effulgence, preparing to receive the dislodged soul, and convey it to that bliss, the sure expectation of which sustained it in this trial, to nature so big with terror. Abraham once more kissed Isaac, dropping only one tear on his blooming cheek, which no tear of his now wetted; yet hove their convulsed hearts with sensations, by few felt, and by these not to be described.

Isaac now composedly placed himself on the wood, as a nearer approach to the fruition of his hopes. Abraham, with worshipping eye, thus addressed his God: Lord, I am now ready; my heart has girded itself with iron; it sighs no more; reluctant nature is silent; behold, every faculty, passion, and power in me, are all obedience to thy sacred will. I give up thy best gift; the comfort, the delight of my life, the stay of my sanctity, I lay at thy feet; with my own hand I sacrifice my all to thee! O splendid ideas! let my mind have one fleeting libation of your delights, irradiate it with one momentary ray, before ye leave me for ever. For ever; for soon, instead of that joy which in the morning gladdened my waking mind, and often mingled with my nightly dreams, my portion will be settled affliction. Soon will Mamre, where, my dear Isaac, thy sweet voice so often charmed me, soon will its oaks, where the Messiah himself promised thy birth, instead of hymns hear only lamentations; for all who knew thee will bewail thee. How was my heart moved within me, at thy endearing accents when thou called me father! but that sweet sound never more shall I hear—I shall no more hear Isaac's sweet voice. Thou, O God, gavest him to me, and even now seest how I delighted in him. Very gracious art thou to man, and in a happy hour on the tables of destiny has thou written his life: The angels rejoiced at his nativity, and mortals to their offspring wish the fate of him, who sees his son growing up in every virtue. But, O Creator, Isaac has thou eminently distinguished; so refined a soul! Such superior faculties! Such heavenly temper! Such piety! such early wisdom! and this peerless youth was mine; I brought him up; he called me father. Behold him and all his virtues crowned in this resignation—by my hand is he to die; but, O sovereign Creator, I complain not—shall I dare to complain of thee?—rather thanksgivings become my lips! Yes, my soul, O bounteous God, shall thank thee for such a child, and his life so long preferred! Blessed be thou, Father of mercies, for each day of his precious life, for every rupture, when in him, with anticipating ideas, I saw the future Redeemer, the Saviour of my fallen progeny. O

Creator, these praises I offer for thy goodness; and do thou propitious accept the sacrifice from my obedient hand.

Thus spake the magnanimous patriarch, and, turning his eyes on his resigned son, took up the sacrificial knife.

Now the eternal Father looked down on earth, and seeing the probatory sacrifice so near execution, he said to the angels, who watch around the sanctuary: Abraham has stood the severe trial; in obedience to me, he would not have spared his own son. Behold him ready with the sacrificing instruments. Whom among you shall I send, to with-hold his arm, and carry him a renewal of my benediction.

Eloah stepping forth, prostrated himself at the throne: be it me.[9] Jehovah, my heart overflows with joy, that thou restores the son to the father; and his obedience thus richly recompenses! O with what ecstatic amazement will he listen to the glad tidings! O, thou Creator of all things, since man came from thy forming hands; since I saw the first human pair tread thy paradise in the beauty of the divine image, never has such a benevolent joy for man so warmed my heart. O permit me to shoot to the earth, and to thy tried servant announce the word of life, which stands manifest in thy benign aspect.

He spake: and in the Deity's visage reading his purport, the seraph instantly, with flight a thousand times swifter than the whirl of the extreme spheres round the heaven of heavens, swift as the thoughts of cherubs, darted towards the earth. He had reached it, when Abraham stood as intranced, in a posture for slaying his son, who bowed on the altar. Time to seraphs is not as to us; the interval which to man slides away unperceived, they fill up with grand achievements. Such was the seraph's instantaneous descent. Over the patriarch stood God's resplendent messenger, whose celestial effulgence diffused an ample glory round him; and now from the irradiated air he called:

Abraham, Abraham! The patriarch raised his head, and seeing the heavenly form, started, and from his trembling hand dropped the knife: but soon Eloah's benign looks removed the tumultuous impressions of his majesty, and inspired elevating hopes: for Abraham having prostrated himself in religious awe, Eloah thus called to him: Rise, thou blessed of the Lord, never didst thou from heaven receive a more welcome message: God has tried thine obedience, and thou has proved it sincere: in submission to his command, thou wouldst not have spared a beloved son; of this thy devotedness to the divine will, that son is now the reward, embrace him. Isaac, arise; come from the altar, and embrace thy father: praise God in effusions of joy, of love.

The patriarch, rising, with extended arms, and streaming eyes, heavenwards, wept gratitude and transport; his emotions precluded

---

9. "Eloah" in Hebrew translates to "god," in this case a high-ranking angel sent to preserve Issac's life.

speech; his paternal heart was too narrow for the impetuous flush; yet shone his countenance with heavenly joys. As a martyr, stedfast to sacred truth, lingers under tortures, the relief of immediate death being denied, till at length his vital powers exhausted, his languorous eyes close in the final sleep, and the disencumbered soul at once sees itself released, at once, amidst the gratulatory peans of exulting angels, that inebriated with the blissful change, with the commencement of beatitude, she speechless sinks on the bosom of the raptured seraph who attended her on earth. Little less transported was the affectionate father, when beyond all his hopes, and with such august circumstances, and, as it were, from the shadow of death, his dear Isaac was restored to him. With redoubled fondness he embraces the youth, who, lost in beholding the angel, observed not his father; exalted ideas dilate his raptured soul, and kneeling respectful, yet with steady eye, he viewed the radiant essence; the beautiful Elhanan he also saw hanging over him with looks of applause; soon he becomes sensible of his father's fondness, and, as conscious of breach of duty, delayed not the most impassioned returns, falls at his feet, rises, and throwing his arms about him, kisses away the tears from the patriarch's venerable cheeks; then his ecstacy gradually subsiding, thus vented itself: Oh, father, from what ecstacy am I again fallen to earth! a change scarce supportable, did it not restore me to the embraces and heavenly discourse of parents whom I can never sufficiently honour? Already on angels wings I was soaring in the regions of light, in near approach to the Deity. This angel, so glorious, who has notified the Lord's gracious pleasure concerning us, is but one of the innumerable choirs, in whose blessed society I was entering on an endless eternity. As I lay on the altar, at the first gleam, which indicated the seraph's approach, O father, I rejoiced in assured hope, that the celestial spirits were come to conduct my soul to their residence; on his nearer approach, I imagined even to hear the sound of that chariot in which our pious forefather Enoch[1] was taken up to heaven. My heart, I can attest it, leaped for joy: But my heart deceived me, and God has determined otherwise. I see myself again in the flesh; yet, which greatly alleviates my concern, in thy embraces. Being yet not ripe for heaven, I must remain in this preparatory life, with constant devotion and piety, the better to be fitted for that of suturity. Hail, my much honoured father, to whom I am thus miraculously restored! thou earth also, hail! willingly from heaven do I return to thee, as the God of heaven has ordained: In all things concerning me, his sacred will be done.

Thus spoke the youth, now wholly intent on his father, who thus addressed Eloah: Divine messenger, thou highest among Jehovah's

---

1. In Genesis 5:24, God takes Enoch to heaven to spare him death.

ministers! not sweeter sound the harps of angels, preludes of bliss, to the expiring just, than thy tidings to me! Oh, it darts new spirit through my whole frame! never did I feel the life of the soul in such power! never did my inward parts dissolve in such melting raptures! O God Shaddai, how shall I thank thy loving kindness! Can dust thank the Sovereign of the cherubs! What can I; but to my kindred and strangers, unwearied, make known thy mighty acts! Thy judgments are a great deep; let the silence of an affected heart praise thee; unutterable are thy glories; rich art thou in mercies. O Jehovah, mighty and gracious has thou shewn thyself to the children of Adam! the proud thou strikes down to the dust, and the humble thou crownest with praise and honour. Thou makest the afflicted to shout for joy; thou settest the captive free. Thou makes the aged a mother of children; thou restores that which was lost! I am now a second time a father; and sweeter is the name to my ears, than when Isaac first lisped it. O blessed day! of all others thou shalt be to me the chief festival. No such happiness did thy morning promise me; thou art the first of that happy life of my renewed youth, which this divine event presages. O golden day, sanctified be thou above all days; be every anniversary of thee signalized by some beneficent wonder; may smiling hours usher thee in; may the sun heighten thy lustre with its brightest rays. On thee may a happy mother, before mourning her sterility, bring forth two comely boys, whose virile years shall increase her joy by valorous deeds! on thee may the adventrous hero bring back the outrageous enemy's spoils: To the youth deliver the bride undefil'd; to fathers, sons. On thee may the voice of joy ring throughout the festive earth. Hail also Moriah! where God has so wonderfully shewn his mercy to me! Stand thou a perpetual monument of his goodness; from thee may the exuberance of God, like dew, descend on blooming Sharon; in remotest futurity shall angels resort under thy umbrageous cedars, and sometimes the divine presence hover over thee, as brooded the creative spirit over the primeval chaos.

Abraham, having thou spoken, gazing around the awful spot, perceived a young ram with his horns entangled in a bush. Pleased that he should not depart without an act of formal worship, he hastens, and drags the reluctant creature to the altar. Whilst with the smoke of the burnt-offering, ascended the sacrificer's grateful praises, Elhanan, with reverential affection, thus bespoke the sublime Eloah:

Divine seraph, how I venerate thy benevolence to man, for his sake to come down from before the throne! Never, no not when thou wait among the angelic choir, have I seen thy face beam a more graceful smile, than at these affectionate embraces of such a son and father. That they are not unworthy of thy regard, is well known to thee. Intuition is thy superior endowment; a look makes known to thee more than a succession of time gradually unfolds to me. Am I not happy in being Isaac's guardian! how beautiful is human virtue in such a form; how amiable the serenity of innocence! My love of the youth deceives me, or Eloah has in charge fresh blessings for him, which will be fresh joys to me.

Eloah thus answered: Kindly seraph, what thou hopest the wing of time is already bringing on Isaac, so has the Lord written in the books of fate, shall to his descendants be the model of human happiness. Hadst not thou seen in Haran's plains a damsel comparatively to others as a rose among the thorns; and well-principled as beautiful, of softest manners and elevated faculties: This peerless damsel is destined for thy ward; then behold the felicity of connubial love, founded on harmony of virtuous sentiments, complacent, decent, and permanent. Thus shall they form each other's joy. Farther, Jehovah himself will visit his dwelling; and the youth of heaven delight in those mansions where the praises of the Lord resound from pure lips.

Thus held the blessed spirits discourse; and when the fume of the consumed victim ceased to ascend, Eloah, with auspicious voice, again called to Abraham:

Abraham, hear the word of the Lord: Thus, saith Jehovah, who in his right hand holdeth the heavens, and in his left the worlds which move by his breath: By myself I swear to thee, thy sanctity being so pleasing in my sight, so pure from the common ways of men, and so unreserved thy obedience, that, at my command, thou wouldst have slain thy beloved son: behold thy race shall be great and honourable before me, above all the generations of the earth; innumerable as the stars of the heavens, or the sands of the sea, it shall possess the gates of its enemies; it shall be called the chosen of the Lord. Yes, from thy seed shall salvation be derived to all the nations of the earth. Thus declares the God of destiny, whose promise stands immoveable as the mountain of the Lord. But can I hide from Abraham the good which my sovereign has appointed for him: No, I will impart to him what I have seen of futurity. Observe then, thou blessed of Jehovah, his wonderful dealings towards thee. Seven times was I permitted to look into God's sanctuary; there on adamantine columns hang the golden tables of divine decrees; and among many other events I read, that out of thy posterity shall arise a King, surpassing all the monarchs of the cast in wisdom and magnificence; he on this mount shall erect a stately temple to Jehovah; in it the glory of God shall reside, visible to man, till the Messiah come; then shall all types be done away. On this consecrated mount, where God had ordered thee to sacrifice Isaac, the Mediator shall give himself as a piacular oblation[2] for lapsed Adam's race; here shall the earth drink in his redeeming blood. Then rent shall be the veil which separateth God from men;

---

2. A sacrificial offering.

then the whole earth becomes no less consecrated than this hill; God is reconciled to all; alike present to all; and all worshiping him in spirit and truth will he hear. Behold this is the branch from thy root, the present hope of the righteous, and in whom all the ends of the earth will one day bless themselves: through him whom, from the foundation of the world, Jehovah chose as restorer of the earth, through him the Messiah shall the earth be renewed in its primeval beauty: truth and peace shall descend from heaven; the desert shall blossom as the rose; to the Sandy waste shall be given the glory of Lebanon, and the excellency of luxurious Sharon streams of honey shall he burst from the rock, and salient springs refresh the parched wilderness. To Sion God's elect shall resort in jubilant troops; with endless joy and divine triumph shall they be filled; the voice of grief and pain shall no more be heard. Then rejoice, ye heavens, and leap for joy, thou earth; shine forth, pre-eminent above other stars, for the Lord Jehovah is thy redeemer. What I have now imparted to thee, Abraham, these eyes saw in the books of irreversible futurity. Hail favourite of heaven! hail respectable ancestor of the Messiah! of man's salvation incarnate! thine are the promises of God; thou dwellest under the shadow of the most High: angels cannot wish thee more.

The patriarch prostrate, melting with reverence and joy, heard Eloah's prophetic relation: close to him lay Isaac, rejoicing in his father's honour, and the redemption of his descendants. Now Eloah raised himself heaven-wards; on spreading his resplendent plumage, an air of fragrance filled the whole air. Already has he passed the sun: Elhanan followed with rapid joy, and at every star on which his effulgence beamed, the expanse rang with the melody of congratulating angels.

Whilst the patriarch remained, with his son, on Moriah, an ambrosial gale, effect of the celestial appearance, rustled among the leaves: Of God's unsearchable ways, of his greatness, which passeth all knowledge, of his superabundant goodness, and of their homage and duties, they converted. Then hastening down the mountain, they returned to their attendants, whom also the enlivening odours, emaning from the celestial essence, had filled with new joys; all, elate in spirit, let out on their return to Mamre, and the way seemed to vanish under their feet.

THE END OF CANTO III

＊　＊　＊

WILLIAM GODWIN

From Enquiry Concerning Political Justice[†]

Book IV

CHAP. VI. OF SINCERITY.

*In favourable tendencies in respect to—innocence—energy—
Intellectual improvement—and philanthropy. History—and effects
of insincerity.—Sincerity delineated.—Character of its adherents.*

It was farther proposed to consider the value of truth, in a practical
view, as it relates to the incidents and commerce of ordinary life,
under which form it is known by the denomination of sincerity.

The powerful recommendations attendant upon sincerity are obvious. It is intimately connected with the general dissemination of
innocence, energy, intellectual improvement and philanthropy.

Did every man impose this law upon himself, did he regard himself as not authorised to conceal any part of his character and conduct, this circumstance alone would prevent millions of actions from
being perpetrated, in which we are now induced to engage by the
prospect of secrecy and impunity. We have only to suppose men
obliged to consider, before they determined upon an equivocal
action, whether they chose to be their own historians, the future
narrators of the scene in which they were acting a part, and the most
ordinary imagination will instantly suggest how essential a variation
would be introduced into human affairs. It has been justly observed
that the popish practice of auricular confession is attended with
some salutary effects. How much better would it be, if instead of an
institution thus equivocal, and which has been made so dangerous
an instrument of ecclesiastical despotism, every man were to make
the world his confessional, and the human species the keeper of his
conscience?

There is a farther benefit that would result to me from the habit
of telling every man the truth, regardless of the dictates of worldly
prudence and custom. I should acquire a clear, ingenuous and
unembarrassed air. According to the established mode, of society,
whenever I have a circumstance to state, which would require some
effort of mind and discrimination to enable me to do it justice and
state it with the proper effect, I fly from the task, and take refuge in
silence or equivocation. But the principle which forbad me concealment, would keep my mind for ever awake and for ever warm. I

[†] From William Godwin, *Enquiry Concerning Political Justice, and Its Influence on Morals and Happiness* (Philadelphia: Bioren and Madan, 1796), pp. 261–83. The Philadelphia edition was based on the second London edition, corrected.

should always be obliged to exert my attention, left, in pretending to tell the truth, I should tell it in so imperfect and mangled a way as to produce the effect of falshood. If I spoke to a man of my own faults or those of his neighbour, I should be anxious not to suffer them to come distorted or exaggerated to his mind, or to permit what at first was fact, to degenerate into satire. If I spoke to him of the errors he had himself committed I should carefully avoid those inconsiderate expressions which might convert what was in itself beneficent into offence; and my thoughts would be full of that kindness and generous concern for his welfare, which such a talk necessarily brings along with it. Sincerity would liberalise my mind, and make the eulogiums I had occasion to pronounce, clear, copious, and appropriate. Conversation would speedily exchange its present character of listlessness and insignificance for a Roman boldness and fervour; and, accustomed, at first by the fortuitous operation of circumstances, to tell men of things it was useful for them to know, I should speedily learn to study their advantage, and never rest satisfied with my conduct, till I found how to spend the hours I was in their company, in the way which was most rational and improving.

The effects of sincerity upon others would be similar to its effects upon him that practised it. How great would be the benefit, if every man were sure of meeting in his neighbour the ingenuous censor, who would tell him in person, and publish to the world, his virtues, his good deeds, his meanesses and his follies? We have never a strong feeling of these in our own case, except so far as they are confirmed to us by the suffrage of our neighbours. Knowledge, such as we are able to acquire it, depends in a majority of instances, not upon the single efforts of the individual, but upon the consent of other human understandings sanctioning the judgment of our own. It is the uncertainty of which every man is conscious as to his solitary judgment, that produces for the most part zeal for proselytism, and impatience of contradiction. It is impossible I should have a true satisfaction in my dispositions and talents, or even any precise perceptions of virtue and vice, unless assisted by the concurrence of my fellows.

An impartial distribution of commendation and blame to the actions of men, would be the most operative incentive to virtue. But this distribution at present scarcely in any instance exists. One man is satirised with bitterness, and the misconduct of another treated with inordinate lenity. In speaking of our neighbours we are perpetually under the influence of sinister and unacknowledged motives. Every thing is disfigured and distorted. The basest hypocrite goes through the world with applause; and the purest character is loaded with unmerited aspersions. The benefactors of mankind are frequently the object of their bitterest hatred, and most unrelenting ingratitude. What encouragement then is afforded to virtue? Those who are smitten with the love of distinction, will rather seek it in external splendour and unmeaning luxury, than in moral attainments. While those who are led to benevolent pursuits by the purest motives, yet languish under the privation of that honour and esteem, which would give new energy to rectitude, and ardour to benevolence.

A genuine and unalterable sincerity would not fail to reverse the scene. Every idle or malignant tale now produces its effect, because men are unaccustomed to exercise their judgment upon the probabilities of human action, or to possess the materials of judgment. But then the rash assertions of one individual would be corrected by the maturer information of his neighbour. Exercised in discrimination, we should be little likely to be misled. The truth would be known, the whole truth and the unvarnished truth. This would be a trial that the most stubborn obliquity would be found unable to withstand. If a just and impartial character were awarded to all human actions, vice would be universally deserted, and virtue every where practised. Sincerity therefore, once introduced into the manners of mankind, would necessarily bring every other virtue in its train.

Men are now feeble in their temper, because they are not accustomed to hear the truth. They lay their account in being personally treated with artificial delicacy, and expect us to abstain from repeating what we know to their disadvantage. But is this right: It has already appeared that plain dealing, truth spoken with kindness, but spoken with sincerity, is the most wholesome of all disciplines. How then can we be justified in thus subverting the nature of things and the system of the universe, in breeding a set of summer insects, upon which the breeze of sincerity may never blow, and the tempest of misfortune never beat?

In the third place, sincerity is in an eminent degree calculated to conduce to our intellectual improvement. If from timidity of disposition, or the danger that attends a disclosure, we suppress the reflections that occur to us, we shall neither add to, nor correct them. From the act of telling my thoughts I derive encouragement to proceed. Nothing can more powerfully conduce to perspicuity than the very attempt to arrange and express them. If they be received cordially by others, they derive from that circumstance a peculiar firmness and consistency. If they be received with opposition and distrust, I am induced to revise them. I detect their errors; or I strengthen my arguments, and add new truths to those which I had previously accumulated. It is not by the solitary anchorite, who neither speaks, nor hears, nor reads the genuine sentiments of man, that the stock of human good is eminently increased. The period of bold and unrestricted communication, is the period in which the materials of happiness ferment and germinate. What can excite me to the pursuit of

discovery, if I know that I am never to communicate my discoveries?
It is in the nature of things impossible that the man, who has determined never to utter the truths he may be acquainted with, should be
an intrepid and indefatigable thinker. The link which binds together
the inward and the outward man is indissoluble, and he that is not
bold in speech, will never be ardent and unprejudiced in enquiry.

What is it that at this day enables a thousand errors to keep their
station in the world; priestcraft, tests; bribery, war, cabal, and whatever else excites the disapprobation of the honest and enlightened
mind? Cowardice; the timid reserve which makes men shrink from
telling what they know; and the insidious policy that annexes persecution and punishment to an unrestrained and spirited discussion
of the true interests of society. Men either refrain from the publication of unpalatable opinions, because they are unwilling to make a
sacrifice of all their worldly prospects; or they publish them in a frigid
and enigmatical spirit, stripped of their true character and incapable
of their genuine operation. If every man to-day would tell all the truth
he knew, it is impossible to predict how short would be the reign of
usurpation and folly.

Lastly, a still additional benefit attendant on the practice of sincerity, is good humour, kindness and benevolence. At present men meet
together with the temper, less of friends, than enemies. Every man
eyes his neighbour as if he expected to receive from him a secret
wound. Every member of a polished and civilised community goes
armed. He knows many things of his associate which he conceives
himself obliged not to allude to in his hearing, but rather to put on
an air of the profoundest ignorance. In the absence of the person
concerned, he scarcely knows how to mention his defects, however
essential the advertisement may be, lest he should finally incur the
imputation of a calumniator. If he mention them, it is under the seal
of secrecy. He speaks of them with the sentiments of a criminal,
conscious that what he is saying he would be unwilling to utter before
the individual concerned. Perhaps he does not fully advert to this
artificial character in himself; but he at least notes it with infallible
observation in his neighbour. In youth, it may be, he accommodates
himself with a pliant spirit to the manners of the world; and, while
he loses no jot of his gaiety, learns from it no other lessons than those
of selfishness and chearful indifference. Observant of the game that
goes forward around him, he becomes skilful in his turn to elude the
curiosity of others, and smiles inwardly at the false scent he prompts
them to follow. Dead to the liberal emotions of a disinterested sympathy, he can calmly consider men as the mere neutral instruments of
his enjoyments. He can preserve himself in a true equipoise between
love and hatred. But this is a temporary character. The wanton wildness of youth at length subsides, and he is no longer contented to

stand alone in the world. Anxious for the consolations of sympathy and frankness, he remarks the defects of mankind with a different spirit. He is seized with a shuddering at the sensation of their coldness. He can no longer tolerate their subterfuges and disguises. He searches in vain for an ingenious character, and loses patience at the eternal disappointment. The defect that he before regarded with indifference, he now considers as the consummation of the most damning vice. What wonder that under these circumstances moroseness, sourness and misanthropy become the ruling sentiments of so large a portion of mankind?

How exactly would the whole of this be reversed by the practice of sincerity? We could not be indifferent to men whose custom it was to tell us the truth. Hatred would perish from a failure in its principal ingredient.—No man could acquire a distant and unsympathetic temper. Reserve, duplicity and an artful exhibition of ourselves take from the human form its soul, and leave us the unanimated memento of what man might have been; of what he would have been, were not every impulse of the mind thus stunted and destroyed. If our emotions were not checked, we should be truly friends with each other. Our character would expand: the luxury of indulging our feelings, and the exercise of uttering them, would raise us to the stature of men. I should not conceive alarm from my neighbour, because I should be conscious that I knew his genuine sentiments. I should not harbour bad passions and unsocial propensities, because the habit of expressing my thoughts would enable me to detect and dismiss them in the outset. Thus every man would be inured to the sentiment of love, and would find in his species objects worthy of his affection. Confidence is of all others the surest soil of mutual kindness.

The value of sincerity will be still farther illustrated by a brief consideration of the nature of insincerity. Viewed superficially and at a distance, we are easily reconciled, and are persuaded to have recourse to it upon the most trivial occasions. Did we examine it in detail, and call to mind its genuine history the result could not fail to be different. Its features are neither like virtue, nor compatible with virtue. The sensations it obliges us to undergo are of the most odious nature. Its direct business is to cut off all commerce between the heart and the tongue. There are organs however of the human frame more difficult to be commanded than the mere syllables and sentiments we utter. We must be upon our guard, or our cheeks will be covered with a conscious blush, the aukwardness of our gestures will betray us, and our lips will falter with their unwonted task. Such is the value of the first attempt, not merely of the liar, but of him who practises concealment, or whose object it is to put the change upon the person with whom he happens to converse. After a series of essays we become more expert. We are not, as at first, detected by the person from whom we intended to withhold what we knew; but we fear detection. We feel uncertainty and confusion; and it is with difficulty we convince ourselves that we have escaped unsuspected. Is it thus a man ought to feel? At last perhaps we become consummate in hypocrisy, and feel the same confidence and alacrity in duplicity, that we before felt in entire frankness. Which, to an ordinary eye, would appear the man of virtue; he who by the depth of his hypocrisy contrived to keep his secret wholly unsuspected, or he who was precipitate enough to be thus misled, and to believe that his neighbour made use of words for the purpose of being understood?

But this is not all. It remains for the deceiver in the next place to maintain the delusion he has once imposed, and to take care that no unexpected occurrence shall betray him. It is upon this circumstance that the common observation is founded, "that one lie will always need a hundred others to justify and cover it." We cannot determine to keep any thing secret, without risking to be involved in artifices, quibbles, equivocations and falsehoods without number. The character of the virtuous man seems to be that of a firm and unalterable resolution, confident in his own integrity. But the character that results from insincerity, begins in hesitation, and ends in disgrace. Let us suppose that the imposition I practised is in danger of detection. Of course it will become my wisdom to calculate this danger, and, if it be too imminent, not to think of attempting any farther disguise. But, if the secret be important and the danger problematical, I shall probably persist. The whole extent of the danger can be known only by degrees. Suppose the person who questions me return to the charge, and affirm that he heard the fact, as it really was, but not as I represent it, from another. What am I now to do? Am I to asperse the character of the honest reporter, and at the same time, it may be, instead of establishing the delusion, only astonish my neighbour with my cool and intrepid effrontery?

What has already been adduced may assist us to determine the species of sincerity which virtue prescribes, and which alone can be of great practical benefit to mankind. Sincerity may be considered as of three degrees. First, a man may conceive that he sufficiently preserves his veracity, if he take care never to utter any thing that cannot be explained into a consistency with truth. There is a plain distinction between this man, and him who makes no scruple of uttering the most palpable and direct falsehoods. Or, secondly, it may happen that his delicacy shall not stop here, and he may resolve, not only to utter nothing that is litterally untrue, but also nothing which he knows or believes will be understood by the hearer in a sense that is untrue. This he may consider as amounting for the most part to an adequate discharge of his duty; and he may conceive that there is little mischief in the frequently suppressing information which it was in his power to supply. The third and highest degree of sincerity consists in the most perfect frankness, discards every species of concealment or reserve, and, as Cicero expresses it, "utters nothing that is false, and withholds nothing that is true."

The two first of these by no means answer the genuine purposes of sincerity. The former labours under one disadvantage more than direct falshood. It is of little consequence to the persons with whom I communicate, that I have a subterfuge by which I can to my own mind explain my deceit into a consistency with truth; while at the same time the study of such subterfuges is more adverse to courage and energy, than a conduct which unblushingly avows the laxity of its principles. The second of the degrees enumerated, which merely proposes to itself the avoiding every active deception, seems to be measured less by the standard of magnanimity than of personal prudence. If, as Rousseau has somewhere asserted,[1] "the great duty of man be to do no injury to his neighbour," then this negative sincerity may be of considerable account: but, if it be the highest and most indispensable business of man to study and promote his neighbour's welfare, a virtue of this sort will contribute little to so honourable an undertaking. If sincerity be, as we have endeavoured to demonstrate, the most powerful engine of human improvement, a scheme for restraining it within so narrow limits cannot be entitled to considerable applause. Add to this, that it is impossible in many cases to suppress information without great mastery in the arts of ambiguity and evasion, and such a perfect command of countenance as shall prevent it from being an index to our real sentiments. Indeed the man who is frequently accustomed to seem ignorant of what he really knows, though he will escape the open disgrace of him who is detected in direct falshood or ambiguous imposition, will yet be viewed by his neighbours with coldness and distrust, and esteemed an unfathomable and selfish character.

Hence it appears, that the only species of sincerity which can in any degree prove satisfactory to the enlightened moralist and politician, is that where the frankness is perfect, and every degree of reserve is discarded.

Nor is there any danger that such a character should degenerate into ruggedness and brutality. Sincerity, upon the principles on which it is here recommended, is practised from a consciousness of its utility, and from sentiments of philanthropy. It will communicate frankness to the voice, servour to the gesture, and kindness to the heart. Even in expostulation and censure, friendliness of intention and mildness of proceeding may be eminently conspicious. There should be no mixture of disdain and superiority. The interest of him who is

---

1. *Emile*, liv. ii. [Godwin's note].

258 WILLIAM GODWIN

corrected, not the triumph of the corrector, should be the principle of action. True sincerity will be attended with that equality which is the only sure foundation of love, and that love which gives the best finishing and lustre to a sentiment of equality.

Appendix, No. I.

ILLUSTRATIONS OF SINCERITY.

Question proposed.—Erroneous maxims upon this head refuted.— General principles and theories estimated.—An injurious distinction exposed.—Limitations of sincerity.—Arguments, affirmative and negative.—Inference.—Conclusion.

There is an important enquiry which cannot fail to suggest itself in this place. "Universal sincerity has been shewn to be pregnant with unspeakable advantages. The enlightened friend of the human species cannot fail ardently to desire the time when each man shall speak truth with his neighbour. But what conduct does it behove us to observe in the interval? Are we to practise an unreserved and uniform sincerity, while the world about us acts upon so different a plan? If sincerity should ever become characteristic of the community in which we live, our neighbour will then be prepared to hear the truth, and to make use of the communication in a way that shall be manly, generous and just. But at present we shall be liable to waken the resentment of some, and to subject to a trial beyond its strength the fortitude of others. By a direct and ill-timed truth we may not only incur the forfeiture of our worldly prospects, but of our usefulness, and sometimes of our lives."

Ascetic and puritanical systems of morality have accustomed their votaries to give a short answer to these difficulties, by directing us "to do our duty, without regard to consequences, and uninfluenced by a consideration of what may be the conduct of others." But these maxims will not pass unexamined with the man who considers morality as a subject of reasoning, and places its foundation in a principle of utility. "To do our duty without regard to consequences," is upon this principle a maxim completely absurd and self-contradictory. Morality is nothing else but a calculation of consequences, and an adoption of that mode of conduct which, upon the most comprehensive view, appears to be attended with a balance of general pleasure and happiness. Nor will the other part of the precept above stated appear upon examination to be less erroneous. There are many instances in which the selection of the conduct I should pursue, altogether depends upon a foresight of "what will be the conduct of others." To what purpose contribute my subscription to an object of public utility, a bridge, for example, or a canal, at a time when I cer-

tainly foreknow that the subscription will not be generally countenanced? Shall I go and complete such a portion of masonry upon the
spot as, if all my neighbours would do the same, would effect the
desired purpose, though I am convinced that no one beside myself
will move a finger in the undertaking? There are various regulations
respecting our habits of living, expenditure and attire, which, if generally adopted, would probably be of the highest benefit, which yet,
if acted upon by a single individual, might be productive of nothing
but injury. I cannot pretend to launch a ship or repel an army by
myself, though either of these might be things, absolutely considered, highly proper to be done.

The duty of sincerity is one of those general principles which
reflection and experience have enjoined upon us as conducive to the
happiness of mankind. Let us enquire then into the nature and origin of general principles. Engaged, as men are in perpetual intercourse with their neighbours, and constantly liable to be called upon
without the smallest previous notice, in cases where the interest of
their fellows is deeply involved, it is not possible for them upon all
occasions to deduce through a chain of reasoning the judgment
which should be followed. Hence the necessity of resting places for
the mind, of deductions already stored in the memory, and prepared
for application as circumstances may demand. We find this necessity
equally urgent upon us in matters of science and abstraction, as in
conduct and morals. Theory has also a farther use. It serves as a perpetual exercise and aliment to the understanding, and renders us
competent and vigorous to judge in every situation that can occur.
Nothing can be more idle and shallow than the competition which
some men have set up between theory and practice. It is true that we
can never predict from theory alone the success of any given experiment. It is true that no theory, accurately speaking, can possibly be
practical. It is the business of theory to collect the circumstances of
a certain set of cases, and arrange them. It would cease to be theory,
if it did not leave out many circumstances; it collects such as are
general, and leaves out such as are particular. In practice however
those circumstances inevitably arise, which are necessarily omitted
in the general process; they cause the phenomenon in various ways
to include features which were not in the prediction, and to be diversified in those that were. Yet theory is of the highest use; and those
who decry it may even be proved not to understand themselves. They
do not mean that men should always act in a particular case without
illustration from any other case, for that would be to deprive us of all
understanding. The moment we begin to compare cases and infer, we
begin to theorise; no two things in the universe were ever perfectly
alike. The genuine exercise of man therefore is to theorise, for this
is in other words to sharpen and improve his intellect; but not to

become the slave of theory, or at any time to forget that it is by its very nature precluded from comprehending the whole of what claims our attention.

To apply this to the case of morals. General principles of morality are so far valuable, as they truly delineate the means of utility, pleasure or happiness. But every action of any human being has its appropriate result, and the more closely it is examined, the more truly will that result appear. General rules and theories are not infallible. It would be preposterous to suppose that, in order to judge fairly, and conduct myself properly, I ought only to look at a thing from a certain distance, and not consider it minutely. On the contrary, I ought, as far as lies in my power, to examine every thing upon its own grounds, and decide concerning it upon its own merits. To rest in general rules is sometimes a necessity which our imperfection imposes upon us, and sometimes the refuge of our indolence; but the true dignity of human reason is as much as we are able to go beyond them, to have our faculties in act upon every occasion that occurs, and to conduct ourselves accordingly.

There is an observation necessary to be made, to prevent any erroneous application of these reasonings. In the morality of every action two things are to be considered, the direct, and the remote consequences with which it is attended. There are numerous modes of proceeding which would be productive of immediate pleasure, that would have so ill an effect upon the permanent state of one or many individuals, as to render them in every rational estimate, objects, not of choice, but aversion. This is particularly the case in relation to that view of any action whereby it becomes a medium enabling the spectator to predict the nature of future actions. It is with the conduct of our fellow beings, as with the course of inanimate nature: if events did not succeed each other in a certain order, there could be neither judgment, nor wisdom, nor morality. Confidence in the order of the seasons and the progress of vegetation, encourages us to sow our field in expectation of a future harvest. Confidence in the characters of our fellow men, that they will for the most part be governed by the reason of the case, that they will neither rob, nor defraud, nor deceive us, is not less essential to the existence of civilised society. Hence arises a species of argument in favour of general rules not hitherto mentioned. The remote consequences of an action, especially as they relate to the fulfilling or not fulfilling the expectation excited, depend chiefly on general circumstances, and not upon particulars; belong to the class, and not to the individual. But this makes no essential alteration in what was before delivered. It will still be incumbent on us, when called into action, to estimate the nature of the particular case, that we may ascertain where the urgency of special circumstances is such as to supersede rules that are generally obligatory.

To return to the particular case of sincerity. Sincerity and plain dealing are obviously in the majority of human actions the best policy, if we consider only the interest of the individual, and extend our calculation of that interest only over a very short period. No man will be wild enough to assert, even in this limited sense, that it is seldomer our policy to speak truth than to lie. Sincerity and plain dealing are eminently conducive to the interest of mankind at large, because they afford that ground of confidence and reasonable expectation which are essential both to wisdom and virtue. Yet it may with propriety be asked, "Whether cases do not exist of peculiar emergency, where the general principle of sincerity and speaking the truth ought to be superceded?"

Undoubtedly this is a question to the treatment of which we should advance with some degree of caution and delicacy. Yet it would be a strange instance of inconsistency, that should induce us, right or wrong, to recommend a universal frankness, from an apprehension of the abuses which may follow from an opposite doctrine; and thus incur a charge of deception, in the very act of persuading our neighbours that deception is in no instance to be admitted.

Some persons, from an extreme tenderness of countenancing any particle of insincerity, at the same time that they felt the difficulty of recommending the opposite practice in every imaginable case, have thought proper to allege, "that it is not the propagation of truth, but of falshood we have to fear; and that the whole against which we are bound to be upon our guard, is the telling truth in such a manner as to produce the effect of falshood."

This will perhaps be found upon examination to be an injudicious and mischievous distinction. In the first place, it is of great benefit to the cause of morality that things should be called by their right names, without varnish or subterfuge. I am either to tell the simple and obvious truth, or I am not; I am to suppress, or I am not to suppress: this is the alternative upon which the present question calls us to decide. If suppression, concealment, or falshood can in any case be my duty, let it be known to be such; I shall at least have this advantage, I shall be aware that it can only be my duty in some extraordinary emergence. Secondly, whatever reason can be assigned for my not communicating the truth in the form in which it originally suggests itself to my mind, must, if it be a good reason, ultimately resolve itself into a reason of utility. Sincerity itself is a duty only for reasons of utility; it seems absurd therefore, if in any case truth is not to be communicated in its most obvious form, to seek for the reason rather in the secondary principle of sincerity, than in the paramount and original principle of general utility. Lastly, this distinction is of a nature that seems to deserve that we should regard it with a watchful and jealous eye, on account of its vague and indefinite application. If the question were respecting the mode of my communicating truth, there could not perhaps be a better maxim, than that I should take care so to communicate it, that it might have the effects of truth and not of falshood. But, it will be extremely dangerous, if I accustom myself to make this the test whether I shall communicate it or no. It is a maxim that seems exactly fitted to fall in with that indolence and want of enterprise which in some degree or other are characteristic of all human minds. Add to which, it is a maxim which may be applied without the possibility of limitation, There is no instance in which truth can be communicated absolutely pure. We can only make approximations to such a proceeding, without ever being able fully to arrive at it. It will be liable to some misconstruction, to some want of clearness and precision, to the exciting some passions that ought to lie for ever dormant. This maxim therefore will either prove too much, or is one to which no recourse must be had but after such an investigation of the capacities of the human mind in each individual instance, as to make the idea of introducing a general maxim by way of compendium ridiculous.

Having cleared the subject of those ambiguities in which it has sometimes been involved, let us proceed to the investigation of the original question; and for this purpose it may be useful to take up the subject a little higher, and recur to the basis of moral obligation.

All just reasoning in subjects of morality has been found to depend upon this as its fundamental principle, that each man is bound to consider himself as a debtor in all his faculties, his opportunities and his industry to the general welfare. This is a debt which must be always paying, never discharged. Every moment of my life can be better employed, or it cannot; if it cannot, I am in that very instance, however seemingly inconsiderable, playing the part of a true patriot of human kind; if it can, I then inevitably incur some portion of delinquency. Considering the subject in this point of view, there are two articles, which will always stand among the leading principles of moral decision, the good to result from the action immediately proposed, and the advantage to the public of my preserving in existence and vigour the means of future usefulness. Every man, sufficiently impressed with a sense of his debt to the species, will feel himself obliged to scruple the laying out his entire strength and forfeiting his life, upon any single instance of public exertion. There is a certain proceeding which in itself considered I ought this day to adopt; change the circumstances, and make it unquestionable that, if adopted, my life will be the forfeit, will that make no change in my duty? This is a question which has been previously anticipated.

In the mean time to render the decision in the subject before us still more satisfactory, let us suppose a case in which the uttering a falshood shall be the only means by which I can escape from a menace of instant destruction. Let it be that, which is said to have occurred in the war of la Vendée in 1793, where the royalists ordered one of their prisoners at the point of the bayonet to cry *Vive le roi*, while he, instead of complying, exclaimed *Vive la republique*, and immediately perished covered with a hundred wounds. Was his conduct under these circumstances commendable and just? Ought he, according to the purest principles of morality, to have acted as he did, or otherwise? Strict sincerity required that he should adopt the conduct which led to the immediate forfeiture of his life. Let us state the several arguments that offer themselves on both sides of this question.

The advantages affirmed of sincerity in general will be found equally to hold in this instance. All falshood has a tendency to enervate the individual that practises it. With what sentiments of mind is he to utter the falshood in question? Shall he endeavour to render it complete, and effectually to mislead the persons to whom it relates? This will require a systematical hypocrisy, and an incessant watchfulness left his features and gestures should prove so many vehicles of his real opinion. Shall he comply with the requisition in the pure spirit of formality, rather implying that he does not think it advisable directly to shock their prejudices, than that he has any anxious desire to impose the thing that is not? It may happen that this indolent compliance will not suffice to avert the danger with which he is threatened. But, if it do, then what he is openly assuming is to play a feeble and imbecil character, destitute of that energy, firmness and decision which are the only qualities worthy of a man. It must be a calamitous state of human action which imposes so despicable an alternative. Add to this, that by such a conduct he is contributing his part to the cutting off the intercourse between men's tongues and their sentiments, infusing general distrust, and trifling with the most sacred pledge of human integrity. To affirm that I am of one opinion, when in reality I am of another, is an action from which the human mind unconquerably revolts. To avow the truth with a fearless disregard of consequences, has something in it so liberal and magnanimous, as to produce a responsive feeling in every human heart. Nor is it to be forgotten that the threatened consequences can scarcely in any instance be regarded as certain. The intrepidity of his behaviour, the sobriety and dignified moderation of his carriage, and the reasonableness of his expostulations, may be such as to disarm the bitterest foe.

Let us consider the arguments on the other side of the question. And here it may be observed, that there is nothing really humiliating in the discharge of our duty. If it can be shown that compliance in the instance described is that which it is incumbent to yield, then without doubt we ought to feel self-approbation and not censure in the yielding it. There are many duties which the habits of the world make us feel it humiliating to discharge, as well as many vices in which we pride ourselves; but this is the result of prejudice, and ought to be corrected. Whatever it be that our duty requires of us, the man who is sufficiently enlightened will feel no repugnance to the performance. As to the influence of our conduct upon other men, no doubt, so far as relates to example, we ought to set an example, of virtue, of real virtue, not of that which is merely specious. It will also frequently happen in cases such as that above described, that the memory of what we do will be entirely lost; our proceeding is addressed to prejudiced persons, who will admit no virtue in the man they hate or despise. Is it probable that the effect of my virtue in la Vendée will be more extensively beneficial to society, than all my future life, however industrious and however pure? Cases might easily have been put of private animosity, where my generous self-devotion would scarcely in any instance be heard of. No mistake can be more painful to an impartial observer, than to see an individual of great utility irretrievably thrown away upon a trivial adventure. It may also be worth remarking, that the most virtuous man that lives, is probably guilty of some acts of insincerity in every day of his life. Though therefore he ought to be careful not lightly to add to the catalogue yet surely there is something extremely contrary to reason in finding the same man deviating from a general rule of conduct for the most trifling and contemptible motives, and immediately after repelling an additional deviation at the expence of his life. As to the argument drawn from the uncertainty of the threatened consequences, it must be remembered that some degree of this uncertainty adheres to all human affairs; and that all calculation of consequences, or in other words all virtue, depends upon our adopting the greater probability and rejecting the less.

No doubt considerable sacrifices (not only of the imbecility of our character, which ought in all instances to be sacrificed without mercy, but) of the real advantage of life, ought to be made, for the sake of preserving with ourselves and others a confidence in our veracity. He who, being sentenced by a court of judicature for some action that he esteems laudable, is offered the remission of his sentence provided he will recant his virtue, ought probably in every imaginable case to resist the proposal. Much seems to depend upon the formality and notoriety of the action. It may probably be wrong to be minutely scrupulous with a drunken bigot in a corner, who should require of me an assent to his creed with a pistol at my breast; and right peremptory to refuse all terms of qualification, when solemnly proposed by a court of judicature in the face of a nation.

If there be cases where I ought not to scruple to violate the truth since the alternative consists in my certain destruction, it is at least as much incumbent on me when the life of my neighbour is at stake. Indeed, the moment any exception is admitted to the general principle of unreserved sincerity, it becomes obviously impossible to fix the nature of all the exceptions. The rule respecting them must be, that, wherever a great end manifest evil arises from disclosing the truth, and that evil appears to be greater than the evil to arise from violating in this instance the general barrier of human confidence and virtue, there the obligation of sincerity is suspended.

Nor is it a valid objection to say, "that by such a rule we are making every man a judge in his own case." In the courts of morality it cannot be otherwise; a pure and just system of thinking admits not of the existence of any infallible judge to whom we can appeal. It might indeed be farther objected, "that by this rule men will be called upon to judge in the moment of passion and partiality, instead of being referred to the past decisions of their cooler reason." But this also is an inconvenience inseparable from human affairs. We must and ought to keep ourselves open to the last moment to the influence of such considerations as may appear worthy to influence us. To teach men that they must not trust their own understandings, is not the best scheme for rendering them virtuous and consistent. On the contrary, to inure them to consult their understanding, is the way to render it worthy of becoming their director and guide.

Nothing which has been alleged under this head of exceptions, produces the smallest alteration in what was offered under the general discussion. All the advantages, the sublime and illustrious effects, which attend upon an ingenuous conduct, remain unimpeached. Sincerity, a generous and intrepid frankness, will still be found to occupy perhaps the first place in the catalogue of human virtues. This is the temper that ought to pervade the whole course of our reflections and actions. It should be acted upon every day, and confirmed in us every night. There is nothing which we ought to reject with more unalterable firmness than an action that by its consequences reduces us to the necessity of duplicity and concealment. No man can be eminently either respectable, or amiable, or useful, who is not distinguished for the frankness and candour of his manners. This is the grand fascination by which we lay hold of the hearts of our neighbours, conciliate their attention, and render virtue an irresistible object of imitation. He that is not conspicuously sincere, either very little partakes of the passion of doing good, or is pitiably ignorant of the means by which the objects of true benevolence are to be effected.

ANONYMOUS

[The Yates Family Murders]†

To the EDITOR *of the* NEW-YORK WEEKLY MAGAZINE.
SIR,
The inclosed Account I transmit to you for publication, at the particular request of a friend, who is well acquainted with the circumstances that gave rise to it.—It is drawn up by a female hand, and she here relates respecting Mr. Y——what she knew of him herself, and what she had heard of him in her father's family, where he had been an occasional visitant; as I have no reason to believe that this transaction has ever appeared in print, you will be pleased to give it a place among your original compositions.

ANNA.

NEW-YORK, *May* 17, 1796.

An Account

OF A MURDER COMMITTED BY MR. J—— Y——,
UPON HIS FAMILY, IN DECEMBER, A.D. 1781.

The unfortunate subject of my present essay, belonged to one of the most respectable families in this state; he resided a few miles from Tomhanick, and though he was not in the most affluent circumstances, he maintained his family (which consisted of a wife and four children,) very comfortably.—From the natural gentleness of his disposition, his industry, sobriety, probity and kindness, his neighbours universally esteemed him, and until the fatal night when he perpetrated the cruel act, none saw cause of blame in him.

In the afternoon preceding that night, as it was Sunday and there was no church near, several of his neighbours with their wives came to his house for the purpose of reading the scripture and singing psalms; he received them cordially, and when they were going to return home in the evening, he pressed his sister and her husband, who came with the others, to stay longer; at his very earnest solicitation they remained until near nine o'clock, during which time his conversation was grave as usual, but interesting and affectionate: to his wife, of whom he was very fond, he made use of more than commonly endearing expressions, and caressed his little ones alternately:—he spoke much of his domestic felicity, and informed his sister, that to render his wife more happy, he intended to take

---

† Anonymous, "An Account of a Murder Committed by Mr. J——Y——, upon His Family, in December, A.D. 1781," *New-York Weekly Magazine; or Miscellaneous Repository,* July 20 and 27, 1796. Reprinted in Philadelphia *Minerva,* August 20 and 27, 1796.

her to New-Hampshire the next day; "I have just been refitting my sleigh," said he, "and we will set off by day-break."—After singing another hymn, Mr. and Mrs. J—s—n departed.

"They had no sooner left us (said he upon his examination) than taking my wife upon my lap, I opened the Bible to read to her— my two boys were in bed—one five years old, the other seven;—my daughter Rebecca, about eleven, was sitting by the fire, and my infant aged about six months, was slumbering at her mother's bosom. —Instantly a new light shone into the room, and upon looking up I beheld two Spirits, one at my right hand and the other at my left; —he at the left bade me destroy all my *idols*, and begin by casting the Bible into the fire;—the other Spirit dissuaded me, but I obeyed the first, and threw the book into the flames. My wife immediately snatched it out, and was going to expostulate, when I threw it in again and held her fast until it was entirely consumed:—then filled with the determination to persevere, I flew out of the house, and seizing an axe which lay by the door, with a few strokes demolished my sleigh, and running to the sable killed one of my horses—the other I struck, but with one spring he got clear of the stable.—My spirits now were high, and I hasted to the house to inform my wife of what I had done. She appeared terrified, and begged me to sit down; but the good angel whom I had obeyed stood by me and bade me go on, "You have more idols, (said he) look at your wife and children." I hesitated not a moment, but rushed to the bed where my boys lay, and catching the eldest in my arms, I threw him with such violence against the wall, that he expired without a groan!—his brother was still asleep—I took him by the feet, and dashed his skull in pieces against the fire-place!—Then looking round, and perceiving that my wife and daughters were fled, I left the dead where they lay, and went in pursuit of the living, taking up the axe again.—A slight snow had fallen that evening, and by its light I descried my wife running towards her father's (who lived about half a mile off) encumbered with her babe; I ran after her, calling upon her to return, but she shrieked and fled faster, I therefore doubled my pace, and when I was within thirty yards of her, threw the axe at her, which hit her upon the hip!—the moment that she felt the blow she dropped the child, which I directly caught up, and threw against the log-fence—I did not hear it cry—I only heard the lamentations of my wife, of whom I had now lost sight; but the blood gushed so copiously from her wound that it formed a distinct path along the snow. We were now within sight of her father's house, but from what cause I cannot tell, she took an opposite course, and after running across an open field several times, she again stopped at her own door; I now came up with her—my heart bled to see her distress, and all my *natural feelings* began to revive; I forgot my duty, so powerfully did her moanings and pleadings affect me, "Come then, my love (said I) we have one child left, let us be thankful for that—what is done is right—we must not repine, come let me embrace you—let me know that you do indeed love me." She encircled me in her trembling arms, and pressed her quivering lips to my cheek.—A voice behind me, said, "This is also an idol!"—I broke from her instantly, and wrenching a stake from the garden fence, with one stroke levelled her to the earth! and lest she should only be stunned, and might, perhaps, recover again, I repeated my blows, till I could not distinguish one feature of her face!!! I now went to look after my last sublunary treasure, but after calling several times without receiving any answer, I returned to the house again; and in the way back picked up the babe and laid it on my wife's bosom.—I then stood musing a minute—during which interval I thought I heard the suppressed sobbings of some one near the barn, I approached it in silence, and beheld my daughter Rebecca endeavouring to conceal herself among the hay stacks.—

At the noise of my feet upon the dry corn stalks—she turned hastily round and seeing me exclaimed, "O father, my dear father, spare me, let me live—let me live,—I will be a comfort to you and my mother—spare me to take care of my little sister Diana—do—do let me live."—She was my darling child, and her fearful cries pierced me to the soul—the tears of *natural pity* fell as plentifully down my cheeks, as those of terror did down her's, and methought that to destroy *all* my idols, was a hard task—I again relapsed at the voice of complaining; and taking her by the hand, led her to where her mother lay; then thinking that if I intended to retain her, I must make some other severe sacrifice, I bade her sing and dance—She complied, terribly situated as she was,—but I was not acting in the line of my duty—I was convinced of my error, and catching up a hatchet that stuck in a log, with one well aimed stroke cleft her forehead in twain—she fell—and no sign of retaining life appeared.

I then sat down on the threshold, to consider what I had best do— "I shall be called a murderer (said I) I shall be seized—imprisoned— executed, and for what?—for destroying my idols—for obeying the mandate of my father—no, I will put all the dead in the house together, and after setting fire to it, run to my sister's and say the Indians have done it—" I was preparing to drag my wife in, when the idea struck me that I was going to tell a *horrible lie*; "and how will that accord with my profession? (asked I.) No, let me speak the truth, and declare the good motive for my actions, be the consequences what they may."

His sister, who was the principal evidence against him, stated— that she had scarce got home, when a message came to Mr. J——n, her husband, informing him that his mother was ill and wished to see him; he accordingly set off immediately, and she not expecting him home again till the next day, went to bed—there being no other person in the house. About four in the morning she heard her brother Y—— call her, she started up and bade him come in. "I will not (returned he) for I have committed the unpardonable sin—I have burnt the Bible." She knew not what to think, but rising hastily opened the door which was only latched, and caught hold of his hand: let me go, Nelly (said he) my hands are wet with blood—the blood of my Elizabeth and her children:—She saw the blood dripping from his fingers, and her's chilled in the veins, yet with a fortitude unparalleled she begged him to enter, which—as he did, he attempted to seize a case knife, that by the light of a bright pine-knot fire, he perceived lying on the dresser—she prevented him, however, and tearing a trammel from the chimney, bound him with it to the bed post—fastening his hands behind him—She then quitted the house in order to go to his, which as she approached she heard the voice of loud lamentation, the hope that it was some one of the family who had escaped the effects of her brother's frenzy, subdued the fears natural to such a situation and time, she quickened her steps, and when she came to the place where Mrs. Y——lay, she perceived that the moans came from Mrs. Y——'s aged father, who expecting that his daughter would set out upon her journey by day break, had come at that early hour to bid her farewel.

They alarmed their nearest neighbours immediately, who proceeded to Mrs. J——n's, and there found Mr. Y—— in the situation she had left him; they took him from hence to Tomhanick, where he remained near two days—during which time Mr. W–tz–l (a pious old Lutheran, who occasionally acted as preacher) attended upon him, exhorting him to pray and repent; but he received the admonitions with contempt, and several times with ridicule, refusing to confess his error or *join* in prayer—. I say *join* in prayer, for he would not kneel when the rest did, but when they arose he would prostrate himself and address his "father," frequently saying "my father, thou knowest that it was in obedience to thy commands, and for thy glory that I have done this deed." Mrs. Bl——r, at whose house he then was, bade some one ask him who his father was?—he made no reply—but pushing away the person who stood between her and himself, darted at her a look of such indignation as thrilled horror to her heart—his speech was connected, and he told his tale without variation; he expressed much sorrow for the loss of his dear family, but consoled himself with the idea of having performed his duty— he was taken to Albany and there confined as a lunatic in the gaol, from which he escaped twice, once by the assistance of Aqua Fortis, with which he opened the front door.

I went in 1782 with a little girl, by whom Mr. Bl——r had sent him some fruit; he was then confined in dungeon, and had several chains on—he appeared to be much affected at her remembrance of him, and put up a pious ejaculation for her and her family—since then I have received no accounts respecting him.

The cause for his wonderfully cruel proceedings is beyond the conception of human beings—the deed so unpremeditated, so unprovoked, that we do not hesitate to pronounce it the effect of insanity—yet upon the other hand, when we reflect on the equinimity of his temper, and the comfortable situation in which he was, and no visible circumstance operating to render him frantic, we are apt to conclude, that he was under a strong delusion of Satan. But what avail our conjectures, perhaps it is best that some things are concealed from us, and the only use we can now make of our knowledge of this affair, is to be humble under a scene of human frailty to renew our petition, "Lead us not into temptation."

May, 27, 1796.

ERASMUS DARWIN

From Zoonomia; or, the Laws of Organic Life[†]

Diseases [Class III.1.2]

* * *

ORDO I.

INCREASED VOLITION.

GENUS II.
WITH INCREASED ACTIONS OF THE ORGANS OF SENSE.

In every species of madness there is a peculiar idea either of desire or aversion, which is perpetually excited in the mind with all its connections. In some constitutions this is connected with pleasurable ideas without the exertion of much muscular action, in others it produces violent muscular action to gain or avoid the object of it, in others it is attended with despair and inaction. Mania is the general word for the two former of these, and melancholia for the latter; but the species of them are as numerous as the desires and aversions of mankind.

---

† From Erasmus Darwin, *Zoonomia; or, the Laws of Organic Life. Part Second. A New Edition; with an Introductory Address, and a Short Appendix, by Charles Caldwell, M.D.* (Philadelphia: Dobson, 1797), pp. 447–53, 462–63. Originally published in London in 1794; an American edition of the first volume was prepared by Brown's friends Elihu Smith and Samuel Mitchill and printed in New York in 1796.

In the present age the pleasurable insanities are most frequently induced by superstitious hopes of heaven, by sentimental love, and by personal vanity. The furious insanities by pride, anger, revenge, suspicion. And the melancholy ones by fear of poverty, fear of death, and fear of hell; with innumerable others.

> Quicquid agunt homines, votum, timor, ira, voluptas, Gaudia, discursus, nostri est farrago libelli.
>
> JUVEN. I. 85.[1]

This idea, however, which induces madness or melancholy, is generally untrue; that is, the object is a mistaken fact. As when a patient is persuaded he has the itch, or venereal disease, of which he has no symptom, and becomes mad from the pain this idea occasions. So that the object of madness is generally a delirious idea, and thence cannot be conquered by reason; because it continues to be excited by painful sensation, which is a stronger stimulus than volition. Most frequently pain of body is the cause of convulsion, which is often however exchanged for madness; and a painful delirious idea is most frequently the cause of madness originally, but sometimes of convulsion. Thus I have seen a young lady become convulsed from a fright, and die in a few days; and a temporary madness frequently terminates the paroxysms of the epilepsia dolorifica, and an insanity of greater permanence is frequently induced by the pains or bruises of parturition.

Where the patient is debilitated a quick pulse sometimes attends insane people, which is nevertheless generally only a symptom of the debility, owing to the too great expenditure of sensorial power; or of the paucity of its production, as in inirritative, or in sensitive inirritated fever.

But nevertheless where the quick pulse is permanent, it shews the presence of fever; and as the madness then generally arises from the disagreeable sensations attending the fever, it is so far a good symptom; because when the fever is cured, or ceases spontaneously, the insanity most frequently vanishes at the same time.

The stimulus of so much volition supports insane people under variety of hardships, and contributes to the cure of diseases from debility, as sometimes occurs towards the end of fevers. And, on the same account, they bear large doses of medicines to procure any operation on them; as emetics, and cathartics, which, before they produce their effect in inverting the motions of the stomach in vomiting, or of the absorbents of the bowels in purging, must first weaken the natural actions of those organs.

---

1. Juvenal, *Satires*, 1.85–86: "Whatever people do—prayers, tears, anger, pleasure, joys, interactions—is the fodder of my little book."

From these considerations it appears, that the indications of cure must consist in removing the cause of the pain, whether it arises from a delirious idea, or from a real fact, or from bodily disease; or secondly, if this cannot be done, by relieving the pain in consequence of such idea or disease. The first is sometimes effected by presenting frequently in a day contrary ideas to shew the fallacy, or the too great estimation, of the painful ideas. 2dly. By change of place, and thus presenting the stimulus of new objects, as a long journey. 3dly. By producing forgetfulness of the idea or object, which causes their pain; by removing all things which recal it to their minds; and avoiding all conversation on similar subjects. For I suppose no disease of the mind is so perfectly cured by other means as by forgetfulness.

Secondly, the pain in consequence of the ideas or bodily diseases above described is to be removed, first, by evacuations, as venesection, emetics, and cathartics; and then by large doses of opium, or by the vertigo occasioned by a circulating swing, or by a sea-voyage, which, as they affect the organs of sense as well as evacuate the stomach, may contribute to answer both indications of cure.

Where maniacs are outrageous, there can be no doubt but coercion is necessary; which may be done by means of a strait waistcoat;[2] which disarms them without hurting them; and by tying a handkerchief round their ancles to prevent their escape. In others there can be no doubt, but that confinement retards rather than promotes their cure; which is forwarded by change of ideas in consequence of change of place and of objects, as by travelling or sailing.

The circumstances which render confinement necessary, are first, if the lunatic is liable to injure others, which must be judged of by the outrage he has already committed. 2dly. If he is likely to injure himself; this also must be judged of by the despondency of his mind, if such exists. 3dly. If he cannot take care of his affairs. Where none of these circumstances exist, there should be no confinement. For though the mistaken idea continues to exist, yet if no actions are produced in consequence of it, the patient cannot be called insane, he can only be termed delirious. If every one, who possesses mistaken ideas, or who puts false estimates on things, was liable to confinement, I know not who of my readers might not tremble at the sight of a madhouse!

The most convenient distribution of insanities will be into general, as mania mutabilis, studium inane, and vigilia; and into partial insanities. These last again may be subdivided into desires and aversions, many of which are succeeded by pleasurable or painful ideas, by fury or dejection, according to the degree or violence of their

2. Straightjacket.

exertions. Hence the analogy between the insanities of the mind, and the convulsions of the muscles described in the preceding genus, is curiously exact. The convulsions without stupor, are either just sufficient to obliterate the pain, which occasions them; or are succeeded by greater pain, as in the convulsio dolorifica. So the exertions in the mania mutabilis are either just sufficient to allay the pain which occasions them, and the patient dwells comparatively in a quiet state; or those exertions excite painful ideas, which are succeeded by furious discourses, or outrageous actions. The studium inane, or reverie, resembles epilepsy, in which there is no sensibility to the stimuli of external objects. Vigilia, or watchfulness, may be compared to the general writhing of the body; which is just a sufficient exertion to relieve the pain which occasions it. Erotomania may be compared to trismus, or other muscular fixed spasm, without much subsequent pain; and to cramp of the muscles of the leg, or other fixed spasm with subsequent pain. All these coincidences contribute to shew that our ideas are motions of the immediate organs of sense obeying the same laws as our muscular motions.

The violence of action accompanying insanity depends much on the education of the person; those who have been proudly educated with unrestrained passions, are liable to greater fury; and those, whose education has been humble, to greater despondency. Where the delirious idea, above described, produces pleasurable sensations, as in personal vanity or religious enthusiasm; it is almost a pity to snatch them from their fool's paradise, and reduce them again to the common lot of humanity; lest they should complain of their cure, like the patient described in Horace,

>————Pol! me occidistis, amici,
>Non servastis, ait, cui sic extorta voluptas,
>Et demptus per vim mentis gratissimus error![3]

The disposition to insanity, as well as to convulsion, is believed to be hereditary; and in consequence to be induced in those families from slighter causes than in others. Convulsions have been shewn to have been most frequently induced by pains owing to defect of stimulus, as the shuddering from cold, and not from pains from excess of stimulus, which are generally succeeded by inflammation. But insanities are on the contrary generally induced by pains from excess of stimulus, as from the too violent actions of our ideas, as in common anger, which is an insanity of short duration; for insanities generally, though not always, arise from pains of the organs of sense; but convulsions generally, though not always, from pains of

---

3. Horace, *Epistles*, 2.2.138–140: "Damn it, friends, I'm done for, not saved; you've wrenched my pleasure from me, forced me to shed the delusion that was my delight."

the membranes or glands. And it has been previously explained, that though the membranes and glands, as the stomach and skin, receive great pain from want of stimulus; yet that the organs of sense, as the eye and ear, receive no pain from defect of stimulus.

Hence it follows, that the constitutions most liable to convulsion, are those which most readily become torpid in some part of the system, that is, which possess less irritability; and that those most liable to insanity, are such as have excess of sensibility; and lastly, that these two circumstances generally exist in the same constitution. These observations explain why epilepsy and insanity frequently succeed or reciprocate with each other, and why inirritable habits, as scrophulous ones, are liable to insanity, of which I have known some instances.

In many cases however there is no appearance of the disposition to epilepsy or insanity of the parent being transmitted to the progeny. First, where the insanity has arisen from some violent disappointment, and not from intemperance in the use of spirituous liquors. Secondly, where the parent has acquired the insanity or epilepsy by habits of intoxication after the procreation of his children. Which habits I suppose to be the general cause of the disposition to insanity in this country.

As the disposition to gout, dropsy, epilepsy, and insanity, appears to be produced by the intemperate use of spirituous potation, and is in all of them hereditary; it seems probable, that this disposition gradually increases from generation to generation, in those families which continue for many generations to be intemperate in this respect; till at length these diseases are produced; that is, the irritability of the system gradually is decreased by this powerful stimulus, and the sensibility at the same time increased. This disposition is communicated to the progeny, and becomes still increased, if the same stimulus be continued, and so on by a third and fourth generation; which accounts for the appearance of epilepsy in the children of some families, where it was never known before to have existed, and could not be ascribed to their own intemperance. A parity of reasoning shews, that a few sober generations may gradually in the same manner restore a due degree of irritability to the family, and decrease the excess of sensibility.

From hence it would appear probable, that scrophula and dropsy are diseases from inirritability; but that in epilepsy and insanity an excess of sensibility is added, and the two faulty temperaments are thus conjoined.

SPECIES.

1. *Mania mutabilis.* Mutable madness. Where the patients are liable to mistake ideas of sensation for those from irritation, that is,

imaginations for realities, if cured of one source of insanity, they are liable in a few months to find another source in some new mistaken or imaginary idea, and to act from this new idea. The idea belongs to delirium, when it is an imaginary or mistaken one; but it is the voluntary actions exerted in consequence of this mistaken idea, which constitute insanity.

In this disease the patient is liable carefully to conceal the object of his desire or aversion. But a constant inordinate suspicion of all people, and a carelessness of cleanliness, and of decency, are generally concomitants of madness. Their designs cannot be counteracted, till you can investigate the delirious idea or object of their insanity; but as they are generally timid, they are therefore less to be dreaded.

Z. Z. called a young girl, one of his maid servants, into the parlour, and, with cocked pistols in his hands, ordered her to strip herself naked; he then inspected her with some attention, and dismissed her untouched. Then he stripped two of his male servants in the same manner, to the great terror of the neighbourhood. After he was secured, with much difficulty he was persuaded to tell me, that he had got the itch, and had examined some of his servants to find out from whom he had received it; though at the same time there was not a spot to be seen on his hands, or other parts. The outrages in consequence of this false idea were in some measure to be ascribed to the pride occasioned by unrestrained education, affluent wealth, and dignified family.

Madness is sometimes produced by bodily pain, particularly I believe of a diseased liver, like convulsion and epilepsy; at other times it is caused by very painful ideas occasioned by external circumstances, as of grief or disappointment; but the most frequent cause of insanity arises from the pain of some imaginary or mistaken idea; which may be termed hallucinatio maniacalis. This hallucination of one of the senses is often produced in an instant, and generally becomes gradually weakened in process of time, by the perpetual stimulus of external objects, or by the successions of other catenations of ideas, or by the operations of medicines; and when the maniacal hallucination ceases, or is forgotten, the violent exertions cease, which were in consequence of it, and the disease is cured.

Mr. ———, a clergyman, about forty years of age, who was rather a weak man, happened to be drinking wine in jocular company, and by accident swallowed a part of the seal of a letter, which he had just then received; one of his companions seeing him alarmed, cried out in humour, "It will seal your bowels up." He became melancholy from that instant, and in a day or two resused to swallow any kind of nourishment. On being pressed to give a reason for this refusal, he answered, he knew nothing would pass through him. A cathartic was given, which produced a great many evacuations, but he still persisted, that nothing passed through him; and though he was frightened into taking a little broth once or twice by threats, yet he soon ceased intirely to swallow any thing, and died in consequence of this insane idea.

Miss ———, a sensible and ingenious lady, about thirty, said she had seen an angel; who told her, that she need not eat, though all others were under the necessity of supporting their earthly existence by food. After fruitless persuasions to take food, she starved herself to death.—It was proposed to send an angel of an higher order to tell her, that now she must begin to eat and drink again; but it was not put into execution.

Mrs. ———, a lady between forty and fifty years of age, imagined that she heard a voice say to her one day, as she was at her toilet, "Repent, or you will be damned." From that moment she became melancholy, and this hallucination affected her in greater or less degree for about two years; she then recovered perfectly, and is now a cheerful old woman.

Mrs. ———, a farmer's wife, going up stairs to dress, found the curtains of her bed drawn, and on undrawing them, she believed that she saw the corps of her sister, who was then ill at the distance of twenty miles, and became from that time insane; and as her sister died about the time, she could not be produced to counteract the insane hallucination, but she perfectly recovered in a few months.

Mrs. ———, a most elegant, beautiful, and accomplished lady, about twenty-two years of age, had been married about two months to an elegant, polished, and affluent young man, and it was well known to be a love-match on both sides. She suddenly became melancholy, and yet not to so great a degree, but that she could command herself to do the honours of her table with grace and apparent ease. After many days intreaty, she at length told me, that she thought her marrying her husband had made him unhappy; and that this idea she could not efface from her mind day or night. I withstood her being confined, as some had advised, and proposed a sea-voyage to her, with expectation that the sickness, as well as change of objects, might remove the insane hallucination, by introducing other energetic ideas; this was not complied with, but she travelled about England with her friends and her husband for many months, and at length perfectly recovered, and is now I am informed in health and spirits.

These cases are related to shew the utility of endeavouring to investigate the maniacal idea, or hallucination; as it may not only acquaint us with the probable designs of the patient, from whence may be deduced the necessity of confinement; but also may some time lead to the most effectual plan of cure.

I received good information of the truth of the following case, which was published a few years ago in the newspapers. A young farmer in Warwickshire, finding his hedges broke, and the sticks carried away during a frosty season, determined to watch for the thief. He lay many cold hours under a hay-stack, and at length an old woman, like a witch in a play, approached, and began to pull up the hedge; he waited till she had tied up her bottle of sticks, and was carrying them off, that he might convict her of the theft, and then springing from his concealment, he seized his prey with violent threats. After some altercation, in which her load was left upon the ground, she kneeled upon her bottle of sticks, and raising her arms to heaven beneath the bright moon then at the full, spoke to the farmer already shivering with cold, "Heaven grant, that thou never mayest know again the blessing to be warm." He complained of cold all the next day, and wore an upper coat, and in a few days another, and in a fortnight took to his bed, always saying nothing made him warm, he covered himself with very many blankets, and had a sieve over his face, as he lay; and from this one insane idea he kept his bed above twenty years for fear of the cold air, till at length he died.

M. M. As mania arises from pain either of our muscles or organs of sense, the arts of relieving pain must constitute the method of cure. Venesection.[4] Vomits of from five grains to ten of emetic tartar, repeated every third morning for three or four times; with solution of gum-ammoniac, and soluble tartar, so as to purge gently every day. Afterwards warm bath for two or three hours a day. Opium in large doses. Bark. Steel.

Dr. Binns gave two scruples (40 grains) of solid opium at a dose, and twenty grains four hours afterwards; which restored the patient. Dr. Brandreth gave 400 drops of laudanum to a maniac in the greatest possible furor, and in a few hours he became calm and rational.

PROGNOSTIC.

The temporary quick pulse attending some maniacal cases is simply a symptom of debility, and is the consequence of too great exertions; but a permanent quick pulse shews the presence of fever, and is frequently a salutary sign; because, if the life of the patient be safe, when the fever ceases, the insanity generally vanishes along with it, as mentioned above. In this case the kind of fever must direct the method of curing the insanity; which must consist of

4. Surgical blood letting.

moderate evacuations and diluents, if the pulse be strong; or by nutrientia, bark, and small doses of opium, if the pulse be weak.

Where the cause is of a temporary nature, as in puerperal insanity, there is reason to hope, that the disease will cease, when the bruises, or other painful sensations attending this state, are removed. In these cases the child should be brought frequently to the mother, and applied to her breast, if she will suffer it, and this whether she at first attends to it or not; as by a few trials it frequently excites the storgè, or maternal affection, and removes the insanity, as I have witnessed.

When the madness is occasioned by pain of the teeth, which I believe is no uncommon case, these must be extracted; and the cure follows the extinction of the pain. There is however some difficulty in detecting the delinquent tooth in this case, as in hemicrania, unless by its apparent decay, or by some previous information of its pain having been complained of; because the pain of the tooth ceases, as soon as the exertions of insanity commence.

When a person becomes insane, who has a family of small children to solicit his attention, the prognostic is very unfavourable; as it shews the maniacal hallucination to be more powerful than those ideas which generally interest us the most.

* * *

7. *Spes religiosa.* Superstitious hope. This maniacal hallucination in its milder state produces, like sentimental love, an agreeable reverie; but when joined with works of supererogation,[5] it has occasioned many enormities. In India devotees consign themselves by vows to most painful and unceasing tortures, such as holding up their hands, till they cannot retract them; hanging up by hooks put into the thick skin over their shoulders, fitting upon sharp points, and other self torments. While in our part of the globe fasting and mortification, as flagellation, has been believed to please a merciful deity! The serenity, with which many have suffered cruel martyrdoms, is to be ascribed to this powerful reverie.

Mr. ———, a clergyman, formerly of this neighbourhood, began to bruise and wound himself for the sake of religious mortification, and passed much time in prayer, and continued whole nights alone in the church. As he had a wife and family of small children, I believed the case to be incurable; as otherwise the affection and employment in his family connections would have opposed the beginning of this insanity. He was taken to a madhouse without effect, and after he returned home, continued to beat and bruise himself, and by this kind of mortification, and by sometimes long fasting, he at length

5. The performance of more than is required.

became emaciated and died. I once told him in conversation, that "God was a merciful being, and could not delight in cruelty, but that I supposed he worshipped the devil." He was struck with this idea, and promised me not to beat himself for three days, and I believe kept his word for one day. If this idea had been frequently forced on his mind, it might probably have been of service.

When these works of supererogation have been of a public nature, what cruelties, murders, massacres, has not this insanity introduced into the world!—A commander, who had been very active in leading and encouraging the bloody deeds of St. Bartholomew's day at Paris, on confessing his sins to a worthy ecclesiastic on his death-bed, was asked, "Have you nothing to say about St. Bartholomew?" "On that day," he replied, "God Almighty was obliged to me!"—The fear of hell is another insanity, which will be spoken of below.

* * *

SAMUEL LATHAM MITCHILL

[On the Illusions of the Human Senses][†]

Dear Sir,

I regret that I cannot find for you a copy of my pamphlet published at Albany in 1789 on the *Illusions of Human Senses*.[1] I must therefore endeavor to give you an abstract of it from my notes and from memory, together with such ideas on the subject as have occurred to me upon deeper reflection, since that time.

The Principle which I endeavored to establish was this: "that conditions of body occur in which the Organs of Sense do from internal causes and without the aid of external agents take upon themselves a configuration or impression, similar to that which is usually induced by the action of material Objects & Occurrences from without."

1. This sometimes happens when the Person whose Sensations are thus perverted is himself quite conscious of the deception, and can

---

† Samuel Latham Mitchill to Alexander Anderson, March 6, 1796. Collections of the New-York Historical Society. Printed by permission. Mitchill, along with Brown's friends Elihu Smith and Edward Miller, co-founded and edited the first American medical journal, *The Medical Repository*, and prepared the first part of Erasmus Darwin's *Zoonomia* for an American edition. Beginning in 1798 Mitchill was also Brown's fellow member of both the Friendly Club and the Mineralogical Society. Alexander Anderson (1775–1870) was Mitchill's medical student at Columbia College and published an inaugural dissertation on chronic mania in 1796.
1. No copy of this pamphlet is known to exist; it is not included in Charles Evans's bibliography of early American imprints.

then counteract in a good degree the influence of these false suggestions upon the mind by the effects of will and the exercise of Judgement. Now and then this singular state of one or more of the Senses comes on in a Person who is in other Respects well in Health; and in such cases the change wrought is generally feeble and fugitive. The Spectra left upon the Retina after looking at the Sun or any other bright or high-coloured body are of this sort; and the Case of our late Professor Nicoll,[2] as he related it to me, was a very remarkable one, wherein the Ears as well as the Eyes were strangely affected while he was perfectly aware of the imposition. High-wrought Imagination and Poetic fancy seem to belong to this Head.

2. Another memorable instance of such illusions is, when beside this affection of the Sensorial Organs there is a belief wrought, at least for the time being, of the Reality of what appears. The whole of the phenomena of dreaming, Incubus, and of delirium, are of this kind. In dreaming, the shapes and colours of things seen, the distinctness of notes and voices, and even in some instances the pleasurable and painful perceptions referable to the Sense of Feeling, oftentimes surpasses any thing that can be impressed upon the Eye, Ear, or touch, even by real Objects, in a State of Wakefulness. A belief of their actual existence is from the Senses so operated upon, impressed upon the mind; but this belief instantly vanishes on waking; and the whole series of events that just before seemed with so much distinctness to be present is confessed to be an Illusion.

In Nightmare and Delirium too, the person who raves, tho firm in the persuasion for the present, that things are truly as he fancies them, acknowledges his Error and stands self convicted as the fit is over. The false suggestion in the Ailments, are, as in dreaming, founded in morbid conditions of the Organs of Sense induced without the customary operation of external bodies.

3. A third case is where the images presented to the Sensorium by morbid sensation are not only "not" present, but where they are wholly different from any thing which exists; and have consequently no prototype in Nature. Wicked persons & such as are highly superstitious and enthusiastic, whose minds are under deep concern, or are violently agitated, and whose Organs of Sense are irritable, are very often the Subject of this illusion. Hence Devils in all imaginable forms, Angels in every possible variety of Shape, Spectres, ghosts and apparitions, are frequently seen by persons suffering this form of Disease, and Visions, Revelations and extraordinary Communications made to them. They see invisible things; they hear

2. Samuel Nicoll (1754–1796), Mitchill's fellow member of Columbia College's medical faculty in the 1790s.

sounds not audible. The irritable condition of the Eyes suggests to them inward light beaming with celestial influence upon them with the notions of fire and flames threatening them with infernal torture and anticipating the pains of Hell. There is nothing Hideous, deformed or monstrous which may not thus be presented to the Mind originating in distempered Sense, and giving rise to fallacious Experience.

4. There is yet another example of morbid Sensation wherein the impressions made upon the Senses from "inward causes" are stronger than those occasioned by external occurrences. And this condition of the organs is so permanent and obstinate that it continues during the time of wakefulness and is not to be dispelled by any effort of the will. When this happens in a single point or in a few respects, it constitutes partial Insanity. When false perceptions ensue on many objects they constitute general or total mania. The fury of such madness will depend upon the vividity of force of the distempered sensation. Its duration will be proportional to the permanent or indelible nature of the impression. And here there is generally the strongest of the truth of the false Perception. From this erroneous principle proceed an endless variety of odd deductions and applications, flowing however in many instances, logically enough from the premises.

I consider the State of Body to which Mania belongs as a morbid Sensation, wherein without corresponding Exciting powers from without, a condition of some or other of the Organs of Sense is indeed from inward causes similar to what usually happens from the operation of external agents and which probably would be brought on by these. Let the causes of this be what they may whether they be imagined to be in the Brain, in the Arterial System, or in the Organs of Sense, such is the Law of Animal Economy that false Sensations suggest unreal perceptions, and they give rise to groundless Motions; and thus a belief, persuasion, or conviction is produced and upon the evidence of the Senses too, of the Existence of non-entities & all manner of unreal representations.

As to the Seat of Madness, I have strong doubts of its being in the Brain. The disorder of the thinking powers is secondary and I believe always subsequent to vitiated Sensations. The Organs of Sense, then, or Sentient Extremities of the Nerves, which have been considered by Darwin,[3] with great appearance of Truth, to be the Seats of Thought, are, I apprehend, particularly and primarily diseased in Madness. Dissections of the Brain in Manias have thrown little or no light upon the Malady; and the Brain has been found excessively deranged in its Structure of Diseases, as Distension, Supportation, Concussion, and in other Ailments, without

3. Erasmus Darwin (1731–1802), author of *Zoonomia* (1794) (see p. 270 in this vol.).

producing any corresponding Disorder of Mind; and I consider it vain and fruitless to search the Brain for the cause of Mania. As it is grounded in false Sensation, the Organs of Sense must be examined with a view to detect the mischief there. The principle internal Stimulus acting upon the Sentient Extremities of the Nerves is the Blood; and if an irregular distribution of blood, its Circulation with too great or too little force, in quantity too large or too small, are capable of inducing Disorder or morbid changes in the Organs of Sense, then a large share of Maniacal Affection is inherent in the Sanguiferous System.[4]

I am, dear Sir, with much esteem and regard yours

Saml L. Mitchill
New York, March 6 1796

ANONYMOUS

[A Case of Spontaneous Combustion][†]

Letter respecting an Italian priest, killed by an electric commotion, the cause of which resided in his own body.

We read in one of the journals of Florence, an extract of a letter from mr. Joseph Battaglia, surgeon at Ponte Bosio, which contains the following relation, as curious as it is interesting to those who apply to the study of philosophy.

Don G. Mac Bertholi, a priest residing at mount Valere in the district of Livizzano, went to the fair of Filetto, on account of some business which he had to transact, and after spending the whole day in going about through the neighbouring country, in order to execute commissions, in the evening he walked towards Fenille, and stopped at the house of one of his brothers-in-law, who resided there. No sooner had he arrived, than he desired to be conducted to his apartment, where he put a handkerchief between his shoulders and his shirt, and, when every body retired, he began to repeat his breviary. A few minutes after, a loud noise was heard in mr. Bertholi's chamber; and his cries having alarmed the family, they hastened to the spot, where they found him extended on the floor, and surrounded by a faint flame, which retired to a greater distance in proportion as it was approached, and at length disappeared entirely.

---

4. Circulatory system.
† From *The American Museum, or, Universal Magazine* (Philadelphia) 11.4 (April 1792); 146–49.

Having conveyed him to bed, such assistance as seemed necessary was given him. Next morning I was called, and after examining the patient carefully, I found that the teguments of the right arm were almost entirely detached from the flesh, and hanging loose, as well as the skin of the lower part of it. In the space contained between the shoulders and the thigh, the teguments were as much injured as those of the right arm. The first thing, therefore, to be done, was to take away those pieces of skin; and, perceiving that a mortification was begun in that part of the right hand which had received the greatest hurt, I scarified it without loss of time; but notwithstanding this precaution, I found it next day, as I had suspected the preceding evening, entirely sphacelous.[1] On my third visit, all the other wounded parts appeared to be in the same condition. The patient complained of an ardent thirst, and was agitated with dreadful convulsions. He voided by stool bilious putrid matter, and was distressed by a continual vomiting, accompanied with a violent fever and delirium. At length the fourth day, after a comatose sleep of two hours, he expired. During my last visit, while he was sunk in the lethargic sleep of which I have spoken, I observed with astonishment, that putrefaction had already made so great progress, that his body exhaled an insupportable smell. I saw the worms which issued from it crawling on the bed, and the nails of his fingers drop of themselves; so that I thought it needless to attempt any thing farther, while he was in this deplorable condition.

Having taken care to get every possible information from the patient himself, respecting what had happened to him, he told me, that he had felt a stroke, as if somebody had given him a blow over the right arm, with a large club, and that at the same time, he had seen a spark of fire attach itself to his shirt, which in a moment was reduced to ashes, though the fire did not in the least injure the wristbands. The handkerchief which he had placed upon his shoulders, between his shirt and his skin, was perfectly entire, without the least appearance of burning, his drawers were untouched, but his nightcap was destroyed, though a single hair of his head was not hurt.

That this flame, under the form of elementary fire, burnt the skin, reduced the shirt to ashes, and entirely consumed the night cap, without in the least touching the hair, is a fact which I affirm to be true: besides, every symptom that appeared on the body of the deceased, announced severe burning. The night was calm, and the circumambient air very pure: no bitumenous smell could be perceived in the chamber, nor was there the least trace of fire or of smoke. A lamp, however, which had been full of oil, was found dry, and the wick almost in ashes. We cannot reasonably suppose this

1. Gangrenous.

fatal accident to have been occasioned by any external cause; and I have no doubt, that if Maffei were still alive, he would take advantage of it, to support an opinion which he entertained, that lightning is sometimes kindled within the human body, and destroys it.

The above observations respecting mr. Maffei naturally bring to our remembrance the fate of the unfortunate countess Cornelia Bandi, of Verona, concerning whom the canon Bianchini has published the details collected by dr. Cromwel Mortimer, fellow of the royal society of London, with some similar facts, to which we may add others more recent, such as the observations which mr. Merille and mr. Muraire inserted in the *Journal de Medicine*, for the months of February and May, 1783.

The authors of these different observations, almost of the same nature, remark, that those subjected to such accidents were for the most part advanced in years, remarkably fat, and had been much addicted to the use of spiritous liquors, either in their drink, or applied in frictions to the body; whence they have concluded, that these people had perished by their whole substance spontaneously taking fire, the principal feat of which had been the entrails or the epigastric viscera, and that the exciting cause was naturally found in the phlogiston of the animal humours, called forth by that of the spiritous liquors combined with the latter.

It is indeed known, and it is an interesting article in the doctrine of the ancient philosophers, which modern physiologists have above all well elucidated, that the material principle of animal heat is an internal fire, capable of acquiring, when excited by several adventitious causes, a certain force and energy, which produce a degree of conflagration in the animal body, carried sometimes even to incineration.

But the case of the unhappy mr. Bertholi, presents particular circumstances, which distinguish it from the preceding observations, and seem to refer to another principle than that of a spontaneous burning. Indeed mr. Battaglia seems decidedly inclined to attribute this phenomenon to that cause; but to his opinion we may oppose doubts, founded upon the following considerations: first, it is demonstrated, that this priest, whose age and constitution we are unacquainted with, experienced a strong electric shock; that he perceived, at the same time, a spark of fire, by which his shirt, his drawers, and his cap were entirely consumed, without injuring his hair, his wristbands, or the handkerchief placed between his shoulders and his shirt; that a sphacelus soon after appeared in his right hand, which had principally sustained the shock, and that there was, besides, a laceration of the skin of the whole arm, and the corresponding side of the body, without the least apparent symptom of pain in the patient, who was found, after the accident, surrounded by a light flame, which vanished on the approach of the people of the house. But these different marks indicate much less the effects of a fire kindled internally, than the destructive action of a flame coming from a highly electric atmosphere; though it is reasonable to think, that this igneous matter, or phlogiston, which we have supposed to be the principle of animal heat, increased by the electric fire of the atmosphere, and strengthened by the latter, concurred in part by its expansion to produce those effects which were observed on the body of the patient. In the second place, besides the speedy putrid degeneration of the solids and fluids, this dissolution of the vital chain, which connects the particles one with another, or establishes their cohesion, and which, in the like cases, shows itself more particularly on the tissue of the flesh, was observed on mr. Bertholi, as it has been observed on animals subjected to the electric spark, in a number of well-known experiments, and particularly in those made by the illustrious abbe Fontana.

Are there then fulminating atmospheres, or lightning without detenation, and noise, as formidable in their effects as ordinary thunder? And is this a scourge of a new kind, which man, already exposed to so many causes of destruction, which surround and attack him, has also to dread? This is a problem, the solution of which might have been looked for from dr. Franklin, that eminent philosopher and politician, who drew from nature the secret of the thunder, and who, after exploring the interests of mankind, as well as the meteors of the air, was one of the grand conductors of the glory and liberty of his country.

As the following phenomenon seems to be somewhat similar to that above related, it may not be improper to subjoin it here. "On the 21st of April, 1781, the first battalion of the brigade of Savoy set out from Tortona, in order to go to Arti, at a time when the weather was excessively hot. On the 22d, having made rather a forced march, the soldiers suffered a great deal from the ardour of the sun, so that at the village of Serre, where they halted, one of them, named Bocquet, a man twenty-five years of age, whose skin being hard and thick, had not perspired, sent forth a loud cry, which seemed to announce some very extraordinary commotion, and instantly fell down. Mr. Bianet, surgeon-major to the regiment, being instantly called, found the patient in convulsions. When he was carried to the hospital, the upper part of his body to the thighs, appeared to be withered and black, and in a gangrenous state. Mr. Bianet employed scarifications, but without effect; it was impossible to make him swallow any thing; and it was found necessary to abandon him to his dismal fate. His body soon exhaled a putrid smell, and he died at the end of five hours. That his disorder might not be communicated to others, he was interred, together with his clothes. Upon enquiry after his

death, it was found, that this man was addicted to the constant use
of spirituous liquors, and that he had even drank of them to excess
during the march.

[Dobson's *Encyclopaedia*: "Ventriloquism"][†]

Ventriloquism, an art by which certain persons can so modify their
voice, as to make it appear to the audience to proceed from any
distance, and to any direction. Some faint traces of this art are to
be found in the writings of the ancients; and it is the opinion of
M. de la Chapelle, who in the year 1772 published an ingenious work
on the subject,[1] that the responses of many of the oracles were
delivered by persons thus qualified to serve the purposes of priestcraft and delusion. As the ancient ventriloquists, when exercising
their art, seemed generally to speak from their own bellies, the
name by which they were designed was abundantly significant; but
it is with no great propriety that modern performers are called *ventriloquists*, and their art *ventriloquism*, since they appear more frequently to speak from the pockets of their neighbours, or from the
roof or distant corners of the room, than from their own mouths or
their own bellies.

From Brodeau, a learned critic of the 16th century, we have the
following account of the feats of a capital ventriloquist and cheat,
who was valet de chambre to Francis the First. The fellow, whose
name was *Louis Brabant*, had fallen desperately in love with a
young, handsome, and rich heiress; but was rejected by the parents
as an unsuitable match for their daughter, on account of the low-
ness of his circumstances. The young lady's father dying, he made a
visit to the widow, who was totally ignorant of his singular talent.
Suddenly, on his first appearance, in open day, in her own house,
and in the presence of several persons who were with her, she heard
herself accosted, in a voice perfectly resembling that of her dead
husband, and which seemed to proceed from above, exclaiming,
"Give my daughter in marriage to Louis Brabant: He is a man of
great fortune, and of an excellent character. I now endure the inexpressible torments of purgatory, for having refused her to him. If
you obey this admonition, I shall soon be delivered from this place
of torment. You will at the same time provide a worthy husband for
your daughter, and procure everlasting repose to the soul of your
poor husband."

[†] From *Encyclopaedia; or, A Dictionary of Arts, Sciences, and Miscellaneous Literature*,
    vol. 18 (Philadelphia: Dobson, 1798), pp. 639–41. Dobson's *Encyclopaedia* was adapted
    from the third edition of the *Encyclopaedia Britannica*.
1. *Le Ventriloque* (1772). See p. 148, n. 1 in this Norton Critical Edition.

The widow could not for a moment resist this dread summons, which had not the most distant appearance of proceeding from Louis Brabant; whose countenance exhibited no visible change, and whose lips were close and motionless, during the delivery of it. Accordingly, she consented immediately to receive him for her son-in-law. Louis's finances, however, were in a very low situation; and the formalities attending the marriage contract rendered it necessary for him to exhibit some show of riches, and not to give the ghost the lie direct. He accordingly went to work upon a fresh subject, one Cornu, an old and rich banker at Lyons; who had accumulated immense wealth by usury and extortion, and was known to be haunted by remorse of conscience on account of the manner in which he had acquired it.

Having contracted an intimate acquaintance with this man, he, one day while they were sitting together in the usurer's little back parlour, artfully turned the conversation on religious subjects, on demons, and spectres, the pains of purgatory, and the torments of hell. During an interval of silence between them, a voice was heard, which to the astonished banker seemed to be that of his deceased father, complaining, as in the former case, of his dreadful situation in purgatory, and calling upon him to deliver him instantly from thence, by putting into the hands of Louis Brabant, then with him, a large sum for the redemption of Christians then in slavery with the Turks; threatening him at the same time with eternal damnation if he did not take this method to expiate likewise his own sins. The reader will naturally suppose that Louis Brabant affected a due degree of astonishment on the occasion; and further promoted the deception, by acknowledging his having devoted himself to the prosecution of the charitable design imputed to him by the ghost. An old usurer is naturally suspicious. Accordingly the wary banker made a second appointment with the ghost's delegate for the next day; and, to render any design of imposing upon him utterly abortive, took him into the open fields, where not a house, or a tree, or even a bush, or a pit, were in sight, capable of screening any supposed confederate. This extraordinary caution excited the ventriloquist to exert all the powers of his art. Wherever the banker conducted him, at every step his ears were saluted on all sides with the complaints and groans not only of his father, but of all his deceased relations, imploring him for the love of God, and in the name of every saint in the kalendar, to have mercy on his own soul and theirs, by effectually seconding with his purse the intentions of his worthy companion. Cornu could no longer resist the voice of heaven, and accordingly carried his guest home with him, and paid him down 10,000 crowns, with which the honest ventriloquist returned to Paris, and married his mistress.—The catastrophe was fatal. The secret was afterwards blown, and reached the usurer's ears, who was so much affected by the loss of his money, and the mortifying railleries of his neighbours, that he took to his bed and died.

This trick of Louis Brabant is even exceeded by an innocent piece of waggery played off not 40 years ago by another French ventriloquist on a whole community. We have the story from M. de la Chapelle, who informs us, that M. St. Gill the ventriloquist and his intimate friend, returning home from a place whither his business had carried him, sought for shelter from an approaching thunder storm in a neighbouring convent. Finding the whole community in mourning, he inquired the cause, and was told that one of their body had died lately, who was the ornament and delight of the whole society. To pass away the time, he walked into the church, attended by some of the religious, who showed him the tomb of their deceased brother, and spoke feelingly of the scanty honours they had bestowed on his memory. Suddenly a voice was heard, apparently proceeding from the roof of the quire, lamenting the situation of the defunct in purgatory, and reproaching the brotherhood with their lukewarmness and want of zeal on his account. The friars, as soon as their astonishment gave them power to speak, consulted together, and agreed to acquaint the rest of the community with this singular event, so interesting to the whole society. M. St. Gill, who wished to carry on the joke still farther, dissuaded them from taking this step; telling them that they would be treated by their absent brethren as a set of fools and visionaries. He recommended to them, however, the immediately calling of the whole community into the church, where the ghost of their departed brother might probably reiterate his complaints. Accordingly all the friars, novices, lay-brothers, and even the domestics of the convent, were immediately summoned and collected together. In a short time the voice from the roof renewed its lamentations and reproaches, and the whole convent fell on their faces, and vowed a solemn reparation. As a first step, they chanted a *De profundis* in a full choir; during the intervals of which the ghost occasionally expressed the comfort he received from their pious exercises and ejaculations on his behalf. When all was over, the prior entered into a serious conversation with M. St. Gill; and on the strength of what had just passed, sagaciously inveighed against the absurd incredulity of our modern sceptics and pretended philosophers on the article of ghosts or apparitions. M. St. Gill thought it now high time to disabuse the good fathers. This purpose, however, he found it extremely difficult to effect, till he had prevailed upon them to return with him into the church, and there be witnesses of the manner in which he had conducted this ludicrous deception.

A ventriloquist, who performed feats somewhat similar to these, made his appearance in Edinburgh, and many of the other towns of

Scotland, a few months before the writing of this article. He imitated successfully the voice of a squeaking child, and made it appear to proceed from whatever place he chose; from the pockets of the company, from a wooden doll, with which he held many spirited conversations; from beneath a hat or a wine-glass, and out of any person's foot or hand. When the voice seemed to come from beneath a glass or hat, it was dull and on a low key, as sounds confined always are; and what evinced his dexterity was, that when the glass was raised from the table during the time of his speaking, the words or syllables uttered afterwards were on a higher key, in consequence, one would have thought, of the air being readmitted to the speaker. This part of the experiment failed, however, when the management of the glass was at a distance committed to any of the company; but as the room was not well illuminated, we are inclined to attribute this failure to the ventriloquist's not being able to perceive at what precise instant of time the glass was removed from the table. The same artist imitated the tones of a scolding old woman, disturbed at unreasonable hours by a person demanding admission into her house; but this exhibition did not to us appear masterly. The tones of the old woman and the child were not accurately discriminated: the child was a young scold, and the scold spoke like an angry child. We have heard that, when in Edinburgh, the same practitioner astonished a number of persons in the Fishmarket, by making a fish appear to speak, and give the lie to its vender, who affirmed that it was fresh, and caught in the morning; and whether this fact was really performed or not, we cannot doubt, from what we saw and heard him do, but that he was fully equal to its performance.

Our ventriloquist was an illiterate man; and though sufficiently communicative, could not make intelligible to us the manner in which he produced these acoustic deceptions. Indeed if he had, we should hardly have described the practical rules of the art to the public; for though it is proper to make the existence of such an art universally known, it will readily occur to every reflecting mind, that the attainment of it should not be rendered easy to those who, like Louis Brabant, might make it subservient to the purposes of knavery and deception. The speculative principles on which it is founded must be obvious to every man who has studied the philosophy of the human mind, and has ever witnessed the feats of mimickry.

It has been shown elsewhere (see METAPHYSICS, no. 47, 48.), that, previous to experience, we could not refer sound to any external cause; that it does not therefore give immediate indication of the place or distance of the sonorous body; and that it is only by the association of place with sound that the latter becomes an indication of the former. This being admitted, nothing seems requisite to fit a man for becoming an expert ventriloquist but a delicate ear, flexibility of the organs of speech, and long practice of those rules which repeated trials would enable him to discover. A delicate ear perceives every difference which change of place produces in the same sound; and if a person possessed of such an ear have sufficient command over his organs of speech, to produce by them a sound in all respects similar to another proceeding from any distant object, it is evident that to the audience the sound which he utters must appear to proceed from that object. If this be the true theory of ventriloquism, it does not seem to be possible for the most expert ventriloquist to speak in his usual tones of conversation, and at the same time make the voice appear to come from a distance; for these tones must be supposed familiar to his audience, and to be in their minds associated with the ideas of his figure, place, and distance. Hence the ventriloquist whom we saw appeared to speak from various places only in the tones of the squeaking child, while Louis Brabant and M. St. Gille, in their great feats, imitated the voices of ghosts, to which no man could be familiar, and where terror would greatly contribute to the deception. There can, however, be no doubt, but that if, by a peculiar modification of the organs of speech, a sound of any kind can be produced, which in faintness, tone, body, and in short every other sensible quality, perfectly resembles a sound delivered from the roof of an opposite house; the ear will naturally, without examination, refer it to that situation and distance, the sound which the person hears being only a sign, which he has from his infancy been constantly accustomed, by experience, to associate with the idea of a person speaking from a house-top. It is evident too, that when there is no particular ground of suspicion, any small disparity between the two sounds will not be perceptible. But if our theory be just, that experience or habit which misleads a person who has seldom heard the ventriloquist, and is a stranger to his powers, at length sets another person right who is acquainted with them, and has been a frequent witness of their effects. This was actually the case of M. de la Chapelle, with whom the illusion at length ceased, in consequence of repeated visits to M. St. Gille: so that while others, ignorant of his talent, and possessed only of their old or habitual experience with regard to articulate sounds, considered his voice as coming from the top of a tree, or from a deep cellar under ground; our author, well acquainted with the powers of the ventriloquist, and having acquired a new kind of experience, at once referred it directly to the mouth of the speaker.

JOHN ROBISON

From Proofs of a Conspiracy†

Chap. II.

THE ILLUMINATI.

I am now arrived at what I should call the great epoch of Cosmopolitism, the scheme communicated to Baron Knigge[1] by the *Marches di Constanza*. This obliges me to mention a remarkable Lodge of the Eclectic Masonry, erected at Munich in Bavaria,[2] in 1775, under the worshipful Master, Professor Baader. It was called *The Lodge Theodore of Good Counsel.* It had its constitutional patent from the Royal York at Berlin, but had formed a particular system of its own, by instructions from the *Loge des Chevaliers Biensaisants* at Lyons, with which it kept up a correspondence. This respect to the Lodge at Lyons had arisen from the preponderance acquired in general by the French party in the convention at Willemsbad. The deputies of the Rosaic Lodges, as well as the remains of the Templars, and *Stricten Observanz*, all looking up to this as the mother Lodge of what they called the *Grand Orient de la France*, consisting (in 1782) of 266 improved Lodges, united under the *D. de Chartres*.[3] Accordingly the Lodge at Lyons sent Mr. Willermooz as deputy to this convention at Willemsbad. Refining gradually on the simple British Masonry, the Lodge had formed a system of practical morality, which it asserted to be the aim of genuine Masonry, saying, that a true Mason, and a man of upright heart and active virtue, are synonymous characters, and that the great aim of Free Masonry is to

---

† From John Robison, *Proofs of a Conspiracy against All the Religions and Governments of Europe, Carried on in the Secret Meetings of Free Masons, Illuminati, and Reading Societies* (New York: Forman, 1798), pp. 82–99. This was a reprint of the fourth London edition of Robison's work, which was originally published in 1797.
1. Baron Franz Friedrich Knigge (1752–1796), author of *Ueber den Umgang mit Menschen* (1788), which was translated into English as *Practical Philosophy of Social Life; or, the Art of Conversing with Men* (London, 1794; Troy, N.Y.: Penniman, 1805). Knigge was, according to Robison, a notorious Illuminatus, seduced into the order by the Marquis of Constanza.
2. In the southeast of what is now Germany. In the seventeenth and eighteenth centuries, it was an electorate of the Holy Roman Empire. "Lodge of the Electic Masonry": freemasonry is a fraternal order, organized into local lodges, which spread through Europe and North America in the sixteenth and seventeenth centuries. Though its roots lay in radical Protestantism, the order was used for the transmission of secret knowledge (including both mysticism and secular Enlightenment thought) and often became embroiled in state politics.
3. Louis Philippe d'Orléans, duke of Orléans (1782–1785) carried the hereditary title Duke of Chartres. "Templars": a military order allied with Roman Catholicism in the twelfth century; active participants in the Crusades. In the early fourteenth century King Philip IV of France disbanded the order and executed many of its members. Legends abounded for centuries that members, sworn to secrecy, had taken the order underground.

promote the happiness of mankind by every mean in our power. In pursuance of these principles, the Lodge Theodore professedly occupied itself with economical, statistical, and political matters, and not only published from time to time discourses on such subjects by the Brother Orator, but the Members considered themselves as in duty bound to propagate and inculcate the same doctrines out of doors.

Of the zealous members of the Lodge Theodore the most conspicuous was Dr. Adam Weishaupt, Professor of Canon Law in the university of Ingolstadt.[4] This person had been educated among the Jesuits; but the abolition of their order made him change his views, and from being their pupil, he became their most bitter enemy. He had acquired a high reputation in his profession, and was attended not only by those intended for the practice in the law-courts, but also by the young gentlemen at large, in their course of general education; and he brought numbers from the neighbouring states to this university, and gave a *ton* to the studies of the place. He embraced with great keenness this opportunity of spreading the favorite doctrines of the Lodge, and his auditory became the seminary of Cosmo-politism. The engaging pictures of the possible felicity of a society where every office is held by a man of talents and virtue, and where every talent is set in a place fitted for its exertion, forcibly catches the generous and unsuspecting minds of youth, and in a Roman Catholic state, far advanced in the habits of gross superstition (a character given to Bavaria by its neighbours) and abounding in monks and idle dignitaries, the opportunities must be frequent for observing the inconsiderate dominion of the clergy, and the abject and indolent submission of the laity. Accordingly Professor Weishaupt says, in his Apology for Illuminatism, that Deism,[5] Infidelity, and Atheism are more prevalent in Bavaria than in any country he was acquainted with. Discourses, therefore, in which the absurdity and horrors of superstition and spiritual tyranny were strongly painted, could not fail of making a deep impression. And during this state of the minds of the auditory the transition to general infidelity and irreligion is so easy, and so invit-

---

4. Johann Adam Weishaupt (1748–1830), philosopher and law professor at the University of Ingolstadt, was the founder of the Order of the Illuminati. Weishaupt was involved in an effort to wrest control of the university from the Jesuits, who had made it a center of the Counter-Reformation during the seventeenth century, before being banned by Pope Clement XIV in 1773. Weishaupt initiated the secret order supposedly to gain influence and spread knowledge apart from state and church authority. In 1784 Karl Theodor, elector of Bavaria, fearing sedition, banned the Illuminati, forcing Weishaupt to flee the electorate. Though the Illuminati were effectively stamped out, Robison's and other exposures fueled fears that the conspiracy endured in secret and aimed to overturn all government and religion in Europe and America.

5. A belief system, prevalent among Enlightenment thinkers, in which a Divine Architect is credited with creation, but the world exists according to natural law, without divine interference.

ing to sanguine youth, prompted perhaps by a latent wish that the restraints which religion imposes on the expectants of a future state might be found, on enquiry, to be nothing but groundless terrors; that I imagine it requires the most anxious care of the public teacher to keep the minds of his audience impressed with the reality and importance of the great truths of religion, while he frees them from the shackles of blind and absurd superstition. I fear that this celebrated instructor had none of this anxiety, but was satisfied with his great success in the last part of this talk, the emancipation of his young hearers from the terrors of superstition. I suppose also that this was the more agreeable to him, as it procured him the triumph over the Jesuits, with whom he had long struggled for the direction of the university.

This was in 1777. Weishaupt had long been scheming the establishment of an Association or Order, which, in time, should govern the world. In his first fervour and high expectations, he hinted to several Ex-Jesuits the probability of their recovering, under a new name, the influence which they formerly possessed, and of being again of great service to society, by directing the education of youth of distinction, now emancipated from all civil and religious prejudices. He prevailed on some to join him, but they all retracted but two. After this disappointment Weishaupt became the implacable enemy of the Jesuits; and his sanguine temper made him frequently lay himself open to their piercing eye, and drew on him their keenest resentment, and at last made him the victim of their enmity.

The Lodge Theodore was the place where the above mentioned doctrines were most zealously propagated. But Weishaupt's emissaries had already procured the adherence of many other Lodges; and the Eclectic Masonry had been brought into vogue chiefly by their exertions at the Willemsbad convention. The Lodge Theodore was perhaps less guarded in its proceedings, for it became remarkable for the very bold sentiments in politics and religion which were frequently uttered in their harangues; and its members were noted for their zeal in making proselytes. Many bitter pasquinades, satires, and other offensive pamphlets were in secret circulation, and even larger works of very dangerous tendency, and several of them were traced to that Lodge. The Elector often expressed his disapprobation of such proceedings, and sent them kind messages, desiring them to be careful not to disturb the peace of the country, and particularly to recollect the solemn declaration made to every entrant into the Fraternity of Free Masons, "That no subject of religion or politics shall ever be touched on in the Lodge;" a declaration which alone could have procured his permission of any secret assembly whatever, and on the sincerity and honor of which he had reckoned when he gave his sanction to their establishment. But repeated accounts of the same kind increased the alarm, and the Elector ordered a judicial enquiry into the proceedings of the Lodge Theodore.

It was then discovered that this and several associated Lodges were the nursery or preparation-school for another Order of Masons, who called themselves the ILLUMINATED, and that the express aim of this Order was to abolish Christianity, and overturn all civil government. But the result of the enquiry was very imperfect and unsatisfactory. No Illuminati were to be found. They were unknown in the Lodge. Some of the members occasionally heard of certain candidates for illumination called MINERVALS, who were sometimes seen among them. But whether these had been admitted, or who received them, was known only to themselves. Some of these were examined in private by the Elector himself. They said that they were bound by honor to secrecy: But they assured the Elector, on their honor, that the aim of the Order was in the highest degree praise-worthy, and useful both to church and state: But this could not allay the anxiety of the profane public; and it was repeatedly stated to the Elector, that members of the Lodge Theodore had unguardedly spoken of this Order as one that in time must rule the world. He therefore issued an order forbidding, during his pleasure, all secret assemblies, and shutting up the Mason Lodges. It was not meant to be rigorously enforced, but was intended as a trial of the deference of these Associations for civil authority. The Lodge Theodore distinguished itself by pointed opposition; continuing its meetings; and the members, out of doors, openly reprobated the prohibition as an absurd and unjustifiable tyranny.

In the beginning of 1783, four professors of the Marianen Academy,[6] founded by the widow of the late Elector, viz. Utschneider, Cossandey, Renner, and Grunberger, with two others, were summoned before the Court of Enquiry, and questioned, on their allegiance, respecting the Order of the Illuminati. They acknowledged that they belonged to it, and when more closely examined, they related several circumstances of its constitution and principles. Their declarations were immediately published, and were very unfavorable. The Order was said to abjure Christianity, and to refuse admission into the higher degrees to all who adhered to any of the three confessions. Sensual pleasures were restored to the rank they held in the Epicurean[7] philosophy. Self-murder was justified on Stoi-

---

6. Now Malbork, a town in northern Poland, Marienburg was founded in the thirteenth century by the Teutonic knights, and is the site of a Gothic fortress dating to 1274. In the eighteenth century Marienburg belonged to the kingdom of Prussia.

7. A philosophical system, derived from the Greek philosopher Epicurus (341–271 B.C.E.), which embraces the simple pleasures of the material world and resists notions of divine intervention.

cal[8] principles. In the Lodges death was declared an eternal sleep; patriotism and loyalty were called narrow-minded prejudices, and incompatible with universal benevolence; continual declamations were made on liberty and equality as the unalienable rights of man. The baneful influence of accumulated property was declared an insurmountable obstacle to the happiness of any nation whose chief laws were framed for its protection and increase. Nothing was so frequently discoursed of as the propriety of employing, for a good purpose, the means which the wicked employed for evil purposes; and it was taught, that the preponderancy of good in the ultimate result consecrated every mean employed; and that wisdom and virtue consisted in properly determining this balance. This appeared big with danger; because it appeared that nothing would be scrupled at, if we could make it appear that the Order could derive advantage from it, because the great object of the Order was held as superior to every consideration. They concluded by saying that the method of education made them all spies on each other and on all around them. But all this was denied by the Illuminati. Some of them were said to be absolutely false; and the rest were said to be mistakes. The apostate professors had acknowledged their ignorance of many things. Two of them were only Minervals, another was an Illuminatus of the lowest class, and the fourth was but one step farther advanced. Pamphlets appeared on both sides, with very little effect. The Elector called before him one of the superiors, a young nobleman, who denied these injurious charges, and said that they were ready to lay before his Highness their whole archives and all constitutional papers.

Notwithstanding all this, the government had received such an impression of the dangerous tendency of the Order, that the Elector issued another edict, forbidding all hidden assemblies; and a third, expressly abolishing the Order of Illuminati. It was followed by a search after their papers. The Lodge Theodore was immediately searched, but none were to be found. They said now that they had burnt them all, as of no use, since that Order was at an end.

It was now discovered, that Weishaupt was the head and founder of the Order. He was deprived of his Professor's chair, and banished from the Bavarian States; but with a pension of 800 florins, which he refused. He went to Regensburg, on the confines of Switzerland. Two Italians, the Marquis Constanza and Marquis Savioli, were also banished, with equal pensions (about L. 40) which they accepted. One Zwack, a counsellor, holding some law-office, was also banished. Others were imprisoned for some time. Weishaupt went afterwards

8. Relating to a philosophical system dating to the third century B.C.E. in which philosophers exercise refined moral judgments by subordinating emotion to reason.

into the service of the D. of Saxe Gotha, a person of a romantic turn of mind, and whom we shall again meet with. Zwack went into the service of the Pr. de Salms, who soon after had so great a hand in the disturbances in Holland.

By destroying the papers, all opportunity was lost for authenticating the innocence and usefulness of the Order. After much altercation and paper war, Weishaupt, now safe in Regensburg, published an account of the Order, namely, the account which was given to every *Novice* in a discourse read at his reception. To this were added, the statutes and the rules of proceeding, as far as the degree of *Illuminatus Minor*, inclusive. This account he affirmed to be conform to the real practice of the Order. But this publication did by no means satisfy the public mind. It differed exceedingly from the accounts given by the four professors. It made no mention of the higher degrees, which had been most blamed by them. Besides, it was alleged, that it was all a fiction, written in order to lull the suspicions which had been raised (and this was found to be the case, except in respect of the very lowest degree.) The real constitution was brought to light by degrees, and shall be laid before the reader, in the order in which it was gradually discovered, that we may the better judge of things not fully known by the conduct of the leaders during the detection. The first account given by Weishaupt is correct, as far as I shall make use of it, and shows clearly the methods that were taken to recommend the Order to strangers.

The Order of ILLUMINATI appears as an accessory to Free Masonry. It is in the Lodges of Free Masons that the Minervals are found, and there they are prepared for Illumination. They must have previously obtained the three English degrees. The founder says more. He says that his doctrines are the only true Free Masonry. He was the chief promoter of the *Eclectic System*. This he urged as the best method for getting information of all the explanations which have been given of the Masonic Mysteries. He was also a *Strict Observanz*, and an adept Rosycrucian.[9] The result of all his knowledge is worthy of particular remark, and shall therefore be given at large.

"I declare," says he, "and I challenge all mankind to contradict my declaration, that no man can give any account of the Order of Free Masonry, of its origin, of its history, of its object, nor any explanation of its mysteries and symbols, which does not leave the mind in total uncertainty on all these points. Every man is entitled, therefore, to give any explanation of the symbols, and any system of the

9. A member of a secret society that originated in early-seventeenth-century Germany with the publication of manifestoes announcing the teachings of Christian Rosencreutz, a mystical figure who had supposedly lived in the fourteenth century; regarded as a hoax by some, Rosicrucianism nevertheless was an important movement of the radical Reformation and laid the groundwork for the emergence of freemasonry.

doctrines, that he can render palatable. Hence have sprung up that variety of systems which for twenty years have divided the Order. The simple tale of the English, and the fifty degrees of the French, and the Knights of Baron Hunde, are equally authentic, and have equally had the support of intelligent and zealous Brethren. These systems are in fact but one. They have all sprung from the Blue Lodge of Three degrees; take these for their standard, and found on these all the improvements by which each system is afterwards suited to the particular object which it keeps in view. There is no man, nor system, in the world, which can show by undoubted succession that it should stand at the head of the Order. Our ignorance in this particular frets me. Do but consider our short history of 120 years.—Who will show me the Mother Lodge? Those of London we have discovered to be self-erected in 1716. Ask for their archives. They tell you they were burnt. They have nothing but the wretched sophistications of the Englishman Anderson, and the Frenchman Desaguilliers. Where is the Lodge of York, which pretends to the priority, with their King Bouden, and the archives that he brought from the East? These too are all burnt. What is the Chapter of Old Aberdeen, and its Holy Clericate? Did we not find it unknown, and the Mason Lodges there the most ignorant of all the ignorant, gaping for instruction from our deputies? Did we not find the same thing at London? And have not their missionaries been among us, prying into our mysteries, and eager to learn from us what is true Free Masonry? It is in vain, therefore; to appeal to judges; they are no where to be found; all claim for themselves the sceptre of the Order; all indeed are on an equal footing. They obtained followers, not from their authenticity, but from their conduciveness to the end which they proposed, and from the importance of that end. It is by this scale that we must measure the mad and wicked explanations of the Rosycrucians, the Exorcists, and Cabalists. These are rejected by all good Masons, because incompatible with social happiness. Only such systems as promote this are retained. But alas, they are all sadly deficient, because they leave us under the dominion of political and religious prejudices; and they are as inefficient as the sleepy dose of an ordinary sermon.

"But I have contrived an explanation which has every advantage; is inviting to Christians of every communion; gradually frees them from all religious prejudices; cultivates the social virtues; and animates them by a great, a feasible, and *speedy* prospect of universal happiness, in a state of liberty and moral equality, freed from the obstacles which subordination, rank, and riches, continually throw in our way. My explanation is accurate, and complete, my means are effectual, and irresistible. Our secret Association works in a way that nothing can withstand *and man shall soon be free and happy.*

"This is the great object held out by this Association: and the means of attaining it is Illumination, enlightening the understanding by the sun of reason, which will dispel the clouds of superstition and of prejudice. The proficients in this Order are therefore justly named the Illuminated. And of all Illumination which human reason can give, none is comparable to the discovery of what we are, our nature, our obligations, what happiness we are capable of, and what are the means of attaining it. In comparison with this, the most brilliant sciences are but amusements for the idle and luxurious. To fit man by Illumination for active virtue, to engage him to it by the strongest motives, to render the attainment of it easy and certain, by finding employment for every talent, and by placing every talent in its proper sphere of action, so that all, without feeling any extraordinary effort, and in conjunction with and completion of ordinary business, shall urge forward, with united powers, the general task. This indeed will be an employment suited to noble natures, grand in its views, and delightful in its exercise.

"And what is this general object? THE HAPPINESS OF THE HUMAN RACE. Is it not distressing to a generous mind, after contemplating what human nature is capable of, to see how little we enjoy? When we look at this goodly world, and see that every man *may* be happy, but that the happiness of one depends on the conduct of another; when we see the wicked so powerful, and the good so weak; and that it is in vain to strive, singly and alone, against the general current of vice and oppression; the wish naturally arises in the mind, that it were possible to form a durable combination of the most worthy persons, who should work together in removing the obstacles to human happiness, become terrible to the wicked, and give their aid to all the good without distinction, and should by the most powerful means, first fetter, and by fettering, lessen vice; means which at the same time should promote virtue, by rendering the inclination to rectitude, hitherto too feeble, more powerful and engaging. Would not such an association be a blessing to the world?

"But where are the proper persons, the good, the generous, and the accomplished, to be found? and how, and by what strong motives, are they to be induced to engage in a task so vast, so incessant, so difficult, and so laborious? This Association must be gradual. There *are* some such persons to be found in every society. Such noble minds will be engaged by the heartwarming object. The first task of the Association must therefore be to form the young members. As these multiply and advance, they become the apostles of beneficence, and the work is now on foot, and advances with a speed encreasing every day. The slightest observation shows that nothing will so much contribute to increase the zeal of the members as secret union. We see with what keenness and zeal the frivolous business of Free Masonry is conducted, by persons knit together by the secrecy of their union. It is needless to enquire into the causes of this zeal which secrecy produces. It is an universal fact, confirmed by the history of every age. Let this circumstance of our constitution therefore be directed to this noble purpose, and then all the objections urged against it by jealous tyranny and affrighted superstition will vanish. The Order will thus work silently, and securely; and though the generous benefactors of the human race are thus deprived of the applause of the world, they have the noble pleasure of seeing their work prosper in their hands."

Such is the aim, and such are the hopes of the Order of the Illuminated. Let us now see how these were to be accomplished. We cannot judge precisely of this, because the account given of the constitution of the Order by its founder includes only the lowest degree, and even this is suspected to be fictitious. The accounts given by the four Professors, even of this part of the Order, make a very different impression on the mind, although they differ only in a few particulars.

The only ostensible members of the Order were the Minervals. They were to be found only in the Lodges of Free Masons. A candidate for admission must make his wish known to some Minerval; he reports it to a Superior, who, by a channel to be explained presently, intimates it to the Council. No notice is farther taken of it for some time. The candidate is carefully observed in silence, and if thought unfit for the Order, no notice is taken of his solicitation. But if otherwise, the candidate receives privately an invitation to a conference. Here he meets with a person unknown to him, and, previous to all further conference, he is required to peruse and to sign the following oath.

"I N. N. hereby bind myself, by mine honor and good name, forswearing all mental reservation, never to reveal, by hint, word, writing, or in any manner whatever, even to my most trusted friend, any thing that shall now be said or done to me respecting my wished-for reception, and this whether my reception shall follow or not; I being previously assured that it shall contain nothing contrary to religion, the state, nor good manners. I promise, that I shall make no intelligible extract from any papers which shall be shewn me now or during my noviciate. All this I swear, as I am, and as I hope to continue, a Man of Honor."

The urbanity of this protestation must agreeably impress the mind of a person who recollects the dreadful imprecations which he made at his reception into the different ranks of Free Masonry. The candidate is then introduced to an *Illuminatus Dirigens*, whom perhaps he knows, and is told that this person is to be his future instructor. There is now presented to the candidate, what they call a table, in which he writes his name, place of birth, age, rank, place of residence, profession, and favorite studies. He is then made to read several articles of this table. It contains, 1st. a very concise account of the Order, its connection with Free Masonry, and its great object, the promoting the happiness of mankind by means of instruction and confirmation in virtuous principles. 2d. Several questions relative to the Order. Among these are, "What advantages he hopes to derive from being a member? What he most particularly wishes to learn? What delicate questions relative to the life, the prospects, the duties of man, as an individual, and as a citizen, he wishes to have particularly discussed to him? In what respects he thinks he can be of use to the Order? Who are his ancestors, relations, friends, correspondents, or enemies? Whom he thinks proper persons to be received into the Order, or whom he thinks unfit for it, and the reasons for both opinions?" To each of these questions he must give some answer in writing.

The Novice and his Mentor are known only to each other; perhaps nothing more follows upon this; if otherwise, the Mentor appoints another conference, and begins his instructions, by giving him in detail certain portions of the constitution, and of the fundamental rules of the Order. Of these the Novice must give a weekly account in writing. He must also read, in the Mentor's house, a book containing more of the instructions of the Order; but he must make no extracts. Yet from this reading he must derive all his knowledge; and he must give an account in writing of his progress. All writings received from his Superiors must be returned with a stated punctuality. These writings consist chiefly of important and delicate questions, suited, either to the particular inclination, or to the peculiar taste which the candidate had discovered in his subscriptions of the articles of the table, and in his former rescripts, or to the direction which the Mentor wishes to give to his thoughts.

Enlightening the understanding, and the rooting out of prejudices, are pointed out to him as the principal tasks of his noviciate. The knowledge of himself is considered as preparatory to all other knowledge. To disclose to him, by means of the calm and unbiased observation of his instructor, what is his own character, his most vulnerable side, either in respect of temper, passions, or prepossessions, is therefore the most essential service that can be done him. For this purpose there is required of him some account of his own conduct on occasions where he doubted of its propriety; some account of his friendships, of his differences of opinion, and of his conduct on such occasions. From such relations the Superior learns his manner of thinking and judging, and these propensities which require his chief attention.

Having made the candidate acquainted with himself, he is apprised that the Order is not a speculative, but an active association, engaged in doing good to others. The knowledge of human character is therefore of all others the most important. This is acquired only by observation, assisted by the instructions of his teacher. Characters in history are proposed to him for observation, and his opinion is required. After this he is directed to look around him, and to notice the conduct of other men; and part of his weekly rescripts must consist of accounts of all interesting occurrences in his neighbour-hood, whether of a public or private nature. Cossandey, one of the four Professors, gives a particular account of the instructions relating to this kind of science. "The Novice must be attentive to trifles: For, in frivolous occurrences a man is indolent, and makes no effort to act a part, so that his real character is then acting alone. Nothing will have such influence with the Superiors in promoting the advancement of a candidate as very copious narrations of this kind, because the candidate, if promoted, is to be employed in an active station, and it is from this kind of information only that the Superiors can judge of his fitness. These characteristic anecdotes are not for the instruction of the Superiors, who are men of long experience, and familiar with such occupation. But they inform the Order concerning the talents and proficiency of the young member. Scientific instruction, being connected by system, is soon communicated, and may in general be very completely obtained from the books which are recommended to the Novice, and acquired in the public seminaries of instruction. But knowledge of character is more multifarious and more delicate. For this there is no college, and it must therefore require longer time for its attainment. Besides, this assiduous and long continued study of men, enables the possessor of such knowledge to act with men, and by his knowledge of their character, to influence their conduct. For such reasons this study is continued, and these rescripts are required, during the whole progress through the Order, and attention to them is recommended as the only mean of advancement. Remarks on Physiognomy in these narrations are accounted of considerable value." So far Mr. Cossandey.

During all this trial, which may last one, two, or three years, the Novice knows no person of the Order but his own instructor, with whom he has frequent meetings, along with other Minervals. In these conversations he learns the importance of the Order, and the opportunities he will afterwards have of acquiring much hidden science. The employment of his unknown Superiors naturally causes him to entertain very high notions of their abilities and worth. He is counselled to aim at a resemblance to them by getting rid by degrees of all those prejudices or prepossessions which checked his own former progress; and he is assisted in this endeavour by an invitation to a correspondence with them. He may address his Provincial Superior, by directing his letter *Soli*, or the General by *Primo*, or the Superiors in general by *Quibus licet*. In these letters he may mention whatever he thinks conducive to the advancement of the Order; he may inform the Superiors how his instructor behaves to him; if assiduous or remiss, indulgent or severe. The Superiors are enjoined by the strongest motives to convey these letters wherever addressed. None but the General and Council know the result of all this; and all are enjoined to keep themselves and their proceedings unknown to all the world.

                    *   *   *

TIMOTHY DWIGHT

The Duty of Americans at the Present Crisis[†]

                    *   *   *

About the year 1728, Voltaire,[1] so celebrated for his wit and brilliancy, and not less distinguished for his hatred of christianity and his abandonment of principle, formed a systematical design to destroy christianity, and to introduce in its stead a general diffusion of irreligion and atheism. For this purpose he associated with himself Frederic the II, king of Prussia, and Mess. D'Alembert and Diderot,[2] the principal compilers of the Encyclopedie; all men of talents, atheists, and in the like manner abandoned. The principal parts of this system were, 1st. The compilation of the Encyclopedie;[3] in which with great art and insidiousness the doctrines of Natural as well as Christian Theology were rendered absurd and ridiculous; and the mind of the reader was insensibly steeled against conviction and duty. 2. The

---

† From Timothy Dwight, *The Duty of Americans, at the Present Crisis, Illustrated in a Discourse Preached on the Fourth of July, 1798* (New Haven, Conn.: Thomas and Samuel Green, 1798), pp. 10–15. Dwight (1752–1817) was president of Yale College and a former teacher of Brown's friend Elihu Smith. Along with his brother, Theodore Dwight, and the Massachusetts minister Jedidiah Morse, he was a major American promoter of conspiracy theories about the Bavarian Illuminati at the turn of the nineteenth century.
1. The pen name of François-Marie Arouet (1694–1778), French Enlightenment philosophe.
2. Denis Diderot (1713–1784), French art critic and philosophe. Jean le Rond d'Alembert (1717–1783), French mathematician and philosphe. Together D'Alembert and Diderot oversaw the compilation of a seventeen-volume *Encyclopédie*, with contributions from over 140 writers.
3. "The celebrated French Dictionary of Arts and Sciences, in which articles of Theology were speciously and decently written, but, by references artfully made to other articles, all the truth of the former was entirely and insidiously overthrown to most readers, by the sophistry of the latter" [Dwight's note].

overthrow of the religious orders in Catholic countries; a step essentially necessary to the destruction of the religion professed in those countries. 3. The establishment of a sect of philosophists to serve, it is presumed, as a conclave, a rallying point, for all their followers. 4. The appropriation to themselves, and their disciples, of the places and honours of members of the French Academy, the most respectable literary society in France, and always considered as containing none but men of prime learning and talents. In this way they designed to hold out themselves, and their friends, as the only persons of great literary and intellectual distinction in that country, and to dictate all literary opinions to the nation.[4] 5. The fabrication of Books of all kinds against christianity, especially such as excite doubt, and generate contempt and derision. Of these they issued, by themselves and their friends, who early became numerous, an immense number; so printed, as to be purchased for little or nothing, and so written, as to catch the feelings, and steal upon the approbation, of every class of men. 6. The formation of a secret Academy, of which Voltaire was the standing president, and in which books were formed, altered, forged, imputed as posthumous to deceased writers of reputation, and sent abroad with the weight of their names. These were printed and circulated, at the lowest price, through all classes of men, in an uninterrupted succession, and through every part of the kingdom.

Nor were the labours of this Academy confined to religion. They attacked also morality and government, unhinged gradually the minds of men, and destroyed their reverence for every thing heretofore esteemed sacred.

In the mean time, the Masonic Societies, which had been originally instituted for convivial and friendly purposes only, were, especially in France and Germany, made the professed scenes of debate concerning religion, morality, and government, by these philosophists,[5] who had in great numbers become Masons. For such debate the legalized existence of Masonry, its profound secresy, its

---

4. "So far was this carried, that a Mr. Beauzet, a layman, but a sincere christian, who was one of the forty members, once asked D'Alembert how they came to admit him among them? D'Alembert answered, without hesitation, "I am sensible, this must seem astonishing to you; but we wanted a skilful grammarian, and among our party, not one had acquired a reputation in this line. We know that you believe in God, but, being a good sort of man, we cast our eyes upon you, for want of a philosopher to supply your place." Brit. Crit. Art. Barruel's Memoirs of the History of Jacobinism. August 1797" [Dwight's note]. In addition to John Robison's *Proofs of a Conspiracy,* Dwight's chief source on the Illuminati is the Abbé Augustin Barruel's four-volume expose, *Memoirs Illustrating the History of Jacobinism* (1797–1798).

5. "The words *Philosophism* and *Philosophists* may in our opinion, be happily adopted, from this work, to designate the doctrines of the Deistical sect; and thus to rescue the honourable terms of Philosophy and Philosopher from the abuse, into which they have fallen. *Philosophism* is the love of *Sophisms,* and thus completely describes the sect of Voltaire: A *Philosophyist* is a lover of *Sophists.* Brit. Crit. Ibid." [Dwight's note].

solemn and mystic rites and symbols, its mutual correspondence, and its extension through most civilized countries, furnished the greatest advantages. All here was free, safe, and calculated to encourage the boldest excursions of restless opinion and impatient ardour, and to make and fix the deepest impressions. Here, and in no other place, under such arbitrary governments, could every innovator in these important subjects utter every sentiment, however daring, and attack every doctrine and institution, however guarded by law or sanctity. In the secure and unrestrained debates of the lodge, every novel, licentious, and alarming opinion was resolutely advanced. Minds, already tinged with philosophism, were here speedily blackened with a deep and deadly die; and these, which came fresh and innocent to the scene of contamination, became early and irremediably corrupted. A stubborn incapacity of conviction, and a flinty insensibility to every moral and natural tie, grew of course out of this combination of causes; and men were surely prepared, before themselves were aware, for every plot and perpetration. In these hot beds were sown the seeds of that astonishing Revolution, and all its dreadful appendages, which now spreads dismay and horror throughout half the globe.

While these measures were advancing the great design with a regular and rapid progress, Doctor Adam Weishaupt, professor of the Canon law in the University of Ingolstadt, a city of Bavaria (in Germany) formed, about the year 1777, the order of Illuminati. This order is professedly a higher order of Masons, originated by himself, and grafted on ancient Masonic Institutions. The secrecy, solemnity, mysticism, and correspondence of Masonry, were in this new order preserved and enhanced; while the ardour of innovation, the impatience of civil and moral restraints, and the aims against government, morals, and religion, were elevated, expanded, and rendered more systematical, malignant, and daring.

In the societies of Illuminati doctrines were taught, which strike at the root of all human happiness and virtue; and every such doctrine was either expressly or implicitly involved in their system.

The being of God was denied and ridiculed.

Government was asserted to be a curse, and authority a mere usurpation.

Civil society was declared to be the only apostasy of man.

The possession of property was pronounced to be robbery.

Chastity and natural affection were declared to be nothing more than groundless prejudices.

Adultery, assassination, poisoning, and other crimes of the like infernal nature, were taught as lawful, and even as virtuous actions.

To crown such a system of falshood and horror all means were declared to be lawful, provided the end was good.

In this last doctrine men are not only loosed from every bond, and from every duty; but from every inducement to perform any thing which is good, and, abstain from any thing which is evil; and are set upon each other, like a company of hellhounds to worry, rend, and destroy. Of the goodness of the end every man is to judge for himself; and most men, and all men who resemble the Illuminati, will pronounce every end to be good, which will gratify their inclinations. The great and good ends proposed by the Illuminati, as the ultimate objects of their union, are the overthrow of religion, government, and human society civil and domestic. These they pronounce to be so good, that murder, butchery, and war, however extended and dreadful, are declared by them to be completely justifiable, if necessary for these great purposes. With such an example in view, it will be in vain to hunt for ends, which can be evil.

Correspondent with this summary was the whole system. No villainy, no impiety, no cruelty, can be named, which was not vindicated; and no virtue, which was not covered with contempt.

The means by which this society was enlarged, and its doctrines spread, were of every promising kind. With unremitted ardour and diligence the members insinuated themselves into every place of power and trust, and into every literary, political and friendly society; engrossed as much as possible the education of youth, especially of distinction; became licensers of the press, and directors of every literary journal; waylaid every foolish prince, every unprincipled civil officer, and every abandoned clergyman; entered boldly into the desk, and with unhallowed hands, and satanic lips, polluted the pages of God; enlisted in their service almost all the booksellers, and of course the printers, of Germany; inundated the country with books, replete with infidelity, irreligion, immorality, and obscenity; prohibited the printing, and prevented the sale, of books of the contrary character; decried and ridiculed them when published in spite of their efforts; panegyrized and trumpeted those of themselves and their coadjutors; and in a word made more numerous, more diversified, and more strenuous exertions, than an active imagination would have preconceived.

To these exertions their success has been proportioned. Multitudes of the Germans, notwithstanding the gravity, steadiness, and sobriety of their national character, have become either partial or entire converts to these wretched doctrines; numerous societies have been established among them; the public faith and morals have been unhinged; and the political and religious affairs of that empire have assumed an aspect, which forebodes its total ruin. In France, also, Illumination has been eagerly and extensively adopted; and those men, who have had, successively, the chief direction of the public affairs of that country, have been members of this society.

Societies have also been erected in Switzerland and Italy, and have contributed probably to the success of the French, and to the overthrow of religion and government, in those countries. Mentz was delivered up to Custine by the Illuminati; and that General appears to have been guillotined, because he declined to encourage the same treachery with respect to Manheim.

Nor have England and Scotland escaped the contagion. Several societies have been erected in both of those countries. Nay in the private papers, seized in the custody of the leading members in Germany, several such societies are recorded as having been erected in America, before the year 1786.[6]

It is a remarkable fact, that a large proportion of the sentiments, here stated, have been publicly avowed and applauded in the French legislature. The being and providence of God have been repeatedly denied and ridiculed. Christ has been mocked with the grossest insult. Death, by a solemn legislative decree has been declared to be an eternal sleep. Marriage has been degraded to a farce, and the community, by the law of divorce, invited to universal prostitution. In the school of public instruction atheism is professedly taught; and at an audience before the legislature, Nov. 30, 1793, the head scholar declared, that he and his schoolfellows detested a God; a declaration received by the members with unbounded applause, and rewarded with the fraternal kiss of the president, and with the honors of the fitting.[7]

I presume I have sufficiently proved the fulfilment of the second part of this remarkable prophesy; and shewn, that doctrines and teachers, answering to the description, have arisen in the very countries specified, and that they are rapidly spreading through the world, to engage mankind in an open and professed war against God. I shall only add, that the titles of these philosophistical books have, in various instances, been too obscene to admit of a translation by a virtuous man, and in a decent state of society. So fully are these teachers entitled to the epithet unclean.

Assuming now as just, for the purposes of this discourse, the explanation, which has been given, I shall proceed to consider the import of the Text.

6. "See Robison's Conspiracy and the Abbe Barruel's Memoirs of the history of Jacobinism" [Dwight's note].
7. "See Gifford's Letter to Erskine" [Dwight's note]. John Gifford, *A Letter to the Hon. Thomas Erskine; Containing Some Strictures on His View of the Causes and Consequences of the Present War with France* (Philadelphia: Cobbett, 1797). Gifford was founder of the London-based *Anti-Jacobin Review*; Erskine had been a defense lawyer for Thomas Paine on charges of libel stemming from the publication of *The Rights of Man* (1791).

The Text is an affectionate address of the Redeemer to his children, teaching them that conduct, which he wills them especially to pursue in this alarming season. It is the great practical remark, drawn by infinite Wisdom and Goodness from a most solemn sermon, and cannot fail therefore to merit our highest attention. Had he not, while recounting the extensive and dreadful convulsion, described in the context, made a declaration of this nature, there would have been little room for the exercise of any emotions, beside those of terror and despair. The gloom would have been universal and entire; a blank midnight without a star to cheer the solitary darkness. But here a hope, a promise, is furnished to such as obey the injunction, by which it is followed; a luminary like that, which shone to the wise men of the east, is lighted up to guide our steps to the Author of peace and salvation.

BLESSED, even in this calamitous season, saith the Saviour of men, *is he that watcheth, and keepeth his garments, lest he walk naked, and they see his shame.*

* * *

CHARLES BROCKDEN BROWN

Outline of *Wieland*†

ACT I.

Wieland was of saxon origin. He was born 1700. He was
apprenticed in London at the age of 15. He contracted a
gloomy & religious spir[r]it, from the perusal of the works
of the first reformers. He built up a system of his own. The
Savoyard protestant faith was his. See Chambers
Cyclopædia. At the age of 22. He retired to America,
with a view to enjoy his tenets unmolested. He was
an orphan, with enough secured to him, to purchase an
estate in [his] [own] country. He bought ground & built
an house, on Schyylkill. He lived a batchelor & farmer
till 1734. Then married a girl of 18. With out fortune,
[but ⟨?⟩] amiable and devout. ✗ They died 1749. Their son

---

† From Elijah Brown's Notebook (No. 14), Brown Family Papers, Historical Society of Pennsylvania. Printed by permission of the Historical Society of Pennsylvania. The transcription follows that of the editors of the Kent State Edition of Brown's novels, where it appears with a facsimile of the notebook pages in volume 1, pp. 423–441.

10. Yr's old. Their daughter 6—a guardeaness. Their
mothers sister, a maiden lady, living in the city.
A Domestic education, not devout, was enjoyed by them
Devotional impressions were already made upon the

$$\text{Rimband} \langle ? \rangle$$
$$\text{Charlotte}$$

son, he, at the age of 21. Married, a woman of 23.. $\overset{2}{X}$

    Ch.2.

Her character, as little devotional, as Carolines. Considerable resemblance of character. Between the woman.
Gayety of spirits in them. A certain gravity & gloom-
iness in them. In solitude deepening, in society & in
consequence of efforts, yieelding. Affectionate, guileless
inoffensive. After [4 ⟨?⟩] 6. yrs. wedlock, happy, serene,
enjoying 4 children. The oldest six yrs old.

    An orphan girl. [13 ⟨?⟩] 14. yrs of age. Adopted &
cherished by Charles.
Marcrieve is introduced to them. A form & mind, cultivated
enlightened. Arrived at Philadelphia from Hull. Single
& unknown. Resides in lodgings— Walks on the schuylkill
Is sometimes seen near Carfield.

Ch. 4.

    One occasion wanders here at night. Takes his post
at the summer house. Philip & Charles come hither,
to plan a certain affair. They are overheard by
Marcrieve. They fear Charlottes disapprobation. This
is ventrilloqually given. A voyage to Europe, to Saxony,
to claim an estate—Charlotte & Caroline at that time
together at Cardale.

Ch. 3.

    previously, to this, Marcrieve, in the temple, sees
Charles approaching. Desires his absence. Therefore calls
to him from behind.—

          5
    Marcrieve introduced. Characterized, parallel
between him & Charles. Deportment. Conversation.

   6
Suppresses his story. Conjectures founded on the hints

         7.8.9.10.

afforded them.— Scenes tending to impress charles
with an opinion of Invisible influence. Designed mere
ly to encite surprize. & sport with credulity. 3 of these
goes a journey—whither he conceals. July 6.

Act. 2nd

[The scenes] Words audible to Charles alone. Assumes

—————————————————————— 1

the character of guardian Angel. Warns of danger to a

rise from going into his chamber

2

Commands him to save a tenants house from the flames.

3^{rdly}—Summer house, the scene; Death, conditional, on

performing some precept to be given

a month forward.

Act 2nd

11 Evening Aug: 6. Carol. Charl. & Charles together
Tranquility, pleasure, conjugal & parental tenderness. Accompanies his sister home. [Returns.]

12. Return. Conference.

13. Carol. visits. & [inspects] examines.

14. Returns. M^{r}. Hatsel & four neighbours. Confined in Philad prison.

15. Arraignment. & incidents.

16. 17. 18. 19. 20.— Confessional speech.

4. 5.

2 Rupture from prison. [Connivance of Caroline.] goes to Menham. Endeavours to gain access to Philip. Kills a faithful Negro who withstands him. Philip escapes. Maniac searches his chamber. Flies to Carlhill. Knocks at the door rouses his sister. Conference from a window. Persuades her to descend. About to do so when seized by officers whom Philip has sent & conducted. Borne to his dungion—

1.2.3

1: Rupture. Connivance of Caroline. Finds her in her chamber midnight. Expostulation. Saved by her presence of mind. Escapes. Search after him descried ⟨desired?⟩

1. prohibition. & reconveyed to prison.

2. Injunction.

3. Warning.

10.

Scene. Summer House. Time 12 oClock.

11 oclock

Returns to his family;   to his chamber. Deportment.
Conversation to his wife & children. Affectionate, solemn forboding misfortune. The hour having arrived, of 12—
goes to Summer house

Vocal sounds, light, figure.
Dialogue. Forewarns against Idolatry. 12 to 4.
                                    in-
4. Hours. Destroys 1 some favourte animate object.
an organ.

               2. greyhound.

                        200.

               3. children 2.

               4. [Wife]. Ward.
omen
Command   5. [Ward]. Wife.
Repugnan⟨c⟩e
               6. Sister.

Resolute
[Interval of]
Repenting

   [Marcrieve.] birth, education. Acquaintancè 2 ⟨sign for with?⟩
Conway. In love with a beautiful woman <u>but</u>
Conway he introduces to her. Louisa seduced by

      Ludloe.
[Conway] & prevailed upon to aid him in persua
ding M. to concur with C. scheme

      Carwin,
  [M.] made unintentionally instrumental in

terrifying M^{rs}. C. Efforts of this kind ineffectual.
prevailed upon fully to adopt the scheme of

destroying M^{rs}. C. by means of faith. This done.
likewise her daughter. Residing at a distance.
                             Colvill
     Discovers the perfidy of Louisa.   accused
                                 by
Ludloe   11.
[Conway] of murdering M^{rs}. C. Circumstantial evidence

strong. Before trial, escapes prison, by changing cloathes
with Louisa. Comes to Am.
Inducements. Affluence. Marriage with Louiza who
is poor. Relief of distress.

Tales. passions pourtrayed.   3[8]7.   38.1–2/3.
Hallucination   2–3 .1/3.

        ulation

Somnamb.	Mimicry	4⟨7?⟩ 6 2/3.
person. Simil	[personal Similitude.]	
Melanæma		12.
Hallucinat.	Ventriloquizm	8. 13 1/3.
Love of Country	Dissimulation.	

24.

Conflagration. of Mil. preparations. Naval. Timber—Hemp
                                          {Ships.

Carwin.
Colvill.
Ludloe.
Conway. Sen.
Conway. Jun.
pleyel.
Weiland Ch.

_____ Char.
_____ Car.

Tales. { 1. life.
        { 2. particular transaction, some moral.

Misfortune.   Self depravity   } Moral.
                Another's depravity }

           physical. _____ { Direct.
                       { Indirect.

             Death.   gr. 20   20.6.
            Pain.   Rwt. 24. ⟨?⟩
         personal.   Onz —12.

Thou, omnipotent & holy! Thou wast the prompter of my deed.
My hands were but instruments of thy will. I know not what
is crime. Of what action caused ⟨?⟩ evil is the ultimate result. Thy
knowledge as thy power is reverenced ⟨?⟩ I lean ⟨?⟩ upon thy promise
I cheearfully sustain the load of pain or of [infaming] hatred wh.
erring ⟨?⟩ men may lay upon me. In thy ⟨the⟩ arms of thy protection
I entrust my safety. In the fullness of thy justice I confide for
my reward.

   You say that I am criminal. Presumptuous man! Thou deserv
             rightious ⟨?⟩
est that the arm of vengeance should crush thee. Thus impious
ly to usurp the prerogative of thy creator! To count thus rashly on

the comprehension of thy views: on the fall ⟨*sic*⟩ pervading property of thy foresight!

I am not commissioned to be thy punisher. Tis well for thee, I am not. The learning ⟨?⟩ thou has defied ⟨?⟩ & spurned is common to resen⟨t⟩ment. A Space is allowed thee for repentance.

If I were, how would thy shadowy security vanish. I am fettered & surrounded. [Were not ⟨?⟩] I cannot reach thee where thou art, but let the commission be given, & in spite of chains & walls & inter posing multitudes, my hands should snatch thee from thy seat &hurl thee to death.

5. Male & 5 female Characters.
Extremes of virtue & vice, in both sexes
Virtue matured by suffering. Vice triumphant

pleyel followed. by Carwin. Former passes the S.H. Latter stops & descends & recals P. by mimicing Leon: laughter. p. cautiously descends; listens to a diallogue. An half-hour elapses. P. goes to his chamber. Talks with Wieland in the morning. Returns to town to M^rs. B. Meets Carwin leaving the house. C. left a letter for Leonora. pleyel opens it. Confirmed by it in his mistake

Leonora returns. Stops at her brothers	
Balfour.	Thorold.
[Menro.] Carlowe.	Carlowe.
[Lorimer.] Wortley	Percival.
Windham. [Smither ⟨?⟩]	Audley.
Davis. Dudley	Harley.
Cleeves.	Maude.
Avonedge.	Cecil.
	Sydney.

CHARLES BROCKDEN BROWN

Letter to Thomas Jefferson, December 15, 1798[†]

Sir:

After some hesitation a stranger to the person, though not to the character of Thomas Jefferson, ventures to entreat his acceptance of the volume by which this is accompanied. He is unacquainted with the degree in which your time and attention is engrossed by your public office; he knows not in what way your studious hours

---

† Original manuscript in the Thomas Jefferson Papers, Library of Congress.

are distributed and whether mere works of imagination and invention are not excluded from your notice. He is even doubtful whether this letter will be opened or read or, if read, whether its contents will not be instantly dismissed from your memory; so much a stranger is he, though a citizen of the United States, to the private occupations and modes of judging the most illustrious of his fellow citizens.

To request your perusal of a work which at the same time is confessed to be unworthy of perusal will be an uncommon proof of absurdity. In thus transmitting my book to you I tacitly acknowledge my belief that it is capable of affording you pleasure and of entitling the writer to some portion of your good opinion. If I had not this belief, I should unavoidably be silent.

I am conscious, however, that this form of composition may be regarded by you with indifference or contempt, that social and intellectual theories, that the history of facts in the processes of nature and the operations of government may appear to you the only laudable pursuits; that fictitious narratives in their own nature or in the manner in which they have been hitherto conducted may be thought not to deserve notice, and that, consequently, whatever may be the merit of my book as a fiction, yet it is to be condemned because it is a fiction.

I need not say that my own opinions are different. I am therefore obliged to hope that an artful display of incidents, the powerful delineation of characters and the train of eloquent and judicious reasoning which may be combined in a fictitious work, will be regarded by Thomas Jefferson with as much respect as they are regarded by me.

No man holds a performance which he has deliberately offered to the world in contempt; but, if he be a man of candor and discernment, his favorable judgment of his own work will always be attended by diffidence and fluctuation. I confess I foster the hope that Mr. Jefferson will be induced to open the book that is here offered him; that when he has begun it he will find himself prompted to continue, and that he will not think the time employed upon it tedious or uselessly consumed.

With more than this I dare not flatter myself. That he will be pleased to any common degree, and that, by his recommendation, he will contribute to diffuse the knowledge of its author, and facilitate a favorable reception to future performances, is a benefit far beyond the expectations, though certainly the object of the fondest wishes of

Charles B. Brown.

CRITICISM

CRITICISM

Early Estimates

WILLIAM DUNLAP

From The Life of Charles Brockden Brown[†]

* * *

In 1798, he published Wieland. This powerful and original romance, excited attention and brought the author into the notice of all readers of works of this description. Few novels or romances have been written, which seize so strongly upon the imagination and feelings of the reader, hurry him from the realities which surround him, bury in oblivion his joys or sorrows, and fix his whole attention on the images which the author presents before him, as Wieland. In this work, the author, rejecting those events which flow from causes well known and constantly in operation, among men in society, which form the best and most useful groundwork for this species of composition, and discarding the hacknied machinery of castles, banditti and ghosts, took a new and untrodden ground. He made the events of his story depend upon, and flow from, two of those wonderful phenomena of the moral and physical world, which though known and established, were still mysterious and undefined, and though vouched for by unquestionable authorities, are of such rare occurrence, as not to be familiar, or even fully accounted for. Self-combustion is an awful and mysterious phenomenon of nature. The author of Wieland, by means of an instance of the extinction of life, and bodily decomposition, which he relates as having happened to the father of his hero, accounts for a predisposition to the reception of insane and pernicious images, in the mind of Wieland. The author then calls to his aid, a second mysterious and wonderful phenomenon, the existence of which is not so well attested as the first, ventriloquism; and by endowing one of his characters with this stupendous power, a power which when once exerted, is incalculable

† From William Dunlap, *The Life of Charles Brockden Brown, Together with Selections from the Rarest of His Printed Works, from His Original Letters, and from His Manuscripts before Unpublished* (Philadelphia: Parke, 1815), pp. 12–15.

in its effects, he excites his hero to the commission of acts, which though they have their prototypes in authentic records, are of a character so horrible as to border on the shocking, and in some measure defeat the end of the inventor, by lessening the attraction of the story.

Wieland, stimulated by what he considers supernatural premonition, murders his wife and children, and finally undeceived in part, and the high wrought tone of feeling which supported him under a consciousness of well doing, and of immediate communication with Heaven, being let down by a glimpse of the truth, he commits suicide. The causes of these dreadful effects, appear supernatural until the denouement or explanation takes place.

The author had doubtless a right to assume these wonderful appearances of nature as a basis for his fabrication. To his active imagination and fertile mind, they suggested the materials for erecting a superstructure of the greatest magnitude, and the most awful importance. Man, frail, ignorant and dependant, is prone to superstition. In all ages those natural phenomena, which are beyond the reach of our knowledge, have been deemed supernatural. The explosion of the electric fluid, has been heard with awe, as the voice of the Creator of the Universe; and its effect upon animal life, an effect as natural as that of fever or hunger, though less common, has been called his judgment, or the immediate display of his anger. In like manner, the expansion of subterraneous gases, and the misery occasioned by their rending the surface of the earth on spots where cities have been erected, has been ascribed to the jealousy or anger of the all-benevolent God, of our love and gratitude. As the causes of these effects became known, they ceased to be thus regarded. But a phenomenon so extraordinary, and apparently contrary to the known laws of nature as self-combustion, though easily explained to the philosopher, cannot but, even at this time, hold the mind in awful pause. The power of the biloquist, never yet explained, if it really exists, may be so used as to produce effects, which must necessarily unhinge the mind and force it to fall into the belief of supernatural interposition. Here Mr. Brown had possession of engines wherewith to work, of the most powerful and novel kind, and he made great use of them; but a doubt has been suggested of the propriety or policy of resorting to such tremendous agents in the conduct of a novel. It is true that they are in nature, but to the generality of mankind, they appear more strange, if not more unnatural, than ghosts or spectres. The instances of self-combustion or ventriloquism,[1] are so rare, that a work whose events are founded

---

1. "It must not be supposed, that by ventriloquism, I mean the bungling tried which jugglers have called by that name" [Dunlap's note].

on such materials, accords less with popular feelings and credulity, than if supernatural agency had been employed. In all ages and in all nations, tales of ghosts, of sorcery and witches, of genii, of demons, of local deities, and of familiar spirits; in short of communication with an invisible world of powerful and incorporeal beings, has received popular credence, and been familiar to man from his cradle to his grave. When the agency of such beings is used in a poem or a tale, if we do not believe, we at least are not shocked. On the other hand to the mass of readers, the natural causes of which we are speaking, are so indefinite and so little understood, that disappointment is experienced when they are brought forward to account for appearances which the reader had previously supposed to be supernatural. It is perhaps always unsatisfactory, to find that causes which had purposely been made to convey an idea of more than mortal agency, are merely natural. The reader will remember the denouement of "the family of Montorio," and the waxen doll which inspires such high and mysterious ideas in Mrs. Radcliffe's "Mysteries of Udolpho."[2]

Notwithstanding these strictures upon Mr. Brown's agents, the writer is disposed to class Wieland among novels of the highest order. It has a well conducted fable, the incidents of which all tend to its progress and developement, and the style is pure, strong and eloquent.

The great cause of all the evils, which befal Wieland and his family, Carwin the biloquist, is a character approaching to the sublime, from the mystery thrown around him, and yet at times inspiring sentiments of disgust, and even contempt. The author does not give us the history of this personage, and thus, as was always his custom, left an opening for a continuation, or for another romance. Accordingly Mr. Brown afterwards began, and partly published "Memoirs of Carwin the Biloquist." This very interesting fragment, the reader will find well worthy of perusal, and will regret that the author did not finish a work so replete with novelty and interest.

* * *

2. Anne Radcliffe. *The Mysteries of Udolpho* (London: Robinson, 1794). Dennis Jasper Murray [Charles Robert Maturin] *Fatal Revenge; or, the Family of Montorio: A Romance* (London: Longman, 1807).

320

ANONYMOUS

[On Brown's Novels]†

Little remains to be said on the subject of literary biography. The usual complaint is that the life of a man of letters is almost necessarily wanting in incident, and when the writer has made this general apology for a meagre narrative, he too often feels at liberty to be as deficient in every thing as may suit his ignorance, indolence, or want of discrimination. He is unable perhaps to collect such facts in the life of a scholar as are commonly called remarkable, and hence infers that there is nothing in it worthy of public notice. Perhaps he is able to collect a few anecdotes, which he records with a proper regard to the order in which they occurred, but without shewing their connexion with the character of the man. It seems as much a matter of course to place a memoir at the beginning of his works, as a stone and epitaph over his remains, and they generally tell us the same thing,—how much we honour and how little we know of him. It is hardly possible that a faithful, judicious history of a literary man should not be full of amusement and important instruction; but it cannot be made so by relating only what is common to him and every one else, or what would be equally interesting if told of another. Most of the events of his life, (if they may be called such,) in which we are concerned, pass within himself rather than abroad. We would see how his experience affected his judgments, purposes and feelings; we want to know, principally, the history of his mind; what gave him a strong, unconquerable inclination to a certain pursuit, what retarded his progress or enabled him to subdue difficulties, what influenced him in the selection of his subjects and in his peculiar views of them, and what were the little incidental aids to the accomplishment of some great work, which appears to have grown up as silently and independently as the oak under the open sky. We want his conversation when most unguarded and unconstrained, for we would see his character and power when there was no effort, nor disguise, nor anxiety about the effect of his opinions upon his fame or upon society. We would know his character thoroughly, for it may serve to explain and qualify his opinions, weaken our false confidence in him, or animate and strengthen our just attachment, give the practical force of example to instruction, and that peculiar attraction to his opinions which every thing possesses that belongs to one whom we understand and love.

† From *North American Review* 9.24 (June 19):58–77. This overview of Brown's work comes from a review of William Dunlap's *Life of Charles Brockden Brown.*

The man of letters, in one sense, may always be his own biographer, if he writes from honest feeling and conviction only, without any attempt to pass for what he is not; for his character will then be wrought into his opinions, and we shall at least be familiar with the man, though not with his history. But this is not enough—we want his history; and no one can write it so well as himself, if he has but an ordinary share of honesty. His opportunity of close self-inspection, his secret knowledge of what has formed his character—trifles perhaps in our eyes, but in fact the only important incidents of his life; his strong sense of the danger of indulging too much in habits of speculation and abstraction, that solitude is sometimes filled with worse temptations than the city; his remembrance of his anxieties and indifference, his disappointments and triumphs, and it may be of his indignant misanthropy when the world misjudged or slighted him;—all these are his and his only. And if they are fairly used and disclosed to us, his narrative will be a lesson of morals, of character, of intellectual philosophy; not a formal and abstract one, but living and practical; what we hear from him has been passed through; the heart warmed it before it was told, and we derive its good instruction for ourselves, from a discriminating view of all the details. And even where his self-love tempts him to hide or extenuate, his anxiety may betray as much as a confession, and throw further light upon his character.

If he has left no memoir of his life, a judicious biographer will present us with his journals, letters, conversation, and especially record the events and occupations to which he recurred most frequently, as having had a decisive influence upon his happiness, ambition or ways of thinking. His literary history will also be preserved as far as possible; all his projects, failures, and success, his mode of life, his rivalries, friendships and antipathies; even the price he obtained for a work, and the editions it passed through, with or without his alterations. Some of these facts are always interesting as they affect or illustrate his character; and the rest may be so from their connexion with a great man, and for the light they may throw upon the literature or distinguished characters of his age.

The work before us contains little that is new, of any value, except a few of Brown's letters, and some extracts from his journal, which occupy but a very small place. The selections fill nearly the whole book, and all of any consequence had been already published. The Life appears to be only an apology or pretence for republishing these, and it is certainly a very poor one. But Brown himself would be the last man to complain of this. He never seems to have laboured with a view to do justice to his powers; he left his fame to accident, and would not have expected a friend to do more for it, after his death, than he had done while living. His life appears to have been always

desultory, and his mind never under steady discipline. His feeble
health withheld him from the common amusements of children,
and this drove him to books and his own thoughts for companions and
diversion. Diligent study wore down the little strength he had, and
then we find him alone in the fields, seeking health from exercise,
but in fact acquiring a love of solitude and habits of abstraction, till
he became, for a season at least, 'an eccentric, isolated being loathing the common pursuits and topics of men.' His mind was always
active and curious, acquiring largely but irregularly and with no distinct object in view. His literary ambition seems to have been above
his opportunities and situation, and sometimes discovers an ignorance of his powers and uncertainty in his taste. For a large part of
his short life he appears as a sad enthusiast, a sceptical inquirer, a
dissatisfied observer, a whimsical projector of better things for society than he could ever bring to pass, or in a calm moment wish to
realize, even if his own views had been completely carried out; turning his mind to various pursuits with rash eagerness; planning epics,
studying architecture, forming literary associations, discussing legal
questions with his fellow students, and abandoning the profession of
his choice before he had felt either its vexations or excitements, or
even framed a tolerable excuse for his conscience or an answer to the
persuasions of his friends. Such was his hurried, mingled, undirected
life. From all that surrounded and excited him, he shrinks within
himself to mourn in secret. 'As for me, I long ago discovered that
nature had not qualified me for an actor on this stage. The nature of
my education only added to these disqualifications, and I experienced
all those deviations from the centre, which arise when all our lessons
are taken from books, and the scholar makes his own character the
comment. A happy destiny indeed brought me to the knowledge of
two or three minds which nature had fashioned in the same mould
with my own, but these are gone. And, O God! enable me to wait the
moment when it is thy will that I should follow them.'

Such strong sensibility as his could not be safe unless all his powers had acted together, and in its diseased state it absolutely prevented this. He wanted something from without to draw his attention
from himself, and make him a sober, practical thinker; he needed
regular employments that always tended to something, and produced
some visible effect; he had yet to learn what man was made of and
why he was placed here, and that the same world which offended the
sensitiveness of the weak, was a fine school for character and might
be a nursery for the tenderest feeling. He tells us with what rapture
he communed with his own thoughts in the gloom of woods, and
'peopled it with the beings of his fancy, till the barrier between
himself and the world of spirits seemed burst by the force of meditation;' but it was in vain that he promised himself that he could

come back to society, to the concerns of life and his appropriate duties, to converse with the world in its own language and upon its favourite subjects.

From the slight view which is given of Brown's character in these volumes (and we know it only from this source) we should judge him to have been, nothwithstanding his infirmities, a friend worthy of all trust; one who could never be spared, and least of all abandoned. His sufferings neither repelled nor wearied. He was a sincere and unobtrusive sufferer. It was a principle with him to conceal what he endured. 'I sincerely lament that I ever gave you reason to imagine I was not happy. The discovery could not take away from the number of the wretched, but only add to it. When I cannot communicate pleasure, I will communicate nothing. Do I wish friendship only to make myself a burden? Let me share in your joys and sorrows, and bear all my misfortunes myself.' We may call this an error, for why should sympathy be unavailing? But with him it was the fruit of a generous spirit. There was no coldness, nor misanthropy, nor repining in his intercourse with the world. He did not refuse pity because he was above it, but he could not endure to wear in the presence of others the wretched singularity of a broken, dissatisfied spirit; to be marked out as one who could only spread clouds over his home and the hearts that loved him.—His mind was perfectly fair, quick to discern and urge what was best for his friend, even though he should give counsel which reproached himself. He was humbled by his weakness, but he was unwilling to rise in his own estimation from the good opinion of others, till he felt that he deserved it. His self-diffidence, however, reminded him that he might not be the fairest judge of his own conduct, and though he might dread approbation, he knew the worth of it.

His life was pure, but he says that frail health had made him an exile from temptation, that his virtue was under the protection of nature; he is grateful for his infirmities, and thinks he loved intellectual glory because he had no resource but in intellectual pleasure. A gentle, subdued spirit appears in his whole character. He expected little from the world, but seems every day growing more and more prepared for its ills, more zealous to do something in its service, and more willing to trust in its reasonable promises. His life was short, but a few years before his death it was active and happy. His importance was increasing, and his claims to the remembrance of after times were secured. His character was unchanged in death. The following affecting account of his last hours was communicated by his wife to the biographer.

He always felt for others more than for himself; and the evidences of sorrow in those around him, which could not at all times be suppressed, appeared to affect him more than his own sufferings. Whenever he spoke of the probability of a fatal termination to his disease, it was in an indirect and covered manner, as "you must do so or so when I am absent," or "when I am asleep." He surrendered not up one faculty of his soul but with his last breath. He saw death in every step of his approach, and viewed him as a messenger that brought with him no terrors. He frequently expressed his resignation; but his resignation was not produced by apathy or pain, for while he bowed with submission to the divine will, he felt with the keenest sensibility his separation from those who made this world but too dear to him. Towards the last he spoke of death without disguise, and appeared to wish to prepare his friends for the event which he felt to be approaching. A few days previous to his change, as sitting up in the bed, he fixed his eyes on the sky, and desired not to be spoken to till he first spoke. In this position and with a serene countenance, he continued some minutes, and then said to his wife, "when I desired you not to speak to me, I had the most transporting and sublime feelings I ever experienced. I wanted to enjoy them, and know how long they would last."

Brown died in 1809 at the age of thirty nine. For ten years before his death he had been an indefatigable author by profession, at first in New York and afterwards in Philadelphia, his native city. During this period he conducted and was principal contributor to three periodical works, of which we have seen at least fifteen volumes. To these we must add his political pamphlets, his unpublished manuscripts and his six novels. Wieland, Ormond, Arthur Mervyn, and Edgar Huntly are the earliest and best known, and to these we shall confine our remarks. Clara Howard and Jane Talbot, his two latest tales, are so very inferior to and unlike the others, that they require no particular notice.

Brown owes his reputation to his novels. He wrote them indeed principally for his amusement, and preferred publishing them when unfinished to labouring upon them after they had lost their interest to himself: they are proofs or signs of power rather than the result of its complete and steady exertion; but they shew the character of his mind and will justify our curiosity to examine it. In attempting this, we do not feel as if we were bringing forward a deserving but neglected author; he has received honourable notice from distinguished men abroad, and his countrymen discerned his merits without waiting till a foreign glory had shone on and revealed them. Still he is very far from being a popular writer. There is no call, as far as we know, for a second edition of any of his works. He is rarely spoken of but by those who have an habitual curiosity about every thing literary, and a becoming pride in all good writing which appears amongst ourselves. They have not met with the usual success of leaders in matters of taste, since, with all their admiration, they have not been able to extend his celebrity much beyond themselves. Some will explain this by saying that he wrote too rapidly, or that his subjects are too monstrous or at least too extraordinary for common sympathy. But the thoughts of great minds, when earnestly at work, are rarely improved by deliberation and change, and a powerful imagination can imprison us with any thing that is not spiritless, or incapable of suggesting something like reality to the mind. No reader would leave Wieland unfinished notwithstanding its self-combustion and ventriloquism, nor Edgar Huntly because of its sleep-walking. If we do not return to them, it is to avoid suffering, and not that they want fascination, and a terrible one, if we are willing to encounter it more than once.

Some have ascribed his want of popularity to his placing the scenes of his novels in our own country. What are the embarrassments from this cause, which the American novelist must be prepared for, and how far has Brown overcome or avoided them?—Our busy streets, and the commodious apartments of our unromantic dwellings are, it is thought, very unsuitable for the wonders and adventures which we have been accustomed to associate exclusively with the mouldering castles and unfrequented regions of older countries. Our cities are large, but new, and they constantly suggest to us the gainful habits and the secure homes of a recent and flourishing population; the labouring and happy are seen every where and not a corner or recess is secret. The deserted street at midnight produces no awful sense of solitude or danger, and the throng that passes us by day would scarcely suggest the thought that any one was alone in the crowd, buried in contemplation and perhaps brooding over mischief in darkness. We hear of crimes, but they usually appear so vulgar and selfish, so mean or cruel, that the imagination almost sleeps under abhorrence or disgust; we regard them as public evils, and think it enough to leave them to the benevolent reformer and the laws of the land. We hear of conspiracies and circumvention, but they are directed at our gains or good name and put us upon our guard; we think of the injury and its prevention, more than of the terrible power, dark purposes and inextricable toils of the contriver. The actions we esteem great, or are prepared to witness and encourage, are the useful rather than the heroic, such as tend to make society happier, not such as disturb or darken it. Our pride, good sense and warmest wishes are satisfied, but the imagination is not kindled, nor could it lend any lustre to what we approve. The writer then who frames a story to call forth extraordinary and violent interest, and lays the scene amongst ourselves, must encounter the difficulty of creating an illusion, where his events and characters are broad exceptions to all we witness or should expect, and where our imaginations are kept from wandering, and from deceiving us into a faint conviction of reality, by the mention of some place or circumstance which is too stubbornly familiar and unpoetical for any thing but common incidents and feelings. We are speaking of that kind of tale-writing in which Brown delights, the romantic; and we have ascribed the difficulty of succeeding in it here, not to the entire absence of romantic incident, situation and characters, but, which is just as unfortunate for the writer, to the want in his readers of romantic associations with the scenes and persons he must set before us, if he makes a strictly domestic story.

But there is another and an extremely popular kind of fictitious writing, which makes the fable subservient to the developing of national character, or of the manners, usages, prejudices and condition of particular classes. Besides truth, spirit and a nice discrimination of peculiarities in the sketches of individuals, a single picture is widely applicable, and gives us much knowledge of the state of society at the time, and what is still higher, an increased and nearer knowledge of mankind. These sketches are not caricatures, merely grotesque delineations of strange individuals, such as amuse or distress us chiefly for their total separation from the crowd to which we belong. They represent classes; they shew us some peculiar operation of familiar principles, in men who received their natures from our common author, and their distinctive characters from limited external influences. A source of sympathy is thus opened between the remotest nations; we read with delight of those who are separated from us by their institutions and manners as well as climate, not that they are represented as beings formed of another mould and with different capacities from ourselves, but because they resemble us in every thing except that distinguishing character and those prevailing tastes which are ascribable to the peculiar circumstances in which they are placed. We love to see the common world moulding the mind a thousand ways, and multiplying our studies and pleasures without lessening our sympathy and attachments.

How far may this kind of fictitious writing be expected to succeed among us? This cannot depend upon the genius only of authors; at least, mere invention is out of the question. The object is to present what exists, to appeal to men's observation and daily experience. We might possibly be more delighted with a merely poetical creation, than with a history of living men and a sketch of ordinary society, but these would lose all their attraction and value, when they profess to describe realities, while in fact they are occupied principally with an imaginary world.—Our state of society at present offers very imperfect materials for a novel, of the kind which has just been alluded to. If we admit that there is here a *lower class*, its peculiarity would not be found in character so much as in vulgarity of manners and narrowness of opinion; and a foreigner would be as little delighted as ourselves with the most lively record of corrupt speech, of coarse or indelicate customs, of sturdy insolence towards the rich, and indifference or contempt for those who consented to be poor, where competency was so easy and so privileged. If such a sketch should be true, it would be so only of individuals, whose influence is scarcely felt amongst ourselves, and whose peculiarities would give strangers very little knowledge of the effect of our institutions or pursuits upon our opinions and character.

We come next to a large and invaluable order, composed of sensible, industrious, upright men, whose whole experience seems at war with adventure, and whose chief distinction is in their unmolested happiness, and perfectly independent modes of living. They are exactly fitted to make society secure and prosperous, and to teach us the importance of good habits and principles; with more firmness and efficiency than variety, sprightliness or vehemence in their characters; free from wild superstitions; not much in the habit of forming poetical associations with the objects they are most familiar with; using, occasionally, highly picturesque expressions, without betraying the feelings in which they originated; affected by many sober and rooted prejudices, which are inseparable perhaps from strong, unpolished character and are even its protection, but such as might appear to more advantage in a book that was only to make us wiser, than in one designed also for our diversion. With such a class of men, we should find more instruction than entertainment, more to gratify our kind feelings and good sense than to fill our imaginations. To visit them in their own homes would please us more than to read of them in a novel; they might offer little to call forth discrimination and acute remark, but a great deal of general happiness and virtue for a good mind to approve and imitate.

If we should look for what are called the higher classes of society, the wealthy, fashionable and ostentatious, whose manners, parade and intrigues in the older countries have given birth to some of the finest modern tales; we might be in a great measure disappointed. We should, indeed, find splendor, luxury and refinement, and possibly an incomplete imitation of foreign fashions; but little of the exclusive spirit of an established order, which owed its existence to something peculiar in our state of society, and had secured respect for its claims from those who are most impatient of superiority and all separate pretensions. More years, practice and affluence might be necessary to render the class more distinct, character more various, peculiarities more graceful and easy, vice and folly more finished and creditable, and affectation less insupportable than uncouth sincerity.

No doubt, it is impossible to give a just account of society, whatever be its state, without affording some entertainment, or at least
knowledge. Man is always our best study, and our most fruitful subject whether we hate or love him. If a writer would be a despot, with
power never to be shaken or questioned, let him become the fearless
and exact historian or painter of real life. If he would be the most
efficient moral teacher, let him tell men what they are and what is
thought of them; let him take us from the crowd where there is too
much motion for thought, where each is countenanced and sheltered
by the other, with an example on all sides for his follies or vices, and
where the very sense of fault dies because there is none to condemn;
let him shew us our conduct in a silent picture, when there is nothing
to dim our perceptions, or mislead our judgments, when the music
has ceased which put us all in the same motion, attracted us to one
object, and made every man happy without a thought of the cause
or the manner. We may then learn the real spirit and business of
society, with much to laugh at and something to lament as well as
approve. In every class amongst ourselves there are fine subjects
for the moral and satirical observer, which have already called forth
much grave and light rebuke, and many short, lively sketches of
domestic manners, national customs and individual singularities.
But our common every-day life hardly offers materials as yet for a
long story, which should be full of interest for its strong and infinitely various characters, fine conversation and striking incident,
for conflicting pretensions and subtile intrigues in private life, and
which should all appear to be exactly in the ordinary course of
things, and what every one would feel to be perfectly true, without
being obliged to verify it by particular and limited applications. And
genius is not apt to employ itself upon subjects where it feels embar-
rassed by the want of materials. It does not indeed court novelties, as
if it thought nothing else would do, nor shun what common minds
might think unpromising or impossible. It follows its own wishes,
and chooses what it can manage to advantage; what provokes its
energy and is yet within its controul.

Brown had the courage to lay the scenes of his stories at home,
but no one will charge him with a disgusting familiarity. He has not
even attempted to draw a peculiar American character; he seeks for
many of his most important persons abroad, or among those who
had lived and been educated abroad, where the character had been
formed and opinions decidedly fixed, under better influences perhaps for his purposes than existed or at present could be expected to
exist here, while many things in our situation and prospects would
offer a good field for a new and striking exhibition of his characters.
The scene is rarely in common life or for ordinary events. Sometimes he begins with a simple, domestic narrative, as in Ormond,

which has no very distinct reference to our state of society, but which exhibits merely, though with great spirit, the unwearied solicitude of a daughter for a weak, sinful and helpless father, the victim of a young impostor whom he had received to his confidence. We are constantly expecting something more important, though without an intimation what it will be. At length some terrific being—little less than omnipotent, of strong mind and feelings, utterly and deliberately perverted—is introduced, and thence forward rules the destinies of every one else, without exhibiting very definite purposes, or adopting any distinct plan of operations. His power is usually of a moral kind; he establishes an inquisition to put the mind to torture; looks, tones, persuasions, threats and dark insinuations are his instruments. Our chief interest is not in the events, nor at all dependent upon the conviction that we ever saw the place or the man. We are not thinking of accustomed modes of living or our ordinary experience, but are held captive by the force of character, the intensity of intellectual suffering, the unrelenting perseverance of a bad spirit disappointed. A spell is thrown over our imaginations, and our belief is at least strong enough for sympathy.

Sometimes the events are placed so far back, that they belong to a somewhat different race from ourselves, at least with different pursuits, pleasures and dangers; but we are not in a strange country; what was then a wilderness is now covered with our own flourishing settlements; the savage and beast of prey are scarcely heard of; the wild, adventurous character of the recent settler has become softened by regular and secure industry, and we feel as if we were reading of our antiquities.

Sometimes the author takes advantage of a recent event amongst ourselves, as in Wieland, which is too shocking to receive any aid from exaggeration, or to lose any interest from its notoriety. A father is tempted by apparent communications from above to murder his family. The rapture and exultation with which he contemplates his triumph over his fond weakness in obedience to heaven, very often reach the sublime. This is equalled perhaps by his utter prostration when he learns that he has been deceived. The author connects this event with just such beings as should be concerned in it; he makes it illustrative of character and dependent upon it; and though it might appear rare and monstrous enough for a lie instead of a wonder, he contrives by the earnestness and argumentative cast of reflection, the depth, sincerity and torture of feeling, the suitableness of every circumstance and the apparent inevitableness of all that occurs, to chain us to a more revolting narrative than perhaps ever before made the smallest pretensions to truth.

Sometimes his stories rest chiefly upon recent events of public concern. We refer particularly to the pestilence that has more than once wasted our principal cities; and here he is so willing to confine himself to mere truth, that he proposes to make his narrative of practical use, by preserving such incidents as appeared to him most instructive amongst those which fell under his own observation. He enters the city; the streets are still, the dwellings deserted or occupied by the sick. There is such terrible distinctness in his description of the calamity, so much of vulgar suffering which cannot be relieved, and of disgusting, selfish inhumanity in the timid, too rarely contrasted with a generous self-exposure, that we are sometimes oppressed and sickened; the reality seems too near. But in connexion with this, there is sufficient horror and wildness for the imagination. We feel that all this suffering is crowded into one spot, where the poor and wretched are almost alone amongst the deserted mansions of the wealthy and in the scenes of recent gayety. The victim is left in a dark, closed dwelling, as if to die in his tomb, with no one near but the safe plunderer. The day and night are equally still— there are no sounds but of the dying and the hearse. The fugitive, whom we thought secure, perishes in a purer air; and to make our sense of hopelessness and desolation still more complete, we see the sun shining as brightly and the grass-walks as fresh in the morning, as if the happy were there to enjoy them.

We can offer only these few remarks upon the course Brown has followed in the selection of his subjects and the use of his materials. Though his scenes lie at home, yet in his four principal tales, we can say with some confidence, that there is little which is too humble and familiar for interest, or so monstrous and unusual that he has not been able to recommend it sufficiently to our belief for all his purposes.

We have alluded to the singular or improbable character of his persons and incidents; and it is the first thing that presents itself on reading his four principal tales. He selects minds that are strangely gifted or influenced, as if for the pleasure of exploring some secret principles of our nature, disclosing new motives of conduct, or old ones operating in a new direction; and especially that he may have an opportunity, the necessity of which we are to admit, of accounting at large for every thing that is resolved upon or done; as if he had discovered springs of action which could not be understood in the usual way, by our observation of their effects, but only from a minute, philosophical discussion of impulses and motives by the parties concerned, after a cool, thorough self-inspection, and a detailed enumeration of rapid and subtile thoughts which incessantly gleamed across their minds in the storm. In the language of one of his characters, 'I cannot be satisfied with telling you that I am not well, but I must be searching with these careful eyes into causes and labouring to tell you of what nature my malady is. It has always been so. I have always found an unaccountable pleasure in dissecting, as it were, my heart, uncovering, one by one, its many folds, and laying it before you as a country is shown in a map.' This scrutiny into the feelings is given with such an air of probability and conclusiveness, or at least sincerity, that we are disposed to admit the existence of the most extraordinary beings, and then their opinions, purposes, conduct, and influence over others are quite satisfactorily explained, without supposing any other despotism over the will but that which is to be found in the power of involuntary thoughts.

But this accounting for every thing is often excessively irksome. A ludicrous importance is given to trifles; the vast mind is seen busied, amazed and anxious about incidents or intimations that are wholly inadequate to the concern they give or the effects which are traced to them, and which ordinary men would be ashamed to notice. What would be nothing elsewhere is every thing here. The feelings not only appear to obey the impulse they receive and tend unerringly to their object, but in a state of excitement and tumult, they are excellent philosophers; they shew the mind's perfect consciousness of all that is passing within; they appear to prescribe their own operations, pass through anticipated changes, and remember that they are afterwards to render an account of themselves. The reader would be better pleased if the mind's rapid conclusions were given, and an opportunity left for his own sagacity to account for them from observation of the whole character.

Brown's principal characters are designed chiefly for our imaginations and ingenuity. They study and delineate themselves with exemplary diligence and fidelity. This is not done that they may grow better, or give us a moral lesson; they are perfectly satisfied with the study, and succeed in engaging us to watch them. They are of a contemplative turn, forever hunting for materials of thought rather than motives to action, not so much from irresolution or speculative indolence, as from a love of thinking and feeling deeply at all times, and associating every thing around them with their own minds. They defer as far as possible the day when the deed shall be done which is to deprive them of something to brood over; they are anxious to operate upon the minds of others rather than upon their conduct, to keep them in suspense, and divert them from the purpose which they themselves have inspired, as soon as they see it ripening into action. They would envy no man the calm assurance and prompt determination, which spring from a general consciousness of good intentions and a quick insight into the subject of his thoughts. They have a perverse love of perplexity and doubt, and of needless though not vulgar difficulties; and to gratify this, a false and bewildering consequence is given to their own most common feelings and the most obvious conduct in others. They have not been enough exposed to the world to acquire a contempt for their singularities; they feel as if they were very peculiar and must attract as much attention as they bestow upon themselves, and especially that mischief must lurk in every thing which appears mysterious to them. Then they plunge into solitudes and heap conjectures upon conjectures about endless possibilities. 'Thought is first made a vehicle of pain,' and then life is not worth enduring; but they live on, for to die would be as fatal as torpor to the wild dreamer, and a disposition to make evils supportable would be just as bad.

But the time for action at last comes—we could not anticipate what would be done, nor comprehend why any thing should be done—there is all at once a rushing and thronging of incidents; the bright heavens are suddenly darkened; a strange accumulation of unforeseen ills falls upon a single deserted being. His innocent actions are most ingeniously misconceived or misrepresented; he is made the blind instrument of all the woe he suffers or inflicts; his sad delusions are made use of to draw him to the most atrocious deeds; the means of vindication to the injured or of correction to the erring are always near but never possessed. It is of no consequence to the author whether you were prepared by the early view of a doubtful character for his conduct afterwards; whether he fulfils his promise or breaks it. He chooses to make men as intense in action as they were before in reflection. He conjures up at once a terrible scene for mighty agents; if one perishes, he supplies the place by infusing new strength and other purposes into him who remains. And the attention is so much engrossed, the imagination is so filled by what is passing now, that we care not for its connexion, if there be any, with the past or future; we want no more, and least of all such explanations as are sometimes given. We seem to have had a disturbed dream; we suddenly reached the precipice, plunged, and awoke in falling, rejoiced that it was an illusion and that it has passed away.

A writer so engrossed with the character of men and the ways in which they may be influenced; chiefly occupied with the mind, turning every thing into thought, and refining upon it till it almost vanishes, might not be expected to give much time to descriptions of outward objects. But in all his tales he shews great closeness and minuteness of observation. He describes as if he told only what he had seen in a highly excited state of feeling, and in connexion with the events and characters. He discovers every where a strong sense of the presence of objects. Most of his descriptions are simple, and many might appear bald. He knew perhaps that some minds could be awakened by the mere mention of a water-fall, or of full orchards and cornfields, or of the peculiar sound of the wind among the pines.— We have alluded to the distinctness and particularity with which he describes the city visited with pestilence; the dwelling-house, the hospital, the dying, the healed, all appear before our eyes; the imagination has nothing to do but perceive, though it never fails to multiply and enlarge circumstances of horror, and to fasten us to the picture more strongly by increasing terror and sympathy till mere disgust ceases.—The most formal and protracted description is in Edgar Huntly, of a scene in our Western wilderness. We become acquainted with it by following the hero night and day, in a cold, drenching rain-storm, or under the clear sky, through its dark caverns, recesses and woods, along its ridges and the river side. It produces throughout the liveliest sense of danger, and oppresses the spirits with an almost inexplicable sadness. Connected with it are incidents of savage warfare, the disturbed life of the frontier settler, the attack of the half-famished panther, the hero's lonely pursuit of a sleep-walker, and his own adventures when suffering under the same calamity. The question is not how much of this has happened or is likely to happen; but is it felt; are we for the time at the disposal of the writer, and can we never lose the impression he leaves? Does it appear in its first freshness when any thing occurs which a busy fancy can associate with it? Does it go with us into other deserts, and quicken our feelings and observation till a familiar air is given to strange prospects? If so, the author is satisfied. To object that he is wild and improbable in his story is not enough, unless we can shew that his intention failed or was a bad one.

Brown delights in solitude of all kinds. He loves to represent the heart as desolate; to impress you with the self-dependence of characters, plotting, loving, suspecting evil, devising good, in perfect secrecy. Sometimes, when he would exhibit strength of mind and purpose to most advantage, he takes away all external succour, even the presence of a friend who might offer at least the support of his notice and sympathy. He surrounds a person with circumstances precisely fitted to weaken resolution by raising vague apprehensions of danger, but incapable of producing so strong an excitement as to inspire desperate and inflexible energy. The mind must then fortify itself, calmly estimate the evil that seems to be approaching, and contemplate it in its worst forms and consequences in order to counteract it effectually.—He is peculiarly successful in describing a deserted house, silent and dark in the day-time, while a faint ray streams through the crevices of the closed doors and shutters, discovering in a peculiar twilight that it had been once occupied, and that every thing remained undisturbed since its sudden desertion. The sentiment of fear and melancholy is perhaps never more lively, nor the disturbed fancy more active than in such a place, even when we are strangers to it; but how much more, if we have passed there through happiness and suffering, if the robber has alarmed our security, or if a friend has died there and been carried over its threshold to the grave. The solemnity of our minds is unlike that which we feel when walking alone on the sea-shore at night, or through dark forests by day, for here there is no decay, nothing that man had created and which seems to mourn his absence: there is rapture as well as awe in our contemplations, and more of devotion than alarm in our fear.

Brown's mind is distinguished for strong, intense conception. If his thoughts are vast, he is still always master of them. He works with the greatest ease, as if his mind were fully possessed of his subject, and could not but suggest thoughts with freedom and rapidity. In the most monstrous and shocking narrative, he writes with the utmost sincerity, as if he laboured under a delusion which acted with a mischievous but uncontrollable power. He never, indeed, shews a desire to complete a story, nor draws a character so much for what it is to effect in the end, as for the development of mind. The present incident is perhaps fine in itself, and answers the author's purpose, and gives room for the display of great strength; but it has little or no connexion with others. With the greatest solicitude to tell us every thing that passes in the mind before a purpose is formed, he is very careless as to any continuity or dependence in the events which lead to or flow from that purpose. He sometimes crowds more into one day than we should have expected in many, and at others leaps over so large an interval as to make the narrative improbable to all who are not in the secret. His characters cannot be relied upon: notwithstanding their strength and apparently stubborn singularities, they accommodate themselves readily to the author, sometimes losing all the importance with which they were at first invested, and at others accomplishing something beyond or opposite to what was expected, and almost what we can believe to be within the compass of human power in the agent or weakness in the sufferer. This incompleteness of views and inconsistency of characters is not owing to carelessness or haste in the writer; he had never determined how things should end, nor proposed to himself any prevailing object when he began, nor discovered one as he advanced. We generally close a story with a belief that as much more might be said. He was engrossed by single, separate scenes, such as invention suggested from time to time; and while we can account from this fact for our feeling little solicitude about the story as a whole, we must at the same time form a high estimate of an author's power, who can carry us through almost disconnected scenes without any considerable failure of interest. He seems fond of exciting and vexing curiosity, but when he fails of satisfying it, it is more, we believe, from forgetfulness than design.

There is very little variety in his writings; at least in those where his genius is most clearly discerned. He loves unusual, lawless characters, and extraordinary and tragic incident. There should not be a moment of calm brightness in the world, unless as it may serve to heighten the effect of approaching gloom and tempest. The inno-cent are doomed to suffer, as if virtue were best capable of enduring and shone most conspicuously in trial, or at least drew the largest sympathy. This suffering is of the mind; bodily pain and death appear but moderate and vulgar evils, and rather a refuge than pun-ishment for the triumphant criminal, who has rioted in mischief till he is weary, and willing to die for repose since his work is ended. In these sad views of life, which make society worse than the wilder-ness and men's sympathy and promises little better than a mockery, there is no apparent design to mislead the world, or covertly con-demn its opinions and awards, but merely to take a firm hold of the heart, by appeals to its pity, terror, indignation or wonder. He wants the universality and justice of a fair observer of the world. He thinks too much in one way, and that a narrow one. His views are of one kind, and shew that he thought more than he observed.

His style is clear, simple and nervous, with very little peculiarity, and not the slightest affectation or even consciousness of manner; rarely varying to suit the subject, or to distinguish conversation from narrative or description. It uniformly bears marks of a serious, thoughtful mind, remembering its excitement and suffering rather than experiencing them. There are, now and then, some attempts at playfulness and humour, but they are wholly unsuccessful, and sometimes ludicrous and offensive. There are few striking sentences which the reader would unconsciously retain for the beauty of their structure, or any peculiar terms; we have the thought without the expression. We should not pronounce Brown a man of genius, nor deny him that distinction, from his style. It might have been acquired by care and study, but it is the result only and never betrays the pro-cess. There is no attempt at what is too vaguely called fine writing; no needless ornament, no sacrifice of spirit and energy from a weak ambition of harmony or finish, no use of a strictly poetical term to excite the imagination, when another and a simpler one will convey the meaning more definitely. He uses words merely to express his own thoughts, and not to multiply our associations. He never allows them to outstrip, or, which is nearly the same thing, to take the place of feeling and truth. He appears to be above the common tempta-tion to exhibit tokens of more passion than is felt, merely on account of 'the imaginary gracefulness of passion,' or to decorate scenes with borrowed beauties till they have lost every thing which could distin-guish them, or even persuade us that we were in our own world.

It has been our object in these remarks, to point out some of Brown's prominent defects and excellences. We never intended to

make an abstract of his stories; and such extracts as we could admit
would do little justice to the author.—His readers will observe
every-where that he was an ardent admirer of Godwin, though not
his slave. Godwin himself has pronounced him a writer of distinguished genius and acknowledged himself in his debt.—The uses
and evils of criticism can no longer be felt by him; the dead are
beyond our judgment. It is for the living that their opinions and
genius should be inquired into; and it is hardly less dishonourable
to let the grave bury their worth than consecrate their errors.

ANONYMOUS

Blackwood's Edinburgh Magazine on Brown, I[†]

* * *

In truth, so far as we know, there are two American authors only
whose genius has reason to complain of British neglect—and with
a very great deal of reason both unquestionably may do so—namely,
Charles Brockden Brown and Washington Irving.

The first of these has been dead for several years; and the periodical works, by his contributions to which he was best known in
America during his lifetime, have long since followed him: but his
name yet lives, although not as it ought to do, in his novels. The earliest and the best of them, *Wieland, Ormond, Arthur Mervyn,* and
Edgar Huntly, are to be found in every circulating library, both in
America and England; but notwithstanding the numbers who must
thus have read them, and the commendations they have received
from some judges of the highest authority, (above all from Godwin,
whose manner their author imitated in a noble style of imitation)—
they are never mentioned among the classical or standard works of
that species of composition. It is wonderful how much of thought,
power, invention, and genius, are for ever travelling their cold unworthy rounds between the shelves of circulating libraries, and the tables
or pillows of habitual novel-readers. The works of Brown, and of
many other writers, scarcely his inferiors, are perused day after day,
and year after year, by boys and girls, and persons of all ages, whose
minds are incapable of discriminating the nature or merits of the
food they devour, without being read once in many years by any
one who has either judgment or imagination to understand while he
is reading them, or memory to retain the smallest impression of their

---

† From "On the Writings of Charles Brockden Brown and Washington Irving," *Blackwood's Edinburgh Magazine* (February 1820): 554–55.

contents after he has laid them aside; while some fortunate accident not unfrequently elevates, for a considerable length of time, into every thing but the highest order of celebrity and favour, writings of the same species, entirely their inferiors in every quality that ought to command the public approbation. We earnestly recommend these novels of Brown to the attention of our readers. In all of them, but especially in *Wieland*, they will discern the traces of a very masterly hand. Brown was not indeed a Godwin; but he possessed much, very much, of the same dark, mysterious power of imagination which is displayed in *Caleb Williams, St Leon,* and *Mandeville;*[1] much also of the same great author's deep and pathetic knowledge of the human heart; and much of his bold sweeping flood of impassioned eloquence. There are scenes in *Wieland* which he that has read them and understood them once, can never forget—touches which enter into the very core of the spirit, and leave their glowing traces there for ever behind them. Wild and visionary in his general views of human society, and reasoning and declaiming like a madman whenever the abuses of human power are the subjects on which he enlarges—in his perceptions of the beauty and fitness of all domestic virtues—in his fine sense of the delicacies of love, friendship, and all the tenderness, and all the heroism of individual souls,—he exhibits a strange example of the inconsistency of the human mind, and a signal lesson how easily persons naturally virtuous may, if they indulge in vague bottomless dreamings about things they neither know nor understand, become blind to many of the true interests of their species, and be the enemies of social peace and happiness, under the mask of universal reformers. The life of this strange man was a restless and unhappy one. The thoughts in which he delighted were all dark and gloomy: and in reading his works, we cannot help pausing every now and then, amidst the stirring and kindling excitements they afford, to reflect of what sleepless midnights of voluntary misery the impression is borne by pages, which few ever turn over, except for the purpose of amusing a few hours of listless or vicious indolence.

* * *

1. Novels by William Godwin, published in 1794, 1799, and 1817, respectively. In the preface to the last, Godwin expressed his admiration for and indebtedness to *Wieland*.

ANONYMOUS

Blackwood's Edinburgh Magazine on Brown, II[†]

BROWN—CHARLES BROCKDEN.—This was a good fellow; a sound, hearty specimen of Trans-Atlantic stuff. Brown was an American to the back-bone—without knowing it. He was a novelist; an imitator of Godwin, whose Caleb Williams made him. He had no poetry; no pathos; no wit; no humour; no pleasantry; no playfulness; no passion; little or no eloquence; no imagination—and, except where panthers were concerned, a most penurious and bony invention—meagre as death,—and yet—lacking all these natural powers—and working away, in a style with nothing remarkable in it—except a sort of absolute sincerity, like that of a man, who is altogether in earnest, and believes every word of his own story—he was able to secure the attention of extraordinary men, as other people (who write better) would that of children;—to impress his pictures upon the human heart, with such unexampled vivacity, that no time can obliterate them: and, withal, to fasten himself, with such tremendous power, upon a common incident, as to hold the spectator breathless.

His language was downright prose—the natural diction of the man himself—earnest—full of substantial good sense, clearness, and simplicity;—very sober and very plain, so as to leave only the *meaning* upon the mind. Nobody ever remembered the words of Charles Brockden Brown; nobody[1] ever thought of the arrangement; yet nobody ever forgot what they conveyed. You feel, after he has described a thing—and you have just been poring over the description, not as if you had been reading about it; but, as if you, yourself, had seen it; or, at least,—as if you had just parted with a man who *had* seen it—a man, whose word had never been doubted; and who had been telling you of it—with his face flushed. He wrote in this peculiar style, not from choice; not because he understood the value or beauty of it, when seriously and wisely employed—but from necessity. He wrote after his peculiar fashion, because he was unable to write otherwise. There was no self-denial in it; no strong judgment; no sense of propriety; no perception of what is the true source of dramatic power (distinctness—vividness.) While hunting for a subject, he had the good luck to stumble upon one or two (hav-

---

† From Anonymous [John Neal], "American Writers. No. II," *Blackwood's Edinburgh Magazine* (October 1824): 421–425.
1. "Or, as the QUARTERLY would say—Not anybody" [original note].

ing had the good luck before, to have the yellow fever) that suited his turn of expression, while he was imbued, heart and soul, with Godwin's thoughtful and exploring manner: and these one or two, he wore to death. The very incidents, which were often common-place, are tossed up, over and over again—with a tiresome circumstantiality, when he is not upon these particular subjects.—He discovered, at last perhaps, as many wiser men have done—when there was no use in the discovery—that it is much easier to suit the subject to the style, than the style to the subject;—no easy matter to change your language, or cast off your identity—your individuality—but 'mighty easy,' as a Virginian would say, to change your theme.

Brown was one of the only three or four professional authors, that America has ever produced. He was the first. He began, as all do, by writing for the newspapers—where that splendour of diction, for which the Southern Americans are so famous—is always in blast: He was thought little or nothing of, by his countrymen; *rose*, gradually, from the newspapers to the magazines, and circulating libraries; lived miserably poor; died, *as* he lived, miserably poor; and went into his grave with a broken heart.

He was born in Philadelphia; lived in Philadelphia—or—as his countrymen would say, with more propriety, 'put up'—(as he *did*—with everything—literal starvation—and a bad neighbourhood, in the dirtiest and least respectable part of the town)—'tarried'—lingered in Philadelphia; and had the good luck—God help him—to die in Philadelphia, while it was the 'ATHENS OF AMERICA'—the capital city, in truth, of the whole United States.

*   *   *

By great good luck, surprising perseverance, and munificent patronage—for America—poor Brown succeeded—(much, as the Poly-glott Bible maker succeeded, whose preface always brings the tears into our eyes—in burying all his friends—outliving all confidence in himself—wasting fortune after fortune—breaking his legs, and wearing out his life, in deplorable slavery, without even knowing it.)—Even so, poor Brown succeeded—in getting out—by piecemeal, a small, miserable, *first* edition—on miserable paper (even for *that* country)—a *first* volume of one or two of his works—the second *volume* following, at an interval—perhaps of years—the second *edition* never—never, even to this hour.—Yet will these people talk of their *native* literature.

* * *—there has *not ever* been, any second edition, of anything that Brown ever wrote—in America, we mean. We say this, with some positiveness (notwithstanding the most unprofitable uproar lately made about him there,—for which we shall give the reasons, before we have done with Brother Jonathan[2] cut where it may—hit or miss)—because we *know*, that, very lately, it was impossible to find, even in the circulating libraries of his native city (Philadelphia) any complete edition of his works:—Because we *know*, that, when they are found, anywhere (in America) they are odd volumes—of the *same* edition, so far as we can judge—printed 'all of a heap'—or samples or some *English edition*:—Because a young Maryland lawyer told OURSELF, not long ago, that he had been offered an armful of Brown's novels—(by a relation of Brown's family)—which were lying about in a garret, and *had* been lying about, in the same place, the Lord knows how long—if he would carry them away—or, as he said, 'tote 'em off, ye see.' But, being a shrewd young fellow—not easily 'cotch;' having heard about an executor *de son tort*, for meddling with a dead man's goods—and suspecting some trick (like the people, to whom crowns were offered, on a wager, at sixpence a-piece,) he cooked his eye—pulled his hat over one ear—screwed up his mouth, and walked off, whistling 'Tain't the truck for trowsers, tho'—

Some years ago, WE took up CHARLES BROCKDEN BROWN; disinterred him; embalmed him; did him up, decently; and put him back again—(that is—one of US did so.)—Since then, poor Brown has had no peace, for his countrymen. We opened upon the North American creature—making him break cover; and riding after him, as if he were worth our while. *Then*—but never till then—(we were the first)—did they give tongue, on the other side of the Atlantic.—We puffed him a little. They have blown him up—'sky-high.'—We went up to him, reverently—they, head-over-heels. We flattered him somewhat—for he deserved it; and was atrociously neglected. But they have laid it on with a trowel.—He would never have been heard of, but for us.—They are determined, now, that we shall never hear of anything else.—We licked him into shape: they have slobbered him—as the anaconda would a buffaloe (if she could find one)—till one cannot bear to look at him. We pawed him over, till he was able to stand alone—in his own woods—they—till he can neither stand nor go; till we should not know our own cub, if we saw him.

The talking about him began, clumsily enough—and, as usual, with a most absurd circumspection, in the North American Review: All the newspapers followed—of course—all the magaxines—tag, rag, and bob-tail: And then, just in the nick of time, came out proposals from a New-Yorker, to publish a handsome edition of BROWN'S NOVELS; at less, we believe, than one dollar (4s. 6d.) a-volume—

---

2. A fictional personification of the Unites States, a counterpart to England's personification as John Bull.

'worthy of him—worthy of the age—and—worthy of America,' —by *subscription*.

There the matter ended. Nothing more was done—of course. The family were scattered—very likely to the four winds of heaven;—and what if there *was* a niece living in Philadelphia—*that* was no business of theirs. They talked about his books; but nobody thought of subscribing. They called him the "Scott" of America—and there the matter ended.

It was one thing to make a noise; another to pay money. His countrymen had kicked up a dust, about his grave—talked of the "star-spangled banner"—and what more would ye expect of *his* countrymen? The whole community were up in arms—people were ready to go a pilgrimage to his birth-place—if there were no toll to pay—but not one in a million can tell, to this hour, where he was born—where he lived—where he died—or what he has written. They had ransacked the circulating libraries, anew; looked into such of his novels, as they could find, most of them for the first time, and the "balance," for the last time; dried out the grease—righted the leaves—wrote over the margins—dog-eared what was agreeable—hurried through a part—skipped the rest—smuttied their fingers—paid a 'fippenny bit' a-head—and what more would you have?

They had bragged of their national spirit, as being unexampled—(they were right—it *is* unexampled): of their national genius, which had been able to *"extort"* praise from us—in spite of our teeth;—they had made a plenty of noise about poor Brown; hurraed, like fine fellows, for American literature—and what more would any reasonable man—who knows them thoroughly—desire?

*   *   *

EDGAR HUNTLY was the second essay—ORMOND, the last.[3] About WIELAND we are not very certain. These three are unfinished, irregular, surprising affairs. All are remarkable for vividness, circumstantiality, and startling disclosures, here and there: yet all are full of perplexity—incoherence—and contradiction. Sometimes, you are ready to believe that Brown had made up the whole stories, in his own mind, before he had put his pen to the paper; at others, you would swear that he had either never seen, or forgotten, the beginning, before he came to the end, of his own story. You never know, for example, in Edgar Huntly, whether——an Irishman, whose name we forget—a principal character, is, or is *not*, a murderer. Brown, himself, seems never to have made up his own mind on that point. So—in Wieland—you never know whether Brown is, or is not, in earnest—whether Wieland was, or was not, supernaturally

3. *Ormond* preceded *Edgar Huntly*; both were published in 1799.

made away with. So—in Ormond—who *was* the secret witness?—to what purpose?—What a miserable catastrophe it is—Quite enough to make anybody sick of puling explanations.—Now, all this mystery is well enough, when you understand the author's *intention*. Byron leaves a broken chain—for us to guess by—when his Corsair is gone.[4] We *see* that he scorns to explain. Byron is mysterious—Brown only perplexing. Why?—Because Brown undertakes to explain; and fails. Brown might have refused as Byron did. We should have liked him, if he had, all the better for it; as we do Byron. But we shall never forgive him, or any other man, dead or alive, who skulks out of any undertaking, with an air—as if not be, but other people are to be pitied.——We have our eye on a case, in point; but—no matter now.

Brown wanted material. What little he found, though it had all the tenuity of pure gold, he drew out, by one contrivance and another, till it disappeared in his own hands. So long as it would bear its own weight, he would never let go of it; and, when it broke—he would leave off spinning, for a time, as if his heart had broken with it. He would seem to have always taken up a new piece before he had thrown off the old one (we do not mean that Old One, whom it is rather difficult for any author to throw off, after he has once given himself up to, the harlotry of the imagination)—to have clung, always, to one or two favourite ideas—the Ventriloquist—and the yellow fever——as if they were his nest-eggs: one might have written, with as much propriety, at the *end* of any story that he ever wrote, as in almost any part of it—after the fashion of Magazines— "TO BE CONTINUED." This grew, of course, out of a system which prevailed, then—and is now taking a new shape in the twopenny publication of costly works, by the number. He was a storyteller by profession.

* * *

He was a magazine writer; and rather 'cute. There was no stealing *his* bait. If you nibbled, you were in, for the whole—like a woman in love—hook, trap, and all. Money-lenders; gamblers; and subscribers to a story—which is *"to be continued,"* nobody knows how long, are all in the same pickle. They must lend more; play higher; and shell out, again—or all that has been done, goes for nothing. You must have the last part of a story—or the first, is of no use to you: (this very article, now, is a pretty illustration)—our author knew this. He never let go of more than one end of a story, at a time—even when he had sold out. It is amusing to see how entirely he would forget where his own traps lay—while he was forging bait; his own hooks, while he was counterfeiting the flies.

4. In George Gordon, Lord Byron's *The Corsair, A Turkish Tale* (1814).

* * *

So with WIELAND: In every case, you leave off, in a tense—a sort of uncomfortable, fidgetting, angry perplexity—ashamed of the concern, that you have shown—and quite in a huff with him—very much as if you had been running yourself to death—in a hot wind—after a catastrophe—with the tail soaped.

Yet, our conclusion respecting CHARLES BROCKDEN BROWN, is this. He was the Godwin of America. Had he lived here—or anywhere, but in America—he would have been one of the most capital story-tellers—in a serious way, that ever lived. As it is, there is no one story of his, which will be remembered or read, after his countrymen shall have done justice to the genius that is really among them. They have enough of it—and of the right sort—if they will only give it fair play. Let them remember that no man will be great, unless he work hard; that no man will work hard, unless he is obliged—and that those who do so work, cannot afford to work for nothing, and find themselves. It would be well for his countrymen to profit by—not imitate—we despise imitation even of what is excellent—it would be well for them to profit by his example. We want once more, before we die, to look upon the face of a real North American. God send that we may!

* * *

ANONYMOUS

Brown's Novels—*Wieland*[†]

Brown's Novels.—WIELAND.—As Mr. Goodrich, of Boston, has just published a new and complete edition of the works of the late Charles Brockden Brown, some remarks on the several productions of that native novelist would perhaps be acceptable to our readers. Mr. Brown may, with propriety, be ranked with the fathers of American literature, if not placed at their head—as he was the first among our countrymen who became an author by profession. He was a native of Philadelphia, his parents belonging to the society of Friends; and he was no less beloved for the unvarying amiability of his character, than admired for the fertility and splendour of his genius. His constitution was naturally inclining to the consumption, and he felt a sacrifice, in the prime of his years, to that fearful malady, which so

[†] *The New-York Mirror: A Weekly Gazette of Literature and Fine Arts* 4.42 (May 12, 1827): 335.

often marks out youth, virtue, and genius, for its prey. Mr. Brown
has generally been considered a disciple of the school of Godwin: in
the tone which pervades his productions, a considerable resemblance
to the latter may be discovered, but our countryman was undoubtedly superior in greatness of conception and delineation. Still his
works, brilliant as they are in many parts, ought rather to he looked
upon as proofs of what he might have been, than specimens of what
he was. He wrote with the most careless rapidity, dispatching the
sheets immediately from the desk to the printing office, so that his
chapters were usually issued from the press as fast as they were written. This sufficiently accounts for their many imperfections; but,
at the same time, it excites our astonishment, that works penned in
this hasty manner, should be generally wrought up to such a high
degree of excellence. In selecting the themes for his stories, and the
scene of their action, Mr. Brown endeavoured to explore ground
which had as yet been untrodden by adventurers in the regions of
romance. He interwove with his tales many of the most terrific and
mysterious things in nature and art; and the characters, which he
delineates with peculiar force, belong not to "the common herd of
vulgar men," but to a singular and isolated branch of the human
family—beings who live in a world of their own, and, in good or evil
pursuits, are wayward and eccentric. The first romance produced
from the pen of this gifted writer, was "Wieland," which we select
for the subject of our present remarks. The story is, in a great measure, founded on two of the most unaccountable of natural and artificial phenomena—the spontaneous combustion of the human body,
and the art of ventriloquism. Instances of the first have so rarely
occurred, that some of our readers are perhaps unacquainted with
its existence. It is, however, well known in the philosophic world,
that, by some strange operation of nature—supposed to condense or
multiply animal heat—the corporal frame of our species may take
fire and partly consume, without any extraneous cause. An accident
of this kind occurs in the early part of the story, and is described
with a degree of power suited to the awful nature of the subject.
There is also introduced into the narrative a person, who, besides the
most consummate powers of mimicry, possesses the faculty of ventriloquism in the highest perfection; and is able, by throwing his
voice into every variety of tone, to make it appear to sound from any
spot, either near or moderately distant from the speaker. By the exertion of this physical talent, oral communications, apparently supernatural, are produced: he thus holds a controlling power over those
about him, and carries on the delusion till Wieland (the nominal
hero of the tale) becomes insane, in consequence of the continued
deception; and, in obedience to the commands of imagined inspiration, imbrues his hands in the blood of his wife and offspring. The

plot of the story is intricate, and involves much mystery, which is gradually and ingeniously unravelled. The catastrophe, and the incidents which bring it about, are related in a manner which few authors can equal; but they are of so appalling a description, that we would advise none of weak nerves or morbid sensibility to peruse the fearful narration. This tale has more dramatic regularity than any that were afterwards written by its author; but, in general merit, it is surpassed by several.

The Modern Critical Revival

BERNARD ROSENTHAL

The Voices of *Wieland*†

Nina Baym's "A Minority Reading of *Wieland*" forcefully demonstrates the structural problems of *Wieland* as seen from the perspective of the contemporary critical theories applied to it.[1] While one might wish, for the sake of Brown's reputation, that modern approaches lack validity for a late eighteenth-century writer of fiction, the fact is that one finds even harsher charges leveled at *Wieland* in Brown's own time.[2] The most virulent complaints of the earlier critics centered on the perceived gimmickry of Brown, such as the use of spontaneous combustion. But hostile critics reserved their greatest disdain for Brown's trick of ventriloquism as a device for unraveling the mysteries of the tale. If one may indeed sympathize with a reader's disappointment at finding the solution to a mystery as nothing more than a parlor stunt gone wrong, the irony remains that the power of the novel as seen by Brown's friendly critics depends on the existence of some natural phenomenon to explain a misguided belief in supernatural agencies. In one sense, then, the division of opinion over Brown's artistry hinges on the success or failure of his use of voices. Regarded as the mere solution to a mystery, ventriloquism surely must disappoint most readers. But I want to argue that Brown's employment of ventriloquism, as well as his alleged use of spontaneous combustion, had purposes having little to do with

---

† From *Critical Essays on Charles Brockden Brown*, ed. Bernard Rosenthal (Boston: G. K. Hall & Co., 1981): 104–125. Copyright ©1981 by Bernard Rosenthal. Reprinted by permission. Page numbers in square brackets refer to this Norton Critical Edition.
1. Nina Baym, "A Minority Reading of *Wieland*," in *Critical Essays on Charles Brockden Brown*, ed. Bernard Rosenthal (Boston: G. K. Hall., 1981): 87–103 [Editor's Note].
2. *Wieland* seems to have gone unnoticed in England when first published. Subsequently, reviews were mixed with particularly savage ones in *The Ladies' Monthly Museum*, n.s., 9 (December, 1810), 338–39 and *Gentleman's Magazine*, 81 (April, 1811), 364. Both reviews were anonymous. Others were mixed, and the only genuinely enthusiastic review appeared anonymously in *Critical Review*, s. 3, 22 (February, 1811), 144–63. Brown seems to have fared better in America. See Harry Warfel, *Charles Brockden Brown* (Gainesville: University of Florida Press, 1949), pp. 110–11.

the solving of mysteries. Brown had a polemic message, the danger
of morality based on revealed religion; and he employed a literary
methodology that suggested rather than explained, a methodology
that in the hands of a literary genius like Hawthorne would be per-
fected and would receive the label of "Romance."[3] As Hawthorne
often does, Brown turns to an event from the past to set a shadow of
gloom upon the present. In *Wieland*, the dark spell originates from
an earlier religious discovery.

The tale has scarcely begun when the elder Wieland happens upon
"a book written by one of the teachers of the Albigenses, or French
Protestants."[4] Declining the opportunity to dwell on the lurid associations connected with the Albigenses, Brown perhaps relied on
popular beliefs about them to suggest the motif of religious fanaticism central to *Wieland*.[5] Thought to be an offshoot of Manichean
theology, the Albigenses were conflated in popular thought with the
Cathari and the Camisards.[6] Among the beliefs attributed to them

3. I use the term here in the sense that Hawthorne does in his preface to *The House of
the Seven Gables*. For an important consideration of Brown and Romanticism see Sydney J. Krause, "Romanticism in *Wieland*: Brown and the Reconciliation of Opposites"
in *Artful Thunder*, ed. Robert J. DeMott and Sanford Marovitz (Kent: Kent State University Press, 1975), pp. 13–24. See also Robert Strozier's suggestive essay, "*Wieland*
and Other Romances: Horror in Parentheses," *Emerson Society Quarterly*, No. 50 (1st
quarter, 1968), pp. 24–29. For associations with Hawthorne and others, see Donald
A. Ringe, *Charles Brockden Brown* (New York: Twayne Publishers, Inc., 1966), pp.
42–43.
4. *Wieland*, ed. Sydney J. Krause and S. W. Reid (1798; Kent: Kent State University Press,
1977), p. 8[9].
5. Brown's outline for *Wieland* is published in the Kent State edition (pp. 420–41) [307–
12] and contains a notation to "See Chambers Cyclopaedia" for reference to Wieland's
religious faith (p. 427) [307], specifically in connection with the Savoyard sect. I have
examined the 1788 and the 1741 editions of *Chambers' Cyclopedia* and have found no
reference to the Savoyard sect in either one. However, the entry for "Albigenses,"
taken here from the 1788 edition, warrants notation: "The Romanists tax the *Albigenses* with abundance of heterodox opinions; as, for instance, that there are two
Gods, the one infinitely good, and the other infinitely evil; that the good God made the
invisible world, and the evil one that which we live in; with the rest of the Manichean
tenets.
"But this seems to be one of those pious frauds allowed particularly in that church,
which esteems it a kind of merit to blacken heretics, and those whom they chuse to call
so." Ephraim Chambers, *Cyclopedia: or, An Universal Dictionary of Arts and Sciences*,
vol. 1 (London, 1788). The 1741 entry differs in some details, particularly in its assertion that the Albigenses "maintained marriage unlawful" (vol. 1). Both emphasize the
dualism cited above as "Manichean tenets," and both suggest that the Albigenses may
not have necessarily held the views ascribed to them by their persecutors. No mention
is made in the 1741 edition of the third name associated with Wieland's religion, the
Camisards, although a brief and relatively insignificant entry appears in the 1788 edition. Although I cannot verify whether Brown followed up his stated intention in the
outline to check this source, the entry cited regarding the Albigenses is similar to that
appearing in other sources and does offer a reliable indication of the connotations carried by reference to that sect. The reliability of these perceptions regarding the Albigenses is not germane to Brown's use of the name. Its attraction seemed to be in the
popular beliefs about the Albigenses.
6. Scholars of Brown have tended to scant the sources of Wieland's theology and their
implications for the novel. Some notable exceptions, however, may be found. David Brion
Davis, *Homicide in American Fiction, 1798–1860: A Study in Social Values* (Ithaca: Cor-

were the views that Satan and the God of the Old Testament were one, that marriage was sinful and should be renounced, and that a select group known as "perfecti" belonged to a higher class of men worthy of salvation. One need not dwell long on these ideas to find associations with the demented killer of his family in Brown's novel.

If such a religion would seem bizarre to a person from Brown's theological culture, so much the better for his purposes. The intrinsic danger of religion, not merely theological excess, might be demonstrated more emphatically. To follow any scripture rather than to follow rational morality risked surrendering sober, wise judgment to the elder Wieland's "empire of religious duty" (p. 9) [10]. The excesses of a man slaughtering his family in response to divine revelation likewise demonstrated the inherent danger of human conduct rooted in religious duty. The issue here is not merely one of religious excess, but rather of a fundamental perception regarding revealed religion as inherently leading to such excess, whether in the purported beliefs and actions of the Albigenses or in the murder of Wieland's family. In his letter of October 24, 1795, to Joseph Bringhurst, Brown had set forth an intellectual premise on revealed religion that would be played out in the fiction of *Wieland*.[7]

In Brown's novel, the elder Wieland takes his new religion to America, prospers, does missionary work, builds a temple, and lives

---

nell University Press, 1957), p. 88 makes the connection between "religious fanaticism" and Wieland's interest in the Albigenses. Various critics have made passing references to the Manichean aspects of *Wieland*, particularly Richard Chase in *The American Novel and Its Tradition* (Garden City; Doubleday and Company, 1957), p. 38. The most serious and extensive examination of the Manichean aspect of *Wieland* may be found in Carl Nelson, "Brown's Manichean Mock-Heroic: The Ironic Self in a Hyperbolic World," *West Virginia University Philological Papers*, 20: 26–42. For an especially suggestive note on the Camisards and the use of voices, see Bruce E. Kirkham, "A Note on *Wieland*," *American Notes and Queries*, 5 (1967), 86–87.

7. See Rosenthal, "Introduction," in *Critical Essays on Charles Brockden Brown*, pp. 11–16. The notion that *Wieland* treats religious excess is so commonplace in the critical canon that no special citation is needed here. I am, of course, distinguishing between religious excess and reliance on revealed religion per se, the idea Brown attacks in his letter to Bringhurst. The idea that Theodore Wieland's problem stems from misguided religion rather than religion itself may be found, for example, in James E. Mulqueen, "The Plea for a Deistic Education in Charles Brockden Brown's *Wieland*," *Ball State University Forum*, 10 (1970), 77. In a different approach Larzar Ziff asserts that "stigmatizing religious fanaticism is inadequate because Wieland's training is singularly free from any sectarianism." "A Reading of *Wieland*," *PMLA*, 77 (1962), 54. While Ziff is clearly correct in pointing out that Wieland belongs to no special sect, Brown is explicit in associating the younger Wieland's approach to theology with that of his father, who does follow a sect. See *Wieland*, p. 23 [21]. For the view that "Brown was testing theological ideas," see Warfel, p. 97.

In emphasizing as I do the association of *Wieland* with Brown's theological concerns, I do not mean to imply that the story has no other textual or intellectual sources. Much has been written about influences on *Wieland*. For a particularly suggestive essay regarding possible links to the German poet C.M. Wieland, see John G. Frank, "The Wieland Family in Charles Brockden Brown," *Monatshefte*, 42 (1950), 347–53.

bound in guilt for having failed to execute a divine injunction. Whether the elder Wieland had been commanded to slay his family is problematic. Brown, in Clara's narrative, writes that the "duty assigned to him was transferred, in consequence of his disobedience, to another, and all that remained was to endure the penalty" (p. 13) [13]. Brown does not assert that the injunction was passed to the son, but no ambiguity exists as to the son's compulsion to obey a command he believed to be divine. Nor does Brown leave ambiguous the text that originally impels the elder Wieland, the words "'Seek and ye shall find'" (p. 8) [10]—good, orthodox Christianity of a kind that trusts the individual to learn from the Bible and to obey the commandments derived from religious study.[8]

By following this advice, the younger Wieland embarks on a course resulting in the slaughter of his family. Brown prepares the reader for so terrifying an act through inviting speculations on the supernatural resulting from the strange death of the elder Wieland. Although the book never does explain what happened to him, the label of "spontaneous combustion" has stuck to the event from the earliest readings to the present. A more skillful writer like Hawthorne would learn the trick of romance whereby alternative explanations are offered for an event that belongs to imaginative understanding rather than to literal translation. For example, does any reader of *The Scarlet Letter* believe that witches flying overhead attract the attention of Mistress Hibbins? Do readers fail to understand that such an event, otherwise ludicrous, in Hawthorne's hands conveys the sense of the demonic that haunts Hester? Unfortunately, readers often miss Brown's early employment of what Hawthorne would call "Romance" and take literally what is merely a suggestion in a footnote (p. 19) [18], this, even though the words "spontaneous combustion" never appear in Brown's novel.[9]

On the night of his death, the elder Wieland goes to the temple. His wife first thinks a pistol has been fired (p. 16) [16]. Her brother rushes to the scene to find some extraordinary light, but no flame (p. 17) [17]. Wieland's "body was scorched and bruised. His right arm exhibited marks as of having been struck by some heavy body"

---

8. The reference to "Seek and ye shall find" is noted by A. Carl Bredahl, Jr. in an essay that treats the lines from another perspective. "Transformation in *Wieland*," *Early American Literature*, 12 (1977), 177–92. The specific reference to the injunction appears on p. 179.

9. The association with "spontaneous combustion" appears from the earliest critical reception of *Wieland* to contemporary criticism, as, for example, in John Cleman's essay, valuable for its addressing the issue of ambiguity, "Ambiguous Evil: A Study of Villains and Heroes in Charles Brockden Brown's Major Novels," *Early American Literature*, 10 (1975), 190–219. The assumption has been questioned by David Ketterer, *New Worlds for Old: The Apocalyptic Imagination, Science Fiction, and American Literature* (New York: Anchor Books, 1974), p. 173. The best comment to date on the issue of "spontaneous combustion" in *Wieland* appears in Mulqueen, p. 72.

(p. 18) [17]. His clothing is in ashes, but his hair and his slippers are unaccountably intact. Now at this point in the story, Wieland the religious fanatic has every reason to explain his experience as divine retribution. Stories from him about avenging angels, or even spontaneous combustion, would be quite in character. At least this would be the case if something more secular had not happened. Yet Wieland's own explanation belongs neither to mysteries of religion nor of science.[1] Here is the dying man's testimony:

> By his imperfect account, it appeared, that while engaged in silent orisons, with thoughts full of confusion and anxiety, a faint gleam suddenly shot athwart the apartment. His fancy immediately pictured to itself, a person bearing a lamp. It seemed to come from behind. He was in the act of turning to examine the visitant, when his right arm received a blow from a heavy club. At the same instant, a very bright spark was seen to light upon his clothes. (p. 18) [17]

This is Wieland's testimony, which Brown never does clarify. If the victim is to be believed, the fire that burned him fell first on his clothes and did not come from within as it would in spontaneous combustion. The elliptical reference to such an explanation is from Clara, who was not there. Moreover, Wieland claims to have been hit by a club. Granted that Clara's uncle feels "that half the truth had been suppressed" (p. 18) [17], neither it nor the other half is ever told. The reader has only the word of the victim who essentially says a light shone, a club hit him, and a spark ignited his clothing. A rational hypothesis would not be hard to construct. Only the "sudden vanishing" of the cloud at the approach of the uncle seems contrary to reasonable explanation. As for the rest, it lends itself to speculations about an intruder with a lamp who attacked Wieland, hit him on the arm and deliberately or accidentally ignited his clothing with the lamp's fire. The blow on the arm is a detail of the story to which Brown never returns. Nor does Clara, as she incorporates the mystery at the temple into the family myth of something unnatural having happened to the father. Clara asks the questions early that will engage the reader throughout. "Was this the penalty of disobedience? this the stroke of a vindictive and invisible hand? Is it a fresh proof that the Divine Ruler interferes in human affairs, mediates an end, selects and commissions his agents, and enforces, by unequivocal sanctions, submission to his will?" (p. 19) [18]. Clara follows

1. Although seeing "spontaneous combustion" as one of Brown's exceptions, John Cleman perceptively observes that "the instances of non-human evil, or harm not the result of human action, are rare in Brown's major novels, and the examples that do appear are never left without a sense of the human connection," p. 193. For one of the rare recognitions of alternative possibilities to spontaneous combustion, see Ringe, pp. 143–44, n. 10.

these questions with the speculation hinting at spontaneous combustion, but the latter possibility will play no further role in the novel. The former will become its center. And Clara, not the rational person some readers have wanted her to be, will to the end have almost as much faith in divine voices as does her tormented brother.[2]

The initial event having left its legacy of supernatural intimations to the six-year-old Clara and to her brother, it is scarcely to be wondered that they become susceptible to the tricks of ventriloquism that Carwin plays. After an idyllic childhood, only vaguely haunted by the horrendous past, the children enter adulthood with marriage for Wieland and hints of romance with Pleyel for Clara. Amidst a life uninterrupted by labor, the foursome live in their almost Arcadian world until a voice is heard calling Wieland back from the temple. The reader subsequently learns that Carwin had played the trick of ventriloquism, initiating a series of deceptions that accounts for all of the voices except for the ones that command Wieland to kill his family. Whether this voice emanates from Carwin, as early critics assumed it did, will be examined subsequently. But setting that voice aside, the reader receives an acceptable—though unsatisfying to many—explanation for all the others.

Acceptable, that is, if certain assumptions are granted: Clara is a reliable narrator as is Carwin and both may be believed. Granting the validity of Clara's experiences with voices and Carwin's confession, all mysteries except the central one are explained by ventriloquism. By the central mystery, I mean the one involving the elder Wieland's death and the younger Wieland's subsequent behavior independent of Carwin's tricks. For when Carwin has completed his explanations, the reader is left with some puzzles that cannot be explained merely on the basis of Wieland's presumed madness. The unaccountable blow on the arm of the elder Wieland offers one problem.

Another intriguing puzzle arises from Clara's discovery of the murdered Catharine's body. What is one to make of Clara's initial response?

> To die beneath his [Clara is assuming Carwin as the murderer] grasp would not satisfy thy enemy. This was mercy to the evils which he previously made thee suffer! After these evils death was a boon which thou besoughtest him to grant. (p. 151) [115]

2. The association of Clara with reason is a traditional one in critical responses to *Wieland*, with various commentators observing that her reason unguided by sound religious principles is insufficient. For a refreshing recognition of the degree to which Clara departs from reason, see Michael Bell, "The Double-Tongued Deceiver: Sincerity and Duplicity in the Novels of Charles Brockden Brown," *Early American Literature*, 9 (1974), p. 148.

Readers need not have prurient imaginations to take for granted that Clara can be suggesting nothing other than rape. Does she see something that she will not narrate? Or does Brown raise the specter in order to encourage the false lead that Carwin was guilty?[3] Certainly nothing in Wieland's account suggests that he raped his wife before murdering her, and Brown never returns to clarify this issue.

A third unaccountable mystery involves the light Clara sees in her bedroom window as she approaches her house just prior to discovering Catharine's body. She sees the light, and then "after flitting to and fro, for a short time, it vanished. I turned my eye again toward the window, and perceived that the light was still there; but the change which I had noticed was occasioned by a change in the position of the lamp or candle within" (p. 145) [110–11]. When she reaches her room, she posits, as she often does, supernatural causes, encouraged this time by the mystery at the foot of the stairs. "Neither lamp nor candle was to be found," she narrates (p. 149) [113]. A person comfortable with rational explanations might simply have assumed that the bearer of light has merely departed the room taking the lamp or candle. But Clara's mind does not run toward the rational. Nor is Clara a discerning auditor in hearing Carwin's explanation. "'A light stood on the table'" in her room, Carwin says (p. 213) [158]. He makes no comment as to whether he ever touched or moved it, except to say that he turned it out and quickly left the room upon hearing Clara's approach. Now it would certainly be reasonable if Carwin had walked around the room holding the light he had discovered and even fled with it to see his way out. But why put out a light and then take it with him? It makes no sense; or, to be more conservative, it invites questions from Clara that are never asked. Indeed, from the account given there is no reason to believe that Carwin ever moved the light, and thus the mystery of the moving light in Clara's room is never resolved.

Without considering whether other unaccountable events occur in the story, one may contemplate the implications of the three unexplained episodes: the blow on the arm, which nothing in the story

---

3. In his splendid historical essay on Brown in the Kent State edition of *Wieland*, Alexander Cowie, in arguing that Clara holds "latent incestuous longings" for her brother, addresses in a note Brown's willingness to write about sexual topics: "It would seem to be an anomaly that Brown, an almost prudish person by most tokens, should have made so much comment, in his publications, on sexual freedom and sexual aberrations, including, in *Stephen Calvert*, a reference to a relationship between man and wife in which the husband exhibits 'propensities . . . that have not a name which' the wife 'can utter'" (*Wieland*, p. 332). Although the note is somewhat misleading in that the reference is actually to the husband's homosexual relationships, Cowie's point remains germane. Brown, of course, also deals with the issue of rape elsewhere in his fiction. For the incident in *Stephen Calvert* cited by Cowie, see William Dunlap, *The Life of Charles Brockden Brown* (Philadelphia: James P. Parke, 1815), II, 400.

contradicts; the hinted rape of Catharine, which creates a contradiction between Wieland's account and Clara's; and the light in the bedroom, which poses Carwin's credibility against Clara's. If one grants that these incidents create narrative problems for the reader, it seems reasonable to assume that Brown either hurried past these incidents and simply left aesthetic flaws or that they are consistent with some as yet undiscussed explanation. I would like to offer a hypothesis for the latter view. For it seems to me that these three minor anomalies are symptomatic of the ambiguity that suffuses Brown's novel; that they fit his pattern of showing how untrustworthy the senses are, particularly—for Brown, I believe, was writing a polemic novel—regarding *all* varieties of religious experience.[4] He was testing in fictional form the argument he offered his friend Bringhurst. The hypothesis of the dangers of all morality based on religious forms, not merely religious excess or religious fanaticism, was being played out in a novel that *required* anomalous and unexplained occurrences. While the line between controlled ambiguity and aesthetic inconsistency may indeed be thin, Brown does seem to strive for the former. A better writer might have achieved his end more convincingly, but even Melville has not escaped from readers of *Pierre* who mistake ambiguity for a variety of literary sins. And Brown did not write at that level of genius. Still, the patient reader will find the purposes of *Wieland* to be clear and the ambiguities and anomalies integral to the polemic against morality based in religious thought.

As indicated earlier, the tragedy of *Wieland* finds its roots in the religious conversion of the elder Wieland. That he chooses a bizarre theology—at least by the standards of his culture—merely highlights the danger of all religion. The man who will follow a "good" voice of God rather than his own moral senses will be capable of following any voice. For all the reader knows, Wieland was struck dead in the temple by a human intruder, or struck on the arm by one and then set on fire, externally ignited, if Wieland's own account is to be believed. But scarcely does the event occur, when Clara, not her father, raises the question of divine retribution (p. 19) [18].

Theodore Wieland from the outset shares his father's religious temperament and habits. Unlike Clara, he studies theology and worries about "preparation and provision" (p. 23) [21] for the next

4. The issue of sensory experience has perhaps elicited more discussion in criticism of *Wieland* than any other subject. I cite only two of the many perceptive comments on this topic. See the introduction by Robert E. Hemenway and Joseph Katz to Paul Allen, *The Late Charles Brockden Brown* (Columbia: J. Faust & Co., 1976), p. liv; and J.V. Ridgely, "The Empty World of Wieland," in H. Kenneth Baldwin and David K. Kirby, eds. *Individual and Community: Variations on a Theme in American Fiction* (Durham: Duke University Press, 1975), p. 3.

life in a way consistent with the religious mode rejected by Brown in his letter to Bringhurst. Clara herself does not look for faith based "in the weighing of proofs, and the dissection of creeds" (p. 22) [20], although as subsequent events show she is much given to a belief in the supernatural and to explanations of events not rooted in rational thought. The advocate of rational thought is Pleyel. "Pleyel was the champion of intellectual liberty, and rejected all guidance but that of his reason" (p. 25) [23], which may be open to debate but which is at least generally true. Catharine seems to have no thoughts on anything; Her primary function in the novel is to give Theodore something to murder and Carwin a voice to imitate.

In response to the first voice heard, the one calling Theodore back from the temple, Pleyel suggests "a deception of the senses" (p. 34) [29], while Theodore flatly rejects such an explanation (p. 36) [31]. Clara fears that Pleyel's view might be right (p. 35) [30], but she essentially reserves judgment. And very soon thereafter, a switch in perceptions occurs, which shatters the symmetry of Theodore as the voice of religion, Pleyel as the voice of reason, and Clara as inclined toward the latter and fearing the former (p. 35) [30]. For the second voice, announcing the death of Pleyel's fiancée, quickly ends the reliance on rational causes. Pleyel, without questioning the source of the voice, simply accepts the idea that she is dead. And Clara makes clear her belief in the supernatural. "That there are conscious beings, beside ourselves, in existence, whose modes of activity and information surpass our own, can scarcely be denied" (p. 45) [38]. She assumes that the voice heard by Theodore and Pleyel is supernatural but benign (p. 46) [38]. She will generally believe this about the voice throughout the book. And if Clara needed confirmation on the validity of the voice, she received it upon learning that Theresa, Pleyel's fiancée, was indeed dead (p. 48) [40]. That this subsequently proved to be untrue is consistent with Brown's method of unexplaining events almost as rapidly as he explains them, a technique most extensively and explicitly employed in *Arthur Mervyn*, where, as Emory Elliott shows, the reader receives two versions of reality with little basis for choosing between them.[5]

At this point in the story, immediately after the second voice, Carwin is introduced. The reader should not ignore Clara's account of him as monstrous (p. 49) [41], particularly when considering that the lines are written after all the facts had been heard.[6] Clara

5. See Emory Elliott, "Narrative Unity and Moral Resolution in *Arthur Mervyn*," in *Critical Essays on Charles Brockden Brown*, 142–143.
6. The matter of Clara's retrospective narration causes numerous uncertainties as to whether a given perception by her is one as seen from the present looking back or as seen at the time of the occurence. Ringe has given some attention to this matter, pp. 45–47, although a full analysis of the subject awaits a separate essay devoted to that topic.

regards Carwin as responsible for "the evils of which it is but too certain that [he was] the author" (p. 50) [41]. And the third experience with voices, the sounds of murderers in her closet (including the voice of one who claims he will deserve "'perdition'" if he commits "'more'" than murder [p. 58] [48]), certainly does little to mitigate Clara's harsh judgment of Carwin. But the fourth voice, the one calling for someone to assist Clara (p. 59) [49], further confirms her views that an outside agency with benevolent intentions is at work (pp. 59–60) [49]. Since this is a retrospective telling, it accounts only for her feelings at the time, but subsequent events will show that in spite of Carwin's confession, in spite of her hatred for him, she does not abandon the belief in an outside agency that would seem untenable in view of the explanations subsequently given by Carwin. At least if Carwin clarifies everything. But he does not.

Consider the fifth voice. Clara, asleep in her summer house, dreams of her brother's leading her to an abyss. Suddenly, a voice calls and a hand grasps her. The voice, according to his confession, is Carwin's (p. 204) [152]. The hand, unmentioned in the confession, presumably belongs to the dream. Clara, awakened by the voice, hears the sound "of him who had proposed to shoot, rather than to strangle" (p. 63) [51], the voice recalled from her bedroom closet. It cautions Clara away from the summer house and threatens her father's fate, presumably learned by Carwin from Clara's maid. At this point, a key incident occurs. Clara "perceived a ray flit across the gloom and disappear. Another succeeded, which was stronger, and remained for a passing moment" (p. 63) [52]. Clara's response to what she sees invites alternative choices for the reader of *Wieland*:

> The first visitings of this light called up a train of horrors in my mind; destruction impended over this spot; the voice which I had lately heard had warned me to retire, and had menaced me with the fate of my father if I refused. I was desirous, but unable, to obey; these gleams were such as preluded the stroke by which he fell; the hour, perhaps, was the same—I shuddered as if I had beheld, suspended over me, the exterminating sword. (p. 64) [52]

The original account of Wieland's death in the temple had left the reader with only one mystery not accountable by some rational explanation—even if one resorted to the spontaneous combustion unsupported by Wieland's dying testimony. This was the mystery of the light. Now Clara sees the same light. Granted that the appearance of the original light came to her through second-hand description. Nevertheless, her own senses, distraught though they may be, see a light like that which preceded the destruction of her father. If the light is indeed the same, speculations of Carwin's presence in the temple when her father was murdered are invited. If the similarity of lights represents only Clara's runaway imagination, is there any reason to believe it runs away here only? In other words, if Clara is so taken in by her imagination at this point that the reader cannot believe her, then why trust her observations or her history elsewhere? But if she is right about the light, then Carwin may have had something to do with the death of her father. Brown does not pick up this idea, although in the true spirit of later "romancers" he suggests possibilities, he uses that which cannot be taken literally to tell truths otherwise untellable. He has, in a sense, discredited Clara and Carwin even as he eventually explains every event between them. To not tell and tell is the essence of romance.

Clara comes to believe that occurrences have been explained. "It was only by subsequent events, that I was fully and incontestibly assured of the veracity of my senses" (p. 65) [53]. Yet the evidence of her own tale has contradicted her, and since the reader only knows the tale through her the mysteries of plot really never do become clarified. Nor should they, any more than Melville should have clarified the meaning of his whale, or Hawthorne the true state of Mistress Hibbens's witches. As with Melville and Hawthorne, Brown uses extraordinary, inexplicable events to arrive at truths in fiction.

Because Brown was writing a book about the dangers of religion in view of the unreliability of human senses, he could not let go of the strategy that swung expectations back and forth between natural and supernatural causes. If he does not pursue fully the possibilities of Carwin's culpability in the murder of Clara's father, he nevertheless sends his heroine back and forth between reliance on the natural and the supernatural for explanations, and in suggesting the former he keeps suspicion focused on Carwin. When Clara has safely escaped the summer house, she tries to make sense of events that have occurred. Her thoughts are of human rather than supernatural explanations. She believes the voice that warned her away from the summer house to be human (p. 66) [53], and she very clearly raises the possibility that this may be the same voice that was behind the death of her father. "Was then the death of my father, portentous and inexplicable as it was, the consequence of human machinations?" (p. 66) [54]. Only readers sucked into Brown's vortex of the supernatural could believe otherwise, and this has included quite a few of them. Perhaps it is necessary to emphasize here that I am not building a case for the conviction of Carwin. Whether he was even old enough to have been the murderer of Wieland is not clear from Brown's story. But I am trying to emphasize how easily the reader may overlook "human machinations" as causes for apparently inexplicable events and that searching for spontaneous combustion as a cause may suggest an irony that Brown could not have anticipated in writing his book about the dangers of religion. Could he have ever guessed how fully science would replace religion as a new theology, that just as people in his generation looked for miracles in the supernatural world, another generation would seek them in the natural one? The scientific paradigm that emerged in the nineteenth century and which has dominated the twentieth century simply overwhelmed his point about "human machinations." The idea needs to be retrieved in the reading of *Wieland*, and the person examining Brown's book must select from three and not two possibilities in considering the story's central mystery.[7]

Carwin himself, when first apprized by the Wielands and Pleyel of the family tragedy, pleasantly surprises Clara by not ridiculing their story and by encouraging the belief in divine voices although he claims his own experience has always found stories so attributed to be ultimately explainable in human terms (p. 74) [59]. Indeed, Carwin toys with the group by actually giving them the explanation of ventriloquism for all the voices so far heard, except at the summer house. That voice is not discussed at all, presumably because Clara has not told anyone of it in response to its warning of dire consequences. Not certain whether the voice was natural or supernatural, she listens nevertheless. But in apparently telling the truth, Carwin finds an audience of skeptics. In response to Carwin's general discussion of similar occurences, Wieland insists on "the probability of celestial interference" (p. 75) [60], while Pleyel holds to the "testimony . . . of his senses" (p. 75) [60]. Clara apparently swings back to belief in the supernatural, since she allies her opinions with her brother's (p. 75) [60]. And when Carwin offers specific speculations regarding the voices heard by the group, they find his thoughts "insufficient to impart conviction to us" (p. 76) [60]. Carwin has offered the simplest and most plausible of explanations, but none of them, particularly Clara and Wieland, can believe in events unshrouded by mystery.

Clara's temptation toward her brother's sensibility of explanations by supernatural causes, as well as her obsession with her father's death, must not be scanted. Clara's thoughts turn often toward her father's death, as they do just before the closet scene in her bedroom, where, expecting to find her brother she finds Carwin instead (p. 83) [66]. Much has justifiably been made of this closet scene and

7. Critics perceptive enough not to accept the death of the elder Wieland as a clarified event have tended to see two choices—theological or scientific—for the reader rather than three. For example, see Joe Lee Davis, John T. Frederick, and Frank Luther Mott, eds. *American Literature, An Anthology and Critical Survey* (New York: Charles Scribner's Sons, 1948), I, 232.

its relation to Clara's dream of her brother's luring her to the abyss.[8] Its invitation to psychological criticism and its introspective search for the nature of human senses as well as its intrinsic drama have contributed to the interest in it. I simply want to emphasize something simple and obvious here. Clara assumes that the voice warning her away from the closet, as well as the same voice she had earlier heard, is "divine" (p. 89) [70]. Like her brother, she believes in voices from other worlds.

Carwin plays on the belief when discovered in the closet. Clara has opened the door, in defiance of the voice warning her away, and has discovered Carwin. What is a man to say when thus exposed in a woman's closet? Writing on the edge of farce, but never crossing over into it, Brown has him demand explanations of her! "'What voice was that which lately addressed you?'" (p. 89) [71] he asks in the first words that pass between them in this bedroom encounter. Or, more accurately, the first words, since Clara actually says nothing. Carwin does all the talking, pretending, if we are to believe his later confession, that the voice was not his but a "'sound . . . beyond the compass of human organs'" (p. 90) [71]. Affirming that the voice belongs to his "'eternal foe'" (p. 90) [71], Carwin emphasizes that he is helpless before that power.[9] As if Clara is not sufficiently confused, the fast-talking Carwin then argues that there would be no harm done in any case if he executed his illicit designs, since only her "'prejudices'" make them injurious (p. 90) [71]. Clearly, Clara has no wish to engage in social discourses about chastity to say nothing of divine voices. Her only response to Carwin's verbal counterattack upon being discovered is to wonder at her own frame of mind. "I used to suppose that certain evils could never befall a being in possession of a sound mind," she narrates (p. 90) [72]. The reader may want to question how sound her mind is at this point.[1]

Carwin might have left after his attack on chastity as a "'chimera still worshipped'" (p. 90) [71], for Clara was in no mood to do anything but stand and wonder. But Carwin makes a final verbal assault before lapsing into self-pity and leaving. He tells Clara that he cannot harm her. "'The power that protects you would crumble my sinews, and reduce me to a heap of ashes in a moment, if I were

8. See, for example, the introduction by Sydney J. Krause and S.W. Reid to the paperback edition of the Kent State text, *Wieland, or The Transformation* (Kent: Kent State University Press, 1978), pp. xix–xx. * * *
    For a view of the closet scene "as a metaphor for the entire action of this strange tale," see William H. Manly, "The Importance of Point of View in Brockden Brown's *Wieland*," *American Literature*, 35 (1963), p. 319.
9. The idea of the double personality used so successfully later by Poe, as in "William Wilson," seems suggested by Brown, but not explored.
1. Bredahl, p. 189, observes that Clara's confusions eventually bring her to the brink of suicide, as he compares her state of mind with her brother's. Frank, p. 253, sees her as faring much better, "since she shows the victory by reason and deism."

to harbour a thought hostile to your safety'" (p. 91) [72]. Now Car-win has just told her that he contemplated taking "'away the spoils of [Clara's] honor'" (p. 90) [71], and the reader has some sorting of information to do. Did Brown forget what he had just written? Did Carwin forget what he had just said? Was Clara incapable of catch-ing the obvious flaw? But most importantly, how does one assess Carwin's "heap of ashes," a phrase that so clearly evokes the death of Wieland? On the latter question, one might speculate that Car-win, knowing the fate of Wieland, has played on it to terrorize her. Or one may guess that he too is mad and believes in avenging spir-its. Or that he is sane and believes in them.

The point of these questions is not to argue their answer. Such matters in a well-executed romance do not trouble the reader, and if it is true that Brown attempts in *Wieland* the elliptical style of romance that finds fulfillment in Hawthorne and Melville, the flaw is not in the inconsistencies but in the level of execution. The terrible events are not the spoken ones, but those hinted at. The terror of the chapter resides not in threats of ravishment or murder, but in the possibility that we live in a world where unnamed powers can reduce us to "a heap of ashes." And both the burning Wieland and Carwin's evocation of the event encourage the gloom that pervades Brown's novel; they hint at the "blackness" Melville saw in Haw-thorne.[2] As Clara observes: "Something whispered that the happi-ness we at present enjoyed was set on mutable foundations. Death must happen to all. Whether our felicity was to be subverted by it tomorrow, or whether it was ordained that we should lay down our heads full of years and of honor, was a question that no human being could solve" (pp. 54–55) [45]. In a book that advocated reliance on this world and the understandings to be derived from it for one's actions, the next world could only emerge as a dangerous illusion and not as a consoling thought. Whether wrought by a human intruder, by some natural phenomenon, or even by divine ordination, the death of Wieland prefigured Clara's fears, articulated perhaps in the "heap of ashes" image. Carwin presumably lied in playing with Clara on the story of her father's death. But in the lie he told the truth.

Clara's thoughts do not entertain the possibility of a world unreg-ulated by higher powers. Like her father and her brother, she tries to guess at the intentions of supernatural forces, to read divine minds. In sorting out her experience with Carwin at the closet, she continues to refer to a "divinity" (p. 96) [76] that spoke to her. More-

---

2. Herman Melville, "Hawthorne and His Mosses" (1850), in Edmund Wilson, *The Shock of Recognition* (New York: Farrar, Straus and Cudahy, 1955), pp. 187–204. See also the very perceptive observations by Pamela J. Shelden about the vision of the world that emerges from *Wieland*. "The Shock of Ambiguity: Brockden Brown's *Wieland* & the Gothic Tradition," *Literary Arts Journal*, 10 (1977), 17–26. See also Ziff, p. 52.

over, she affirms that "to yield to my fears is to deserve that they should be realized" (p. 96) [76]. This observation is doubly ironic, since it describes what happens to her brother who does yield, even as it also describes the realization of her own fears whether she yields to them or not. For the nightmare of her brother as monster is spurned by her as a cause for serious anxiety, yet the terrible dream materializes, even if Clara's abyss is not literal.

But before Clara's nightmarish confrontation with her brother occurs, Brown unfortunately turns his attention to the deviltry that voices play in Clara's love life. Perhaps because conventions of the day required it, Brown integrated into his tale of madness and cosmic ambiguity the courting of Clara and Pleyel. If this aspect of *Wieland* does little to enhance the sustained power of the tale, it does bring to an everyday level the consequences of relying merely on appearances. Maybe the part of Brown who saw himself as a "moral painter" felt obliged to work this lesson into a situation familiar to readers of novels addressed to the misunderstandings of lovers.[3] More probably, he anticipated an audience that expected a love motif, and he gave them one along with a set of voices to precipitate the misunderstanding between Clara and Pleyel. As the explanations and accusations emerge, the story loses its central focus on the mystery of the past and its intimations of terror in the future. It also loses some consistency in story line that will not be explained by suggestions of the romantic mode. For example, as Pleyel gives his long account of why he has lost faith in Clara's virtue, she actually reflects on Carwin's powers in setting up the misleading situation. But this occurs at a point in the book prior to her knowledge of Carwin's ability (p. 133) [103]. And, shortly after, with no suspicion that he has been duped and with every reason to believe that Clara is at the summer house (having just spoken with her there, or so he thinks), Pleyel goes to Clara's bedroom to confirm the fact that she is not there (p. 135) [104].

However, Brown picks up the thread of his story once more when he places Clara back in her bedroom in response to Carwin's note. Clara, questioning her own wisdom in returning to meet her would-be ravisher, contemplates her belief in the protection of voices and assumes them supernatural (p. 147) [112]. But shortly afterward she qualifies her narrative. Just after hearing the voice calling her back from her room and seeing a glimpse of a face, she observes: "I now speak as if no remnant of doubt existed in my mind as to the supernal origin of these sounds; but this is owing to the imperfection of my language, for I only mean that the belief was more permanent,

3. In his "Advertisement" for *Wieland*, Brown refers to "moral painters" in connection with his own intentions. See *Wieland*, p. 3 [4].

and visited more frequently my sober meditations than its opposite"
(p. 148) [113]. This is a telling statement, since the reader might
otherwise think that early references to "divine" sounds were figura-
tive. They were not. Clara is removing whatever ambiguity may have
existed about her own belief in supernatural voices. If she sometimes
departs from that belief, more often she holds to it. Whether Brown
wanted to suggest that a more rational Clara might have helped avert
tragedy can only be a matter of speculation. The story really does not
make this point. It simply gives the reader the true state of Clara's
mind on the issue of divine commandments in preparation for her
encounter with Wieland as the high tragedy of the story unfolds with
unresolvable ambiguity.

Upon seeing Clara in her room, Wieland soon becomes distracted
by a commandment he receives. Neither Clara nor the reader has any
evidence of voices, so the presumption must be that Wieland is now
simply mad or that divine voices actually speak to him. Assuming the
latter as implausible, one infers the former. Brown gives us no reason
to do otherwise, and since no voice is heard to urge on the killing of
Clara, one would think that Carwin is exonerated from a direct link
to the other murders. Yet Wieland's account of his actions offers the
reader the third alternative as stated earlier by Clara's uncle: "'Carwin, perhaps, or heaven, or insanity, prompted the murderer . . .'" (p.
161) [122]. That Wieland is insane by the time he threatens Clara
seems uncontestable. But the matter of his other murders is not so
clear. As Wieland tells his story of the event precipitating the murder
of his family, a sudden light came upon him.[4] The reader has seen
something of this light in the temple of the elder Wieland and at
Clara's summer house. The possibility of its human sources cannot
be ruled out, nor is it necessarily only in Wieland's mind. Upon opening his eyes after the burst of light, Wieland still sees it, "'but, anon,
a shrill voice from behind called upon me to attend'" (p. 167) [126].
Whether the voices heard by madmen are always "shrill" is uncertain
at best. But there is no reasonable doubt that Carwin at times speaks
that way, at least if we believe his confession that the earlier voices
were his. Wieland himself has heard three voices previously, once
when alone and going to the temple, once with Pleyel, and once at
his house when the voice called for assistance to Clara. The first two
voices Wieland heard came as the sound of Catharine. The third had
no association with anyone he knew. In its anonymity the most strik-

---

4. Although nothing in the story suggests anything false to me about the confession, I do
call attention to the fact that Wieland's confession comes to Clara from her uncle who
received the transcription from an unidentified person; this confession, of course,
along with the rest of the tale, comes to the reader through the perception of Clara.
Those concerned with the reliability of narration in *Wieland* may want to scrutinize
further this matter. See p. 163 [123].

ing characteristic was "piercing shrillness" (p. 59) [49], perhaps similar to the "piercing" voice Clara heard in approaching the closeted Carwin (p. 147) [112]. This third voice, with its "shrillness," was heard by others besides Wieland. So the sound at that time is not a trick of his imagination.

Is it wholly unreasonable to assume that the "shrill" voice commanding him to murder his family might be identical to the "shrill" voice heard earlier? It is not, and the idea that Carwin, a confessed liar, created the voice commanding murder remains a possibility, if not the certainty that early critics of *Wieland* assumed.[5] The indescribable sight that Wieland next sees argues for his madness, but this is not inconsistent with the notion that Carwin's "shrill" voice might have commanded the murders. Again, I want to emphasize that the issue is not Carwin's guilt or innocence. Rather it is the ambiguity of the event; it is Brown at his best, I believe, controlling the narrative so that the reader, unable to guess the source of this voice—coming from inner madness, outer chicanery, or even divinity—can scarcely dismiss the plausibility of Wieland's lapse into insanity, particularly with his predilection toward divine injunctions. Under the best of circumstances, Brown seems to be saying, rational conduct in this world is not easily maintained. Add the dimension of reliance on religion, and abandoning the norms of civilization becomes an event only awaiting the circumstances that will precipitate it.

Brown will not let the reader escape this association, nor will he allow one to see the issue merely as religious *excess*. It is reliance on religion per se that allows the situation. The unpenitent Wieland defends himself, like Carwin in the closet, not by apologizing for his actions, but by accusing. "'You say I am guilty. Impious and rash! thus to usurp the prerogatives of your Maker! to set up your bounded

5. One must not, of course, rule out the possibility that a demented Wieland merely chose for his delusion a voice he had heard earlier. The question of whether Carwin commanded the murders is an old one. Most of the early critics, particularly those disliking the book, took Carwin's guilt for granted. A few examples of opinion in the twentieth century, presented chronologically, reflect the modern range of views on this subject. Martin S. Vilas sees "pure malice" from Carwin and holds him responsible for the voice: *Charles Brockden Brown: A Study of Early American Fiction* (Burlington: Free Press Association, 1904), p. 21. According to Ziff, "Wieland's homicidal actions result, finally, from causes which are inexplicable scientifically," p. 54. Arthur Kimball argues that to ask whether the villain is Carwin or the insanity of Wieland is to ask the wrong question; he also offers a useful survey of opinion on the subject. See *Rational Fictions: A Study of Charles Brockden Brown* (McMinville: Linfield Research Institute, 1968), pp. 44–49. Bell writes that "Wieland's insanity . . . turns out to have arisen from his own mind and not from Carwin's deceptions . . ." (p. 144). Ridgely takes the view "that the voice which Wieland heard was *not* that which had addressed [Clara] and the others on previous occasions" (p. 10). Finally, Robert. W. Hobson points the argument back toward earlier views in raising "the possibility that Carwin's influence on Wieland is more direct than Mr. Cambridge will allow. Indeed, it appears that Carwin may be as guilty of murder as Wieland." See "Voices of Carwin and Other Mysteries in Charles Brockden Brown's *Wieland*," *Early American Literature*, 10 (1975), 307–09.

views and halting reason, as the measure of truth!'" (p. 176) [132]. This is precisely the issue Brown debated with Bringhurst. Does not religion, by its nature, preclude our relying on our own reason? And who can predict the consequences when we abandon the rules of this world for the communications of another? The soundness of Brown's argument on this point of theology may be contested, as Bringhurst obviously did. But its soundness is not the issue. It is its application to *Wieland*.

Nor will Brown allow us the comfort of seeing the whole matter as an aberration of Wieland's, since Clara's uncle tells the story of her grandfather plunging to his death in response to voices from a dead brother (pp. 178–79) [134]. This does not invite the explanation of congenital madness in the Wieland family, since the grandfather here is on the maternal side. And Clara, ever wavering between natural and supernatural explanations, casts her lot with the latter as she tries to absorb what she has experienced.

> My opinions were the sport of eternal change. Some times I conceived the apparition to be more than human. I had no grounds on which to build a disbelief. I could not deny faith to the evidence of my religion; the testimony of men was loud and unanimous: both these concurred to persuade me that evil spirits existed, and that their energy was frequently exerted in the system of the world. (p. 180) [135].

This is Clara relying on religion and not reason. Whereupon she proceeds to divide the world of spirits into benign and malign agencies. Their existence is a matter of certainty and not speculation for Clara. "That conscious beings, dissimilar from human, but moral and voluntary agents as we are, some where exist, can scarcely be denied" (p. 181) [136]. And this leads her to the mystery she cannot fathom. "Carwin was the miscreant whose projects were resisted by a minister of heaven. How can this be reconciled to the stratagem which ruined my brother? There the agency was at once preternatural and malignant" (p. 181) [136].

The "answer" to this will appear as the disappointing ventriloquism which historically has seemed so unsatisfactory to critics of *Wieland*. But if the solution hinges on gimmickry, the issue posed is as old as Christianity. Why does a benevolent heaven allow evil voices? Wieland's father had found his answer in the Albigensian heresy as popularly understood—the division of the world into a Manichean scheme of good and evil, a god for each. Clara seems to believe her father's heresy as she juggles events into this dualistic scheme. Then, suddenly, she finds a "new channel" of thought (p. 181) [136]. Clara reasons that "there was truth in this [Wieland's] appeal" to God (p. 181) [136], "and nothing but unerring proof of divine approbation could sustain his mind in its present elevation" (p. 181) [136]. Put another way, the "new channel" emerges in the recognizable form of the Christian synthesis whereby the duality of good and evil becomes subsumed under the unity of heaven's just purposes. In this "new channel," Clara has left the Albigensian heresy and has acknowledged the Christian requirement to accept the will of heaven. Consequently, for the moment at least, she takes the side of her brother! No "transformation" in a book carrying that subtitle proves more remarkable. Such is the power of reasoning from heaven's word.[6]

Attempts to persuade Clara that her brother is simply mad do not succeed. She reverts to uncertainty as to whether he is "a faithful servant of his God, the victim of hellish illusions, or the dupe of human imposture . . ." (p. 187) [140]. Clara wants to visit him, but her uncle opposes the plan in part with the argument that a visit from her might restore him to sanity and thus shake "his confidence is divine approbation and future recompense" (p. 187) [140]. Although his true reason for discouraging the visit is to protect Clara, he speaks the truth in warning about the fatal consequences of shattering his religious belief. Wieland has committed his life to religion, and he has based his morality on the promise of future reward, a central belief of Christianity and an issue fundamental to the dialogue between Brown and Bringhurst. The wisdom of Clara's

---

6. William Hedges has called attention to Clara's "idolizing Wieland as Christlike" in response to his "supreme sacrifice" resulting from obedience "to orders he took to be divine." "Charles Brockden Brown and the Culture of Contradictions," *Early American Literature*, 9 (1974), p. 121. This suggestion by Clara that Hedges notes warrants careful consideration on two grounds. It very clearly emphasizes how thoroughly Clara's thought is conditioned by religious predispositions. It also invites associations of Wieland with the "perfecti," cited in my essay's opening discussion of the Albigenses. Of the many notions attributed to this group, a particularly significant one held that Satan, the Old Testament Jehovah, created the material world and that most individuals are beyond redemption because they were Jehovah's creatures. According to Appleton's *American Cyclopaedia*, however, "there is also a higher class of men, whose souls are the fallen angels, and for the redemption of whom the God of light sent the angel Jesus, who taught them that they were of a higher nature, and that by despising everything material they could emancipate themselves from the prince of this world." Those in this group were presumably the "perfecti." See Appleton's *American Cyclopaedia*, ed. George Ripley and Charles A. Dana (New York: D. Appleton and Company, 1873), vol IV, 116. While I can identify no specific source in which Brown might have found such information, the view described here was an old one and widely available in Brown's day. His specific association early in the story of the elder Wieland's discovery of Albigensian theology, along with the younger Wieland's affinity with his father's theology, surely offers a possible theological frame of reference for Wieland's destruction of his attachments to the world. Certainly, Clara sees him as above and apart from other mortals. "Infatuated wretch that I was!" she exclaims. "To set myself up as a model by which to judge of my heroic brother!" (p. 225) [167]. Note also on the same page: "A new soul appeared to actuate his frame, and his eyes to beam with preternatural lustre."

Those interested in pursuing the subject of Manichean theology, of which the Albigensian heresy represented a late historical form, should begin with Hans Jonas, *The Gnostic Religion: The Message of the Alien God and the Beginnings of Christianity*, second edition, revised (Boston: Beacon Press, 1963).

uncle would be justified in the fate of Wieland as would Brown's argument to Bringhurst.

But before this climatic scene emerges, the reader is taken once more into the ambiguity of Clara's perceptions about Carwin, whom she can never see properly because her vision is through a prism of spirits. Thus the reader can never fully know just what role Carwin had, since he can be understood only through the distorted understandings of Clara.

For reasons never clarified by Brown, the tide of Clara's reasoning begins to shift toward focusing blame on Carwin—this, even before his confession and on the basis of no appropriate information. Terrorized by the thought of being hunted to death by Wieland, who does so in heaven's name and in the cause of virtue, Clara leaps at the prospect of somehow focusing her search for causes on Carwin. "In this paroxysm of distress, my attention fastened on him as the grand deceiver; the author of this black conspiracy; the intelligence that governed in this storm" (p. 190) [142]. By the time she meets Carwin, once more in her bedroom, she assumes that he somehow "urged" (p. 196) [146] Wieland on to his crimes. That she has no basis for this insinuation is beside the point. More germane is that for the moment she surrenders her belief in his guilt for two reasons: Carwin's denial even of having heard of the murders and her own recollection of the voice that previously saved her from Carwin (p. 196) [146]. Clara simply will not abandon her belief in the supernatural. With none to blame, and having faced horror beyond her capacity to comprehend or even to fit into some consoling scheme, she asks only to be left to her own despair.

But Carwin has come to confess. Readers of *Wieland* have readily accepted that confession of ventriloquism, even if they have often regretted Brown's inability to do better. Clara is less easily convinced. Bluntly, she asserts that "his tale is a lie, and his nature devilish" (p. 216) [161]. Her response bears careful consideration. Upon first hearing Carwin's claim that it was his voice and face she heard and saw, Clara arrives at a plausible response. "But if Carwin's were the thrilling voice and the fiery visage which I had heard and seen, then was he the prompter of my brother, and the author of these dismal outrages" (p. 197) [147]. The reader may recall that earlier scene, one which indeed comes close to the method of Hawthorne. Clara says upon seeing the face that "the lips were stretched as in the act of shrieking; and the eyes emitted sparks, which, no doubt, if I had been unattended by a light, would have illuminated like the corruscations of a meteor" (p. 148) [112]. It is a tableau hinging on an "if," but as true to reality as the "A" in the sky of *The Scarlet Letter* that tells the truth, even if its reality rests in the illusion of the romancer's art. The "fiery visage" Clara has seen invites inconclusive specula-

tions on its association with the death of Wieland and the precipitation of his son's murders. On the basis of her own senses, Clara has
every right to doubt Carwin.

Carwin's story has less mystical problems. He insists to Clara that
he did not cause Catharine's death, "yet had I not rashly set in
motion a machine, over whose progress I had no controul, and which
experience had shewn me was infinite in power?" (pp. 215–216)
[160]. Maybe. But how would he know? By his own testimony he has
claimed that he did not even know Wieland was a "'lunatic'" (p. 196)
[146]; he had no idea of his involvement in Catharine's murder until
Clara told him on the very occasion of the conversation now trans-
piring. Brown is inconsistent or Carwin is lying. "'The perpetrator
of Catharine's death was unknown to me till now; nay, it is still
unknown to me'" (p. 216) [160]. This is Carwin speaking almost
immediately after admitting that he had "'set in motion a machine'"
(p. 215) [160]. How one responds to this clear contradiction no doubt
depends on how one responds to Brown as an artist. While I readily
grant that he writes careless lines and has inconsistencies of narrative, he was in my opinion too good a writer to make this kind of slip
up, to inadvertently juxtapose such contrary evidence. The flaw is in
Carwin's story and not in Brown's artistry. Clara does not reason it
all out, but she understands "a lie" when she hears it here.[7]

What then of the rest of Carwin's story? Some perhaps is true;
some perhaps false. Brown's point is that the event is beyond comprehension; his explanation is for an audience that must have answers,
while his "moral" is that where no answers exist, one must not insist
upon false ones. Neither Clara nor the reader really can decide
whether Carwin prompted Wieland to his murders. If *Wieland* is
a successful "Romance" directed to another point, the resolution of
such a detail does not matter. Certainly, though, one can understand
the belief in Carwin's guilt by those who wish to solve such problems.
When Wieland tries to hear voices with Carwin and Clara in the
room, there are none (p. 218) [162]. Only when Carwin leaves the
room does a voice sound, this time to save Clara from Wieland.

Before the story's final voice rescues Clara, she finds herself alone
with her brother; the nightmare of the summer house has been
transformed into the reality of Wieland in her bedroom ready to send
her to the abyss of death. Brown masterfully weds this pathetic,
tragic moment to the "moral" he wants to teach. "'I have acted poorly
my part in this world,'" Wieland tells his sister, apparently doubting for the moment the righteousness of his acts. "'What thinkest
thou? Shall I not do better in the next?'" (p. 224) [166]. Here Brown

7. For another perspective on Carwin, see David Lyttle, "The Case Against Carwin,"
Nineteenth Century Fiction, 26 (1971), 257–69.

relentlessly fixes on the issue he had debated with Bringhurst. What kind of morality can we expect if it is contingent on rewards and punishments in an afterworld? For all his misery, Wieland remains faithful to future judgments for present conduct. He does not reject this religious construct; he merely seems to acknowledge that he may not have followed heaven's rules after all. "'The cup is gone by,'" he says, "'and its transient inebriation is succeeded by the soberness of truth'" (p. 224) [166]. But only the "truth" that he may have been deceived. He does not question the morality of rewards and punishments. Indeed, he shakes himself free of the tormenting doubt to affirm his purity on the grounds that "'I believed that my God was my mover!'" (p. 224) [166].

How does Clara react to this from the murderer of Catharine and her children? With admiration and with doubt over the capacity of her own reason or anyone's reason to judge wisely. But this must not be seen as an attack by Brown on reason or on its limitations. Rather it is an attack on reason rooted in beliefs of the supernatural. It is also of course not a condoning of Wieland's actions. But in the ambiguity of admiration for her "heroic brother" (p. 225) [167] and the horror of what has happened, Clara can resort only to cursing Carwin.

Wieland is more certain in his beliefs, his wavering faith having returned. He claims that his silent prayers had after all been answered, and that he understands Carwin to be evil. But Carwin's evil has been commissioned by God, and that is sufficient for Wieland. To Carwin, Clara appeals for help, and the voice that subsequently saves her is presumably his. But Clara, after Wieland's suicide concludes the tragic sequence, has gone beyond concerns of whose voice belonged to whom.

> Talk not to me, O my revered friend! of Carwin. He has told thee his tale, and thou exculpatest him from all direct concern in the fate of Wieland. This scene of havock was produced by an illusion of the senses. Be it so: I care not from what source these disasters have flowed; it suffices that they have swallowed up our hopes and our existence.
>
> What his agency began, his agency conducted to a close. He intended, by the final effort of his power, to rescue me and to banish his illusions from my brother. Such is his tale, concerning the truth of which I care not. (p. 233) [172–73].

The reader does well to be guided by Clara's final assessment (at least before the tacked-on chapter).[8] The questions of Carwin's reliability, of how the elder Wieland died, and of other matters belong

---

8. For a history of this chapter, see Alexander Cowie's comments in *Wieland*, pp. 322–23.

to truths of fiction rather than to truths of life. Her lack of concern for the "truth" is in the spirit of romance where the details of narrative matter less than the implications behind them. For the "truth" has been told, and the monstrousness of a world that abandons the reason Brown believed in has been revealed.

The remainder of *Wieland*, the chapter apparently coming as an afterthought on Brown's part, has pained his admirers who understandably wish he had left well enough alone. An aspect of the story, the Louisa Conway motif that had been touched upon and dropped is here picked up and explained in the form of a tale of seduction and murder that bears little need for critical analysis. One may speculate that Brown felt obliged to tie up a loose end, or perhaps that he wanted to give his audience something brighter and more conventional, something to make the book more marketable. These must remain speculations.

But one observation about this chapter must be made. Brown returns in it to his moral lesson and ties the Maxwell story to the Wieland tale by observing that "it will not escape your notice, that the evils of which Carwin and Maxwell were the authors, owed their existence to the errors of the sufferers" (p. 244) [181]. That is, what applies in religious conduct applies in social conduct also. However extraneous the chapter may appear, it manages to take the moral of a religious tale and show its application to that of a conventional seduction story. Neither the Stuarts nor the Wielands ever did understand the correct moral obligations that this world requires of us, and the final sentence of the book implicitly applies to the Stuarts as well as to the Wielands and to the Bringhursts. "If Wieland had framed juster notions of moral duty, and of the divine attributes; or if I had been gifted with ordinary equanimity or foresight, the double-tongued deceiver would have been baffled and repelled" (p. 244) [181]. Here is no argument for atheism, since it acknowledges "divine attributes." But it is an argument for understanding that the voice of God must be obeyed only as it is consistent with human morality based in reason.

Brown was a man of the eighteenth century, so of course his assumptions about the efficacy and power of reason are tied to beliefs then held about the ways in which people learn and sense their world. The critic who seeks to understand Brown's premise need not accept it or the morality that the book attacks. But the critic is obliged to come to terms in some way with the ambiguities and contradictions of the tale or to acknowledge *Wieland* as an unsatisfactory novel. Read as a book hinging on the gimmick of ventriloquism, it indeed disappoints the reader. As a story that explores the limits of understanding, the ambiguity of perception, it justifies some of its most extravagant praise. At its best *Wieland* captures the wonder of romance and transforms improbabilities into vehicles for conveying truths otherwise beyond the capacity to tell. The theme of illusion and reality, so central to the writings of Hawthorne, Melville, and Poe, found its first American expression in *Wieland*. It was expressed well.

WALTER HESFORD

"Do you know the author?": The Question of Authorship in *Wieland*†

"The author!" said he: "Do you know the author?"
"Alas!" I answered, "I am too well acquainted with him."[1]
The author in question is the author—the originator, the perpetrator—of a mass murder. Clara, our narrator, is sure she knows who that is. Her interrogator, Clara's uncle, is sure he knows, but sure Clara does not. Neither character's assurance proves wholly warranted. Authorship in Charles Brockden Brown's *Wieland or The Transformation* is difficult to determine, so "Do you know the author?" remains a central open question in the novel, one that the reader is asked to ponder along with the narrator.

Perhaps without intending to, critical readers have successfully kept the question open. They agree, to be sure, that Brown wrote, authored, *Wieland*, but argue about the author, the initiator, of the bloody, confusing action of the novel. Is it the elder Wieland, who initiates a destructive behavioral pattern from which his children cannot escape; or Theodore Wieland, who, prompted by his God or daemon, sacrifices his family; Carwin, the mysterious biloquist whose talent works confusion and catalyzes violence; or Clara Wieland, whose repressed guilt and incestuous desires provide her with motivation and who, indeed, writes our story with a pen sharpened by a knife steeped in her brother's blood? Some readers posit cultural or literary authorship: fingers are pointed at Calvinism, rationalism, sentimentalism, isolationism, utopianism, or pastoralism as the villain Brown would have us discover; scholars contend that the Bible, *Hamlet, Paradise Lost*, and *Faust* (among other works) are the texts that "father" the action in *Wieland*. Still other readers focus atten-

---

† From *Early American Literature* 17.3 (winter 1982–83): 239–48. Copyright © 1983 by the University of North Carolina Department of English. Used by permission of The University of North Carolina Press, www.uncpress.unc.edu. Page numbers in square brackets refer to this Norton Critical Edition.
1. Charles Brockden Brown, *Wieland or The Transformation; Memoirs of Carwin the Biloquist* (Kent, Ohio, 1977), p. 160 [121]; hereafter cited parenthetically in the text.

tion on the act of reading and writing, holding this act responsible for all that happens for good or ill in the novel.[2]

Most of these sometimes contradictory readings help establish the meaning of *Wieland*. What remains to be suggested, I think, is that the novel itself caters to diverse responses to the question "Do you know the author?," caters to diverse readings and the proffering of multiple meanings, because it works to deconstruct the idea of single authorship, and, with it, belief in a single, authoritative source of meaning and action. It reveals a disconcertingly modern, decentered world, one not centered on answers supplied by any authority, but rent by, and rendered through, questions.

The preeminent author *Wieland* implicitly calls into question is the Judeo-Christian God, the traditional originator and center of being and meaning in Western culture. In illustrating his first definition of "author" ("The first beginner or mover of anything; he to whom anything owes its original"), Samuel Johnson cites passages from Hooker, Milton, and Newton which bear witness that God is the *true* author of man and nature. Noah Webster's first definition of "author" also testifies to God: "One who produces, creates, or brings into being; as God is the author of the universe."[3] As author, God may be said to work in three modes. First, he (I will justify this egregiously sexist use of the pronoun toward the conclusion of my paper) according to tradition, is the true author of the Bible, the book that authenticates as it records his active identity; second, God is the author of man's being, and ratifies his authorship through an

---

2. Dazzled, puzzled student readers of *Wieland* first stimulated my preoccupation with the problem of authorship in the novel. The early criticism that raises this question tends to focus primarily on Theodore Wieland and his religious mania, with secondary attention to Carwin as a devious artist-seducer. Recently, the focus has been on Clara. James R. Russo, for example, in "'The Chimeras of the Brain': Clara's Narrative in *Wieland*," *Early American Literature*, 16 (1981), 60–88, argues that Clara is directly or indirectly the author of *all* the mayhem in the novel, an argument I find more intriguing than convincing.

   Two excellent cultural readings of *Wieland* are: Larzer Ziff, "A Reading of *Wieland*," *PMLA*, 77 (1962), 51–57; and Donald Ringe, chap. 2: "*Wieland*," *Charles Brockden Brown* (New York, 1966), pp. 25–48.

   Among those which explore literary pretexts are: Joseph Soldati, "The Americanization of Faust: A Study of Charles Brockden Brown's *Wieland*," *ESQ: A Journal of the American Renaissance*, 20 (1974), 1–14; Wayne Franklin, "Tragedy and Comedy in Brown's *Wieland*," *Novel*, 8 (1975), 147–63; and Michael T. Gilmore, "Calvinism and Gothicism: The Example of Brown's *Wieland*," *Studies in the Novel*, 98 (1977), 107–18.

   Three readers who focus on the act of reading and writing are: Michael D. Bell, "'The Double-Tongued Deceiver': Sincerity and Duplicity in the Novels of Charles Brockden Brown," *Early American Literature*, 9 (1974), 143–63; Mark Seltzer, "Saying Makes It So: Language and Event in Brown's *Wieland*," *Early American Literature*, 13 (1978), 81–91; and Cynthia S. Jordan, "On Rereading *Wieland*: 'The Folly of Precipitate Conclusions,'" *Early American Literature*, 16 (1981), 154–74.

   For a full bibliography of *Wieland* criticism through 1978 see Patricia L. Parker, *Charles Brockden Brown: A Reference Guide* (Boston, 1980).

3. Samuel Johnson, *A Dictionary of the English Language* (1755; rpt. New York, 1967), I. Noah Webster, *An American Dictionary of the English Language* (1829; rpt. New York, 1970), I.

historic human incarnation; and third, God is the author of the universe and reveals himself in the Book of Nature as well as in the
Bible and in man. All three modes of God's authorship fall under
scrutiny in *Wieland*.

A reading of a biblical verse sets in motion, authors, the "prehistory" of the central drama of *Wieland*—a prehistory that haunts this
drama itself. The gloomy, purposeless existence of "the young elder
Wieland" is transformed one Sunday afternoon when his eyes chance
to light upon the words "Seek and ye shall find" in a book that "by
some accident had been opened and placed full in his view" (p. 9) [10].
The scene somewhat resembles the one celebrated in the opening of
Georg Poulet's "Phenomenology of Reading," in which an open book
lies waiting for a reader to rescue it from objectivity and restore it to
the world of human significance, to life.[4] But the biblical verse the
elder Wieland lights upon seems to have a compelling life of its own,
would appear to have more control over the reader than a phenome-
nologist would want to grant. The words in sight are extraordinarily
powerful, having a privileged position (owing to the authority of their
speaker, Jesus) within a text, the Bible, "whose centrality, potency,
and dominating anteriority inform," according to Edward Said, "all
Western literature"; "the displacing power in all texts," Said asserts,
"derives finally from the displacing power of the Bible. . . ."[5] This
book, which the elder Wieland comes to view as "the fountain,
beyond which it was unnecessary to trace the stream of religious
truth" (pp. 8–9) [10], does indeed seem to displace all other authority
in his life and govern his decision to journey to America, where he
engages in the common effort of displacing Native American culture
with a Bible-based logocentric culture.

Contact with the Indians collapses his effort, dislodges his center. The failure of his mission—which typifies the common failure
of the spiritual errand into the wilderness—is one of the circumstances that casts ironic shadows upon the supposed authority of
the Bible and its supposed author. The script written by the likes of
Capt. John Smith, promoting not the kingdom of God but economic
success, ultimately has more authority in America than Revelation.
The elder Wieland handily transforms himself from a failed missionary into a successful capitalist, exploiting cheap land and slave labor,
though repressed guilt over his failure eventually works itself out
explosively.

The authority of the word of God is called into question not only
by the elder Wieland's inability to live it out constructively in Amer-

4. Georg Poulet, "Phenomenology of Reading," *New Literary History*, 1 (1969), 53.
5. Edward W. Said, "The Text, the World, the Critic," in *Textual Strategies: Perspectives in Post-Structuralist Criticism*, ed. Josué V. Harari (Ithaca, N.Y., 1979), p. 179. Said acknowledges his debt to Northrop Frye.

ica, but also by circumstances surrounding the initial reading of the biblical verse. First, that he read it by pure (or sinister) "accident" suggests that whether or not God's word addresses us at all, let alone with authority, is purely (or sinisterly) accidental. Second, the way in which the elder Wieland takes in the word is partly predetermined by his gloomy, depressed, genetically poetic disposition. And third, his reading of the Bible is shaped by the doctrine of a radical French Protestant sect, the Camissards; it was a book by a Camissard apostle that happened to be open to a page containing the injunction, "Seek and ye shall find." When the elder Wieland searched the Bible itself,

> Every fact and sentiment in this book were viewed through a medium which the writings of the Camissard apostle had suggested. His constructions of the text were hasty, and formed on a narrow scale. Everything was viewed in a disconnected position. One action and one precept were not employed to illustrate and restrict the meaning of another. Hence arose a thousand scruples to which he had hitherto been a stranger. He was alternately agitated by fear and by ecstasy. He imagined himself beset by the snares of a spiritual foe, and that his security lay in ceaseless watchfulness and prayer, (p. 9 [10])

Our narrator would have us see that the elder Wieland grossly misreads the Bible. Yet is his misreading much greater, say, than that which authorized the plan of some seventeenth-century English Puritans to establish a Zion in America? It seems probable that one will read the Bible through the medium of one's personality and culture. Thus God's book may be received as merely a text among other texts, without special authority, subject to the same phenomenological interpretation—or misreading—as any other work.

One might argue that a right reading of, at least, "Seek and ye shall find" is possible, and that it involves identification with Jesus, the speaker, who, according to Christian biblical tradition, spoke and acted with the authority of one who embodied—who was— the word of God. To identify with Jesus involves recognizing oneself as a son of God, as a being under divine authorship. It is precisely such a sense of himself which blesses and burdens the younger Wieland (appropriately, ironically, named Theodore), who seems to inherit from his father a passion to seek and find oneness with God. His decision to sacrifice his family to that end is premised on a corollary to the supposition that God is the author of his being: "The author of my being," he reflects in his murder confession, "was likewise the dispenser of every gift with which that being was embellished. The service to which a benefactor like this was entitled, could not be circumscribed" (p. 166) [125]. His desire to serve his benefactor had long been frustrated, for God the Author had long remained silent and hidden; "Alas!" cries Wieland, "thou hidest thyself from my view" (p. 167) [125]. In his desperation to see, to *know* his author, he conjures up God's commanding presence, conjures up a voice that commands him to sacrifice his bourgeois domestic version of happiness in order to ratify his true identity.

One thinks of Abraham's sacrifice. Yet it is hard to ascribe to the God whose son says "Seek and ye shall find" authorship for what Wieland does. (For one thing, Wieland forgets that, according to Judeo-Christian tradition, his family members are also authored by God, and are not his gifts to dispose of; for another, he, unlike Jesus, forgets his humanity in his thrust to become one with the divine.) The issue of authorship is also confused by Wieland's devotion to classical as well as biblical authorities. He literally worships Cicero, and passionately defends his rhetorical sincerity; when he starts hearing mysterious voices, he becomes obsessed with the daemon of Socrates, who, according to Plato's *Apology of Socrates*, was a divine presence who kept Socrates from doing what he should not do, but who could never be construed as an author, as one who initiated action.[6] Theodore, however, seems to think his action authorized by this daemon as well as by God, by classical as well as by Judeo-Christian command. Indeed, toward the end he is willing to think that he committed murder under the influence of a demonic daemon, but one who acted under the authority of God. It is when this last authorial illusion is swept away that he becomes closest to the one who said, "Seek and ye shall find." He is transformed, our narrator tells us, into "the *man of sorrows*" (p. 230) [170], the man Jesus revealed himself to be on the cross as he lived out his humanity and fulfilled prophetic tradition, abandoned by his author, his father. But while the abandonment of Jesus is, according to Christian tradition, temporary, Wieland's transformation into the man of sorrows is, we are led to conclude, his last one. No author resurrects him for a happy ending.

The author who closes Theodore Wieland's life is his sister, Clara, who first provides him with the penknife with which he kills himself, and then, as our narrator, concludes his story with her pen. Though deeply, psychologically, bound to her father and, consequently, to her brother, she, by her own account, grew to maturity thinking herself a freer agent than they, and not so keen on considering herself under God's authorship. She notes that her religion (and that of her friend, Catherine Pleyel) "was the product of lively feelings, excited by reflection on our own happiness, and by the grandeur of external nature" (p. 22) [20]. Her belief, then, is in a deity

6. Plato, *The Apology of Socrates*, ed. A. M. Adams (Cambridge, 1979), pp. 43–44.

who authors happiness within and nature without. Even this vague attribution of authority becomes suspect when her placid existence is disturbed and when nature proves to be a not very clear or firm text upon which to ground one's faith.

This happens with the entrance of Carwin, the biloquist, whose presence evokes strong, disturbing passions in Clara, and whose projected voices undermine all the characters' trusted versions of reality. Not knowing that he is the author of these voices, Clara and her circle invite him to speculate on their origin: "if he did not persuade us," writes Clara, "that human beings are, sometimes, admitted to a sensible intercourse with the Author of nature, he, at least, won over our inclinations to the cause. He merely deduced, from his own reasonings, that such intercourse was probable; but confessed that, though he was acquainted with many instances somewhat similar to those which had been related by us, none of them were perfectly exempted from the suspicion of human agency" (p. 74) [59]. Carwin here quite cleverly clouds the issue of authority. First by suggesting that the Author of nature perhaps revealed himself in ways natural law could not account for, he calls into question a basic Enlightenment premise that in nature one could read all that this Author had written, and arrive thereby at a clear perception of his being and will. Then he works to undermine his own argument for special revelation by holding out "the suspicion of human agency." Thus through Carwin's agency, the question "Do you know the author?" becomes more problematic.

Of course Carwin has a vested interest in obscuring the origin of the voices, as they are his, not God's. Michael D. Bell has argued that, in *Wieland*, Brown substantiates the late eighteenth-century fear of novels by having God's voice, God's authority, usurped by Carwin, who, in his duplicitous ability to spin fiction upon fiction, creating and destroying reality, is a prototypical novelist, a prototypical modern author.[7] Although Bell's argument has weight, it must also be noted that if Carwin has pretensions to displacing God as author, his own authority is also questionable.

Judging by entries in both Johnson's and Webster's dictionaries, it was common during Brown's lifetime to distinguish an author from a mere compiler or translator. To be an author was to be a "beginner, former, first mover" (Webster). In "Memoirs of Carwin the Biloquist," Brown has Carwin discover and develop his talent by listening to the echoes his voice produces in nature. His biloquial, fictive accomplishments are thus a translation of a natural phenomenon. When he puts his abilities to work on the people he wishes to manipulate, test, or dazzle, it is often their own voices he compiles and

7. Bell, p. 148.

imitates. If, then, we claim Carwin as a prototypical author, we need to grant that human authorship is a matter of compiling, imitating, or translating sources—not of authentically beginning or generating something new.

Carwin, as human author, comes closest to usurping God's role when he twice projects his voice so that the injunction "Hold! hold!" enters Clara's ears as if it were some divine command (pp. 62, 85) [51, 67]. Yet a variety of circumstances make this usurpation ironic. Carwin does not claim that he was the first to put the words "Hold! hold!" into God's mouth; this was, he says, the "mode in which heaven is said by the poet, to interfere for the prevention of crimes" (p. 203) [152]. Brown informs us in a footnote that Carwin has in mind Shakespeare's lines "—Peeps through the blanket of the dark and cries / Hold! hold!" It is Lady Macbeth who utters this pious sentiment that a divine, authoritative voice might intervene thus to prevent murder, a sentiment the action of the play proceeds to prove false; as often in his tragedies, Shakespeare undermines his characters'— and his audience's—notion that God or the gods intervene for good or ill in human affairs. Brown, in *Wieland*, also undermines the notion of divine, authorial intervention, and at the same time, if Carwin be considered exemplary, makes human authorship problematic: his divine "command" is a quotation, one borrowed, ironically, from the lips of one who also urges murder; and his "command" in one instance is not heeded and in neither instance has its intended effect.

Carwin's authorial efforts frequently have an unintended effect. Frequently they turn on him, deconstructing the web of fiction he has spun for his own happiness. He does not even intend to begin spinning the rhetorical text which entangles the Wieland circle. He reactivates his "dangerous talent," which he had "a thousand times . . . vowed never again to employ," out of "force of habit and the influence of present convenience" (p. 200) [149]. Once he starts spinning, he works compulsively, as if some "daemon of mischief" were in control of him (p. 201) [150]; and once he abandons his web, it continues to spin on by itself, destructively out of control. Thus if Brown gives us in Carwin a portrait of an author, it is of one who has not even authority over his own fiction, not even over himself.

Carwin is only one of several authors in *Wieland*. Most of the major characters, from the pious elder Wieland to the impious Pleyel, weave texts of one sort or another. Pleyel, whose self-satisfied, rationalistic version of reality Carwin cannot resist destroying, sees Clara as a model of virtue and devotes himself to writing down her every feature and trait: "'I found [he tells her] no end and no bounds to my task. No display of a scene like this could be chargeable with redundancy or superfluity. Even the colour of a shoe, the knot of a ribband, or your attitude in plucking a rose, were of moment to be recorded. Even the arrangements of your breakfast-table and your toilet have been amply displayed'" (p. 122) [94]. Pleyel's intended audience for his composition is his intended bride, whom he hopes will model herself on his version of Clara. The ironies here are manifold. Pleyel's intended bride could hardly be expected to view the proffered model with pleasure or submit to its authority. Pleyel's attention to Clara's every habit evinces an attraction to which he is blind. He is blind as well to her attraction to him, and to other aspects of her personality which make her a more complex, more human person than Pleyel's exalted, supposedly exact literary version of her suggests. When he is led to believe that his version is false, the "real" Clara immediately becomes the object of his scorn. The ease with which Carwin's fictive involvement with Clara deconstructs Pleyel's model points to the fragility of such supposedly authoritative portraits of virtue eighteenth-century writers were fond of holding up for their readers' edification and encouragement. And that Pleyel dismisses his ideal version of Clara only to adopt the equally inauthentic, debased version of her points to the difficulty of arriving at authentic understanding.

The author in *Wieland* who mediates whatever authentic understanding the reader achieves is, of course, Clara. She wants to deliver a tale that will elucidate the past and "inculcate" a clear-cut moral (p. 5) [7]. Her narrative, however, as she herself notes, "May be invaded by inaccuracy and confusion." "What but ambiguities, abruptnesses, and dark transitions," she pleads, "can be expected from the historian who is, at the same time, the sufferer of these disasters?" (p. 147) [112]. The events of the tale she tells, even as they transform her supportive environment into a treacherous one, transform her, by her own accord, into that much-celebrated, much-lamented creature, the unreliable narrator. Ironically, the very unreliability of the narrative affords it a certain authenticity, as it enables the narrative to render formally ambiguities of personality and experience and to underscore the difficulty of ascribing definite authorship.

The course of events she experiences and unfolds erodes Clara's Enlightenment faith that one's senses, if healthy, afford a clear, reliable understanding of reality upon which one can then act with authority (see p. 35) [30] and leaves her sorting out the ambiguities of authorship right to the end of her tale. Even as she accuses Carwin of plotting her family's destruction, she entertains the possibility that her brother might in fact have received divine authority. In the last paragraph she still insists that Carwin, the "double-tongued deceiver," is the author of the horrid history she has reported, but also acknowledges its origin in her brother's moral and religious perspective and in her own flawed character. The cumulative effect of her deliberations is to make her one with the reader as she struggles to make meaning of the text.

As God is "he," so the reader is "she." In our traditional, patriarchal, authoritarian culture the author of our being and authoritative center and disseminator of meaning is masculine, while the passive recipient of the seed of meaning, the passive reader of the given script, is feminine.[8] *Wieland*, as it deconstructs models of authority, classical and Judeo-Christian, Calvinist and Enlightenment, divine and human, leaves the making of meaning in the hands of the reader, who will either be overwhelmed by the ambiguities or become actively involved in the process of interpretation. If a reader becomes involved, she perforce becomes something of an author, a constructor of meaning, herself, and, as such, a threat to the established "fathers" of meaning. While Brown's Clara is literary kin to such fictional English writer-heroines as Pamela and Clarissa, she is cultural kin to such real colonial American women interpreter/authors as Anne Hutchinson, who threatened the Puritan fathers by speaking as one with authority, Anne Bradstreet, whose heart kept rising without authority toward genuine poetry, and Mary Rowlandson, whose involvement in her own story and in the process of interpretation informs her captivity narrative with "ambiguities, abruptnesses, and dark transitions." Like Clara, Rowlandson loses her complacent, well-authorized version of reality as she drinks the "dregs of the cup, the wine of astonishment," that the events she narrates force on her.[9] Like Rowlandson, Clara provides herself and her reader with a happy ending and a firm moral, but one which does not satisfactorily settle the question raised in and through her story—the question of authorship.

That Brown leaves unsettled the question "Do you know the author?" testifies to his aesthetic and intellectual honesty, all the more so because of cultural pressures to fix on an author. "The author," asserts Michel Foucault, "is . . . the ideological figure by which one marks the manner in which we fear the proliferation of meaning."[1] The proliferation of meaning does, indeed, follow the disappearance from the world of *Wieland* of an ideological authoritative presence. Brown's novel may reflect his culture's anxieties over this disappearance: we may hear in Clara's assertion that her narrative shows "the immeasurable evils that flow from an erroneous or imperfect discipline" (p. 5) [7] longings for a life led in true and per-

---

8. See Naomi Schor, "Fiction as Interpretation / Interpretation as Fiction," in *The Reader in the Text*, ed. Susan R. Suleiman and Inge Crosman (Princeton, 1980), p. 182. Schor, along with others, links the "new," antiauthoritarian, "negative" hermeneutics to feminism.
9. Mary Rowlandson, "The Sovereignty and Goodness of God . . . ," in *So Dreadful a Judgment: Puritan Responses to King Phillip's War, 1676–77*, ed. Richard Slotkin and James K. Folson (Middletown, Conn., 1978), p. 395.
1. Michel Foucault, "What is an Author?" *Textual Strategies*, p. 159.

fect submission to an authoritative, central, and centering religious and ethical tradition. On the other hand, *Wieland* may challenge sentimental and potentially dangerous allegiance to authority: much of the woe that befalls its characters can be traced to their commitment to some false author or some nonexistent center of meaning. Whether the unauthorized, decentered world imaged forth in the novel affords the reader happiness is debatable. It certainly affords her work, as the proliferation of interpretations of *Wieland* attests.

EDWIN SILL FUSSELL

Wieland: A Literary and Historical Reading[†]

> I entreated him to tell me . . . what progress had been made in detecting or punishing the author of this unheard-of devastation. "The author!" said he; "Do you know the author?"
> "Alas!" I answered, "I am too well acquainted with him. The story of the grounds of my suspicions would be painful and too long."[1]

Dark Transitions

Born January 17, 1771, in the proprietary colony of Pennsylvania, a presumably loyal subject of the crown; five years old when the American Revolution broke out; twelve years old when the Treaty of Paris was signed; eighteen years old when the Constitution was ratified: if not in 1776 or 1783 then certainly in 1789, Charles Brockden Brown underwent a change of political allegiance and was henceforth a citizen of the United States of America. Although his opinion or preference was never consulted in these matters, it is likely he thought about them, thought about them to most purpose when he was writing and publishing *Wieland; or The Transformation. An American Tale* in 1798. At some point during those twenty-seven nationally turbulent yet spectacularly developmental years he strangely had become a different person, as his patria ceased to be one comparatively clear thing and became quite another thing, not clear at all. Indubitably, there had been a transformation. He took the word for his first subtitle and his theme.

† From *Early American Literature* 18.2 (fall 1983): 171–86. Copyright © 1983 by the University of North Carolina Department of English. Used by permission of The University of North Carolina Press. www.uncpress.unc.edu. Page numbers in square brackets refer to this Norton Critical Edition.
1. Charles Brockden Brown, *Wieland and Memoirs of Carwin the Biloquist*, ed. S. W. Reid, Sydney J. Krause, and Alexander Cowie, Bicentennial Edition (Kent, Ohio, 1977), p. 160 [121]; quotations will hereafter be cited parenthetically in the text.

His second subtitle was also his theme, for of course he was engaged in the creation of an American literature—his need to define and embody the typifying communal experience of that new polity, to write the nation into an existence more deeply and genuinely constitutional than the merely assertive and legalistic, to give it a character, a personality, and a soul. What if on reflection it appeared as if an earlier generation of writers, the polemical patriots, as one might call them, had in very fact or inflamed fancy written a predecessor patria out of existence and what if it were the very patria Brown had been born to? Then the creation of the new literature must somehow depend on the destruction of the old patria, it must admit and assess the extent and the cost of that disallegiance, only then to incorporate that destructive knowledge and, with it, to move on. The new American writer must by birth and profession inhabit the old world and the new. To be an American he must have been transformed. Born into the Society of Friends, it must also have been second nature for Brown to ask how it was that the most glorious nation God ever shone his face at happened to commence in widespread hatred, mass murder, willful blindness, possible psychosis.

His ambivalences were many and in themselves doubtful, including a bit of the hysterical and paranoid bewilderment of those polemical patriots, with their mixed motives of *ad fontes* and stand-pat; his own mixed attitudes toward that precedent generation, which had altered his nationality for him and landed him in his present plight (whether they were to be thanked or cursed, they could hardly be ignored); was it by their doing that he now found himself in the odd position of asking for, and answering the call for, an American literature, when indeed there was no such thing, nor easy prospect of it, the best available models (the English) being anathema? It was a most quixotic undertaking.[2] The revolution was itself so literary in a sort—not his sort—that literature encapsulated the other dilemmas and might justly have been seen as the direct or indirect cause of them. The national agony in letters, and thus in national identity, was owing to writers, and Brown's particular agony was both the fault of the tribe and a unique problem of his own. Writing was the imaginable source of woe, yet still more writing was the only exit from woe. And so he wrote a diatribe against writing but within that context he split the indictment in order to show an irresponsible writer wreaking havoc and wretchedness on a hapless populace while quite another kind of writer—his kind—was quietly restoring a semblance of reason and peace to such of those people as chanced to survive. *Wieland* is a furious contest between villainous confused Carwin

2. It may be further quixotism to attribute the shortcomings of early American literature to subservience to such imports as sentimentality, Gothicism, or Scotch Common Sense philosophy. Early American literature is its own sufficient cause.

and our doughty daughter of the American Revolution, Clara Wieland, Brown's narrator. Clara wins, but the price of her victory is exile. Having finished her novel, she removes to Europe, never more to confront the monstrosity of these States.

An author so circumstanced as Brown could hardly avoid thinking of himself as tantamount to the historical process yet by no means in control of it. Especially in her guise as Columbian Fair, sufferer and inditer of the new American literature, Clara Wieland in her fictive torments is Charles Brockden Brown in his, and the language she lavishes on her situation can easily be applied to the author of her being:

> My ideas are vivid, but my language is faint; now know I what it is to entertain incommunicable sentiments. . . . Yet I will persist to the end. My narrative may be invaded by inaccuracy and confusion; but if I live no longer, I will, at least, live to complete it. What but ambiguities, abruptnesses, and dark transitions, can be expected from the historian who is, at the same time, the sufferer of these disasters? (P. 147) [112]

Clara Wieland tells us that when her father died she was "a child of six years of age. The impressions that were then made upon me, can never be effaced" (p. 19) [18]. Clara's course runs nicely parallel with her creator's and they both run parallel with their broader constituency. Clara's lover, Pleyel, "urged, that to rely on the exaggerations of an advocate, or to make the picture of a single family a model from which to sketch the condition of a nation, was absurd" (p. 30) [27], but it is just this exaggeration and absurdity upon which *Wieland* is constructed and from which it derives its wild yet public power. As Clara says, "How will your wonder, and that of your companions, be excited by my story! Every sentiment will yield to your amazement. If my testimony were without corroborations, you would reject it as incredible. The experience of no human being can furnish a parallel" (p. 6) [7–8]. The experience of Charles Brockden Brown can, and the experience of the youthful United States can. They are all three the same.

Devils and Dupes

"Ventriloquism" is an old word but Brown had "biloquist" a decade before the *OED*.[3] "One who can speak with two different voices"

---

3. Ventriloquism further appears in the fragmentary "Memoirs of Carwin the Biloquist" (1803–05) (*Wieland*, pp. 252–53, 259). Also of special interest are Brown's variations in formula, as "my biloquial faculty" (p. 259), "my bivocal projects" (p. 276), "my bivocal faculty" (p. 284), and "some bivocal agency" (p. 308). Ventriloquism, but without the American literary theme, is in *Arthur Mervyn; or Memoirs of the Year 1793*, ed. Sydney J. Krause, S. W. Reid, Norman S. Grabo, and Marvin L. Williams, Jr., Bicentennial Edition (Kent, Ohio, 1980), p. 194, and in *Ormond; or the Secret Witness*, ed. Ernest

naturally suggests moral obliquity, all the more as it is only one person who speaks, and it may also suggest a literary situation in which
a newly nationalized writer must talk both English and American,
using the same lexicon and syntax for roughly opposite, and even
inimical, ends. The latter duality dates as far back as the revolutionary slang-whangers (Irving's and Paulding's term, in *Salmagundi*),
especially those poetical satirists who concocted anti-British invectives in the metrical modes of Dryden and Pope. "'Yes, said I, this, it
is plain, is no fiction of the fancy'" (p. 44) [37]. Indeed, it is not. It is
literary history. "I have not formed this design upon slight grounds,
and . . . I will not be finally diverted from it" (p. 49) [41]. Pleyel says
the first and Clara the second. *Wieland* is full of helpful hints. After
all, ventriloquism comes in two stages, the imitation of the voice
and the physical (geographical) displacement of it, both stages making apt analogies with literary creation in the art of the novel. They
are two stages of mimesis.[4] In addition to "ventriloquism" and "biloquism," these also are loaded words in *Wieland*: "narrative," "narrator," "tale," "plot," "writing," "audience," "war," and "author." (In the
present essay, hardly a quotation but contains one or more of them.)
Whether viva voce or by the pen, each of the following is an "author":
the grandfather Wieland, the Wieland father, the Wieland of the
title, Pleyel, Carwin, and, encompassing all these as well as herself,
Clara Wieland. Except for the first named, in Brown's novel each of
them is reversibly an audience. Finally, in *Wieland* the vox humana
and the scribal habit are perpetually being confounded. "'You saw
me in the very act of utterance'" (p. 214) [159], Carwin says to Clara,
with more pertinence to theme than to any ordinary view of things.

Talkers and listeners, writers and readers, not only reverse but
concatenate. "Such was my brother's narrative. It was heard by us
with different emotions. Pleyel did not scruple to regard the whole
as a deception of the senses" (p. 34) [29].[5] On this occasion Carwin
was first the narrator and Wieland was his audience but then
Wieland becomes the narrator and Clara and Pleyel are his audience. Pleyel is also a narrator in his own right, in addition to being
a secret audience (reader) of Clara's secret journal (about him).
Perhaps for better reasons than we have supposed, the writer of the
day is by the nature of his calling reclusive, or as the wife remarks

---

Marchand (New York, 1937), pp. 95–96. These two novels were published in 1799 and
1799–1800, respectively.
4. Ventriloquism as a mode of imitation is strenuously discussed in a chapter called "Animal Magnetism" by James Fenimore Cooper in *Gleanings in Europe; France*, ed. Robert
E. Spiller (New York, 1928).
5. "This scene of havock was produced by an illusion of the senses. Be it so: I care not from
what source these disasters have flowed; it suffices that they have swallowed up our
hopes and our existence" (p. 233) [172]. But no more than Scotch Common Sense philosophy is Lockean psychology the subject of *Wieland*. It is a condition of the subject.

in Crèvecoeur's *Letters From An American Farmer* (1782), "Let it be as great a secret as if it was some heinous crime. . . . I would not have thee, James, pass for what the world calleth a writer; no, not for a peck of gold, as the saying is."

Crèvecoeur's *Letters* and Brown's *Wieland* resemble each other in thematic progression from idyl through regrettable action to paradise lost—one view of the American Revolution, not necessarily Loyalist. "The storm that tore up our happiness, and changed into dreariness and desert the blooming scene of our existence, is lulled into grim repose," as Crèvecoeur has it. "How had my ancient security vanished!" (p. 60) [49] is perhaps the briefest of Brown's many perorations on the modalities of pathos, and a good question. According to Huckleberry Finn, "That's the peculiarity of a revolution—there ain't anybody intending to do anything when they start in."[6] (Who is "anybody" and who are "they"?) It is plain enough what kind of view *Wieland* takes of incontinent authors and their instigations— a dim one. Clara expostulates to and about Carwin: "And thou, O most fatal and potent of mankind, in what terms shall I describe thee? What words are adequate to the just delineation of thy character? How shall I detail the means which rendered the secrecy of thy purposes unfathomable? . . . Let me tear myself from contemplation of the evils of which it is but too certain that thou was the author" (pp. 49–50) [41]. This is not the view of the author commonly found in English literature nor is it yet that fearful conservative distaste for the imagination (Scotch Common Sense philosophy) supposedly universal in American colleges and universities—Brown attended none of them—which is considered responsible for the dearth of imagination in our early national literature. Brown's view of literature in this novel is far worse than that, more inclusive, more realistic, purely American, distinctly a product of postrevolutionary backlash, composed in about equal parts of horror and contempt. By unholy cross with such attributes of omniscience as "the author of creation" and "the author of our being," the concept of author is raised to almost infinite powers but with no commensurate responsibility or benevolence. He is, in a word, the devil.

Writers As the Bane of Our Existence

According to *Wieland*, writers do not merely reflect and record the disasters of social disruption; they are positively the prime cause of it. No matter that he peddles his wickedness by voice rather than by pen, Carwin clearly stands in for the American writer in times not so very long ago when he was busy producing his diabolical revolution.

---

6. "Tom Sawyer's Conspiracy," in *Hannibal, Huck & Tom*, ed. Walter Blair (Berkeley, Calif., 1969), p. 168.

Brown's attitude toward him is as threatened and disdainful as that of the farmer's wife in Crèvecoeur toward the whole lot of them. As Clara frames the charge with her customary vehemence: "His tale is a lie, and his nature devilish. As he deceived me, he likewise deceived my brother, and now do I behold the author of all our calamities!" (p. 216) [161]. The tone is biblical, prophetic, and angry; the word "author" recurs like clockwork.

Nor are disclaimers by way of intention of any use. The personages of Brown's fiction are strictly accountable for the results of their behavior, let their intentions be what they might, and this simplistic moral asperity is applied with special rigor to anyone engaged in the act of writing, or indeed of communicating by whatsoever means with other persons, the latter being held defenseless in a degree.[7] Carwin's extenuations are feeble bleats and are as quickly dismissed. "'Had I not rashly set in motion a machine, over whose progress I had no controul, and which experience had shewn me was infinite in power? . . . This is the extent of my offenses'" (pp. 215–16) [160]. It is too much to be borne, the extent is so boundless. Men are supposed to be responsible for what they set in motion, all the more so as the machine—speech, writing, publication in any form—is indirect in operation. "'Carwin may have plotted,'" Clara's uncle tries to interpose, insouciant and reasonable, "'but the execution was another's'" (p. 161) [122]. Clara, herself a writer, will never be brought to agree. What she knows is that the writer will be held responsible for whatever the audience takes it into its sweet head to do. She will herself so hold, in continuous outrage. It avails Carwin no whit to mumble, "'I meditated nothing'" (p. 201) [150]. He is simply damned by virtue of damage irretrievably done. Few will fully share Brown's judgments of these matters but none will deny their necessitarian clarity and sweep.

It is all Clara can do to write about it. "Yet have I not projected a task beyond my power to execute? If thus, on the very threshold of the scene, my knees faulter and I sink, how shall I support myself, when I rush into the midst of horrors such as no heart has hitherto conceived, nor tongue related? I sicken and recoil at the prospect" (p. 49) [41]. Nearly all such remarks in *Wieland* may be understood, really must be understood, in various applications extending from

7. It is not only in sentimental novels of seduction that the nubile young are led astray; our highly rationalistic Clara also succumbs. "The impulses of love are so subtile," she reasons, "and the influence of false reasoning, when enforced by eloquence and passion, so unbounded, that no human virtue is secure from degeneracy" (p. 241) [178]. Neither is all degeneracy sexual, any more than all eloquence and passion are spent in the pursuit of erotic happiness. Thus Carwin is "the grand deceiver" but he is also "the author of my peril . . . the author of this black conspiracy; the intelligence that governed in this storm. Some relief is afforded in the midst of suffering, when its author is discovered or imagined; and an object found on which we may pour out our indignation and our vengeance" (pp. 189–90) [142]. Author, author, author—it is all his fault, and always.

the most limited to the most inclusive. The horrors from which Clara sickens and recoils are the family murders, or they are Carwin, the cause of them, or they are the American writer in his capacity as inflammatory revolutionist, or they are the problems of American literature *tout ensemble*. (Such readers as wish may still have Carwin as a ventriloquistical clown.)

Yet we must be equally mindful that Clara never ascribes to her own writing any such baleful effect on a potential audience as she so stridently ascribes to Carwin. And in his "Advertisement," or preface, Brown strikes a perfectly normal tone of self-confidence and self-esteem, touched with becoming modesty. "The following Work is delivered to the world as the first of a series of performances, which the favorable reception of this will induce the Writer to publish. His purpose is neither selfish nor temporary. . . . The incidents related are extraordinary and rare." Notably Brown capitalized "Work" and "Writer," asserted the purity and permanence of his achievement, and for good measure sent a copy crosstown to Thomas Jefferson, the vice president, with a long letter, which Jefferson answered briefly but politely.[8] As for the ambiguity of reference, there is something curiously reciprocal, maybe perverse, in the American writer answering his own demand for an American literature with an American Work or Works, and it may be the perversity of the situation that partly accounts for the unceasing animosity against Carwin. It is, as almost always, Clara crying out: "'O wretch! once more hast thou come? Let it be to abjure thy malice; to counterwork this hellish stratagem. . . . Testify thy innocence or thy remorse: exert the powers which pertain to thee, whatever they be, to turn aside this ruin. Thou art the author of these horrors! . . . I adjure thee, by that God whose voice thou hast dared to counterfeit'" (p. 227) [169]. It is not in the long run Carwin, however, but Clara who turns aside this ruin, she who exorcises the horrors of him by writing about them—by writing about his writing, as one might say. It is plain enough that Clara exists for us, as does Brown, only as she writes. "A few words more and I lay aside the pen for ever. . . . I have justly calculated upon my remnant of strength. When I lay down the pen the taper of life will expire: my existence will terminate with my tale" (p. 221) [164]. In that termination American literature is born. These are the birth pangs.

Exchanges of Writers and Readers, with Some Culpability of the Audience

Two generations earlier the grandfather, an unmoved mover, began it all. He was a composer, and he was a writer—gifted with a famous

8. Both letters are in David Lee Clark, *Charles Brockden Brown: Pioneer Voice of America* (Durham, N.C., 1952), pp. 163–64.

writer's name—and even yet Clara can hardly confront one of his ballads without its suggesting "a new topic in the horrors of war" (p. 55) [46]. "War" is one of those black-magic words of *Wieland* but it is not the French and Indian War that is in question but a worse one, closer to home.[9] The father emigrates to the American plantations and devotes his religious fanaticism to converting the Indians through Scripture, i.e., the written word: "[T]o disseminate the truths of the gospel among the unbelieving nations" (p. 10) [11], which sounds innocuous until we remember how gullible some people are and wonder how it will be when Thomas Paine is scattering his atheistical firebrands among our amber fields of grain. As father Wieland is also a writer, he constitutes one more splendid reason for disbelief in the whole train of unreliable narrators, especially as the American writer might be conceived—it must have been tempting in 1798— as having imported dangerous doctrine from Europe only in his mad success to export it back again. *Wieland* is a tissue of dubieties concerning causation: "There was somewhat in his manner that indicated an imperfect tale. My uncle was inclined to believe that half the truth had been suppressed" (p. 18) [17]. This is the father Wieland. He has written an autobiography that sounds like an early American masterpiece, idealized; in Clara's language, "the narrative was by no means recommended by its eloquence; but neither did all its value flow from my relationship to the author. Its stile had an unaffected and picturesque simplicity. The great variety and circumstantial display of the incidents, together with their intrinsic importance, as descriptive of human manners and passions, made it the most useful book in my collection" (p. 83) [66].

That author's son, titular hero of *Wieland*, brother to Clara, is a chip off the old block, the new or proto-American through and through, madness multiplied. "His brain seemed to swell beyond its continent. . . . His words and motions were without meaning. . . . I beheld the extinction of a mind the most luminous and penetrating that ever dignified the human form. . . . I had not time to reflect in what way my own safety would be affected by this revolution, or what I had to dread from the wild conceptions of a mad-man. . . . Confused clamours . . ." (pp. 153–54) [116–17]. The diction is suggestive: "continent" and "without meaning" and "extinction" and "revolu-

9. "These events took place between the conclusion of the French and the beginning of the revolutionary war" ("Advertisement"). The statement is plausible only if taken to mean that one war leads to another, with private disasters in between. In the text proper, there are echoes of a war actually going on, and the only question is, which one? "The Indians were repulsed on the one side, and Canada was conquered on the other" (p. 26) [23] is diversionary or maladroit, for it is hard to know how "furnishing causes of patriotic exultation" to the British Empire fits "An American Tale." In the same passage, Brown refers to "revolutions and battles." There were no revolutions in the French war but in 1798 the American Revolution was still active—violently so—in Brown's imagination.

tion." Out of these clamors the younger Wieland writes literally a criminal confession. Upon reading it, Clara (now audience, now speaker) tells us: "The images impressed upon my mind by this fatal paper were somewhat effaced by my malady. They were obscure and disjointed like the parts of a dream. I was desirous of freeing my imagination from this chaos" (p. 175) [131]. This document, which she does and does not wish to read, she calls a "tale" and a "narrative" (pp. 175, 176) [132]. Even its author admits that it will hardly be believed. This is the same he who at the beginning of *Wieland* was so "diligent in settling and restoring the purity of the text" (p. 24) [22], the text being Cicero. Of him, Clara's uncle says to her, she for a while supposing him to mean Carwin, "'Thou art anxious to know the destroyer of thy family, his actions, and his motives. Shall I call him to thy presence, and permit him to confess before thee? Shall I make him the narrator of his own tale?'" (p. 162) [123]. Hearing Carwin's voice, and acting on it, Wieland was audience; now he is author to the shattered Clara, who doubles as audience and writer both.

The parade of narrators and auditors continues unabated. Pleyel, the lover she will lose and regain, literally takes notes on Clara his inamorata, even she so novelistically inclined, she so nationally representative: "'I was desirous that others should profit by an example so rare. I therefore noted down, in writing, every particular of your conduct. . . . Here there was no other task incumbent on me but to copy; there was no need to exaggerate or overlook, in order to produce a more unexceptionable pattern. . . . I found no end and no bounds to my task. No display of a scene like this could be chargeable with redundancy or superfluity'" (p. 122) [94]. Perhaps one reason he notes her down *in writing* is that she so often appears to partake not only of the American literary enterprise but of the republic itself. In that last passage she is referred to as a "scene." "'Here, said I, is a being, after whom sages may model their transcendent intelligence, and painters, their ideal beauty. Here is exemplified, that union between intellect and form, which has hitherto existed only in the conceptions of the poet'" (p. 121) [94]. Comparable remarks were frequently made about the Constitution, with its new institutions; like them, Clara was worth writing down; Pleyel sounds like an infatuated version of *The Federalist Papers*. "'I have marked the transitions of your discourse, the felicities of your expression, your refined argumentation, and glowing imagery; and been forced to acknowledge, that all delights were meagre and contemptible, compared with the audience and sight of you.'" Listening and looking are again conflated. "'I have contemplated your principles, and been astonished at the solidity of their foundation, and the perfection of their structure'" (pp. 121–22) [94], and now she is just like a poem of some length. All this was written in the administration of John Adams.

Clara points out that Pleyel's narrative is in turn dependent on an antecedent telling, which in turn depends on the rather mindless susceptibilities of a previous audience. "Here Pleyel paused in his narrative, and fixed his eyes upon me. Situated as I was, my horror and astonishment at this tale gave way to compassion for the anguish which the countenance of my friend betrayed. I reflected on his force of understanding. . . . Carwin had constructed his plot in a manner suited to the characters of those whom he had selected for his victims" (p. 133) [103]. Pleyel persists in being an arrant gull: "'I can find no apology for this tale. Yet I am irresistibly impelled to relate it. . . . Why then should I persist! yet persist I must'" (p. 134) [103]. He must, they all must, because of Charles Brockden Brown's unrelenting purposes. His is that kind of a world.

Clara not only composes the entire novel in a series of letters (chapters) lacking salutation or signature, but in it she tells of composing still another document, the secret tale of her abortive passion for Pleyel. "I was tempted to relinquish my design"—of returning to her house—"when it occurred to me that I had left among my papers a journal of transactions in short-hand. I was employed in this manuscript on that night when Pleyel's incautious curiosity tempted him to look over my shoulder. . . . I had regulated the disposition of all my property. This manuscript, however, which contained the most secret transactions of my life, I was desirous of destroying" (pp. 190–91) [143]. Not only does Pleyel look over her shoulder, but Carwin takes the key to her chamber, lets himself in, and reads the whole thing. Like Pleyel, he is a great admirer of the native American character, or muse, so bountifully burgeoning in young Clara: "'Your character exhibited a specimen of human powers that was wholly new to me. . . . I perused this volume with eagerness. The intellect which it unveiled, was brighter than my limited and feeble organs could bear. . . . You know what you have written. You know that in this volume the key to your inmost soul was contained. If I had been a profound and malignant imposter, what plenteous materials were thus furnished me of stratagems and plots!'" (pp. 205–06) [153]. Who but Charles Brockden Brown could conceive an imposter who was "profound"? Like nearly every other character in the novel, Carwin is an audience as well as an author, but he is a very immoral audience, specifically a peeping Tom and an eavesdropper. He is also a plagiarist, once removed: "'I exerted all my powers to imitate your voice, your general sentiments, and your language. Being master, by means of your journal, of your personal history and most secret thoughts, my efforts were the more successful'" (p. 210) [156]. If in the early years of the republic, writing was a most dangerous business, and reprehensible as well, reading was about as bad. They went together and were together suspect. The story of suspicions was painful and long.

Carwin as American Revolutionary
and Postrevolutionary Writer

As given to us in Clara's narration, Carwin is first and foremost a voice, a sweet talker, and mighty irresistible. She reports his verbal advent in language suggesting the advent of the new American literature as well: "The words uttered by the person without, affected me as somewhat singular, but what chiefly rendered them remarkable, was the tone that accompanied them. It was wholly new." It will never be easy to say in an old language (English) what the new tone is, but Clara patriotically plows ahead: "I cannot pretend to communicate the impression that was made upon me by these accents, or to depict the degree in which force and sweetness were blended in them. They were articulated with a distinctness that was unexampled in my experience." If Clara's description owes something—not much— to the traditions of sensibility, we will value its transcendence the more, here put to new uses, public, literary, historical. Clara goes on. "The voice was not only mellifluent and clear, but the emphasis was so just, and the modulation so impassioned, that it seemed as if an heart of stone could not fail of being moved by it. It imparted to me an emotion altogether involuntary and incontroulable. When he uttered the words 'for charity's sweet sake,' I dropped the cloth that I held in my hand, my heart overflowed with sympathy, and my eyes with unbidden tears" (pp. 51–52) [43]. Clara's reaction is vastly in excess of its cause, and once more it would seem that the Work or Works of literature are likely to be dangerous, lies and deception, wonderfully sweet, reducing the audience to abject debaucheries of pleasing emotion, with loss of reason, loss of will.

At first, Carwin seems the nearly ideal audience for "the tale" of "the inexplicable events that had lately happened" (p. 73) [59], i.e., the death of the elder Wieland, but soon we find roles reversed, and the others are captive audience to his "disquisition," to his "narratives" ("all the effects of a dramatic exhibition"), and in general to "the exquisite art of this rhetorician." Yet even Clara in her admiration observes that "his narratives, however complex or marvellous, contained no instance sufficiently parallel to those that had befallen ourselves, and in which the solution was applicable to our own case" (pp. 74–75) [59–60], as was so regularly complained of English fiction of the times by American literary patriots, especially such as were out of patience with republican women who swooned over dukes. Brown's fable manages to glance at nearly all the literary hopes and fears of that brusque but unconfident epoch. If *Wieland* were an allegory, it would be nonsense for Carwin to represent the American writer, in his worst badness, while at the same time bringing to mind the preposterous irrelevance of English literature. But in Brown's loose fable he can suggest all manner of thing, perhaps most how transitional the literary situation was, with the muse forever migrating to these shores, or about to, momentarily delayed, weary of wing, inevitable, and even so late as Whitman's "Song of the Exposition" (1871). Let Carwin be vague, multiple, forward looking. As Pleyel says to Clara: "'It would be vain to call upon Carwin for an avowal of his deeds. It was better to know nothing, than to be deceived by an artful tale'" (p. 127) [98]. Pleyel is promptly deceived by an artful tale. As a general rule, Carwin's victims are remarkably complicit in their own duping, and even Providence— novelistic Providence—is made to conspire: "Carwin's plot owed its success to a coincidence of events scarcely credible. The balance was swayed from its equipoise by a hair" (p. 139) [106].

Through the melodramatic rhetoric, Carwin enacts what seems to be Brown's conception of the revolutionary and even the postrevolutionary American writer, he who wrought great evil—but maybe in the fullness of time he will wreak some good—without quite willing it, by possessing powers whose extent neither he nor his audience might have understood in advance. Perhaps it was part of Brown's purpose to persuade a later audience, with these analogues of military and political events only a little while back, of the awesomeness of literary power in a society where the written word was so boundlessly on the march; perhaps he meant also to suggest a heightened moral responsibility on the part of himself and his fellows, whence benefit might yet evolve from sin, as in *Paradise Lost*. Culpable Carwin is a veritable model of literary laceration, a classic case against the dire effects of literature out of control, an exemplary enactment of late eighteenth-century American political and literary hysteria, culminating in the American Revolution, now slowly receding in the popular mind. "'I will fly. I am become a fiend, the sight of whom destroys. Yet tell me my offense! You have linked curses with my name; you ascribe to me a malice monstrous and infernal. I look around; all is loneliness and desert! . . . My fear whispers that some deed of horror has been perpetrated; that I am the undesigning cause. . . . My actions have possibly effected more than I designed. . . . I come to repair the evil of which my rashness was the cause, and to prevent more evil. I come to confess my errors'" (pp. 195–96) [146]. To whom Clara cries: "Wretch!" Continuing on, ever loquacious, righteously wronged, at the top of her bent: "Who was it that blasted the intellects of Wieland? Who was it that urged him to fury, and guided him to murder? Who, but thou and the devil, with whom thou art confederated?" (p. 196) [146]. She continues to vilify "the author of these dismal outrages" and he poorly replies: "'Wretch as I am, am I unworthy to repair the evils that I have committed? . . . I have deceived you: I have sported with your terrors: I have plotted to destroy your reputation. I come now to remove your errors; to set you beyond the reach of similar fears; to rebuild your fame as far as I am able.'" His best line is: "'All I ask is a patient audience'" (p. 197) [147].

Whether or not Clara is in some of her permutations the young nation herself, it is surely that young nation, more or less represented by the Wieland family and what happens to them, that is most damaged by Carwin's acts of imitation. As in Crèvecoeur, it is not so much an individual who is outraged and devastated as it is an entire family, with suggestions of the countryside around. Carwin's is the true voice of the American bard imposing his own exile for monstrous unspeakable crimes against the people, and it sounds as if he is talking about the American Revolution: "'I had acted with a frenzy that surpassed belief. I had warred against my peace and my fame: I had banished myself from the fellowship of vigorous and pure minds: I was self-expelled from a scene which the munificence of nature had adorned with unrivalled beauties, and from haunts in which all the muses and humanities had taken refuge'" (p. 211) [157]. He even seems to blend with the audience of the bard and is not only he who incites to violence but those incited. It is impossible to imagine Brown in 1798 or any other time an unreconstructed Loyalist, but it is easy to imagine him a good enough Quaker to wonder if that transformation from colonial to national condition might have been accomplished with less violence.

Writing and Action and Writing

For history, the inclusive point is that writing is both the cause and the effect of action; in this instance, the American Revolution was at least partly caused by writers, then that revolution, now won, necessitates an American literature to justify it and to ensure its fruits to posterity. There is plainly in *Wieland* just such a cause-effect-cause triad where Charles Brockden Brown in the process of helping create a national literature records in analogue how the opportunity and obligation of doing so arose from a war of rebellion induced by his literary precursors. It is rather a matter for definition, as there can hardly be an American literature, in the full sense of the term, until there is a United States of America. Historians of ideas notwithstanding, colonial American history is colonial American history.

With respect to the polemics of political uprisings, *Wieland* surely takes cognizance of the well-known fact that literary produce as a cause of war increases with the increase in the reading public— at least the violence is sooner likely to come to a boil. But as the audience is also more widely spread, so the more various and complex is likely to be the interplay between expression and physical

action and the more various and complex the timing of these interactions, so that our awareness of the relations of history and literature (neither of them a simple cause of the other, nor a simple effect
of some third cause, seldom specified, but locked in their reciproci-
ties) must also be correspondingly more various and complex. In
the new, comparatively democratic society, more and more persons
were not only readers but writers, and literature was no longer the
preserve or responsibility of a ruling class; then if guilt should come
into question, as it certainly does in *Wieland* the guilt can be gen-
erously shared, which is maybe a comfort. With public rhetoric
abounding, it must have been evident that the line between speaking and writing was increasingly blurred, the line between the political speech delivered orally to a small crowd and that same speech set
in print and delivered up at large. Would that wider readership be
more or less inflamed? Who could know ahead of time? Historians
might be able to tell us later. Who would then be responsible? Everybody, if they wanted to live.

Fortunate as we are to have so revealing a document as *Wieland*, it
seems the rankest folly to read it mainly as a Gothic novel or other
divertissement in the annals of literary types. Spontaneous combustion, religious mania in a homicidal degree, ventriloquism—the
topics are not especially American, they are not even topics of adult
interest. It seems a terrible confession of weakness in historical reasoning to define the field of American literature in political terms,
precisely in terms of the break with the parent country, followed
by the desire to create an independent culture, primarily in literature,
the most accessible of the arts for a new nation, and then go looking
for the evidence in the junkyards of universal infantilism, psychologically or existentially construed. *Wieland* is more important to us
than that. It is conceivably the major literary landmark between the
Declaration of Independence and the appearance of *The Pioneers* by
James Fenimore Cooper in 1823, and the reasons for its importance
must be of the same order as the claim. What is hardest to grasp, yet
at the heart of the rest, is that in *Wieland* Charles Brockden Brown
was writing about writing, including his own, i.e., about that American literature not yet in existence but coming into existence as he
confronted and incorporated the stiffest resistance imaginable, his
own impossibility. It sounds more Alexandrine than it is, human
achievements, both individual and collective, so conspicuously effec-
tuating themselves in present actions that look to the future at the
same time as they ride the waves of the past, and all in one unitary
mode.

SHIRLEY SAMUELS

[Patriarchal Violence, Federalist Panic, and *Wieland*]†

* * *

Charles Brockden Brown's *Wieland; or The Transformation*, published the year the Alien and Sedition Acts[1] were passed, might be read as their novelistic response, but also counterpart. Like the qualities of America that attract the "alien," the very charm of the Wieland's idyllic community has attracted Carwin, the alien called from afar. In each case, the attractiveness of order invites the intrusion of disorder. However, the novel does not unilaterally assign guilt to Carwin as the alien intruder, and indeed often questions whether we should instead blame, as the narrator, Clara, sometimes believes we should, the interior of the home itself, or, more particularly, "the immeasurable evils that flow from an erroneous or imperfect discipline" (5) [7]. *Wieland* presents alternative versions of educational and religious beliefs but frames the presentation with this announcement of a moral to be derived from the effects of such an "imperfect discipline": these very "freedoms" of thought and belief may have caused the destruction of the Wieland family. Despite its gothic sensationalism, the novel, like Weems's pamphlet,[2] often appears more significant as an educational tract, one which contains lessons about the contemporary disputes over religious infidelity, a strictly circumscribed education, the chastity of women, and the status of institutions, preeminently the institution of the family.

After the death of their parents, Clara and Wieland have a premature and, in Federalist[3] terms, unnatural independence. They are "subjected to no unreasonable restraints," indeed are virtually free from any external restraints at all, and are "saved from the corruption and tyranny of colleges and boarding schools," becoming "superintendants of [their own] education" (20, 21) [19]. Clara's terms for her upbringing could have been taken from colonial pamphlets

† From *Early American Literature* 25.1 (1990): 46–66. Copyright © 1990 by the University of North Carolina Department of English. Used by permission of The University of North Carolina Press. www.uncpress.unc.edu. Page numbers in square brackets refer to this Norton Critical Edition.
1. Four bills signed into law by President John Adams in 1798, under threat of war with France. They were designed to stem criticism of the Adams administration and resulted in the prosecution and conviction of some opposition publishers [Editor's note].
2. Mason Weems, "God's Revenge against Adultery" (1815), a pamphlet that warns against the dangers of religious and sexual infidelity [Editor's note].
3. The party of President John Adams. The opposition party, the Democratic-Republicans, was led by Vice President Thomas Jefferson [Editor's note].

about the benefits of independence from Britain.[4] The dangers of infidelity, however, would have been apparent to anxious contemporaries: "Our education had been modelled by no religious standard. We were left to the guidance of our own understanding and the casual impressions which society might make upon us. . . . We sought not a basis for our faith" (22) [20]. In other words, the Wieland children are educated in the style of the Enlightenment, a style derived in the eighteenth century from the formulations of Locke and Rousseau. One function of the novel might be to question how successfully this style functions on American soil.

Clara's utopian upbringing has created a hazardous situation both because it has attracted Carwin and because it has not been supplemented by the kind of institutions that were increasingly perceived as necessary in the young republic. Indeed, Clara judges that she has had a "perverse and vicious education," especially because she has not been "qualified by education or experience to encounter perils" (80, 150) [63, 115]. In *The Discovery of the Asylum*, David Rothman asserts that the late eighteenth-century American fear of contamination by France was in the process of becoming a fear of contamination by anything in the "world"; to counter this fear, the family had to be protected and protective and to "inoculate" the child against society. As we have seen, the rise of institutions of social control in this period, like the orphan asylum and even the school, is modeled on and supported by such an insular notion of the family. The institution compensated for the failure of the family, supplemented and even instructed the family, from which it was presumed to have derived (85, 121, 234, 152–53). One of *Wieland*'s functions as a tutelary tract might be to prepare the way for the notion that institutions are a necessary supplement to the family. Without the formal institutions of education, religion, "benevolent societies," orphanages, or prisons, the new republic would be susceptible to the chaos unleashed within the Wieland family.[5]

In *Wieland*, that chaos is blamed on Carwin, whose intrusion has excited sexual tensions in Clara and Pleyel and an insane and murderous religious enthusiasm in Wieland. Published while the fear of contagion by the alien was at its height, the novel foments and yet tries to explain away the threat by both blaming Carwin for introducing sexuality, disorder, and violence into the Wieland family, and explaining that introduction as nothing more than an enhance-

---

4. Cf. Fliegelman's discussion of the relation of novels and political programs in the eighteenth century.
5. While Tompkins finds a "plea for the restoration of civic authority" in *Wieland* (61), I do not find the novel quite so programmatic; still, I concur with her emphasis on political and historical context.

ment of sexual and familial tensions already present.[6] Carwin is an intruder, an alien called "from afar" by what he perceives as the almost "divine" qualities of Clara and her brother. But he also embodies an instability already present within the Wieland family. Introduced as an external threat, the alien, Carwin, instead stands (in) for an internal one, the infidelity of religious and institutional beliefs that the novel at first appeared to celebrate.[7] If the family had been properly inoculated against him, he could have had no effect on them.

The extent to which the family can be seen as a haven from the outside world is made problematic on the historical front as well. Although *Wieland*'s action takes place "between the conclusion of the French and the beginning of the revolutionary war," Clara finds that "revolutions and battles, however calamitous to those who occupied the scene, contributed in some sort to our happiness, by agitating our minds with curiosity, and furnishing causes of patriotic exultation. Four children . . . exercised my brother's tenderness" (3, 26) [4–5, 23]. The unabashed segue between the "scene" of war and the family scene does not disturb Clara and would pass by the reader were it not that what seems continuous to her appears discontinuous to us. While Clara apparently intends that the violence outside should emphasize the harmony within the family, the introduction of the children is instead the introduction of violence: they are to be the object not of Wieland's "tenderness," but of violence "calamitous to those who occupied the scene." Both the absent battles and the present children mysteriously "contributed in some sort to our happiness," while both agitate minds with curiosity about violence. If Clara conflates the revolutions of nations and the transformations of families, this conflation of national and familial violence further confirms the extent to which the novel registers

6. There has been much critical attention to the sexual attraction Clara feels for Carwin and for her brother. Davis, for example, claims that "Carwin had saved Clara from an incestuous relation with her brother" (*Homicide*, 90). What has not been focused on is the parallel between that sexual tension and the representations of deism and revolution in sexual terms during this period. Instead, many critics read the novel as psychological or moral commentary. Cowie, for example, asserts that "at times *Wieland* seems more like an exposure of the author's unconscious than a reasoned attempt to communicate with the reader logically" (327). For other standard critical treatments of the novel, see Bell, Gilmore, or Ziff. For a suggestive reading of incest in other novels of the period, see Dalke.

7. Suggesting the unlocatable threat of the Bavarian Illuminati (with which secret organization he is often linked, especially because of his apprenticeship under Ludloe in *Carwin the Biloquist*), it is Carwin's mysterious appropriation of voices, voices that are "inexplicably and unwarrantedly assumed," and, even more importantly, his assumption of the desires that go along with those voices, that makes Clara fear him most. Pleyel has already accused Clara of being in love with Carwin when he hears the conversation between them that Carwin projects. Wieland has already prepared himself to hear the voices that he hears. For the history of the threat of the Illuminati in America, see Stauffer.

contemporary national concerns in its depiction of familial turmoil. The novel emphasizes the violence within the family while ascribing that violence to the intrusion of a violent force, but that very force seems immanent rather than intrusive, and the efforts to name it as "alien" only emphasize its immanence.

The clearest instances of the intrusion of the alien into the family may be the explicit "otherworldly" experiences of the novel, the spontaneous combustion of the elder Wieland and the "inspiration" of the younger. While the younger Wieland begins by seeking a "ground of his belief" in the "history of religious opinions," Clara finds in the Calvinist "ground" her brother stands on nothing but "props" that can be only a temporary support: "Moral necessity, and calvinistic inspiration, were the props on which my brother thought proper to repose" (23, 25) [21, 23]. Unfortunately for Wieland, the shakiness of his "ground" points to an "obvious resemblance between him and my father" (23) [21]. In other words, we are warned that his attempt to reason toward faith by combining "calvinistic inspiration" with the "history of religious opinion" will produce infidelity and madness. The conflation of Wieland's attempt to reason toward faith (apparently an oblique reference to Paine) and the horrific effects of his sudden access to God (reminiscent of some of the excesses of the Great Awakening) appears as a reference to the conflict earlier described between Timothy Dwight, the grandson of that arch-Calvinist Jonathan Edwards, and Thomas Paine, the archdeist. Paralleling the twin downfalls of the Weems pamphlet, the novel shows the pitfalls of either position. Neither the inspired Wieland nor the rationalist Pleyel represents a form of belief that can effectively function against the hazards of the early Republic. By demonstrating the weakness of either extreme, the novel enacts a desire for the norm. And the champion or hero of this enactment may finally be not the reasonable Pleyel, or even Clara, but Carwin. His voice forces a questioning of perceived realities and underscores the abnormalities already present within the Wieland family. Carwin can be seen as an "alien" who introduces himself surreptitiously into households and exposes abnormalities as part of a regularizing or normalizing strategy.

Before examining further the effects of Carwin's presence in *Wieland*, I want to examine the context of this presence by returning to the terms of the pairing established in Weems's pamphlet, where deism and revivalism were both excesses that led to disaster. Specifically, I want to trace the religious, legal, and sexual implications of Wieland's destruction of his family by looking at the crime both in the novel and in two possible sources for the novel. The novel's presentation of Wieland's brutal murders brings together, in the arena of the family, anxieties about law and religion. Set in a period when the nation was haunted alike by fears of the removal of an institutionalized God perceived in deism and of the direct access to Him promised in the revivalism of the Great Awakening, the novel also works effectively to collapse the difference between these categories and to relocate the threat as an intrusive violation into the family.

When Clara reads Wieland's confession, which she transcribes as evidence within her own first-person narrative, she discovers his belief that in murdering his family he has obeyed a personal call to faith. Like the court he appears in, Wieland once wanted to "settle the relation between motive and actions, the criterion of merit, and the kinds and properties of evidence" (23) [21]. Now he professes to be thankful for the chance "to testify my submission to thy will" (165) [124]. Incongruously presenting a personal narrative of conversion in the world of the court, Wieland represents himself and his motives for the murder of his family in the terms of the conversion narrative that was required for admittance into the Puritan congregation.[8] But his story of conversion, instead of gaining him admittance into the "congregation," causes him to be cast out, and in a way that emphasizes the conflict between "legal" and "religious" explanations that the novel examines.

Wieland's appeal to a transcendent deity was soon to become, in the eyes of the law, an insanity defense. Even in the 1790s, as the novel presents the case, Wieland's perceived madness saves him from the gallows, although not from institutionalization. David Brion Davis has discussed the change in the early republic from the Calvinist concentration on sin or sinful thought as worthy of punishment to the focus on actual crime and its origin in "parental neglect and faulty emotional growth [rather than] inherent depravity or a conscious choice of evil." According to this view, the early republic witnessed a basic shift in notions of responsibility and communal legitimations and also a shift in notions of character. The structure of social institutions, modeled on the family, becomes the locus of the moral and emotional "nurture" and formation of the subject: "there was a growing conviction that crime was a disease . . . to be prevented by improved education and social reform" (*Homicide* 9, 22). Adapting to this shift to the jurisdiction of the family, Timothy Dwight preached that "murder in the proper sense is begun in . . . the early and unrestrained indulgence of human passions. This indulgence,

---

8. The language of Wieland's account of his journey to God also incongruously echoes several passages in Jonathan Edwards's "Personal Narrative." In this conversion narrative, Edwards reports that as he "walked abroad alone . . . for contemplation . . . God's excellency appeared in every thing" (60). Wieland too reports walking outside alone: "My mind was contemplative. . . . The author of my being was likewise the dispenser of every gift with which that being was embellished" (166) [125].

therefore, Parents, and all other Guardians of children, are bound faithfully to restrain" (*Theology* 3:356). The conversion narrative has given way to the legal confession, innate character to education and growth, and penitence to the penitentiary. In one respect this transformation was itself dramatically ratified in the separation of church and state represented by the ratification of the Constitution and the dispersal of the authority of the church into the related institutions of education, law, and the family. The novel plays out the anxieties that this change in jurisdiction has produced.

More particularly, the novel dramatizes the change from judging Wieland's crime according to his faith (Wieland castigates his judges for their failure to recognize divine rather than legal jurisdiction: "Impious and rash! thus to usurp the prerogatives of your Maker!") to judging it according to a legal conception of sanity. Still the novel betrays a rather uncertain jurisdiction over the topic of madness. In part this is due to the uncertainty of causal relations in a novel that foregrounds the problem of cause and effect.[9] The notion that madness is both motive and cause for Wieland's crime poses rather than solves the problem of motive, complicating what it means to have motives. Clara's uncle reassures her that "there could be no doubt as to the cause of these excesses. They originated in sudden madness, but that madness continues, and he is condemned to perpetual imprisonment" (177) [133]. Rather than solving the crux of Wieland's motives, the weak causal links of this statement beg the question. What is the connection between the continuation of Wieland's madness ("but") and his imprisonment ("and")? If the "cause" or origin of Wieland's "excesses" is "madness," does his imprisonment represent an attempt to cure him or to contain the effects of his delusions? The notion that character can change is exhibited most problematically here: if Wieland's madness no longer continued, would he be freed?

An excess of belief has led to Wieland's crimes, but what may appear as a simple conflict between religious and legal explanations is further complicated by references to the family. Curiously, in addition to his marked submission to a divine vision, Wieland appeals to the community, and he makes that appeal in terms that suggest he recognizes yet another version of the constituted self. Turning to the audience at his trial, he asks, "Who is there present a stranger to the character of Wieland? Who knows him not as an husband—as a father—as a friend?" (164) [123]. His appeal to the community's "knowledge" of him in familial terms is at once an escape from the confines of legal and religious definitions of the citizen or congregant

---

9. For interesting discussions of the frailty of cause and effect relations in the novel see Scheick and also Seltzer. For a history of nineteenth-century American treatments of insanity, see Caplan.

and a move to the heart of those definitions. If Wieland is "known" as a member of his family, he is placed safely within both legal and religious discourses. His actions in murdering his family have been as much a confirmation of his belief in the value of family as a denial.

Wieland contains a family destroyed from within, though agency is ascribed to outside forces. A similar displacement occurs in one of the presumed sources for *Wieland*. James Yates was sitting in front of his fire in 1781 reading the Bible when he suddenly heard a voice commanding him to destroy his idols. He threw his Bible into the fire; then, upon further admonition from the voice, he killed his wife and four children. His next thought was to set the house on fire so that it would appear that the Indians had done the deed ("I shall be called a murderer for destroying my idols—for obeying the mandate of my father—no, I will put all the dead in the house together, run to my sister's and say the Indians have done it!"),[1] but he was thoroughly convinced that his actions were justified since they had been dictated by a divine voice and decided that it was better to have the deed known as a confirmation of his devoutness. Axelrod has argued that by taking "'communion' with the wilderness" Yates internalizes the threat of the Indians and acts as they would presumably have acted (59).[2] But if Yates, as a sort of afterthought, displaces his violence onto the Indians, his justifications for his actions, and indeed the acts themselves, explicitly invoke a rather different perspective. Yates's justifications, and his presentation of himself as wavering between a family of "idols" and "divine" injunctions to destroy them (reminiscent of Puritan iconoclasm), suggest that he has not so much incorporated the threat of the Indians as violently externalized the closely linked internal problems of belief and the family.

Another analogue for *Wieland* may be the *Narrative for William Beadle* (reprinted several times in the 1790s), which gives an account of a murder-suicide that took place in the last year of the American Revolution. This analogue has not been heretofore noted and is worth looking at in some detail for the clues it may provide about *Wieland*. Beadle was a retailer ruined because of the failure of

---

1. *New York Weekly Magazine*, July 1796, vol. 2, no. 55, p. 20. Blaming the Indians has a long history in the United States. In a perhaps similar way, William Bradford blamed internal problems in the Plymouth colony on the external threat of the Indians, who usefully alleviated the psychological threats of faith by posing a physical one. As long as he could blame the Indians for tensions within the colony, he could ignore the divisive internal battles over commerce, settlement, and religion. See also Slotkin: "The crowning irony of the witchcraft delusion is that the Puritans' hysterical fear of the Indian devils led them to behave precisely like the Indians" (142).
2. This source was recognized as early as 1801 by an anonymous reviewer in the *American Review and Literary Journal*. Axelrod comments further that "the blackest irony of James Yates's actions is that in performing what he sees as God's will he commits an atrocity worthy of the stereotyped godless American Indian" (58).

continental specie toward the end of the war. One morning in 1782, he killed his wife and four children and then himself. Beadle left letters in which "he professes himself a deist" and claimed that "the deity would not willingly punish one who was impatient to visit his God and learn his will from his own mouth face to face": "That it is God himself who prompts and directs me . . . I really believe" (20, 21, 31). Conflating the concepts of deism and revivalism, Beadle apparently meant that the promise of direct access to God enabled him to perceive his premeditated murders as righteous acts, and hence his mind, like Wieland's "was contemplative" before the murders (15).[3]

The narrative of Beadle's life was presented by its editor as a testament to the "shocking effects of pride and false notions about religion," but it also and perhaps more strikingly shows the power of the unstable tension between family and world in the early Republic (10). When Beadle originally began to fail, "he adopted a plan of the most rigid family economy, but still kept up the outward appearance of his former affluence" (6). More than an understandable attempt to retain status, Beadle's version of "family economy" is transformed into the necessity of family sacrifice. Beadle's family went hungry because "he was determined not to bear the mortification of being thought poor and dependent," but his considerateness did not stop there: "since it is a father's duty to prepare for his flock, he thought it better to consign them over to better hands" (21, 24). His wife had been having premonitory dreams of the murders, perhaps because Beadle had been in the habit of bringing a butcher knife and an axe to bed with him every night. Beadle wrote of her premonitions, but claimed that "heaven" thought "his purpose was right": God "now directs me and supports me" (18). He wondered whether he could justify killing his wife; finally he decided that it "would be unmerciful to leave her behind to linger out a life in misery and wretchedness which must be the consequence of the surprising death of the rest of the family, and that since they had shared the smiles and frowns of fortunes together, it would be cruelty to her, to be divided from them in death" (15).

Beadle's fear of being alienated from the community, through poverty, or the family, through death, was dramatically realized when the community had to dispose of his body. No one wanted to be responsible: "at last it was performed by some Negroes, who threw him out of the window, with the bloody knife tied on his breast" (20). Having found suitably marginal characters as undertakers and a thoroughly marginal means of egress, the community became per-

3. Another parallel to *Wieland* occurs with a servant girl who survives the massacre of the family: Beadle sends her on an errand during his murderous activities at home; in *Wieland*, she hides in the closet.

turbed about interring the body: "After some consultation, it was thought best to place it on the banks of the river between the high and low water mark; the body was . . . bound with cords upon a sled, with the clothes on it as it was found, and the bloody knife tied on his breast, without coffin or box, and the horse he usually rode was made fast to the sled." After a gruesome funeral procession, "the body was tumbled into a hole dug for the purpose like the carcase of a beast" (12). Despite the communal attempts to eliminate Beadle and even to eradicate his identity as a human being, the multiply outcast Beadle returned yet again: some children discovered his body washed up by the river, and it was finally reburied by a crossroads.

Finally, then, the difference that Beadle enforces between outward appearance and an inner "rigid family economy" sets up an unbearable distinction between the family and the world. Although Beadle's explanation of his actions invokes a peculiar form of deism, in fact the confusion between revivalism and deism he exhibits appears equivalently in the Weems pamphlet and in other discussions of the early republic that create a striking correspondence between the effects of these religious excesses. The editor of Beadle's account, Stephen Mix Mitchell, asks, in terms reminiscent of *Wieland*, if it is possible that "a man could be transformed from an affectionate husband and an indulgent parent to a secret murderer, without some previous alteration, which must have been noticed by the family or acquaintance?" (16). The "previous alteration" that effected a transformation in Beadle seems again, as with Yates and Wieland, to have been caused by exposure to religious excess. What appears in these accounts to be on the one side an affirmation of devout Calvinist orthodoxy and on the other an affirmation of deistic reasoning that curiously allows for direct access to God turns out to be much the same thing when put into practice: deism and Calvinist revivalism are represented as significant, and significantly similar, threats to the family. What may be most disturbing, however, about these "alterations" is that they cannot finally be blamed on an alien intrusion; instead, the family-republic, like the Wieland family that serves as its "model," is caught in the grip of transformations in which it discovers that the alien is already within.

In *Wieland*, the direct result of excessive styles of belief is not only the violence we have been discussing, but also, and perhaps more importantly in terms of the scene of the family, irregular sexual desires. Specifically, as several critics have noted, incest appears as an almost unmistakable element of both Wieland's actions and Clara's responses. In this final and most disturbing version of naming inner desires as alien in order to expel them, Clara performs a double action, at once projecting the violence of her brother's actions onto Carwin, and discovering Carwin in threatening scenes (with sexual overtones) where she has anticipated her brother.

Wieland and Carwin are repeatedly linked by Clara. Even the possibility of a connection between the antinomian beliefs that Wieland appeals to when he explains the murder of his family (by which one may be freed from moral law by virtue of grace) and the Albigensian beliefs for which her father apparently died (in which God and Satan are manifestations of the same force) provides a link between what Clara perceives as godlike qualities in Wieland and the apparently satanic qualities of Carwin. Both Carwin and Wieland undergo "transformations," though their characters remain ambiguous and even interchangeable.[4] When Clara opens closets expecting to find her brother, or steps back from pits her brother has beckoned her toward, she finds Carwin. When she discovers the murders her brother has committed, she blames Carwin. Although she explains them as antipodes, the "virtues" of her brother may not finally be distinguishable from those of Carwin: the alien and the infidel are the same.

Further, Clara's obsessive concern with the placing of responsibility, the assumption of guilt, and the assignation of blame, her attempts to discover who is guilty and how that guilt shall be determined and judged, appear connected to her own displacement of a sense of guilt. Near the end of her narrative, Clara "acknowledge[s] that my guilt surpasses that of all mankind" (223) [165]. One critic asserts plausibly that Clara's "repressed guilt and incestuous desires provide her with motivation" for the crimes that Wieland commits, and argues that she "writes our story with a pen sharpened by a knife steeped in her brother's blood" (Hesford 239). Clara's fascination with Carwin as he interferes with her fantasy life, mingled with her immediate assumption of his agency in the destruction of her family, points to her desire to have a scapegoat for her own desires. She identifies with Wieland's "transformation" to the extent that she asks, "Was I not likewise transformed from rational and human into a creature of nameless and fearful attributes? Was I not transported to the brink of the same abyss? Ere a new day should come, my hands might be embrued in blood" (179–80) [135]. In spite of her attempt to maintain Carwin as a supernaturally gifted "double-tongued deceiver," Clara manages to castigate herself. Though she calls Carwin the "phantom that pursued my dreams," she suspects that he might be one of the "phantoms of my own creation" (157, 83) [120, 66].

Clara responds immediately to Carwin's voice: her eyes fill with "unbidden tears" and are later "rivetted" upon the portrait she makes of him (52, 53) [43, 44]. Though his features are "wide of beauty," it

4. Pleyel mentions Carwin's "*transformation* into a Spaniard" (68) [55].

seems curiously their very characteristic of being "outside" beauty and the inversion of usual standards in the "inverted cone" of his face that attracts her, so that she "consumed the day in alternately looking out upon the storm and gazing at the picture" (53, 54) [44, 45]. She cannot "account for [her] devotion to this image"—though she allows the reader to suppose it a sign of the "first inroads of a passion incident to every female heart"—and similarly cannot explain why, although the outside storm passes, "thoughts ominous and dreary" overwhelm her as she continues to look at the picture (54) [45]. Rather than pointing to a romantic infatuation, these signs point to her participation in or even invocation of Carwin's existence at the same time as the associations she makes with him seem importantly connected to her own desires. Looking at Carwin's portrait, she thinks of death, specifically dwelling upon the foreshadowed deaths of her brother and his children. This oscillation between the portrait and the storm is reiterated when, in her retrospective tracing of the events that led to the deaths of her brother's children, she remembers Carwin as "the intelligence that operated in this storm" (190) [142]. The storm that raged outside has been internalized. Still, she does not finally know whether Carwin is "an object to be dreaded or adored" and moves to blame him with a tentative assertion: "Some relief is afforded in the midst of suffering, when its author is discovered or imagined" (71, 190) [57, 142].

Indeed, Clara's attempts to "discover" or "imagine" (activities that she appears to confuse in the novel) the "author" of the deeds she has been so appalled by seem finally rather disingenuous. Like Beadle, she has tried to separate the "inviolate asylum" of the home from the dangers of the world, and, like Beadle, she finds that the scene of the home is already the scene of destruction. (It seems quite telling that Clara hears murderers in her closet.) While she claims that "that dwelling, which had hitherto been an inviolate asylum, was now beset with danger to my life," her mistake is to think that it has ever been an "inviolate asylum" (60) [49].[5]

Clara's efforts to fix blame and determine judgments are part and parcel of the attempts to maintain familial and social boundaries that may be seen to structure the action of *Wieland*. Although Clara and Wieland turn their father's restrictive and rigidly regulated retreat (the temple where he meets his demise) into a haven for free discourse (a new infidelity), it quickly becomes a place where transgressions are foregrounded. Carwin turns the temple into a zone of terror by his voice projections, but his intrusion should have been expected. Clara speaks of the meetings that take place there as free

5. These reactions again seem directly connected to the contemporary American fears of Revolution. For an interesting treatment of the novel in this historical context, see Fussell.

from societal interference and of Carwin as the destroyer of their peace, but rather than being simply the double-tongued deceiver that she calls him, rather than being simply an intruder or foreign violator of the pastoral American scene, Carwin's very abnormalities expose the shaky underpinnings of the family "asylum." By his intrusion into what Clara has presented as normal domestic scenes, he emphasizes or highlights underlying incongruities and potent desires. Although he systematically invades all Clara's retreats, including her body (albeit through the surrogate servant Judith, and through the ventriloquized sexual conversation that Pleyel "overhears"), Carwin might be seen as exposing Clara's general policy of concealment. In her shaded retreat by the river, Clara dreams of terrifying incest; Carwin wakes her. Clara's bower already resembles a sexual recess; Carwin forces her to confront the mingled invitation and threat of her brother's and her own sexuality.

In *Wieland*, then, the family is initially presented as a retreat, or "sweet and tranquil asylum" (193) [144], from the intrusions of the outside world, but the distinction between home and world, radically personified by the figure of the intruding Carwin, gets blurred as the destruction seen to lurk without gets discovered within. Clara concludes her account of her family with a typically mixed acknowledgment of the flaw that lay within: "the evils of which Carwin [was] the author, owed their existence to the errors of the sufferers." No violence could have been introduced into the family "if their own frailty had not seconded these efforts" (244) [181]. What Clara still manages to assume in this statement is Carwin's "authorship" of an account which she herself has written. Even as Clara cannot fully recognize the implications of her involvement as the author of the account of her family or see the family as the source of its own destruction, the novel presents her failed perceptions as part of a prevailing faulty perception in the early republic. For the family to keep its identity as an "asylum," the outside world must be posited as a threat. At the same time, the imitation of the family in social institutions designed to assume or supplement its functions provides a way out of the unbearable tension created between inside and outside by such an insular view of the family. *Wieland*'s message may finally be that for the family to be a haven from the excesses of radical democracy, deism, and revivalism, it must be inoculated, by way of these social institutions, at once with and against the "outside" world. Following the lead of Charles Brockden Brown, the American novel continued to explore the boundaries of the family and to suggest styles of education that would be appropriate for maintaining the family as the support for such an "outside" world, a world represented as all that is alien to the tranquil space, the "inviolate asylum," of the family.

WORKS CITED

"An Account of a Murder Committed by Mr. J——— Y———, upon His Family, in December, A. D. 1781." Reprinted in *Philadelphia Minerva* 2.81, 82 (August 20 and 27, 1796).

Axelrod, Alan. *Charles Brockden Brown: An American Tale*. Austin: Univ. of Texas Press, 1983.

Bell, Michael Davitt. "'The Double-Tongued Deceiver': Sincerity and Duplicity in the Novels of Charles Brockden Brown." *Early American Literature* 9 (1974): 143–63.

Bradford, William. *Of Plimoth Plantation, 1620–47*. Ed. Samuel Morison. New York: Modern Library, 1981.

Brown, Charles Brockden. *Wieland, or The Transformation; an American Tale*. Bicentennial ed. Ed. Sydney Krause, S. W. Reid, and Alexander Cowie. Kent, Ohio: Kent State Univ. Press, 1977.

Caplan, Ruth. *Psychiatry and the Community in Nineteenth-Century America*. New York: Basic Books, 1969.

Cowie, Alexander. "Historical Essay." In Charles Brockden Brown, *Wieland*. Kent, Ohio: Kent State Univ. Press, 1977.

Dalke, Anne. "Original Vice: The Political Implications of Incest in the Early American Novel." *Early American Literature* 23 (1988): 188–201.

Davis, David Brion. *Ante-Bellum Reform*. New York: Harper and Row, 1967.

———. *Homicide in American Fiction, 1798–1860*. Ithaca: Cornell Univ. Press, 1957.

Dwight, Timothy. *Theology Explained and Defended, in a Series of Sermons*. New York, 1846. Cited by Davis (*Homicide* 8).

Edwards, Jonathan. "Personal Narrative." *Representative Selections*. Ed. Clarence Faust and Thomas Johnson. New York: Hill and Wang, 1965. 57–72.

Fliegelman, Jay. *Prodigals and Pilgrims: The American Revolution Against Patriarchal Authority, 1750–1800*. Cambridge: Cambridge Univ. Press, 1982.

Fussell, Edwin. "*Wieland*: A Literary and Historical Reading." *Early American Literature* 18 (1983): 171–86.

Gilmore, Michael. "Calvinism and Gothicism: The Example of Brown's *Wieland*." *Studies in the Novel* 9 (1977): 107–18.

Mitchell, Stephen Mix. *Narrative of the Life of William Beadle*. Windsor, Vt.: Spooner, 1795.

Paine, Thomas. *The Life and Major Writings of Thomas Paine*. Ed. Philip Foner. Secaucus, N.J.: Citadel, 1974.

Rothman, David. *The Discovery of the Asylum: Social Order and Disorder in the New Republic*. Boston: Little, Brown, 1971.

Scheick, William. "The Problem of Origination in Brown's *Ormond*."

406   CHRISTOPHER LOOBY

Critical Essays on Charles Brockden Brown. Ed. Bernard Rosenthal. Boston: G. K. Hall, 1981. 126–41.

Seltzer, Mark. "Saying Makes it So: Language and Event in Brown's *Wieland.*" *Early American Literature* 13 (1978): 81–91.

Slotkin, Richard. *Regeneration through Violence: The Mythology of the American Frontier, 1600–1860.* Middletown, Conn.: Wesleyan Univ. Press, 1973.

Stauffer, Vemon. *New England and the Bavarian Illuminati.* New York: Columbia Univ. Press, 1918.

Tompkins, Jane. *Sensational Designs: The Cultural Work of American Fiction, 1780–1860.* New York: Oxford University Press, 1985.

Weems, Mason. "God's Revenge Against Adultery." (1815) Rpt. in *Three Discourses.* New York: Random House, 1929.

Ziff, Larzer. "A Reading of *Wieland.*" *PMLA* 77 (1962): 51–57.

CHRISTOPHER LOOBY

[Ciceronian Elocution in *Wieland*]†

* * *

The Saxon myth—the construal of political history in terms of an imaginary genealogy of constitutional and legal forms—finds a counterpart in one of the more intriguing details of *Wieland.* Some of the obsessive concentration with which Brown addressed the complex coherence of issues of language, speech act, law, and history can be gauged by attending to a textual anomaly that might easily be dismissed as minor or accidental, but seems to me to be too unusual to be inadvertent even if Brown does not make much of it. Clara tells us that her brother "was an indefatigible student" and that among the authors he was fond of reading "the chief object of his veneration was Cicero" (p. 24) [22]. This locates Theodore quite firmly within the political-moral ideology of the day, which endorsed civic virtue as it had been elaborated in classical literature and as that elaboration had been transmitted through English Whig political ideology. But Theodore's participation in such a nostalgic ideology is taken to rather unusual lengths: "He was never tired of conning and rehearsing [Cicero's] productions. To understand them was not sufficient. He was anxious to discover the gestures and cadences with which they ought to be delivered" (p. 24) [22].

† From *Voicing America: Language, Literary Form, and the Origins of the United States* (Chicago: University of Chicago Press, 1996), pp. 158–65. Copyright © 1996 by The University of Chicago. All rights reserved. Reprinted by permission. The author's parenthetical references are to the Kent State edition of *Wieland.* Page numbers in square brackets refer to this Norton Critical Edition.

Theodore's attempt to hallucinate the voice of Cicero and mimic
it may recall Franklin's similar practice of trying to reproduce and
assume fully an alien discourse, as I have described that practice
above (see Looby, *Voicing America*, chapter 2). It recalls also the
fantasmatic relation that political leaders of the revolutionary era
enjoyed to the heroes of classical antiquity. And it bears an obvious
relation to the theme of ventriloquism: Theodore effectively wants to
play Charlie McCarthy to Cicero's Edgar Bergen, to adopt not only
the moral and political sense of his philosophy but the whole paralin-
guistic apparatus of Cicero's tone, gesture, cadence, and pronunciation as he is able to reconstruct it inferentially. Brown's presentation
of the American revolutionaries' attempt to revive a classical theory
of politics and rhetoric of virtue in the form of a ventriloquistic reas-
sumption of vocal performance is surely parodistic: it implies that
such a politics of nostalgia is an attempt to recreate what is inaccessible, and that such an ambition of recreation is absurd, artificial,
and anachronistic.

Theodore's project of resumption has another aspect. "Not contented with this, he was diligent in settling and restoring the purity
of the text. For this end, he collected all the editions and commentaries that could be procured, and employed months of severe study
in exploring and comparing them. He never betrayed more satisfaction than when he made a discovery of this kind" (p. 24) [22]. One of
Nietzsche's aphorisms has it that "only that which has no history is
definable."[1] Theodore's efforts to restore a definitive text are attempts
to collapse history, to retreat from time's vicissitudes to an original
stability, represented here figurally by the model of a pure text that
has been corrupted over the centuries. This wish for an original
purity, for a text identical to itself, can only be realized by means of
inference and conjecture, and can only fabricate an ideal unity from
the concrete experience of collating discrepant present texts: nothing
will ever make it certain that the restored text actually is identical
to the lost original. Perhaps Theodore's attachment to "Moral necessity, and calvinistic inspiration" guides him in these endeavors; Pleyel,
the "champion of intellectual liberty" whose "gaiety was almost boisterous" and who was "prone to view every object merely as supplying materials for mirth," was capable of ridiculing Wieland's efforts
and even bluntly contesting "the divinity of Cicero" (p. 25) [23]. The
carefully presented opposition of the temperaments and behaviors of
Wieland and Pleyel functions here to suggest the most conspicuous
ideological oppositions within the political culture of the new nation:
on the one hand, the rather literal classical republicanism in alliance

1. Friedrich Nietzsche, *On the Genealogy of Morals, Ecce Homo*, trans. Walter Kaufmann
et al. (New York: Vintage Books, 1969), p. 80.

with a residual Puritanism, and on the other hand, the radical free-thinking of the secular Enlightenment. Whether an intellectual collation and emendation comparable to Theodore's textual reconstruction could restore the pure original American text from these conflicting contemporary political texts could only seem doubtful in 1798 at the height of Federalist-Republican controversy.

A test of the possibility of such a mediation and melioration comes right along in *Wieland*. When the companions are enjoying the spring air in the temple one day (having converted its use from religious worship to secular colloquy, with a new idol—a bust of Cicero—presiding over the scene), Theodore and Pleyel are "bandying quotations and syllogisms."

> The point discussed was the merit of the oration for Cluentius, as descriptive, first, of the genius of the speaker; and, secondly, of the manners of the times. Pleyel laboured to extenuate both these species of merit, and tasked his ingenuity, to shew that the orator had embraced a bad cause; or, at least, a doubtful one. He urged, that to rely on the exaggerations of an advocate, or to make the picture of a single family a model from which to sketch the condition of a nation, was absurd. (p. 30) [26–27]

Robert Ferguson reminds us that Cicero was "every early American lawyer's favorite symbol of oratorical excellence and professional virtue."[2] The *Pro Cluentio*, however, has a peculiar status among Cicero's famous defenses: it records Cicero at his most brilliantly specious. The defense of Cluentius is a tour de force, in which Cicero successfully defended a remarkably weak case, by "throwing dust in the eyes of the jury," as he admitted himself.[3] Cicero described an extraordinarily tangled series of protogothic events (murder, poisoning, bribery, seduction), and did so in a nonsequential way that didn't clarify but only further obscured the relation of one event to another. Brown chose to make this oration, of all of Cicero's speeches, the object of *Wieland's* and Pleyel's disagreement; the analogies between the course of events described by Cicero and those described therein by Brown is apparent to any reader, as is the comparable disconnectedness of the narration. And the self-reflexive metacommentary on legal oratory (ad-vocacy) in Cicero's oration also bears evident relation to Brown's own concerns: Cicero reflects within this speech on the ethical status of his own discourse, the morality of advocacy. He concludes that the advocate has no need to believe

2. Robert A. Ferguson, *Law and Letters in American Culture* (Cambridge, Massachusetts: Harvard Univ. Press, 1984), p. 142.
3. Cicero, *The Speeches: Pro Lege Manilia, Pro Caecina, Pro Cluentio, Pro Rabirio, Perduellionis*, trans. H. Grose Hodge, Loeb Classical Library (Cambridge, Massachusetts: Harvard Univ. Press, 1927), p. 212.

in the truth of the argument he makes, and is free even to make an argument that, in its construction of the facts, controverts an argument he made in a previous trial which concerned the same events.[4] He is not committed, that is, to the view that there is one true world, one univocal set of facts. And although Cicero decries the cheap lawyerly practice of appealing blatantly to prejudice, he repeatedly does so rather flagrantly, and in addition appeals to legal technicalities even after having promised not to do so. He talks around the issues constantly, strays from the point persistently, and in countless ways makes of his oration a catalogue of devices of rhetorical mystification and outright dishonesty. As an extravagantly self-contradictory text, it makes an apt object for disputes among its readers.

Theodore admires the oration. (It turns out to be a good model for his own oration at his trial for murder later on.) Pleyel, on the other hand, doesn't admire it: he especially resists Theodore's claim that the events narrated by Cicero can be taken to represent the conditions of Roman civilization at the time, and in particular that a single family can stand synecdochically for an entire nation. Again, it's hard not to think that Brown is giving indirect clues to the reader of his own novel, at once raising the possibility of a familial-national allegory and then casting doubt on it. What follows from this disagreement among the characters—a disagreement that incites, as it were, an undecidable question in the reader about the representative status of the Wielands *vis-à-vis* American society—is a series of narrative diversions and displacements that is characteristic of Brown's narrative method and that raises persistently the problematics of historical continuity, temporal linearity, and logical consequentiality that is everywhere at stake in this novel.

Theodore's and Pleyel's dispute about the representative status of Cluentius and his family goes unresolved because it is deflected by a new disagreement before any resolution is reached.

> The controversy was suddenly diverted into a new channel, by a misquotation. Pleyel accused his companion of saying *"polliceatur"* when he should have said *"polliceretur."* Nothing would decide the contest, but an appeal to the volume. My brother was returning to the house for this purpose, when a servant met him with a letter from Major Stuart. He immediately returned to read it in our company. (p. 30) [27]

"Misquotation" again suggests the inevitable deflection or error inherent in a present resumption of the text of the past. And there is nothing accidental about the site of this purported misquotation— *polliceatur* or *polliceretur.* The Latin translates two forms of the verb

4. Ibid., pp. 371, 369–70.

"to promise," which is used in an ethically dubious fashion in at least three places in *Pro Cluentio* (pp. 294, 296, 394). Promising is an instance of what Austin called a performative utterance; it is, in fact, the classic case of a performative, an act of speech that does not so much *refer* to something as *do* something.[5] To speak a promise is to perform that promise. In Cicero's defense of Cluentius the word is used twice to refer to a false promise (Staienus promises money to certain judges for acquitting Oppianicus, without intending to pay it) and once when Cicero himself makes a promise to his listeners (to base a legal defense on statutory technicalities in future trials, even though—he claims falsely—he is not doing so in the present trial). The promise, as a representative performative utterance, does several things relevant to the themes of *Wieland*: it forms a contract, and hence is a verbal act fundamental to a legal order, and in doing so it forges a connection between present and future, entailing a future obligation and an expectation upon the parties to the promise. It thus effects a narrative order, actually establishing the temporal relation of intentionality that preforms a historical structure of narrative continuity. This is the kind of social contract that Burke endorsed: a relation of obligation between generations.[6] In contrast, the social contract of Rousseau was primarily a synchronic contract, an agreement among contemporaries. Burke insisted that the contractual relations that constituted a political order be extended over time, and that in fact social order depended upon the diachronic stability of such contractual relations. In direct opposition to such a traditionalist view, we might think of Jefferson's famous dictum that "the earth belongs . . . to the living," that past generations could not entail any obligations upon their descendants.[7] Only such a view—a fundamental delegitimation of received norms—could make possible the kind of reimagining of social relations that Jefferson and other revolutionary leaders proposed. Pleyel, as the radical freethinker in this crowd, can be taken to stand in for Jefferson here, and Theodore—who seeks to resolve the dispute by an appeal to the text, by a return to an original authority—thereby becomes a stand-in for an indistinct Federalist point of view. Pleyel, the "champion of intellectual liberty," has a position on promises (on the verbally instituted relations of legal obligation that ensure a transtemporal stability to social arrangements and thereby make a continuous and intelligible history possible) that is similar to Jefferson's refusal of all that such promises imply. Theodore's contrasting position, if not quite Feder-

5. J. L. Austin, *How to Do Things with Words*, 2d ed., J. O. Urmson and Marina Sbisà, eds. (Cambridge, Massachusetts: Harvard Univ. Press, 1975), pp. 9–11 and passim.
6. Edmund Burke, *Reflections on the Revolution in France* (with Thomas Paine, *The Rights of Man*) (Garden City, New York: Anchor/Doubleday, 1973), pp. 108–111.
7. Thomas Jefferson, *Writings* (New York: Library of America, 1984), p. 959.

alist, might remotely correspond to Madison's, who, in his reply to Jefferson's disavowal of received obligations, held that it was morally and practically necessary to assume a tacit contract between generations. If you held to Jefferson's position, Madison thought, you might finally disestablish all political legitimacy ("Would not a Government so often revised become too mutable to retain those prejudices in its favor which antiquity inspires, and which are perhaps a salutary aid to the most rational Government in the most enlightened age?"):[8] you required that consent be constantly reiterated by every member of a nation whenever any child was born. Pragmatically, in the face of such an impossibility, it was necessary to assume and institute a default position (as it were) in the system of consent, to hold that in the absence of any challenge to the legitimacy of the state, tacit consent had in fact been given ("I find no relief from these consequences, but in the received doctrine that a tacit assent may be given to established Constitutions and laws, and that this assent may be inferred, where no positive dissent appears").[9]

Now such a structure of tacit consent can readily be construed as a form of ventriloquism—a claim that someone has always already spoken for you, a myth of the alienation of one's "voice" in an always already preempting "general voice"—or, rather, an assumed alienation of one's "voice" in a text, a textualized *vox populi* that took the form in the new United States of the rhetorical we in its founding documents. Such a mythic general voice effectively makes any political disagreement, then, into a matter of misquotation, and requires that such disagreement be resolved by a resort to the original text.

In *Wieland* this textual recourse—Theodore's intended referral to his edition of *Pro Cluentio*—is diverted, however, and the reconciliation promised by it is deferred and never thereafter accomplished. Instead of the text of Cicero, Theodore returns to the group in the temple with a just-delivered letter from Major Stuart, which he reads to his friends. A rainstorm quickly ensues, and forces the group back into the house (Major Stuart's letter is carelessly left behind in the temple), where they soon enter upon another dispute about a description of a cataract in the recently read letter. Textual recourse is the proposed method for resolving this dispute, too: "To settle the dispute which thence arose, it was proposed to have recourse to the letter" (p. 31) [27]. And—it begins to be obvious that Brockden Brown's repetitions are *not* careless—this recourse to the text is *again* diverted. The series of interlocked recourses, which keeps tracing unsuccessfully back along a track of displacements—displacements that have

---

8. James Madison, *The Papers of James Madison,* ed. Charles F. Hobson et al. (Charlottesville: Univ. of Virginia Press, 1981), vol. 13, p. 19.
9. Ibid., p. 20.

taken us from the purported pure text of Cicero's oration through variant corrupt texts, to disputed quotation (displacement of a written text in oral citation of it), to suddenly interpolated letter, to disputed recollection of the letter's contents—this labyrinth of displacements and attempted returns is now further diverted by the first intervention of the biloquist. The intrusive voice of Carwin is thus the last in this local series of verbal dislocations. When Theodore leaves his friends to go to the temple and retrieve the Stuart letter, his performance of this retrieval is inhibited by what sounds to him like his wife's voice outdoors as he climbs the hill to the temple. This first action of the displaced, counterfeited voice that will figure so importantly in the novel inaugurates here a new series of vocal and verbal substitutions.

*   *   *

PAUL DOWNES

Constitutional Secrets: "Memoirs of Carwin" and the Politics of Concealment[†]

> It is an eminent advantage incident to democracy, that . . . its inherent tendency is to annihilate [secrets].
> William Godwin, *An Enquiry Concerning Political Justice*[1]

> It is said, that you are afraid of the very Windows, and have a Man planted under them to prevent Secrets and Doings from flying out.
> William Paterson, Letter to William Ellsworth, a delegate at the Constitutional Convention in Philadelphia, August 23, 1787.[2]

William Godwin's antipathy towards secrets could be said to inaugurate a long tradition of equating democracy with publicity, a tradition that has received further elaboration in recent accounts of the American Revolution. The renewed attention to a Habermasian "public sphere" and to a late-eighteenth-century civic culture of print has focused attention on the relationship between the emergence of modern political forms and a marked proliferation of unfettered political expression. The growth of a discursive space distinct from

† From *Criticism: A Quarterly for Literature and the Arts*, 39.1 (winter 1997): 89–117. © 1997 Wayne State University Press, with the permission of Wayne State University Press. Page numbers in square brackets refer to this Norton Critical Edition.
1. *An Enquiry Concerning Political Justice: and its Influence on Modern Morals and Happiness*, [1793] (New York: Penguin, 1985) 531.
2. Quoted in *A Rising People* (Philadelphia: Library Company of Philadelphia, 1989) 274.

that of the state yet capable of commenting critically upon the state is said to have facilitated an opening up of opportunities for political participation and to have contributed to an erosion of the structural secrecies of a pre-modern political world.[3]

But Michael Warner, in his very influential study of the relationship between print culture and the American Revolution raises an important question about the subject of the public sphere. "If the discourse of publicity allows individuals to make public use of their reason," Warner asks, "what will individuals be like, and what will count as reason?"[4] Publicity, this question suggests, should not simply be seen as offering possibilities for the (pre-existing) individual to bring him- or herself into the light of the political day, but as a mode of production for a new way of being an individual. Rather than offering a transparent link between the individual and the realm of the political, publicity should perhaps be seen as a new way of extending the play of revelation and concealment in the field of political intervention. With this in mind, I want to look at the obsession with secrecy in post-revolutionary American politics and, in particular, at the function of secrecy in the production of the new constitutional citizen. I am interested, in other words, in shifting attention away from the sphere of civic publicity so ably described by Warner and others, and onto the space of democratic citizenship, a space which can also be figured by the enclosure of the ballot box. With its indication of the individual's simultaneous concealment and revelation as citizen and its emphasis on the passage from oral to written voting practices, the ballot box indicates the relationship between secrecy, writing and the democratic revolution that I would like to trace in the following pages. If the democratic revolution signals a transformation in the economy of political power, I argue, the citizen's accession to this power cuts a path through an irreducible experience of secrecy. Against Godwin, I want to propose that democracy rather than doing away with Monarchy's or Aristocracy's secretive political practices, in fact introduced the possibility of a "democratized" secrecy by deploying its constitutive relationship to the democratic subject, the citizen.

No early-American novelist was as preoccupied with secrets as Charles Brockden Brown. Taken together, his most compelling pieces of writing comprise a dissertation on secrecy; his novels trace the character of the secret holder and the penetrator of secrets, and they find their narrative propulsion in the labyrinthine endlessness of the quest to uncover secrets. It's not surprising then, that his stories have

3. Jurgen Habermas, *The Structural Transformation of the Public Sphere*, [1962] trans. Thomas Burger (Cambridge, Mass.: MIT Press, 1989).
4. *The Letters of the Republic: Publication and the Public Sphere in Eighteenth-Century America* (Cambridge, Mass.: Harvard University Press, 1990), xiii.

often been read as literary products of a reactionary post-Revolutionary paranoia, expressing a "Federalist" fear that "complicated motives and unknown agents are always threatening to overthrow an apparent order."[5] Stephen Watts goes even further, and suggests that the obsession with secrets in Brown's work responds to the personal and social incoherence generated by an emerging capitalist order. The "deceptions and fluidities of bourgeois individualism," writes Watts, produced the "fragmented self" that "haunted the roads and waterways, the libraries and parlors, the marketplaces and churches of the early American republic."[6] It is this kind of capitalist freak, suggests Watts, that Charles Brockden Brown so vividly portrays in, for example, "Memoirs of Carwin the Biloquist."

But what keeps critics returning to Brown's fiction is a familiar uncertainty: Brown's stories cite, or ventriloquize, an obsession with secrets, and we can never be sure whether it is the citation or the obsession that most needs to be read. In this regard, "Carwin the Biloquist" (1798/1803–05) is exemplary. Not only does the story pit one secret holder against another in an explicit struggle over the individual and political ends of concealment, but it does so while telling a story about ventriloquism. Carwin, the secret imitator—and the narrator of Brown's unfinished story—is brought face to face with Ludloe, the representative of a zealous and insistently clandestine political sect. And while Ludloe offers Carwin access to the kind of enlightened political philosophy that had once fascinated Brown himself, it is nevertheless Carwin's reluctance to embrace the sect that arrests both our attention and, it would seem, the story's plot. Carwin's hesitation provides another example of Brown's continued importance as a source of insight into the transformation of the political subject in the late-eighteenth century United States. Brown's story, as I hope to show, helps us to think about the modern democratic subject's relationship to secrecy. When Carwin breaks his father's law and enters the uncharted seclusion of the Pennsylvania Wilderness, he initiates a movement of independence which will culminate in the obstinate refusal to let go of a fascinating secret. It is this very commitment to secrecy, however, that will distinguish Carwin from the two paternal figures (his unenlightened father and the Godwinian Ludloe) whose mutually determined opposition defines the limits of a static revolutionary antagonism.

---

5. Beverly Voloshin, "*Edgar Huntly* and the Coherence of the Self," *Early American Literature* 23.3 (1988) 263; Jay Fliegelman, whose line on Brown is by no means a narrow one, writes of *Wieland*'s "terrifying post-revolutionary account of the fallibility of the human mind and, by extension, of democracy itself," and of that novel's sensitivity to "larger fears about the Jacobinization of the impressionable American mind" ("Introduction," Charles Brockden Brown, *Wieland and Memoirs of Carwin the Biloquist* [New York: Penguin, 1991] vii, xi).
6. Steven Watts, *The Romance of Real Life: Charles Brockden Brown and the Origins of American Culture* (Baltimore: Johns Hopkins University Press, 1994) 193.

1

In an 1815 letter to Thomas Jefferson, John Adams reminisced on the American Revolution with characteristic hyperbole. The American innovation in politics, he exclaimed, had replaced the "fictitious miracles" with which Priests and Kings ruled the world, with the "laws [of] nature." In America, he wrote, "authority is originally in the People" and is no longer brought down from heaven by the holy ghost in the form of a dove, in a phyal of holy oil."[7] In fact, as early as 1765, Adams had insisted on the de-mystifying tendencies of the American people, when he contrasted what he called the "two greatest tyrannies . . . the canon and the feudal law" with the American settlers' "love of universal liberty."[8] The colonists, he continued, possessed "an utter contempt of all that dark ribaldry of hereditary, indefeasible right—the Lord's anointed—and the divine, miraculous original of government with which priesthood had enveloped the feudal monarch in clouds and mysteries" (454).[9]

But the revolution against mystery and dark ribaldry ushered in an era that commentators have singled out for its paranoid sense of secret machinations, and its heated and haunted political imagination.[1] Political debate conjured up a covert world of secret aristocrats and Jacobin conspirators as republicans and federalists sought to define each other in terms of their post-revolutionary relationship to French radicalism and English reaction. According to one recent history of the period, the most extreme positions in this debate had something in common: "each indeed was enveloped in ideological nightmares."[2] For arch-Federalists, the nightmare was given shape by the publication of Scotsman John Robison's *Proofs of a Conspiracy*

7. *The Adams-Jefferson Letters: The Complete Correspondence Between Thomas Jefferson and Abigail and John Adams* (Chapel Hill: University of North Carolina Press, 1959) 445. Compare Adams's reference to miracles here with Madison's suggestion to Jefferson that the Constitutional Convention had achieved "[nothing] less than a miracle" (*The Papers of James Madison*, ed. William T. Hitchinson et al. [Chicago, Charlottesville, 1962] 10, 208).
8. John Adams, *The Works of John Adams*, ed. Charles Francis Adams. 10 vols. (Boston: Little Brown, 1850–1856) 3:454.
9. Thomas Paine is also eloquent on the revelatory dimension of the American Revolution. England's constitution, he wrote, was suited "for the dark and slavish times in which it was erected." On the other hand, of the American experiment, he proclaimed, "the sun never shone on a cause of greater worth" (*The Thomas Paine Reader*, ed. Michael Foot and Isaac Kramnick [New York: Penguin, 1987] 82).
1. Richard Buel is not alone in describing the period in terms of a "mood of grim foreboding" that hung over the early Republic on account of the "specter[s]" of "'great secrecy'" frequently conjured up by wary politicians (*Securing the Revolution: Ideology in American Politics, 1789–1815* [Ithaca: Cornell University Press, 1972] 174–5). Linda Kerber refers to the early national period as "one of the most intellectually traumatic in modern times" (*Federalists in Dissent: Imagery and Ideology in Jeffersonian America* [Ithaca: Cornell University Press, 1970] xxi). See too the first chapter of Bill Christophersen's *The Apparition in the Glass: Charles Brockden Brown's American Gothic* (Athens: University of Georgia Press, 1993).
2. Stanley Elkins and Eric McKitrick, *The Age of Federalism: The Early American Republic, 1788–1800* (New York: Oxford University Press, 1993) 583.

Against all the Religions and Governments of Europe, Carried on in the Secret meetings of Free Masons, Illuminati, and Reading Societies.[3] This tract inspired New England Federalists and Anglophiles, including Jedediah Morse and Timothy Dwight to publish their own highly influential pamphlets on the conspiratorial Jacobin threat to the stability of the new Republic.[4] Their hysteria fueled many a New England sermon and found a ready audience in a period that produced some of the Nation's most xenophobic and repressive legislation, the Alien and Sedition Acts of 1798.

At the same time, as François Furet has shown, an obsession with secrecy was central to the ideology of those figures most feared by federalists, the French radicals and their American sympathizers. Furet argues that the concept of the secret plot appealed to a "democratic conviction that the general, or national, will could not be publicly opposed by special interests" (53). The discourse of the secret plot, explains Furet was "marvelously suited to the workings of revolutionary consciousness" (53):

> there was no need to name the perpetrators of the crime and to present precise facts about their plans, since it was impossible to determine the agents of the plot, who were hidden, and its aims, which were abstract. In short, the plot came to be seen as the only adversary of sufficient stature to warrant concern, since it was patterned on the Revolution itself. Like the Revolution, it was abstract, omnipresent and pregnant with new developments; but it was secret whereas the Revolution was public, perverse whereas the Revolution was beneficial, nefarious whereas the Revolution brought happiness to society. It was its negative, its reverse, its anti-principle. (53–4)

In post-Revolutionary America, however, the most powerful political voices maintained a careful distance from "French" radicalism and thus directed their suspicion towards what were frequently called the excesses of democracy. If the "dark ribaldry" of ancient institutions had, in Adams' words "enveloped the feudal monarch in clouds and mysteries," George Washington feared in 1786 that the various excesses of democracy (figured most significantly by Shay's Rebellion) might leave "the great body of the people . . . so . . . enveloped in darkness, as not to see rays of a distant sun through all this

---

3. Robison's book was printed in Edinburgh in 1797 and reprinted in New York the following year.
4. Richard Hofstadter, *The Paranoid Style in American Politics, and Other Essays* (New York: Knopf, 1965) 10–14; and Vernon Stauffer, *New England and the Bavarian Illuminati* (New York, 1918). Curiously, Robison's book is one of the documents circulated by contemporary militia movements in the United States. It is certainly intriguing to think of the leading New England clergyman, Yale President, and notorious denouncer of secret internal threats to the Nation, Timothy Dwight "passing on" John Robison's book to suspected Oklahoma City bomber Timothy McVeigh.

mist of intoxication and folly."[5] And James Madison added rhetorical force to his condemnation of majority factions in the *Federalist Papers* by referring to the *"secret* wishes of an unjust and interested majority" (X, 128).

But of course it was not only the Shaysites, Jacobins, and anarchists who seemed to want to keep post-revolutionary Americans in the dark. In September of 1786 a small gathering of state representatives met in Annapolis, Maryland ostensibly to discuss trade on the Potomac. James Madison, one of the representatives from Virginia, already had his sights set on a more consequential series of national discussions. The report that the commissioners finally delivered to their respective state governments contained a carefully worded proposal that would eventually succeed in precipitating the constitutional convention of 1787. "Your commissioners," the report announced with remarkable management of the rhetoric of disembodied compulsion, "cannot forbear to indulge an expression of their earnest and unanimous wish, that speedy measures may be taken to effect a general meeting of the states, in a future convention, for the same and such other purposes, as the situation of public affairs may be found to require."[6] The French Minister, Louis (Guillaume) Otto, reporting back to his country on the document produced by the Annapolis assembly, seems to have been acutely suspicious of what he called the commissioners' "secret motives" and "pretext[s] for introducing innovations." The calculated "infinity of circumlocutions and ambiguous phrases," which the commissioners employed, noted Otto, gave to their report "an obscurity which the people will penetrate with difficulty."[7]

This practiced obscurity continued to inform the progress of the Constitution's formation. Indeed, three of the five rules agreed upon at the start of the Convention pertained to secrecy, forbidding copies to be taken of any entries in the journal and requiring that "nothing spoken in the House be printed, or otherwise published, or

5. Quoted in Albert B. Hart, *American History Told by Contemporaries*, 3 (New York: Macmillan, 1897) 190.
6. Quoted in Jonathan Elliott, ed., *The Debates in the Several State Conventions, on the Adoption of the Federal Constitution, as Recommended by the General Convention at Philadelphia in 1787*, 1 (Philadelphia, 1881), 151.
7. Quoted in Hart, 185–187. Madison maintained a careful secrecy concerning the progress of the new constitution. In the *Federalist Papers*, too, his anonymity led him to write only speculatively about what had gone on in the convention. His use of a cipher with which to communicate secretly with Jefferson would also seem to be evidence of a certain delight in secrecy. In 1784, when Madison reported to Jefferson in Paris that the hostility of Patrick Henry would block the calling of a state constitutional convention, Jefferson replied, partly in a numerical cipher: "If one could be obtained, I do not know whether it would do more harm than good. While Mr. Henry lives another bad constitution would be formed and forever on us. What we have to do I think is devotedly to 252.746 for his death." This letter is quoted in Irving Brant, *James Madison: The Virginia Revolutionist* (New York: Bobbs-Merrill, 1941) 188. The code was later decoded for posterity by Jefferson's secretary.

communicated without leave."[8] "The members of the Convention," wrote William Blount in 1787, "observe such inviolable secrecy that it is altogether unknown out of doors what they are doing" (Burnett, 691).[9] In his final speech to the Convention, Benjamin Franklin spoke of the opinions he had entertained of the proposed constitution's errors. "I have never whispered a syllable of them abroad," he announced proudly, "Within these walls they were born, and here they shall die."[1] When the Convention finally issued its report in September of 1787, the Deputy Secretary of Congress breathed a sigh of relief and declared that "the important secret is now exposed to public view" (694).

Of course, the surreptitious procedures of the Federalists did not go unnoticed by their contemporaries. Massachusetts Congressman Stephen Higginson was among the many who suggested a "plot" originating "in Virginia with Mr. Madison";[2] and Madison's caution did not prevent him from suggesting to Thomas Jefferson that "the public is certainly in the dark with regard to [the imminent constitution]." "I do not learn however," he later added, with more than a hint of apprehension, "that any discontent is expressed at the concealment" (60).[3] Jefferson was not entirely assuaged. "I am sorry," he wrote John Adams in August of 1787, "[that] they began their deliberations by so abominable a precedent as that of tying up the tongues of their members."[4]

Not surprisingly, the secrecy of the convention figures repeatedly in letters from the delegates to their friends and family outside of Philadelphia. George Mason, for example, explained his support for the convention's silence in a 1787 letter to his son. The secrecy of the debates was "a proper precaution," he suggested, "to prevent mistakes and misrepresentations until the business shall have been

---

8. Max Farrand, ed., *The Records of the Federal Convention of 1787*, 3 vols. (New Haven: Yale University Press, 1911) 1:15. Furthermore, the debates in Congress for September 26 and 27, the days devoted to discussion of the proposed Constitution drawn up in Philadelphia, were officially censored from the Records.

9. George Mason wrote of the need to "keep our doors shut" in order to protect "the public eye" from the "crude and indigested" shapes which the "business" might at first assume (Farrand, *Records*, 3:28). The reference to "closed doors" and "out of doors" picks up on a phrase frequently used in this period to designate the soverign people in their capacity as ultimate source of legitimate political power. In much revolutionary rhetoric, the people were only to be found "out of doors," at the site of an excess that could not be contained by any structure, the site of actions open to the light of the sun that Thomas Paine liked to refer to as shining upon the American cause (see note 9 above). The motif of the door also recurrs in one of Madison's more nervous missives from the Convention: "The labor is great indeed," he told William Short, "whether we consider the real or imaginary difficulties within doors or without doors" (Farrand, *Records*, 3, Appendix A, 37).

1. Benjamin Franklin, "Speech in the Convention," September 17, 1787, in Nina Baym *et al* ed., *The Norton Anthology of American Literature* (New York: Norton, 1989): 388–90.

2. Ralph Ketcham, *James Madison: A Biography* (New York: Macmillan, 1971) 185.

3. Madison to Thomas Jefferson, July 18, 1787, in Madison, *Papers*, 10:105–6.

4. *The Political Writings of Thomas Jefferson*, ed. Edward Dumbauld (New York: Macmillan, 1955) 136.

completed, when the whole may have a very different complexion from that in which the several crude and indigested parts might in their first shape appear if submitted to the public eye."[5] This mildly gothic sense of rather unsightly and disturbing goings on within the Convention room recurs in Alexander Martin's letter to Governor Caswell of North Carolina. It is best for the convention to keep its proceedings hidden, wrote Martin, "till their deliberations are moulded for the public Eye . . . lest unfavourable Representations might be made by imprudent printers of the many crude matters and things daily uttered and produced in this Body."[6] Many years later, Jared Sparks recorded notes from a visit with James Madison in his journal, notes which included references to the secrecy of the convention. It was best for the convention to "sit with closed doors," recorded Sparks, "because opinions were so various and at first so crude that it was necessary they should be long debated before any uniform system of opinion could be formed. Meantime the minds of the members were changing, and much was to be gained by a yielding and accommodating spirit."[7] Sparks continues: "Had the members committed themselves publicly at first, they would have afterwards supposed consistency required them to maintain their ground, whereas by secret discussion no man felt himself obliged to retain his opinions any longer than he was satisfied of their propriety and truth, and was open to the force of argument. Mr. Madison thinks no Constitution would ever have been adopted by the convention if the debates had been public" (479). Intriguingly, Madison's account, as Sparks records it, suggests that rather than shielding delegates from persuasion and influence, the secrecy of the convention gave full play to the "force" of persuasion.[8] And if this secrecy concealed the "yielding" of delegates, it also concealed what Franklin

5. Farrand, 3, Appendix A, 28.
6. Farrand, 3, Appendix A, 64. Of course, some of the debates taking place behind the convention's closed doors concerned precisely the shape of a "man," what counts as a person, and the astonishing possibility of "three-fifths of a person." For an excellent discussion of this debate, see Paul Finkelman, "Slavery and the Constitutional Convention: Making a Covenant with Death," in *Beyond Confederation: Origins of the Constitution and American National Identity*, ed. Richard Beeman *et al* (Chapel Hill: University of North Carolina Press, 1987): 18–225. The precise content of the debates and the interests and prejudices that members defended in secret are less important to me here than the fact of the secrecy itself and its place in the formation of the Constitution. After all, racist and pro-slavery rhetoric hardly needed a cloak of secrecy in late-eighteenth-century America.
7. Farrand, 3, Appendix A, 478–479. For more on the word "crude" that crops up repeatedly in these accounts of the Convention, see Garry Wills, *Explaining America: The Federalist* (Garden City, New York: Doubleday, 1981) 243–44. As a term often used in scientific discussions of the chemistry of digestion, "crude" both signalled the founders' relationship to Scottish scientific analogizing in political discourse, and went some way towards producing political voice (the unanimous voice of the convention) as a form of *ventriloquism* (literally, a speaking from the stomach).
8. If we were looking for a way to read some kind of erotics into the monumentally cerebral (some would say "dry") history of the formation of the Constitution, we might begin here with this secret yielding to the other's force.

called the "sacrifice" of opinion that members might have to consider
in the name of the new Nation. Reminding delegates of the "salutary
effects and great advantages" that would follow from "our real or
apparent unanimity" (389), Franklin (via James Wilson, who read
the sickly Franklin's written speech to the members) appealed to
delegates to put their names to the proposed constitution and thereby
"make *manifest* [their] *unanimity*" (390). Above all else, the success
of the convention depended on the achievement of a unanimous voice
with which to present the constitution to the people. This voice,
which, as origin of the law, would eventually succeed by appearing
to come from nowhere was discovered in, produced by, secrecy.[9]

Thus, in the 1790s, secret political maneuvering became an object
of acute public apprehension even as it was put to work in the name
of law, order and the consolidation of revolutionary achievement.
But for many interpreters this secrecy continues to have a decidedly
conservative profile. The post-revolutionary obsession with secrecy
was the result, suggests Linda Kerber of a "common Federalist fear
that the Jeffersonians were insufficiently conscious of the precari-
ousness of revolutionary accomplishments, and that this laxity might
well prove disastrous" (174). And Jefferson's dissatisfaction with the
secrecy of the Convention reverberates in Joshua Miller's attempt
to account for the failures of American democracy. The devious federalist combination of highly secretive political maneuvers with a
rhetoric of "popular sovereignty," argues Miller, secured power for
an elite class while "transform[ing] the body politic into a specter."[1]
Conservatives deployed secrecy, these accounts suggest, in order to
circumvent some of the democratic consequences of Revolutionary
success. Such a line of interpretation received one of its most memorable articulations in Richard Hofstadter's 1965 study, "The Paranoid Style in American Politics." Hofstadter identified a tendency
to convert feelings of persecution into "grandiose theories of conspiracy" in the history of post-Revolutionary American politics. The
spokesman of the paranoid style shares many characteristics with
the "clinical paranoid," writes Hofstadter, but whereas the latter feels
conspiracy to be directed specifically against him, the former "find
[hostility and conspiracy] directed against a nation, a culture, a way
of life whose fate affects not himself alone but millions of others" (4).
Despite acknowledging that this "style" has been adopted by activists

9. Derrida writes, in "Before the Law": "It seems that the law as such should never give
rise to any story. To be invested with its categorical authority, the law must be without
any history, genesis, or any possible derivation. That would be *the law of the law*." In
Acts of Literature, ed. Derek Attridge (New York: Routledge, 1992) 191.
1. Joshua Miller, "The Ghostly Body Politic" The *Federalist Papers* and Popular Sovereignty" *Political Theory* 16.1 (1988): 115. The possibility of a wholly fleshly "body politic" that Miller's account suggests, is surely as fantastic and undesirable as the ghostly
citizen of his gothic imagination.

belonging to a variety of political movements (from anti-Masonic and anti-Catholic movements to certain elements of abolitionism and of course McCarthyism), Hofstadter, whose own political and intellectual allegiances are strongly shaped by the McCarthy experience, maintains that, "the term 'paranoid style' is pejorative, and it is meant to be; the paranoid style has a greater affinity for bad causes than good" (5).

Hofstadter's pathologizing paradigm is one that Gordon Wood, perhaps the most widely read contemporary historian of the Revolutionary period, finds unsatisfactory. In "Conspiracy and the Paranoid Style: Causality and Deceit in the Eighteenth Century," Wood suggests that the paranoid characterization fails to do justice to late-eighteenth century Americans. Far from representing a pathology, Wood argues, the obsession with secret political activities marked an enlightened response to "the expansion and increasing complexity of the [eighteenth century] political world."[2] As the century went on, he explains:

> there were more people more distanced from one another and from the apparent centers of political decision making. . . . The more people became strangers to one another and *the less they knew of one another's hearts*, the more suspicious and mistrustful they became, ready as never before in Western history to see deceit and deception at work . . . [this] Society was composed not simply of great men and their retainers but of numerous groups, interests, and 'classes' whose actions could not be *easily deciphered*. Human affairs were more complicated, more interdependent, and more impersonal than they had ever been in Western history. (410–11, my emphases)

Where the tradition that he critiques introduces psychologizing, clinical terminology to explain historical behavior, Wood stresses the external pressures of number, distance and class interest. Com-

---

2. Gordon Wood, "Conspiracy and the Paranoid Style: Causality and Deceit in the Eighteenth Century," *William and Mary Quarterly*, 39.3 (1982): 410. While it tends to be read for its contribution to our understanding of conspiracy fascination in revolutionary and post-revolutionary America, Wood's essay is perhaps more invested in the vicissitudes of contemporary historiographical methodology. Wood makes it quite clear that in his work he wishes to repudiate historiography muddled by "modern notions of psychic strain" and instead show that conspiratorial thinking was not clinical, pathological, bizarre, but an element of the way of thinking of "'reasonable people,' indeed the most enlightened minds of the day" (406). Wood's neo-conspiratorial approach here has a methodological ethics attached to it: a commitment to the historical specificity of particular individuals. It is by recovering the specificity of individual experience and defending it against the distortions of anachronistic historiography that the historian, in Wood's opinion, does his true work (40). Clearly it is a certain concept of the historian that Wood is also rescuing from charges of paranoia. On the other hand, what Wood calls an enlightened desire to trace everything to first causes, Furet identifies with a revolutionary demand that "every historical fact . . . be reduced to a specific intention and to a subjective act of will" (53).

plexity is the key term here, and it serves to link a widespread concern with secrets and plots to a historical reality, rather than to an anachronistic diagnosis.

Interestingly, Wood's explanation has some precedent in the period which he addresses. His argument participates in the logic of a theory that argued against the viability of large republics on the grounds that in such republics interests become too diverse, and the homogeneity vital to order disappears. This anti-federalist argument drew heavily upon the writings of Baron de Montesquieu. "In an extensive republic," wrote Montesquieu, "the public good is sacrificed to a thousand private views. In a small one, the interest of the public is more obvious, better understood, and more within the reach of every citizen."[3] Wood's emphasis on the explanatory importance of "the growing number of persons and interests participating in politics" (430) follows Montesquieu, then, in equating the disunity of interests with number. Wood's article does register some discomfort with a neo-Montesquiean account of the demographic sources of a conspiratorially-minded populace. Wood refers to the *"growing* gap" (my emphasis) between intentions and actions in the expanding public sphere of the eighteenth century, a formulation which would seem to suggest the possibility of an originary gap. And, indeed, this is something that his essay explicitly suggests. Conspiratorial modes of interpretation, notes Wood, "rested on modes of apprehending reality that went back to classical antiquity" (409). "There was nothing new," he continues, "in seeing intrigue, deceit, and cabals in politics. From Sallust's description of Catiline through Machiavelli's lengthy discussion in his *Discourses*, conspiracy was a common feature of political theory" (409). Nevertheless, Wood returns to his central contention by asserting that the difference between the operation of conspiracy theory in modern as opposed to pre-modern politics, is merely a difference of scale: classical and Renaissance conspiracies, he writes, occurred "within the small ruling circles of a few great men—in limited political worlds where everyone knew everyone else" (410). The apparent relationship between modern democratic political organization and a heightened discourse of secrecy, this account suggests, is merely a contingent effect of social and economic expansion.

3. Baron de Montesquieu, *The Spirit of the Laws*, trans. Thomas Nugent (New York: Collier-Macmillan, 1949) 8, 16. Samuel Beer suggests that this position is Machiavellian first (Samuel H. Beer, *To Make A Nation: The Rediscovery of American Federalism* [Cambridge, Mass.: Harvard University Press, 1993]). The expanding public was, according to Machiavelli, made "unwieldy" and hard to "manage" by the "animosities and tumults" of too many participants (qtd. in Beer, 90). "The fundamental problem," Beer writes, "was not class conflict but pluralism" (90). As Beer helps us to see, this position shares assumptions with those political theories that justify dictatorial rule on the grounds that, as Thomas Aquinas wrote, "many, as such, seek many things, whereas one attends only to one" (Beer, 91).

Wood's theory of the obsession with conspiracy leaves us with an important question about the political philosophy of one of the most careful thinkers of the revolutionary period. Why, if it is true that suspicion and uncertainty expand with an expanding society, would James Madison argue, as he did in the famous *Federalist* #10, that an extended republic would be more likely to safeguard liberty and order than a narrow one? Political historians have long recognized the originality of Madison's defense of large-scale Federalism against the classical critique exemplified by Montesquieu's *Spirit of the Laws*, a defense he carries out, most notably, in Federalist #10 and in a 1787 letter to Thomas Jefferson.[4] Defending the constitution proposed by the Philadelphia convention, Madison contests that the proliferation of interests and factions in an extended political state can, contrary to classical political philosophy, form the basis for *preserving* individual rights and protecting against the tyranny of majority. The advantage of the Constitutional Republic's "extensive sphere," Madison contends, consists (in part) in "the greater security afforded by a greater variety of parties, against the event of any one party being able to outnumber and oppress the rest" (128). The fact that a large republic produced a proliferation of "strangers" who, to use Wood's phrase, knew less of "one another's hearts," is not denied by Madison so much as it is exploited to demonstrate the obstacles to tyranny in such a diverse society. In his letter to Jefferson, which he wrote to complement Jefferson's receipt of the results of the Convention, Madison went into more detail in order to explain some of the key Philadelphia resolutions. In discussing the constitutional negative on the laws of the States, Madison knew he had to take pains to counter his friend's suspicions. "It may be asked," Madison writes, "how private rights will be more secure under the Guardianship of the General Government than under the State Governments, since they are both founded on the republican principle which refers the ultimate decision to the will of the majority, and are distinguished rather by the extent within which they will operate, than by any material difference in their structure" (212). A full answer to this question, Madison continues, would "unfold the true principles of Republican Government." Those who contend that a democratic government can only operate "within narrow limits," he writes, "assume or suppose a case which is altogether fictitious: "[t]hey found their reasoning on the idea, that the people composing the Society, enjoy not only an equality of political rights; but that they all have precisely the same interests, and the same feelings in every respect. . . . We know however that no Society did or can consist of so homogenous a mass of Citizens" (212). Here, Madison rejects, as

4. The letter to Jefferson is dated 24 October, 1787 (*Papers*, 10, 206–219).

a founding political principle, the idea that any community, no matter how small or homogenous, can be said to "share the same feelings in every respect." This rejection is thus also a rejection of any account of political development that nostalgically emphasizes a falling away from simpler and more harmonious beginnings.

Madison's examples of the kinds of differences that counter such an idea of homogeneity begins by citing economic differences, between "rich and poor; creditors and debtors; a landed interest, a monied interest, a mercantile interest, a manufacturing interest" (letter, 213), but in his letter to Jefferson, Madison gives as much space to distinctions founded on "accidental differences in political, religious or other opinions, or an attachment to the persons of leading individuals." "However erroneous or ridiculous these grounds of dissention and faction, may appear to the enlightened Statesman, or the benevolent philosopher," Madison continues, "the bulk of mankind, who are neither Statesmen nor Philosophers, will continue to view them in a different light" (213). What is most intriguing about this catalogue of differences, is not just Madison's reluctance to dismiss their importance for political thought, but also the implicit suggestion that some of these differences indicate a more intimate dislocation.

As Samuel Beer has recently pointed out, Madison's theory of faction (a faction that is "latent," "sown in the nature of man," 124) is intimately connected to what he called "self-love." "As long as the connection subsists between his reason and his self-love," wrote Madison in Federalist #10, "[the citizen's] opinions and his passions will have a reciprocal influence on each other; and the former will be objects to which the latter will attach themselves" (123–124). If Montesquieu's political theory sought to found government on a renunciation of the self's disruptive self-love ("which is ever arduous and painful," Montesquieu writes, and "requires a constant preference of public to private interest"),[5] Madison's begins with the impossibility, or the refusal, of that renunciation. Beer explains: "Madison focused his attention on a source of republican disorder inherent in human nature: self-love . . . Even if *ex hypothesi*, a society small enough to be composed only of persons with identical and equal interests could be found or created, self-love would still persist. Conflict would be ruled out only if we also supposed that its members had vanquished self-love and lived wholly according to the dictates of self-sacrificing virtue" (259–60).

The crucial aspect of Madison's argument then, is not what seems to be a more pessimistic attitude towards the possibility of civic virtue, but its suggestion that an irreducible resistance to "self-

5. *Spirit*, Book 4, chs. 5 and 3.

sacrificing virtue" might itself correspond to something politically valuable. The aim of the Federalist project as he sees it, after all, is not simply to get rid of faction; it is "To secure the public good and private rights against the danger of such a faction, *and at the same time* to preserve the spirit and the form of popular government" (125, emphasis added). "Liberty is to faction," Madison continued, "what air is to fire, an aliment without which it instantly expires." Madison seems here to suggest that just as number and social complexity guard against the destructive aspects of faction, so the tendency to faction bears an integral relationship to the "spirit" of popular government. In Madisonian political philosophy, in other words, the spirit of democratic politics is indissociable from an originary non-self-identity of the political subject.[6] It is not the tension between a disruptive "self-love" and virtuous citizenship that defines Madison's political subject; rather, it is the curious tension marked within the concept of "self-love" itself: the splitting that occurs within the unit of the citizen, between, in Madison's formulation, a self that loves and the self that that self loves.[7] Selfhood, indeed, would be produced as the object of a disembodied affection. "Self-love" does not merely name an impulse at odds with love of nation, state or the common good; it names a constitutive disjunction in the self, a "latent" factionalism. "Self-love" is one way of naming that which ambiguates the singularity of the individual as source of political authority, wisdom, and virtue.[8] If there is a profound sense of the unknowability of "one another's hearts" (to use Wood's phrase) in the post-revolutionary United States, the *Federalist* (and James Madison in particular) suggests that this unknowability may be constitutive of both the Republican State and the state of the individual. The Constitutional citizen, is a secret to himself; he is, first and foremost, "secreted."[9]

6. I think it would be possible to show that it is this primary self-difference at work in Madison's theory that is recognized as "blockage" in his theory of the constitutional state by such scholars as Robert Dahl. See Dahl's *A Preface to Democratic Theory* (Chicago: University of Chicago Press, 1956).

7. One might also consider here Madison's remarks on irreducible "sources of . . . obscurity" in the domains of language and the natural sciences in the fascinating (and very un-Hamiltonian) *Federalist #37* (245).

8. This ambiguated singularity of the source and recipient of political authority is registered in other ways in The *Federalist*. In arguing for the Constitution as a means of making National politics a popular politics, Hamilton writes of "the persons of the citizens—the only proper objects of government" (#15, 149). In paper number 39, Madison writes of Republican government as one which "derives all its powers directly or indirectly from the great body of the people" (255). As "object" *and* origin of political power, the people are registered here (and elsewhere) in strikingly awkward formulations: "the persons of the citizens" or "the great body of the people."

9. Franklin, of course, was a pioneer and master of the modern deployment of secret agency: his attempt to start a subscription library was only one democratic project that taught Franklin to "put myself as much as I could out of sight" in the proposing of the scheme. See *The Autobiography and Other Writings*, ed. with an Introduction by Kenneth Silverman (New York: Penguin, 1986) 87 and 131. With this in mind, one might want to address the suggestions that Franklin was a double agent during the Revolutionary war.

But why would one still want to defend this Madisonian theory of republicanism against the kind of argument proposed by Gordon Wood in his 1982 article? In the first place, to guard against a familiar yet worrying component of Wood's argument. Wood's albeit somewhat qualified assertion of the relationship between modern social complexity and the rise of conspiratorial modes of thinking shares too much with those theories of political organization that identify harmony with the tendency towards more localized, ultimately more homogenous social bodies. The sentimental allusion to the possibility of "knowing one another's hearts" signals (even if Wood would not want to be associated with it) a recognizable tendency to invoke figures of bodily union in any portrayal of the harmony of small groups. Theories of the incohesion of complex social organizations, in other words, need to guard against becoming theories of the essential cohesion of the body, of the identity between interest and bodily integrity or bodily relation, theories, in other words, of the political privilege of blood, family, and ethnicity. One of the effects of an attempt to rethink the positive social effects of an extended political space, made up of a multitude of interests (including those that Madison noted might seem to arise out of "accidental," "erroneous or ridiculous" grounds of difference)[1] is to disable the temptation towards theories of essential identity as the grounds for successful democratic government. And it is as a contribution to the disruption of this temptation that I want to invoke Madison's articulation of the self-different subject of "self-love," (and of "artificial" and "accidental" attachments) and the contentious Constitutional republic.

In *Common Sense* Thomas Paine wrote of "something exceedingly ridiculous in the composition of monarchy": "it first excludes a man from the means of information, yet empowers him to act in cases where the highest judgment is required. The state of a king shuts him from the world, yet the business of a king requires him to know it thoroughly; wherefore the different parts, unnaturally opposing and destroying each other, prove the whole character to be absurd and useless."[2] Paine here condemns monarchy's institutionalization of a rupture in the conversion of empirical knowledge into executive decision, a rupture that constitutes the absurdity (what was most often called the "arbitrariness") of the English monarch. But what Paine here calls the King's "different" and "unnaturally opposing parts" can also be seen to be at play in Madison's constitutional democracy. Paine's picture of the absurdity of monarchy is simultaneously an analysis of monarchy's power, its highly effective *spell*, and it is that power that the American Revolution, Madison's theory

---

1. See the letter to Jefferson, in Madison, *Papers*, 10, 213.
2. Thomas Paine, *Common Sense*, ed. Isaac Kramnick (New York: Penguin, 1988), 69.

suggests, wants to reconfigure for democracy. Hazarding a daring translation, Madison made precisely this point in his letter to Jefferson: *"Divide et impera,"* wrote Madison, "the reprobated axiom of tyranny, is under certain qualifications, the only policy, by which a republic can be administered on just principles" (Letter to Jefferson, 214). Madison's formulation recognizes, quite powerfully, that the divisiveness deployed by the tyrant sovereign is not to be destroyed and buried by democracy; rather, democracy will abrogate this power for the democratic state: it is the sovereign subject of democracy whose experience of power will be simultaneously an experience of self-division.[3]

I want, then, to suggest that the democratic subject, promised by the modern (American) Revolution has a new and vital relationship to secrecy. Perhaps the Revolution can even be said to have democratized secrecy, to have begun to deploy its constitutive relationship to the democratic subject, the citizen. If the "arbitrariness" of monarchical forms of government names a secret relation to reason at the source of political power, democracy, rather than simply abolishing this arbitrariness, this secrecy at the origin of political decision making, displaces it, re-inscribes it across a new topography of political legitimacy. The democratization of secrecy that is ambivalently marked in the political and literary discourse of the post-revolutionary period would consist not in the transfer of any particular property of secrecy—any particular secrets—but in an institutionalization of the definitive obscurity, the definitive non-self-identity, of the democratic subject of power, the obscurity that distances the citizen from him or herself in the act of political intervention. If the Federalist Constitution seems to betray the "spirit" of '76 and to succeed only in turning the "body politic into a specter," as Miller puts it, perhaps we need to reassess our understanding of the ontology (what Jacques Derrida might call the "hauntology") of the democratic subject.[4] Such a reassessment cannot avoid a detour through the ballot box.

3. Similarly, the concept of the division of powers will be translated under Constitutional Republicanism into a separation not designed to represent differences between classes of subjects but to institutionalize separation itself as a means to limit the possibility of representative tyranny. See J.G.A. Pocock, *Virtue, Commerce, and History: Essays on Political Thought and History Chiefly in the Eighteenth Century* (Cambridge: Cambridge University Press, 1985). Pocock writes: "[separation of powers] ensured that the representatives could not corruptly consolidate themselves to monopoize the government. We have seen how separation of powers emerged with conjoint sovereignty to give parliamentary monarchy its republican shadow; in this way too the oppositions of eighteenth-century Britain left their legacy to the American republic" (271). It is for its literary exploration of precisely these kind of "shadows" and monarchic "legacies" that Brown's work remains vital. Secrecy and separation are of course etymologically related ("Secret fr. L *Secretus,* past part, of *secernere* to separate": see *Webster's Third New International Dictionary of the English Language* [Springfield, Mass.: Merriam-Webster, 1986] 2052).
4. Jacques Derrida, *Specters of Marx: the State of the Debt, the Work of Mourning, and the New International* (New York: Routledge, 1994) 10.

2

One of the more visible ways in which the democratization of secrecy took place in the late-eighteenth century United States was through transformations in electoral practice. Robert Dinkin explains:

> by the end of the Revolutionary era, voting procedures had been substantially reformed. Many arbitrary practices had been eliminated. Elections had become more regular and frequent, representation in the legislature more just and equitable, polling places more numerous and accessible, and balloting more orderly and secret. While a few states still clung to some of their old ways, which limited popular participation and control, the majority of them had moved in a more democratic direction.[5]

These lines contain most of the key words we might associate with democracy: representation, justice, equity, accessibility, and popular participation. But in addition, and as if it were merely one more link in this revolutionary chain, Dinkin makes reference to secrecy. British precedent had determined that most elections in colonial America were held by the method of "viva voce," that is to say, voice vote. One of the democratic revolution's successes, however, was the institutionalization of a certain secrecy at the site of origin of democratic legitimation. The revolution in the name of the "people-out-of-doors" realized itself by giving its citizens an indoors, a ballot box, ultimately a voting booth.[6] Democracy gave the citizen a secret space where he could be alone with him (later her-) self.

Why was the secret ballot so essential to the progress of democracy? It's advocates pointed to the numerous practices of fraud associated with public voting: the use, for example, of bribes, threats and rewards. The secret ballot was necessary, it would seem, because voters were in danger of casting a vote that was not (in some way) their "true" vote.[7] The secrecy of the ballot box was necessary, it was suggested, to avoid the citizen's susceptibility to influence, his tendency to fail to voice his true opinion, his tendency to misrepresent himself. The fear generated by public voting was that the purity and

5. Robert J. Dinkin, *Voting in Revolutionary America: A Study of Elections in the Original Thirteen States, 1776–1789* (Westport, Connecticut: Greenwood Press, 1965) 106. A 1769 meeting in New York City "to protest the abuses of open voting and to advocate the secret ballot" was held, Williamson notes, "under the shadow of the Liberty Pole" (Williamson, 77–8).
6. What Madison might have called—as he did when referring to the citizen contemplating in private—the "closet" (see his letter to Thomas Jefferson, October 24, 1787 in *Papers*, 10, 213).
7. The anti-democratic dimension of dominant sentimental discourse in this period is given some focus here by critics of the secret ballot who defended the *viva voce* system for providing that, "every Elector is at Liberty to declare the Sentiments of his Heart publicly, which is the Glory of the British Constitution . . ." ("J.W., a Squinter on Public Affairs," *Connecticut Courant*, March 5, 1770. Quoted in Williamson, 42).

singularity of the citizen's desire, the originary and only legitimate desire of democratic politics, would be compromised by scheming individuals or interest groups. The secret ballot would preserve the democratic citizen from that which might cause him to betray his civic responsibility. In 1785, Madison told Caleb Wallace that "as to the mode of suffrage I lean strongly to that of the ballot, notwithstanding the objections which be against it.[8] With a rare flourish of (mixed) metaphor, Madison continued: "It appears to me to be the only radical cure for the Arts of Electioneering which poison the very fountain of Liberty. The States in which the Ballot has been the Standing mode are the only instances in which elections are tolerably chaste and those arts are in disgrace" (354).

But the secrecy of the secret ballot perhaps keeps another secret. The institutionalization of secret voting marks a revolutionary recognition: the "people," democracy's ultimate source of legitimacy, can only be found, democracy discovers, in the inaccessibility of the secret ballot; which is also to say, in writing, for in this period the term "secret ballot" is used interchangeably with the term "written ballot" in order to emphasize its distinction from the *viva voce* procedure. What the ballot's hinge also conceals (and thereby reveals) is the citizen's written relationship to himself, to his own political will.[9] The secret ballot restages in miniature, so to speak, every time a vote is cast, the drama of closed-door political origination that was the Philadelphia Convention. The insistent secrecy of the Constitutional Convention (and indeed of the procedures leading up to the Convention) is remarked in the secret performance of the citizen's elective authority.[1] The ballot box, site of the unseen and of the written, offers us an architecture of the democratic citizen's political subjectivity. In this closet, the doubled citizen of democracy (doubled by

8. Madison, *Papers*, 8, 354.
9. While Michael Warner's very influential *The Letters of the Republic: Publication and the Public Sphere in Eighteenth-Century America* (Cambridge, Mass.: Harvard University Press, 1990) argues for the interpretive importance of "print culture" for any understanding of late-eighteenth-century America, his argument frequently acknowledges that many of the features assigned to "Print" function just as pertinently when considered under the more general rubric of writing. Moreover, it is writing's relationship to secrecy that I find most interesting in Warner's claim that, "writing became the hinge between a delegitimizing revolutionary politics and a nonrevolutionary, already legal signification of the people; it *masked* the contradiction between the two" (104, my emphasis).
1. Jacques Derrida points out that for Rousseau in the *Contrat social*, "the instance of writing must be effaced to the point where a sovereign people *must not even write to itself*, its assemblies must meet spontaneously, without 'any formal summons'" (*Of Grammatology*, trans. Gayatri Chakravorty Spivak [Baltimore: Johns Hopkins University Press, 1976] 302. The intriguing introduction to Crèvecoeur's *Letters From an American Farmer* might be another place to look for figurations of the anxiety generated by writing in the new republic. The fictional author's hesitation upon being asked for a written account of life in the New World by his friend, the Abbé Raynal is fueled, in part, by his wife's opposition. "If thee persistest in being such a foolhardy man," she says, "for God's sake let it be kept a profound secret among us" (J. Hector St. John de Crèvecoeur, *Letters From an American Farmer and Sketches of Eighteenth-Century America*, ed. with an Introduction by Albert E. Stone [New York: Penguin, 1986] 47).

what Madison in Federalist #10 calls his "self-love," or by what Rousseau recognized as the citizen's status as both giver and receiver of
the law) sends himself an anonymous letter; with his secret, written vote, he envelops himself into the text of democracy.[2]

3

How does a Charles Brockden Brown character experience independence? Or, to give this question a more specifically political
inflection, how does Brown figure the transfer of power announced
by democratic revolution? I want to show how these questions cross
paths with a discussion of secrecy by taking a close look at Brown's
unfinished supplement to *Wieland*, "Memoirs of Carwin the Biloquist" (1798/1803–05). The story is narrated by the second son of
a smallholding farmer in pre-revolutionary rural Pennsylvania. Like
Edgar Huntly, another of Brown's impetuous protagonists, Carwin
stands to inherit little from his family, and his socio-economic uncertainty adds a degree of practical anxiety to what he himself calls
a "restless" and "unconquerable" curiosity.[3] "My attention," Carwin
tells us, "fastened upon everything mysterious or unknown" (247)
[183]. Carwin is at pains to distinguish himself from his "unenlightened" family. While his brother never progressed beyond learning
to sign his name or spell out a chapter in the bible, "my character,"
he insists, "was the reverse" (247) [183]. His brother's ideas "never
ranged beyond the sphere of his vision," while Carwin, the writer
and lover of books, possessed a "fancy [which] teemed with visions
of the future" (247) [183]. His father, not unpredictably, determines
to restrain Carwin's thirst for knowledge, and thus "the most vigilant
and jealous scrutiny was exerted" in an attempt to "keep me within . . .
limits" (247) [183]. Carwin's rebellious tendencies, then, take the
form of intellectual indulgences, indulgences that are often marked
by a tendency to exceed "the period assigned" for any of his father's
tasks. His story begins with just such an act of filial disobedience.

2. For Rousseau's analysis see the *Contrat social* in *Oeuvres complètes*, 4 vols., ed. B. Gag-
nebin and M. Raymond (Paris: Editions Gallimard, 1959–) 3: 351–470.
3. *Wieland and Memoirs of Carwin*, (Kent, Ohio: Kent State University Press, 1993), 247.
Brown began work on "Memoirs of Carwin" while *Wieland* was still in press, and Alexander Cowie has argued that "Memoirs of Carwin" was intended "as a sequel or an interpolated addition to *Wieland*." "It probably should not," he adds, "be read as a prologue"
("Historical Essay" in 1977 edition of *Wieland, and Memoirs of Carwin* [Kent State University Press] 337). Near the end of *Wieland*, Carwin makes reference to having sought
"retreat in the wilderness" from the wild events of *Wieland*, where he "might henceforth
employ myself in composing a faithful narrative of my actions." "I designed it," he adds,
"as my vindication from the aspersions that had rested on my character, and as a lesson to
mankind on the evils of credulity on the one hand, and of imposture on the other" (1977,
212) [158]. In the preface ("Advertisement") to *Wieland*, the author writes: "The memoirs
of Carwin alluded to at the conclusion of the work, will be published or suppressed
according to the reception which is given to the present attempt" (3) [5]. The story then
has the intriguing status of already-written and yet-to-come within the text of *Wieland*.

Carwin has been assigned to bring his Father's cattle home from a far pasture. Discovering that the cattle are gone, Carwin exercises his curiosity in an attempt to determine the cause of the broken fence through which the cows escaped. Recognizing that his first duty should have been to return with the news, an anxious Carwin gathers his thoughts. "I was terrified at the consequences of my delay," he recalls, "and sought with eagerness how they might be obviated. I asked myself if there were not a way back shorter than that by which I had come." (249) [184]. Thus, Carwin attempts to follow a short-cut home through uncharted territory. Carwin's strange career begins with this detour, this decision to follow a passage whose "practicability was to be known only by experiment" (249–250) [185][4].

Brown's famous preface to *Edgar Huntly* stressed the significance of the wilderness to his literary project, and "Memoirs of Carwin" provides another opportunity to test this significance. Brown's wilderness marks the site of the unwritten, the uncharted, the mazy and impassable. But as the site of new spatial and temporal possibilities, the wilderness also offers Carwin the possibility of both exceeding the period assigned for his task *and* arriving home in time; breaking his father's law yet remaining within the law. Carwin's short cut, in other words, represents another of Charles Brockden Brown's attempts to theorize the paradoxical movement of revolution. To traverse the "abrupt points" and "gloomy hollows" of this "unbeaten" terrain is to chart a supplement to the legal landscape, and thereby return to the father.

Following a familiar logic of the supplement, however, Carwin's detour through the wilderness generates further displacements. The unfamiliar landscape begins to unnerve him, and he falls prey to anachronistic trepidation. "By a defect common in everyone's education," he tells us, "goblins and specters were to me the objects of the most violent apprehensions" (250) [185]. Hence, Carwin feels the necessity to find another detour, a detour around his apprehension.[5] The "terrors," that the wilderness brings on, Carwin notes, can be "lessened by calling the attention away to some indifferent

4. Brown's story shares something, then, with contemporary stories of formative disobedience, notably Franklin's accounts of his quarrels with his father and brother in the *Autobiography* and Stephen Burroughs' story of petty theft and deception at the start of his "notorious" memoirs (Franklin, *Autobiography*, and Burroughs, *Memoirs of Stephen Burroughs* [Boston: Northeastern University Press, 1988]).
5. In fact, it is difficult to decide, finally, if the specters and goblins he is afraid of are not displaced indications of the disconcerting paradoxicality of Carwin's experimental detour: going into the wilderness in order to stay within the law. Something of this paradoxicality seems to be registered in Brown's own attitude towards the practice of law. His friend and biographer William Dunlap wrote that the young Brown gave up the profession his family had encouraged him to train for because "he could not reconcile it with his ideas of morality to become indiscriminately the defender of right or wrong; thereby intimating, if not asserting, that a man must, in the practice of the law,

object," and thus he begins to "amuse" himself by "hallowing as loud as organs of unusual compass and vigour would enable me" (250) [185]. Carwin utters "the words which chanced to occur to me," and thus repeats "in the shrill tones of a Mohock savage . . . 'Cow! cow! come home! home! . . .'" (250) [185]. Carwin imitates an Indian voice and thereby calls his attention away. His anxiety is placated by a practice of self- distraction that requires an accomplished artifice and an "indifferent object."

No sooner is he calmed, however, than Carwin is re-frightened, this time by the echo that reverberates from the rocks "which on either side towered aloft": "I was startled by this incident, and cast a fearful glance behind, to discover by whom it was uttered. The spot where I stood was buried in dusk, but the eminences were still invested with a luminous and vivid twilight. The speaker, however, was concealed from my view" (250) [185]. Boxed in by the towering rocks, Carwin hears himself again and for the first time, and the experience is both disturbing and thrilling. Hearing his *own* voice "at a distance . . . not uttered by another . . . but by myself," Carwin imagines a further possibility. "The idea of a distant voice, like my own," he recalls, "was intimately present to my fancy" (252) [187]; "To talk from a distance, and at the same time, in the accents of another, was the object of my endeavours, and this object . . . I finally obtained" (253) [188].[6] With this achievement, Carwin begins a new stage of his life. From this point on he will begin to plot his break from his father, a break that will finally take him to Europe and introduce him into the world of radical international politics.

But Carwin's discovery of his secret voice cannot be read simply as the culmination of an act of (revolutionary) resistance to authority. Certainly, Carwin discovers his voice when he is both temporally and spatially (geographically) outside the law: he has entered the Pennsylvania wilderness that *Edgar Huntly*, and indeed Carwin's "chance" imitation, marks as Indian territory, while under the threat of punishment for having exceeded the designated time for his task. But it is equally true to say that Carwin discovers his voice in the course of an attempt to return to legitimacy and retrospec-

---

not only deviate from morality, but become the champion of injustice" (William Dunlap, *The Life of Charles Brockden Brown* [Philadelphia: James P. Parke, 1815] 40).

6. The importance of the "Mohock" reference in this passage deserves its own study. The "indifference" of this choice in the mediation of Carwin's revolutionary anxiety could be interestingly compared with, for example, the use of Indian imitation in the Boston tea party and the false alibi of Indian insurgency used by the Confederate government to justify sending financial aid to those attempting to suppress Shay's rebellion, the symbolic exploitation of Native Americans in patriotic poems and plays, the revolutionary arrogation of Chief Logan's speech to the British, etc. The figure of the Native American emerges here as a particularly economic revolutionary device. While helping to mask acts of unsettling violence, the appropriated Indian also registers, once again, the Revolution's yearning for an origin "out of doors."

tively nullify his disobedience. If, as I am suggesting, Carwin's narrative recounts an origin story for his independence, it does so by suggesting that independent subjectivity coincides with an apparently impossible temporal and spatial position. This subject founds itself in the supplement of legitimacy, in an outside that is also an inside, both too late and in time. And, of course, in secret.

Brown's interest in this scene, in other words, can be explained by noting its correspondence with one way of describing the success of the American political revolution.[7] Michael Warner has recently written of the new republic's need to find a "hinge" between "a delegitimizing revolutionary politics and a nonrevolutionary, already legal signification of the people" (104). For Warner, this "hinge" was to be found in the unique efficacy of print: its structural anonymity "masked the contradiction" (104). For this reason, Benjamin Franklin becomes for Warner (as for others) an exemplary figure in any account of the American Revolution. Franklin's recognition of the efficaciousness of print's anonymity marked his biography as proto-revolutionary: "Franklin's career," writes Warner, "is preeminently that of the republican man of letters, the citizen of print" (77). Franklin succeeded in performing the role of republican statesman; he was able to "embody representational legitimacy," Warner suggests, by making a career out of the "involution of republicanism and print" (73). Given this paradigm, Brown's pastoral narrative would seem to be almost perversely archaic. What could be further from the cultural context of the modern American revolutionary than Carwin's gloomy wilderness? What could be more anathema to the theory of the revolution's indebtedness to print anonymity, than a tale of vocal (theatrical?) prowess?

In fact, Carwin's story is a uniquely distorted version of the kind of story that identifies the achievement of independence with the discovery of one's own voice. This latter position has been given renewed attention in recent years, in part as a way of countering the attention neo-Hebermasians have given to late-eighteenth century print culture.[8] Christopher Looby, for example, writes of a "distinct countercurrent in the literature of the period that valorizes the grain of the voice in addition to, or instead of, the silence of print" (3). He continues: "Precisely because the new nation's self-image was characterized by its difference from a traditional (quasi-natural) conception of the nation, indeed by the conscious recognition of its historical

7. See Fliegelman, *Prodigals and Pilgrims*.
8. On the importance of the voice and public speaking in Revolutionary America, see Jay Fliegelman, *Declaring Independence: Jefferson, Natural Language, and the Culture of Performance* (Stanford: Stanford University Press, 1993), and Christopher Looby, *Voicing America: Language, Literary Form, and the Origins of the United States* (Chicago: University of Chicago Press, 1996).

contingency that was produced by the abrupt performativity of its inception, vocal utterance has served, in telling instances, as a privileged figure for the making of the United States" (3–4). Carwin's "biloquism," however, fails to fall comfortably into either an oratorical theory of revolutionary assertion or a print-based civic interpretation. Rather, his othered voice, the voice of disembodiment and imitative repetition, effectively challenges the opposition between print anonymity and vocal utterance that would seem to dominate these recent discussions. Carwin discovers that the individualizing properties of voice are indissociable from the masking, self-distancing properties of what Michael Warner calls "writing's unrestricted dissemination" (40). Carwin's secret is not just that his voice comes to him as an originary appropriation of the native American's voice (the Mohock's cry), but that this homeless voice simultaneously produces him as the independent subject of appropriation.

Biloquism's oddity ought to remind us that an investment in the anonymity of print discourse and in the individualizing dimensions of oratory are mutually determining investments. It should not be surprising that the Revolutionary period can be read as the site of both an expanded print sphere and a vital oratorical culture. The effective importance of an anonymous intervention can only be measured against the figure of the public speaker and vice versa. What Carwin and the discourse of the revolutionary period give us to consider is the possibility that democratic transformation crucially extended the field of *political* intervention, which is to say the field of interventions in the name of interests or positions that can only ever be *represented*. To participate in democracy's expansion is to find one's voice as a voice of representation. Following the logic of the ballot box, the democratic citizen, the member of the "people out of doors," necessarily and inevitably conceals himself into political power. The impossible, or aporetic space and time of Carwin's revolution gives Carwin both a voice and a secret and the two are mutually dependent on one another. The wilderness, in other words, the dusky space in which Carwin finds himself surrounded, the place where he tries to placate anachronistic and superstitious fears, the place where as he disobeys he nevertheless seeks re-legitimation, this wilderness that Brown chose to replace the castles of the tired European gothic novel is also a defamiliarizing figuration of that most banal of democratic constructions: the ballot box.

4

The second part of "Carwin the Biloquist" follows the young man's precarious independence as it is put to the test in the form of an encounter with a radical, international political organization. After a series of botched attempts to use his biloquism to advantage, he is

taken under the wing of a wealthy Irishman named Ludloe who
takes Carwin with him when he returns to the old world.[9] Carwin's
encounter with Ludloe brings the singularly secretive Carwin up
against an insistently clandestine political movement. While the
story refuses to be explicit about the exact nature of Ludloe's or his
sect's politics, we are encouraged to hear echoes of Rousseau and
particularly Godwin in Ludloe's pronunciations. The sect holds, for
example, that "the absurd and unequal distribution of power and
property gave birth to poverty and riches, and these were the source
of luxury and crimes" (276) [206]. "Man," Ludloe tells Carwin, "is
the creature of circumstances . . . his progress has been stopped by
the artificial impediment of government" (276) [207]. In the utopian community that the sect hopes to found, "justice should be
universally understood and practised; the interest of the whole and
of the individual should be seen by all to be the same" (277) [207].[1]
More importantly, perhaps, Ludloe's organization calls to mind the
movements that attracted the period's most profound political anxieties (the Jacobins, Illuminati and freemasons). Finally, however, all
the sect's political conviction seems to pale in comparison to its primary preoccupation with secrecy. Ludloe, who wants to induct Carwin into the sect, begins by passing on a series of solemn injunctions.
He tells Carwin: "A number of persons are leagued together for an
end of some moment . . . Among the conditions of their alliance are
mutual fidelity and secrecy . . . Their existence depends on this: their
existence is known only to themselves. This secrecy must be obtained
by all the means which are possible." (281) [210]. "Compared with
this task," Ludloe warns Carwin, "the task of inviolable secrecy, all
others are easy" (282) [211]. Well, all others except one: the pro-
spective member must also "disclose every fact in his history, and
every secret of his heart" (284) [212]. And "if secrecy were difficult
to practise," remarks Carwin, "sincerity, in that degree in which it
was here demanded, was a task infinitely more arduous . . . Any
particle of reserve or duplicity would cost me my life" (284) [213].
Ludloe explains that a member may decide to leave the fraternity,
but if he chooses to do so he must maintain his commitment to its
absolute secrecy: "Admit not even a doubt as to the propriety of hiding [the secret of the society] from all the world," he warns, "There

9. Thus when Brown brings Carwin to bear on the young Americans in *Wieland*, he gives
   a twist to the popular, xenophobic identification of threats to the new Nation with
   European corruption: what the United States fears and thrills to, Brown's work suggests, is an alienated return of their revolutionary selves.
1. One could dwell here on the Godwinian and other motifs in Ludloe's philosophy. For
   example, his commitment to the justice of "spontaneity," his antipathy towards con-
   tracts and promises, his veneration of "sincerity," and his commitment to a "new model
   of society" grounded in rational enquiry. His library also contains "Aristotle's republic,
   the political romances of sir Thomas Moore, Harrington, and Hume" and other works
   on "political economy and legislation," in all of which Ludloe found "nothing but error
   and absurdity" (298) [223].

are eyes who will discern this doubt amidst the closest folds of your heart, and your life will instantly be sacrificed" (282) [211].

The double imperative of Ludloe's sect, to remain secret yet hold no secrets from one another, underlines the extent to which a certain commitment to secrecy corresponds to a profound unease about secrets.[2] The need to keep its existence secret from the outside world that the sect will defend to the death, is protected in the name of a society that will have banished secrets forever: "the interest of the whole and of the individual should be seen by all to be the same" (277) [207].

But Carwin resists. He holds onto his secret. Moreover, his resistance to Ludloe's sect is made not in the name of an alternative philosophy, but under the sway of what he calls a "perverse" attachment to his own secret, his defining secrecy. "My character had been, in some degree, modelled by the faculty which I possessed," he remarks, and "by some fatal obstinacy" he resolves to conceal it from Ludloe (297) [223]. This attachment, he suggests, follows "no conceivable reason" (304) [229]. It is as if in holding on to his secret, and to the secret of his "inconceivable reason" (what Madison might have called his "accidental attachment") Carwin holds on to himself, or to the possibility of a self. His secret produces him as a (independent) subject.

In Carwin and Ludloe, then, Brown brings together two different relationships to secrecy, two different ways of conceiving secrecy. Ludloe's resistance to secrecy, his sect's ethics of disclosure, participates in what I would call a revolutionary sentimentality. Secrecy, in this scheme of things, marks the line of a border that protects the sanctity of an enlightened community, a community in which the particular and the general are no longer distinguishable. But Brown's portrayal of Ludloe's sect would lead us to suspect that the assertion of this reconciliation coincides with the invocation of a border, a border whose secret policing finally shares too much in common with the invisible borders of ethnic separation. Ludloe's politics rejects secrecy as a constitutive component of its individual members by asserting that they are all one, as if they are all of one blood (and the familial model is referenced in the sect's fraternal and patriarchal invocations of brotherhood and inheritance). To share a secret is to belong, to be outside is not to share the secret and the maintenance of this distinction would appear to demand all the sect's attention. In his typically too quick, yet nevertheless unique portrait of Ludloe's political philosophy, Brown gives us a late-eighteenth-century

---

2. And along with secrets, the sect would do away with the various arts of delusion (rhetorical persuasion) that are, not surprisingly, associated with the "seductive and bewitching powers of women" (292) [219].

critique of Godwinian democratic theory's troubled relationship to secrecy.

Carwin, on the other hand, remains the subject of the border he crossed at the start of his story. I want to claim Carwin as an insistently *democratic* subject because of his attachment both to his enlightenment faith in the "empire of reason" *and* to his own inscrutability, his "own" surprising voice. Brown's young American approaches independence by participating in the democratic displacement of monarchic arbitrariness. The King's defining unreasonableness becomes the citizen's inscrutability, his own difference from reason in the exercise of power as secrecy, power as nonknowledge. In *Wieland* Carwin will be repeatedly invoked as an author figure, a dramatist and plotter, an inventor of characters and of other people's lives, he who casts (characters, voices, spells), and it is also this relation to the literary, to fiction with all its attendant investments in authorial obfuscation that I would contend marks a post-revolutionary, democratic subjectivity. Distancing himself from himself in the moment of revolution, Carwin tricks himself into independence. The secret that Carwin, like the ballot box, conceals for us is the secret of the citizen's enveloped self.

NANCY RUTTENBURG

[The Voice of the People in *Wieland* and *Memoirs of Carwin*]†

* * * Theodore Wieland is the enlightened and brilliant scion of a melancholic religious enthusiast and radical antinomian, a German immigrant to America by way of England. His untimely and mysterious death in Wieland's childhood, apparently by spontaneous combustion, is connected in family legend to his conviction that he would suffer for having failed to obey divine commands whose import he never divulges. For his "thrilling melancholy," the younger Wieland resembles his father; in other respects, he seems largely to have distanced himself from his father's religious enthusiasm as well as his fate, for although he shared his father's thoughts insofar as "[m]oral necessity, and calvinistic inspiration, were the

---

† From *Democratic Personality: Popular Voice and the Trial of American Authorship* (Stanford, CA: Stanford University Press, 1998), pp. 212–58. Copyright © 1998 by the Board of Trustees of the Leland Stanford Jr. University. All rights reserved. Used with the permission of Stanford University Press, www.sup.org. The author's parenthetical citations refer to the Penguin Classics edition, ed. Jay Fliegelman (1991). Page numbers in square brackets refer to this Norton Critical Edition.

props on which [he] thought proper to repose," yet his "mind . . . was enriched by science, and embellished with literature" (25, 28, 26) [23, 25, 21]. As a mark of this difference, Wieland, a devotee of Cicero, converts the gazebo in which his father solitarily worshiped his god and later died his violent death into a neoclassical "temple" where he and his only associates—a self-styled "congregation" of childhood playmates composed of his wife Catharine, her brother and his closest friend Pleyel, and his devoted sister Clara—carry on a daily round of enlightened and strictly "theoretical" conversation (17, 23) [17, 19]. This pleasant routine, the privilege of the agriculturalist whose "fortune exempted him from the necessity of personal labour," remains unimpaired until Wieland hears what he takes to be the voice of God commanding him to prove his religious faith by sacrificing his wife, his four children, his foster daughter, and his beloved Clara, who alone escapes to narrate the tale (23) [24]. In the novel's penultimate scene, Wieland, having escaped from prison, has cornered Clara in her bedroom and is about to kill her when yet another voice imperiously informs him that he had been mistaken in the aural representation to which he had uncritically consented and had thus killed in error. In response, he commits suicide with his sister's penknife which she, preparing to wield it against her brother in self-defense, has just dropped. Before Wieland heard the voice urging him to murder, other members of the "congregation" had heard mysterious voices in and around their isolated compound whose import they tirelessly debate and which slowly erode their Lockean faith in the epistemological adequacy of visible reality to inform the understanding and thus the will. As it turns out, all of these voices, with the possible exception of the murderous voice of God that only Wieland hears, were generated unbeknownst to them by a stranger who from "curiosity" they had recently admitted into their exclusive circle, an itinerant "rustic," the fantastically eloquent (and inaptly named) Frank Carwin (81) [57].

* * *

Considering the literally unspeakable isolation to which they all eventually succumb, the characters of *Wieland* are so incestuously intimate before the arrival of Carwin, their doubling (as in each of Brown's novels) is so relentless and their emotional attachments so hyperbolic, that for clarity's sweet sake (apologies to Carwin) the novel is best approached with reference to the concept of artistic space.[1] The Mettingen estate in which the main action of the novel

1. The concept of artistic space is elaborated by Iurii M. Lotman in "Problema khudo-zhestvennogo prostranstva v proze Gogolia" (The problem of artistic space in the prose of Gogol). Interestingly, Lotman's analysis of Gogol's representation of the estate, or "the inside world," in his story "The Old-fashioned Landowners" recalls Brown's repre-

occurs, including its immediate prehistory (the elder Wieland's death as Clara narrates it), offers a literary representation of the space beyond formal observance—the spectral space, the "third ontological domain," the "interval between"—that religious conservatives and, before them, spectral evidence theorists had found so troubling to imagine.[2] Chauncy had identified the space beyond formal observance with religious enthusiasm and its accompanying malaise, a pathological melancholy. As such, it was the site not only of intellectual febrility but of spiritual blindness and deafness, the result of an uncharitable and ultimately blasphemous refusal to concede the epistemological adequacy of the visible world for discovering invisible realities and, at the same time, an inability to distinguish legitimate from illegitimate inner voices. It was the sphere in which the religious itinerants, "disorderly walkers of unpeaceable froward and turbulent Spirits," ranged at will, unauthorized individuals with apparently unbounded authority over "the mob," but with no discernable or stable identity.[3] It was the space of seduction in which "*silly Women*" surrendered their integrity to the unscrupulous changeling and became seducers in turn.[4] It was the space given over to the unnatural domination of the better by the vulgar classes and was thus identified as the revolutionary site dedicated to the overturning of established values and meanings. For spectral evidence theorists (for whom the conservatives of the Great Awakening, as rationalists, had little respect), the spectral realm or space beyond formal observance was likewise associated with the radical calling into question of the visible world, with a revolutionary power of dissemblance, with the menacing proliferation of the representational possibilities of individual personality, and with transgressions of sacrosanct boundaries. The fear latent in the conservative abhorrence of enthusiasm as it recapitulated the earlier fear of spectrality was that it promoted a state of visible invisibility associated with a vocal-characterological power of misrepresentation that corrupted virtue, understood as the integrity of visible character and invisible identity, by destroying the

---

sentation of Mettingen: "The inside world is achronic. On all sides, it is isolated; it has no direction; and nothing occurs within it. Actions refer neither to the past nor to the present, but represent multiple repetitions of one and the same thing. . . . Unchangingness is a property of . . . inside space, and change is possible only as the catastrophic destruction of this space" (428, 429, my translation). Lotman's analysis is also relevant for his focus upon "the path" versus "the road," an opposition whose moral valence approaches Brown's "mazy path" versus the "blissful" or "forth-right path." For an analysis of doubling and its relation to coincidence, see Norman S. Grabo, *The Coincidental Art of Charles Brockden Brown*. See also Roland Hagenbüchle, "American Literature and the Nineteenth-Century Crisis in Epistemology," pp. 138–51, and William J. Scheick, "The Problem of Origination in Brown's *Ormond*."

2. On the "third ontological domain," see Lorraine Daston, "Marvelous Facts," p. 99.
3. Bartlett, *False and Seducing Teachers*, p. 42.
4. Bartlett, *False and Seducing Teachers*, p. 29; cf. pp. 38–49.

common ground of consent to legitimate authority through the corruption of the individual mind.

* * *

Carwin, then, acts as the facilitator of a crisis of credibility that
reaches a critical stage soon after he materializes and that will deci-
mate the congregation in one forty-eight-hour period during which
Wieland will hear and act upon the voice urging him to murder and
Pleyel will abandon Mettingen in a fury, convinced that Clara, whom
he has known all his life, is the "most specious, and most profligate
of women" (119) [81]. Arguably, it is the latter, relatively minor and,
indeed, almost comic delusion that allows the former to play itself
out: had Pleyel remained on the grounds, it is difficult to imagine
how Wieland would have carried out the murders of Catharine and
their children. Moreover, Pleyel's jealous abdication draws Clara to
his home in the city in hopes of vindicating herself from his suspicions of her infidelity, a withdrawal that permits a failure of observation which also gives Wieland free scope. Pleyel's pique is important,
too, in that the trial of Clara's character that he stages provides the
immediate context for her next encounter with Carwin as well as
her (and our) discovery of the bodies of Wieland's victims, and thus
testifies to the transformation "of a mind the most luminous and
penetrating that ever dignified the human form" (175) [117].

* * *

The trial and her subsequent stopover at her aunt's home mark the
first time in the novel that Clara has ventured outside of Mettingen
which, up until Carwin's accession and Pleyel's abandonment, had
provided her with everything she needed to sustain her self-image
in her own eyes and the eyes of her closest friends. In the scene in
which she receives Carwin's written invitation to return to her home,
she is stranded outside its sustaining environment, denied an old
friend's belief in the integrity of her visible character, abandoned to
her own devices and in a state of inner turmoil. She thus realizes
that to return to Mettingen will be to descend into the fearful pit
toward which Wieland had beckoned her, Carwin enticed her, and
Pleyel traced her. She decides to do so less because the power of the
plot or the plotter is driving her there, but because only there can
she affirm and even consecrate the destruction of her visible character accomplished during her trial, discard the principles by which
she had always governed herself, and consent to die to her former
integrity in order to reemerge as the poet and commence her "deadly
toils" (164) [110]. * * * Clara will expose and condemn the machinations of the disembodied author by becoming one herself and in
the penultimate scene of the book will compel Carwin to undertake

precisely the reversal of this action, the ventriloquistic repudiation of ventriloquism. By unwittingly refuting Pleyel's portrait of her as one for whom language was merely ornamental, Clara anticipates her transformation into an author who intends to take an active role in a plot already launched by identifying and then wresting control from the elusive plotter. It is crucial to explore this process by which she redefines herself as counterplotter rather than hapless character: her redefinition will provide the immediate context for the novelistic presentation of her brother's parallel transformation into a murderer, as well as for the peculiarities of that presentation.

Clara's resurrection in the novel as a counterplotter who intends at all costs to expose and thus to eliminate the author of evil is not accomplished instantaneously upon her decision to return to Mettingen and confront Carwin in her bedroom. Instead, it occurs in stages that correspond with the two posttrial returns she will make to her bedroom, separated by an interval of delirium and then recovery. The bipartite pattern of return, with its interval of psychological disintegration, is thus structured like the trial itself: the specter of character assassination is in this way always present, a consideration that explains Clara's obsession with vindication. Clara's bedroom, then, the "stage," she reflects, "on which that enemy of man shewed himself for a moment unmasked," emerges as the drastically attenuated space within which the remainder of the action will occur—the deadly struggle between Clara, Carwin, and Wieland to control the unfolding of events (220) [144]. As the former symbol of her independence, her bodily integrity, and her principled rejection of the irrational, as well as the site of her (private) writing, Clara's bedroom is reconfigured by Carwin's summons to become the pit which has all along threatened her with engulfment and effacement (the literal fate of Wieland's favorite child, his foster daughter) and within which she must now vindicate herself by reclaiming it as her own domain. On her first return, she discovers her sister-in-law's body (and is then taken by people who arrive on the scene to Wieland's home to view the bodies of his five children). On the second occasion, she returns to collect and destroy her journal before departing with her uncle for Europe, and encounters there for the last time both Carwin, who finally confesses his role in the demise of Mettingen, and Wieland, who finally attempts his long-intended murder of Clara. Each of the two returns coincides with the death of a member of the original circle, first Catharine and then Wieland; in the second and final return Clara both witnesses and supervises the elimination of Wieland and Carwin as her rival authors. The complex orchestration of each return suggests that they be individually examined as stages in Clara's developing determination to wrest authorial power—both the power to plot and the power to determine the significance of events—from Carwin and, to the degree he wields it, her brother, and thus to transcend the limitations of her role as exemplary character even as she assiduously claims for herself the victim's part.

What I am calling Clara's first return, however, is itself a considerably complex event that occurs as the second in a sequence of three scenes so similar in structure, time, and locale that they appear to constitute an oddity or defect within the plotting of *Wieland*, a stutter or apparent refusal of the plot to advance, almost a slippage of the characterological doubling so prevalent in the novel into the domain of plot. The first scene in the sequence is Clara's pretrial encounter with the disembodied voice and then, because she disregards its warning, with Carwin in her closet; this event becomes part of the fabric of misrepresentation within which Pleyel is entangled only to extricate himself by defecting from novelistic space altogether. This scene bears significant resemblances to what occurs the next evening (the second scene; the first return), when Clara returns to her house at Carwin's summons and encounters the disembodied voice as she is ascending the staircase to her room. Because she again disregards its warning, even though she describes having done so the night before as "imbecility" and "infatuation," she is led to discover Catharine's ravished and strangled body upon her bed: thus is Catharine eliminated from the novel (160) [107–8]. The third scene in this sequence occurs in chronological time between the first and second scenes, shortly before Clara's return to her house. It features Wieland's decisive encounter with a disembodied voice as he is ascending the staircase to Clara's room which will lead him to lure Catharine to Clara's house moments later, immediately before Clara's return, in order to murder her. Aside from the prominent role played by the disembodied voice in these scenes, they are further connected by the antinomian desire explicitly articulated by both Clara and Wieland to see and be unambiguously guided by the invisible speaker they both regard as "divine." This desire is fulfilled in the last two scenes when they independently see from the staircase leading up to Clara's bedroom a "fiery visage" that gives off significant light and which they apprehend in the act of speaking (224) [147]. In the first, pretrial scene, although Clara strives but fails to discern the speaker, she is granted a partial or "toke[n]" confirmation of what Cotton Mather had called "the *Reality of Invisibles*" (98).[5] Her meditations upon this shadowy revelation of "the genius of [her] birth" (108) [74], as well as the ambient circumstances of her occluded vision, forcefully recall Nathaniel Hawthorne's self-depiction at the conclusion of the "Custom-House" sketch in which he figures his own transformation into a writer. A closer look at these intra- and intertextual echoes

5. Cotton Mather, *Diary*, 1:23.

may help supplement our understanding of the authorial role that Clara determines to assume (and, as an essential feature of her self-representation, determinedly repudiates) following Pleyel's trial of her integrity in which the authority and legitimacy of her visible character is categorically denied.

Although Clara fears a repetition of the previous night's terror if she returns to her room to grant Carwin a midnight interview, two significant differences between the first (pretrial) and the second (posttrial) scenes deserve notice: the gratification in the second scene of the antinomian desire to see and be guided by her angel that she expresses and is denied in the first scene; and the conversion of her penknife from an instrument of self-destruction in the first scene to an instrument of self-defense in the second. In the first scene, Clara arms herself with her penknife not to "plunge it into the heart of my ravisher," as she concedes her reader may assume, but to commit suicide and thus "to baffle my assailant, and prevent the crime by destroying myself" (111) [76–77]. Although she had always considered such an expedient to be a particularly abhorrent species of female cowardice, when the time came to act offensively she admits that it did not "once occu[r] to me to use [the penknife] as an instrument of direct defense" (111) [77]. In the second scene, she arms herself in advance with the penknife offensively, to serve as "my safeguard and avenger" in order to fight to the death: "The assailant shall perish, or myself shall fall" (166) [111]. As she envisions it, the assailant shall perish by becoming visible: "I would see this man," Clara continues, clutching the penknife, "in spite of all impediments; ere I died, I would see his face, and summon him to penitence and retribution; no matter at what cost an interview was purchased" (167) [111]. The seizing of her penknife in the second scene is clearly connected, then, not with her earlier determination to see her beneficent angel, whose airy presence is sporadic and even irrelevant (Clara survives even though she disregards his warnings) and whose absence may signify, as Clara wryly points out upon her return, either the absence of danger or simply his own absence from the scene of danger (167) [111]. Rather, in seizing the penknife as she approaches her dark house she determines to see "this man," "the grand deceiver; the author of this black conspiracy; the intelligence that governed in this storm"; and having seen this impenetrable intelligence, she intends to convert him, by means of her weapon and his mortality, to an "object . . . on which we may pour out our indignation and our vengeance" (167, 217) [111, 142].

As it signifies a reversal of her previously held "principles" and "motives," the conversion of the penknife into a weapon of aggression and knowledge rather than self-destruction signifies a reversal of her pretrial antinomian desire to see transcendent authority. In the second scene, she searches for the revelation not of the divine will in order to obey it, as Wieland continues to do, but of the author's plot in order to appropriate it.[6] On the night before her trial, as she stood suspended in her moonlit room between her closed closet door and the disembodied speaker's shrieked warning against opening it, she had awaited precisely the visual confirmation of invisible realities she would receive the next night, a confirmation which we may designate the quintessential spectral moment when the invisible emerges momentarily into visibility. Recalling Mather at the bedside of his possessed houseguests, Clara had been struggling to pierce the moonlit emptiness of her room with "penetrating glances" in a desperate attempt to see her invisible advocate, "[h]e that hitherto refused to be seen" (98) [68]. But instead of observing "distinguishable" form, she observes only that the effect of the moonlight was to erode the "means by which we are able to distinguish a substance from a shadow, a reality from the phantom of a dream" (98, 99) [68]:

> Solitude imposes least restraint upon the fancy. Dark is less fertile of images than the feeble lustre of the moon. I was alone, and the walls were chequered by shadowy forms. As the moon passed behind a cloud and emerged, these shadows seemed to be endowed with life, and to move. The apartment was open to the breeze, and the curtain was occasionally blown from its ordinary position. This motion was not unaccompanied with sound. I failed not to snatch a look, and to listen when this motion and this sound occurred. My belief that my monitor was posted near, was strong, and instantly converted these appearances to tokens of his presence, and yet I could discern nothing. (98) [68]

Her strong belief in the presence of her "monitor" in the first scene sustains only a partial conversion to visibility: absence yields to tokens of presence, but not to presence itself.

On the next night, after her disastrous meeting with Pleyel, poised to ascend her dark staircase, penknife at the ready, Clara once again hears the anticipated "divine injunction" to halt (cf. 160) [108]. The disarticulating shock of the sound causes her to turn her head in

6. Cf. Fussell, "*Wieland*," who sees Brown as having written "a diatribe against writing" for, if nothing else, writing may be seen as having instigated the American Revolution which then placed upon Brown the imperative to write the new nation. However, "within that context he split the indictment in order to show an irresponsible writer wreaking havoc and wretchedness on a hapless populace while quite another kind of writer—his kind—was quietly restoring a semblance of reason and peace to such of those people as chanced to survive. *Wieland* is a furious contest between villainous confused Carwin and our doughty daughter of the American Revolution, Clara Wieland, Brown's narrator. Clara wins, but the price of her victory is exile. Having finished her novel, she removes to Europe, never more to confront the monstrosity of these States" (172–73).

time to see a "head thrust and drawn back" very swiftly in the act of utterance: thus is her previous night's desire to see the divine monitor unexpectedly gratified.[7] "[T]he immediate conviction was," Clara explains, recalling again Mather's awed testimony, at a moment equally fraught, to the materialization from invisibility of a spectral iron spindle and a scrap of sheet, "that thus much of a form, ordinarily invisible, had been unshrouded" (168) [112]. The materialization of her spectral monitor, however, does not cause Clara to reverse her steps as it commands her to do. Disregarding its shrieked admonition as she had the previous evening, she hastens forward to "the verge of the same gulf" that had plagued her since her summerhouse nightmare and is amazed at her audacity given this miraculous materialization of divine beneficence. "Was it possible for me not to obey?" Clara asks incredulously. "Was I capable of holding on in the same perilous career? Yes. Even of this I was capable!" (169) [113]. The question here is less what possessed Clara to disobey, but rather, given her possession of the penknife and her unwillingness to relinquish it even at a divine behest, what authorial model (that is, what model of self-authorization) does her act of disobedience, undertaken despite the gratification of her antinomian wish of the evening before for direct communion and guidance, enact?

Toward the conclusion of the "Custom-House" sketch that introduces *The Scarlet Letter* (1850), Hawthorne portrays himself similarly (albeit more sanguinely than Clara in the first scene) contemplating the effects of moonlight upon the solitary observer in a darkened and familiar room. His reflections, however, are intended to suggest that the call to authorship occurs precisely in this environment, announced by presences only partially realized rather than either fully materialized or wholly spiritualized. Like Clara, Hawthorne recognizes the moonlit room to be a mediate space between substance and shadow, "a neutral territory, somewhere between the real world and fairy-land, where the Actual and the Imaginary may meet, and each imbue itself with the nature of the other." As Clara remarks upon the imagistic fertility of this territory, Hawthorne explicitly associates it with literary creation by representing himself awaiting within its bounds the accomplishment of two simultaneous and interdependent transformations. The transformation of the government bureaucrat into the writer of romance occurs when the scarlet letter, which the bureaucrat had found buried in the dust of the Salem customhouse attic, is transformed from a fossilized metonymy into narrative. This resurrection and renewal of the unsignifying remainder of

---

7. I use the adjective "disarticulating" to convey Clara's description of the impact the disembodied voice has upon her body: "It appeared to cut asunder the fibres of my brain, and rack every joint with agony" (97) [67].

a historically spent plot occurs when the bureaucrat, waiting patiently in the moonlight, succeeds in "pictur[ing] forth" from the shadows cast in "the little domestic scenery of the well-known apartment" those spectral presences who embody the fullness of its symbolic trajectory: the requisite act of picturing forth proposes that the resurrection Hawthorne contemplates is less an affair of the resurrected body than of the resurrector's "intellect." Although Walt Whitman would more unambiguously insist on the simultaneous coming-into-being of poet and poem, Hawthorne in this self-portrait refrains from representing himself as the creator of his imaginary visitors. He portrays himself rather as one who awaits alone, in the darkness, the miraculous and mundane realization of a double impossibility—the spiritualized materialization of independent subjects, bearers of the letter's symbolic meanings, who are yet the products of his intellect. This stance represents a full-blown literary reconceptualization of religious antinomianism: Hawthorne insists that what occurs in the moonlit parlor, the space fertile of images, is less a feat of authorial will than it is the shadowy realization, produced by faith and grace (the former, Hawthorne insists, is impotent without the latter), of a third ontological domain. Within this "genial atmosphere" a mixed medium both foreign and familiar, the would-be writer may finally be granted the opportunity to "get acquainted with his illusive guests" whom he welcomes as his characters-to-be.[8]

The same realization that charms Hawthorne in his vocational limbo repels the deeply emplotted Clara who is disinclined to be guided or authorized by a materialized intelligence which she suspects to be, even in part, "pourtrayed by my fancy" (168) [113]. Despite her "conviction" in the second scene that the invisible was indeed miraculously emerging in her presence into visibility, Clara cannot dismiss the inference of her observation that "the cry was blown into my ear, while the face was many paces distant": precisely because the shriek's "airy undulation" had palpably delivered a "shock" to her nerves, she must doubt whether "the spectacle I beheld," the face of the speaker, "existed in my fancy or without" (168) [112]. The discrepancy compels her to conclude that the invisible content realized in this instance was less that of divine intelligence than of human imagination: "thirs[ting]" above all "for knowledge and for vengeance," she does not confer authority upon her vision because her desire is to illuminate, and thus to obliterate, the chiaroscuro of romance that Hawthorne relishes but for which she emphatically has no patience (217) [142]. And yet, as for Hawthorne, her encounter with the hybrid, objective-subjective vision denotes her transformation into an author. At least at this moment, if she does

8. Nathaniel Hawthorne, *The Scarlet Letter*, pp. 40, 39, 40, 50, 39.

not positively affiliate herself with some understanding of authorship, she unhesitatingly refutes the antinomian version of authorized
agency to which she, as her father's daughter, has been strongly
attracted and which her brother has already fully embraced, with the
disastrous consequences that Clara is about to discover. Her unmistakable refutation here of antinomianism as an authorial stance
that rejects representation or any structure of mediation as illegitimate (as Wieland will act, and even plot, and yet claim not agency
but mere instrumentality) is a momentary conviction: although she
cannot hold steadfastly to it, it will nevertheless enable her to survive her encounter with her brother and both pronounce and determine the novel's final word. We may say provisionally, then, that
Clara's refutation of literary antinomianism—here enacted if not
articulated—ensures the possibility of literary narrative.

What she perceives as the hybridity of the spectacle on the staircase, her suspicion that it may be in part a self-projection, causes
her to question its legitimacy and thus to reject its authority over
her actions. Yet paradoxically, this rejection leads her to anticipate
adopting a similarly compromised authorial stance: "What but ambiguities, abruptnesses, and dark transitions," she laments, "can be
expected from the historian who is, at the same time, the sufferer
of these disasters?" (167) [112]. The representational failures that
she predicts will ensue from her insistent identity of historian and
sufferer, subject and object, author and character betray her reluctance altogether to repudiate the antinomian excuse: I authored, but
not I.[9] If these failures attest to her continuing victimization, they
also attest to her innocence of authorship, and therefore the innocence of her narrative account of events—both its credibility and
(relatedly) the unobjectionable nature of the role she herself played
in its unfolding. Clara's authorial stance is thus quite distinctive in
its indeterminacy. If she does not, like Hawthorne, dissemble with
a coy literary antinomianism what she well knows to be the aggression and potential violence of authorship, neither does she betray
Carwin's nihilistic glee upon discovering in his wilderness maze
that he was both the source and the referent of all objective variety.
And yet the very temerity with which she bluntly rejects the command of the supernal other suggests that despite her much-protested
veneration of her enthusiastic brother who, in murdering, claims to
have passed "the test of perfect virtue" and whom she represents as

---

9. As Wieland insists that God authored his acts, Clara will insist that "the author of evil"
authored, or at least provoked, hers. Paul De Man's "Excuses" analyzes "the devious-
ness of the excuse pattern" by showing how it "occurs within an epistemological twilight zone between knowing and not-knowing" (287, 286). It thus provides a provocative
gloss upon this point, as well as upon the very similar excuses for spying on Clara copiously produced by both Pleyel and Carwin.

a Christic *"man of sorrows,"* and despite her claim, in the denouement, to "part[ake] of Wieland's credulity, sh[ake] with his amazement, and pan[t] with his awe," it is Carwin's prerogative to plot, and
not the "peace of virtue, and the glory of obedience," enjoyed by
Wieland, that she covets (200, 263, 262, 201) [132, 170, 133].

Thus in the second scene, gripping her penknife in anticipation
of compelling repentance, Clara rejects the authority of the materialized specter in order to keep an appointment with a fully corporeal
assailant. This expectation of embodiment is perversely realized in
her discovery not of Carwin but of the disfigured corpse of her sister-
in-law, "the companion of my infancy, the partaker of all my thoughts,
my cares, and my wishes"—in a word, her double (172) [115]. If the
advent of Carwin may be correlated with the increased spectraliza-
tion of Clara, a fantastic expansion of her characterological reach
into the authorial domain, it hastens Catharine's reversion to the
"clay" with which she has all along been approvingly identified (88)
[61]. Having on the staircase assumed the authorial initiative to
determine the course of events only to discover herself irrevocably
"severed" in Catharine's death from the possibility of returning to
her former self (even if Carwin could be made to unravel the maze
and recall Pleyel), the old characterologically correct Clara defini-
tively dies in the death of Catharine, an event she had both promoted
and anticipated by consenting to relinquish her former principles of
self-governance (172) [115]. The effacement of Wieland's hyperboli-
cally loved but otherwise superfluous foster daughter, the last sight
Clara sees before lapsing into the lengthy delirium that separates her
first and second posttrial returns to her bedroom, provides a fitting
emblem or visual epitaph for this death.

Clara's delirium is, of course, a response to her shocking discovery of the carnage Wieland has wrought from the sublime disengage-
ment of Mettingen society, its unwavering devotion to maintaining
the bloodlessness of the theoretical. It is also, like her briefer moment
of psychological discomposure after the trial at Pleyel's, an interval
during which she reconstitutes herself as an author—by default, she
insists, as the only way of controlling proliferating and increasingly
dangerous misrepresentations. Her determination to return surreptitiously a second time to her bedroom in order to retrieve from her
closet her encoded journal containing "the most secret transactions
of my life" is thus inherently an authorial gesture (218) [143]. Her
desire to retain undisputed and exclusive possession of the text will
fulfill itself, however, only when she has choreographed the fatal
confrontation of Wieland and Carwin from which she emerges as
the lone (authorial) survivor. In order to understand the dynamics of
this confrontation, especially given Clara's tendency to represent
herself as backing into authorship, it is worthwhile to examine the

confessional statements, which are also statements of authorial intent, given by both Wieland and Carwin in advance of the final scene.

As are all other competing voices in this first-person narrative, Wieland's confession (a speech delivered in court and "faithfully recorded" by an auditor) is mediated and even expurgated by Clara; the reader's perusal of it is limited by her inability to absorb its shocking details (185) [123]. Yet the assumptions and strengths of antinomian authorship emerge clearly from that portion of Wieland's "tale" that Clara does include in her narrative: his account of what led him to murder his family and his refusal to acknowledge the legitimacy of his judges' censure (185, 200) [123, 132]. Wieland is in fact the only authorial figure in the narrative (Brown included) who is free of the obsessive need to vindicate himself before his auditors or readers and who forthrightly condemns it as an "ignoble" task (186) [123]. Although his judge had commanded him "to confess or to vindicate his actions" (185) [123], Wieland delivers with prophetic authority a conversion narrative whose unassailable legitimacy inheres in what the narrator represents as the full gratification of the convert's desire for privileged and direct access to transcendent being. Encountering the fiery visage on the staircase, Wieland does not pause, as his sister will, to register any spatial discrepancy of voice and face, any cognitive irregularities that might betray an enthusiastic penchant to take "internal motions" for the will of God. Because he believes that the vision represented the fulfillment of his search for the revelation of God's will, that he had been granted "[t]he blissful privilege of direct communication" and heard "the audible enunciation" of the transcendent author's "pleasure," that in seeing the illuminated face and hearing its murderous command his senses had been "salute[d]" with an "unambiguous token" of presence, he is "acquitted at the tribunal of his own conscience" and is therefore unconcerned by, and even disdainful of, the capital conviction about to be rendered by the jury (189, 206) [125, 136]. In his view, the matter had been straightforward: once the command had been uttered, "nothing remained but to execute [the decree]" and thereby prove his "virtue" (190) [126]. There was no reason to consider "the purity of [his] intentions" because, outside of his desire to conform himself to transcendent being, he had none: presuming to consider neither the rationale for nor the consequences of the divinely mandated act, the merely instrumental self that performed it was, in the performance, utterly vanquished (200) [132]. The ignominious end artificially and belatedly engineered outside of the spiritual logic of the act by the moral pygmies of the law who set up their "bounded views and halting reason, as the measure of truth" confirms rather than undermines his authority (201) [132].

Wieland's claim to moral infallibility is further supported by the fact that he narrates his "tale" before an "audience . . . of thousands whom rumours of this wonderful event had attracted": the reach of his speaking voice, then, exceeds Carwin's own (185, 184) [123, 122]. His persuasive power is similarly amplified: Clara's uncle, representing the scene of his direct address to "[j]udges, advocates and auditors," claims that Wieland's aspect, like Carwin's when appropriating the voice and then the form of divinity, "denoted less of humanity than godhead" and that his audience, like Nathan Cole listening to Whitefield, was "panic-struck and breathless with attention" (185) [123]. Clara and her uncle, too, find the conviction in the narrator's voice (as he makes the kinds of "simple and solemn declarations" Carwin repeatedly intends and fails to make to Clara) so compelling that it permits the speaker to transcend his textualization in order to convey to his readers the physical immediacy and the rhetorical power and authenticity of original utterance: here is the perverse vindication of the Cicero project (156) [105]. That Wieland's textual voice reclaims the authority and presence of the body is somewhat sadistically suggested by her uncle when he asks a horrified Clara, before handing her the trial documentation, if she would like him to call "the destroyer of thy family . . . to thy presence" (185) [123]. Eschewing vindication, textualization, and interpretation, Wieland speaks with such unshakable conviction to the gathered multitudes that they condemn him only "reluctantly," and Clara, having read, is quick to follow suit (200) [132]. As Wieland claims that no one can know "what is crime" because no one dare judge the decrees of Omnipotence, so Clara wonders if it is "indisputably certain" that the "murderer" of Catharine and her children "was criminal" (201, 206) [132, 136]. Despite the revolting details of the murders she learns from Wieland's manuscript, including the machinations by which he lures Catharine to her bedroom in order to kill her unobserved, Clara immediately judges his capital conviction "cruel and unmerited" and attempts to recast him as a killer whose innocence, both in kind and degree, dwarfs the banal probity—the mere blamelessness—of those who presume to judge him (202) [133]. Clara's beatification of Wieland will reach its apotheosis when, coming face to face with him in her bedroom upon her second return, she "violen[tly]" throws to the floor her penknife with which she had intended to kill her brother—"a brother thus supreme in misery; thus towering in virtue!"—and in so doing tacitly invites him to take it up (254) [165].

Thus does Clara's trauma-induced lassitude not bring quiescence: before she can "take up" the new life she introduces in a jarring concluding chapter which offers a conventionally comic resolution of the Mettingen massacre, she must take up the pen which she had thought to have "forever laid aside" (267) [173]. This final movement, the taking up of the pen, begins with her reading of her brother's unre-pentant confession. Even as it makes explicit the attractions of anti-nomian authorship—decisive action without accountability—and suggests to her that by both sympathy and heredity she may ally her-self with it, Wieland's statement revitalizes her determination to dis-cover the author as that object upon whom, in place of the murderous innocent, she may pour out her indignation and vengeance. Like all quests in this novel, beginning with the elder Wieland's, Clara's par-takes of the paradigmatic structure of ventriloquism: the novel fun-nels itself down, life by superfluous life, to its most frequently asked question—"Who is the author?"—which is thrown out only to be mechanically returned by the inevitable wall, moving ever closer to confront the questioner with its own blank interrogative. In the pen-ultimate chapter, the question is posed for the last time, with less wonder than desperation, in Clara's evacuated bedroom, a stagelike square of dim light in a waste of dark and depopulated space. Here will occur, as the final scene of the novel proper, that authorial awak-ening produced when the otherness at the heart of voice is elimi-nated, when the asker acknowledges, through her actions if not her overt admission, that the respondent, the culprit, the fiery visage, the author, is herself. Clara here repeats in the blasted interior of what had been presented as ideal social space Carwin's savage experiment in the wilderness maze by which he elicits, in order to appropriate and deploy, the infinite variety of voice.

The novel's denouement can only arrive when one character—whether the enthusiast, the ventriloquist, or the victim—eliminates the others in a contest that can only be fratricidal and is thereby identified, through this process of elimination, as author. Seeking a collective resolution to their competing and still outstanding claims, into Clara's bedroom each of the novel's remaining charac-ters "penetrate[s] unobserved," self-liberated and thus "restored" to narrative life from various forms of characterological invisibility: Clara from delirium and the close guardianship of her well-meaning uncle, Carwin from a self-imposed exile of shame, and Wieland from incarceration (215) [141]. If Wieland seeks to triumph by killing and Carwin by explaining and rebuilding, Clara's motivation for return-ing is less clear as she takes (like the young Carwin) "an irregular path" to her old haunt (219) [143]. Like her opinions about what has occurred and who is responsible, her intentions in returning are the "sport of eternal change": initially, she intends to regain possession in order to destroy her private journal; having seized her journal, she then decides to destroy herself, but is prevented when the entrance of Carwin into the room reminds her that her more pressing desire, since her trial at Pleyel's, has been to discover the author and to pun-ish him rather than herself (205) [135]. Obligingly, at the moment she prepares to end it all by penetrating to "the recesses of life" with her lancet, Carwin, who has been all along her prime authorial suspect, emerges from the room's shadowy depths, Hawthorne's gentleghost as Frankenstein's monster: "the shadow moved; a foot, unshapely and huge, was thrust forward; a form advanced from its concealment, and stalked into the room. It was Carwin!" (221, 222) [145].

After reading her brother's confession, Clara had bitterly, tentatively identified Carwin as that peculiar "genius" able to subject demons to his control in order to marshal their "supernatural aid" in his diabolical schemes (206) [136]. As she imagines his role in the demise of the Mettingen congregation, he emerges as the practitioner of what can only be described as spectral humanism: that is, although he willfully engages the help of specters—"conscious beings, dissimilar from human, but moral and voluntary agents as we are"—in order to perpetrate evil, he dismisses with the disdain of the rationalist the trappings of witchcraft along with its accompanying theological rationale (206) [136]:

> The dreams of superstition are worthy of contempt. Witchcraft, its instruments and miracles, the compact ratified by a bloody signature, the apparatus of sulpherous smells and thundering explosions, are monstrous and chimerical. These have no part in the scene over which the genius of Carwin presides. (206) [136]

Meeting her again in her "solitary and dismantled" room, Carwin will attempt to disabuse Clara of her notions of his control over events to claim instead the innocence of one who—although he freely admits to having deceived, sported with another's terrors, and plotted to destroy another's reputation—was criminal only insofar as he was curious (223, 225, 235) [146, 147, 153].[1] Although he insists that his culpability is limited to his uncontrolled curiosity, he claims to have returned in order to confess himself "a repentant criminal" who offers to let Clara "denounce punishment" as a means of removing her errors and rebuilding her reputation (225) [147]. Clara renounces her fantasies of Carwin's preternatural powers only when he confesses to her the secret he keeps from Ludloe on pain of death, his purely mechanical and acquired ability "to speak where he is not,"

---

1. Carwin's admission that his culpability must be limited to his uncontrolled curiosity makes him the victim—of the false and seducing teacher, as so many Old Lights had warned would occur if curiosity was indulged. Curiosity, in their view, ended in conviction. Another consideration to add: Carwin admits to Clara as part of his confession that after she had seen his face in the act of utterance on her staircase, he had fled Mettingen, like Adam discovered in his transgression, "covered with the shame of this detection" (244) [159]. Clara's vision of Carwin in the ventriloquistic act, then, is the equivalent of Carwin's illicit scrutiny of Clara's diary, the materialization of her "inmost soul" whose "possession" gives Carwin the benefit of a knowledge of Clara "more accurate" than "conjugal intimacies" (235, 234) [153].

and even then she will prove herself perfectly willing to resuscitate them when convenient (249) [162].

In his confession, Carwin offers a view of ventriloquism as a form of authorship which, although it lacks anything like a transcendent rationale, yet bears a parodic resemblance to the antinomian authorship of Wieland. For both men, authorship is the activity of a moment, whose extension is limited by the absence of authorial intention on the one hand, and on the other by the almost instantaneous dissolution of the authorial impulse, making the agent remarkably careless of consequences. If Wieland's authorship entailed the spare narrative sequence of a decree desired, received, multiply enacted, and fulfilled, Carwin in acting "meditated nothing" beyond the immediate "gratification which I derived from these exploits." Much like the brother and father whose conceptual limitations he strove to exceed and despite the extent of his powers, his "views were bounded to the passing moment, and commonly suggested by the momentary exigence" (229) [150]. Whereas Wieland, the antinomian author, is subjected to the unquestionable commands of an unrepresentable deity, Carwin is "subjected to the empire of mechanical and habitual impulses" (244) [159]. As Wieland, having acted, was instantly relieved of his agency by an infinitely powerful God, Carwin, having acted, was instantly relieved of his agency by the "machine" he himself had "rashly set in motion [and] over whose progress," he confesses, "I had no controul, and which experience had shewn me was infinite in power" (246) [160]. Both view themselves as "the undesigning cause" of events for which they bear no true responsibility and for which they disavow any personal role (223) [146]. If anything, Carwin represents himself as less an author even than Wieland: he is the unstable embodiment of the unrepresentable principle by which plots are generated solely for the sake of their generation. Clara, then, in attempting to follow Cotton Mather's train into the invisible world where she hopes to surprise criminal authorial intent at the instant in which it assumes a material form, finds not Mephistopheles, not the hyperrational orchestrator of the spectral hosts, not the cosmic contriver, but a cowering and snaggletoothed rustic—"[u]nfortified by principle, subjected to poverty, stimulated by headlong passions"—who is himself the victim of his own fantastic eloquence, "a tool of wonderful efficacy" that he happens to possess but is unfit to use (227, 225) [148, 147].[2]

2. Carwin's description of himself here fulfills the recipe for vulgarity to which conservatives from Old Lights to Federalists subscribed. His account of his powers here differs from his more confident description of the ventriloquist's art that he provides the Mettingen congregation upon first learning from them of the strange voices (86–87) [60–61]. In an article from 1806 entitled "What Is Literary Genius?" Brown, in refuting the idea that geniuses are born and not made, insists that "Man *creates* by *imitation*" (253). Moreover, he claims that genius is the product of chance events. "When men of letters

At the conclusion of Carwin's confession, the irrepressible Wieland makes his entrance upon the stage, despite Clara's uncle's assurance that she "will never more behold the face of this criminal, unless he be gifted with supernatural strength" (185) [123]. Wieland, of course, will not hesitate to act and cannot be appeased until his authorship has run its sacrificial course; moreover, his incarceration has compounded his power: beyond enthusiasm, he has revealed his possession of the exhorter's ability to penetrate into houses and the specter's ability to "shake off his fetters" and "restor[e] himself to liberty" no matter how his body is enchained (215) [141]. Upon Wieland's entrance and Carwin's speechless and wobbly-kneed exit, Clara securely grips the penknife which she has had concealed in the folds of her skirt (254) [165]. This detail in itself constitutes her wordless response to her questions and prediction after reading Wieland's confession: "Was I not likewise transformed from rational and human into a creature of nameless and fearful attributes? Was I not transported to the brink of the same abyss? Ere a new day should come, my hands might be embrued in blood" (204–5) [135]. But unlike Wieland and Carwin, Clara has not yet discovered a mode of guiltless authorship, has not found a way to arrange for, let alone justify, the alienation of her voice or her actions. Even if one refrains from plotting outright, even if one confines oneself to unraveling another's maze—to disemplotting and deauthorizing—can one do so with clean hands?

The only possibility for doing so is if Wieland and Carwin both voluntarily resign their authorial claims, if Carwin's ventriloquism and Wieland's enthusiasm—identities that encompass their entire sphere of action—come to a simultaneous end and self-sacrificially allow Clara, who has refused the offices of strategy and rationale, to survive them both.[3] Her solution for effecting the deauthorization of her rivals without literally killing them is, as it occurs to her in the heat of the moment, an ingenious one. Redeeming the ethical promise of Carwin's stated intention to restore her life, Clara forces him to ventriloquize himself: she commands him to tell Wieland, in the accents of transcendent being before which both sister and brother will shudder, that the voice of transcendent being has been and is

---

reflect on the manner of their own attainments, and on the literary history of others, they discover that the faculties of the mind are not *gifts* of nature, but effects of human causes, or *acquisitions* of art." "Every man of common organization," then, "has the power of becoming a man of genius, if to this he add a solitary devotion to his art, and a vehement passion for glory" as well as "the capacity of long attention"; "nature is more impartial than some of her children allow" (249). In this respect, Carwin exemplifies Brown's democratic idea of the genius.
3. Clara more forthrightly expresses her will to survive her brother, as when (on p. 260) [169] she marvels that with all her tribulations, "still I consent to live!" while she finds (on p. 263) [171] that, given her brother's comparable woes, she cannot wish for the "continuance of [his] being."

being counterfeited. In so doing, Carwin is compelled to "conduct his inscrutable plots to [their] consummation" and is thus self-canceled: he has given his last performance on this stage (262) [170]. * * * Carwin's voice of transcendent being denies its own reality even while relying upon and commanding the awed belief of the listener in its transcendental status; this untenably paradoxical denial necessarily constitutes its last utterance. Clara permits Carwin to sustain the fiction of his authorship just long enough for him to remove Wieland's sustaining belief in transcendent being. Wieland, who will allow only transcendent being—even self-confessed as fraudulent—to deauthorize him, takes his own life in an insupportable moment of lucid incoherence, cutting his throat[,] * * * the victim of antinomian delusion. Rendered voiceless through his own utterance, Carwin at the novel's end has "hid[den] himself in a remote district of Pennsylvania," where, Clara surmises (willing the realization of her earlier benign fantasy), he "is now probably engaged in the harmless pursuits of agriculture," silently pondering "the evils to which his fatal talents have given birth" and, an unlikely convert to Jeffersonian virtue, wordlessly envisioning "[t]he innocence and usefulness of his future life" (273) [177]. The suicide of her brother saves Clara from committing fratricide, and the sprinkling of her hands with his blood thus serves to consecrate her as the text's sole survivor and bereft victim to whom nothing is left but to tell the tale of a singular fate bearing no connection to a general, representative truth. Thus does Clara author and yet retain the privileged status of a character who may legitimately bewail that her life must end when the pen is laid down.[4]

Her recourse to metaventriloquism having spared her the use of her penknife, Clara is thus left holding the pen in a gesture of ambiguous proprietorship upon whose unrepresented resolution her innocence, and thus her vindication, ultimately depends. After the elimination of Wieland and Carwin, Clara insists on inhabiting the scene of so many agentless crimes and continuing to write, which she represents as her affliction: authorship is the symptom of "a perverse constitution of mind," and its products the necessarily "abortive creations" whose author merely "suffer[s]" them until some outside force—if not relatives recalling her to her duty, then a fiery apocalypse which forces her to leave Mettingen once and for all— relieves her from their tyranny (268, 269) [174, 175]. Clara's restoration to her right mind, her redemption from the criminal psychosis

4. One might say that Clara has appropriated for herself a strategy she had initially attributed to Carwin, that he "had constructed his plot in a manner suited to the characters of those whom he had selected for his victims" (153) [103]. And this, of course, echoes Moses Bartlett, *False and Seducing Teachers*, pp. 22–26 (where he argues that the carnally minded are especially susceptible) and pp. 38–44 (where he notes the resemblance between false teachers and their followers).

of authorship, is signaled by her offer at her narrative's end of an impossibly conventional conclusion that represents, as Norman Grabo has pointed out, Clara's only honorable authorial exit.[5] For those aspirants to authorship who will succeed her, her legacy is not the reinscription of literary norms that her story has made untenable but rather her achievement of a fantastic naïveté as she represents herself panting with awe at a fiction of her own devising, the transcendent voice that disarms her brother "*as if* the God whom I invoked were present" (258, emphasis added [168]). What will prove useful to future aspirants to national authorship is Clara's gift of a secularized antinomianism to a future literary corpus that makes possible, as a sign of the fiction's legitimacy, not the representation of truth but rather a moment of presence, of direct communication, that is both staged and authentic.

Bibliography

Bartlett, Moses. *False and Seducing Teachers.* New London: 1757.

Brown, Charles Brockden. "What Is Literary Genius?" *Literary Magazine and American Register* (1806): 247–54.

Daston, Lorraine. "Marvelous Facts and Miraculous Evidence in Early Modern Europe." *Critical Inquiry* 18 (1991): 93–124.

DeMan, Paul. "Excuses." In *Allegories of Reading: Figural Language in Rousseau, Nietzsche, Rilke, and Proust*, 278–301. New Haven, CT: Yale University Press, 1979.

Fussell, Edwin Sill. "*Wieland*: A Literary and Historical Reading." *Early American Literature* 18 (1983): 171–86.

Grabo, Norman S. *The Coincidental Art of Charles Brockden Brown.* Chapel Hill: University of North Carolina Press, 1981.

Hagenbüchle, Roland. "American Literature and the Nineteenth-Century Crisis in Epistemology: The Example of Charles Brockden Brown." *Early American Literature* 23 (1988): 121–51.

Hawthorne, Nathaniel. *The Scarlet Letter and Selected Writings.* Ed. Stephen Nissenbaum. New York: Modern Library, 1984.

Lotman, Iurii M. "Problema khudozhestvennogo prostranstva v proze Gogolia." (The problem of artistic space in the prose of Gogol.) *Izbrannye stat'I v trekh tomakh, t. I, Stat'i po semiotike i tipologii kul'tury*, 413–47. Tallin, Estonia: Aleksandra, 1992.

Mather, Cotton. *Diary of Cotton Mather.* 2 vols. New York: Frederick Ungar Publishing Co., n.d.

Scheick, William J. "The Problem of Origination in Brown's *Ormond*." In *Critical Essays on Charles Brockden Brown,* ed. Bernard Rosenthal, 126–41. Boston: G. K. Hall, 1981.

5. See Grabo, *The Coincidental Art of Charles Brockden Brown*, pp. 23–29.

LEIGH ERIC SCHMIDT

[Enlightenment, Ventriloquism, and *Wieland*]†

* * *

From late antiquity through the early decades of the eighteenth century, ventriloquism was deeply embedded in Christian discourses about demon possession, necromancy, and pagan idolatry. The term itself, in its Latin derivation, meant literally "one who speaks from the belly," and it long held a place among many other specialized markers for different types of divination, prophecy, and conjuring. As Reginald Scot explained in *The Discoverie of Witchcraft* (1584), "*Pythonists*" or "*Ventriloqui*" speak in a "hollowe" voice, much different from their usual one, and are "such as take upon them to give oracles" or "to tell where things lost are become." In demonological discussions, such nomenclature was used to refer to those who were overcome by "a familiar spirit," who spoke during trances or fits in an apparently diabolical voice, or who claimed soothsaying powers.[1]

Much of the formative discussion of ventriloquy in the Christian tradition focused on the story of the Witch of Endor recounted in 1 Samuel 28, in which King Saul disguises himself and visits a sorceress in hopes of summoning up the ghost of Samuel and discerning the future of his battle against the Philistines. With the help of the necromancer, Saul hears the prophet Samuel speak from beyond the grave—an apparent success for the soothsayer that made for considerable anxious commentary in the patristic literature and long afterward: Why would God allow necromancy, a practice repeatedly abominated, to be used for divine purposes? Was this whole scene not accomplished through the power of the devil? Was this apparitional voice of Samuel real and prophetic, or only a diabolical illusion created by the enchantress to trick a weakened

---

† Reprinted by permission of the publisher from "How to Become a Ventriloquist," in *Hearing Things: Religion, Illusion, and the American Enlightenment* by Leigh Eric Schmidt, pp. 138, 140–141, 143–145, 147–152, Cambridge, Mass.: Harvard University Press, Copyright © 2000 by the President and Fellows of Harvard College. Page numbers in square brackets refer to this Norton Critical Edition.
1. Reginald Scot, *The Discoverie of Witchcraft* (London, 1584; rpt. London: Rowan and Littlefield, 1973), 101. For multiple uses of the term in late antiquity and in medieval Europe, see Valentine Vox, *I Can See Your Lips Moving: The History and Art of Ventriloquism* (Tadworth, Surrey, 1981; North Hollywood, Calif.: Plato Publishing, 1993), 11–39. The early modern vocabulary for soothsaying and divination was very rich; other terms used for a person given to prophetic, demonic, or ventriloquial speech included "ob," "python" or "pythonist," "engastrimyth," and "gastriloquist." Two other related terms for divination by the belly included "gastromancy" and "hariolation." See Thomas Blount, *Glossographia; Or, A Dictionary, Interpreting All Such Hard Words, Whether Hebrew, Greek, Latin, Italian, Spanish, French, Teutonick, Belgick, British or Saxon, as Are Now Used in Our Refined English Tongue* (London: Newcomb, 1656) as well as the pertinent entries in the *Oxford English Dictionary*.

Saul? The story bundled many crucial theological issues together, but among the most intriguing to centuries of interpreters was the question about the source of the ventriloquized voice—namely, who was speaking and by what means or powers.[2]

In the early modern versions of this debate about Samuel's ghost, interlocutors swung, as in the larger controversies over witchcraft, between those who saw the power of the demonic and the supernatural on display and those who supported increasingly materialistic or skeptical explanations. Reginald Scot's work, a leading harbinger of dissent from long-standing demonic readings, shifted the blame, comparing the woman's powers to that constant Protestant bugbear of Catholic "magic": "Let us confesse that *Samuell* was not raised . . . and see whether this illusion may not be contrived by the art and cunning of the woman, without anie of these supernaturall devices: for I could cite a hundred papisticall and cousening practises, as difficult as this, and as cleanlie handled." Amid his detailed explanations, Scot speculated that the diviner was a cunning ventriloquist who "abused *Saule*" with her "counterfeit hollow voice." In the opposite camp, Joseph Glanvill, who, as a member of the Royal Society, was committed to establishing an empirical base for the defense of Christian supernaturalism, argued that it was "a *real* Apparition" and thought that the ventriloquial explanation was nonsense: "It cannot certainly in any reason be thought, that the Woman could by a natural knack, speak such a Discourse as is related from *Samuel*, much less that she could from her Belly imitate his Voice, so as to deceive one that knew him as *Saul* did." For Glanvill—as with the Mathers, Henry More, and George Sinclair—the contention that necromancers, witches, and demoniacs were mostly frauds was mere sophistry. Diabolical as well as prophetic utterances were part of a biblical world of spirits, apparitions, and wonders that Glanvill and his various allies stood ready to defend against the incipient challenges of skeptical critics.[3]

The scriptural debate over the Witch of Endor and the sources of Samuel's voice had its lived counterpart in the "sacred theater" of possession that haunted seventeenth-century Protestants and Catholics alike.[4] In the context of such dramatic religious phenomena, "ventriloquy" was one of the terms used to debate whether or not

2. For background on the problems the Witch of Endor created for Christian commentaries, see Valerie I. J. Flint, *The Rise of Magic in Early Medieval Europe* (Princeton: Princeton University Press, 1991), esp. 18–21, 54–56; Lynn Thorndike, *A History of Magic and Experimental Science*, 8 vols. (New York: Columbia University Press, 1923–1958), 1: 352, 448, 470–471.
3. Scot, *Discoverie*, 114, 121; Joseph Glanvill, *Saducismus Triiumphatus; Or, Full and Plain Evidence Concerning Witches and Apparitions*, 2 vols. (London: J. Collins, 1681), 2: 64.
4. On possession as "sacred theater," see Clarke Garrett, *Spirit Possession and Popular Religion: From the Camisards to the Shakers* (Baltimore: Johns Hopkins University Press, 1987), esp. 4–6, 86–87.

Satan was speaking through the possessed. Was it a "familiar spirit" who made people roar out in low and unnatural voices, speak in languages heretofore unknown to them, taunt ministers and godly neighbors, or mimic the cries of animals in what amounted to an infernal menagerie? Or were those afflicted with such voices, bellowings, and barkings fraudulent or diseased? As the Reverend John Whiting reported of a Hartford woman, Ann Cole, in 1662, she "was taken with strange fits, wherein she (or rather the devil, as 'tis judged, making use of her lips) held a discourse for a considerable time." One of the signs that the devil was indeed speaking "vocally" in another New England woman, Elizabeth Knapp, was that she often uttered her "reviling" expressions without "any motion at all" of her mouth and lips—"a clear demonstration," Increase Mather thought, "that the voice was not her own." Those who held to the supernaturalist position heard, in these "grum, low" voices from sometimes motionless lips, highly compelling evidence for the fearful presence of demons.[5]

Skeptics were inevitably contemptuous of all such trickeries of the voice, all the supposed fraud of demoniacs and soothsayers. In *A Perfect Discovery of Witches* (1661), Thomas Ady described ventriloquism as a commonplace scam used by impostors to make people "beleeve that they are possessed by the Devil, speaking within them, and tormenting them, and so do by that pretence move the people to charity."[6] In *Leviathan* (1651), Thomas Hobbes, arguing for the prevalence of religious impostures, was predictably scathing about vocal artifice, describing ventriloquism as a means by which enchanters were "able to make very many men believe" that their own voice "is a voice from Heaven." If the construct still required further sharpening, already it was being whetted for use against pious fraud. As another British exposer of demonic displays explained in 1718, "Some Counterfeits can speak out of their Bellies with a little or no Motion of their Lips. They can change their Voices, that they shall not be like their Own. They can make, that what they shall say be heard, as if it was from a different Part of the Room, or as if it came

5. For these well-known cases, see David D. Hall, ed., *Witch-Hunting in Seventeenth-Century New England: A Documentary History, 1638–1692* (Boston: Northeast University Press, 1991), 149, 202, 207–211, 225–229; Increase Mather, *An Essay for the Recording of Illustrious Providences* (Boston: n.p., 1684), 140. For English and European examples, see C. L'Estrange Ewen, *Witchcraft and Demonianism* (London: Heath Cranton, 1933), 148–149, 336, 452; Michael MacDonald, *Mystical Bedlam: Madness, Anxiety, and Healing in Seventeenth-Century England* (Cambridge: Cambridge University Press, 1981), 198–202; Jean Bodin, *On the Demon-Mania of Witches*, trans. Randy A. Scott (Toronto: Centre for Reformation and Renaissance Studies, 1995), 109. For a reading of these New England cases that insightfully highlights the vocality of possession, including its ventriloquial dimensions, see Jane Kamensky, *Governing the Tongue: The Politics of Speech in Early New England* (New York: Oxford University Press, 1997), 150–179.
6. Thomas Ady, *A Perfect Discovery of Witches* (London: Brome, 1661), 78.

from their own Fundament." "Such persons are call'd," he said, "*Engastriloques*, or *Ventriloquists*."[7]

For all the sneering of skeptics, these discussions long remained torn. The lexicographer Thomas Blount captured this ambivalence in his entry under "ventriloquist" for his *Glossographia* (1656)— "one that has an evil spirit speaking in his belly, or one that by use and practice can speake as it were out of his belly, not moving his lips." In the late 1740s John Wesley, given his own first-hand experiences with the possessed and with exorcising prayer, easily placed the term in a frame similar to Glanvill's, suggesting that rationalistic critics who saw mere guile in extraordinary religion were wrongheaded. In one American replay of the debate in 1773, Congregationalist Ezra Stiles, a notable bearer of Enlightenment learning in New England, tried to convince a rabbi in Newport, Rhode Island, of the wisdom of a theatrical explanation for necromantic voices: "He had not heard of Ventriloquism before and still doubted it." In another American rendition in 1810, Frederick Quitman, a Lutheran minister who was ashamed of lingering Christian "superstitions," suggested that the Witch of Endor be interpreted as "a ventriloquist, who could speak in a manner unobserved by the spectators." Another preacher, Robert Scott, quickly countered Quitman's exegesis with a public rejoinder affirming the divine reality of the apparition and the voice. Ventriloquism remained embroiled in theological debates about the diabolical, the revelatory, and the magical, even as skeptics sought to turn it into a consummate example of staged religious imposture.[8]

The decisive turn toward the Enlightenment construction of ventriloquism was made in 1772 by Joannes Baptista de La Chapelle

7. Thomas Hobbes, *Leviathan; Or, The Matter, Form, and Power of a Commonwealth Ecclesiastical and Civil*, in *The English Works of Thomas Hobbes of Malmesbury*, 11 vols. (London: Bohn, 1839–1845), 3: 434; Francis Hutchinson, *An Historical Essay Concerning Witchcraft* (London: Knaplock, 1718), 8–9.
8. Blount, *Glossographia*, s.v. "ventriloquist"; John Wesley, *Letter to the Author of "The Enthusiasm of Methodists and Papists Compared"* (1749), in *The Works of the Rev. John Wesley, A.M.*, 14 vols. (London: Wesleyan Conference, 1872), 9: 7; Franklin Bowditch Dexter, ed., *The Literary Diary of Ezra Stiles, D.D., L.L.D., President of Yale College*, 3 vols. (New York: Scribner's 1901), 1: 386, 403; Frederick H. Quitman, *A Treatise on Magic; Or, On the Intercourse between Spirits and Men* (Albany: Balance, 1810), 45–48; Robert Scott, *Letters to the Rev. Frederick H. Quitman, Occasioned by His Late Treatise on Magic* (Poughkeepsie, N.Y.: Adams, 1810), 26–29. Demonic taunts, altered voices, and motionless lips remained common in accounts of exorcism in the twentieth century, so again what is at issue is not the expunging of religious frameworks, but the development of increasingly powerful alternative discourses. In one instance from Wisconsin in 1928, the officiating priest noted that there "was not the slightest sign that the lips moved" in the possessed girl, that it "was possible for these evil spirits to speak in an audible manner from somewhere within the girl." See the cases in Adam Crabtree, *Multiple Man: Explorations in Possession and Multiple Personality* (New York: Praeger, 1985), 95–106 (quotation is on p. 97). See also Michael Cuneo, "Exorcism in American Culture: Two Case Studies," paper presented 5 March 1999, Center for the Study of American Religion, Princeton University.

(1710–1792). That year, La Chapelle—mathematician, pedagogue, acoustician, and participant in the leading scientific societies of France and England—published his 572-page opus *Le Ventriloque, ou L'Engastrimythe* in London and Paris. Part of the much wider currents within the Enlightenment striving to establish a natural history of pious frauds, La Chapelle's treatise took its place in that stream of works fed by writers such as Hobbes, Fontenelle, van Dale, Charles Blount, John Trenchard, and David Hume. As a mathematician of respected standing and as an inventor who relished showing the practical applications of his learning, La Chapelle was well positioned to join the philosophical band in "the propagation of universal reason." Prior to this massive tome on ventriloquism, his most widely circulated work, the two-volume *Institutions de géométrie*, was a quintessential Enlightenment textbook and Cartesian blueprint. It presented the instruction of children in mathematics as the best means for enshrining the purity of reason and for inculcating the habits of exactitude that would lead to ever greater knowledge of nature. Though always wanting to restrain the vagaries of prejudice and the religious imagination, La Chapelle regularly gave free reign to his own technological fantasies, showing how mathematical reasoning issued in one solution after another for the operative needs of the state—in mining, communications, and warfare. His inventiveness included the grand design of a cork-filled flotation device that he labeled *L'homme-bateau*, useful not only as a lifesaver for shipwrecked travelers, but also as a clandestine conveyance for soldiers.[9]

It was his applied geometry, notably his *Traité des sections coniques* (1765), that led La Chapelle into the domain of acoustics—a field in which he distinguished himself as an investigator of the physics of speaking trumpets, the main heir of Samuel Morland's mantle. His acoustic research on the improvement of these voice-carrying devices made him, in effect, a natural to take up the mechanics of deceptive religious voices. Scientific instruments could augment the range at which human utterances were heard; the voice was manipulable and extendable; it was capable of being duplicated and disjoined from the body of the speaker. The experimental knowledge behind a "machine" like the *Porte-voix* was apt preparation for a rationalistic interpretation of revelatory voices and mediumistic phenomena: the subtle art of propagating these mysterious sounds could likewise be penetrated.

9. Joannes Baptista de La Chapelle, *Institutions de géométrie*, 2 vols. (Paris: Debure, 1757), 1: 10–18, 39–45; Joannes Baptista de La Chapelle, *Traité de la construction théorique et practique du scaphandre, ou du bateau de l'homme* (Paris: Debure, 1775). In the latter work (pp. 1–8) La Chapelle also uses the occasion to reassert his basic propositions about ventriloquism.

La Chapelle was well positioned to correct the defects of the ear, to become a consummate demystifier of the auditory.[1]

Though now all but forgotten—not gaining even a mention in any of the standard genealogies of the Enlightenment's production of a critical study of religion—La Chapelle's *Le Ventriloque* was a peculiarly influential work. It provided much of the basic analysis of these sorts of vocal phenomena across Europe and North America for the next century. Translated into Dutch (1774), Italian (1786), and Russian (1787), it was widely disseminated and even more widely abstracted. His book was the main source for the 1797 entry on ventriloquism in the *Encyclopaedia Britannica* (and its ensuing American incarnation); it was cited by Charles Brockden Brown as the background on the subject for his major fictional creation of Carwin, the rogue ventriloquist, in *Wieland* (1798) and in the serialized, fragmentary sequel *Memoirs of Carwin the Biloquist* (1803–1805); it provided all of the material for one of the first American expositions of the art, a small pamphlet published in Morristown, New Jersey, in 1799; it influenced a mix of philosophical interpreters, from Dugald Stewart to David Brewster to Eusèbe Salverte; and its stories even became staples of popular how to guides by the mid-nineteenth century. La Chapelle, more than anyone else, reinvented ventriloquism as a generalized category for the rationalistic explanation of religion's most puzzling vocal phenomena. He gave it renewed currency as an idea; others would then turn his philosophical observations into a system of rational recreation, a widely recognized form of stage entertainment.[2]

La Chapelle, beginning his work in the skein of the age-old Christian debate about the Witch of Endor and the apparitional voice of Samuel, wanted to cut through the whole theological tangle. Defending the view that the soothsayer was a studied impostor with the ability to feign voices and to pass them off as supernatural, La Chapelle expanded this archetypal case of necromantic fraud into a

1. Joannes Baptista de La Chapelle, *Traité des sections coniques, et autres courbes anciennes* (Paris: Debure, 1765), i–ii, 113–120, 203–206; Johann Beckmann, *A History of Inventions and Discoveries*, trans. William Johnston, 4 vols. (London: Longman, Hurst, Rees, Orme, and Brown, 1817), 1: 166.
2. For the author's notation on La Chapelle in *Wieland*, see Charles Brockden Brown, *Wieland; Or, The Transformation and Memoirs of Carwin, the Biloquist*, ed. Emory Elliott (Oxford: Oxford University Press, 1994), 181n–182n [148n1]. For the 1799 pamphlet, see *Amusement-Hall; Or, A Collection of Diverting Stories, and Extraordinary Facts, with an Account of the Art of Ventriloquism, and Other Entertaining Matter* (Morristown, N.J.: n.p., 1799), 10–19. For the influence on Salverte, see Eusèbe Salverte, *The Occult Sciences: The Philosophy of Magic, Prodigies and Apparent Miracles*, trans. Anthony Todd Thomson, 2 vols. (Paris, 1829; London: Bentley, 1846), 1: 157–162, 283–284. Brewster, Stewart, and the popular guides are discussed below. Suggestive of their wide dispersion in gentlemanly circles of learning, La Chapelle's tales of Saint-Gille's exploits also caught the attention of Yale's Ezra Stiles, who extracted them at length. See "Anecdotes Relative to Ventriloquism," 23 May 1782, Ezra Stiles Papers, Beinecke Rare Book and Manuscript Library, Yale University.

blanket explanation that moved from the artifice of the ancient oracles (following van Dale and Fontenelle) to the credulity and fanaticism of his contemporaries. He moved the debate out of the biblical
narratives, the scriptural commentaries, and the theological territory
of demonology into the domains of experimental observation, acoustic inquiry, and anatomical dissection. (It was the anatomy of the
mouth and throat, not the belly, argued La Chapelle, that deserved
examination in the search for the "causes" of this vocal phenomenon.) Ventriloquism, he concluded, was an art, a practiced technique
of modulation, misdirection muscular control; it required neither
supernatural assistance nor any special endowments of nature.
Locating two contemporaries who had developed ventriloquial
skills for their own amusement—one a Viennese baron who dabbled
in puppetry and mimicry, and the other a local grocer named Saint-
Gille who always enjoyed a good practical joke—La Chapelle built
his explanatory framework on scientific report and empirical observation particularly of the grocer. To understand religious imposture, La Chapelle did not need to view the possessed or the inspired;
instead, all he required was close observation of an impish illusionist. That was a fateful shift of perspective.[3]

La Chapelle insisted that Saint-Gille was an honest man and hence
a reliable source, but the shopkeeper certainly had a roguish streak,
confounding people with his amateur illusions time and again. One
story, aptly titled "Les Religieux dupés," was particularly important
for La Chapelle's purpose of establishing his point that ventriloquism
was a generative force of religious delusion, that it was an important
technique for creating "an appearance of revelation." Taking refuge
in a monastery during a storm, Saint-Gille learns that the brothers
are in mourning over the recent death of one of their members; visiting the tomb in the church, Saint-Gille projects a ghostly voice pur-
porting to be that of the dead friar—one that laments the indifferent
prayers of his fellows for his suffering soul in Purgatory. Soon the
ventriloquist has the whole community praying for forgiveness, falling on the floor in fear and astonishment, and trying desperately to

3. After ventriloquism became popular on stage, various others followed up La Chapelle's
treatise with their own investigations of the acoustics and physiology of the art. See,
for example, John Gough, "Facts and Observations to Explain the Curious Phenomenon of Ventriloquism," *Journal of Natural Philosophy, Chemistry, and the Arts* 2 (June
1802): 122–129; F. M. S. Lespagnol, *Dissertation sur l'engastrimisme* (Paris: Didot
Jeune, 1811); Anthelme Richerand, *Elements of Physiology*, trans. G. J. M. De Lys
(Philadelphia: Dobson, 1813), 506–507; "Voice," *Boston Medical Intelligencer*, 22 July
1823, 39; "Ventriloquism," *Boston Medical Intelligencer*, 31 August 1824, 67; John
Mason Good, *The Book of Nature* (Boston, 1826; Hartford: Belknap and Hamersley,
1845), 257–262; George Smith Sutton, *A Treatise on Ventriloquism, with Extracts from
the Opinions of Several Authors Respecting that Extraordinary Gift of Human Faculty*
(New Haven: n.p., 1833); Robert Tolefree, Jr., "The Voice and Its Modifications (More
Particularly Ventriloquism) Briefly Considered," *American Journal of Science and Arts*
26 (1834): 76–83.

make amends to their lost brother. Overawed by the divine evidences he finds in the spectral voice, the prior even tells Saint-Gille that such apparitions effectively put to flight all the skeptical reasonings of the philosophers. But then Saint-Gille, La Chapelle reports in all seriousness, lets the duped in on the trickery—telling them that it had all been done by the art of ventriloquy, that he himself is the all-too-human source of this oracle. In the consummate act of the enlightened magician, Saint-Gille takes the devout back to the church and turns it into the scene of their awakening from illusion, showing them his techniques of mystification. La Chapelle, reaffirming the ease with which the senses are deceived and the need for critical reason, drew out the doubled moral of the story: "The art of the ventriloquists is excellent for establishing and destroying superstition."[4]

That farcical story became La Chapelle's most renowned scene, reproduced from one commentary to another, with its anti-Catholic dimensions taking on an added edge when repeated in Britain and North America. La Chapelle's formal experiments with Saint-Gille, monitored by two other observers from the Académie Royale des Sciences, conjured up similar conclusions. In one test, Saint-Gille's talents were employed to convince a credulous woman that she heard the voice of a spirit, and then the researchers laboriously persuaded her of the real source of her illusion (the gendered aspects of this exhibition—the men of reason, the woman of superstitious faith—were all too transparent). To La Chapelle, the point of such demonstrations was that he had found one of the originating causes of religious phantasms and that now, so identified, ventriloquism could be turned with delicious irony from being a buttress of superstition to a tool of the Enlightenment. The study of nature had yielded up the secrets of the sorcerer's power, as well as the ancient springs of political and religious despotism, and now those demystified illusions could be turned into a Baconian theater, a didactic exhibition that would enact rationality's triumph over superstition and truth's routing of fraud. Other writers on the subject would improve the details of La Chapelle's anatomy and add to his data, but most would repeat his basic conviction: ventriloquism was a primeval font of religious error that was capable of being turned from the purposes of occult mystery to modern éclaircissement.[5]

La Chapelle's experimental observations had immediate relevance to the much larger battle against religious enthusiasm. This was especially evident in appropriations among the Scottish Common-

4. Joannes Baptista de La Chapelle, *Le Ventriloque, ou l'engastrimythe* (London and Paris: Duchesne, 1772), 341, 471–478.
5. Ibid., xxi, 323–360, 419–422, 438–439.

Sense philosophers. Dugald Stewart, in his *Elements of the Philosophy of the Human Mind* (3 vols., 1792–1827), placed his consideration of ventriloquism at the end of a long section on "sympathetic imitation" in which he considered the human propensity for copying others and the weighty influence that the imagination has on the body. Here, joining a train of medical writers, he took up "the contagious nature of convulsions, of hysteric disorders, of panics, and of all different kinds of enthusiasm" and turned to the joined importance of imitation and imagination to explain these varied phenomena. In crowded and noisy assemblies, whether political or religious, people were given to "spasmodic affections"; "their senses and their imagination" overstimulated, they were incapable of the "cool exercise" of the "reasoning powers." Animal magnetism was Stewart's leading example of people's susceptibility to such "theatrical representations," but that was part of a longer train of popular enthusiasms and religious frenzies (such as the Quakers, the French Prophets, and the massive evangelical revival at Cambuslang) for which sympathy, contagion, and "mechanical imitation" provided guiding categories of explanation. The Scottish Enlightenment was hardly any more moderate than the French when it came to efforts to retune the resonances of popular Christian piety.[6]

Ventriloquism was relevant to this discussion for Stewart because of the crucial role that "the imagination of the spectator or of the hearer" played in the human susceptibility to both deception and enthusiasm. Whereas some wanted to emphasize the formal acoustic dimensions of vocal illusions, for Stewart the point was the way in which the ventriloquist "manages the imaginations of his audience" through suggestion, misdirection, counterfeiting, and theater. Stewart accented the complicity of the deceived, the ways in which their own imaginations were excited, making up for any gaps in the artifice, finally yielding, "without resistance, to the agreeable delusions practised on [them] by the artist." The ventriloquist was thus like the mesmerist or the revivalist in bringing the imaginations of his spectators under his own skillful management. In his *Letters on Natural Magic*, David Brewster picked up on Stewart's point, attesting that the susceptibility of the human imagination to fall for such vocal illusions was immense, the superstitious person being "the willing dupe of his own judgment." "The influence over the human mind which the ventriloquist derives from the skillful practice of his art," Brewster concluded, "is greater than that which is exercised by any other species of conjuror." Stressing the ventriloquist's enormous power to manipulate people's superstitious imaginations, Brewster

6. Dugald Stewart, *The Works of Dugald Stewart*, 7 vols. (Cambridge: Hilliard and Brown, 1829), 1: 108, 137–151, 159.

suggested that the accomplished artist had "the supernatural always at his command," being able to "summon up innumerable spirits" and to make them "unequivocally present to the imagination of his auditors." Such vocal artifice was, in short, the priest's treasure and the enthusiast's downfall.[7]

No one made more sophisticated use of La Chapelle's propositions about ventriloquism and religious illusion than did the American novelist Charles Brockden Brown, whose *Wieland; Or, The Transformation* and *Memoirs of Carwin, the Biloquist* centered on just such themes. Brown, like Tom Paine, journeyed from a Quaker upbringing into deistic skepticism, and Carwin's ventriloquist act was one emblem of Brown's religious disavowals. The Wieland family, steeped via their father in a long history of radical Protestant sectarianism, proves an easy target for Carwin's deceptions after his arrival at their tranquil home. Clara and her brother Theodore, for all their cultivation of republican virtue and education, retain active religious imaginations and are all too ready to attribute supernatural agency to Carwin's mysterious voices. The pious Theodore, after all, has long sought "the blissful privilege of direct communication" with God, "of listening to the audible enunciation" of divine speech. Clara, somewhat more cautious, is torn by the appearance of the marvelous, but ultimately lacks "grounds on which to build a disbelief." Carwin, too late, will provide the naturalistic basis for presuming "auricular deception" through his learned exposition of ventriloquy, or biloquism (Brown uses the two terms interchangeably). Earlier Carwin, tipping his hand, has tried to make the Wielands aware of "the power of mimicry," but they remained impervious to his "mode of explaining these appearances," incapable of absorbing such knowledge.[8]

7. Ibid., 3: 166–171; David Brewster, *Letters on Natural Magic* (London: John Murray, 1842), 167, 171–172. For the point that the illusion was less about acoustics than the misdirection of the imagination, Stewart was drawing especially on an anonymous review of John Gough's "An Investigation of the Method Whereby Men Judge, by the Ear, of the Position of Sonorous Bodies, Relative to Their Own Persons." The assessment had appeared in *Edinburgh Review* 2 (April 1803): 192–196.

8. Brown, *Wieland*, 32, 69–70, 152, 165 [30, 60, 125, 135]. *Wieland* is among the most widely commented upon novels of the early national era, but scholars have been imprecise in contextualizing the book's central illusionist practice of ventriloquism and the religious implications that flow from it. For a basic contextualization of this dimension of the novel, see "Historical Essay," in Charles Brockden Brown, *The Novels and Related Works of Charles Brockden Brown*, ed. Sydney J. Krause, S. W. Reid, and Alexander Cowie, vol. 1, Bicentennial edition (Kent State: Kent State University Press, 1977), 325–326. Readings that I have found especially insightful for my purposes include: Jay Fliegelman, *Prodigals and Pilgrims: The American Revolution against Patriarchal Authority, 1750–1800* (Cambridge: Cambridge University Press, 1982), 235–248; Jane Tompkins, *Sensational Designs: The Cultural Work of American Fiction, 1790–1860* (New York: Oxford University Press, 1985), 40–61; Steven Watts, *The Romance of Real Life: Charles Brockden Brown and the Origins of American Culture* (Baltimore: Johns Hopkins University Press, 1994). esp. 54–58, 82–89, 184–185; Bernard Rosenthal, "The Voices of *Wieland*," in *Critical Essays on Charles Brockden Brown*, ed. Bernard Rosenthal (Boston: G. K. Hall, 1981), 104–125. Watts does an especially fine job of locating

Similar credulity within Carwin's own family started him in the cultivation of this art. "A thousand superstitious tales were current in the family," Carwin avers in the *Memoirs*. "Apparitions had been seen, and voices had been heard on a multitude of occasions. My father was a confident believer in supernatural tokens. The voice of his wife, who had been many years dead, had been twice heard at midnight whispering at his pillow." Seeing in such popular Christian beliefs an opening to manipulate his father, Carwin feels emboldened to move from simple mimicry and the ventriloquizing of distant voices to feigning utterances of the dead as well as the divine. Traveling through Spain, Carwin becomes a master at manipulating Catholic "superstitions," very much on the model of Saint-Gille, but his vocal artifice proves equally powerful over the imaginations of faithful Protestants. Put to the test, both his own family and the Wielands fail badly at suspicion; Carwin's studied art dupes them all (with bloody consequences for the Wielands, as Theodore is eventually thrown into such religious madness by this eruption of voices that he murders his wife and children). The whole violent mess, the apparently repentant Carwin tells Clara as he reveals his technical knowledge of natural magic, provides a potent "lesson to mankind on the evils of credulity," on the fatality of religious illusions.[9]

The reimagining of ventriloquism offered a way for rationalists and deists to scorn the continuing ferment of religious enthusiasm and prophecy—all the innovative voices of evangelical awakening, all the personal discoveries of divine calling amid these outpourings of the Spirit. "No other instrument" but deft ventriloquy was necessary to "institute a new sect," Carwin learns from a European mentor—a dismissive point that La Chapelle had made directly as well. "Can you doubt that these were illusions?" Clara's uncle asks her with appropriate skepticism after hearing about the voices. "Neither angel nor devil had any part in this affair." The philosophical knowledge of ventriloquism provided a basis for canniness and disbelief, an assumption of suspicion, as well as a game of disenchantment. It offered both a naturalistic vocabulary and a distancing amusement that helped support a stance of incredulity in the face of the clamoring voices of religious inspiration and the sweeping rise of revivalistic fervor. In this respect, at least, Brown's work was less a tale of Federalist alarm or Edwardsian depravity than

the novel within Brown's wider deistic suspicions about revealed religion. For a subsequent romance featuring a rogue ventriloquist who plays on the "superstitions" of the credulous, see Henry Cockton, *Life and Adventures of Valentine Vox, the Ventriloquist* (London: R. Tyas, 1840). A more famous descendant of Carwin is L. Frank Baum's Wizard of Oz, who also used ventriloquism as a technique of mystification. See L. Frank Baum, *The Wonderful Wizard of Oz* (New York: Signet Classic, 1984), 100–103, 156–157.
9. Brown, *Wieland*, 194, 234 [158, 189].

one of solidarity with Jeffersonian suspicion over the perils of popular Christian piety.[1]

Brown, however, still played on both sides of the fence as he exposed the inner contradictions of the new learning: Enlightenment dreams that philosophical experiments with ventriloquism would unmask popular superstitions blended into the new masquerades made possible with such rational forms of recreation. The mesmerizing impostor Carwin was less interested in taming the enthusiastic imagination than in manipulating "the ignorant and credulous" for his own ends of wealth, power, and pleasure. In Carwin, Brown created the sort of charlatan who bared the irrationality hidden in La Chapelle's embrace of the illusionist Saint-Gille as a philosophical ally. In this juggling of the Enlightenment and magic, reason easily slipped into humbug, and such subversions from within made the natural philosopher's hope of containing the eruptive voices of popular Christianity all the more a pipe dream.[2]

The uses to which La Chapelle's theory could be put ultimately extended far beyond such "local" applications within European and North American Christianity. It offered a naturalistic lens on religions across the board and came specifically to provide a way of making sense of indigenous conjurers encountered through colonial contact. La Chapelle and his varied heirs had all seen ventriloquism as part of that ancient conspiracy of priestly magicians, as one of the chief means employed among Egyptians, Greeks, and other pagans to produce oracular illusions. Dugald Stewart, though, made a significant extension of the construct by concluding his remarks on the subject in *Elements of the Philosophy of the Human Mind* with an account of Captain George Lyon's travels among the Eskimos. Lyon's story was then picked up by David Brewster in his *Letters on Natural Magic*, quickly becoming part of the ventriloquist's echo chamber.

Stewart and Brewster read Lyon's "curious" narrative of exploration with their new explanatory tools, ready to incorporate these "savages" and their "male wizards" into the natural history of superstition. Lyon himself had licensed this reading, finding "all the effect of ventriloquism" in the various imitations that he saw enacted among the Eskimos by "an ugly and stupid-looking young glutton." Speaking wryly of a diviner's possession by a spirit named Tornga and the hollow voice that replaced the shaman's own, Lyon reported what he heard in diction shaped by his knowledge of ventriloquism: "Suddenly the voice seemed smothered, and was so managed as to sound as if retreating beneath the deck, each moment becoming more distant, and ultimately giving the idea of being many feet below the cabin,

---

1. Ibid., 163, 243; La Chapelle, *Le Ventriloque*, 341, 478.
2. Brown, *Wieland*, 243 [196].

when it ceased entirely." Brewster, Stewart, and Lyon saw no mystery in the conjurer's powers, no threat of difference, no hint of the ecstatic or the demonic, only the natural curiosity of the ventriloquist's illusion, only what Euro-American stage magicians had by now rendered a harmless and humorous simulation. "The Eskimaux of Igloolik," it turned out, were simply, as Brewster said, "ventriloquists of no mean skill." Philosopher and explorer joined together to make ventriloquism a vagrant hypothesis available for explaining Eskimo "wizards" as readily as Delphic oracles or sectarian enthusiasts.[3]

This rational recreation as a framework for encounter lingered. Decades later one of the major ethnographers among the Chukchees and Eskimos still included in his massive field report a section on "ventriloquism and other tricks" in his discussion of religious practices. "The Chukchee ventriloquists," he observed, "display great skill, and could with credit to themselves carry on a contest with the best artists of the kind of civilized countries . . . It is really wonderful how a shaman can keep up the illusion." As with the Enlightenment fabrication of shamanism and fetishism as global constructs, universalizing the category of ventriloquism allowed the learned to take "possession" of such indigenous practices in the stock terms of imposture and credulity. It enabled them to perform their own interpretive sleight-of-hand of transforming the strange into the familiar, ritual into art(ifice).[4]

As wildly vagrant as the excursions of Stewart and Brewster were, ventriloquism's use as a construct for advancing rationality and embarrassing superstition continued to widen. In a lengthy American tract called *Ventriloquism Explained* (1834), with a laudatory preface by the Amherst geologist Edward Hitchcock, the avowed hope was the further "diffusion of Scientific principles" of material causation and the negation of all the old wonders—ghosts, visions, voices, prognostications. The focus was especially on refining the judgment of the young, so that they would avoid being deceived by the slippery talk of mountebanks as well as the supernatural tales of

3. Brewster, *Letters*, 5, 176–178; Stewart, *Works*, 3: 171–173; Dugald Stewart, "Observations on Ventriloquism," *Edinburgh Journal of Science* 9 (1828): 250–252. For the original account, see George Francis Lyon, *The Private Journal of Captain G. F. Lyon H.M.S. Hecla, during the Recent Voyage of Discovery under Captain Parry* (London: Murray, 1825), 149–150, 359–374.
4. Vladimir Bogoraz, *The Chukchee*, in *Memoirs of the American Museum of Natural History*, vol. 11 (Leiden, 1904–1909; New York: AMS, 1975), 435–439. See also Sutton, *Treatise*, 26–29; Elisha Kent Kane, *Arctic Explorations in the Years 1853, 1854, 1855*, 2 vols. (Philadelphia: Childs and Peterson, 1856), 2: 126–127; W. H. Davenport Adams, *Curiosities of Superstition, and Sketches of Some Unrevealed Religions* (London: Masters, 1882), 274–278; Daniel G. Brinton, "The Folk-Lore of Yucatan," *Folk-Lore Journal* 1 (1883): 249. On the construction of shamanism, see Gloria Flaherty, *Shamanism and the Eighteenth Century* (Princeton: Princeton University Press, 1992). On the making of fetishism, see Frank E. Manuel, *The Eighteenth Century Confronts the Gods* (Cambridge, Mass.: Harvard University Press, 1959), 184–209.

"colored servants." Here, one more time, were La Chapelle's stories of Saint-Gille's religious dupes and Dugald Stewart's appropriation of Captain Lyon's travels. Some years later, in 1851, La Chapelle's abusive pranks were given an even more explicitly racial spin in the anecdote of one performer who supposedly disrupted a black revival meeting with a series of thrown voices. "Les Religieux dupés" had become, in this American incarnation, "Blitz and the Darkies," though, tellingly, illumination was not offered to the "cullered bred-deren." Instead, the narrator invited his ostensibly white reader to share a good laugh at the irredeemably credulous; the ventriloquist, having broken up the meeting, left them with "their eyes rolled heav-enward." Though one of the earliest ventriloquists, Richard Potter, was possibly the son of a slave mother and a white master, stage ven-triloquism remained a predominantly Euro-American technique, a theatrical chiaroscuro in which the "white magic" of enlightened ingenuity was contrasted with "dark" superstition.[5]

* * *

LAURA H. KOROBKIN

Murder by Madman: Criminal Responsibility, Law, and Judgment in *Wieland*[†]

* * *

Criminal law and evidence are key concepts in *Wieland*, a highly forensic novel in which every reader and every character is cast as a juror at whose "bar" evidence of crime is presented for judgment.[1]

5. *Ventriloquism Explained; And Juggler's Tricks, or Legerdemain Exposed; With Remarks on Vulgar Superstitions* (Amherst: J. S. and C. Adams, 1834), unpaginated preface, x, 9, 39–40, 56, 77–78, 82–83, 114–115; "Blitz and the Darkies," *Flag of the Union*, 1 Febru-ary 1851, reprinted in *Everybody a Ventriloquist: A History of Ventriloquism, with Instruc-tions and Anecdotes Combined* (Philadelphia: Brown's, 1856), 24–25. On Potter's racial identity (he is said to have passed as "an East Indian," which would have been useful for selling his magic, and to have carefully concealed his own background), see John R. Eastman, *History of the Town of Andover, New Hampshire, 1751–1906*, 2 vols. (Concord, N.H.: Rumford, 1910), 1: 425–427; Pecor, *Magician on the American Stage*, 69–71. When one ventriloquist advertised a special show in 1802 for black Philadelphians, he was forced to cancel the performance. See Pecor, *Magician on the American Stage*, 88–89.
† From *American Literature* 72.4, pp. 721–50. Copyright, 2000, Duke University Press. All rights reserved. Used by permission of the publisher. The author's parenthetical citations refer to the Penguin Classics edition of the novel, ed. Jay Fliegelman, 1991. Page numbers in square brackets refer to this Norton Critical Edition.
1. For example, Clara presents the difficult evidentiary problems related to the possible causes of her father's death as if to an inquest jury: asking "'[W]hat is the inference to be drawn from these facts?'" (21) [18], she marshals evidence and argues the options; describing the voices in her closet, Clara positions readers as jurors who may reject her "testimony" as "the immediate witness" (74–75) [53]; presenting Pleyel's accusation against her, Clara refers to "evidence," to his ears being "witness" and his own "convic-

Surprisingly, especially in light of Brown's extensive legal training, detailed explorations of the novel's legal aspects have been virtually absent from critical discussions. While many critics have noted that *Wieland* deals with law and features a courtroom confession, none has fully explored how central legal concepts are to the way the novel works, choosing instead to analyze issues of causation, motivation, and individual responsibility in terms of contemporary discourses about religion, politics, and philosophy.[2]

Brown spent six years reading law in the offices of Alexander Wilcocks, a Philadelphia practitioner.[3] In 1793, he disappointed his family by rejecting the law and embarking on what he hoped would be a successful career as a man of letters in New York.[4] As Robert Ferguson has shown, Brown had come to despise what he called in one novel the law's "endless tautologies, its impertinent circuities, its lying assertions and hateful artifices."[5] Yet *Wieland* is a novel obsessed with law, saturated with the vocabulary of evidence, testimony, proof, inference, corroboration, and judgment, and Brown's then recent

---

tion" (118) [81], then complains that "'[h]e had judged me without a hearing'" (120) [82]; soliciting her "vindication," Clara's brother says, "'You speak before a judge who will profit by any pretence to acquit you: who is ready to question his own senses when they plead against you'" (124) [85]; and defending herself to Pleyel, Clara worries that her narrative will not "'be permitted to outweigh the testimony of his senses'" because she has "'no witnesses to prove my existence in another place,'" and because "'[she] cannot summon Carwin to [her] bar, and make him the attestor of [her] innocence, and the accuser of himself'" (126) [86]. When Clara goes to Pleyel's house "to plead the cause of [her] innocence, against witnesses the most explicit and unerring" (131) [89], their interchange is presented as a trial, ending in Pleyel's verdict of "conviction" based, he claims, on "'evidence which took away the power to withhold [his] faith'" (154–55) [104].

2. Robert A. Ferguson is the one critic who has considered *Wieland* in light of Brown's legal background, yet he analyzes none of the legal doctrines the novel engages. Instead, he asserts generally that Brown trivializes the law, finding it inapplicable to real problems, and that his "repeated theme is the inability of law to control or even to define behavior," a position this article challenges (*Law and Letters in American Culture* [Cambridge: Harvard Univ. Press, 1984], 138–39). Psychological readings include Norman S. Grabo, *The Coincidental Art of Charles Brockden Brown* (Chapel Hill: Univ. of North Carolina Press, 1981), and Toni O'Shaughnessy, "'An Imperfect Tale': Interpretive Accountability in *Wieland*," *Studies in American Fiction* 18 (spring 1990): 41–54; religious angles have been explored by Michael T. Gilmore, "Calvinism and Gothicism: The Example of Brown's *Wieland*," *Studies in the Novel* 9 (summer 1977): 107–18; Shirley Samuels, "*Wieland*: Alien and Infidel," *Early American Literature* 25 (1990): 57–60; and Marshall N. Surratt, "'The Awe-Creating Presence of the Deity': Some Religious Sources for Charles Brockden Brown's *Wieland*," *Papers on Language and Literature* 33 (summer 1997): 310–24; enlightenment philosophy has been carefully analyzed by Roland Hagenbüche, "American Literature and the Nineteenth-Century Crisis in Epistemology: The Example of Charles Brockden Brown," *Early American Literature* 23 (1988): 121–51, 125, and Jay Fliegelman, introduction to *Wieland*, vii–xlii; and political readings have been offered by, among others, Fliegelman, Samuels, and Nicholas Rombes, "'All was Lonely, Darksome, and Waste': *Wieland* and the Construction of the New Republic," *Studies in American Fiction* 22 (spring 1994): 37–46.

3. See Ferguson, *Law and Letters*, 129–30.

4. Ibid., 129–34.

5. "Endless tautologies" is from Brown's *Ormond* (Peterborough, Canada: Broadview, 1999), 51. This passage is cited in part by Ferguson in his useful description of Brown's distaste for law (*Law and Letters*, 132).

emergence from the world of courtrooms and legal treatises requires that we take the text's forensic positioning seriously. Every incident is presented to us in legal language; every character speaks as if he or she has been up all night reading trial practice manuals; every page echoes with the "testimony of the senses," the "inferences" to be drawn from the "evidence" of outward appearance, the "conviction" of a character's "guilt" reached by one who ear-"witnesses" damning "evidence."

Indeed, *Wieland* is structured by the idea of the trial—the law's procedural mechanism for recovering past events, for resolving conflicting narrative versions of such events by making factual determinations, and for using those determinations to make judgments that assign various forms of liability. To recognize the novel's immersion in difficult evidentiary questions such as those surrounding the cause of the senior Theodore Wieland's death[6] or Pleyel's accusations of Clara's sexual corruption[7] is only part of the story. Also missing from critical discussions is an exploration of the novel's deep engagement with both the necessity for—and the problems of—judgment. Just as characters make cases before each other's "bars," a series of cases is presented to the bar of every reader-juror's judgment.[8]

Like Nabokov's Humbert Humbert, Clara Wieland deploys an insistently forensic rhetoric that situates her narrative as both a witness's testimony of what she has seen and heard (with all the biases and limitations implied by such an "interested" role), and a lawyer's final argument to the jury (assembling and arguing her view of the case). From the start, she leaps back and forth between these roles, worries about the obvious conflict of interest between them, yet stays within the parameters of what would work at a trial in her attempts to resolve narrative problems. "'If my testimony were without corroborations,'" Clara declares, "'you would reject it as incredible. The experience of no human being can furnish a parallel'" (6) [7–8]. Concerned that reader-jurors will reject as inherently unbelievable evidence outside their own experience, Clara the lawyer promises to bolster the credibility of Clara the witness by introducing consistent, objectively acceptable evidence from other sources.[9] That

6. Clara treats readers as an inquest jury returning a verdict on the cause of death. Problematically, reasonable causal inferences (fire, gunshots or an explosion, a blow from a heavy object) cannot be made from familiar phenomenal evidence (lights, loud noises, ashes, and bruises); the best Clara can offer is a choice between supernatural causes and the psuedo-scientific theory of self-combustion (18–21) [16–18].

7. Pleyel hears what he infers is Clara's voice speaking licentiously to Carwin (132–44) [89–98]. The inference is reasonable but incorrect; Carwin later explains that he mimed her voice to test and deceive Pleyel (239–41) [156–57]. Pleyel's jealousy and fury cause him to misinterpret other evidence, including a letter Clara writes to Carwin (142–43) [96]. While there is ample evidence, it is difficult to interpret correctly because its sensory nature makes it apparently trustworthy and because Pleyel's premature judgment against Clara warps his response.

8. These cases include, most notably, the investigation into the cause of Wieland Sr.'s death and the accusation of sexual impropriety against Clara.

she is unable to do so successfully—that she is not believed by those around her, that Carwin escapes judgment, and that she ultimately abandons her forensic roles—does not invalidate the legitimacy of her quest. Instead, it shifts to us the responsibility to complete her task: by positioning his readers as jurors, Brown implicates us from the start in Clara's project of assessing evidence and reaching a verdict. The novel invites us to do a better job than she did at sorting out the credible from the incredible—in short, to accept responsibility for judgment despite its extraordinary difficulties and thus to make possible an ethical, if not a perfectly coherent, world.

In designing *Wieland*'s plot, and especially in constructing the complex relationship between Carwin's ventriloquism and Wieland's violence, Brown drew, I believe, on provocative examples and maxims from two prominent legal works, Sir William Blackstone's *Commentaries on the Laws of England* (1765–1769) and Sir Geoffrey Gilbert's *The Law of Evidence* (1754).[1] By transforming what were meant as theoretical examples into fully realized situations, Brown relied on Blackstone and Gilbert while using the resources of fiction to pull the rug out from under their complacent analyses. In the universe of Brown's novel, it is often impossible to apply the rules of evidentiary assessment taught by legal experts. There is evidence galore, but the normative relationships between evidence and inference, effect and cause, corroboration and truth, have broken down: identifiable voices do not belong to those who seem to be speaking; corroborated newspaper reports are false; sounds, lights, words all mislead. More frightening still, the instrument used to assess this evidence—the supposedly rational human mind—is shown to be warped, fragile, and malleable. Even Clara, though she struggles valiantly to maintain the rule of law and its requirement of individual accountability, ultimately abdicates all her forensic roles, including, most importantly, the role of judge.

Though Brown used the novel to mock the law's procedural ineffectiveness, he also carefully designed a plot that demonstrates how key principles of law and evidence can supply the conceptual links that restore accountability in a fragmented world. As in a courtroom, the law helps reader-jurors complete their job because it provides rules for determining responsibility. This is not to say that *Wieland*

---

9. For example, Clara bolsters her own credibility through a corroborating witness when she says that her description of the circumstances surrounding her father's death is not based on her observations as an unreliable six-year-old but on the oft-repeated recollections of her uncle, a doctor, whose "testimony is peculiarly worthy of credit, because no man's temper is more sceptical, and his belief is unalterably attached to natural causes" (21) [18].

1. Sir William Blackstone, *Commentaries on the Laws of England*, 4 vols. (1765–1769; reprint, Chicago: Univ. of Chicago Press, 1979); and Sir Geoffrey Gilbert, *The Law of Evidence* (1754; reprint, New York: Garland, 1979). All citations are to these editions and appear parenthetically in the text as *CLE* and *LE*, respectively.

champions the legal system as it functioned in Brown's day or that it celebrates enlightenment rationality and the inherent order of the universe. Much of the novel's achievement lies precisely in its complexity, its ability to attack assumptions about the rational readability of the world while affirming the possibility of ethical judgments grounded in an assessment of the effect our acts have on others. If there is a message in the novel for the newly formed republic, it may be that Americans should assess policies by their actual impact in the world, both expected and unexpected, rather than by a politician's character, ideas, or articulated intentions. The surprising twists and turns that characterize the real world consistently escape the narrowing limits of intention; while statements about motive can be proposed to excuse or define actions, the actual consequences of those actions stand as the final and only valid determinant of their value.

* * *

In fashioning his plot, Brown drew not only on Blackstone but on recent American cases of violent religious mania. Critics have long connected Brown's mention in the novel's "Advertisement" of "an authentic case, remarkably similar to that of Wieland" (4) [4], with the tragedy of James Yates, a fanatical religious separatist who in 1781 killed his wife and four children, believing that he was obeying God's directly communicated commands.[2] Shirley Samuels has added the similar case of William Beadle, and Marshall Suratt recently suggested additional sources in the less violent religious manias of David Brainerd and Ludwig von Zinzendorf.[3] Such analyses, while useful, present Wieland's religious fanaticism as a closed system in which what is ultimately most disturbing about Wieland's blissful violence is, in Samuels's phrase, the discovery that the "alien is already within."[4] But if we look closely at the novel, it is clear that whatever else may be true about Wieland's horrifying acts, they are not produced solely by his own inner demons.

Like every other character in the novel, Theodore Wieland has been struggling with a difficult evidentiary problem. Obsessed with the challenge of proving God's existence and knowing his will, Wieland asks, as Emerson will, why he does not enjoy an original relationship with the universe, why he does not have direct rather than circumstantial evidence of God's existence. But where Emerson sees direct evidence in every horizon, leaf, and flower, Wieland cannot move from evidence to inference, cannot look at the phenome-

2. See Samuels, "Alien and Infidel," 57–58; and Suratt, "The Awe-Creating Presence," 312–13.
3. See Samuels, "Alien and Infidel," 58–60; and Suratt, "The Awe-Creating Presence," 314–20.
4. Samuels, "Alien and Infidel," 60.

nal world and infer from it the necessary existence of a divine spirit
and his own role in the divine plan. When disembodied voices are
heard, especially an oracular voice announcing the death of Pleyel's
missing German fiancée, Wieland begins to believe that God's voice
might be heard by man. This possibility engenders an intense, vulnerable, and volatile emotional state. According to Wieland's own
narrative, he walked toward Clara's house on the night of the murders filled with a "torrent of fervid conceptions," raptures, and a consciousness of joy and gratitude toward God (188–89) [125]. Suddenly
he stretched out his arms and exclaimed out loud:

> "O! that I might be admitted to thy presence; that mine were
> the supreme delight of knowing thy will, and of performing it!
> The blissful privilege of direct communication with thee, and
> of listening to the audible enunciation of thy pleasure!
>
> "What task would I not undertake, what privation would I not
> cheerfully endure, to testify my love of thee? Alas! thou hidest
> thyself from my view: glimpses only of thy excellence and beauty
> are afforded me. Would that a momentary emanation from thy
> glory would visit me! that some unambiguous token of thy pres-
> ence would salute my senses!" (189) [125]

Had there been no external, vocalized response, no demand for a
death and a victim, it is likely that Wieland's religious fervor, though
continuing, would have flowed as it had so far, in nonviolent directions. But there is a response. Moments after his plea for an "audible
enunciation of thy pleasure," his passionately expressed desire to
"testify" his love for God by undergoing a difficult "task," Wieland
sees exactly the "momentary emanation" of divine "glory" he has
asked for, a luminous vision confronting him as he descends the
stairs after finding Clara's room empty. The words of this beaming
visage respond precisely to Wieland's yearnings: "Thy prayers are
heard. In proof of thy faith, render me thy wife. This is the victim I
chuse. Call her hither, and here let her fall" (190) [126]. Filled with
elation, Wieland brings his wife to the house, where with some difficulty he manages to strangle her. Shortly thereafter, he hears the
voice demanding that he sacrifice his children as well, and he does so.

Does Carwin impersonate the voice of God and demand that
Wieland "render" his wife as a chosen victim who must fall in death?
The answer, I think, is yes. While Carwin assures Clara that he has
"slain no one" and "prompted none to slay" (225) [147], Brown carefully strews throughout the novel the facts reader-jurors need to
identify the gaps and inconsistencies in Carwin's self-serving narrative. To begin with, Carwin's general credibility could not be worse.
He displays sympathy and speaks persuasively, but Brown makes
sure we also know that he is not only a practiced liar, a schemer, and

a master manipulator of language but also an immoral seducer and an inveterate meddler in the affairs of others, a ventriloquist who has already preyed on many victims' weaknesses. He is also, he admits, driven by irresistible curiosity to test the virtue of those who seem to be models of rectitude. Specifically, he confesses that Judith's reports of her mistress's goddess-like fearlessness induced him to test Clara's courage by pretending to be a rapist and murderer hiding in her closet (230) [150]. He admits that he schemed to hoodwink Pleyel into believing in Clara's sexual profligacy because to deceive "'a man of cold resolves and exquisite sagacity . . . would be the sweetest triumph I had ever enjoyed'" (239) [156]. Even though this trick, if successful, would make Pleyel believe Clara sexually depraved and would lead him to reject her love, Carwin could not resist it, consoling himself with the likelihood that the deception would be short-lived. In each case, though aware of the "dangerousness of that instrument" (235) [153] he employs and resolves not to use again, he cannot resist the urge to experiment, to test the virtue of those whose perfections he resents, to use intimate knowledge picked up through eavesdropping to devise schemes that exploit his victims' weaknesses. Knowing this, we can reasonably infer that when he hears Wieland's impassioned plea, Carwin cannot resist such a seemingly direct invitation and he uses his powers to answer it on its own terms.[5] Characteristically, too, he also cannot resist demanding a sacrifice so great that it tests the limits of his victim's receptivity, although he claims later that he believed its very outrageousness would make the artifice obvious. This strategy parallels the one Carwin explains to Clara that he employed in deceiving Pleyel: while admitting that his vocal mimicry is so persuasive that it must be believed, Carwin defends himself by claiming that he expected Pleyel to reject the overheard conversation as incredible because its lasciviousness was so uncharacteristic of Clara (240) [156–57].

The details of time and place carefully distributed throughout the novel prove that Carwin met Wieland at Clara's house at eleven o'clock on the night of the murders, heard his anguished prayer, and decided, with horrible consequences, to answer it. On that night,

5. Interestingly, Carwin's almost uncontrollable addiction to such experimentation brings him close to the controversial "irresistible impulse" test for criminal insanity first proposed in the 1840s and sometimes used in the twentieth century. Nineteenth-century commentators such as Fitzjames Stephen considered it not a definition of insanity but a means for rendering the criminal act involuntary and therefore not willful (see Nigel Walker, *Crime and Insanity in England*, 2 vols. [Edinburgh: Edinburgh Univ. Press, 1968], 1:104–9; subsequent references to this text will appear parenthetically with the abbreviation C1). The idea that lack of control over one's actions would relieve a man of criminal responsibility was thus not available when Brown was writing in the 1790s. Yet Brown's fascination with the connection of mental states to accountability suggests one more complication to Carwin's relation to the consequences of his actions.

Carwin had asked Clara by letter to meet him at eleven o'clock at her house (156) [105]. Her narrative states that when "the preconcerted hour had arrived" she was at her brother's house waking up Louisa Conway, who informed her that Wieland was not home (163) [110]. Wieland's courtroom confession explains that he was missing because, when Clara did not arrive from her visit to the city, he went to her house long after the usual hour for bed (188) [124–25]. While Carwin's initial narrative, designed to exculpate him, denies any encounter with Wieland on the night of the murders, he does admit that he was at Clara's house "at the appointed hour" of eleven (242) [158].

The eleven o'clock meeting is also specifically admitted by Carwin months later, again at Clara's house, when Wieland appears just after Carwin has finished the story of his ventriloquistic powers. Attempting to shock her brother out of his madness and prevent him from murdering her, Clara rephrases what she has heard, telling Wieland that Carwin "'counterfeited the voice and face of an angel, for the purpose of destroying thee and me. . . . He is able to speak where he is not'" (249) [162]. Wieland then asks Carwin a direct question: "'The visage—the voice—at the bottom of these stairs—at the hour of eleven—To whom did they belong? To thee?'" (249) [163]. Carwin falters, tries to speak, and finally manages to whisper, "'I meant nothing—I intended no ill—if I understand—if I do not mistake you—it is too true—I did appear—in the entry—did speak. The contrivance was mine, but—'" (250) [163]. Clearly, Wieland's question and Carwin's answer refer not to the similar vision and voice Clara experienced later the same evening, just before discovering the mutilated body of her sister-in-law, but to an encounter at eleven o'clock on Clara's stairs, when the voice demanded the sacrifice of Wieland's wife. Carwin's hesitancy may be because he is now admitting before Clara precisely the encounter with Wieland he had earlier denied. Certainly Carwin is capable of producing the vision Wieland saw: he has already confessed to using an identical face and voice in crying, "'Hold!'" to Clara (168, 224) [112, 147], and, soon after Carwin confesses the imposture to Wieland, Wieland (though briefly believing Carwin to be a demon) recognizes him and tells Clara that "'the visage and voice which urged me to the sacrifice of my family, were his'" (257) [167].

In short, the source of the first "divine" injunction, the one demanding the sacrifice of Catherine Wieland, was the ventriloquized voice of a reckless Carwin and not a projection from Wieland's warped mind. As reader-jurors assessing the credibility of witnesses and the weight of evidence, we must pay careful enough attention to the factual details in the text to reject Carwin's earlier exculpatory narrative, something a surprising number of critics—even those who challenge Clara's credibility—have failed to do.[6] Carwin is a quick-witted liar; realizing that Clara holds him liable for the murders, he shapes his story to separate himself from Wieland's acts. He is clever enough to adopt a sympathetic stance of grief and contrition, and to admit to a range of lesser crimes such as seduction, in order to establish a level of credibility that will make Clara believe his account of the greater crime, the capital crime of murder. Of course the evidence presented to us is confusing. But if encouraging readers to become critical, sharp-minded jurors is part of Brown's project, then our skill at sifting that evidence and rejecting the self-serving and inconsistent components of Carwin's narrative is a key test of our adequacy as readers. As we learn the lesson in judgment Brown offers us, our control over the bewildering data of daily life is not effaced but increased.

As Carwin confesses that the vision Wieland saw was his "contrivance," he attempts to excuse his behavior by assuring Clara that he "meant nothing" and "intended no ill" (250) [163]. If Carwin's motives were not malevolent, should we exonerate him from liability for the disastrous consequences of his actions? In a parallel gesture, Wieland explains at his murder trial that his motives were pure and religious. What credence should we give to either testimony? Before deliberating, juries are instructed in the relevant law by the trial judge. If we as reader-jurors are to render a true verdict, we need to know not only the novel's facts but also the relevant law on motive, malice aforethought, and insanity. While fiction is deeply concerned with questions of motive—with psychological drives and emotional intensities—the law, as we will see, is not. To assess its difficult cases, *Wieland* invites us to consider the law's methods as well as the novel's.

Blackstone tells us that "the killing must be committed with malice aforethought to make it the crime of murder" (*CLE*, 4:198). In law, malice is not "spite or malevolence to the deceased in particular" but "any evil design in general; the dictate of a wicked, depraved, and malignant heart" (*CLE*, 4:198), and it may be expressed or implied. The law does not require that the criminal have a motive for the murder, and no evidence of motive need be presented at a criminal trial.[7] It is not necessary that the accused consciously

6. Grabo, for instance, attacks Clara as disturbed and unreliable, but he accepts Carwin's "confession" as an honest, believable explanation that "exculpates" him "entirely" (*Coincidental Art*, 14, 20).

7. In law, motive and intent are different: "Motive is the moving cause, that which induces an individual to act; intent is the purpose or design with which the act is done. Motive has to do with the desire; intent involves only the will" (Francis Wharton, *Wharton's Criminal Law*, 12th ed., 3 vols. [Rochester, N.Y.: Lawyer's Cooperative,

wish the victim harm, if he "with a sedate and deliberate mind" engages in "a concerted scheme to do him some bodily harm" (*CLE*, 4:198). The required mental element is an intent to do the act that results in the victim's death, not a malevolent or vicious desire to hurt her or him. Though there is no reason to believe that Carwin wishes the deaths of Wieland's family, there is also no reason to believe that he doesn't, and though he adopts a stance of horrified surprise when told of their deaths, the deliberateness of his imposture, combined with the clear demand that the victim "fall," constitutes the kind of "concerted scheme to do . . . bodily harm" that should meet the law's definition of malice.

If Carwin's "inciting" Wieland toward murder is a perfect illustration of Blackstone's "murder by madman," his specific demand for Catherine's death without any particular wish for its accomplishment is an especially horrifying example of the outer limits of malice aforethought. Critics may accept Carwin's claim that he acted "without malignant intentions, but without caution" (226) [147–48] as sufficient to exonerate him, but Brown would have known that a lack of desire to produce disastrous consequences will not efface culpability so long as the accused intentionally performed acts that were likely to produce those consequences. Carwin's willingness to admit a lack of "caution" does not improve matters, for, like the man who shoots a gun in the direction of a crowd while claiming that he didn't intend to hurt anyone, he displays a reckless disregard for the consequences of his actions that is equivalent to an intent to produce those consequences.

In short, the law will not permit us to escape responsibility for the damage we do by letting us use the limits of our conscious mental states to deny the link between our acts and their consequences. The legal definition of malice will effect the linkage that the individual disavows. Except in certain circumstances, then (one of which, not at all coincidentally, is insanity), the law assigns responsibility based on acts and consequences, which can be known, not on mental states, which cannot.

Carwin seems to believe that so long as his intentions extended only to his acts and not to their disastrous effects, he should be exonerated. He sees his acts of ventriloquism as if they exist only at

---

1932], 1:208 n. 20). In a subsection entitled "Motive need not be shown," Wharton states that "as a general rule" "the proof of motive for the commission of the offense charged does not show guilt, and that a want of proof of such motive does not establish the innocence of the accused" (1:211). Asserting that "motive is not an essential element of a crime," Rollin M. Perkins notes that though evidence of motive is relevant and may be introduced "whenever it is clearly established that he committed [the deed] with whatever state of mind is required for the *mens rea* of the particular offense, all the requisites of criminal guilt are present, even if no possible motive for the deed can be shown. In fact, in such a case, even proof of a good motive will not save a defendant from conviction" (*Criminal Law* [New York: Foundation Press, 1969], 828–33).

the moment the voice is counterfeited, rather than as embedded in an ongoing context with consequences involving other people tomorrow or next week. Though he can manifest terror and sympathy, and his voice alone elicits Clara's tears, he seems at the core strangely lacking in emotions and a sense of human connectedness. Like Twain's mysterious stranger, he travels from another world, sets up tests and traps for undesigning humans, and then watches coolly to see how they respond. Like the malarial plague in Brown's *Arthur Mervyn*, Carwin destroys lives and then moves on, leaving in his wake a destabilized community struggling to cope with the effects of a fatal toxin. Even if we accept Carwin's motive as quasi-scientific curiosity rather than malevolence, his conscious detachment from his acts ("I meant nothing—I intended no ill") does not entitle him to dissociate himself from the carnage his acts produced.

While many critics have argued that *Wieland*'s separation of unpredictable consequence from original stimulus undermines all notions of human accountability, I think Brown's point is more complex. As the causal connection between Carwin's original imposture and the violence it engenders becomes more attenuated, as it reaches toward Wieland's suicide and Clara's collapse, the significance of that first intervention should not be obliterated. Congratulating Carwin on his "strange sense of honesty," Grabo concludes that because Carwin begins a process whose effects he cannot control, he has "in a sense, no responsibility."[8] This seems to me quite wrong. Carwin's responsibility may be located at a double remove—because Wieland's hands rather than Carwin's close around Catherine's neck and because he may not consciously desire her death—but the law's key contribution to the novel is a conceptual scheme that closes the gaps separating Carwin from Catherine's corpse. Carwin wants us to attend to questions of intent and motive, to his subjective mental state before he acted, and if we follow his invitation we find ourselves caught up in indecipherable states, in excuses, in what cannot be known. But while Brown's novel vividly presents this psychological ambiguity, it also uses legal principles to suggest that it is possible, and, for the assignment of culpability, preferable, to assess acts on the basis of their external, knowable consequences. Carwin orchestrates his dazzling vision and verbal demand for a victim for maximum impact; when that victim falls, the responsibility is his.

In "inciting" Wieland to murder, Carwin counts on the direct sensory impact of his vision to make its authenticity seem irrefutable. As Hagenbüchle and others have noted, Brown uses Carwin's stratagems to demonstrate weaknesses in the philosophical theories of Locke and others who argued that all knowledge derives from the senses. By showing how easily the senses can be misled,

8. Grabo, *Coincidental Art*, 10.

Brown also challenges related legal principles that privilege sensory evidence. To attack the senses' absolute reliability, however, is not to suggest that the truth can never be confidently determined. With effort and attention, reader-jurors can be quite sure that Carwin's imposture is a deliberate trick. Not the world, but the evidence, is misleading; when accurate evidence is available, reliable verdicts can be reached. Eighteenth-century courtrooms evinced a strong preference for direct sensory evidence. Brown probably learned about evidence from Gilbert's influential *The Law of Evidence*. Instead of describing the law of evidence himself, Blackstone simply reprints a few maxims and refers his readers to Gilbert's "excellent" work.[1] The 1788 edition of *The Law of Evidence* printed in Philadelphia, where Brown was reading law, was the only American edition of any treatise on evidence before 1802.[2] Gilbert begins by noting the different degrees of certainty about facts,

> from perfect Certainty and Demonstration, quite down to Improbability and Unlikeliness, even to the Confines of Impossibility; and there are several Acts of the Mind proportion'd to these Degrees of Evidence, which may be called the Degrees of Assent, from full Assurance and Confidence, quite down to Conjecture, Doubt, Distrust and Disbelief. . . .
>
> Now to come to the true Knowledge of the Nature of Probability, tis necessary to look a little higher, and see what Certainty is, and whence it arises.
>
> All Certainty is a clear and distinct Perception, and all clear and distinct Perceptions depend upon a man's own proper Senses, for this in the first Place is certain, and that which we cannot doubt of if we would, that one Perception or Idea is not another, that one Man is not another; that what belongs to one Man, does not belong to another, and when Perceptions are thus distinguish'd on the first View, it is called Self-Evidence or Intuitive Knowledge. (*LE*, 1–2)

By creating a divine visitation that Wieland experiences with his "own proper senses," Carwin provides the only kind of evidence that can elicit Wieland's "full assurance and confidence," his complete "certainty" about the vision's actuality.[3] Ironically, of course,

9. Hagenbüchle, "Crisis in Epistemology," 124.
1. Blackstone calls Gilbert's treatise "a work which it is impossible to abstract or abridge without losing some beauty and destroying the charm of the whole" (*CLE*, 3:367).
2. Morris L. Cohen lists all books on evidence published in the United States before 1860 (*Bibliography of Early American Law*, 6 vols. [Buffalo, N.Y.: William S. Hein, 1998] 2: 131–58); according to Cohen, Crukshank's Philadelphia edition of Gilbert is the only one before 1802 (2:134).
3. Carwin's imitation of Clara's voice in the ruse against Pleyel works the same way: just as Wieland overcredits the "divine" vision because he sees and hears it with his own senses, so Pleyel refuses to credit Clara's narrative declarations of sexual purity because they contradict evidence of her sexual corruption he has "earwitnessed." Though Clara insists that her offenses "exist only in your own distempered imagination" (133) [90],

Brown designs the vision precisely to disprove what Gilbert says we "cannot doubt of if we would," for here one perception is another (Wieland perceives a divine emanation instead of a trick; he hears a voice in one place that is sent from somewhere else), one man is another (the divine presence is really Carwin), and what belongs to one man belongs to another (the voice of God is really the ventriloquized voice of Carwin).

By springing his seemingly incontrovertible vision on a man already infused with a dangerous religious mania, Carwin does more than present a believable, demanding God; he loosens Wieland's fragile hold on reality, pushing him over the edge into madness. At the moment Wieland rushes out of Clara's house to find and sacrifice his wife, Carwin's hoax has accomplished two "transformations" simultaneously: it has created a madman, and it has transformed this madman into an instrument for committing murder. A jury well-instructed in eighteenth-century law would therefore be justified in convicting Carwin as a principal in Catherine Wieland's murder.[4] If the imposture's sensory nature explains its success, its later demystification as a comprehensible hoax shows that attentive reader-jurors can correctly sort out the facts. The vision Wieland sees may be misleading, but it is not essentially ambiguous.

Turning now from Carwin's criminal responsibility to Wieland's, we find a different set of complications. Let us take the murders first. At his trial, Wieland presents a shocking spectacle. A loving husband and father, intelligent, educated, thoughtful, and religious, he is convinced that his willingness to bludgeon and strangle his family to death demonstrates the completeness of his religious devotion and the success of his search to know and obey God's will. As he declares in court when asked why he should not be executed:

> "If my judges are unable to discern the purity of my intentions, or to credit the statement of them which I have just made; if they see not that my deed was enjoined by heaven; that obedi-

---

she knows she must do battle with "proof" that, "though fallacious, is not implausible" (134) [91]. When she asks why Pleyel failed to "compare the evidence of sight with that of hearing," he replies only that he had strong proof and "yielded not but to evidence which took away the power to withhold my faith" (154) [104].

4. The evidence about the voices demanding the deaths of Wieland's children and Louisa Conway, and, later, Clara and Pleyel, is much less clear. Did Carwin lurk in Clara's house to see the results of his first imposture, then try a second one? Or was Wieland's now fully delusional insanity the source? Just as Brown carefully provides multiple, consistent sources for everyone's whereabouts at eleven o'clock, Wieland himself provides the only narrative of later "divine" demands. Carwin's liability might still be argued on a theory that, having caused Wieland's madness, Carwin is liable for all damage traceable to that madness, including his suicide. While the argument for Carwin's moral responsibility is strong, the chain of cause and effect is probably too thin to support a criminal conviction. But the distinction between deaths for which a culpable criminal can be identified and prosecuted and those for which the evidence is insufficient is very much the point, and careful reader-jurors learn that difference.

ence was the test of perfect virtue and the extinction of selfishness and error, they must pronounce me a murderer. . . . You say that I am guilty. Impious and rash! Thus to usurp the prerogatives of your Maker! to set up your bounded views and halting reason, as the measure of truth!" (200–201) [132]

Wieland assumes that the judges see only two possibilities: either he is a holy man, chosen by God to perform these acts, or he is a murderer. Knowing that they have already rejected the former, he assumes they will condemn him to death as the latter. With great fervor, he challenges the court's authority, arguing that the judges usurp what should be God's privilege. Their refusal to take into account any explanations from outside the phenomenal, material world and their presumptuous rejection of his testimony that God appeared to him demonstrate how woefully ill-equipped they are to judge his acts. Wieland's belief in the divinity of the voices he hears is sincere, as is his corresponding belief that the violence he perpetrated in response is pure and admirable. But because he speaks from inside his delusions, he cannot recognize a third possibility: that he is neither a divine instrument nor a murderer but a madman—and a manipulated one at that.

While there was no single legal definition of criminal insanity before the *McNaghten* case in 1842, the most widely used standard was the predominantly moral test for "knowledge of good and evil." First articulated in 1581, it was repeated by judges and legal writers up to the time it became one prong of the two-part *McNaghten* standard.[5] As Michael Dalton put it in 1618, "[I]f one that is *'non compos mentis,'* or an ideot, kill a man, this is no felony, for they have not knowledge of Good and Evil, nor can have a felonious intent, nor a will or mind to do harm."[6] In his *History of Pleas of the Crown* (1736), Sir Matthew Hale similarly grounded the definition of insanity in the ability to distinguish between good and evil (*CI,* 1:40–41).

Two aspects of this test are especially relevant to Wieland. First, an accurate moral sense is the precondition for the law's expectation of individual responsibility. If the legal definition of malice demonstrates the law's resistance to assessing criminal responsibility in terms of interior mental states, the definition of insanity shows that the law will carve out an exception where the absence of a functioning moral consciousness effaces the minimal understanding necessary to assess one's actions. Second, as a practical matter, the moral

5. See Walker's excellent chapter "From Bracton to Hale," in *CI,* 1:35–51, and his discussion of *McNaghten,* 84–103. Under *McNaghten,* the defendant must be laboring under such a disease or defect of mind "as not to know the nature and quality of the act he was doing; or, if he did know it, that he did not know he was doing what was wrong" (Walker, *CI,* 1:100, citing Lord Chief Justice Tindal in *McNaghten*).
6. Walker, *CI,* 1:41, citing Dalton's *The Country Justice* (1618).

test enabled a verdict of not guilty by reason of insanity even if the accused understood and intended his violent act. As Nigel Walker notes, "In all but the exceptional case the madman obviously does mean to kill or at least seriously injure his victim; in other words . . . the will to harm [is] not lacking" (CI, 1:40). So long as courts required evidence that the madman didn't know what he was doing, or had no more awareness than a wild beast, insanity was often impossible to prove. With the "right and wrong" test, however, a man who could speak rationally on some subjects and perform practical tasks, such as buying and loading a gun, could still be found insane. So Wieland, who can competently describe his spiritual quest and the difficult business of killing his wife and children, qualifies as a madman.

Wieland's justification of the murders, proudly claimed as proof of his spiritual perfection, ironically provides the legal system with the evidence it needs to label him a madman. He may be, as Clara suggests, "acquitted at the tribunal of his own conscience" (206) [136] because he no longer feels a gap between God's will and his own, but the very absence of that gap condemns him. His belief that the murders were pure and right proves his absolutely warped sense of what is right and what is wrong. In one of the novel's most salient ironies, Wieland is wholly engaged with assessing his moral and spiritual state, yet his inability to distinguish good from evil condemns him to perpetual imprisonment as a dangerous madman.[7]

In analyzing Wieland's culpability, we must also consider the final death Wieland accomplishes: his own. As Brown would have known, Blackstone considered suicide "among the highest crimes." It is a "double offence," he writes, not only a temporal crime against the king, as all felonies are, but also a spiritual crime, because "no man hath a power to destroy life but by commission from God." The suicide, he informs us with just a hint of dry wit, is guilty of "invading the prerogative of the Almighty and rushing into his immediate presence uncalled for" (CLE, 4:189). Significantly, Blackstone argues that suicide itself is not evidence of insanity, for that would be carrying the excuse too far,

> as if every man who acts contrary to reason had no reason at
> all: for the same argument would prove every other criminal

---

7. Blackstone argues that insane defendants should be acquitted, for "as a vicious will without an act is no civil crime, so . . . an unwarrantable act without a vicious will is no crime at all" (CLE, 4:21). Nevertheless, Brown's Pennsylvania court convicts Wieland; it also remands him permanently to prison, because these "excesses . . . originated in sudden madness, but that madness continues" (202) [133]. While the difference is conceptually significant, its consequence is not, for Blackstone too recommends perpetual imprisonment for dangerous lunatics, and, as Walker notes, "the obvious, indeed often the only place where a troublesome or dangerous lunatic could be securely detained was the gaol" (CI, 1:43).

> *non compos,* as well as the self-murderer. The law very ratio-
> nally judges that every melancholy or hypochondriac fit does
> not deprive a man of the capacity of discerning right from wrong;
> which is necessary . . . to form a legal excuse. And, therefore,
> if a real lunatic kills himself in a lucid interval, he is *felo de se*
> as much as another man. (*CLE,* 4:189–90)[8]

When Wieland attempts to murder Clara, Carwin saves her by once
more impersonating the voice of God, instructing Wieland that "not
heaven or hell, but thy senses have misled thee to commit these acts.
Shake off thy phrenzy, and ascend into rational and human. Be
lunatic no longer" (262) [170]. When Wieland, shocked into rationality, realizes that he has butchered his family meaninglessly, he
snatches up Clara's knife and plunges it into his own neck.

Wieland's impulsive suicide provides a final twist to our discussion of criminal responsibility. For while Wieland's insanity should
excuse him "from the guilt, and of course from the punishment" for
murders committed while insane (*CLE,* 4:25), his suicide, the one
violent act that hurts only himself, is a rational choice made during
a "lucid interval" and is therefore fully punishable under the law.
Thus at the moment of his death—but only then—Wieland is both
a responsible human being and a condemnable felon. But if his
suicidal act makes him a criminal, it also implies concurrent acts of
self-judgment and self-sentencing that make him his own jury and
judge. By executing himself, Wieland embraces the judicial roles he
mocked his judges for performing when he accused them of "usurping" God's "prerogatives." Both a legal and a spiritual wrongdoer,
he commits exactly the crimes against God and law that he accused
the criminal justice system of committing against him.

Significantly, Wieland judges himself differently than the law does.
The law's judges are able to assess the situation dispassionately; in
forbearing to impose the death penalty, they show compassion and
restraint. The lax prison security that fails to prevent Wieland's
escapes does not invalidate their sentence. Like Blackstone, who
opposes executing the criminally insane because it would present
"a miserable spectacle, both against law, and of extreme inhumanity and cruelty, and can be no example to others," (*CLE,* 4:25, citing
Sir Edward Coke), the court refrains from destroying a body uncon-
nected to a rational mind. Though he is now at least minimally
rational, Wieland is incapable of such clear judicial thinking. Overcome with grief and guilt, his agonized consciousness can neither

8. Hale was the first to articulate a theory of "partial insanity," whereby a man could have
   an intact sense of reason on most subjects but be chronically deranged and morbidly
   preoccupied on others; such a man was responsible for acts committed during a "lucid
   interval" (see Walker, *CI,* 1:38, quoting Sir Matthew Hale, *History of the Pleas of the
   Crown* [2 vols. (1736; reprint, London: Professional Books, 1971), 1:30]).

live with his new knowledge nor work out the relationship between insanity and criminal responsibility. Unable to dissociate the delusional self that acted from the rational self that suddenly sees the horror of those acts, he grabs Clara's knife and cuts through what he cannot comprehend. But if Wieland's suicide ends his own suffering, it inflicts new suffering on others, most dramatically on Clara. Her consequent breakdown leads her not only to abdicate her familiar role as judge but, finally, to lead her narrative out of the legal framework she has so persistently constructed. In this essay's final section, I return to Clara's—and the reader's—relationship to law and judgment.

*   *   *

One reason the final chapter is so unsatisfying, despite its reestablishment of order and its love-and-marriage ending, is, I think, Clara's withdrawal from judgment and from her forensic framework. Sadly, she seems to have learned that her only hope for happiness lies in ceasing to insist on evidentiary assessment and adequate verdicts. Her struggle to judge nearly destroys her mind: she is not believed and the criminal justice system fails to try or to punish those responsible. Legal institutions cannot protect the community from further violence, since Wieland escapes his fetters several times with the avowed intention of killing Pleyel and Clara. And Carwin not only manages to hoodwink Clara's correspondent, her friends, and her uncle into believing his specious explanations, he also ends the novel alive and well, having suffered no arrest, trial, or punishment. It is highly unlikely, of course, that he is the "harmless" farmer Clara imagines; more likely, he is wreaking havoc on a new crop of unsuspecting victims.

 Wieland ends, then, with an orchestrated retreat from judgment. Clara resigns as judge and recasts her narrative discourse to eliminate its forensic insistence. And it is easy to see why. Those who have accepted the role of judge, and to whom cases have been presented, have failed to reach appropriate verdicts on each other or themselves. The institutions charged with administering justice have failed to indict the real criminal or secure the dangerous madman. Clara's grounded belief in the culpability of Carwin's agency has been rejected by those she most respects.

 But if Clara cannot sustain the responsibilities she assumes, if she vacates the judge's bench, we who have been seated in it with her from the start must not. Every case that has been presented at the "bar" of one or more characters has also been presented at ours. Testimony has been introduced, attacked, corroborated for us; sensory evidence heard and seen by us; arguments made and challenged. The evidentiary puzzles and deceptions that mislead the characters, then, need not, finally, mislead us. If the evidence is confusing, it is nevertheless possible to sort most of it out. We can decide whose voice expresses Clara's seemingly lascivious desires, whose visage impersonates a demanding God. The bias, passion, grief, and vulnerability to deception that mark each of the novel's interior judges as incapable of objective juridical deliberation do not cancel out the need for judgment. Instead, they present a strong and consistent argument for the necessity of neutral, disinterested judges and jurors who can bring to the act of judging clear, open minds undeformed by any stake in the outcome. This is not to say that *Wieland* paints a reassuring picture of the contemporary criminal justice system or the easy accessibility of valid verdicts. The novel attacks both the era's confidence in universal rational capacity and in the primacy of sensory evidence. The world is a murky, confusing place: interior mental states are ambiguous, deceptive sensory data often plausible. But important principles survive, even under siege, and these provide helpful tools to reconnect what presents itself to us, and to courts, in fragments.

Foremost among these principles are individual responsibility for one's actions and their consequences, maintenance of the link between act and effect despite the ambiguity or narrowness of mental states, and the necessity for objective, disinterested judgment. By bringing to life the concepts of principal and accessory liability, malice aforethought, and insanity, Brown suggests that the law can work effectively to enforce both legal and moral responsibility.

Finally, the contrast between Wieland's morally engaged and heartbreakingly sincere courtroom demeanor and Carwin's heartlessly curious and self-serving fluency is significant. Carwin is guilty of murder, though he lacks what might seem a necessary mental state—a motive or desire to kill—while Wieland is not responsible for his violence precisely because he also lacks a necessary mental state—the ability to appreciate its wrongfulness. Despite the seeming parallel, Carwin's irresponsibility and Wieland's insanity are radically different: where Carwin disavows the destructive consequences of his actions, Wieland is unable to comprehend their immorality. By juxtaposing Carwin and Wieland, Brown highlights the key role of moral awareness in both individual responsibility and the act of judging. Accountability for the consequences of our actions is at bottom a moral rule, for it insists that individuals remain connected to, and responsible for, the damage they do in the world, for the pain they cause. Carwin knows that horrible murders have been committed; what he should have known, and what the law can teach him, is that he has committed them. His dramatic schemes are not neutral or limited experiments but profoundly destructive and immoral crimes. His recklessness and limited foresight may explain, but they cannot justify, his acts. In contrast, Wieland's insanity legally separates him from his acts and their consequences because it robs him of a valid moral consciousness, a standard of right and wrong based on communal norms rather than delusional visions. Clara tries to enforce her judgment against Carwin, but she fails and finally abdicates her crucial juridical role. We, Brown's reader-jurors, are invited to fill it.

EDWARD CAHILL

[Brown's Politics of Imagination]†

On the eve of the series of disasters that will destroy her peace and pleasure, Clara, the narrator of Charles Brockden Brown's novel *Wieland* (1798), prepares to hear her brother, Theodore, recite a tragic tale just arrived from Germany and written by a promising novice Saxon poet:

> The exploits of Zisca, the Bohemian hero, were woven into a dramatic series and connection. According to German custom, it was minute and diffuse, and dictated by an adventurous and lawless fancy. It was a chain of audacious acts, and unheard-of disasters. The moated fortress, and the thicket; the ambush and the battle; and the conflict of headlong passions, were pourtrayed in wild numbers, and with terrific energy. (78) [62]¹

This elegant but ominous scene would seem to project two distinct possibilities: aesthetic pleasure or irrational chaos. On the one hand, like the recitation of Cicero, singing of ballads, and playing of violin and harpsichord that were the typical "occupations and amusements" (23) [21] of the Wieland circle, the tale reflects Brown's allusive romantic and pedagogical tendency, an illustrative example of refinement whose implicit purpose is to both define the tastes of his characters and educate those of his readers. Accordingly, although Brown's German poet suggests the gothic sensibility of Goethe, Schiller, or Christoph Wieland,² the story itself is of no significance; any that represented genteel romance reading and stirred the delicate passions of educated Americans like the Wielands would have

---

† From "An Adventurous and Lawless Fancy: Charles Brockden Brown's Aesthetic State," *Early American Literature* 36.1 (2001): 31–70. Copyright © 2001 by The University of North Carolina Department of English. Used by permission of The University of North Carolina Press, www.uncpress.unc.edu. Page numbers in square brackets refer to this Norton Critical Edition.
1. All references to Brown's novels, as well as the essay *Alcuin*, indicate the Kent State University editions and will be cited parenthetically.
2. Brown's German influence appears to be more one of literary models than philosophical traditions. See Warfel, "German Sources."

sufficed. On the other hand, the story's content and form prefigure both the events and the narrative style of the story Clara is about to tell.[3] The "dramatic series and connection" of the hero's exploits and his "chain of audacious acts" represent a plot barely held together by the "adventurous and lawless fancy" of the tale's narrator: an associative imagination whose train of ideas is as "wild" as the "headlong passions" it seeks to represent.[4] Thus, the Wielands' final exercise of aesthetic sociability, one culminating "six years of uninterrupted happiness" (26) [23], stands as a representation of the wide spectrum of aesthetic experience conceivable in Brown's world. It indicates as much the possibility of moral improvement through pleasure as it does the psychic confusion that follows in Clara's narrative.

The passage is thus an important clue to understanding how the multiple aesthetic registers in Brown's fiction reveal both the complexity and coherence of his diverse representations of imagination, as well as their manifold political implications. Critics of *Wieland* often mistakenly read the violence at the end of the novel as an indictment of the aesthetic forms at the beginning.[5] Although such fatalistic inductions were staples of republican antinovel discourse, the object of Brown's critique in *Wieland* and his other novels is neither the danger nor the failure of aesthetic experience, but rather the wide and contradictory range of its implications and effects. The distinction is crucial. Brown's novels deal with not only the excessive and "distempered" imagination but also with aesthetic education and pleasure, philosophical inquiry and enlightenment, and utopian possibility. Indeed, the principal tension in Brown's novels concerns the imagination's mutable status as both the source of the various possibilities of irrationality and the faculty through which art finds its moral ends. The imagination in Brown's fiction is the site of fanatical delusion and deceptive error, to be sure, but also correct judgment, rational speculation, and transformative sublimity. It is at once the potent source and susceptible object of confusion and crisis, as well as art and idealism. It is, like the novice Saxon poet, vulnerable to tragic dissolution but full of creative potential.

3. Seltzer similarly observes that Clara's description of the German romance "was a model of the novel itself" (88).
4. Brown understood no definitive distinction between the words "fancy" and "imagination," but like other eighteenth-century writers, he sometimes used "fancy" to refer to creative invention, liveliness, or luxuriance of thought, and "imagination" to suggest a more comprehensive and predictable power. For a brief history of the distinction, see Engell 172–83.
5. The Wielands' commitment to art and pleasure has often been seen as symbolic of the moral and epistemological fragility that finally undermines them. Bredahl, for example, calls Clara's world "an elite, aristocratic existence dedicated to worship of the mind, classical ideals, and [her] father . . . an involuted and stagnant world . . ." (181). See also Bell 148; Bennett 60; Butler 131; and Seltzer 89.

Yet we must take care not to reduce this multivalence to merely antithetical correlates of reason and passion. Not only do Brown's novels themselves defy such binaries, but the models of aesthetic experience that inform them often assume the imbrication of reason and passion. As we shall see, the chief problem in the theory of the imagination in the eighteenth century is not so much a *distinction* between the real and the ideal as it is a *confusion* of them: a confusion of perceiving things and imagining ideas. That is, the discourse of the imagination is persistently troubled by an ambivalence about understanding the image in the mind as a perception, impression, or material fact subject to the laws of empirical science—what Jean-Paul Sartre called a "naïve metaphysics of the image" (4)—and as a transcendent act of consciousness beyond the limits of body and world. As they seek to understand affect in rational terms, eighteenth-century theorists of the imagination struggle to negotiate the infinite claims of the mind and the limiting claims of matter. For Brown, such a struggle is realized in both the evanescence of his fiction's narrative reality and the substantiality of his characters' thoughts: the implied correlation between the "chain of audacious acts" described in his fiction and the "adventurous and lawless fancy" that describes them.

Brown's critics have typically found in this thematic and formal confusion the articulation of a general republican aversion to the imagination and a symptomatic representation of a fragile political state. Carl Bredahl refers specifically to "evil" energies of the imagination in Brown's novels (177); and James R. Russo finds Brown's representations of imagination to be consistently illicit and pathological. Similarly, Michael Davitt Bell and Mark Seltzer's otherwise groundbreaking essays on Brown find imagination in the early republic chiefly to be a source of "terror" and "deception" (Bell 145) and blame the chaos in Brown's fiction on a "fear or distrust of art" (Seltzer 160). In this essay, I propose an approach to Brown's fiction that recovers his interest in the moral and philosophical efficacy of aesthetic pleasure, reexamines the sources and significance of his novels' narrative confusion, and foregrounds his investment in the difference between—and the continuity of—the disordered and the transformative imagination. In the midst of the frenetic political and philosophical climate of the 1790s, Brown finds the technologies of aesthetic experience to be highly complex and ambiguous, but he also assumes the imagination's eminent ability to comprehend such complexity and ambiguity, and to elaborate its central relation to national polity and social transformation.

* * *

In the late eighteenth century, imagination conceived as the transcendent perfection of the soul was usually referred to as "genius."

For Brown, like most of his contemporaries, genius denoted the imagination's chief creative power and thus offered a romantic alternative to the rationality of Lockean empiricism. According to Joshua Reynolds, genius begins "where vulgar and trite rules no longer have any place" (97).[6] In his *Critique of Judgment*, Kant took this idea one step further by announcing that "genius is the talent . . . which gives the rule to art" (150). Thus, if genius implied a rejection of the rules of human reason or criticism, it also suggested access to universal ones. Late in his career, Brown defended genius from those who would "put their mark of scorn on every eccentricity of him who lives in that high temperament, in which alone works of genius can be produced." He warned impatiently, "To be in constant terror of exceeding the cold bounds of propriety, to be perpetually on the watch against any extravagance of mind, is not to be a poet" ("Desultory Observations").[7]

However, in his earliest writings, Brown perceived the inherent tensions implied by the imaginative freedom of genius: in particular, the nagging possibility of chaos. In "The Rhapsodist," his first significant work of criticism, published in 1789, Brown writes that "my felicity principally consisted in the liberty I . . . enjoyed to follow the dictates of my own inclination, into whatever seeming error, or absurdity, it might chance to lead me" (*Rhapsodist* 15). Reminiscent of Rousseau's *Reveries of a Solitary Walker* [1778], this wandering free spirit has a definitive fondness for solitude, such that "was he not compelled by the necessities belonging to his nature . . . he would withdraw himself entirely from the commerce of the world" (7). In the sublime tranquility of the Rhapsodist's thoughts, imagination has near-perfect autonomy and integrity. Yet, like the Solitary Walker, and Brown's later solitary pleasure seeker, Arthur Mervyn,[8] the transition from the ideality of rural peace to the reality of urban bustle produces enough "error, or absurdity" to send the Rhapsodist into a "temporary paroxism of frenzy" during which his "fancy was altogether ungovernable" (16). This "black moment of despair" (15) is not quite the baleful pessimism that haunts the entirety of Rousseau's *Reveries*, but it is enough for the Rhapsodist finally to warn of the "warmth of my imagination" unchecked by the "wholesome precepts of experience" (16), and to articulate the balanced formula of rational imagination that begins the essay:

6. On the eighteenth-century discourse of genius, see Engell 78–88, and Abrams 184–225.
7. Brown's familiarity with aesthetic theory in general is evident in his numerous essays in the *Monthly Magazine* and the *Literary Magazine* on taste, genius, beauty, sublimity, and the picturesque. Among these are his "On a Taste for the Picturesque," "American Prospects," "Alliance Between Poverty and Genius," "Reflections on Taste," "Poetry and Painting Compared," "On the Standard of Taste," and "Distinctions Between the Beautiful and the Picturesque."
8. The hero of Brown's 1799–1800 two-part novel, *Arthur Mervyn* [Editor's note].

> A rhapsodist is one who delivers the sentiments suggested by
> the moment in artless and unpremeditated language. His rea-
> soning is always introduced to illustrate the circumstance, and
> the fact to confirm the reason. He pours forth the effusions of
> a sprightly fancy, and describes the devious wanderings of a
> quick but thoughtful mind: But he is equally remote from the
> giddy raptures of enthusiasm, and the sober didactic strain of
> dull philosophy. . . . (5)

However, although here Brown trades Rousseau for a more moderate Addison—an autonomously creative imagination for one shored
up by reason and morality—this represents a tension more than a
renunciation. For all his moral grounding, one of Addison's main
premises was the dependence of imagination on freedom, that "the
Mind of Man naturally hates every thing that looks like a Restraint
upon it" (540). Given this tension, Brown maintains that the Rhapsodist is, like the perfect commonwealth, an abstract ideal, a "just
criterion of excellence," whose visionary impulses will be, for the
"brute" masses, the "object of laughter and ridicule," while "men of
sense will treat this unhappy propensity with a pity mingled with
admiration" (10).

We can understand this problem in formal terms. The reason for
such pity and admiration is what the Rhapsodist calls the "dream"
that mistakes "the incidents of human life" for "the phantastic stages
of a vision," a false perception of resemblance that "exists only in our
own imagination" (6–7). In claiming the moral multivalence of such
imagining, Brown refers implicitly to the ideas of thinkers like Hume
and Hartley, whose principles of association implied a structural
understanding of imagination rather than a wholly abstract one.
Association assumed that sensory "impressions" in the brain are
linked to ideas, which are in turn linked to other related ideas in
order to produce more complex "trains" of association. In *A Treatise
of Human Nature*, Hume described "the liberty of the imagination to
transpose and change its ideas" as a power guided by the "gentle
force" of associative principles (resemblance, contiguity, and cause
and effect) to form through experience coherent ideas of our existence (space and time) on which we may rely (57). Because these
links were based on the logical connection between ideas, association simultaneously suggested a unified vision of the world and
explained differences in taste and perspective. But it also invoked the
possibility that the productive capacity of the imagination to connect
disparate impressions and ideas might be capable of error, and merely
subjective or arbitrary rather than universal or based in reason.
Although association would usually produce regularity in the transition from idea to idea, Hume admitted the powerful effect of the
passions on this process, as well as a distinction between principles

that were "permanent, irresistible, and universal" and others that were "changeable, weak, and irregular" (274). Thus, however much association explained the complexity of mind based on the preeminence of the imagination and according to rational principles, it implied a model of consciousness in which one might share with others neither experience nor understanding of the world, one in which the alienation of total subjectivity would undoubtedly produce "black moments of despair." Brown parodied this tendency in his 1798 sketch "The Man at Home," in which an imaginary writer absurdly aims to trace out an almost infinite number of associations based on the arbitrary topic of a "broom-stick" (*Rhapsodist* 57–58). But he became increasingly interested in the moral implications of associative principles and their importance to literature. For what was at stake, as "The Rhapsodist" implies, was not only whether "the incidents of human life" were similar to "the phantastic stages of a vision," but whether citizens of a republic were to be held together by anything more than the rhetoric of the Constitution.

If anxiety was one response to the idea of association, another was an enthusiasm that engendered further emphasis on the materiality of the imagination, particularly in the work of such thinkers as David Hartley, Hermann Boerhaave, and Erasmus Darwin, three of Brown's most important influences.[9] If Hume resisted the mechanism of association by giving full reign to the passions, Hartley, association's most popular proponent, looked to neurology to render the idea not only immune from skeptical doubts but fundamental to every human feeling, thought, and action. In his major work, *Observations on Man, His Frame, His Duty, and His Expectations*, Hartley posited the unity of mind and matter by giving physiological form to psychological experience. Borrowing the idea of "vibration" from Newton, he argued that the vibrations of a "white medullary substance" of the brain, the spinal marrow, and the nerves are the ultimate source of all sensation, motion, and ideas.[1] Boerhaave, the modernizing Dutch physician and teacher, resembled Hartley in his belief in the relations of mind and body; but concerned with sympathy rather than pure association, he described the bodily effects of the imagination through sympathetic relations with others, such that one

9. Brown's familiarity with the work of these thinkers, which he read with Elihu Hubbard Smith while both were members of the Friendly Club, indicates something of the context of philosophical optimism in which they were generally received. In a letter to Davidson, Brown wrote, "Go on my friend—perseverance shall level every obstacle before thee, and genius and Industry shall unite to place thee by the side of Boerhaave and of Haller," his disciple (L3). Brown's passing references to Boerhaave in "The Rhapsodist," with its discussion of "cacoëthes scribendi, or itch of writing," is described "in the spirit of the eloquent professor of Leyden" (*Rhapsodist* 23–24). The education of Brown's Constantia Dudley in *Ormond* (1799) not as a "musician or pencilist" but as a student in "the school of Newton and Hartley" (33) reflects Brown's rejection of conventional female instruction and his sympathy with writers whose work expressed a new confidence in the understanding of human thought and action.
1. See Krause, "Historical Essay" for *Ormond*, 396–97.

"becomes healthy or sick from the dominion of the passions" ("On the Great"). Brown was also an avid reader of Erasmus Darwin's *Zoonomia*, which provided him with Wieland's "mania mutabilis" (Brown cites Darwin in *Wieland*) and Huntly's "somnambulismus."[2] Darwin calls "mutable madness" a tendency to mistake "imaginations for realities" (2:356), or the confusion of affective "sensations" with physical "irritations." But this apparently neat distinction is belied by the work's larger conflation of imagination and the materiality of physiology. In fact, Darwin's treatise, whose catalogue of diseases includes the admittedly speculative "diseases of association," such as "sympathetic tears" and "trembling from anger," also categorizes "madness" and "sleepwalking" along with less benign diseases like "pity," "sentimental love," and "reverie" (2:317–18). Just as the transcendent imagination slipped all too easily into "black despair," Darwin's expansive system, like Brown's yoking of "diseases and affections," both pathologized the passions and made illness imaginary.

The new discourse of psychic disease did as much to excite imaginations as to explain them. The renown of Darwin's *Zoonomia* was in large part based on its fascinating case studies of mental illness. Equally notable was fifteenth-century physician Thomas Fienus's treatise *De Viribus Imaginations,* which made a sudden reappearance in eighteenth-century England with its marvelous histories of "the force of imagination." Republican magazines regularly printed examples from Fienus's book, such as the tale of a man who, believing himself too large to pass through his door, was forced though it by his physician and quickly died of imaginary agony.[3] Similarly, Isaac Disraeli's *Curiosities of Literature*, a popular eighteenth-century miscellany excerpted and quoted in early American magazines, offered anecdotes of mental delusion collected from such writers as Mallebranche and Montaigne, such as that of a delirious fever patient cured by "swimming" in an imaginary lake. In fact, so many of these anecdotes, both reprinted and original, regularly appeared in American print that they appear to constitute a significant media fad of republican culture.[4]

* * *

2. The protagonist of Brown's 1799 novel *Edgar Huntly,* who like Clara Wieland is a somnambulist [Editor's note].
3. One exceedingly popular piece was "A Physical Dissertation Concerning the Strength of the Imagination in Women with Child upon the Foetus," by James Blundel, M.D., which was often reprinted and redacted in republican magazines and newspapers. See "On the Eccentricities."
4. As Fisher Ames wrote in 1801, "a newspaper is pronounced to be very lean and destitute of matter, if it contains no accounts of murders, suicides, prodigies, or monstrous births" (12).

Jay Fliegelman has argued that the late eighteenth century rejected the older tradition of scholastic education, which taught by "precepts and authority," for the modern Lockean pedagogy, which was based on rational and sensationalistic principles and rendered "by means of example and emulation."[5] One of the effects of this change was a new fear of bad examples. According to the principles of association, good examples would beget good ideas and actions, and bad would beget bad. As d'Holbach, one of Brown's favorite writers, warned: "The brain of man, especially in infancy, is like soft wax, fit to receive every impression that is made upon it" (25). Thus, the young imagination, now eminently vulnerable to accidental "impressions," had to be both rigorously exposed to the most wholesome ideas and assiduously protected from the most sinister. Whether good impressions might be stronger than bad, or vice versa, and how long either might last, were questions for speculation, but also questions whose lack of a definitive answer threatened to turn the moral order of Lockean sensationalism into nightmarish disorder. * * *

Brown examines the mysterious and paradoxical nature of early impressions most completely in *Wieland*. The religious mania of the elder Wieland is attributed to his accidentally encountering a work of French Camissard theology, at which point "the craving which had haunted him was now supplied with an object" (8) [10]. Similarly, the education of his children, Theodore and Clara, which rather ominously occurred "by accident more than design," taught "most branches of useful knowledge" (20) [19], including philosophy, literature, and music, none of which prepared them for the deceptions of Carwin. But the ultimate culpability of these impressions is anything but clear. Clara holds that her narrative "will exemplify the force of early impressions, and show, the immeasurable evils that flow from an erroneous or imperfect discipline" (5) [7]; but we never learn exactly what these "early impressions" are, nor whether they refer to those affecting the elder Wieland or his two children.[6] Nor are we able to distinguish between the force of early impressions and present ones. Like her brother's and father's adult experiences of imaginative deception, Clara's encounters with the subtle manipulations of Carwin's voice make "a deep impression on [her] fancy" (59) [49] that changes the course of her life. Finally, although powerful, not all early and forceful impressions are permanent in *Wieland*. Of Carwin, Clara asks, "What could have obliterated the impressions

5. For Brown's engagement with Lockean ideas, see Fliegelman 237–40; and Voloshin 263–68.
6. Christopher Looby notes that Clara's early impressions concerning her father's religious mania and spontaneous combustion were of second-hand accounts rather than first-hand experience. Because they are "products of reconstructive 'inference'" (153) rather than effects of immediate sensation, they demonstrate Brown's further complication of the Lockean model of ideation.

of his youth, and made him abjure his religion and his country?" (69) [56]. Writing from Montepellier at the end of the narrative, "a thousand leagues from my native soil, in full possession of life and health, and not destitute of happiness," Clara answers the question for herself: "Such is man. Time will obliterate the deepest impressions" (234) [173]. Clara's overcoming the force of early impressions, like Carwin's, comes as a result not only of exile and time but of new impressions: "A swift succession of new objects, and the exclusion of every thing calculated to remind me of my loss, was the only method of cure" (235) [174]. But such newfound pleasure rests on the same unpredictable series of impressions and moral logic of association that led to Clara's tragedy, her peace being restored as arbitrarily and indefinitely as it was destroyed.

So if Brown is making a point in *Wieland* about "the force of early impressions," it is one that undermines the very terms with which it is made. One must avoid "an erroneous or imperfect discipline," but this guarantees no protection from accidental impressions and unknown influences.

*   *   *

Indeed, even the most socially illegitimate uses of the imagination, such as Carwin's deceptive "biloquism," have their mitigating circumstances. In *The Memoirs of Carwin* (1803–5), Brown tells us that young Carwin's passionate literary yearnings face insurmountable opposition from his penurious and narrow-minded father; prohibited from pursuing the study of poetry, Carwin satisfies his aesthetic needs through the baser pursuit of ventriloquism. In the context of *Wieland*, in which Carwin's career as a deceiver makes its well-known and infamous end, Brown's sequel thus offers an originary moment that seems to explain Carwin's vice as the perversion of legitimate creativity. But if corrupted imaginations can be reformed or excused, and if they can coexist provisionally with a rigorous republicanism, then what is the ultimate status of aesthetic pleasure in Brown's novels?

Consider again the example of Clara Wieland. Despite her passion for poetry, music, and polite conversation, Clara, like Constantia,[7] is hardly a sensualist. Rather, she is an "economist of pleasure" for whom "self-denial, seasonably exercised, is one means of enhancing our gratifications" (22) [20]. It is because of this highly disciplined aesthetic attitude and refusal of easy pleasures that Clara's first encounter with Carwin's voice is both so powerful and so dangerous: "I cannot pretend to communicate the impression that was made upon me by these accents, or to depict the degree in which force and sweetness were blended in them. . . . The voice was not only melliflu-

---

7. The heroine of Brown's 1799 novel *Ormond* [Editor's note].

ent and clear, but the emphasis was so just and the modulations so empassioned, that it seemed as if a heart of stone could not fail of being moved by it" (52) [43]. Although the actual impression made by Carwin's voice is finally stronger than those of the education and experience that produced Clara's aesthetic discipline, its nature remains mysteriously incommunicable and finally unknowable. Yet what Clara does articulate about the beauty of Carwin's voice is precisely in the language of aesthetic pleasure, suggesting that, in spite of her being uncontrollably moved by it, she understands it as specifically aesthetic. Although Carwin's voice is intentionally deceptive, it is no less beautiful, and Clara's response no less disinterested and authentic. Her claim that "a heart of stone could not fail of being moved by" Carwin's "emphasis" and "modulations" is in fact an aesthetic judgment—according to Kant, a judgment of beauty assuming "subjective universal validity" (49)—such that the beauty it discerns is neither a function merely of the object (the sound of Carwin's voice) nor of Clara's subjective interpretation of it, but an epistemological reconciliation of object and subject. Yet Clara's claim also implies a social reconciliation of disparate subjects. As Terry Eagleton argues, aesthetic judgment in the eighteenth century signaled "a precious form of intersubjectivity . . . a community of feeling subjects linked by a quick sense of our shared capacities" (75). Which is to say that the exact moment when Clara is most susceptible to the impression of Carwin's voice is also when she is least aware of any danger and most confident of the benign fellowship in the world around her. Although it is punished so cruelly, her experience of pleasure is itself not guilty but entirely virtuous, and perhaps so compelling that it finally makes Clara vulnerable to the entirely extraneous fact of its viciousness. From this perspective, then, Brown appears both to distinguish aesthetic pleasure from the dangers of irrationality and to join them in a difficult and highly indefinite relation.

*   *   *

Like the "sublime visions of imagination" whose infinite power assumed and enumerated a transforming world, Edmund Burke's theory of the sublime described an empirical response to what Rousseau called the "incomprehensible chaos" of experience. For Burke, the painful experience of being overwhelmed by particular aesthetic objects—for their size, grandeur, or strangeness—yielded a feeling of delight, a positive experience that celebrated the confrontation of danger and resistance to complacency.[8] But if the sublime applauded

8. This is not to say that Burke's empiricism was adequate. Frances Ferguson argues that "Burke's inability or refusal to make a thorough-going distinction between objects and mental objects makes the testimony of the senses its own skeptical double, and mental representations become their own opposites." This "impossibility of sustaining a distinction between objects and representations" (2) resembles Clara's confusion of idea

momentous transformation, it also sought to make sense of it. As Thomas Weiskel argued, "the true function of the sublime is to legitimate the necessary discontinuities in the classical scheme of signification and to justify the specific affective experience which these discontinuities entailed" (17). In this context, we might examine the similarly overwrought language of Clara's transformation, her framing of the events of the narrative and her own thoughts in an insistently personal lamentation of the disruption of her pleasure:

> The storm that tore up our happiness, and changed into dreariness and desert the blooming scene of our existence, is lulled into grim repose (5–6) [7]; But alas! This and every other scheme of felicity and honor, were doomed to sudden blast and hopeless extermination (48) [40–41]; How had my ancient security vanished! (60) [49]; My life had been serene and blissful, beyond the ordinary portion of humanity; but, now, my bosom was corroded by anxiety. . . . I was pushed from my immovable and lofty station, and cast upon a sea of troubles (69) [56]; What a gloomy reverse had succeeded since the ominous arrival of this stranger! (95) [75]; All happiness and dignity must henceforth be banished from the house and name of Wieland (151) [115].

Clara's language may represent what Christopher Looby calls "postrevolutionary nostalgia," a conservative reaction to the "epistemological and linguistic undoing" of the status quo (177). More specifically, it is pattern of formal gesture that gives value and order to otherwise degraded and distorted social conditions. The rhetorical reversals and dramatic pairing of antitheses emphasize the close correlation of aesthetic pleasure and its opposites. In this way, Clara's performance of sublime solitude, like that of Rousseau, is as much an elegiac justification of her dislocation and reconstitution of the social order as it is an expression of confusion and suffering.

If such transformations are not always catastrophic, neither do they necessarily signal the breakdown of an elite, immoral, or otherwise fragile society. To be sure, prior to their crisis and the disorder that inspires it, the Wielands' relation to transformation—to all social and political change—is purely imaginative; but this does not mean they are guilty of antirepublican aesthetic solipsism. Their geographic and psychic distance from the reality of the French-Indian War, for example, figures as a complex symbol of their attitudes about the relation between the imagination and a changing world. As Clara describes it, the war is "at such a distance as to enhance our enjoyment . . . by agitating our minds with curiosity, and furnishing

---

and action because neither Brown nor Burke finally understood the sublime image, as Kant later would, as essentially an act of the mind. See Ferguson 37–95.

causes of patriotic exultation" (26) [23]. The political struggles of the nation are perceived as an object of the imagination without any effective reality beyond the ideas and feelings they produce. Two apparently opposite but related conclusions may be drawn from Clara's remark. The first, a standard view, is that the Wielands do not participate in any social world but the private utopia they have created; when that world is finally interrupted by politics and difference in the form of Carwin, it necessarily collapses. The second, however, assumes that social transformations are experienced chiefly in the mind, that an imaginative relation to the nation is not elitist escapism but *sensus communis*, and in this case, one that reflects an essential understanding of the difference between practical and theoretical ideas of government. Such a conclusion recalls Brown's early claim that "the idea of a perfect commonwealth" is both the object and merely hypothetical product of the imagination rather than an immediate social goal. Thus, whether we see *Wieland* as a pessimistic allegory of national formation or a more uncertain and speculative apprehension of a relation between mind and society finally depends on which conclusion we emphasize. But if the first conclusion implies the inherent dangers of the imagination in a republic, the second implies its absolute necessity. That is, we may either say that war and national politics had no effect at all on the circle at Mettingen, or that they made it possible both by providing a source of aesthetic pleasure and by symbolizing the inherent relation between the imagination and the ideal society.

* * *

The ambiguity of the discourse of national lawlessness helps us better to understand Brown's complex attitude toward the "lawless imagination" so often possessed and professed by his characters, the unrestrained thoughts and desires that propel them chaotically through their plots. The "adventurous and lawless fancy" of Clara's Saxon poet, however ominous, is a source of social pleasure. The "lawless mirth" enjoyed by Clara's friends (23) [21] is described in terms of an invigorating "diversity" rather than chaos: "variegated but not tarnished or disordered." For, like the effect of the French-Indian War on their imaginations, "some agitation and concussion is requisite to the due exercise of human understanding" (23) [21].[9] In a more general way, lawlessness in Brown's characters is both a flaw and a virtue, as well as a condition of personal transformation. It

9. Clara appears to be echoing Hume, who writes: "'Tis a quality very observable in nature, that any opposition, which does not entirely discourage and intimidate us, has a rather contrary effect, and inspires us with a more than ordinary grandeur and magnanimity. In collecting our force to overcome the opposition, we invigorate the soul, and give it an elevation with which otherwise it would not have been acquainted" (2:188).

propels Arthur Mervyn into social confusion, but it allows him to
negotiate successfully the social contradictions of republican culture.
Edgar Huntly's "ungovernable curiosity" leads him into great danger
but allows him to expose to public view a complex and illicit web of
private affairs (29). Felix Calvert's[1] "lawless and wild enthusiasm"
precipitates his bad judgments but shows itself neither worse nor less
credible than the nominally lawful world against which he struggles.

Whether this lawlessness speaks most directly to reactionary paranoia or radical idealism, or a combination of both, is debatable, but
its multivalent impact on Brown's representations of nationhood is
significant. Considering that many of Brown's protagonists leave
their native country, an abandoning of homeland appears to be the
punishment meted out for the failure of the imagination. *Wieland*'s
Clara leaves Pennsylvania for Montpellier; *Edgar Huntly*'s Clithero
flees Ireland to America; *Ormond*'s Constantia finally settles in
England; *Stephen Calvert*'s Felix runs away temporarily to Europe
and permanently to the wilderness of Michigan, thereby "interpos-
ing deserts between me and the haunts of mankind" (72). However,
if irrational imaginings imply having left the *sensus communis*, and if
their lawless nature exposes those who entertain them to a political
discipline that implicitly separates them from their communities, this
may be only a reminder of the gap that remains between the real
world of the early republic and the realm of the imagination, between
the actual and the possible. At the moment when their ideas and
perceptions cease to agree with those of the world around them,
they remove, albeit not entirely by choice, to a place more suitable.
That Clara, Constantia, and Felix ultimately find, quite literally,
peace of mind, suggests that to leave one's nation is not merely to
be deported but to seek another, more adequate world elsewhere.

WORKS CITED

Abrams, M. H. *The Mirror and the Lamp: Romantic Theory and the Critical Tradition*. New York: Oxford Univ. Press, 1953.

Addison, Joseph. *The Spectator*. Ed. Donald Bond. Vol. 3. Oxford: Clarendon Press, 1965.

Ames, Fisher. *Works of Fisher Ames*. Indianapolis: Liberty Press, 1983.

Bell, Michael Davitt. "'The Double-Tongued Deceiver': Sincerity and Duplicity in the Novels of Charles Brockden Brown." *Early American Literature* 9 (1974): 143–63.

Bredahl, A. Carl. "Transformation in *Wieland*." *Early American Literature* 12 (1977): 177–92.

1. A character in Brown's unfinished serial novel *Stephen Calvert* (1799–1800) [Editor's note].

Brown, Charles Brockden. "Annals of Europe and America, for 1806–7." *American Register* 1 (1806–1807).

———. *Bicentennial Edition of the Novels and Related Works of Charles Brockden Brown.* Kent: Kent State Univ. Press, 1977–1987.

———. "Desultory Observations on the Sensibilities and Eccentricities of Men of Genius: With Remarks on Poets." *Literary Magazine* 7.4 (April 1807): 294–96.

———. *Letters of Charles Brockden Brown.* Ed. John R. Holmes and Edwin J. Saeger. In *The Charles Brockden Brown Project: An Electronic Archive and Scholarly Edition,* unpublished.

———. *Literary Essays and Reviews.* Ed. John R. Holmes, Edwin J. Saeger, and Alfred Weber. Frankfurt: Lang, 1992.

———. *The Rhapsodist and Other Uncollected Writings.* Ed. Harry R. Warfel. New York: Scholars' Facsimiles and Reprints, 1943.

Butler, Michael D. "Charles Brockden Brown's *Wieland*: Method and Meaning." *Studies in American Fiction* 4 (1976): 127–42.

Darwin, Erasmus. *Zoonomia.* New York: AMS, 1974.

Disraeli, Isaac. *Curiosities of Literature.* New York: W. F. Widdleton, 1971.

Eagleton, Terry. *The Ideology of the Aesthetic.* London: Blackwell, 1990.

Engell, James. *The Creative Imagination: Enlightenment to Romanticism.* Cambridge: Harvard Univ. Press, 1981.

Ferguson, Frances. *Solitude and the Sublime: Romanticism and the Aesthetics of Individuation.* New York: Routledge, 1992.

Fliegelman, Jay. *Prodigals and Pilgrims: The American Revolution Against Patriarchal Authority, 1750–1800.* Cambridge: Cambridge Univ. Press, 1982.

Hartley, David. *Hartley's Theory of the Human Mind.* Ed. Joseph Priestly. New York: AMS Press, 1973.

d'Holbach, Paul Henri, Baron. *Good Sense, or Natural Ideas.* New York: Vale, 1856.

Hume, David. "Of Refinement in the Arts." In *Essays.* Ed. Eugene F. Miller. Indianapolis: Liberty Fund, 1985.

———. *A Treatise of Human Nature.* Ed. Ernest C. Mossner. London: Penguin, 1984.

Kant, Immanuel. *Critique of Judgement.* Trans. J. H. Bernhard. New York: Hafner Press, 1951.

Looby, Christopher. *Voicing America: Language, Literary Form, and the Origins of the United States.* Chicago: Univ. of Chicago Press, 1996.

"Of the Eccentricities of the Imagination." *Columbian Magazine and Monthly Miscellany,* June 1788.

"On the Great and Extensive Powers of Sympathy." *American Universal Magazine,* January 1798.

Rousseau, Jean-Jacques. *Reveries of the Solitary Walker.* London: Penguin, 1979.

Russo, James R. "'The Chimeras of the Brain': Clara's Narrative in *Wieland*." *Early American Literature* 16 (1981): 60–88.

Seltzer, Mark. "Saying Makes It So: Language and Event in *Wieland*." *Early American Literature* 13 (1978): 81–91.

Voloshin, Beverly R. "*Edgar Huntly* and the Coherence of the Self." *Early American Literature* 23 (1988): 262–80.

Warfel, Harry R. "Charles Brockden Brown's German Sources." *Modern Language Quarterly* 2 (Sept. 1940): 357–65.

Weiskel, Thomas. *The Romantic Sublime: Studies in the Structure and Psychology of Transcendence*. Baltimore: Johns Hopkins Univ. Press, 1976.

DAVID KAZANJIAN

[White Settler Colonialism in *Memoirs of Carwin the Biloquist*]†

Toward the beginning of Charles Brockden Brown's uncompleted novel, *Memoirs of Carwin the Biloquist,* the protagonist relates "events . . . which ascertained my future destiny." Rushing home one day with the news that his father's cows have escaped their field, he takes a shortcut through an unfamiliar rocky pass; in its dark enclosure, he confronts "terrors" and "violent apprehensions" of "goblins and spectres." His response is to "hallow . . . as loud as organs of unusual compass and vigour would enable me . . . the words which chanced to occur to me, . . . repeat[ing] in the shrill tones of a Mohock savage. . . . 'Cow! cow! come home! home!'"[1] As the echoes of these tones in the rocky passage suggest to Carwin the possibility of becoming a "biloquist," Brown's word for a ventriloquist, *Memoirs of Carwin* proceeds to tell the story of the escapades into which biloquism leads him. Serialized in the *Literary Magazine* from 1803 to 1805, *Memoirs of Carwin* is the prequel for Brown's first published novel, *Wieland; or, the Transformation: An American Tale* (1798), providing the story of Carwin's life before he appears as a crucial character in *Wieland*. Since the scene in the rocky passage contains the only appearance of "a Mohock savage" in either text, the figure appears to be incidental; however, "a Mohock savage" is in

---

† From "Charles Brockden Brown's Biloquial Nation: National Culture and White Settler Colonialism in *Memoirs of Carwin the Biloquist*," in *American Literature* 73.3, pp. 459–96. Copyright, 2001, Duke University Press. All rights reserved. Used by permission of the publisher. Page numbers in square brackets refer to this Norton Critical Edition.

1. Charles Brockden Brown, *Memoirs of Carwin the Biloquist*, in *"Wieland" and "Memoirs of Carwin the Biloquist"* (New York: Penguin Books, 1991), 282–84 [183–85]. (In the quotation from *Memoirs*, the last ellipsis is Brown's.) Further references to *Memoirs of Carwin* and *Wieland; or, the Transformation: An American Tale* will be to this edition and will be cited parenthetically in the text as *M* and *W*, respectively.

fact foundational to the plots of both texts, since its "shrill tones" and their echoes produce Carwin's biloquism, which in turn motivates his life-long misadventures. It is a tenuous foundation, however, since the "Mohock savage" appears not as a character but as the echo of ventriloquized "tones" that only "chanced to occur" and could never have been understood by their bovine addressee. As I will suggest, "a Mohock savage" can be read as a tenuous foundation for more than these two plots.

Throughout his life, Brown sought to represent himself as a founder of the proper national literary aesthetic. Literary critics and historians have obliged him for two hundred years, often representing *Wieland* as the first American novel. But this hold on foundational status that Brown and *Wieland* have long maintained is as tenuous as it is persistent. The familiar critical narrative that positions Brown as the founder of American literature overlooks not only William Brown Hill, whose novel *The Power of Sympathy* was published in 1789, nine years before *Wieland*, but also a lengthy list of literary predecessors who raise the very question of what "American" and "literature" might mean: Olaudah Equiano, Phillis Wheatley, J. Hector St. John de Crèvecoeur, Samson Occom, to name just a few of the most well known. *Wieland*'s foundational status as the first American novel can be challenged not only by *The Power of Sympathy* and a host of proto- and quasi-novels but also by the ambiguous status of *Memoirs of Carwin*, which tells of events prior to those of *Wieland* and, although it was published after *Wieland*, seems to have been written before or during *Wieland*'s composition.[2] Indeed, Brown seems to have intended *Memoirs of Carwin* to be part of *Wieland* itself, until Carwin's story "became too unwieldy for inclusion" and so was abandoned and reconceived ("I," xlii–xliii).[3]

In "a Mohock savage," then, we have not only a tenuous foundation for the plot of *Memoirs of Carwin* but also a figure for the tenuousness of an American literary aesthetic itself. A reading of this figure, in turn, opens up a constitutive relationship between aesthetics and politics—in particular, the politics of white settler colonialism at the turn of the nineteenth century. Thus, I will read Brown's "Mohock savage" in *Memoirs of Carwin* as a necessary, and necessarily tenuous, condition of possibility for American literary aesthetics.

2. On when Brown wrote *Memoirs of Carwin*, see his letter of 5 September 1798 to William Dunlap, in Fred Lewis Pattee, introduction to *"Wieland; or, the Transformation," together with "Memoirs of Carwin the Biloquist,"* ed. Pattee (New York: Harcourt, Brace, 1926), xlii–xliii. Further references to Patee's introduction will be cited parenthetically in the text as "I."

3. Pattee offers the following evidence for this conclusion: Brown admits as much in the 5 September 1798 letter to Dunlap; in *Wieland*, Carwin announces his intention to write his version of the story's events, but this version never appears fully in *Wieland*; and sentences with epistolary forms of address appear in *Memoirs of Carwin* but make no sense apart from *Wieland*, since only *Wieland* explicitly takes an epistolary form ("I," xlii–xliv).

*   *   *

As quickly as it is mobilized in *Memoirs of Carwin*, the figure of the
"Mohock" is subsumed by another: the echo. For after Carwin
hears the first "confused and indistinct" echo of his initial "Mohock
savage" utterance, he proceeds, shored up with a newfound confidence, through the rocky passage:

> I continued, for some time, thus to beguile the way, till I reached
> a space more than commonly abrupt, and which required all
> my attention. My rude ditty was suspended till I had surmounted
> this impediment. In a few minutes I was at leisure to renew it.
> After finishing the strain, I paused. In a few seconds a voice as
> I then imagined, uttered the same cry from the point of a rock
> some hundred feet behind me; the same words, with equal dis-
> tinctness, and deliberation, and in the same tone, appeared to be
> spoken. I was startled by this incident, and cast a fearful glance
> behind, to discover by whom it was uttered. . . . The speaker,
> however, was concealed from my view. . . . A few seconds, in a
> like manner, elapsed, when my ditty was again rehearsed, with
> a no less perfect imitation, in a different quarter. . . . Five times
> was this ditty successively resounded. (*M*, 285) [185]

The more distinct echoes of his call puzzle him and renew his terror, until he makes the second crucial judgment of his life and,
once again, banishes his terrors:

> A little reflection was sufficient to shew that this was no more
> than an echo of an extraordinary kind. My terrors were quickly
> supplanted by delight. The motives to dispatch were forgotten,
> and I amused myself for an hour, with talking to these cliffs: I
> placed myself in new positions, and exhausted my lungs and
> my invention in new clamours. The pleasures of this new dis-
> covery were an ample compensation for the ill treatment which
> I expected on my return. By some caprice in my father I escaped
> merely with a few reproaches. I seized the first opportunity of
> again visiting this recess, and repeating my amusement; time,
> and incessant repetition, could scarcely lessen its charms or
> exhaust the variety produced by new tones and new positions. . . .
> My reflections were naturally suggested by the singularity of this
> echo. To hear my own voice speak at a distance would have been
> formerly regarded as prodigious. To hear too, that voice, not
> uttered by another, by whom it might easily be mimicked, but by
> myself! I cannot now recollect the transition which led me to the
> notion of sounds, similar to these, but produced by other means
> than reverberation. Could I not so dispose my organs as to make
> my voice appear at a distance? (*M*, 285–87) [186–87]

Carwin surmounts his subjection to the authority of his traditional
father by "play[ing] the part of judge in matters of taste" (*CJ*, 43) and

by making his second crucial judgment: he decides to master the echo and to teach himself to become a willful producer of the echo's pleasure and delight. This second judgment is structured much like the first. "Naturally" and spontaneously, without being able to "now recollect the transition," Carwin focuses only on the "extraordinary" "singularity of this echo," eschewing mere mimicry in favor of what Kant might have called "genius," or the "innate mental aptitude" that can be neither learned nor mimicked but "*through which* nature gives the rule to art" (*CJ*, 168): "Hence, where an author owes a product to his genius, he does not himself know how the *ideas* for it have entered into his head, nor has he it in his power to invent the like at pleasure, or methodically, and communicate the same to others in such precepts as would put them in a position to produce similar products" (*CJ*, 169). Carwin draws on this rich fund of the echo, reaping a profit from it by subjecting it to his control.

With this second judgment, however, Carwin also begins to drift from Kant's aesthetic ideal and to become more of the scientist, or one who seeks the "power to invent the like at pleasure, or methodically" (*CJ*, 169), by engaging in "incessant repetition" and asking such practical questions as, "Could I not so dispose my organs as to make my voice appear at a distance?" (*M*, 287) [187]. Invoking the language of scientific investigation and mastery even more insistently, Carwin continues:

> From speculation I proceeded to experiment. . . . Gradually I subjected these finer and more subtle motions to the command of my will. What was at first difficult, by exercise and habit, was rendered easy. I learned to accommodate my voice to all the varieties of distance and direction.
>
> It cannot be denied that this faculty is wonderful and rare, but when we consider the possible modifications of muscular motion, how few of these are usually exerted, how imperfectly they are subjected to the will, and yet that the will is capable of being rendered unlimited and absolute, will not our wonder cease? (*M*, 287–88) [187]

For Carwin, the echo suggests an opportunity to rewrite a chance occurrence as a mastered invention. Faced with a second moment of judgment in this rocky passage, one provoked by an echo of his first judgment, he responds with a will to mastery and control, a rewriting of his initial judgment in the idiom of scientific biloquism.

Carwin at this point resembles Kant's "immortal" Newton more than his "poetic" genius. Kant explains the distinction thus:

> [W]e cannot learn to write in a true poetic vein, no matter how complete all the precepts of the poetic art may be, or however excellent its models. The reason is that all the steps that Newton

had to take from the first elements of geometry to his greatest and most profound discoveries were such as he could make intuitively evident and plain to follow, not only for himself but for every one else. On the other hand no *Homer* or *Wieland* can show how his ideas, so rich at once in fancy and in thought, enter and assemble themselves in his brain, for the good reason that he does not himself know, and so cannot teach others. . . . The talent for science is formed for the continued advances of greater perfection in knowledge, with all its dependent practical advantages, as also for imparting the same to others. Hence scientists can boast a ground of considerable superiority over those who merit the honor of being called geniuses . . . [S]uch [poetic] skill cannot be communicated . . . and so with him it dies. (*CJ*, 170)

Kant's comparison between the Greek poet Homer and the eighteenth-century German poet Christoph Martin Wieland speaks not only to the neoclassicism of German aesthetics but also to Kant's emphasis on "the talent for science" over "the talent for fine art." Science seems to name the "transcendence" of fine art, thus reminding us that Kant himself privileged understanding and a critique of pure reason, as well as reason and a critique of practical reason, over aesthetic judgment and its critique (*CJ*, 4). Genius is here characterized by a solipsism haunted by death, whereas science has a transmissibility that pushes it beyond art. It would seem to be Carwin's own effort to proceed "from speculation . . . to experiment" that pushes him beyond the limits of genius and toward the scientific practice of the "diligent observer of circumstances," who through "exercise and habit" is able to consider "all the varieties of distance and direction" and all "the possible modifications of muscular motion" (*M*, 287–88) [187]. In turn, this push gives Carwin an "unlimited and absolute" power more akin to Kant's Newton than to Kant's Wieland (*M*, 288) [187].

Of course, Carwin's biloquism eventually pushes the life of another Wieland beyond his own limits and toward depraved, homicidal insanity in Brown's other novel about Carwin. Indeed, even in the context of *Memoirs of Carwin*, the scientific elements of biloquism begin to make trouble for the poetic, suggesting that Carwin's shift from aesthetic judgment to scientific practice figures the rationalism about which Brown was so skeptical.[4] Carwin's biloquial misadventures in *Memoirs of Carwin* and *Wieland* certainly articulate a Brownian critique of the very rational universality that Brown's Carwin and Kant's Newton or Wieland represent. More

4. See Jay Fliegelman, introduction to the Penguin edition of *"Wieland" and "Memoirs,"* x–xi, xv–xvi.

importantly, however, I want to suggest that the reproducible and reiterative aspect of scientific biloquism, which, by definition, aesthetic genius cannot perform, is called forth by the concealed racial and national form of Carwin's character. For if Carwin's utterance of the "shrill tones of a Mohock savage" retroactively conditions his "character" or "thirst of knowledge," and thus figures the iterative, cultural assimilation of Mohawks being sought in the newly independent United States of the 1790s, then the "incessant" scientific reiterability of Carwin's mastery over the echo of those "shrill tones" figures the *maintenance* required by any policy of assimilation. That is, the condition of possibility for maintaining the universal and natural cast of Carwin's national identity, and thus for concealing its particular racial and national formation, is the systematic and continuing reproduction of its natural universality: "I *learned* to accommodate my voice," Carwin explains (my emphasis). More so than "fine art," scientific biloquism, as a figure for the maintenance of mastery over the echo of "the shrill tones of a Mohock savage," is made necessary by the racialized terms of Brown's national allegory.

In fact, by describing Carwin as a biloquist and not a ventriloquist, Brown seems to have coined a term, and in the process to have performed an important substitution and displacement of "fine art" by "science." The Oxford English Dictionary gives *Memoirs of Carwin* and *Wieland* as the first uses of *biloquist* or *biloquial* in the English language, whereas *ventriloquism* has a history dating back to the sixteenth century. *Ventriloquism*, meaning voices coming from the *venter* or the belly, suggests voices from an unknown origin, or some deep and unbeatable interiority.[5] This unknown origin resonates with the fact that ventriloquism was often understood in the seventeenth and eighteenth centuries to indicate possession by evil spirits or by Satan. Its unknown, satanic quality undoubtedly gave the word *ventriloquism* an antirational, premodern feel for Brown. By coining the term *biloquism*, he suggests a merely doubled voice, a single copy alongside a single original, no matter how many forms the "copy" might take (for Carwin biloquizes many different animal and human voices). In fact, Brown emphasizes that Carwin's voices were produced by a precise "concurrence of teeth, palate and tongue" (*M*, 288) [187], making them a mere trick of the mouth rather than an unknown, supernatural, or preternatural emanation from the *venter*. Brown's Carwin in effect tames the Gothic text of "goblins and spectres" implicit in the word *ventriloquism* by producing a "biloquial" skill of his own mastery out of his "thirst of knowledge." *Biloquism*, more precisely than *ventriloquism*, figures a universally

5. *C-OED*, s.v. "biloquial," "biloquist," "ventriloquism," and "ventriloquist."

reiterable and learnable practice that could reproduce the citizen-subject by preserving the assimilated echo of the "Mohock savage," turning the memory of its threatening particularity into a formal practice of modern citizenship.

Thus, although biloquism can be read as a figure for Carwin's dangerous rationalism, and in turn as part of Brown's critique of Godwinism, the fact that biloquism emerges from Carwin's mastery of the echo of "the shrill tones of a Mohock savage" indicates the prior, concealed racial formation of that critique. That is, Brown's very critique of Godwin is itself conditioned upon the naturalized emergence, assimilation, and continuing mastery of the "Mohock savage." Nonetheless, this incorporation and mastery cannot be said to be absolute, for as the plot of *Memoirs of Carwin* develops, one can still hear echoes of this figure.

As soon as Carwin masters the echo of "the shrill tones of a Mohock savage," he leaves his family and sets out to make a life for himself. Yet he finds it nearly impossible to resist using his biloquism to deceive people into following his wishes, despite his sense that such deception leads him into unethical territory. In one of his earliest experiments with his newfound skill of biloquism, Carwin makes the voice of Ariel, from Shakespeare's *The Tempest*, appear to sing from the sky at a garden party. The scene begins with a woman singing some of Ariel's songs to the assembled guests:

> On a subsequent occasion a select company was assembled at a garden, at a small distance form the city. Discourse glided through a variety of topics, till it lighted at length on the subject of invisible beings. From the speculations of philosophers we proceeded to the creations of the poet. Some maintained the justness of Shakspeare's [sic] delineations of aerial beings, while others denied it. By no violent transition, Ariel and his songs were introduced, and a lady, celebrated for her musical skill, was solicited to accompany her pedal harp with the song of "Five fathom deep thy father lies" . . . She was known to have set, for her favourite instrument, all the songs of Shakspeare [sic]. . . . She ended and the audience were mute with rapture, (*M*, 297–98 [193–94]; second ellipsis is mine)

In *The Tempest*, Ariel sings "Five fathom deep thy father lies" in the midst of the scene that first conveys the differences between Caliban and Ariel (1.2). When Carwin reproduces this song at the garden party in *Memoirs of Carwin*, the guests disregard the fact that Ariel is a slave to Prospero and instead appreciate his songs as objects of beauty in the way that Kant's subject of aesthetic judgment might have done: "I may . . . inveigh . . . against the vanity of the great who spend the sweat of the people on such superfluous things . . . only [this] is not the point now at issue" (*CJ*, 43). Enraptured by a song a slave performs according to his master's bidding, sublating Ariel's airy slavery to an invisible object of aesthetic judgment, the guests formalize the text of colonialism in just the way Carwin does in the rocky passage.

By invoking Ariel in an allegory of U.S. identity, itself made possible by a racial formation—the "shrill tones of a Mohock savage"— Brown mobilizes a trope that Roberto Fernández Retamar diagnoses in his epochal article "Caliban: Notes toward a Discussion of Culture in Our America." In what amounts to a genealogy of one strand of the text of colonialism in the Americas, Retamar argues that the name *Carib* was conflated with the word *cannibal* soon after Columbus publicized the supposedly cannibalistic practices of the Caribs in his *Diario de Navegación*.[6] From Columbus's *Diario de Navegación* to Mannoni's *Psychologie de la Colonisation* and beyond, Retamar continues, the figure of the Carib as cannibal has been opposed to the figure of the Arauaco or Taino Indian, whom Columbus regards as "peaceful, meek, and even timorous and cowardly."[7] For Retamar, the couplet has consistently been used in colonial discourse to suggest that the colonized peoples of the Americas were either irredeemable beasts who ought to be exterminated or noble savages who could be assimilated into modernity as slave-laborers or, later, as cooperative "employees" of the institutions of colonization (for example, temporary allies against other enemies, native colonial administrators, and, finally, the national bourgeoisie).

In Shakespeare's *The Tempest* in particular, Retamar suggests, the figure of the Carib-cannibal anagramatically becomes Caliban, and the figure of the Arauaco becomes Ariel.[8] In Retamar's reading, Caliban, the colonized subject who resists his subjection to the end and suffers dearly for it, is opposed to the airy and sublime Ariel, a cooperative slave who, through his "peaceful, meek and even timorous" ways, is awarded his freedom by his master Prospero. Retamar calls on us to read for the appearance of this couplet in colonial discourse and to attend to its role in discourses and practices of colonization. Although Caliban's very ability to speak is forced on him by Prospero in *The Tempest*, he continues to resist Prospero

6. See Roberto Fernández Retamar, "Caliban: Notes toward a Discussion of Culture in Our America," in *"Caliban" and Other Essays* (Minneapolis: Univ. of Minnesota Press, 1989), 6; and Cecil Jane, ed., *The Four Voyages of Columbus: A History in Eight Documents, Including Five by Christopher Columbus, in the Original Spanish, with English Translations* (New York: Dover, 1988).
7. Retamar, "Caliban," 6.
8. Ibid., 6, 8–9.

and thus, for Retamar, becomes the sign of the possibility of using the language and practices of the colonizer against colonization.[9]

The appearance of Ariel in *Memoirs of Carwin* is all the more interesting given Retamar's reading of the Carib-Caliban and Arauaco-Ariel couplet. As we have seen, Mohawks came to be known as cannibals by colonists in North America, and the very name *Mohock* acquired many of the associations that the Carib-Caliban figure did. Thus, when Carwin cannot help but intervene in the garden party's scene of rapture, and he makes Ariel sing, we must keep track of the echoes of the Caliban-Mohock figure. The scene continues:

> The pause continued, when a strain was wafted to our ears from another quarter . . . The sound proceeded from above. At first it was faint and scarcely audible; presently it reached a louder key, and every eye was cast up in expectation of beholding a face among the pedant clusters. The strain was easily recognised, for it was no other than that which Ariel is made to sing when finally absolved from the service of the wizard.
>
> > *In the Cowslip's bell I lie,*
> > *On the Bat's back I do Fly . . .*
> > *After summer merrily; &c.*
>
> Their hearts palpitated as they listened: they gazed at each other for a solution of the mystery. At length the strain died away at distance, and an interval of silence was succeeded by an earnest discussion of the cause of this prodigy. One supposition only could be adopted, which was, that the strain was uttered by human organs. That the songster was stationed on the roof on the arbour, and having finished his melody had risen into the viewless fields of air. (*M*, 297–98) [194]

Carwin, as he tells us, chooses to sing the song Ariel sings when Prospero announces his intention to set Ariel free ("Quickly, spirit! / Thou shalt ere long be free" [5.1.94–95]).[1] By choosing this song, Carwin once again assimilates the "Mohock savage" by turning the colonized subject into an object for wonder. What is more, he has now rewritten "the shrill tones of a Mohock savage," the Brownian figuration of Caliban, as the "peaceful, meek and even timorous" Ariel. More so than *The Tempest*, *Memoirs of Carwin* completely

---

9. It is crucial to know that Retamar's own project has been critiqued for reading Caliban as an always already *mestizo* figure, thereby erasing the continuing histories and politics of Indians in Latin America. For a brilliant account of the implications of such an erasure, see María Josefina Saldaña-Portillo, "Who's the Indian in Aztlán? Rewriting *Mestizaje,* Indianism, and Chicanismo from the Lacandon," in *The Latin American Subaltern Studies Reader,* ed. Ileana Rodriguez (Durham, N.C.: Duke Univ. Press, 2001) 402–23.

1. It should be noted that Ariel is not actually freed until the last line of the play: "Be free, and fare thou well.—please you draw near."

displaces the figure of Caliban. Carwin develops the Caliban-Mohock into Ariel, just as he has developed his biloquial skill since his first encounter with the echo in the rocky passage. From cannibalistic and savage Caliban-Mohock to sublime Ariel, Carwin performs a forceful rewriting of the text of colonialism in the Americas by formalizing a figure for the troubling and resistive colonized subject, and all that "by no violent transition" (*M*, 297) [194].

Of course, Carwin's performance turns Ariel from a pure object of rapture to an object of both rapture and wonder, even superstition, and this biloquial performance later causes problems for Carwin. The guests at the garden party seem thrown into an extremely rational consideration of the mysterious voice: "an earnest discussion of the cause of this prodigy." In turn, this extreme rationalism paradoxically precipitates a renewed superstition: "That the songster . . . had risen into the viewless fields of air." This extreme and unstable rationalism at the heart of the modernizing narrative can once again be read as Brown's critique of the dangers invoked by modernization and the dissolution of traditional, institutional constraints. In fact, *Memoirs of Carwin* eventually tells us that Ludloe, the evil Godwinian character who eventually leads Carwin astray, is at this garden party and suggests that this is when Ludloe guesses Carwin has a secret skill that he can use to lure Carwin into his secret society (*M*, 300) [195].[2]

In this essay I will not be able to pursue the crucial role Ludloe plays toward the end of this uncompleted novel or examine the precise form taken by a critique of Godwinism based, as is *Memoirs of Carwin's* critique, on the reiterative assimilation and mastery of "the shrill tones of a Mohock savage."[3] Rather, I want to emphasize that

2. Jay Fliegelman describes this interpretation (introduction to *"Wieland" and "Memoirs,"* xxxv–xxxvi).
3. Many critics of Brown do read his critique of rationalism in general, and Carwin's biloquial misadventures in *Wieland* in particular, as a psychological or even protopsychoanalytic allegory of subjectivity meant to challenge the rationalist and sensationalist models of the mind that were so prevalent in the postrevolutionary United States; see, for example. Emory Elliot, *Revolutionary Writers: Literature and Authority in the New Republic, 1725–1810* (New York: Oxford Univ. Press, 1982), introduction; Fliegelman "Introduction"; Peter Kafer, "Charles Brockden Brown and Revolutionary Philadelphia: An Imagination in Context," *Pennsylvania Magazine of History and Biography* 116 (October 1992): 467–98; Patrick Marietta, "Charles Brockden Brown's *Ormond*: A Psychological Portrait of Constantia Dudley," *Journal of Evolutionary Psychology* 5, nos. 1–2 (1984): 112–28; and Patrick Marietta, "The Transformation Myth in *Edgar Huntly," Journal of Evolutionary Psychology* 10, nos. 3–4 (1989): 360–71. In the larger project from which this essay comes, I question this tendency to apply contemporary psychological models to Brown, arguing that Brown's racial and national allegories need to be read as conditions of possibility for modern conceptions of "the psychological" itself. I also attempt to show how homosociality and masculinism emerge toward the end of *Memoirs of Carwin* to keep the assimilation of the "Mohock savage" concealed and, in turn, how that concealment allows homosociality and masculinism to emerge. For an excellent reading of Brown that resists the anachronistic tendency, see Dana Luciano, "'Perverse Nature': *Edgar Huntly* and the Novel's Reproductive Disorders," *American Literature* 70 (March 1998): 1–27, 15–16.

prior to Brown's use of biloquism to critique rationalism, *Memoirs of Carwin* turns the echo of "a Mohock savage" into Ariel. That is, it is not the troublesome Caliban who appears and spooks the garden party's audience into a superstitious fear that questions the very possibility of culture's universal communicability; rather, it is Carwin's mastered Caliban, the airy Ariel whose enslavement is utterly erased in *Memoirs of Carwin*, displaced by aesthetic rapture and scientific mastery. If Caliban had spoken through Carwin, the assimilation of the figure of the Mohock might have been troubled by unassimilated "savagery." Yet the Brownian critique of that rationalization is not voiced by the colonized Caliban-Mohock, and so cannot question America's white settler colonial formation. Rather, by assimilating the "Mohock savage" into Carwin's "character" and transforming that character into biloquism, *Memoirs of Carwin* constructs an early American debate between white settler traditionism and white settler modernity, a debate enjoined by Brown's critics ever since. The very terms of that debate are themselves made possible by Brown's allegory of assimilation and transformation. Perhaps Brown's text explicitly urges us, in Davidson's terms, to take our pick between America the corrupt and America the beautiful. However, we must also learn to read carefully and critically for the echo of the racialized condition of possibility for that choice itself.[4]

Finally, the difference between "the Iroquois" and "that Iroquois *sachem*" in *The Critique of Judgment* can be read. Recalling Kant's passages, hierarchies within Iroquois communities reappear, through the lens of a European philosopher, as the difference between an Iroquois leader in Paris (who, though not refined and not even critical, can humorously encounter and even comment on a European eating house) and common Iroquois, who do not even exist in the same epoch as civilized man, and who are linked to Columbus's name for El Gran Carib Island's unwelcoming inhabitants: "the Caribs." Ariel is welcome to eat in Paris, but Caliban must never even go there. The question of beauty can only be posed once "Caliban" becomes "Ariel," once "the Iroquois" becomes "that Iroquois *sachem*," once "a Mohock savage" becomes the sublime voice of a biloquized Ariel. In turn, the question of biloquism's value can only be debated with civilized terms like *tradition* and *modernity* if the assimilation of that "Mohock savage" remains forgotten.

---

4. For a brilliant reading for echoes, see Gayatri Chakravorty Spivak, "Echo," *New Literary History* 24 (1993): 17–43.

ED WHITE

Carwin the Peasant Rebel†

In 1797 and 1798, Charles Brockden Brown's former teacher Robert Proud published his two-volume *History of Pennsylvania*, an apparently odd text for the early national moment. Proud's lapsarian chronicle was resolutely provincial and focused on the period between 1681 and 1742, explicitly refusing to address the revolutionary turmoil during which it was written. Diminishing the significance of the War for Independence, Proud located the end of "the golden days of Pennsylvania" not in the Philadelphia of 1776 but in the backcountry of the early 1760s.[1] In an appendix titled "A View of the Province of Pennsylvania and of the State in Which It Flourished, Chiefly between the Years 1760 and 1770," he challenged the nascent triumphalist historiography of the Revolution with a jarring emphasis upon the Paxton Riots of 1763–64:

> In the latter part of the year 1763, calling to their aid the madness of the wildest enthusiasm, with which, under pretence of religion, certain most furious zealots, among the preachers of a numerous sect . . . could inspire their hearers, to cover their barbarity, a number of, not improperly named, armed demisavages, inhabitants of Lancaster county, principally from the towns of Paxton and Donegal, and their neighbourhood, committed the most horrible massacre, that ever was heard of in this, or perhaps, any other province, with impunity! (326)

The rioters' goal was that "of extirpating the Heathen from the earth, as Joshua did of old, that these saints might possess the land alone," and to achieve this they "murdered the remains of a whole tribe of peacable, inoffensive Indians, who were British subjects, young and old, men, women and children, situated on Contestogoe manor" (327). Proud then describes the second Paxton massacre at Lancaster, the planned march on Philadelphia, and the arrival at Germantown:

> This lawless banditti advanced, in many hundreds, armed, as far as Germantown, within about six miles of the city, threatening death and slaughter to all, who should dare to oppose them; and, in all probability, they would have effected their bloody purpose, had they not met with such a proper and vigorous opposition from the government, and the inhabitants of Philadelphia, as

---

† From *Revising Charles Brockden Brown: Culture, Politics, and Sexuality in the Early Republic*, ed. Philip Barnard, Mark L. Kamrath, and Stephen Shapiro (Knoxville, Tenn.: University of Tennessee Press, 2004), pp. 41–59. Copyright © 2004 by the University of Tennessee Press. Reprinted with permission. Page numbers in square brackets refer to this Norton Critical Edition.
1. Proud 1: 7. Further citations from Proud are given parenthetically in the text.

they seemed not to expect; which put a stop to their career. But
so far was the contagion spread, and so deeply had the spirit of
faction infected the minds of many, that the weakness of the
government was not able to punish these murderers, nor to
chastise the insurgents! a sorrowful presage of an approaching
change in that happy constitution. (329–30)

For Proud, the episode signaled the "great influx and increase of
such kind of people . . . as experience has abundantly demonstrated
a rod of iron is more proper to rule, than such a mild establishment,
as is better adapted to promote the prosperity of the virtuous and
good, than properly to chastise the most profligate of mankind"
(330). With the Paxton Riots, then, Proud's history identified a fundamental scission in the population produced by rural immigration
and a government conducive to both prosperity and profligacy,
fanaticism, and ungovernability.

What are we to make of Proud's substitution of the Paxton
Riots—an agrarian uprising—for the American Revolution, and his
substitution of class divisions and social breakdown for celebratory
accounts of an organic nation? While it is tempting to read his history as the idiosyncratic narrative of a disaffected Quaker Tory,
Proud's alternative account of the eighteenth century—as a period
of farmers' rebellions in which the American Revolution was better
seen as an extended variant of rural insurrection—was not uncommon at the end of the century. And this understanding itself raises
challenging questions about the role of the American backcountry in
early American culture, about the significance and impact of the rural
subaltern, and about the limitations of today's critical-historiographic
preoccupation with the Revolution.

In this essay I will explore these questions with reference to Charles
Brockden Brown's novel *Wieland*, and I will insist at the outset that
Brown's novel was heavily informed by Proud's *History*.[2] There are
obvious echoes of Proud's narrative in Brown's novel. In both, "the
madness of the wildest enthusiasm . . . under the pretence of religion," instigated by backcountry instigation, results in "the most
horrible massacre" of "peaceable, inoffensive" subjects situated on a
rural manor. Furthermore, Brown carefully located his novel at the
moment of the Paxton Riots. "The sound of war had been heard,"
writes Clara Wieland in reference to the Seven Years' War of 1756–
63, the same global conflict that makes Wieland wary about relo-
cating to Westphalia,

> but it was at such a distance as to enhance our enjoyment by
> affording objects of comparison. The Indians were repulsed

2. These arguments are developed more fully in *Rural Rebellion and the First American
Novels* (in press), ch. 3. Chapter 1 treats the historical sketches, while chapter 4 treats
Arthur Mervyn.

on the one side, and Canada was conquered on the other. Revolutions and battles, however calamitous to those who occupied the scene, contributed in some sort to our happiness, by agitating our minds with curiosity, and furnishing causes of patriotic exultation.[3]

And just as the Wieland circle is curiously contemplating the Seven Years' War, Brown himself was agitating his mind with Proud's book. Critics have noted that Brown's 1799 review of Proud seems dismissive at times, describing the work as that of "the humble, honest, and industrious compiler."[4] But in the review's penultimate paragraph, Brown shows a more suggestive appreciation of Proud's work. "To bring together the stones and rafters that are to constitute the building is little more than manual labour," he states, but "Mr. Proud has, indeed, done more than this. He has distinguished and culled out those blocks and beams that were useful to his purpose, and not only collected them together, but placed them in the order in which they will be successively required by the builder." One critic has paraphrased this paragraph as arguing that "the historian does the groundwork while the writer of 'genius' and 'philosophy' can build structures more grand, more worthwhile."[5] But a more accurate rendering of the construction metaphor would read Proud as somewhere between a contractor and an architect, someone who selects and arranges the best materials—in this case, the constituent regions and populations of Pennsylvania, and the decisive lapsarian episodes of the Paxton Boys' rural agitation. It is up to the builder, Brown, to put them together, to explain spatially and socially how this fall took place.

This must have seemed an important problem in the 1790s, as the United States continued to experience the rural insurrections that punctuated the colonial period: the Carolina Regulations, the Jersey and New York rent riots, and the Paxton Riots were followed by the interprovincial rural-urban conflicts of the revolutionary era and then by the Massachusetts Regulation (a.k.a. Shays' Rebellion), the Whiskey Rebellion, and, in 1799, the Fries Rebellion, the last two largely concentrated in Pennsylvania.[6] The nation fixation of contemporary criticism renders these conflicts largely invisible, insisting as it does that early American fiction rests on "an allegory of America and the dangers that democracy poses."[7] I want to suggest, though,

3. Brown, *Three Gothic Novels* 25 [23]. Further citations are given parenthetically in the text. Citations from "Memoirs of Carwin the Biloquist" come from Brown, *Wieland*.
4. Brown, *Literary Reviews and Essays* 26. Further citations from this review are from the same page.
5. Clark 240.
6. For a general overview of the major conflicts of the period, see Brown, "Back Country Rebellions."
7. Samuels 45. Edwin Fussell writes that Brown was driven by "his need to define and embody the typifying communal experience of that new polity, to write the nation into

an alternative political framework for the emergence of the American novel, one in which attention to geographical and class particularities did not allow writers to start with the benign a priori framework of the nation and to churn out so many allegorical readings of the nation. In ways that I hope to illustrate below, Brown was very much part of the moment's groping for a vernacular sociology attentive to class formations, geography, material conditioning, and social structure that literary critics (usually feminists) have only begun to appreciate. I will even go so far as to call Brown a burgeoning historical materialist—rather than a bourgeois nationalist—struggling, like a later, fellow student of Italian history, Antonio Gramsci, to understand the dynamics of the rural subaltern. Brown's interest was not emancipatory—as a student of Proud, he sought to decipher the backcountry in order to control and correct it—but he sought, nonetheless, a fairly sophisticated engagement with the rural subaltern that has tremendous heuristic value for contemporary criticism. In the remainder of this essay, then, I will explore *Wieland*'s attention to the geography of class ("The German Crescent"); its formulation, under the rubric of biloquism, of the still perplexing nexus of structure, agency, and communication ("The Rural Sovereign"); and the overarching question of understanding subaltern resistance from an elite perspective ("The Pit"). The essay's final section ("At the Precipice") will explore some of Brown's conclusions. Under each of these rubrics, I will be reading Brown's novel as a stab at cognitive mapping, an early American variant of "subaltern studies," that not only might guide a rethinking of early American culture but also offer contributions to the study of subaltern classes in general.

The German Crescent

Every literary text "begins by generating and reproducing its own context . . . taking its measure with a view toward its own projects of transformation"; context is not some purely reflective background but "the rewriting or restructuration of a prior historical or ideological subtext."[8] This seems especially true for Brown's writings, some of which, like the "Sketches of a History of the Carrils and Ormes" or "Sketches of a History of Carsol," display a concern with situating that struggles to break into narrative. *Wieland*'s opening chapters, with their account of three generations of the Wieland family, painstakingly outline a differential geography that proves central to the

existence . . . to give it a character, a personality, and a soul." Fussell 171–72. Christopher Looby's reading of *Wieland* stresses the "deep correspondence between the conceptual grammar of the Gothic plot and the predominant representations of history and politics given in the culture of postrevolutionary America"—representations concerning the nation-state and "the discursive foundation of national legitimacy." Looby 146, 15.
8. Jameson 81.

novel's "transformation." Clara's father, for instance, is orphaned at a young age and removed from his German context to a London apprenticeship which he passes mostly "pent up in a gloomy apartment, or traversing narrow and crowded streets" (7) [9]. A wild child of the London attics, he encounters "a book written by one of the teachers of the Albigenses, or French Protestants," containing "an exposition of the doctrine of the sect of Camissards, and an historical account of its origin" (7–8) [9]. His "craving" now supplied with "an object," he relocates to the New World to serve as a missionary to the "North-American Indians"; upon arriving in Philadelphia, however, he finds himself terrified of the frontier savages, "relinquish[es] his purpose, and purchas[es] a farm on Schuylkill, within a few miles of the city" (9) [11]. Fourteen years of domestic life later, he returns to thoughts of "the conversion of the savage tribes" but achieves "no permanent success" in the face of both the "license of savage passion, and the artifices of his depraved countrymen" (10) [12]. Retiring to his homestead, Mettingen, he lives out his life in rural isolation, "allied himself with no sect," and "shut out every species of society" (10) [12]. His end comes when, having returned to Mettingen from Philadelphia, but also just after his return "from the shores of the Ohio," he experiences his bizarre and mysterious death (13) [14].

What are we to make of this spatial biography? A map of the Elder Wieland's life suggests three distinct zones or arcs in Pennsylvania. First is the small urban zone of Philadelphia, with obvious links to the metropole of London and, at another remove, the Hanseatic port of Hamburg, home of his parents. Here the city is not the center of culture where the subject is at last filled, but the place where culture is taken away (the first Wieland's loss of his feudal background in Hamburg, the idiocy of the London apprenticeship, the second Wieland's loss of fervor in Philadelphia). Thus Brown's explication of the most meaningful cultural dynamics of America will be, in this novel, consigned to the rural spaces already anticipated by the first Wieland's Saxon background. But here we must not speak of a single agrarian space diametrically opposed to the urban, for Brown consistently sketches two distinct rural zones.

At the farthest remove is the region of the backcountry, the "western districts," where the Elder Wieland finally undertakes mission work and finds himself insulted by vulgar farmers and Indians. It is this region, of course, that finds its embodiment in Carwin. But at this point in the novel its other significant expression is the history of the Camissards. From 1702 to 1704, Protestant peasants, artisans, and smallholders had engaged in guerrilla warfare against Catholic authorities, burning over two hundred churches and killing some priests in the Bas-Languedoc region of southern France. This remote rural uprising had ultimately had a strange impact on London, for a

number of the "prophet"-leaders of the movement, including Elie
Marion and Jean Cavalier, had sought refuge in England by 1706.
By late 1707, a movement of English inspirés was taking shape, producing evangelical pamphlets and provoking counterresponses from
alarmed Conformists. By the end of the decade, the "French Prophets" had followers in cities throughout England and Scotland.[9] The
long-term impact of the movement is attested by an anonymous 1742
Boston polemic against it, *The Wonderful Narrative: or, A Faithful
Account of the French Prophets, their Agitations, Extasies, and Inspirations*, which argued that the prophets "were either Imposters, or
under the Power of Delusion, or an overheated Imagination."[1] The
immediate reference, in 1742, is to the Great Awakening, interestingly cast by the pamphleteer as a backcountry phenomenon brought
to the seaports. Brown's own correlation of the Camissards with
Wieland's religious delusions is obvious, but not as a simple ideological phenomenon: the sociogeographical implications are central, for
the backcountry Camissards (who had metaphorized their isolation
in millenarian accounts of the "Desert") exercise their most dangerous influence on an empty and receptive urban culture.

Brown is meanwhile equally interested in that middle rural region
between Philadelphia and the Ohio River, the zone of Mettingen
and the Schuylkill. There, instead of a fanatically unified peasantry
or tribal, Indianized farmers, we find a series of isolated and interchangeable farms à la Crèvecoeur. With no "new objects, new employments, [or] new associates," and forming a church of one (10) [11],
the Elder Wieland embodies less an idiosyncratic isolation than a
particular form of rural life perpetuated in the next generation. Protected from the "corruption and tyranny of colleges and boarding
schools" in Philadelphia, Clara and the younger Wieland quickly
reestablish themselves at Mettingen where they too escape "the
society of others" (19) [19], living a life of agriculture (even if without labor) in separate houses. Such is the zone of Philadelphia
County, ethnically and religiously marked in the eighteenth century
as something of a German Crescent around Philadelphia. Settled by
Lutherans and "German" Pietists, the region was contrasted with
the Presbyterian and crypto-Catholic counties to the west, predominantly settled by Irish, Scots-Irish, and Scottish immigrants. Such
ethnic coding of rural zones was and is an exaggeration of real settlement patterns,[2] but it recurs frequently (e.g., in Crèvecoeur) as an
eighteenth-century Pennsylvanian dichotomy for thinking about

---

9. Here I draw on Schwartz.
1. *Wonderful Narrative* 6.
2. James Lemon has argued against the German/Scots-Irish binary that plagues historiography of early Pennsylvania, but his maps of ethnic settlement show a basic, general-
   izing validity to the assessment. Lemon 69, 77, 49–50.

competing rural cultures. Brown obviously believed this division—
ethno-religious and material, opposing a culture of settled dispersal
with a mobile, disruptive backcountry—illuminated the cultural
dynamics of early America and used it to structure the antagonisms
of his novel, in which the major conflicts are rural. If the city exists,
in *Wieland*, as a site of conflict at all, it is through the arrival and
transformation there of rural forces (e.g., the Elder Wieland in London infected by Camissards or Theodore stewing in a Philadelphia
prison before dashing back to the country). And it is no coincidence
that the Elder Wieland's death is prefaced with references to jour-
neys to "the city" and to "the shores of the Ohio" (13) [14], for it is
in the tense oscillation between these three regions—a disruptive
backcountry, a prismatic city, and an isolated but receptive German
Crescent—that *Wieland* finally explodes.

The German Crescent, then, is the mediating region between the
wild, disruptive, and factional violence to the west and the urban
vacuum to the east; it is the testing ground for cultural and political
developments, and in that sense the bulwark against revolutionary
upheaval. It is so important because it is the locale of seriality, of
isolation and autonomy and interchangeability—all characteristics
that make it the strongest and weakest region of society. It is with
an eye to this politicogeographical problem that we might consider
some of the classic critical puzzles of *Wieland*. For instance, when
Clara muses (upon first hearing of Carwin's thrown voice) that
"there are conscious beings, besides ourselves, in existence, whose
modes of activity and information surpass our own" (43) [38], we
would do better to resist the antinomy—Religion or Nature, Inspiration or Reason?—that has driven so many interpretations of the
novel. What we find, rather, is a historical, geographical problem,
one concerned with the elusive cultural dynamics of the material
landscape of Pennsylvania—spirit-and-science not as an unsolvable
antinomy but as perplexing constituents of a critical rural sociology.
Those creatures "besides ourselves" may be in Cumberland County
rather than in the Celestial Spheres. A similar translation is required
in the intellectual musings of the modern Mettingen over Cicero's
"oration for Cluentius." Many critics have ironized Pleyel's objection
that "to make the picture of a single family a model from which to
sketch the condition of a nation"—as did Cicero—"was absurd" (29)
[27]; with Jane Tompkins, they insist that "[t]his, of course, is exactly
what Brown intended in writing *Wieland*."[3] But we might better
take this objection seriously and side with Pleyel against Wieland,
for the Mettingenites cannot be assessed apart from the geocultural
differences which surround them, as is suggested by the sudden,

3. Tompkins 60.

revealing turn in the conversation toward "a waterfall on the Monongahela" (29) [27]. The other problem facing the community before the arrival of Carwin betrays a similar concern with political geography. In discussing Wieland's inheritance of the Lusatian estate, Pleyel urges Wieland to consider the German principality a utopian community in which he might become an "enlightened proprietor" (35) [32], while Wieland uncharacteristically offers a geopolitical analysis assessing the dangers posed by the contiguous realms of Austria and Prussia through the "horrors of war" (36) [32]. For a moment, and only negatively, he undertakes the kind of analysis needed to understand his coming transformation.

The Rural Sovereign

If the situation of Wieland is the palimpsestic moment of the Paxton Riots and the variegated rural landscape of Pennsylvania, the primary agent of the novel is Carwin, who appears on the scene precisely at the moment of the Cicero discussion. His first words—warning Wieland away from the family temple, expressing Catherine's refusal to relocate to Germany, and announcing the death of the Baroness de Stolberg—are striking on two counts. First, they involve the control of movement, not just in the individual or local sense (not walking to the temple, not going to Europe), but in the deeper social sense of maintaining the isolated seriality of the German Crescent. With the first vocalization, Wieland is kept from the comparative insights made possible by the waterfall description (and the western farmer, Carwin) and is instead directed back to the isolation of the home. With the second, Pleyel is prevented from pursuing relocation to Europe for the possible construction of an alternative rural society. For Carwin to enjoy the Mettingen society, it must remain the dispersed and blinkered pseudo-society he loves to observe.

But more telling is the subjective position Carwin adopts, that of the sovereign. Jean-Paul Sartre, describing the phenomenology of power within modern, serialized ensembles, characterized sovereignty as the identification of a third party granted the power to mediate and direct relations within the collective. While the sovereign may have an exterior existence of some kind, the crucial relationship is that of an interiorization whereby the members of the series understand that justification, direction, agency, and transcendence all come from the sovereign. The sovereign thus "emerges initially as an organ of integration," that, by mediating all relationships, paradoxically "destroys reciprocity wherever it exists" between members of the series.[4] Brown was arguably working out a similar theorization of power-through-the-sovereign, here marked by Car-

4. Sartre 1: 622–23.

win's God-like use of the absolute affirmative and negative ("Yes," "No") and the imperative ("Stop," "go not up," "Be satisfied"). Certainly the exterior voice is interiorized by the characters, and it undermines reciprocity as well, as Wieland, Pleyel, Catharine, and Clara each become more introspective, private, panicked, and distrustful of the others.

Here we find another intersection with the ostensible thematics of religion, as Carwin's biloquism leads the characters to reconsider the role of that most familiar sovereign of their culture—God. Religion is undoubtedly a central concern of Wieland, but less in the sense of ideology or even psychology than as a kind of "feeling of structure"—sovereignty-over-seriality—occurring in significant variations throughout the society.[5] One index of this broader sociological reckoning of "religion" is surely Carwin's initial adoption of the voice of Catharine, the novel's seemingly most ineffectual character and Wieland's most sensational victim. That Brown initially gives the rural sovereign the voice of this most serial woman suggests in part that a reinforced seriality involves the interiorization of the historically specific "feminine" of an oppressive domesticity, suggesting if not a feminine sovereign per se then at least the mediation of isolation through the passivity of "woman." The patriarchs of the German Crescent disperse their women, interiorize that dispersal, and are dispersed themselves.

But Carwin adopts other voices as well—the "hoarse and man-like voices" of scheming murderers, his own voice as an attempted rapist, his voice as an illicit lover. In none of these instances does he revert to the omniscient sovereign voice, but there is no doubt that in adding fictitious personages to the Mettingen community (two murderers, Carwin-as-lover, Carwin-as-rapist), he heightens and extends the sense or seriality while also strengthening the sovereign voice. The characters become increasingly alienated from each other, and increasingly insecure, yet at the same time more attuned to the sovereign guardian directing their actions. When Clara "hears" the scheming killers, she feels her "ancient security [has] vanished" even as, in her flight to Wieland's house, she is rescued by the sovereign voice which rouses the household: "Awake! arise! . . . hasten to succour one that is dying at your door" (56, 55) [49]. Carwin fosters both seriality and sovereignty as complementary forces acting upon Mettingen; his biloquism is not so much the throwing of the "western" voice as it is the creation of two kinds of voices—serial voices and the voice of the sovereign.

Here we might usefully review Brown's construction of Carwin with reference to his unfinished "Memoirs of Carwin the Biloquist," written in 1798. The "second son of a farmer, whose place

<hr/>

5. On the notion of the "feeling of structure" in an eighteenth-century context, see White.

of residence was a western district of Pennsylvania," he stumbles
onto biloquism as a fourteen year old bringing in the cows (281)
[183]. Crawling along a riverside cliff, he "uttered the words which
chanced to occur to me, and repeated in the shrill tones of a Mohock
savage . . . 'Cow! cow! come home! home!'" (284) [185]. This originary moment of biloquism is vintage Brown in combining geography with a host of social coordinates: the western farmboy seeking
a dispersed herd while bisecting the landscape and using the tone
of the Mohawk. Landscape "primitive" communication, and herding
converge in startling insights about structure, culture, and agency
respectively. The fortuitous nature of this convergence underscores
the simultaneously narrow and expansive construction of Carwin,
who is much less and much more than a "self." Never the master
manipulator entirely in control of his speech—the unintended consequences of his biloquism are a central concern of *Wieland* and the
"Memoirs"—"Carwin" is less a Subject marking a social type (e.g.,
"the alien" or "the farmer") than a baffling nexus of geography, voice,
and project. Brown may be hinting at such a reading in *Wieland's*
obsession with "the Dæmon of Socrates"—an obsession that com-
mences after the Mettingenites have twice heard Carwin's voice (45)
[40]. Brown's thinking about the dæmon question was probably
guided by John Dryden's prefatory essay on the "Life of Plutarch" for
the popular 1683 translation of Plutarch's Lives. That essay began
with an attempt to situate Plutarch geographically, then chronologically, before moving on to Plutarch's view that the dæmons are "of
a middle nature":

> [H]e thinks it absurd that there shou'd be no mean betwixt the
> two extreams, of an Immortal and a Mortal Being: That there
> cannot be in nature so vast a flaw, without some intermedial
> kind of life, partaking of them both; as therefore we find the
> intercourse betwixt the Soul and body, to be made by the Ani-
> mal Spirits, so betwixt Divinity and humanity there is this
> species of Dæmons.[6]

Dryden's gloss proceeds to speak of creatures who had "purg'd off
the grossness and fæculency of their earthly being," though they
remained "Spirits which have so much of their terrestrial principles
remaining in them, as to be subject to passions and inclinations"
(253–54).

As a secularized reworking of Plutarch, this is in many respects a
nice approximation of human structures, and we might read Brown's
dæmons as markers of his sociological project. Dryden had noted
that Plutarch believed such dæmons could be found in the "many

6. Dryden 253.

Islands . . . which lie scattering about Britain" (255), and this may
have been a subtext for the elaborate conjunction, in the unresolved
"Memoirs," of the cultural geography of America, Ireland, Spain,
and the newly discovered micro-Britain of the South Pacific; Carwin's raw and immature "vocal powers" (346) [227]; and Ludloe's
secret league "for an end of some moment," perhaps some "new
model of society" (321, 323) [210, 212].[7] Applied to a reading of
Wieland, this megalo-conspiracy is less important than its practical
and muddled counterpart in the German Crescent, and in fact we
might read Brown's failure to finish the "Memoirs" as a sign that
he reached the same limits of understanding reached by Carwin—
aware of the interconnectedness of language, geography, and action
but unable to master the connections in a concerted project.

The Pit

First a variegated landscape of divergent rural classes, and to com-
plicate this geopolitical framework, the mysterious phenomenon of
biloquism, in which voice is refracted off the landscape with unintended consequences: such was Brown's constructive reworking of
the raw materials provided by Proud. The problem to solve: How do
rural insurrections happen, and how can they be stopped? My title
notwithstanding, Brown did not seek to identify the subaltern in
an essentialist fashion (Carwin = subaltern), nor to explain violent
resistance in terms of an intentional group agency motivated by
class interests. He is oddly in agreement with Spivak: the subaltern
cannot really speak in some categorical fashion identical with social
position. Rather, the subaltern's voice is thrown, reverberating off
the contours of his environment and ricocheting off the collective
structures of other differentiated ensembles. To attempt even a pre-
liminary understanding of the subaltern, one must resist collapsing
representation and representation, and map the complicated deflec-
tions of space, intentionality, and reception. Certainly the intellectual cannot grasp that speech, and this holds not only for Wieland,
Pleyel, Clara—and Carwin—but also for Proud and Brown himself. Spivak's solution to the challenge of subaltern speech was a
Derridean-inspired self-reflexiveness about the Western intellectual's

7. The Irish subtext is most important here: while under Ludloe's tutelage, Carwin is
caught between Belfast and Dublin on the one hand, and an estate in County Kerry on
the other. Brown was likely aware of the increasing rural mobilization of southern Ireland and the rural agitations occurring around Kenmare, Dingle, and other towns in
County Kerry; he may have known, too, that Dublin often "acted as a kind of opera-
tional headquarters for much of southern Ireland." Smyth 60, 102, 58. The names of
eighteenth-century Irish agitators—the Whiteboys, the Steelboys, and the Rightboys—
had certainly become pejoratives for backcountry farmers in America. For example,
during the constitutional ratification debates in Pennsylvania, Pelatiah Webster characterized backcountry antifederalists as "Carlisle *white* boys." Bailyn 1: 567.

perception of that speech, a focus on "the mechanics of the constitution of the Other."[8] Brown was more sanguine about capturing
the subaltern, but in some respects he extended Spivak's insight. For
he sought the subaltern through a careful analysis of the social
mechanics of the constitution of the other, with a kind of geographical positioning system. Finding the peasant rebel per se was a mean-
ingless undertaking—you would only find Carwinesque rubes. More
important was to determine how a Carwin could inadvertently make
a Wieland slaughter his own—that is, to grasp that dynamic between
Carwin and the Wielands.

I would suggest that Brown's closest approximation of this dynamic
comes through a series of visions of pits throughout the novel. In
chapter 7, Clara, asleep in a "declivity" along the river (57) [50],
dreams that she is walking to Wieland's home:

> A pit, methought, had been dug in the path I had taken, of
> which I was not aware. As I carelessly pursued my walk, I
> thought I saw my brother, standing at some distance before me,
> beckoning and calling me to make haste. He stood on the oppo-
> site edge of the gulph. I mended my pace, and one step more
> would have plunged me into this abyss, had not some one from
> behind caught suddenly my arm, and exclaimed, in a voice of
> eagerness and terror, 'Hold! hold!' (58) [50–51]

As soon as she awakens, she hears a voice from an adjacent "chasm"
saying "Attend! attend! but be not terrified" (58) [51]; identifying
itself as a "friend" but also as one who "leagued to murder you," the
voice warns her to "Avoid this spot" (59) [51]. Two chapters later,
when Clara tries to open her closet door, the hiding Carwin cries
out "Hold! Hold!" (79) [67]. When Clara persists, Carwin, playing
sovereign and series, exits and tells her that he had intended to rape
her but had been stopped by "the baffler of my best concerted
schemes." "Scanned by the eyes of this intelligence," he adds, "your
path will be without pits to swallow" (85) [71]. The same evening,
Pleyel overhears an obscene conversation between Carwin and
Carwin-as-Clara, causing Clara to reflect later that the "gulf that
separates man from insects is not wider than that which severs the
polluted from the chaste among women" (105) [88]. After Wieland
murders his family, Clara learns about a family suicide in which
another uncle "rushed to the edge of the cliff, threw himself headlong, and was seen no more" (165) [134]. And at the novel's end,
Clara dreams, "My uncle, Wieland, Pleyel and Carwin were successively and momently discerned amidst the storm. Sometimes I was
swallowed up by whirlpools, or caught up in the air by half-seen

and gigantic forms, and thrown upon pointed rocks, or cast among the billows. Sometimes gleams of light were shot into a dark abyss, on the verge of which I was standing, and enabled me to discover, for a moment, its enormous depth and hideous precipices. Anon, I was transported to some ridge of Ætna, and made a terrified spectator of its fiery torrents and its pillars of smoke" (220) [175]. Pits, gulphs, abysses, stormy eddies—even Carwin's face, with its "eyes sunken" and outline "of an inverted cone" (49–50) [44].

If we map out the narrative formula operative in these visions and experiences, we find a recurrent narrative structure taking shape around the geographeme of the pit. In the first four instances of pit narratives, for instance, a character is journeying to some ideal future (the domesticity of the family, fulfillment of a relationship, contemplation in the summer-house). The path to this future is interrupted by a pit or gulph, indicative of catastrophe (death, ruin). But a passage to this catastrophe is itself interrupted by arrival at a precipice, where there is some moment of perception or comprehension, initially in the form of voices ("Hold!" "Attend!"). The ideal narrative is thus blocked not by the pit itself—one could, like Clara's uncle, take the plunge—but by some perception at its edge. After the first instance, the dream in which Clara hears a voice behind her, this perception/warning comes from within the pit. And with the final two instances, products of Clara's delirium occurring, we have a slight modification of this narrative form, as the ideal state is now completely undefined (Clara is now simply standing at the precipice), while the perception comes not from voices but through imperfect vision. Furthermore, the pit has gradually been transformed from a space of ruinous and monistic events to the combination of characters not clearly engaged in any actions but marking the possibility of historical eruptions (the Italian volcano that famously erupted and might erupt again) when a mix of agents are thrown together.

Let me revisit here another favorite conundrum for critics of *Wieland*, the seemingly trivial dispute over a verb tense in an oration by Cicero (34) [27]: did he use the subjunctive "polliceretur" or the indicative "polliciatur"? Many critics have read this little debate as a metonymy for Brown's interest in rhetoric and speech acts.[9] But in the context outlined above, a more fruitful reading might discern a debate contrasting what one might do (the subjunctive) with what one does (the indicative). Perhaps Jane Tompkins's question—"What

9. Robert Ferguson writes that Cicero was a paradigm of oration, that "every [!] early American lawyer's favorite symbol of oratorical excellence." Ferguson 142. This is an overstatement: eighteenth-century readers of Plutarch would find in Cicero a humanized and imperfect orator, one for whom the possibilities of oration were often missed or botched by personal and political circumstances. And in Plutarch, biography is not about exemplars, it is about comparison.

happens in *Wieland?*"—might be usefully reframed: What *might* happen in *Wieland?* For Brown's reiteration and development of these narratives might serve as a guide to readers about the novel's historical lesson. First, Brown prioritizes the subjunctive over the indicative, showing less interest in—even hostility toward—conventional narrative events than in the framework for those events. Thus the pit narratives incorporate naïvely "good" and "bad" examples of narrative (passage to an ideal, catastrophe) within a more complex framework, shifting attention back to the moment before a possible narrative climax to a moment of comprehension and decision. Simple narrative forms are somehow escaped, even defamiliarized, as the characters stand on the cliff observing the narrative conventions of their historical and literary lives. Second, the subjunctive narrative form, and specifically this new moment of comprehension, is concretized metonymically by its insertion in the geographical setting of pit and precipice. This makes geography the location of both the catastrophe interrupting ideal history and of the now elevated moment of comprehension and decision that can interrupt conventional narrative form.

If pits suggest geography and geographical structures suggest history, the narrative pits signal nothing less than the interruption of narrative by "History"—not history cast as curious, discrete events (the Seven Years' War, the Paxton Riots, the American Revolution) but history understood as the structural potential for human actions. We can return for a moment to two already mentioned, "primal" moments of narrative complication: Carwin's discovery of biloquism and the Paxton Riots. In the former instance, we have a naïve pastoral tale (a farmboy fetching the cows) interrupted by a geographical passage (a cliff over a turbulent eddy) at which, using a Mohawk's yell, Carwin discovers structure (that voice can be thrown and redirected within the backcountry landscape). Here the naïve indicative is expanded to become the origin of the subjunctive, in Carwin's biloquism. Carwin's passage into the landscape of the backcountry explodes the pastoral narrative specifically through the mastery of the "Mohock" cry, which will come to motivate the events and nonevents of the novel. The second primal moment, that described by Proud, is doubly layered but in a related fashion. The Paxton Boys naïvely seek expanded prosperity (complete land ownership) within the already idyllic experiment of Pennsylvania but hear the distorting voices of their Presbyterian leaders and plunge into violence. In the sequel to the Indian killings, they march on Philadelphia to "slaughter" its inhabitants but are stopped at the precipice (Germantown) by the "proper and vigorous opposition from the government." Even with Proud's indignity at "what happens" (the killing of Indians), the culmination of his narrative is not a tragic event (the slaughter of Quakers at Philadelphia) but a new geopolitical state in which "good" but naïve narratives (citizens pursue prosperity, government punishes criminals) have broken down. And as troubling here is the transcendence of "bad" naïve narratives (rioters kill innocents) into a new state of perpetual subjunction. For the government does not punish or eliminate the Paxton Boys, it simply makes them "Hold!"— stops them on the brink of action, in fact creating the unbearable yet perpetual possibility of rural violence. We may rethink the "rise and fall" of Pennsylvania, then, in Brown's terms: the moment of ascension marking the happily predictable unfolding of simple events, the moment of descent marking less a cataclysm than a new state of torment, of possible backcountry Ætnas.

At the Precipice

For Brown, then, the subaltern is not a subject or a group, but a materialized, subjunctive relation. The historical state of America in the late 1790s is that of a land of pits—a site of perennial eruptions (the Paxton Riots, Pontiac's Conspiracy, Shays' Rebellion, the Whiskey Rebellion) over which concerned citizens gaze from the precipice. Especially terrifying is the fact that anyone might become part of a subaltern outburst. If *Wieland* is somehow about the Paxton Riots, who represents the Paxton Boys? Carwin of the backcountry or Wieland the family killer? Actually, it is neither: it is the encounter of the backcountry biloquism with German Crescent seriality in the pitted landscape of the rural classes. This is Brown's significant revision of Proud's narrative, which still emphasized the intentional manipulation of settlers by religious leaders; in *Wieland* we have almost the reverse scenario, as settlement (regions, biloquism) manipulate a religious leader of sorts. But where does this leave the eighteenth- or twenty-first-century readers trying to comprehend the subaltern rebellion? Granting that Brown locates the problem in the subjunctive pit, what are the hermeneutics of the pit itself? What should we learn standing at the precipice?

If we take Clara as our cognitive index, the pit visions at least initiate a sense that the serial isolation of the German Crescent is the danger to be avoided, more threatening ultimately than the backcountry voice of Carwin. For the pit visions give her a reflexive sense of the heightened isolation among the Mettingenites (the gulph between her and Pleyel, the abyss between her and Wieland) that is the first step toward a solution. Yet comprehension or mastery of the situation does not seem an option seriously considered in the novel. Brown's landscape is cratered with spaces in which, we should realize, dæmonic structures operate beyond our understanding. Brown may have felt he could clarify this further in Carwin's

"Memoirs," although his failure to complete that work and his turn to *Arthur Mervyn* suggests he took up a different tack, the exploration of the rural-urban axis, the subaltern as movement.

Where did this leave Brown in *Wieland?* The novel has a comic resolution and a tragic one. On the one hand, Wieland, having killed his family and standing at the brink of killing Clara, succumbs to the complexity of structures. Learning from Carwin that he is a "Man of errors!" Wieland's final "transformation" marks a long-awaited perception of complexity (214) [170]. Faced with his own complicity in history, he plunges a penknife into his neck; Clara ceases to morally evaluate the deaths, "indifferent" to questions of guilt; Carwin retreats to "a remote district of Pennsylvania" where he "is now probably engaged in the harmless pursuit of agriculture" (222) [177]. This is the conclusion of wishful thinking—the violent will destroy themselves, the backcountry can move west and diminish in significance, the problem can be dropped. A conclusion fitting for the deluded residents of Mettingen, but Brown trumps this with a more radically tragic conclusion. Clara moves to Europe with her uncle, where Major Stuart (whose daughter Louisa was murdered by Wieland) now reproduces the historical subjunctive: seeking the naïve resolution of his disastrous marriage, he challenges his wife's would-be seducer to a duel on "the banks of a river, about a league from the city." But before the duel, stepping within the portico of Clara's hotel, he is stabbed to death (226) [180]. More important, however, is Clara's new home, for Montpellier, where she is reunited with Pleyel, is just south of the Cévennes, in the Bas-Languedoc region of southern France. We are back in the home of the Camissards, the misunderstanding of whom had initiated her father's passage to America.

WORKS CITED

Bailyn, Bernard, ed. *The Debate on the Constitution: Federalist and Antifederalist Speeches, Articles, and Letters During the Struggle over Ratification.* 2 vols. New York: Library of America, 1993.

Brown, Charles Brockden. *Literary Reviews and Essays: Edited by Alfred Weber, Wolfgang Schäfer and John R. Holmes, Studien Und Texte Zur Amerikanistik.* New York: Peter Lang, 1992.

———. *Three Gothic Novels.* Ed. Sydney J. Krause. New York: Library of America, 1998.

———. *Wieland and Memoirs of Carwin the Biloquist.* Ed. Jay Fliegelman. New York: Penguin, 1991.

Brown, Richard Maxwell. "Back Country Rebellions and the Homestead Ethic America, 1740–1799." *Tradition, Conflict, and Modernization: Perspectives on the American Revolution.* Ed. Richard

Maxwell Brown and Don E. Fehrenbacher New York: Academic, 1977. 73–99.

Clark, Michael. "Charles Brockden Brown's *Wieland* and Robert Proud's *History of Pennsylvania.*" *Studies in the Novel* 20.3 (1988): 239–48.

Dryden, John. "The Life of Plutarch." *The Works of John Dryden*. Ed. Samuel Holt Monk, A. E. Wallace Maurer, Vinton A. Dearing, R. V. LeClercq and Maximillian E. Novak. Berkeley: U of California P, 1971. 239–88.

Ferguson, Robert A. *Law and Letters in American Culture.* Cambridge: Harvard UP, 1984.

Fussell, Edwin Sill. "*Wieland*: A Literary and Historical Reading." *Early American Literature* 18 (1983–84): 171–86.

Jameson, Fredric. *The Political Unconscious: Narrative as a Socially Symbolic Act.* Ithaca: Cornell UP, 1981.

Lemon, James T. *The Best Poor Man's Country: A Geographical Study of Early Southeastern Pennsylvania.* Baltimore: Johns Hopkins UP, 1972.

Looby, Christopher. *Voicing America: Language, Literary Form, and the Origins of the United States.* Chicago: U of Chicago P, 1996.

Proud, Robert. *The History of Pennsylvania, in North America, from the Original Institution and Settlement of That Province, under the First Proprietor and Governor William Penn, in 1681, Till after the Year 1742; with an Introduction, Respecting, the Life of W. Penn, Prior to the Grant of the Province, and the Religious Society of the People Called Quakers;—with the First Rise of the Neighbouring Colonies, More Particularly Called West-New-Jersey, and the Settlement of the Dutch and Swedes on the Delaware. To Which Is Added, a Brief Description of the Said Province, and of the General State, in Which It Flourished, Principally between the Years 1760 and 1770. The Whole Including a Variety of Things, Useful and Interesting to Be Known, Respecting That Country in Early Time, &C. With an Appendix.* Vol. 1. Philadelphia: Zachariah Poulson Jr., 1797.

Samuels, Shirley. *Romances of the Republic: Women, the Family, and Violence in the Literature of the Early American Nation.* New York: Oxford UP, 1996.

Sartre, Jean-Paul. *Theory of Practical Ensembles.* Vol. 1 of *Critique of Dialectical Reason.* Trans. Alan Sheridan-Smith. Ed. Jonathan Ree. Corrected ed. 2 vols. New York: Verso, 1991.

Schwartz, Hillel. *The French Prophets: The History of a Millenarian Group in Eighteenth-Century England.* Berkeley: U of California P, 1980.

Smyth, Jim. *The Men of No Property: Irish Radicals and Popular Politics in the Late Eighteenth Century.* Corrected ed. New York: St. Martin's, 1998.

Spivak, Gayatri Chakravorty. "Can the Subaltern Speak?" *Marxism and the Interpretation of Culture*. Ed. Cary Nelson and Lawrence Grossberg. Urbana: U of Illinois P, 1988. 271–313.

Tompkins, Jane. *Sensational Designs: The Cultural Work of American Fiction, 1790–1860*. New York: Oxford UP, 1985.

White, Ed. "The Value of Conspiracy Theory." *American Literary History* 14.1 (2002): 1–31.

The Wonderful Narrative: or, a Faithful Account of the French Prophets, Their Agitations, Extasies, and Inspirations: To Which Are Added, Several Other Remarkable Instances of Persons under the Influence of the Like Spirit, in Various Parts of the World, Particularly in New-England. In a Letter to a Friend. With an Appendix, Directing to the Proper Use of Such Extraordinary Appearances in the Course of Providence. Boston: Rogers & Fowle, 1742.

BRYAN WATERMAN

[The Illuminati Scare, Social Authority, and Brown's Fiction]†

* * *

The Illuminati Crisis and Public Intellectual Authority

* * *

Scholars have long viewed the Illuminati scare as an important episode in early American history, primarily as it illustrates the extremes of the partisan divisions that preceded and followed Jefferson's election in 1800.[1] But the incident went beyond American politics. A transatlantic affair, it was made possible, in fact, by intellectual networks through which books, bodies, correspondence, and

---

† From *Republic of Intellect: The Friendly Club of New York City and the Making of American Literature* (Baltimore: The Johns Hopkins University Press, 2007), pp. 76–85. Copyright © 2007 The Johns Hopkins University Press. Reprinted by permission. Page numbers in square brackets refer to this Norton Critical Edition.

1. Vernon Stauffer, *New England and the Bavarian Illuminati* (New York: Columbia University Press, 1918); Gary Nash, "The American Clergy and the French Revolution," [*The William and Mary Quarterly*, 3rd series] 22:3 (July 1965): 392–412; Henry May, *The Enlightenment in America* (New York: Oxford University Press, 1976), 252–77; Larry Tise, *The American Counterrevolution: A Retreat from Liberty, 1783–1800* (Mechanicsburg, Pa.: Stackpole Books, 1998), chs. 18–19; Michael Leinesch, "The Illusion of the Illuminati: The Counterconspiratorial Origins of Post-Revolutionary Conservatism," in W. M. Verhoeven, ed., *Revolutionary Histories: Transatlantic Cultural Nationalism, 1775–1815* (New York: Palgrave, 2002), 152–65. For another reading of *Wieland* in the context of the Illuminati crisis, see Charles Bradshaw, "The New England Illuminati: Conspiracy and Causality in Charles Brockden Brown's *Wieland*," *New England Quarterly* (Sept. 2003): 356–77.

criticism crisscrossed the Atlantic Ocean. The actual Illuminati emerged from struggles between clergy and university professors during the European Enlightenment. Founded in 1776 by Adam Weishaupt, a law professor at the Jesuit-controlled University of Ingolstadt, the Illuminati sought to infiltrate and assert control over the government, thereby wresting the school and other public institutions free from clerical control. In the early 1780s the secret society expanded to around 3,000 members, mostly by converting Masonic lodges to its purposes. In the late 1780s, the Bavarian government published a stash of papers it had seized in an effort to stamp out secret societies in general and the Illuminati in particular. The governmental crackdown and exposé put a quick end to the order, but the threat of the group's secret survival has fueled conservative conspiracy theories from the 1780s to the present.

The late 1790s witnessed the major thrust of an international anti-Illuminati crusade, which came in response to the bloody excesses of the French Revolution. An exiled French Jesuit, the Abbé Augustin Barruel, who had already written a book about the persecution of the priesthood during the Revolution, published in 1797 and 1798 a four-volume exposé of the Illuminati that assigned the group direct responsibility for France's political turmoil. Barruel was preceded, for American readers, by John Robison, a professor of natural history at Edinburgh—with whom Samuel Mitchill had been personally acquainted during his education there[2]—who in 1797 published his *Proofs of a Conspiracy against All the Religions and Governments of Europe, Carried on in the Secret Meetings of Free Masons, Illuminati, and Reading Societies*. Both authors took up Edmund Burke's claim that midcentury philosophes had conspired to bring about the popular uprising; according to Barruel and Robison, these thinkers, ultimately through the agency of Masons and the Illuminati, were not only responsible for the overthrow of

---

2. The group's friend [Margaret Bayard] MB documented [Samuel Latham Mitchill's] SLM acquaintance with Robison; see MB to [Samuel Harrison Smith] SHS, 22 June 1798, [Margaret Bayard Smith Papers, Library of Congress] MBSP. She wrote that SLM had verified that Robison was "a man of strictest integrity & his motives certainly were good." She also calls SLM a "disciple" of the very type of "Philosophy" Robison so violently opposed, and so his "certain[ty] that whatever account he gave might be depended upon" should carry special weight. In a later letter, after her fiancé accuses Robison of being motivated by party spirit, she writes again that "Dr. Mitchel who from his own principles would oppose this book, yet assured me that he was a man of integrity, & that whatever he asserted might be depended on as truth, altho' his conclusion might be faulted; Dr. M. was surprised at [Robison's] undertaking such a work, as he did not think very highly of his understanding." SLM had not yet read the book. A year earlier Dr. Rodgers, another New Yorker with ties to Edinburgh, had received a letter from a Dr. Ershine of Scotland, "which spoke highly of the author [Robison] as a man, & recommended his work as calculated to stem the torrent of irreligion which overflowed the world." MB to SHS, 12 July 1798. [Elihu Hubbard Smith] EHS makes no similar notice of SLM's testimony on Robison's behalf.

religion and government in France but also for conspiring to infiltrate and seize control of all the governments in the world, including the fledgling one in the United States.[3]

The American campaign against the Bavarian Illuminati was
driven by close associates of the Friendly Club.[4] The campaign's
most forceful voice belonged to Jedidiah Morse, a 37-year-old clergyman from Massachusetts on whose behalf Smith and Johnson[5]
had testified in a copyright case involving his *American Geography*.[6] Morse in turn served as an informal New England agent for
the *Medical Repository* and would also be called on, in 1799, to help
promote the *Monthly Magazine, and American Review*. Second only
to Morse among anti-Illuminati crusaders were Timothy and Theodore Dwight.[7] Other Congregationalist clergymen and Federalist
politicians and propagandists throughout New England spent the
spring and summer of 1798 delivering alarmist orations and sermons, many of which were immediately sent to print and distributed throughout the country.

Historians typically date the campaign's beginning to a Fast Day
sermon Morse preached on 9 May 1798, in his hometown of Charles-
town, Massachusetts; his jeremiads built on Timothy Dwight's two
forceful sermons at Yale the previous fall, published as *The Nature,
and Danger, of Infidel Philosophy*. On 4 July 1798, Theodore Dwight
thundered against the Illuminati at a Federalist Independence Day
oration in Hartford while his brother did the same in New Haven.
All three described in graphic terms various dangers the Illuminati
posed. Timothy Dwight focused on the role played by his old imagined nemesis, Voltaire. Morse targeted the Freemasons. As the nation
approached the presidential elections that would result in Jefferson's
"Revolution of 1800," Theodore Dwight in particular attempted to
attach the rhetoric and claims of the anti-Illuminati crusade to a
political assault not only on Jefferson's party but on the vice president himself. He did so by imagining himself an Illuminatus. "If I
were about to make proselytes to illuminism in the United States,"
Dwight told his Hartford audience, "I should in the first place apply

---

3. For a useful overview of Robison, see Stauffer, *New England*, 199–214; on Barruel see
   215–28.
4. Brown's circle in New York City for much of the 1790s. Key members included the
   physician and poet Elihu Hubbard Smith, the playwright William Dunlap, and the
   lawyers James Kent and William Johnson [Editor's note].
5. Elihu Hubbard Smith and William Johnson, Brown's fellow club members [Editor's note].
6. See [Elihu Hubbard Smith, *The Diary of Elihu Hubbard Smith, 1771–1798*, ed. James
   E. Cronin (Philadelphia: American Philosophical Society, 1973)] *DEHS*, 319, 325, 331.
7. Timothy Dwight became Yale's president in 1795; his younger brother, Theodore, was
   a Federalist lawyer and newspaper editor. The Dwights were the grandsons of Jonathan Edward and had been close associates of Elihu Hubbard Smith, though their
   relations strained in the late 1790s over religious differences [Editor's note].

to Thomas Jefferson, Albert Gallatin, and their political associates."[8] While Smith shared his friends' Federalist politics to the last, to the point of calling Jefferson, in a letter to a Federalist friend, "jacobinical almost to lunacy,"[9] the Dwights' growing tendency at the end of the decade to conflate Jeffersonians, Jacobins, deists, and atheists must have unsettled him.

During the summer of 1798, the climax of Smith's two-year standoff with Dwight coincided not only with the onset of the Illuminati conspiracy scare but also with Brown's return to New York, where he completed and published *Wieland* and began drafting its sequel, *Memoirs of Carwin the Biloquist*, works that have often been read by critics in relation to the political turmoil of 1798. The Friendly Club's encounter with the conspiracy theories began prior to Jedidiah Morse's Fast Day sermon in May; months earlier, on New Year's Day, Smith took notes in his diary on the appendix to a recent volume of the British *Monthly Review*, which had included excerpts from Barruel's multivolume exposé of the Illuminati. Smith responded skeptically and at length. He questioned Barruel's knowledge "concerning the highest order of Freemasons." How could he have such knowledge without being one? If he had been one, Smith believed "he could not have exposed their secrets." Other questions abounded: why would Masons participate in an atheistic campaign, when Smith had always assumed that they were "friendly to Xtianity"?[1]

William Dunlap[2] also encountered anti-Illuminati propaganda prior to the publication of Morse's Fast Day sermon. On a visit to Dobson's booksellers in Philadelphia in April 1798, Dunlap looked through Robison's volume and pronounced it "at least a curious book" before meeting Brown for tea, where they may have had occasion to discuss what Dunlap had read.[3] From the start, then, club members engaged with these theories in a transatlantic context of countersubversive discourse, anti-Jacobinism in particular; religion, not national partisan politics, was key to their reading, as several of their favorite British Jacobin writers had been—or would soon be—dragged into the fray.

Through the summer of 1798, as Smith traveled through Connecticut to shore up the damage caused by his disclosures to Dwight, the Illuminati dominated conversations as well as Federalist oratory.

8. [Theodore Dwight] ThD, *An oration, spoken at Hartford, in the state of Connecticut, on the anniversary of American independence, July 4th, 1798* (Hartford, Conn.: Hudson and Goodwin, 1798), 30.
9. EHS to Samuel Miles Hopkins, 7 Nov. 1797, in *DEHS*, 390.
1. *DEHS*, 412–13 (1 Jan. 1798).
2. Brown's friend and fellow club member, a painter and playwright [Editor's note].
3. Ibid.; [William Dunlap, *The Diary of William Dunlap (1776–1839), The Memoirs of a Dramatist, Theatrical Manager, Painter, Critic, Novelist, and Historian*, ed. Dorothy C. Barck (1930; reprint, New York: Benjamin Blom, 1969)] *DWD*, 241 (11 Apr. 1798).

Smith first picked up a copy of Robison's *Proofs of a Conspiracy* at his father's house. Upon returning to New York, where he found that Brown had arrived in his absence, Smith read through parts of Timothy Dwight's *The Nature, and Danger, of Infidel Philosophy*, to which he refers in his diary as "Two Sermons." A few days later, Morse delivered to Smith in person a printed copy of his anti-Illuminati Fast Day sermon. By late July, after Brown, Smith, and Johnson carried on "a long conversation, chiefly on a suitable catastrophe" for *Wieland* (for which they were already correcting page proofs of early chapters), Smith had finished reading Robison's book along with Theodore Dwight's Independence Day oration.[4] The proximity to Brown's scene of composition was fortuitous; Dunlap noted in an early August diary entry that Brown was already working on *Wieland*'s sequel, in which he had "taken up the schemes of the Illuminati."[5]

The friends' responses to their countersubversive associates reveal much about key conflicts for intellectual authority in the new nation's public sphere. Some opponents—even staunch Federalists like the New Hampshire editor Joseph Dennie, one of Smith's many correspondents—criticized the clergy for bringing politics to the pulpit.[6] From the perspective of people like the Dwights and Morse, however, religion was the central issue in public life, and politics was simply one arena they saw as especially vulnerable to the influence of infidelity. Although Smith left less in his diary than he had about Barruel to indicate how he read the Morse and Dwight pamphlets or responded to their authors in person, Dunlap was more forthcoming and suggests that for him religion was the central issue. In early August, Dunlap received gift copies of Timothy Dwight's two "Sermons against Infidels" (*Nature, and Danger*), along with Theodore Dwight's Independence Day oration.[7] Dunlap had long expressed concern privately over an emotional distance from his brothers-in-law over religion and politics. In May 1798, when Dunlap first read *Nature, and Danger*, he regarded the sermons as "an intemperate farrago of falshood and abuse." When he finished reading Robison's book in early August, he judged it "a strange mixture of knowledge & prejudice, truth & error, and another proof of the avidity with which we make every circumstance bend to the favorite System." His response to Robison included his exasperation at the "perseverance"

4. *DEHS*, 458 (29 July 1798).
5. *DWD*, 339 (14 Sept. 1798).
6. "Miscellany. For the Farmer's Museum," *Farmer's Museum* (5 Aug. 1799): 1–2. Catherine Kaplan discusses Dennie's repudiation of Morse's theories briefly in "'He Summons Genius . . . to His Aid': Letters, Partisanship, and the Making of the *Farmer's Weekly Museum*, 1795–1800," *Journal of the Early Republic* 23:4 (winter 2003): 545–71, esp. 559–60, as an example of the diversity of Federalist thought on such issues as commerce and religion. Dennie suggested Morse return to his ministry and his practice of geography and leave international politics alone. He suggests too that Morse is motivated by a desire for fame.

with which "these religionists believe or pretend to believe the necessary connection between Religion & morality: with what impudence
[they] inculcate that without Religion a man cannot be virtuous."[8]
Though he maintained a polite face to the Dwights in person, Dunlap set to work on responses to the orations and on a satirical novel
he called *The Anti-Jacobin*, whose title character was a Francophobic
minister modeled on his brother-in-law.[9]

It was one thing to harbor such sentiments in private. It was
another thing altogether to take them public, though Brown, Smith,
and Dunlap had all long contemplated, as Smith put it in his letter
to Theodore, how best to "expose the nakedness & insufficiency of
Religion."[1] To promote their philosophical positions they chose the
novel and the stage as vehicles, already favorite targets of their
ministerial friends.[2] For Timothy Dwight, not only were these literary forms morally dangerous, they were the very opposite of masculine intellectual labor: "When the utmost labor of boys is bounded
by history, biography and the pamphlets of the day, girls sink down
to songs, novels and plays."[3] In Smith's position, in spite of his sincere respect for his former teacher, the clergy had for too long exercised its own stranglehold on the public sphere by pretending to
speak with the voice of God, a voice he did not believe interfered in
human affairs. Brown, Smith, Dunlap, and Johnson, who ironically
appropriated from Dwight the moniker "infidel philosophers" and
appreciated the humorous deflation of religion in Thomas Paine's
infamous *Age of Reason*, conceived of literary professionalism as the
province of moral observers like themselves, which placed them in
direct competition with religious authorities. * * *

The conflict boiled down to epistemological difference. Smith's
premium on discussion helps explain his attitudes toward claims of
divine authority. In an article titled "Prayer," composed in his diary
on his 25th birthday—only a few months before he would write his
manifesto to Dwight—Smith explains that, convinced of the "falsity
of Christianity," he had along the way "ceased to employ the name

7. *DWD*, 323 (6 Aug. 1798).
8. *DWD*, 324 (10 Aug. 1798).
9. For the installments, see *DWD*, 152–59, 163–65, 168, 172, 322, 345 (1 October 1797–
   14 October 1798).
1. EHS to ThD, 22 Nov. 1796, in *DEHS*, 265. The passage is from Smith's long letter to
   ThD. CBB's most recent biographer underestimates the sincerity of his religious crisis
   in the 1790s. See Peter Kafer, *Charles Brockden Brown's Revolution and the Birth of
   American Gothic* (Philadelphia: University of Pennsylvania Press, 2004), ch. 3.
2. As early as 1795, [Charles Brockden Brown] CBB had contemplated an anti-Christian
   novel, scraps of which survive in what Steven Watts called the "Ellendale" fragments.
   See Steven Watts, *The Romance of Real Life: Charles Brockden Brown and the Origins
   of American Culture* (Baltimore: Johns Hopkins University Press, 1994), 57–58.
3. [Timothy Dwight] TD, *Travels in New England and New York* (New Haven: Timothy
   Dwight, 1821), 1:515. This portion of TD's work was composed sometime between 1796
   and 1805.

of Christ" in his prayers. Later, satisfied with the deist doctrine that "the Supreme Being" did not intervene in human affairs, he stopped "petitioning" God for favors and simply offered "praise & thanksgiving." Tempted to quit praying altogether, he continued to praise God for some months "because I would be satisfied of the reasonableness of discontinuing it, before I should actually" do so. The passage ends with a birthday resolution: "[P]eriodical exercise of this kind is inconsistent with the notions I entertain of the structure & constitution of the Universe, & henceforth I am resolved to discontinue it." Prayer ultimately becomes unacceptable for Smith; not only does God apparently not hear prayer, but more importantly he does not speak in return. To someone for whom inquiry depends on the "brisk breeze of discussion," such a being was of no use.[4]

Talking Dogs and the Public Sphere: Publicity, Conspiracy, and Religious Voices in Brown's First Fictions

Smith's portrait of a silent and possibly nonexistent God anticipates the premise for *Wieland*, Brown's first published novel, in which a stranger named Carwin enters the Wieland family's rural Pennsylvania family circle and supplants its conversation, unbeknownst to them, with an impersonation of God's voice. And to disastrous effect: the group hears a series of mysterious voices that culminates in young Theodore Wieland's conviction that God has commanded him to murder his wife, children, and sister in Abrahamic acts of sacrifice. (He succeeds in all but the last before he becomes convinced of his deception and kills himself.) When modern critics consider Brown's hints in *Wieland* and in its unfinished sequel that Carwin, the villainous ventriloquist, is a proselyte to a secret society that resembles the Bavarian Illuminati, the typical response has been to read the novel as aligned with countersubversives like the Dwights.[5]

---

4. Smith, *Diary*, 213 (September 4, 1796), 122 (Smith to Susan Bull Tracy, January 10, 1796) [Editor's note].
5. *Memoirs of Carwin the Biloquist* appeared in serial form in CBB's *Literary Magazine, and American Register* between Nov. 1803 and Mar. 1805, although a substantial portion was completed, apparently, in the fall of 1798. On these dates, see Michael Cody, *Charles Brockden Brown and the* Literary Magazine: *Cultural Journalism in the Early American Republic* (Jefferson, N.C.: McFarland, 2004), 184n13. In *Wieland*, after the disastrous effects of Carwin's agency are all too clear, a character named Ludloe shows up in Philadelphia hunting for Carwin, who is "engaged in schemes, reasonably suspected to be, in the highest degree, criminal, but such as no human intelligence is able to unravel" (130) [100]. In *Memoirs*, the action of which takes place prior to the events narrated in *Wieland*, Carwin counters by disclosing that Ludloe is an agent for a secret society whose membership requires "inviolable secrecy" under pain of death (282) [211]. If Carwin submits himself to Ludloe's reeducation, he may earn a "post, in which you will be invested with divine attributes, and prescribe the condition of a large portion of mankind" (280) [210]. The sequel ends before we learn if Carwin ever became an initiate.

The connection, on closer examination, is not so easy to make. Brown never used the term "Illuminati" in his novels; readers who posit him as a countersubversive often rely on a more explicit connection between Carwin and the group drawn in Dunlap's diary. In the year of the Alien and Sedition acts, these critics suggest, Brown offered his debut novel as a Federalist brief on the dangers of alien influence; what Carwin has done to the young Wieland family, infidels and aliens may do to the new nation.[6] Another common critical approach exploits the personal link between Brown and the Federalist clergy. One of the most frequent claims critics have made about the Friendly Club, in fact, is that its members were responsible for perceived reactionary elements of Brown's fiction and for what biographers describe as his turn from intellectual radicalism to cultural and political conservatism.[7] Even critics careful to distinguish between political pamphleteering and novel writing draw biographical conclusions regarding Brown's apparent anxieties "about Enlightenment rationalism, foreign infiltration, 'artistic' and marketplace duplicities, and American vulnerability."[8]

But if Friendly Club sources reveal a deeply entrenched skepticism among most of this group toward the Illuminati conspiracy theories, and suggest furthermore that religion, not politics, was the group's chief concern, how should we understand Brown's engagement with the conspiracy scare? Smith's and Dunlap's diaries and correspondence reveal an abundance of evidence to confute claims that the Friendly Club was "largely a Federalist group with ties to New Haven orthodoxy, united in nothing so strongly as their hatred for the French Revolution and Jacobin rationalism."[9] Once we recognize that what most united the club's inner circle—Smith, Brown,

6. Robert Levine, for example, discussing the relationship between the Illuminati scare and *Ormond* (1799), views CBB "in the late 1790s, particularly in his association with the conservative members of New York's Friendly Society, as a Federalist in the making." Robert Levine, *Conspiracy and Romance: Studies in Brockden Brown, Cooper, Hawthorne, and Melville* (New York: Cambridge University Press, 1989), 25. Jane Tompkins, though she mentions neither the [Friendly Club] FC nor the Illuminati, maintains that CBB's novel was Federalist propaganda. Tompkins, *Sensational Designs: The Cultural Work of American Fiction, 1790–1860* (New York: Oxford University Press, 1985), ch. 2. Shirley Samuels reads *Wieland* as antideist as well as anti-Jeffersonian in "Infidelity and Contagion: The Rhetoric of Revolution," [*Early American Literature*] *EAL* 22 (1987): 183–91; "*Wieland*: Alien and Infidel," *EAL* 25:1 (1990): 46–66; and *Romances of the Republic: Women, the Family, and Violence in the Early American Nation* (New York: Oxford University Press, 1996), ch. 2.
7. For example: "The fact that the strongest members of the Friendly Club were staunch Federalists accounts, in part at least, for Brown's gradual conversion to more conservative principles." David Lee Clark, *Charles Brockden Brown: Pioneer Voice of America* (Durham: Duke University Press, 1952), 131. Much of the most recent critical work on CBB questions the narrative of his radical-to-conservative shift. Steven Shapiro, Phillip Barnard, and Mark Kamrath, eds., *Revising Charles Brockden Brown: Culture, Politics, and Sexuality in the Early Republic* (Knoxville: University of Tennessee Press, 2004).
8. Levine, *Conspiracy and Romance*, 42.
9. John Limon, *The Place of Fiction in a Time of Science: A Disciplinary History of American Writing* (New York: Cambridge University Press, 1990), 31. Gordon Wood notes,

Dunlap, and Johnson in particular—was not an antipathy toward
Jacobins or Jeffersonians but a shared derision of established Christianity, we can begin to recognize ways in which this skepticism
fuels Brown's *Wieland* and haunts his entire novelistic career in
significant ways. From this vantage point, *Wieland*, a cornerstone of
the early American literary canon, stands not as a warning cry
against the breakdown of civic authority but as a dramatic illustration of the reasons that religious voices should be suspect sources of
knowledge.[1]

Wieland stands as a warning against the desire for "sensible intercourse" with God;[2] its incomplete sequel, which describes Carwin's
earlier proselytization by an Illuminati-like secret society, makes a
broader warning still; it sets forth a theory of publicity that reveals
how both works engage contemporary debates over public intellectual authority. In *Memoirs of Carwin*, which tells the ventriloquist's
life story leading up to the events recounted in *Wieland*, Brown suggests how publics are conceived and, like those who long to hear
God's voice, are often deceived. Although critics tend to treat the two
works separately, the terms of the sequel's discussion of publicity are
useful for recognizing the religious content and context of Brown's
fictional debut.

From the first of his *Memoirs*, Carwin stands as a rather compelling emblem of publicity. Three episodes illustrate different ways
in which Carwin allegorizes the public sphere. The first comes prior
to his original discovery of his talent for ventriloquism. While hiking
in a canyon one day, singing a "rude ditty," Carwin elicits an unexpected response:

> After finishing the strain, I paused. In a few seconds a voice as
> I then imagined, uttered the same cry from the point of a rock
> some hundred feet behind me; the same words, with equal

---

but does not account for, CBB's difference from the anti-Illuminati conspiracy theorists in "Conspiracy and the Paranoid Style," 436–37.

1. Levine, *Conspiracy and Romance*, ch. 1. Levine is on safer ground when he resists the
   impulse to "reduce [CBB's] writings to a series of political statements, [which] would
   finally only crudely distort his literary intentions and methods" (25). My reading counters, along with arguments for CBB's Federalism, criticism that attempts to make CBB
   into a Calvinist or Quaker apologist, such as Michael Schnell, "'The Sacredness of
   Conjugal and Parental Duties': The Family, the Twentieth-Century Reader, and
   Wieland," *Christianity and Literature* 44:3–4 (1995): 259–73; and Marshall N. Surratt,
   "'The Awe-Creating Presence of the Deity': Some Religious Sources for Charles Brock-
   den Brown's *Wieland*," *Papers on Language and Literature* 33:3 (1997): 310–24; Rich-
   ard P. Moses, "The Quakerism of Charles Brockden Brown," *Quaker History* 75:1
   (1986): 12–25; Joel Porte, "In the Hands of an Angry God: Religious Terror in Gothic
   Fiction," in G. R. Thompson, ed., *The Gothic Imagination: Essays in Dark Romanticism*
   (Pullman, Wash., 1974), 42–64; Michael Gilmore, "Calvinism and Gothicism: The
   Example of Brown's *Wieland*," *Studies in the Novel* 9:1 (spring 1977): 107–18.
2. [Charles Brockden Brown, *Wieland, or, the Transformation, an American Tale; Memoirs of Carwin the Biloquist. The Novels and Related Works of Charles Brockden Brown*,
   vol. 1 (Kent, Ohio: Kent State University Press, 1977)] CBB, *WMC*, 74 [59].

distinctness and deliberation, and in the same tone, appeared to be spoken. I was startled by this incident, and cast a fearful glance behind, to discover by whom it was uttered. . . . The speaker, however, was concealed from my view. . . . A few seconds, in like manner, elapsed, when my ditty was again rehearsed, with a no less perfect imitation, in a different quarter. . . . To this quarter I eagerly turned my eyes, but no one was visible. . . . Five times was this ditty successively repeated, at intervals nearly equal, always from a new quarter, and with little abatement of its original distinctness and force.[3]

The episode can be read as a publication fantasy; Carwin's voice, behaving like a printed text, enters circulation, leaves his body behind, and reconstitutes him as an audience member as it moves without him, constantly returning from various quarters. This characterization of the experience of disembodied publicity draws on the same trope Smith and his Hartford Wit associates used when they circulated their anonymous neo-Augustan political satires under the title *The Echo*.[4] In both cases, the figure suggests an audience that has sent its own voice into circulation, a circle of audience-author relations typical not only of republican print generally but of the type of magazine publishing the friends would conduct through the first decade of the nineteenth century.[5]

In Carwin's case, as seen in a second episode he narrates, the circle of author-audience relations quickly became one in which he delighted in possessing a "superior power" over his audience. Leaving Western Pennsylvania for Philadelphia in search of education, young Carwin successfully tricks a group of his friends into thinking that his "favourite Spaniel," Damon, can utter "clearly distinguished English words."[6] He prefaces the talking dog trick—which has nothing to do, of course, with the dog's training or skill—with a more above-board routine, as he has taught his pet to respond to "simple monosyllables" and to "comprehend my gestures." "If I crossed my hands on my breast," Carwin explains, "he understood the signal and laid down behind me." This part of the performance, in which Damon played a legitimate part, still aimed to deceive, because the means by which Carwin manipulated the dog's behavior were not apparent to the audience. "[T]o a stranger [his actions] would appear indifferent

3. Ibid., 250 [185–86].
4. Benjamin Franklin V, *The Poetry of the Minor Connecticut Wits* (Gainesville, Fla.: Scholars' Facsimiles and Reprints, 1970).
5. Jon Klancher discusses this mode of magazine publishing and its relationship to the British public sphere in the same period in *The Making of English Reading Audiences, 1790–1832* (Madison: University of Wisconsin Press, 1987).
6. Note CBB's self-referential joke: Damon's name echoes the word *dæmon*, which figures prominently in *Wieland*'s discussion of disembodied voices; the anecdote that immediately follows this one in the *Memoirs* includes a conversation on "the subject of invisible beings," another reminder of *Wieland*'s dæmonic concerns.

or casual," Carwin explains, "[and] it was easy to produce a belief that the animal's knowledge was much greater than in truth, it was." If Carwin exposes himself to his implied auditor (unidentified, but intimately familiar, we are given to believe, with the events of *Wieland*), the scene itself illustrates the creation of credulity; Damon's audience "separated lost in wonder, but perfectly convinced by the evidence that had been produced."[7]

Here, too, Carwin can be seen as an allegory of the republican print sphere; there he sits, a member of the audience, responsible for yet also disconnected from the disembodied voice that successfully claims the audience's belief.[8] Building on a long tradition of reading Carwin as reflecting various attitudes toward American authorship, one recent critic writes that "authorship itself is ventriloquism writ large." Like Carwin, "the author extricates his voice from the physical limitations of the body and the psychosocial contours of his personality and usurps the voices of others in the interests of fabricating a plot."[9] In this scenario, however, unlike some others Carwin orchestrates, his voice does not come out of thin air; it has simply taken possession of an unwitting spaniel. The voice does not, strictly speaking, pretend as it did repeatedly in *Wieland* to be disembodied; it just pretends to come from someone else's body. Significantly, Damon's first utterance is an argument for "the dignity of his species and capacity of intellectual improvement," a shrewd implication that those who speak in the voice of "the people" actually stage an elaborate form of political theater. Playing on his audience's superstitions or gullibility for his own amusement or benefit, Carwin serves less as an emblem of republican publicity than as a warning about insider manipulations of "the public."[1]

A third instance from the *Memoirs* more clearly relates to the events in *Wieland*. At one point Carwin considers feigning a voice from heaven and manipulating his aunt into altering her will in his favor. Although he does not follow through on the plot, at this crucial juncture a character named Ludloe enters the story. Carwin's pursuer and accuser at the end of *Wieland*, Ludloe figures in the prequel

7. CBB, *WMC*, 259–60 [193].
8. Michael Warner, *The Letters of the Republic: Publication and the Public Sphere in Eighteenth-Century America* (Cambridge: Harvard University Press, 1990), and his *Publics and Counterpublics* (New York: Zone Books, 2002), chap. 2; Walter Hesford, "'Do You Know the Author?': The Question of Authorship in *Wieland*," *EAL* 17 (1982–83): 239–48.
9. Nancy Ruttenburg, *Democratic Personality: Popular Voice and the Trial of American Authorship* (Stanford: Stanford University Press, 1998), 267.
1. CBB, *WMC*, 260 [193]. Ruttenburg notes and rightly disagrees with a strain of CBB criticism that reads Carwin as the "democratic threat" posed by "common people." For Ruttenburg, though, Carwin is still *Wieland*'s "common-man protagonist," and an "apt figure for conservative fears of the verbal excesses of democratic personality" (*Democratic Personality*, 185). My argument presumes that Carwin is not so much an outsider but the ultimate expert on the inner workings of publics.

as both a paternal benefactor and as a member of a secret association that conspires to establish a one-world government. As a literary narrative Carwin's *Memoirs* really gains momentum not in these early rehearsals of Carwin's ventriloquial mischief—not even when his dog tricks threaten, as in this third instance, to roll over into *God* tricks. Rather, as Ludloe presses him to confess the origins of his secret skill, Carwin comes to the realization that he is close to giving away his deepest secret. The vocal and verbal talents that confirm Carwin's sense of superiority and his deepest sense of identity become instead a source of vulnerability and paranoia. The secret of his "biloquism," the one secret he keeps from Ludloe, the one that had "modelled" his "character" and that reads easily as an emblem of the public sphere, leads only to insecurity at having peeked behind publicity's screen. Carwin's knowledge of how publics work leaves him always looking over his shoulder. The tricks he has pulled on others, he worries, are bound to return and do him in.[2]

Carwin's refusal to tell Ludloe about his secret skill (about which his implied auditor and the reading audience are already aware) keeps the story interesting. The reader, for whom Carwin's confidant is a surrogate, should identify vicariously with Carwin's anxiety. Rhetorically, Brown implies, a half-disclosed secret generates interest and authority.[3] This fact suggests a relationship between reading audiences and the disclosure of secret knowledge, crucial to understanding Carwin and early American literary culture alike. In the proliferating information economy of the eighteenth century, an advertisement that one possesses secret knowledge grants the bearer superiority, as young Carwin realized, and the transmission of the secret facilitates an imagined author-audience transaction that establishes an imagined intimacy between author and audience. The trick is to gain the reader's confidence by making it seem as if one possesses exclusive information.

If in Carwin's *Memoirs* Brown delineates the manipulation of audience paranoia, in *Wieland* he had already outlined the disastrous effects of linking claims to divine sanction and confidence in the supernatural with such aspirations for social authority. Brown structures *Wieland* on a series of religious pretensions, mishaps, and misunderstandings, beginning with the elder Wieland's discovery of

---

2. CBB, *WMC*, 297 [223]. In his discussion of the sociology of secrets and secret societies, Georg Simmel identifies the secret as the core of modern individual consciousness. See "The Secret and the Secret Society," in Kurt H. Wolff, ed., *The Sociology of Georg Simmel* (Glencoe, Ill.: Free Press, 1950), 307–78.

3. Compare this to the scene in *Wieland* in which Carwin, who has just entered the Wieland family circle, comes close to exposing himself as the source of mysterious voices the other characters have heard by laying out his entire modus operandi; he "was disposed," he tells the friends, "to question whether the voices heard in the temple, at the foot of the hill, and in [the] closet, were not really uttered by human organs" and explains to them "the power of mimickry" and the "illusion of the fancy" (CBB, *WMC*, 75) [60].

a pamphlet, "written by one of the . . . Albigenses, or French Protestants," which lays out "the doctrine of the sect of Camissards." This
book sets him on the path of religious fanaticism that results first in
his emigration to North America and ultimately to his death, when
he apparently bursts into flames while praying. These early moments
in the Wieland family history offer two important insights into the
novel's ultimate attitude toward religion. First, Brown's choice of
religious orientation for the patriarch of this ill-fated family—a line
running from the Camisards to the Albigenses, representing centuries of religious extremism—sets the stage for the novel's later
extended attention to the intervention of good and evil spirits.[4] Second, Brown suggests that the elder Wieland's predisposition to religious delusion—and his spontaneous combustion—may both have
medical explanations. When he stumbled onto the fateful pamphlet,
his "mind was in a state peculiarly fitted for the reception of devotional sentiments" (that is, he was young, poor, and depressed).

Reflecting on her father's devotion and his death, Clara poses two
means of explaining these events: "Was this the penalty of disobedience? [T]his the stroke of an invisible hand? Is it a fresh proof that
the Divine Ruler interferes in human affairs[?]" Or were there natural explanations: "the irregular expansion of the fluid that imparts
warmth to our blood, caused by the fatigue of the preceding day, or
flowing, by established laws, from the condition of his thoughts?"
Here Brown tips his hand toward the latter, citing Italian medical
journals with accounts of similar cases; later he cites Erasmus Darwin's discussion of "mania" in his medical compendium *Zoonomia*,
the first volume of which Samuel Mitchill had prepared in 1796 for
American publication. Darwin's volume includes a discussion of
Mania Spes Religiosa (or "superstitious hope"), including accounts of
people who hear disembodied voices calling them to repentance.

---

4. The early-eighteenth-century Camisards or "French Prophets" were driven from the
same region that had centuries earlier fostered the Albigensian heresy. They resettled
in London, where they set about recruiting converts. Believers in the direct intervention of the Holy Spirit and the constant presence of angels (whom they were occasionally allowed to see), they practiced a form of "trance preaching" or speaking under the
influence of God's spirit. In 1707 a wealthy Camisard follower named Francois Mission
published an account of the Camisard revolt accompanied by convert testimonials; it
was translated into English as *A Cry from the Desart* and distributed liberally in London. The idea of the senior Wieland converting to the Camisard religion (in London,
no less, not long after Camisard leaders had fled there from southern France) packs
even more meaning than the evocation, through the allusion to the Albigenses, of the
same sort of dualism that would preoccupy Wieland junior. In popular thinking, the
Camisards were connected both to Quakers and to Shakers (or Shaking Quakers;
the latter came to the American colonies in 1744). Clarke Garrett, *Spirit Possession and
Popular Religion: From the Camisards to the Shakers* (Baltimore: Johns Hopkins University Press, 1987), 17–21. The Camisard preoccupation with spirit possession, similar in
certain respects to the Quaker notion of the "inner voice," provides another link between
the elder Wieland's faith and CBB's religious upbringing.

Darwin classifies mania in general as "increased actions of the organs of sense." Both generations of Wielands appear to have been so diseased.[5]

If *Memoirs of Carwin* warns about the mechanics of public delusion, *Wieland* argues that a "superstitious hope" in supernatural beings and divine intervention may predispose some to grave error, if not mental disorder. The most concentrated evidence for this reading comes in the novel's climax, when Theodore Wieland, who has already butchered his young family at what he understood to be a divine command, attempts next to murder his sister, Clara, before he finally commits suicide by plunging a penknife into his neck. Just prior to this sensational scene, Carwin spends nearly two chapters defending himself against the implication that he has unleashed this violence. He does so by carefully retelling everything Clara, the novel's principal narrator, has already recounted. When Carwin comes to the part of his story where Clara herself, while sleepwalking, nearly falls over the edge of a cliff, he reveals to Clara that he was in fact her savior; he prevented her plunge by "break[ing] [her] slumbers" with a "powerful monosyllable" repeated twice: "hold! hold!" He chose this word, he explains, in part for literary effect, as it is the "mode in which heaven is said by the poet to interfere for the prevention of crimes." An asterisked footnote quotes the relevant lines from Shakespeare ("—Peeps through the blanket of the dark, and cries/Hold! Hold!"), and Carwin moves forward with his self-defense.[6]

Whether we are to read the footnote as placed there by Clara (a sign of the rigor with which she has tried to make sense of the story she is simultaneously narrating and recovering from) or by Brown (a sign of his own literary acumen) the quotation from Shakespeare reveals a set of concentric circles, layers of quotation, that when peeled back reveal the novel's preoccupation with religious experience and ecclesiastical authority in the production of the early American public sphere. At the outermost ring of these circles, Brown narrates Clara's voice, and one of them provides the authoritative footnote. Clara in turn narrates Carwin's voice. Carwin quotes Shakespeare. Shakespeare gives voice to Lady Macbeth, nervous about Duncan's pending murder and afraid that God will intervene to prevent it. The layers of quotation within quotation most obviously

---

5. CBB, *WMC*, 19 [18]. Erasmus Darwin, *Zoonomia, or, the Laws of Organic Life: vol. I* (New York: T. & J. Swords, 1796), 439, 448, 462.
6. CBB, *WMC*, 203–4 [152]. For the Shakespearean quotation in context, see *Macbeth*, Act I, Scene 5, lines 51–52. The lines are Lady Macbeth's: "Come, thick night,/And pall thee in the dunnest smoke of hell,/That my keen knife see not the wound it makes,/Nor heaven peep through the blanket of the dark,/To cry 'Hold, hold!'"

emphasize the similarities between ventriloquism and authorship, resemblances many critics have recognized as significant. And yet more is at stake here, for at the core of these concentric rings of quotations, occupying the innermost circle, there is no original or originating authorial voice at all, certainly no heavenly interference, as Lady Macbeth had feared, but rather the paranoia of a fictional character who imagines how an intervening God *might* stage "the prevention of crimes." In Shakespeare's play, of course, God fails to intervene, and the murder goes off as planned. Similarly, in Brown's novel the heavens remain silent and readers are left with an open question regarding Carwin's complicity. Whether or not Carwin cast the voice that Theodore Wieland took to be God's, a family has been sacrificed. There was no ram caught in the Wieland family's thickets.

The concentric set of voices in this passage crystallizes *Wieland*'s religious dilemma: will God intervene in human affairs, either to inspire such Abrahamic human sacrifice or to prevent horrific murder in his name? A majority of the novel's characters desire either to be subjected to or to wield the authoritative force of an interventionist God. Theodore wants to see and hear one; Clara believes herself protected by one; Carwin impersonates one; and, in the passage just discussed, Lady Macbeth fears one, as did the senior Wieland. The editorial footnote—which by generic definition exists to provide authoritative commentary—offers an appropriate rejoinder to such a quest. If God won't intervene, the note seems to suggest, then Shakespeare will, or perhaps Erasmus Darwin will, as the novel pits literary-historical parallels and medical explanations for Wieland's behavior against his own religious understandings. The authoritative footnotes replace—displace, perhaps—the voice of God. In *Wieland*, a deist conception prevails of a God a lot like Carwin, who admits to having "rashly set in motion a machine, over whose progress [he] ha[s] no controul." Clara speculates, as she begins to narrate the novel, that the "Deity . . . has chosen his path [and] admits no recal." Her desire for intervention, like Theodore's, has been disappointed, but the violent nature of their joint disappointments suggests that the novel offers a warning as much as it stakes out a theological position. In providing what Brown called, in the preface, "some important branches of the moral constitution of man," *Wieland* argues against the utility—and for the dangers—of faith in divine intervention, and offers pointed parodies of Calvinist Christianity and Quakerism alike in its illustrations.[7]

Carwin, as one historian has convincingly shown, belongs to a tradition of ventriloquists who, unmasked, expose the pretensions

7. CBB, *WMC*, 215–16, 5, 3 [160, 7, 4].

of religious authority. They act, that is, as Enlightenment figures of demystification.[8] But Carwin does even more. He stands for what one recent public sphere theorist calls "publicity's secret,"[9] and does so by commenting not so much on the actual Illuminati conspiracy but on the means by which shrewd narrators like John Robison, Jedidiah Morse, or the Dwight brothers sought to capitalize on fears of conspiracy by claiming secret knowledge. Other satires of the countersubversives worked in similar ways. John Cosens Ogden, an Episcopalian rector in New Hampshire, authored a widely reprinted pamphlet in which he turned the tables and accused Dwight and Morse themselves of being the true secret combination of conspirators. The "New England Illuminati," his pamphlet proclaimed with mock seriousness, was a secret cabal "designed to increase the power and influence of the clergy." Like Brown, Ogden opposed the countersubversive clergy primarily on religious, not political, grounds. Like Dwight, Ogden decried infidelity, but he also argued that Connecticut's establishment laws had authorized an "ecclesiastical state, ruled by the *President* of the *College*, as a *Monarch*."[1] In "tak[ing] up the schemes of the Illuminati," as Dunlap wrote, Brown similarly critiqued the countersubversives and outlined a competition among different kinds of intellectuals over newly significant knowledge industries, the management of public information, and representations of public opinion.

Countersubversives may have been particularly disposed to paranoia about the Illuminati's alleged invasion of America precisely because, as long-standing power and information brokers, they understood the ways in which "the public" was often a representation conceived in secret and put into circulation.[2] In this light, the Illuminati

---

545 8. Leigh Eric Schmidt, *Hearing Things: Religion, Illusion, and the American Enlightenment* (Cambridge: Harvard University Press, 2000), esp. ch. 4.

9. Jodi Dean, *Publicity's Secret: How Technoculture Capitalizes on Democracy* (Ithaca: Cornell University Press, 2002).

1. John Cosens Ogden, *A View of the New England Illuminati: who are indefatigably engaged in Destroying the Religion of the United States; under a feigned regard for their safety—and under an impious abuse of true religion* (Philadelphia: James Carey, 1799), 3, 9. Ogden's reversal is consistent with CBB's inversion of a scenario presented in ThD's *An Oration*: "[T]he spirit of Jacobinism, differs very essentially from all other spirits. The zeal of an enthusiast in religion, though violent, and often pernicious, yet will stop short of acknowledged crime—it will shrink from cool deliberate murder. But the Jacobin is not satisfied with guilt of a common dye. He delights in murdering the wife of his bosom, in destroying the life of a smiling infant, in plunging a dagger into a parent's heart" (25). *Wieland's* plot defiantly counters ThD's claim; Theodore Wieland, "an enthusiast in religion," willingly murders his family when he believes God requires it. It is tempting to consider the possibility that CBB named Theodore Wieland for EHS's zealous friend.

2. If CBB's fiction is less concerned with the existence of an actual order of the Illuminati than it is with popular representations of such conspiracies, such a distinction has particular bearing on the Illuminati scare as it relates to Habermasian discussions of the public sphere. Habermas's original narrative placed European Freemasonry among the cluster of social institutions that helped give birth to the public sphere; Freemasonry in particular typified his notion that "the coming together of private people into a public

scare has a literary context within the transnational republic of intellect, particularly as the circulation of printed sermons and orations,
correspondence, and journalistic criticism all reveals struggles to
define a public sphere that encompassed but was not limited to the
partisan press of the American 1790s. Conservative intellectuals
described the Illuminati, for this reason, as attempting to gain control of the engines of intellectual and literary culture.

This strand of the anti-Illuminati fears was stressed most by
Timothy Dwight, though Robison had laid the groundwork. In
Proofs of a Conspiracy he had printed a letter purportedly written by
one of the order's leaders, which included a declaration that the
Illuminati aimed to "acquire the direction of education—of church
management—of the professorial chair, and of the pulpit. We must
bring our opinions into fashion by every art—spread them among
the people by the help of young writers. . . . We must take care that
our writers be well puffed, and that the Reviewers do not depreci-
ate them; therefore we must endeavor by every mean[s] to gain over
the Reviewers and Journalists . . . [and] the booksellers, who in
time will see that it is their interest to side with us."[3] The letter
demonstrates an acute awareness of the ability of interested parties
to manipulate the institutional bases of the public sphere. Another
purported Illuminati document in Robison's book similarly posited
"[a] Literary Society [as] the most proper form for the introduction
of our Order into any state where we are yet strangers."[4]

Seated as Yale's president, Dwight was extremely anxious to
influence literary culture, especially as it affected the Christian
indoctrination of young people in the new nation. In *The Duty of
Americans, at the Present Crisis*, his 1798 Independence Day sermon, he declared his belief that infidels had already penetrated

---

was . . . anticipated in secret, as a public sphere still existing behind closed doors [as
long as] publicity [still] had its seat in the secret chanceries of the prince." Secrecy, for
Habermas, relates to publicity as both characteristic of its earliest emergence and as an
earlier social form that eventually gave way to "open associations[,] access to which . . .
was relatively easy." Following this account, the transition from courtly secrecy through
secret societies (or "internal" publics) to a democratic public sphere has been a staple
feature of the literature on the public sphere's emergence. Habermas, *The Structural
Transformation of the Public Sphere: An Inquiry into a Category of Bourgeois Society*,
trans. Thomas McCarthy (Cambridge: MIT Press, 1989), 35. John Brooke has similarly
argued that for "thousands of aspiring young men" in the new nation, "an introduction
to—and indoctrination in—the cultural configuration of the public sphere would come
in the blue light of the lodge-room, as they were inducted into the mysteries of Freemasonry." John L. Brooke, "Freemasonry and the Public Sphere in New York State, 1784–
1830," unpublished paper, Organization of American Historians meeting, Louisville,
Ky., 11 Apr. 1991, page 5, quoted by permission.

3. John Robison, *Proofs of a Conspiracy against All the Religions and Governments of
Europe, Carried on in the Secret Meetings of Free Masons, Illuminati, and Reading Societies. Collected from Good Authorities* (New York: George Forman, 1798), 150–51.

4. Ibid., 155.

"every place of power and trust, and [insinuated themselves] into every literary, political, and Friendly society."[5] Following Barruel and Robison, he framed the battle with Jacobin and Illuminati conspirators as a battle for literary eminence in which Voltaire—who had long been Dwight's imagined foe and was also Barruel's special target—plotted to make himself a literary celebrity by controlling the international flow of printed information.[6]

In an 1801 sermon (a late statement in the debates, though Dwight apparently never lost his conviction of the conspiracy's existence) Dwight again emphasized the Illuminati's monopolization of the public sphere: infidel writings "have assumed every form, and treated every subject of thought. From the lofty philosophical discourse it has descended through all the intervening gradations to the news-paper paragraph; from the sermon to the catechism; from regular history to the anecdote; from the epic poem to the song; and from formal satire to the jest of the buffoon."[7] The hierarchical catalog includes high and low genres intended for audiences of elite, middling, and lower classes. And yet, the problem goes beyond the circulation of dangerous printed matter, in spite of his conviction that the Illuminati had successfully infiltrated all media and placed a stranglehold on all genres. Dwight worried even more about the effects of face-to-face "action and influence,"[8] a sign of the distrust bred by the ways in which the conception of a monolithic "public" could conceal secret movements and behind-the-scenes machinations, an explicit vote of no confidence in an anonymous republican print sphere. Brown's analysis of the public sphere, though it stemmed from a different set of concerns, suggested the sources for Dwight's particularly suspicious subjectivity, the fate of those who know that publics are imaginary relationships generated through representations and that they can be manipulated by powerful interests behind the screen.

5. TD, *The Duty of Americans, at the Present Crisis: Illustrated in a Discourse, Preached on the Fourth of July, 1798* (New Haven: Thomas and Samuel Green, 1798), qtd. in Grasso, *A Speaking Aristocracy*, 352. Significantly, TD's concerns here go beyond denouncing the same "self-created" Democratic-Republican societies George Washington famously targeted in his farewell address.
6. TD had sarcastically dedicated his satirical poem *The Triumph of Infidelity* (1788) to Voltaire. See Colin Wells, *The Devil and Doctor Dwight: Satire and Theology in the Early American Republic* (Chapel Hill: University of North Carolina Press, 2002), 34.
7. TD, *A Discourse on Some Events of the Last Century: Delivered in the Brick Church in New Haven, on Wednesday, January 7, 1801* (New Haven: Ezra Read, 1801), 16.
8. TD, *The Duty of Americans*, 17.

548

STEPHEN SHAPIRO

[*Wieland*'s Political Romance and the History of Subjectivity]†

* * *

Wieland *and the Critique of the Moment*

In *Wieland* and its prequel, *Memoirs of Carwin the Biloquist*, Brown composes a tale about the historical transformation of subjectivity and its relation to forms of knowledge to make four interventions within the re-export republic's intellectual field. First, he dissects Franklin's[1] universalizing claims for a seemingly neutral arena of public access as a middle-class, male strategy that uses covert institutionality to structure class and gender violence within the publicized amity of pluralist concerns. Second, Brown finds the Woldwinite[2] cultural politics of rational sentiment as insufficiently attentive to the co-implication of class and gender inequities and naive in its belief that the main obstacle for progressive change is aristocratic privilege rather than the commercial interests of a market society. Additionally, because of the Woldwinites' protoanarchist distrust of stable institutions, they failed to establish progressive institutions that could materially ensure the enactment of their ideals and thus left the social field open to be appropriated by the nascent business and professional interests. Finally, *Wieland* registers Brown's own ambivalence about the suitability of the romance-form as a medium of cultural intervention due to the ensuing ideological appropriation of the conceptual tools on which the political long fiction was based. If "reason" fails in the novel, Brown's point is not that epistemology is fragile, but that the Woldwinite cognitive field on which he grounds his critique was incapable of providing a strong foundation that could protect volunteerist claims for small-scale behavioral modification during times of conservative domination. *Wieland* is at once an attempt to advance the Woldwinite project and a postmortem on its ideals.

Brown conveys these points by structuring *Wieland* with three historical segments, each of which ends with a paradigmatic death

---

† From *The Culture and Commerce of the Early American Novel: Reading the Atlantic World-System* (University Park: The Pennsylvania State University Press, 2008), pp. 229–257. Reprinted by permission. Page numbers in square brackets refer to this Norton Critical Edition.
1. Benjamin Franklin (1706–1790) [Editor's note].
2. An amalgamation of the names Godwin and Wollstonecraft, used here to indicate the political and philosophical program associated with these two prominent English radicals [Editor's note].

of a father by a lateral blow to the body that emblematizes that phase's dominant mode of social regulation, along with an iconic explanatory text, which seeks to answer the question about the origin of violence within the terms available to each moment.

Wieland's first temporality concludes with the wounding flash of Wieland senior (chapters 1–2) at the temple he constructed for his vengeful God. After a restless night of dread, he ascends the sacred mount for what he assumes will be divine punishment. As his "right arm exhibited marks of having been struck" by something like a "heavy club," the father's ensuing spontaneous combustion characterizes a society dominated by notions of absolutist, repressive power and an authority that rules through coercive, extrinsic brands of terror with little regard for an individual's integrity.[3] Wieland senior exists in a realm of sovereignty defined by the subject's extrarational submission to an omnipotent, wrathful divine, and, implicitly, a Leviathan, Hobbesian state. As Wieland's prayer temple is built for solitary worship, his cosmology suggests the uselessness of sympathetic human community. Wieland senior's "scorched and bruised" body, absent of clothes, conveys his notion that the lonely individual is naked before the supernatural force of terrific judgment. His paternal text is the Manichean "doctrine of the sect of Camissards," which frames his death as "the penalty of disobedience" by a divine ruler, who "enforces by unequivocal sanctions, submission to his will."[4]

Wieland's second, and main narrative, unit involves the postabsolutist age of the son, Theodore Wieland, a new model father, sibling to Clara, husband to Catharine, and friend to Pleyal. Theodore's world rests on a model of sovereignty grounded on Lockean associationist (children's) rights and Enlightenment principles of rational sensibility, typified by the section's ur-text, Cicero's jury speeches that Theodore continually studies and performs aloud. The vertical hierarchy of the elder Wieland's mentality is replaced by a horizontal, republican-like equality among the new generation. Just as the manner of Wieland senior's death exemplifies his era, so too does Theodore's. As his father died from a side attack, Theodore falls after he plunges a knife into his neck, causing a "stream that gushed from the wound."[5] Yet since the *idea* of stabbing Wieland and the manual appropriation of a penknife quickly circulates between Clara and Theodore (and both are stained by his gushing blood), the death characterizes their society as one based on principles of mutualist sensibility and the reorganization of power through emulative, shared behavior. The socioepistemological problem for this era is

3. Charles Brockden Brown, *Wieland; or, The Transformation* and *Memoirs of Carwin, the Biloquist*, ed. Emory Elliot (Oxford: Oxford University Press, 1994), 16–17 [17].
4. Ibid., 8, 18 [10, 18].
5. Ibid., 212 [171].

not that of the earlier generation, of having to decipher the obscure intentions of a wrathful God, but the managerial task of maintaining a balanced sensibility. Clara sounds the period's typical question when she wonders if her brother's violence was the result of corporeal derangement caused by an impaired sensibility.

The novel's third historical segment, Clara's second letter (chapter 27), involves Clara Wieland's recovery from suicidal depression and transportation from Mettingen to Montpellier. This section ends when Major Stuart, the father of the girl, Louisa Conway, who was first adopted and then macerated by Theodore, encounters the libertine Maxwell, who had seduced his wife and is attempting to do so with Clara. Stuart challenges Maxwell to a duel, but the trial of masculine honor does not take place, as Stuart is first murdered by a mysterious assassin's stiletto. The covering text for this section's violence is neither sacred nor civic, but medical. Clara's maternal uncle, the surgeon Cambridge, cites Erasmus Darwin's *Zoonomia; or, The Laws of Organic Life* to define the mayhem in Mettingen as resulting from something like hereditary madness rather than from religious transgression or civil imbalance.[6]

The typology of laterally murdered fathers seems less stable in the third section as the bundled elements disaggregate. The dying father is now Major Stuart, who belongs to a family unrelated to the Wielands and represents a throwback to an obsolete social history as he embodies reactionary imperial military honor codes and not the radically transformative ones either of sacral asceticism or secular enlightenment. The epistemic source-text belongs now to an avuncular authority, rather than a patriarchal father or brother, and it is even initially cited out of its phase sequence by appearing before the break of Clara's second letter, which separates the second from the third temporality. This apparent weakening of the schematic seems only to confirm what the majority of critics assume to be the novel's greatest flaw and evidence of Brown's inability to maintain the trajectory of a cohesive narrative structure: the inclusion of the apparently trivial Stuart-Conway family narrative in the novel's last moments. Yet despite the pressure of printer's deadlines, Brown carefully considered the novel's end and discussed the problem with Friendly Club associates even before the urgency of providing copy became real.[7] Brown's dislocation of the narrative's signifying elements accurately conveys his perception about the onset of a modern form of social organization that can remap past relations through

---

6. Erasmus Darwin, *Zoonomia; or, the Laws of Organic Life*, 3rd ed. (London: J. Johnson, 1801).
7. For Smith, Dunlap, and Brown's debate on what might be a suitable conclusion to *Wieland*, see James E. Cronin, ed., *The Diary of Elihu Hubbard Smith* (Philadelphia: American Philosophical Society, 1973), 458.

indirect connections. The nascent mode of social regulation operates through the institutional production of knowledge on a medicalized and interiorized subjectivity, a process that Brown conveys as the series of fatal blows become increasingly weightless and invisible—the bruising club turns into a gushing knife that becomes a stiletto's bloodless prick.

Wieland's three histories of the father, son, and maternal uncle neatly correspond to the characteristics of Foucault's exemplary tripartite sociopenal historiography involving the early modern period, organized around spectacles of regal-divine anger and the terrific monarch's repressive power to take life; an eighteenth-century phase that invokes semiotic sensibilitarianism and rationalized equivalences; and a modern (late eighteenth-nineteenth century) society typified by disciplinary interiority alongside divisions between abnormality/normality in the classification of madness, disease, perversity, and criminality. Brown, however, does more than simply map out, *avant la lettre*, a by now familiar historical narrative. *Wieland* charts the passage from a postfeudal, early modern society and subjectivity to a present-ness initially defined by rational reflection and illuminated eighteenth-century perfectabilitarian humanism and then a disciplined interiority so that Brown can interrogate the pressures on romance within incipient forms of a modern geoculture.

"It is true that I am now changed": Wieland *and the History of Subjectivity*

Wieland begins with a moment in the bourgeois separation from feudal society as the Wieland family's unnamed grandfather is alienated from Saxon nobility due to his mésalliance with a merchant's daughter. A male child is born, and the orphaned youth endures the dubious "freedom of the city" in the dual sense of being liberated from association with a landed estate and free to be exploited in the metropolis's cramped physical and psychic living conditions. Discovering a Grub Street–like religious tract, he becomes an acolyte of a "mournful and contemplative" sect of ascetic Protestantism.[8] After sailing to America and failing to evangelize the native Indians, he settles on a suburban Philadelphia farm, named Mettingen after its first European owner, and builds a temple for solitary worship. When he experiences premonitions of divine retribution, he runs to the temple, and after being struck, spontaneously combusts, leaving little but ashes as the record of his morbid existence.

8. For the French Prophets' history, see Wolf Kinderman, *Man Unknown to Himself: Kritische Reflexion Der Amerikanischen Aufklärung: Crevecoeur—Benjamin Rush— Charles Brockden Brown* (Tübingen: Gunter Narr Verlag, 1993), 133–44.

After their father's holocaust and their mother's ensuing mournful demise, the younger Wielands, Theodore and Clara, fashion themselves in the Enlightenment's postpatriarchal skepticism. Rejecting their father's Hobbesian world of spectacular power, the children receive a Rousseauian autodidact education in Philadelphia, free from the "corruption and tyranny of colleges and boarding-schools."[9] On reaching their majority, the younger Wielands return to Mettingen and renovate it to signal their radical break with the past's exploded values.

The temple's somber isolation becomes reformed as a "place of resort in the evenings of summer" where the younger generation "sung, and talked, and read, and occasionally banqueted."[1] With the raising of a marble bust of Cicero, the temple's deity becomes the spirit of convivial inquiry, rational sensibility, and cosmopolitan attitude, "modeled by no religious standard" but "the guidance of our own understanding and the casual impressions which society might make upon us."[2] Readers of German, Italian, and Latin texts, Theodore and Clara exult in the self-educative play of speech, and their conversations are generated by the mutual pleasure of debate rather than doctrinal controversies. Articulate and innovative, the younger Wielands freely experiment with performative effects, as Theodore endlessly reads Cicero's speeches aloud "to discover the gestures and cadences with which they ought to be delivered."[3]

Refusing to be predetermined by historical trauma, the Wielands recast their textual descent away from their father's Bible to the poetry of their namesake, the German lyricist Christoph Wieland. In this light, Clara considers their father's death as caused not by "the stroke of a vindictive and invisible hand," but by "the irregular expansion of the fluid that imparts warmth to our heart and our blood, caused by the fatigue of the preceding day, or flowing, by established laws, from the condition of his thoughts."[4]

---

9. Brown, *Wieland*, 19 [19].
1. Ibid., 22 [22].
2. Ibid., 20 [20].
3. Ibid., 22 [22].
4. Ibid., 18 [18]. The French articles that Brown cites consider alcoholism as the cause of combustion, and Benjamin Rush had written on the connection of internal agitation and alcoholism in a 1784 essay, "The Effects of Ardent Spirits upon Man." I take if as a sign of Brown's clarity about the sociohistorical typology that *Wieland* uses that he chose not to mention what would have been the received sense of the father's alcoholism, since the theme of secret inebriation would suggest a personality defect, a deviancy that would confuse the early modern, eighteenth-century, and modern period separation on which the romance's larger argument depends. Brown, *Wieland*, 18; Fred Lewis Pattee, "Introduction," to Charles Brockden Brown, *Wieland; or, The Transformation and Memoirs of Carwin the Biloquist* (New York: Harcourt Brace Jovanovich, 1926), xxix–xxx; Larry E. Arnold, *Ablaze! Spontaneous Human Combustion* (New York: Evans, 1995); Warren S. Walker, "Lost Liquor Lore: The Blue Flame of Intemperance," *Journal of Popular Culture* 16, no. 2 (1982): 17–25.

Without the mental encumbrance of gothic fear and thanks to slave labor that grants them leisure, the young Wielands are able to transition from a lifeworld based on divine magic to one of secularized Enlightenment, but their ideals remain untested as they avoid contact with the outside world and its political turmoil. Eighteenth-century pedagogues recommended the study of "Roman eloquence" as training for the responsibility of statecraft, but Theodore's love of Cicero's cadences is merely for the delights of theatricalized verbal dexterity. Like Theodore's "merely theoretical" study of agriculture, Mettingen's political science is purely abstract.[5] When Pleyel suggests that Theodore reclaim his ancestral rights in Saxony, so as to bring the practice of enlightened government to Europe, Wieland rejects the proposal by claiming that any contact with an obsolete mode of hierarchy is intrinsically corrupting.[6] Yet Wieland's philosophic hesitation also evades the ethical imperative to try and resurrect "Saxon liberties" in the homeland of republicanism's mythic origin, the Gothic democracy of the German forest.

Having alienated themselves from their father's history, they assume they can be removed from history itself to form a utopian community free from the violence of social hierarchy. Brown puts these assumptions of trial by staging interrelated crises of disembodiment, where acts of telephony examine access to political emancipation through the rights to participate in public discussion by two kinds of subaltern: plebeian men and bourgeois women. With Carwin's arrival in Mettingen and his ventriloquizing of Catharine Wieland's voice, the romance challenges the republican liberal fiction about the amity of a system based on unmarked voices in the realm of disputation and decision making.[7]

Within this placid horizon, Carwin's appearance in Mettingen sets off the question of class, where Carwin's laboring-class body initially appears as a social grotesque to his social superiors. The disfigured sight of one like Carwin does not itself surprise Clara, since men like him "were frequently met with on the road and in the harvest-field."[8] Easily identified as an itinerant worker, Carwin is unusual to Clara because he has moved beyond a cultural boundary by appearing on her lawn, which is "only traversed by men whose views were directed to the pleasures of the walk, or the grandeur of the scenery."[9] The discrepancy between Carwin's obviously embodied social location

5. Brown, *Wieland*, 19 [19].
6. Ibid., 35 [32].
7. For Carwin as representing plebeian interests, see Ed White, "Carwin the Peasant Rebel," in *Revising Charles Brockden Brown: Culture, Politics, and Sexuality in the Early American Republic*, ed. Philip Barnard, Mark Kamrath, and Stephen Shapiro (Knoxville: University of Tennessee, 2004), 41–59.
8. Brown, *Wieland*, 47 [42].
9. Ibid.

and the implication of his actual standpoint and mellifluous voice confuses Clara. Dazed by the incongruity between the evidence of Carwin's social rank and signs of his aesthetic appreciation and verbal skill, Clara wonders if the separation between manual and mental labor can be maintained within Mettingen's proclaimed tenets of sympathetic egalitarianism.[1] Can Carwin's body, which bears the marks of his lower-class status, remain unremarkable to allow his entry within Mettingen's cultural establishment?

The logical answer would be yes, but Clara literally draws attention to her anxiety about Carwin when she compulsively sketches his face after first seeing him, as if to insist on his debasing corporeality. She then begins singing about "the fate of a German Cavalier, who fell at the siege of Nice."[2] The allusion is to a battle in the First Crusade's attempt to retake Jerusalem for Christian designs. Since Clara is herself of German descent, the metaphor structurally positions Carwin as an Orientalized Muslim, someone whose radical difference, in terms of racialized culture, makes it inappropriate for him to stand within the sanctity of valorized spaces.[3] The fear telegraphed in Clara's citation of the ballad is that if Carwin's ugly looks and ambient social place can occupy the realm of fine taste, through the disembodied realm of aesthetic appreciation, then the lower class might go beyond achieving access into regions that had previously been denied them and seek either to dominate or destroy these institutions in acts conceptualized by their former controllers as those of cultural desecration. Clara's fear is that the inclusion of others will not simply expand her lifeworld's horizons, but radically and somewhat unpleasantly transform them beyond recognition.

That Carwin's alien presence typifies the unpleasant surfacing of class struggle within the republican liberal ideal is a notion signaled by Clara herself. When she first hears a ventriloquized plot on her life, Clara simultaneously assumes class antagonism to be the most likely cause and dismisses this idea based on a self-aggrandizing erasure of her own complicity within social privileges. Insisting that

1. Ibid. "Can an honest ploughman be as virtuous as Cato? Is a man of weak intellects and narrow education as capable of moral excellence as the sublimist genius or the mind most stored with information and science? . . . Poetry is the business of a few, virtue and vice are the affair of all men. To every intellect that exists, one or other of these qualities must properly belong. . . . If must be remembered that a vicious conduct is always the result of narrow views. A man of powerful capacity, and extensive observation, is least likely to commit the mistake, either of seeing himself as the only object of importance in the universe, or of conceiving that his own advantage may best be promoted by trampling on that of others." William Godwin, *Enquiry Concerning Political Justice and Its Influence on Modern Morals and Happiness* (Harmondsworth: Penguin Books, 1985), 303–7. In many ways, *Wieland* can be read as putting Godwin's claims here under pressure to see what its analysis does not recognize.
2. Brown, *Wieland*, 51 [46].
3. Kinderman, *Man Unknown to Himself*, 156–57. Kinderman notes that one effect of this crusade was a mass murder of German Jews, and Carwin's bodily irregularity and denominational indeterminacy also connotes this other category of foreignness.

her frequent acts of charity mean that she is beloved by the region's inferiors, Clara fails to question her implicit assumptions of caste-like hierarchies or consider how these advantages have been gained from property appropriated from the native Indians and now farmed by African slaves.[4]

Clara's refusal to challenge the structure of class that forms the endoskeleton of her mental and material domain results in one of the narrative's crucial missed opportunities. When Clara asks Carwin how he gained access to her private quarters to ventriloquize a plot on her life, Carwin answers that Clara's female servant was easily seduced into being his accomplice as she came from a family of loose morals. The ease with which Clara accepts Carwin's claim is disturbing not only because the servant Judith is never granted the opportunity to confront and deny Carwin's claims, but also because the imputation of female vice originating from Carwin is precisely what Clara herself has been vehemently struggling against in her efforts to overcome the belief that she has been seduced by Carwin. While Clara is outraged by masculine assumptions about her own lack of female propriety, she tacitly accepts the same claims when applied to lower-class women. Had Clara interrogated the invisibility of her assumptions, by giving Judith a chance to testify in her own defense, Carwin's ensuing imposture might have been determined and avoided. This is precisely Carwin's point; he recognizes how Clara's class prejudice will carry the alibi, since himself has always born the brunt of exclusion and the violence inherent in the Franklinian mythos, as Brown makes clear in *Memoirs of Carwin*.

Carwin *and Aspirational Class Frustration*

Although written and published after *Wieland*, *Carwin* makes its context explicit as Brown uses the generic guise of a rogue's exculpatory narrative to emphasize the acts of coercive violence embedded in the seeming neutrality of the public sphere that Franklin claims to support.[5] One ought to hear Frank Carwin's name as an abbreviated version of "Franklin."

In his own autobiography, Carwin describes himself as the second son of a domineering father on a western Pennsylvania farm. Like Franklin in Boston, Carwin finds his desires for education thwarted by a dull brother and a father whose verbal shaming, beatings, and destruction of the boy's hidden books limits Carwin's secularized, upward class mobility.[6]

4. Brown, *Wieland*, 60–61 [53].
5. Sydney Krause, "Historical Essay," in *Wieland; or, The Transformation: An American Tale and Carwin*, ed. Sydney Krause (Kent: Kent State University Press, 1977), 311–48, 336.
6. Brown, *Wieland*, 228 [183].

The limits of Carwin's cloistration within this old regime first erode during a primal Enlightenment scene that uses animal and topographical nature to insinuate the presence of an alternative source of power, which metaphorically suggests how other previously unrecognized bodies, like those of the aspirational bourgeoisie, might contain untapped yet explosive energies for social transformation. After seeing how a cow has managed to escape from his master's pen by a strategic use of initial force—bashing the enclosure's top rail, and then carefully managing his horns simply to lift the remaining rails out from one side of their sockets—Carwin receives a cameo about a revolutionary mechanism for liberty: a burst of necessary violence followed by a longer period of rationalized activity. Following the freed cow to a "gloomy recess" that recalls "goblins and specters," the psychic apparatus of atavistic gothic authority, Carwin shouts into the canyon and hears his voice's echo.[7] As it presents a material explanation for magical beliefs, this desacralizing epiphany encourages Carwin to extrapolate from the action of the geologic crevice and discover the anatomical chamber trick of ventriloquism.

The discovery of his second voice liberates Carwin from an early modern cognitive structure as it dissolves his awe of supernatural power and the patriarch's associated authority. Gaining self-possession by instrumentalizing his body, Carwin realizes that the wonders of the world are mysteries only because their mechanism has not been deduced, and he quickly perceives how this ignorance can be used to manipulate the public realm of disembodied voices, as a metonym for an entire gamut of republican liberal agendas, to appropriate men's "disposal of their industry, their property, and even of their lives."[8]

Carwin sadly discovers his theory of modern power is not so easily materialized when he sneaks upon his sleeping father to ventriloquize his dead mother's voice as a means of persuading his father to allow Carwin to move in with his wealthy aunt in Philadelphia. Just as he is about to enact this symbolic killing of the king, a bolt of lightning fills him with trembling dread and anxiety that traditional authority cannot be surmounted simply by an individual's revolt. Historical change must be collectively organized.

Fortunately for Carwin, his aunt's threat to disinherit her relatives unless the boy is allowed to come to Philadelphia succeeds, and, like a translocated Franklin, Carwin gains the city's freedom to follow his interests and choose his associates outside of clan oversight. When his aunt dies leaving a will that suspiciously grants her fortune to the maid, Carwin is left despondently wandering round the Schuylkill's

---

7. Ibid., 229 [185].
8. Ibid., 243 [196].

banks, as if trying to repeat the resource discovery of the glen's prior revelation. This search for a new empowering "second voice" is rewarded when he meets the older and wealthier Ludloe, who proposes to pay for Carwin to accompany him to Europe. Like Franklin sailing into a foreign land with the help of benevolent older men, Carwin learns that the security of traditional structures can be abandoned only if new ones simultaneously emerge.

In Europe, Ludloe suggests the presence of these structures when he hints at Carwin's possible initiation into a utopian Enlightenment secret society if Carwin commits a series of impostures beginning with masquerading as a Catholic in Spain, posing as a librarian to gain a rich widow's fortune through marriage, and confessing his past secrets. Carwin intuitively realizes this last item will reveal his ventriloquism, which he is reluctant to declare. Instead he becomes fascinated by the discovery of Ludloe's secret library, which contains a book of maps indicating the secret society's planned colony. After Carwin's wandering in the glen and around the Schuylkill, his search for the book's hiding place is the text's third instance of a belief in the possibility of escaping his class origins through an epistemologized geography that contains a secret machinery for operating civil society. As the sequence of Carwin's movements follows the *Autobiography*'s trajectory of Franklin learning personal skills that become increasingly socialized into disciplinary schemes of public institutions, Brown uses Carwin's romantic history of property and sex to stage his initial critiques of Franklinian republican liberalism and its dependence on covert institutionality.

In Brown's eyes, Franklin's confidence in the benevolence of secret institutionality legitimizes modern forms of corruption and violence. Ludloe praises "sincerity" while plotting more elaborate machinations, as his ideal of the equal distribution of wealth first requires that he become rich through fraud. Yet for Brown, contra Mandeville, no public good can emerge from private vice. Carwin uses his ventriloquism to thwart a stagecoach robbery but in so doing scares the horses, which overturn the carriage and cause more physical damage than would have been the case without his intervention.

Furthermore Brown does not see the decomposition of absolutist patriarchal regimes as removing power relays. Instead, the rise of new interests simply reformulates power. As the king/father's absolutist hoard is undermined by a market of circulating wealth, the displacement of one economic mode for another is expressed in modernized gender terms, where capital appears as controlled by widows or females outside of the older sexual economy of the matrimonial traffic in women: Carwin's aunt (who overrides the father's plans for his son), the aunt's female domestic (who is willed her mistress's wealth), or the widow Bennington (who auctions off her dead husband's collection of curiosities to liquidate their value). As women become represented as responsible for a market of mobile capital, *Carwin* details the ensuing perception that in order for men to succeed in the historical transition toward a liberal market, they must redominate women in terms conveyed as libertinage, where the misogyny of male persuasion typifies the new performances of imposture felt necessary to survive in a world made incoherent by the price-setting marketplace.[9]

As a figure between Godwin and Wollstonecraft, on the one hand, and Fourier, on the other, Brown represents a particular moment in the evolving criticism of gender relations. The Woldwinite critique of marriage as nonconsensual slavery analogized gender liberation as the freedom from repressive male force. Here elite women are collocutors with bourgeois men, a move seen in the dialogue in Brown's earlier, Wollstonecraftian *Alcuin*, where both face the restrictions of old regime stratification.[1] Fourier equates the vice of marriage with capitalist—not aristocratic—property relations, a move that foreshadows Marx's and Engels's critique of bourgeois domesticity. Brown is somewhere in the middle as he recognizes how women are structured as the main obstacle to the establishment of male bourgeois desire, while lacking a protosocialist critiques of bourgeois conjugality as a means of economic exploitation in the household.

Last, Carwin's ashamed hesitancy about revealing his ventriloquism suggests the onset of an interiorized self that is constructed through new modes of epistemological transparency even as it simultaneously erects barriers of privacy. Since the confession is to be linked to his entry into a fraternal institution guaranteed by acts of heterosexual domination, Carwin's ventriloquism has the connotations of what the "personal secret" would later become, an indication of sexualized deviancy, which Ludloe's institutionally backed oversight seeks to reform.[2]

The emergence of gender and sexual violence as that which enunciates and delimits the frustration of laboring-class men about their exclusion from the "space" of rational discourse is captured in *Wieland* when Carwin's violation of Clara's house seems to be a case of male sexual aggression. But this is just one of two bedrooms at stake here, and the most contested site is less Clara's boudoir than Carwin's, which is a grotto at the base of the temple mount. This enclosure is Clara's preferred space, a "little demesne" that spatially

9. Elizabeth Jane Wall Hinds, *Private Property: Charles Brockden Brown's Gendered Economics of Value* (Newark: University of Delaware Press, 1997).
1. Charles Brockden Brown, *Alcuin: A Dialogue; Memoirs of Stephen Calvert* (Kent: Kent State University Press, 1987), 67.
2. Eve Kosofsky Sedgwick, *Epistemology of the Closet* (Berkeley and Los Angeles: University of California Press, 1990), 74.

implies the possibility of an alternative social zone in between the hyperbolic privacy of her house and the agoric temple's open-air, public conversations. Its natural enclave suggests a utopian mediation between the competing behavioral demands of what will be seen as highly gendered spheres, a disjunction that Clara often represents in her nightmares of falling into gaps and crevices. Carwin is likewise drawn to the grotto as a therapeutic location that erases poverty's "hardship and exposure," caused by his sleeping mainly in the open air or in slightly insulated summerhouses. Following the sequence of the glen, belly, riverbank, and library, the grotto is a surrogate space that promises to lift away Carwin's class position; there his "sadness was converted into peaceful melancholy," his "slumbers were sound," and his "pleasures enhanced."[3] Carwin's unleashing of ominous acts of ventriloquism in Mettingen begins as a panic response only when the Wielands are about to intrude on this sanctuary and discover his class difference from their situation. Since Carwin recognizes that explicit revelation of his economic subject position will be quickly followed by a forcible eviction from the Wielands' grounds and conviviality, his violence emerges as a preemptive gesture.

As Shirley Samuels concludes from the narrative's violence, "*Wieland*'s message may finally be that for the family to be a haven from the radical excess of radical democracy, deism, and revivalism, it must be inoculated, by way of these social institutions, at once with and against the 'outside' world."[4] Rather than arguing for a nativist prophylaxis against "aliens," Brown implies the reverse: the actual roots of social violence originate from domestic resistance to new bodies and the conservative refusal to remove class asymmetries, despite the rhetoric of sentimental equivalence.

When Clara finally sees Carwin in the act of ventriloquism, his face appears tensed and contorted.[5] Steven Connor notes the orgasmic connotations of Carwin's spasms as the act of throwing his voice alludes to a different kind of male lower body ejaculation.[6] Yet the tortured look has another meaning prior to gendered aggression. At the moment of actual revelation about his real conditions, Carwin registers the pain caused within his attempt to achieve disembodied normativity as a marker of social equality. His facial discomfort makes manifest the hidden injuries of class resulting from his having to mask the disability of his background and conform to Mettingen's behavioral manners, and his divided voice records and

3. Brown, *Wieland*, 186 [151–52].
4. Shirley Samuels, "*Wieland*: Alien and Infidel," *Early American Literature* 25, no. 1 (1990): 46–66, 63.
5. Brown, *Wieland*, 136 [113].
6. Steven Connor, *Dumbstruck: A Cultural History of Ventriloquism* (Oxford: Oxford University Press, 2000), 239.

plays back the Wielands' hypocrisy.[7] Clara comes closest to recognizing Carwin's dilemma, since she also encounters Mettingen's contradictions within the register of gender.

Engendering Violence

After Clara first sees Carwin, her "heart" overflows and she cries "unbidden tears." Inviting the generic overlay of a seduction narrative, Clara retrospectively explains the events by saying that her "mind became the victim of . . . imbecility; perhaps because of . . . the inroad of a fatal passion" that is "incident to every female heart."[8] This tragedy is ostensibly a woman's destiny—to be tyrannized by her sex in ways that violate the gendered expectations of virtuous female behavior. Throughout the novel Clara often bumps against the restraints of feminized gender, such as when she hesitates over proposing marriage to Pleyel, her brother-in-law, because she sees "with the utmost clearness that a confession like that would be the most remediless and unpardonable outrage upon the dignity of my sex."[9] Clara seems less worried about sexual attraction than the power of conventional femininity as a regulatory device.

Clara's weepy response to Carwin's arrival allows Brown to pose the questions he had tentatively raised in *Alcuin:* can erotic affinities be disarticulated from the power hierarchies instituted within normative sex-gender roles so that men and women (and implicitly any other combination) are able to enjoy each other outside of the gothic codes that currently regulate physical intimacy?[1] Is sexual desire between men and women "fated" to retreat into modes that can articulate erotic affinities only through the archaic narratives of mortal seduction and "true love" in ways that allow these codes to reinforce other modes of power inequality, like that of class? Must difference and disempowerment be tautological or is there a third way, a third space, which can guide a progressive way beyond the antimony?

Just as Carwin tried to escape from the codes of "rustic ignorance," Brown similarly uses Clara's seeming control of her address as a test, and best, case for the possibility for women to separate sex

---

7. Though David Lyttle does not explain his argument in terms of class resentment, he believes that Carwin's anger at his father's initial coercion is *Wieland*'s main focus. David Lyttle, "The Case Against Carwin," *Nineteenth-Century Fiction* 26, no. 3 (1971): 257–69, 269.
8. Brown, *Wieland*, 76, 50 [66, 45].
9. Ibid., 75 [65].
1. Bruce Burgett, "Between Speculation and Population: The Problem of 'Sex' in Thomas Malthus's *Essay on the Principle of Population* and Charles Brockden Brown's *Alcuin*," in *Revising Charles Brockden Brown: Culture, Politics, and Sexuality in the Early American Republic,* ed. Philip Barnard, Mark Kamrath, and Stephen Shapiro (Knoxville: University of Tennessee, 2004), 122–48.

from gender and enter public discourse without the burden of "femininity." As she stands on the cusp of breaking free from the past's codifications, Clara woozily oscillates between images of love and death, where her fantasies of affective union often transpose into images of a precipitous fall or drowning.[2] These images of incipient bodily distress presciently convey what she understands as the simultaneous attraction and risk of dispatching the corporealized category of her gendered subjectivity, just as Carwin's disfigurement paradoxically also functions as the source of his attractiveness to Clara, since Carwin's failure to embody bourgeois masculinity signifies his analogous complaint about class domination.[3]

The question of gender equality arises with the first crisis of telephony when Carwin initially ventriloquizes Catharine Wieland's voice so that her husband, Theodore, hears his wife's voice where he does to expect it to be: in the temple's space of debate. This possibility of female disembodiment metaphorizes the problem of women's entry into realms otherwise forbidden by their gendered location, a challenge mainly conveyed through Clara who attempts to bridge the gap between masculine competitive argument and feminine communal nurturing and silent domestic housework.

Living in her own house, Clara maintains closely knit, nearly protolesbian, female affective relations with Mettingen's other women. She feels the connection to her sister-in-law as if it was a personal doubling, and when the Wielands adopt the orphaned Louisa Conway, this suggestively consolidates an all-female household, indicated by the consonantal repetition (Clara-Catharine-Conway), displaces the need for Theodore's paternity.[4]

Clara's inclusion within this privatized female intimacy is matched by her willingness to appropriate the masculine privilege of self-definition. Unlike most female characters in the period's fictions, who are frequently objectified in third-person narration and unable to establish signifying authority, as their personal letters are routinely either misdirected or destroyed, Clara initiates and, despite some challenging moments, maintains control of *Wieland*'s narration. In the literary equivalent of portraiture's direct gaze, she introduces the tale by addressing her reader(s) unreservedly.

Clara begins the romance's dramatic events already on the verge of masculine prerogative: she overcomes the (gentry) custom of male primogeniture as she shares her father's property with her brother

2. Leslie Fiedler, *Love and Death in the American Novel* (Briarcliff Manor, N.Y.: Stein and Day, 1960).
3. Andrew J. Scheiber, "The Arm Lifted Against Me: Love, Terror, and the Construction of Gender in *Wieland*," *Early American Literature* 26, no. 2 (1991): 173–94.
4. Brown, *Wieland*, 25 [24]. It is another mark of Carwin's feminization as a plebeian that his name includes him within the category of the gendered "C" (Clara, Catharine, Louisa Conway).

and manages her own household economy. Clara is under no titular or contractual subordination to Theodore, even if she often defers to his opinion in times of crisis. She appears to be under no pressure to marry and complete the traffic of women's exchange from father to husband. Like her brother, she appreciates fine rhetoric (this is initially what attracts her to Carwin), and the men recognize her as unique among the women for having a "masculine" temperament typified by the qualities of rationality and bravery.[5] She alone among the women participates in the men's conversations. Unlike Catharine, who remains unknowing and overwhelmed by the waves of violence, Clara desires to intervene in the events swirling around her, and she insists on the attempt at activity, rather than reactivity. Even the possibility that she might share the fatal biology of her father's and brother's madness is something of a sign that she could fully inherit her father's traits and participate in masculinized mania, rather than be descriptively erased into her mother's denarratived depression or the silence of Catharine's corpse.

Yet Clara, like Carwin, is unable to divest herself from the discriminating garb of her particular identity and assume the invisibility of equal rights without paying the supplemental cost of personal damage. Carwin's efforts to rise socially results in his being shunted back into what Clara calls the "harmless pursuit of agriculture" as a reconsolidation of his "fatal" class origins. *Wieland*, likewise, consistently presents women's contact with male discursivity as resulting in morbid female distress. While the novel's middleclass men are celebrated for "bandying quotations," as the ventriloquizing ability to inhabit, repeat, and subsume other people's voices, women are characterized as violently silenced when attempting to do likewise. The terror of Catharine's independent voice and other instances of women's agency sets off a trail of female carnage that literally mutes women. Louisa Conway's mother passes away in "solitude and anguish" after her independent flight to America to escape accusations of infidelity; Pleyel's fiancée, the Baroness de Stolberg, who attempts to seek out her lover, is not allowed a single word and is declared dead multiple times in the text; and Judith, Clara's servant, is never given any right of reply to Carwin's unverified accusation of her betrayal of Clara. Clara and Catharine can variously exculpate themselves only if they convince the men that they have never tried to speak in the first instance, and even then Catharine and Louisa end as bloodied pulp and Clara becomes dangerously anorexic. Theodore murders his wife because he believes that his god asked for her sacrifice. The divine injunction to take life did not, however, include a command to so convulse the women's faces that, in Louisa's case,

5. Ibid. 144 [118–19].

"not a lineament remained," and in Catharine's, not flesh enough for
Clara to plant one farewell kiss.[6] The uncalled-for extreme violence
suggests that it was the nongendered organ of women's public voice
that most unhinges Wieland.[7] Consequently, the ungendered zone of
speech must be destroyed so that women can now be recognized only
by their secondary sex characteristics of breasts and other bodily features. Theodore's violence returns women to the subordinating features of their sexed bodies.[8]

The extravagant violence unleashed as a response to Carwin's and
Clara's border crossing is nothing more than the manifestation of
New Mettingen's interior tensions. For despite Mettingen's rhetoric
of sincere fraternity, it is replete with covert maneuvers of imposture
and voyeuristic surveillance. Even before formal reasons emerge to
doubt Carwin, he is constantly watched, probed, and deployed by
Mettingen's agents as a tool to gauge their response. Clara discovers
that underneath the congenial surface of the Wielands' verbal play
and graceful leisure, there is grave competition for rank, and she
finds out that the price for seeking equality is a series of epistemic,
rapelike, invasions of her private quarters, personal affects, and
private diary by Pleyel and Carwin.

Even her brother, Theodore, otherwise disconnected from these
schemes, symbolically repeats these procedures of invasive control
both in his murderous appearances in her bedroom and as his trial
narrative is placed, admittedly by Clara herself, amongst her "finer
clothing," a situation that continues the series of male science penetrating female interiority.[9] Brown has Theodore, as the male least
invested in Pleyel's or Carwin's masculinist games, wield the knife
on his family to indicate that the horror Clara faces is one intrinsic
to the current mode of social regulation and not an individual's
personality defect, a meaning carried by his increasing similarity in
Clara's mind to the other men. Her nightmare of being in a "theatre
of uproar and confusion" where her "uncle, Wieland, Pleyel, and
Carwin" all summon her to fall over a precipice indicates that she
considers the cross-class alliance of patriarchy as greater than their
class differences.[1] So when Theodore appears to attack her, his
tangled locks and dusty clothes repeat her first image of Carwin, as
though all men ultimately share a fundamental physiognomy.[2]

6. Ibid., 145 [120].
7. On rising male anger due to changing gender relations between the sexes in the 1790s,
see Ed Hatton, "'He Murdered Her Because He Loved Her': Passion, Masculinity, and
Intimate Homicide in Antebellum America," in *Over the Threshold: Intimate Violence
in Early America*, ed. Christine Daniels and Michael V. Kennedy (London: Routledge,
1999), 111–33.
8. Scheiber, "'The Arm Lifted Against Me,'" 178.
9. Brown, *Wieland*, 161 [132].
1. Ibid., 216 [174].
2. Ibid., 199 [161].

Clara's indication of the violence percolating within the realm of superficial equanimity signals Brown's first agenda as it reveals how Franklinian republican liberal claims for the amiable conversion of competition into civic weal actually result in the Wielands' catastrophe. As Clara increasingly realizes that the seemingly disinterested realm of neutral interaction is, in fact, a realm of covert alliances based on unrationalized inclinations, she educates herself in the rules of deception and vocal manipulation. A pivotal moment in this process appears when Clara discovers that Pleyel has prejudged her involvement with Carwin, and she rushes to his house to defend herself. Repeating the men's invasiveness, she creeps up behind Pleyel and then performs a ballet of different poses (tears, moody silence, rage, imperious demands) that move in rapid succession from one emotional mask to another as she gauges the relative impact of her performance. This game of deception with Pleyel is noteworthy, not so much in that it perfectly duplicates Carwin's masquerades and Pleyel's traps, but as it reveals Clara learning the tricks of male conversational imposture. Assuming the men's characteristic fusion of violence and information, Clara now "thirsted for knowledge and for vengeance" against Carwin's "black conspiracy," and she increasingly arms herself before conversational encounters with the novel's men, as if to manifest the invisible antagonisms within seemingly pacific dialogue.[3]

As Clara increasingly learns to deploy violence, she survives Mettingen's wreckage, but Brown suggests that this should not be read as a happy end. Despite the expulsion of Carwin and another libertine, *Wieland* ends ambivalently and without readerly joy or satisfaction, despite the generic convention of comedic closure with Clara's and Pleyel's long-delayed marriage. What ought to have been a coherent trajectory of justice evades the reader as Carwin never appears before the bar, preventing us from evaluating his testimony within the juridical public sphere and gauging his relative culpability for events in Mettingen.[4] Additionally, the symbolic promise of Mettingen's enlightenment, as a society radically different from European tyranny and land-based absolutism, disappears as Clara's second letter comes from Montpellier, where she plans to reside permanently. Her return to a European location, which a more lucid Theodore had rejected as a reactionary move, suggests that Clara has given up on the new world of her philosophic ideals. More specifically, she seems to have fallen back into an older social geography and temporality as

3. Ibid., 175, 174 [142].
4. Laura H. Korobkin, "Murder by Madman: Criminal Responsibility, Law, and Judgment in *Wieland*," *American Literature* 72, no. 4 (2000): 721–50, esp. 742.

she settles in a region associated with the evangelical sect that had inflamed her father's imagination.[5]

The atmosphere of voided promise continues as Clara describes her marriage as more akin to a feudal alliance than one based on the consensual intimacy of mutual happiness. In Montpellier Clara's narrative voice is more distant and less emotionally vibrant than it was in Mettingen, and the later Clara is more comfortable with delivering definitive decisions rather than forensic considerations. She has abandoned the values of transparency, sympathy, and mutuality that Mettingen Clara struggled to uphold, as well as the attempt to bridge the gender divide between masculine rationality and feminine sociability as Montpellier Clara relinquishes women's solidarity by existing in a solely male world.[6] Clara may have learned how to maneuver in the hostile waters, but her ethical transgendering and internalization of competitive isolationism means, for Brown, it is Clara's ultimate end in Montpellier, not the penultimate one in Mettingen, that is tragic. To survive she lost her ethical compass and became intellectually dispossessed. Having mistaken the acquisition of (male) power for the ideal of (female) liberation, Clara enacts a social ventriloquism far more substantively aggressive than Carwin's garden-variety imposture.[7]

While Mettingen's false promise of discursive equality was literally a dead-end for Clara, a possible alternative might have existed with the potential union of Clara and Carwin as mutual discontents and fringe members of New Mettingen's male bourgeois sphere. Clara vaguely realizes this possibility of partnership as, despite her surface hostility to Carwin, she continually maintains an affinity for him, evidenced in her otherwise inexplicable willingness to meet him at her house even after events have led her to suspect the dangerous implications of doing so. With Clara's and Carwin's submarine concern for each other, Brown suggests that erotic attraction can act as a productive medium for solidarity by overcoming the social artifices that are constructed between bourgeois women and laboring-class men, a theme that Brown's *Alcuin* had already broached and that *Arthur Mervyn* will reconsider. Because a potential Clara-Carwin mésalliance would have echoed Wieland senior's own cross-class marriage, Brown implies that history does not have to be tragic, since every new phase has a chance to revisit and revise

5. Kinderman, *Man Unknown to Himself*, 137.
6. For an empirical confirmation of this claim, see Larry L. Stewart, "Charles Brockden Brown: Quantitative Analysis and Literary Interpretation," *Literary and Linguistic Computing* 18, no. 2 (2003): 129–38.
7. Andrew J. Scheiber, "'The Arm Lifted Against Me: Love, Terror, and the Construction of Gender in *Wieland*," *Early American Literature* 26, no. 2 (1991): 173–94, 191.

past mistakes, not in the superficial sense of Franklin's errata-correction but through a substantive erasure of all strata divisions.

Clara, however, only inchoately perceives the possibility of "believing" (in) Carwin, and turning the space in between masculine-defined discourse and feminine affect into a productive common grotto shared between middleclass women and male plebeians in a postbourgeois, postpatriarchal society. Clara fails to realize this solidarity because she ultimately holds too tightly to her subjectivity as a property owner and conflates the notion of female enfranchisement with the acquisition of private property and possessive individualism, a move today associated with liberal feminism.[8]

Clara's and Carwin's lost opportunity for coalition stands as Brown's complaint at the petit bourgeois Woldwinites' reluctance to forge cross-class alliances in their political practice and create stable counterinstitutions that could confront insurgent reactionary ideological formations. This gap would substantially diminish the actionable scope of Woldwinite ideals and the durability of the period's progressive designs. Brown's diagnosis on the recent failure of English and Continental radicalism was not that it was an immanent failure of progressive *thought*, but a practical one as bourgeois dissidents did not learn to institutionalize radical ideals as a means of supporting the inclusion of heterogeneous social elements.

Clara vaguely senses the need for new networks of affiliation when she introduces the second seduction narrative of Louisa Conway's mother to indicate her belief that Mettingen's problem was a lack of comparative examples that could determine an empirical normative standard. In this view, her father's mania was caused by an excessive reliance upon the narrow foundation of a single text.[9] Pleyel and Theodore's debate over what should be the ethical lesson learned from Cicero's oration on Cluentius similarly flounders because it is "absurd" to depend on the image of a "single family" since it is difficult to determine if that family is typical or anomalous.[1] Carwin likewise remains a seemingly unsolvable riddle to the Wielands because they had "no ground on which to build even a plausible conjecture" and cannot gather "satisfactory information" to judge Carwin's "uncommon" behavior.[2] Clara's anxiety about narrating her biography is that since no other tale can "furnish a parallel," it faces the danger of seeming useless to her readers and even to herself.

The problem of vulnerable singularity, which the Woldwinites warned against, arises after the Wielands rejected older models of sovereignty (their father's) and refused the "corruption and tyranny"

---

8. Hinds, *Private Property*, 101.
9. Brown, *Wieland*, 8 [10].
1. Ibid., 28 [27].
2. Ibid., 66 [57].

of existing educational structures. After condemning one mode of irrational power as corrupting, they distance themselves from taking responsibility for replacing it with a more egalitarian structure because they believe that a better society will naturally and spontaneously emerge. Their confidence in the Smithian "invisible hand" of social regulation means, however, that they are left in what Joseph Ridgely calls an "empty world" bereft of guidelines for responding to crises or analyzing testimony "before the bar" of reason that the Wielands often invoke.[3]

The failure to concretize an institutional framework means that they frequently retreat to individual responses. Each of the core trio in Mettingen relies on a particular mode for explaining their experience, but the idiosyncratic nature of these approaches means they fall back on the very errors from which the Woldwinites sought to escape. With his intensive reading, behavioral gravity, and belief in "moral necessity and Calvinistic inspiration," Theodore is the one who most reaffirms his father's solitary superstition. This pathway leads to mania. Pleyel is the extreme rationalist, "the champion of intellectual liberty," who rejects "all guidance but that of his reason."[4] This Cartesian worship of his own reason leads to solipsistic "fury," a lighter form of madness typified by a dogmatic unwillingness to consider the potential logical faults in his own explanation of Clara's behavior by submitting them to dialogic conversation. Instead of "celestial interference" or pure reason, Clara relies on the force of associationist sensibility. When Theodore first hears voices, she initially fears that they result from his sense's derangement, and her faith in the moral nature of sensations often leads her to comment on changing light or air conditions. During emergencies she will try to block the atmospheric matrix of sensation, either by shielding her eyes or fainting, as if the body's intake of sensations, not the mind's empirical observations, is what matters in forming a response. Her reliance on environmental causes, however, leads to an immobilizing lack of self-confidence in her intuition and inability to analyze the events around her in a rational and critical fashion.

Since none of the proponents of belief, reason, or sense are willing to converge with the other's mode of decision making, they are left unable to make any decision at all or move forward in crisis. Mettingen's conversations are typically inconclusive, rarely achieve consensus, and frequently end with the participants even more disengaged and mutually suspicious than before. The clarifying purpose of speech is easily frustrated when it becomes evident that nothing

---

3. Joseph Ridgely, "The Empty World of *Wieland*," in *Individual and Community: Variations on a Theme in American Fiction*, ed. Kenneth H. Baldwin and David K. Kuby (Durham: Duke University Press, 1975).

4. Brown, *Wieland*, 23 [23].

can be said one way or the other to dislodge a certain prejudice, as when Clara fails to convince Pleyel of her innocence and Wieland of Carwin's manipulation.

Despite their frequent invocation of rational adjudication, the members of New Mettingen are usually unable to recognize the correct answer for events even when it is set before them. When voices preternaturally float through their milieu, Carwin offers the explanation that it is a fraud based on vocal tricks.[5] The confusion *is* caused by an eavesdropping ventriloquist (Carwin himself), but the Wielands cannot recognize his answer's validity. It does not occur to Theodore to see that that the much-rehearsed defense of Cluentius by Cicero provides obvious explanatory similarities to Mettingen's events. After his successful defense of Cluentius against charges of poisoning his stepfather, Cicero boasted that he had "thrown dust in the eyes of the jurymen" by distracting them with complaints about the accusing mother's sexual misbehavior and avoiding any attempt to clarify whether Cluentius had really plotted the murder or not.[6] Wieland fails to see that Pleyel's accusation of Clara's licentiousness duplicates Cicero's tactics and is himself likewise distracted from pursuing the actual agent of misbehavior—Carwin. Theodore does not learn the text's lesson, which is that seemingly disinterested public speech can deflect analysis from pursuing the truth about violence in its social interior.

As Brown sees it, the disastrous fragmentation of Mettingen's lifeworld results from the Woldwinites' failure to distinguish between social structure and social domination. Consequently, while the Woldwinites have a respect for the agency of the cultural, they failed to consolidate their cultural innovations by moving from the sociocultural back to the political; cultural standards did not become formal counterinstitutions based on a post-ideological, postpublic sphere mechanism, hinted at by Brown with the idea of a shared Clara-Carwin grotto, because the Woldwinites assumed that all forms of institutionality are equally tyrannical.

Without cementing alternative structures of feeling within progressive institutions, the Woldwinites' ideals, as staged in New Mettingen, are fragile, short-lived and easily collapsed backwards. Clara's recognition of Mettingen's need for more stable standards of evaluation points to *Wieland*'s last critique of the Woldwinites, which is that by failing to replace absolutist institutions with postabsolutist ones, they left the field open to be occupied by other nascent ideological groups, an argument conveyed in *Wieland*'s third, post-Mettingen phase of social history.

5. Ibid., 68 [59].
6. Cicero, "In Defence of Aulus Cluentius Habitus," in *Murder Trials*, ed. Michael Grant (Harmondsworth: Penguin, 1975), 113–253, 119, 123; W. Peterson, "Introduction," in *M. Tulli Ciceronis: Pro A. Cluentio Oratio*, ed. W. Peterson (London: Macmillan, 1920).

Brown's final intervention, which acts as a self-diagnosis in the status of romance itself in an age of ideological discipline, works through a technique that he develops. In a para-Woldwinite, proto-Brechtian manner, Brown stages an illustration of *wrested authority* within the narrative voice, where the speaker's local instability and contradictoriness is not a matter of deceit or epistemological ambivalence but registers a dynamic struggle between competing social interests for sovereignty over individual subjectivity and hegemonic control over what constitutes a normative voice. This technique of wrested authority differs from a more familiar use of irony. The latter involves a stable narrative voice that knowingly deploys two levels of signification to convey meaning. Wrested authority refers to how the register of narration is contested by different social interests or perspectives that seek to appropriate control over the mode of commonsensical expression. Brown's singular achievement is his elaboration of a narrative style that can represent the global conditions of transition at the level of aesthetic form.

In this way, the changed tone between Clara's two letters indicates how her earlier ideals have been appropriated and recodified by another set of informing interests. By alienating the reader's tendency to sympathize with the narrator through the unappealing portrait of Montpellier Clara, the competitive survivor, Brown has a narrative device to convey his belief in the increasing containment of early 1790s progressivism by conservatism as a result of its failure to establish institutions that could protect and nurture their progressive ideals, thus allowing the new forces of disciplinary institutionality to opportunistically intervene in the vacuum created by the old regime's obsolescence and potentially ensuing one's fragility.

This appropriation by ideological forces appears with the arrival of figures who superintend Clara's psychic reconstruction, the legal and medical authorities of Hallet and Cambridge. Hallet is the "magistrate and good citizen" who produces the "facts" of Carwin's European criminality and superintends the crime scene, and Thomas Cambridge is the surgeon who treats Clara and interprets Wieland's court testimony. These men represent the new kind of sovereignty grounded in the disciplinary fields of professional knowledge, with Cambridge's name evoking the geography of institutional higher education. They seal their authority by seizing control of the right to explain Mettingen's events through their own language of medicalized case history and legalized confession of motive.

Whereas Theodore revised the totemic text that covers the Wielands from his father's Gnostic psalter to Latin republican rhetoric, Cambridge relocates the Wielands' literary descent to be from Erasmus Darwin's medical directory as he explains the Wieland family's errors through the category of *mania mutabilis*. Rather than seeing violence as caused by divine wrath or sentimental imbalances, Hallet suggests that it is a matter of congenital inheritance, a turn that deflates the need for legal scrutiny on Carwin.[7] Cambridge does produce Theodore's court testimony for Clara to examine, but only as it lends credence to his professional opinion about Wieland's interior dysfunction.

Brown represents this turn to the new disciplinary power with a different organization of the family. Wieland senior represents the regime of absolutist terror configured as analogical to the father's repressive authority. Conversely, Theodore's mode of elder masculinity is one of fatherhood without the father's absolutism as it depends on a world of semiotic equivalences configured as the sibling realm of brothers and a boyish, autonomous daughter. The era of disciplinary knowledge is not based on either patriarchal coercion or sibling appeals to consensus but on the productive creation of categories, like madness, as a means of institutionalizing new forms of control. Brown conveys this transformation from patriarchal domination and fraternal equivalence to professional "benevolent" control as this period's symbolic fathers and brothers are represented in terms of matrilineal avuncularity and cousinage. Hallet is a "distant kinsman" of Clara's mother and Cambridge is the Wielands' maternal uncle.[8] Symbolically transferring the figure of authority from the unbroken paternal line of fathers and brothers to the ancillary maternal axis of uncles and cousins, Brown represents the latter's authority as a light, lateral touch (the stiletto's puncture of Maxwell) that encodes the shift to the "transparent" rule of disciplinary knowledge. While the father/brother axis represents the force of force, the maternal uncle/cousin axis represents the unforced force of regulatory institutional knowledge: ideology.

The representation of ideology as avuncular power also captures Brown's resistance to Franklin's outlook. Christopher Looby and Cynthia Jordan describe how Franklin's *Autobiography* looks to uncle power as an alternative to the older system of patriarchal subordination that decreases the father's force by dispersing it among several uncles.[9] Franklin is named after one uncle and he looks to another, Thomas, as a model for how education can overcome class barriers. Whereas Franklin appreciates the tactical utility of avuncular ideology, Brown, as one inscribed under a (step)uncle's name and its legal aura, sees it as no more democratic than what came

7. Darwin, *Zoonomia*, 4:64.
8. Brown, *Wieland*, 142 [117].
9. Christopher Looby, *Voicing America: Language, Literary Form, and the Origins of the United States* (Chicago: University of Chicago Press, 1996), 105. Cynthia S. Jordan, *Second Stories: The Politics of Language, Form, and Gender in Early American Fictions* (Chapel Hill: University of North Carolina Press, 1989), 28–30.

before. While Brown famously abandoned his law apprenticeship by complaining about the legal profession's duplicity, he soon began to question the innocence of fiction as well.[1]

Is Political Romance Viable?

By the mid-nineteenth century, according to D. A. Miller and Lennard Davis, the novel-form has become a full-blown ideological, disciplinary institution in its own right, capable of regulating its readers.[2] That achievement is only in its initial stage of development at Brown's moment. Yet Brown suggests that the process of wresting knowledge from its original proponents has already begun during the 1790s. Cambridge's use of Darwinian etiology to deliver a diagnosis of quasi-genetic interiority puts considerable pressure to deliver a content that is not entirely present in Darwin's work, which is still rooted in eighteenth-century sensibilitarian physiology. By having Cambridge's academic mistranscription revise Darwin in a more modern way, Brown indicates that a more serious recodification of the eighteenth century's geoculture is occurring, mainly within American universities, the knowledge institutions that the Friendly Club members had initially moved away from but increasingly return to support, often as administrators, after the century's turn.

Throughout the 1790s, disregard for theological pedagogy was carried to an extreme by the period's collegians, who were collectively energized by the modern library of the freethinking Enlightenment. Letters and memoirs of the time attest to the galvanizing popularity on campuses of writers like Wollstonecraft, Godwin, Condorcet, Volney, and especially deist tracts like Paine's *Age of Reason*.[3] Having graduated from the academy, collegians kept up their fascination with deist concerns, a continuity that appears when the *New-York Magazine*, begins to regularly publish articles by Priestly, Wollstonecraft, and Godwin after 1793, when recent graduates took over its pages.

But if conservative academics failed in their first attempts to resist and repress student interest in culturally radical ideas, they then shifted strategy by teaching the topics that students liked, but in a highly conservative redaction. While undergraduates proclaimed a version of sensibilitist moral sense philosophy that they imbibed

1. Harry R. Warfel, *Charles Brockden Brown: American Gothic Novelist* (Gainesville: University of Florida Press, 1949), 36–37.
2. D. A. Miller, *The Novel and the Police* (Berkeley and Los Angeles: University of California Press, 1988); Lennard Davis "Who Put the *the* in the Novel: Identity Politics and Disability in Novel Studies," in *Bending over Backwards: Disability, Dismodernism, and Other Difficult Positions* (New York: New York University Press, 2002), 79–101.
3. Henry F. May, *The Enlightenment in America* (New York: Oxford University Press, 1976), 234.

through Paine and Godwin, the academics realized that there was little to this discourse in itself that made it intrinsically radical. Professors perceived that they could dilute student recalcitrance by splitting rational sentiment from its utopian political claims and proffering it back to students in an anodyne form. By the end of the eighteenth century and throughout the early nineteenth, universities broadly institutionalized a reconstructed version of Scottish moral sense that realigned its claims to support the institutional authority of the pedagogues and market society overall.

A second-wave version of Scottish School sensibilitarian claims, known as moral or common sense, quickly became consecrated as they became canonical texts. Kames's *Elements of Criticism* and Blair's *Rhetoric* were massively reprinted, the latter thirty-nine times before 1835, and used as core texts on a required curriculum.[4] Universities instituted a mandatory senior year course on morals, often taught by the college's president, which safely relied on the professor's interpretation of a single chosen text.[5] As moral sense arguments became "institutionalized in American colleges," whatever radicalism Scottish common sense might have had, especially in the Woldwinites' hands, "had ceased."[6] The top-down version of moral sense read texts in such a way as to shift their arguments from the collective concerns of Smith and Ferguson towards the celebration of the isolated individual and his "immediate conviction of right and wrong, of the reality of the external world, freedom, etc. about which there was no need or warrant for debate or doubt." By emphasizing the individual's prerational perception of right and wrong, moral sense, as Merli Curti argues, was "admirably suited to the needs of conservative-minded intellectuals" because it undercut the conversational intersubjectivity on which Woldwinite and Painite formulations depended.[7]

By narrowing moral sense claims into ones about individual character, rather than a communal sensibility, ideological academics prepared the way for the rise of an interiority that could be disciplined by moralizing professional in ways suited to the emerging geoculture of high capitalism. "The principles of Common Sense were extended to the field of political economy, which was taught as a set of self-evident maxims about the laws of God and the duties of man in the material world . . . the doctrines of laissez-faire were

---

4. Terence Martin, *The Instructed Vision: Scottish Common Sense Philosophy and the Origins of American Fiction* (Bloomington: Indiana University Press, 1961), 24; Andrew Hook, *Scotland and America: A Study of Cultural Relations, 1750–1835* (Glasgow: Blackie, 1975), 75–82.
5. Martin, *Instructed Vision*, 23. Jean V. Matthews, *Towards a New Society: American Thought and Culture, 1800–1830* (Boston: Twayne Publishers, 1990), 39.
6. Martin, *Instructed Vision*, 4–5, 11.
7. Ibid., 3, 4.

taught in textbooks written by American clergymen, which simplified not only Smith's economics but also his morality. Instead of Smith's careful balance between justice and benevolence, the American texts taught the supreme virtue of competitive individualism as a part of the clear dictates of the conscience, implanted by the creator and apprehended through common sense."[8]

The academy's conservative appropriation of sensibility's terms for the benefit of a new manner of competitive capitalism casts its shadow on *Wieland* as the wrested authority within Clara's consciousness conveys Brown's sense that his own terms of social imagination are themselves contested. For the appearance of the medicojuridical authorities, Hallet and Cambridge, not only represents the emergence of refashioned institutions that stage modern ideas, but also the ability of these authorities to ventriloquize the terms of progressivism for conservative propaganda.

Theodore finds it difficult to "think" cogently about the cause of his confusion because he lacks a stable perspective that can validate his thoughts, but Clara cannot ultimately analyze the problem of Mettingen's collapse because her own cognitive apparatus has been gutted by the new medical and legal authorities. Consequently, she becomes easily contained and repackaged in her Montpellier avatar. By charting how Mettingen's common sense becomes smashed to bits, Brown himself doubts the larger efficacy of the weakly institutionalized romance as a force of change and finds it increasingly harder to produce an intellectually robust narrative as the forces of reaction are busily reconstituting the terms of reference on which the Woldwinite narrative depends. The chaotic air of Brown's narrative style conveys a gloomy recognition that his own medium of possible resistance is undergoing colonization even while some, like himself, are attempting to use it as a platform for culturally driven social change. In a contest over the politics of form, the romance is itself being forced to be compliant and become a form of entertainment: in short, to become a novel.

* * *

8. May, *Enlightenment in America*, 349.

Charles Brockden Brown:
A Chronology†

1771   Born January 17 in Philadelphia to Elijah and Mary Armitt Brown, Quakers.

1777   Father exiled to Virginia with nineteen other men, mostly Quakers, by Continental Congress, for refusing to take an oath of loyalty to Pennsylvania's Revolutionary authority and for selling prohibited goods (flour) on the open market rather than under Revolutionary regulations. Elijah Brown returns from Virginia in April 1778.

1781–86   Attends Friends' Latin School in Philadelphia. Studies Greek, Latin, English, and mathematics under headmaster Robert Proud, a former Tory and future historian of Pennsylvania. Classmates include Joseph Bringhurst. At home, parents favor Dissenting British authors, over time including Richard Price, William Godwin, and Mary Wollstonecraft.

1787   Begins legal studies with Alexander Wilcocks. Joins law society, formed for debating and mock courts. Forms Belles Lettres Club, with Bringhurst and other friends, Quakers and non-Quakers, to further literary improvement. Writes poetry.

1789   Publishes "Rhapsodist" essays in *Columbian Magazine*. Wilcocks becomes Philadelphia's city recorder.

1790   Meets Elihu Hubbard Smith, a Connecticut native in Philadelphia for medical study.

1791   With Bringhurst and Smith publishes poetic correspondence (using pseudonyms Henry, Birtha, and Ella) in *Gazette of the United States* and *General Advertiser*. The friends also help found Society for the Attainment of Useful Knowledge. His studies completed, Smith returns to Connecticut.

† Adapted and expanded from John R. Holmes, "Chronology of the Life of Charles Brockden Brown," published on the website of the Charles Brockden Brown Society (brockdenbrownsociety.ucf.edu), and Sidney Krause's chronology in Charles Brockden Brown, *Three Gothic Novels* (New York: Library of America, 1998).

1792   Abandons legal training to pursue literary vocation. Corresponds with Bringhurst about religious doubts; says he prefers Richardson's novels to the Bible as a spur to virtue, and thinks Richardson is "inferior to none that ever lived, as a teacher of virtues and the friend of mankind, but the founder of the Christian Religion."

1793   Spends summer with Smith in Connecticut. Introduced to Smith's literary friends there, including Richard Alsop, Theodore Dwight, and other "Connecticut Wits." Smith edits *American Poems, Selected and Original*, first anthology of American poetry, probably with Brown's help. Smith moves to New York in September; Brown returns to Philadelphia, which suffers a major yellow fever epidemic in the late summer and fall, killing over four thousand. In December, Bringhurst moves from Philadelphia to Wilmington, Delaware.

1794   Visits New York in spring and summer. Meets William Dunlap, playwright and theater manager, and begins to visit theater regularly. Attends meetings of Friendly Club with Smith, Dunlap, and others.

1795   Visits New York in summer. Lays literary plans with Smith and Dunlap. Visits Dunlap's country house in Perth Amboy, New Jersey. Reads William Godwin's *Enquiry Concerning Political Justice* and *Caleb Williams*. Writes Dunlap that he plans to write a novel "equal in extent" to *Caleb Williams* over a six-week period. Unfinished "Philadelphia novel," now known as "Ellendale fragments," includes anti-Christian elements and anticipates *Arthur Mervyn*.

1796   Visits Dunlap in Perth Amboy in July, then moves to New York for seven months. Attends Friendly Club and the theater regularly. Works on "projected novel" and "new political romance," parts of which he reads to friends.

1797   Returns to Philadelphia in March. Plans but does not execute a dramatization of Robert Bage's *Hermsprong*. Reads *Memoirs of Emma Courtney* by Mary Hays. Writes first two parts of *Alcuin*, a Wollstonecraftian dialogue on women's rights, which Smith reads to club members in New York. Survives yellow fever outbreak in Philadelphia in the fall. Completes first novel, *Sky-Walk, or Man Unknown to Himself*, never printed.

1798   *Alcuin* published in April, with Smith's assistance, in New York; serialized (and censored) by James Watters in Philadelphia *Weekly Magazine* as "The Rights of Women." Works on parts III and IV, which will be printed only after his death. Publishes several other serials for Watters' weekly, including "A Lesson on Sensibility," "The Man at Home," "A Series of Original Letters," and the first nine chapters of *Arthur Mervyn*. Begins *Wieland*. Failed relationship with Susan Potts, who does not meet his parents' approval. Moves to New York in July, leaving manuscript of "Sky-Walk" with Watters, who dies in a yellow fever epidemic that fall. "Sky-Walk" manuscript is lost. Completes *Wieland* in New York with assistance from Smith, Dunlap, and William Johnson. Begins *Memoirs of Carwin* and *Memoirs of Stephen Calvert*. In September, shortly after *Wieland* is published, survives a yellow fever epidemic in New York that takes Smith's life and kills two thousand. Flees to Perth Amboy with Dunlap. Travels to New England, then returns to New York in November. Writes *Ormond* during the last few weeks of the year.

1799   Publishes *Ormond* in February. Begins editing *Monthly Magazine and Amerian Review* in New York, assisted by Johnson and other Friendly Club members. Encourages Margaret Bayard and other female friends to write for *Monthly Magazine*. *Arthur Mervyn*, part I published in May. Begins serializing *Stephen Calvert* in *Monthly Magazine* in June. Publishes *Edgar Huntly*. Travels to New England with Johnson in July; visits Smith's family. *Monody* on George Washington's death is read at New York's Park Theatre and published in *Monthly Magazine* in January 1800.

1800   Meets Elizabeth Linn in New York. Resumes serialization of *Calvert* in *Monthly Magazine*. Visits Connecticut again in spring. Publishes *Arthur Mervyn*, Part II. Begins *Clara Howard*. Tells Margaret Bayard "the Godwinian [is] the most perfect system" he knows, but that "were I to marry, I should wish for my wife to be a Christian, with this system engrafted on her." Returns to Philadelphia and joins family mercantile enterprises. *Monthly Magazine* stops publication in December.

1801   Begins correspondence with Elizabeth Linn, daughter of Dutch Reformed minister William Linn and sister of Brown's friend, poet John Blair Linn. Founds and edits *The American Review and Literary Journal*, a quarterly that aims to review every new American publication. Writes for Joseph Dennie's *Port Folio* and attends Tuesday Club with him. Publishes *Clara Howard* in June. *Ormond* issued in London by William Lane's Minerva Press. Visits New York and Albany in summer; travels through Western Massachusetts and Connecticut. Hears Timothy Dwight preach at Yale College. Returns to New York City in July and stays through late summer or early fall. Visits New York again in winter. *Jane Talbot* published in December.

1802 Publishes "Dialogues on Female Accomplishment" in *Port Folio*. Discontinues *American Review* after eight numbers. Grandmother Armitt dies in the spring; Brown named executor.

1803 William Lane's Minerva Press releases London editions of *Arthur Mervyn* and *Edgar Huntly*. Brown publishes anti-Jeffersonian political pamphlets on the Louisiana question. In fall, begins publication of *Literary Magazine, and American Register*. Serializes "Memoirs of Carwin" starting in November. (Ten installments appear between November 1803 and March 1805.)

1804 Publishes London edition of *Jane Talbot* with Minerva Press. Publishes translation of Volney's *Soil and Climate of the United States*, with copious editorial notes and commentary. John Blair Linn dies in August. Brown marries Elizabeth Linn in November in a ceremony performed by her father. Wedding, which his parents refuse to attend, results in censure by Monthly Meeting of the Philadelphia Society of Friends.

1805 Writes biographical sketch of John Blair Linn to be printed with Linn's posthumously published poem *Valerian*. Twin sons, Charles Brockden Brown Jr. and William Linn Brown, born in August.

1806 Dunlap makes extended visit to Philadelphia in spring; Brown travels to Albany to visit in-laws in summer, hoping for relief from symptoms of consumption.

1807 *Literary Magazine* ceases publication following January issue. Publishes political pamphlet *British Treaty of Commerce and Navigation*, critical of Jefferson's Embargo Act. Son Eugene Linn Brown born in July. Begins publishing semi-annual *American Register* in November (runs through 1811, Brown editing first five volumes). Minerva Press issues *Philip Stanley; or, the Enthusiasm of Love*, a slightly altered version of *Clara Howard*, in London.

1808 Begins publishing "Annals of Europe and America" in *American Register*.

1809 Publishes *An Address to the Congress of the United States*, critical of Embargo Act. Publishes "Scribbler" essays in *Port Folio*. Begins work on "System of General Geography," projected for two six hundred-page volumes, never completed. Daughter Mary Brown is born.

1810 Suffers from pulmonary tuberculosis. Dies on February 22, interred in Friends Burial Ground in Philadelphia.

Selected Bibliography

• indicates items included or excerpted in this Norton Critical Edition.

Website

Charles Brockden Brown Society.

Biographies

Clark, David Lee. *Charles Brockden Brown: Pioneer Voice of America*. Durham, NC: Duke University Press, 1952.

Kafer, Peter. *Charles Brockden Brown's Revolution and the Birth of American Gothic*. Philadelphia: University of Pennsylvania Press, 2004.

Watts, Steven. *The Romance of Real Life: Charles Brockden Brown and the Origins of American Culture*. Baltimore: Johns Hopkins University Press, 1994.

Warfel, Harry R. *Charles Brockden Brown: American Gothic Novelist*. Gainesville: University of Florida Press, 1949.

Monographs Primarily on Brown

Axelrod, Alan. *Charles Brockden Brown, An American Tale*. Austin: University of Texas Press, 1983.

Christophersen, Bill. *The Apparition in the Glass: Charles Brockden Brown's American Gothic*. Athens: University of Georgia Press, 1993.

Cody, Michael. *Charles Brockden Brown and the Literary Magazine: Cultural Journalism in the Early American Republic*. Jefferson, NC: McFarland & Company, 2004.

Crain, Caleb. *American Sympathy: Men, Friendship, and Literature in the New Nation*. New Haven, CT: Yale, University Press, 2001.

Grabo, Norman S. *The Coincidental Art of Charles Brockden Brown*. Chapel Hill: University of North Carolina Press, 1981.

Hinds, Elizabeth Jane Wall. *Private Property: Charles Brockden Brown's Gendered Economics of Virtue*. Newark: University of Delaware Press, 1997.

• Shapiro, Stephen. *The Culture and Commerce of the Early American Novel: Reading the Atlantic World-System*. University Park: The Pennsylvania State University Press, 2008.

Slawinski, Scott. *Validating Bachelorhood: Audience, Patriarchy, and Charles Brockden Brown's Editorship of the* Monthly Magazine and American Review. London: Routledge, 2005.

• Waterman, Bryan. *Republic of Intellect: The Friendly Club of New York City and the Making of American Literature*. Baltimore: Johns Hopkins University Press, 2007.

Selected Criticism of Wieland and Memoirs of Carwin

Barnard, Philip, and Stephen Shapiro. "Introduction" and notes. *Wieland, or, the Transformation: An American Tale, with Related Texts.* Indianapolis: Hackett, 2009.

Barnes, Elizabeth. "Loving with a Vengeance: *Wieland*, Familicide and the Crisis of Masculinity in the Early Nation." In *Boys Don't Cry?: Rethinking Narratives of Masculinity and Emotion in the U.S.* Ed. Milette Chamir and Jennifer Travis. New York: Columbia University Press, 2002, pp. 44–63.

Bauer, Ralph. "Between Repression and Transgression: Rousseau's *Confessions* and Charles Brockden Brown's *Wieland*." *American Transcendental Quarterly* 10 (1996): 311–29.

Baym, Nina. "A Minority Reading of *Wieland*." In *Critical Essays on Charles Brockden Brown.* Ed. Bernard Rosenthal. Boston: G. K. Hall, 1981, pp. 87–103.

Bell, Michael Davitt. "'The Double-Tongued Deceiver': Sincerity and Duplicity in the Novels of Charles Brockden Brown." *Early American Literature* 9.2 (1974): 142–63.

Bradshaw, Charles C. "The New England Illuminati: Conspiracy and Causality in Charles Brockden Brown's *Wieland*." *New England Quarterly* 76.3 (2003): 356–77.

• Cahill, Edward. "An Adventurous and Lawless Fancy: Charles Brockden Brown's Aesthetic State." *Early American Literature* 36.1 (2001): 31–70.

Clark, Michael. "Charles Brockden Brown's *Wieland* and Robert Proud's *History of Pennsylvania*." *Studies in the Novel* 20 (1988): 239–48.

Cowie, Alexander. "Historical Essay." In Charles Brockden Brown, *Wieland; or, The Transformation and Memoirs of Carwin the Biloquist.* Volume 1: *The Novels and Related Works of Charles Brockden Brown.* Kent, OH: Kent State University Press, 1977, pp. 311–48.

Crain, Caleb. "Introduction" and notes. In Charles Brockden Brown, *Wieland; or The Transformation: An American Tale and Other Stories.* New York: Modern Library, 2002, pp. xi–xxiv.

Dawes, James. "Fictional Feeling: Philosophy, Cognitive Science, and the American Gothic." *American Literature* 76.3 (2004): 437–66.

Dill, Elizabeth. "The Republican Stepmother: Revolution and Sensibility in Charles Brockden Brown's *Wieland*." *The Eighteenth-Century Novel* 2 (2002): 273–303.

• Downes, Paul. "Constitutional Secrets: 'Memoirs of Carwin' and the Politics of Concealment." *Criticism* 39 (1997): 89–117.

Doyle, Laura. *Freedom's Empire: Race and the Rise of the Novel in Atlantic Modernity, 1640–1940.* Durham, NC: Duke University Press, 2008, ch. 9.

Elliott, Emory. "Introduction" and notes. In Charles Brockden Brown, *Wieland; or, The Transformation and Memoirs of Carwin the Biloquist.* New York: Oxford University Press, 1994, pp. vii–xxx.

Faherty, Duncan. *Remodeling the Nation: The Architecture of American Identity, 1776–1858.* Lebanon: University of New Hampshire Press, 2007, ch. 2.

Fliegelman, Jay. "Introduction" and notes. In Charles Brockden Brown, *Wieland; or, The Transformation and Memoirs of Carwin the Biloquist.* New York: Penguin Books, 1991, pp. vii–xlii.

• Fussell, Edwin Sill. "Wieland: A Literary and Historical Reading." *Early American Literature* 18.2 (fall 1983): 171–86.

Galluzzo, Anthony. "*Carwin's* Terrorist Aesthetic: Charles Brockden Brown's Aesthetics of Subversion." *Eighteenth-Century Studies* 4.2 (2009): 255–71.

Goddu, Teresa A. "Historicizing the American Gothic: Charles Brockden Brown's Wieland." In *Approaches to Teaching Gothic Fiction: The British and American Traditions.* Ed. Diane Long Hoeveler and Tamar Heller. New York: Modern Language Association of America, pp. 184–89.

Hagenbüche, Roland. "American Literature and the Nineteenth-Century Crisis in Epistemology: The Example of Charles Brockden Brown." *Early American Literature* 23 (1988): 121–51.

Harris, Jennifer. "At One with the Land: The Domestic Remove—Charles Brockden Brown's *Wieland* and Matters of National Belonging." *Canadian Review of American Studies* 33.3 (2003): 189–210.

• Hesford, Walter. "Do You Know the Author? The Question of Authorship in *Wieland*." *Early American Literature* 17.3 (winter 1982–83): 239–48.

Hsu, Hsuan L. "Democratic Expansionism in *Memoirs of Carwin*." *Early American Literature* 35 (2000): 137–56.

Hughes, Rowland. "'Wonderfully Cruel Proceedings': The Murderous Case of James Yates." *Canadian Review of American Studies* 38. 1 (2008): 43–62.

• Kazanjian, David. "Charles Brockden Brown's Biloquial Nation: National Culture and White Settler Colonialism in *Memoirs of Carwin the Biloquist*." *American Literature* 73 (2001): 459–96.

• Korobkin, Laura H. "Murder by Madman: Criminal Responsibility, Law, and Judgment in *Wieland*." *American Literature* 72 (2000): 721–50.

Krause, Sydney J. "Charles Brockden Brown and the Philadelphia Germans." *Early American Literature* 39. 1 (2004): 85–119.

Kutchen, Larry. "The 'Vulgar Thread of the Canvas': Revolution and the Picturesque in Ann Eliza Bleecker, Crevecoeur, and Charles Brockden Brown." *Early American Literature* 36.3 (2001): 395–425.

Levine, Robert S. *Conspiracy and Romance: Studies in Brockden Brown, Cooper, Hawthorne, and Melville.* New York: Cambridge University Press, 1989, ch. 1.

• Looby, Christopher. *Voicing America: Language, Literary Form, and the Origins of the United States.* Chicago: University of Chicago Press, 1996, ch. 3.

Manning, Susan L. "Enlightenment's Dark Dreams: Two Fictions of Henry Mackenzie and Charles Brockden Brown." *Eighteenth-Century Life* 21.3 (1997): 39–56.

Norwood, Lisa West. "'I May Be a Stranger to the Grounds of Your Belief': Constructing a Sense of Place in *Wieland*." *Early American Literature* 38 (2003): 89–122.

O'Shaughnessy, Toni. "'An Imperfect Tale': Interpretive Accountability in *Wieland*." *Studies in American Fiction* 18 (1990): 41–54.

Rombes, Nicholas, Jr. "'All Was Lonely, Darksome, and Waste': *Wieland* and the Construction of the New Republic." *Studies in American Fiction* 22 (1994): 37–46.

• Rosenthal, Bernard. "The Voices of *Wieland*" In *Critical Essays on Charles Brockden Brown.* Ed. Bernard Rosenthal. Boston: G. K. Hall, 1981, pp. 104–25.

• Ruttenberg, Nancy. *Democratic Personality: Popular Voice and the Trial of American Authorship.* Stanford, CA: Stanford University Press, 1998, ch. 4.

Samuels, Shirley. *Romances of the Republic: Women, the Family, and Violence in the Literature of the Early American Nation.* New York: Oxford University Press, 1996.

• Samuels, Shirley. "Wieland: Alien and Infidel." *Early American Literature* 25.1 (1990): 45–66.

Schreiber, Andrew J. "'The Arm Lifted Against Me': Love, Terror, and the Construction of Gender in *Wieland*." *Early American Literature* 26 (1991): 173–94.

Seed, David. "The Mind Set Free: Charles Brockden Brown's *Wieland*." In *Making America/Making American Literature.* Ed. Robert A. Lee and W. M. Verhoeven. Amsterdam: Rodopi, 1995, pp. 105–22.

Seltzer, Mark. "Saying Makes It So: Language and Event in Brown's *Wieland*." *Early American Literature* 8 (1978): 81–91.

Shuffelton, Frank. "Juries of the Common Reader: Crime and Judgment in the Novels of Charles Brockden Brown." In *Revising Charles Brockden Brown: Culture, Politics, and Sexuality in the Early Republic.* Ed. Philip Barnard,

582   SELECTED BIBLIOGRAPHY

Mark L. Kamrath, and Stephen Shapiro. Knoxville: University of Tennessee Press, 2004, pp. 88–114.

Temple, Gale. "Carwin the Onanist?" *Arizona Quarterly: A Journal of American Literature, Culture, and Theory* 65 (1): 1–32.

Tompkins, Jane. *Sensational Designs: The Cultural Work of American Fiction, 1790–1860.* New York: Oxford University Press, 1985, ch. 2.

Ven Leeuwen, Evert Jan. "'Though Hermes never taught thee': The Anti-Patriarchal Tendency of Charles Brockden Brown's Mercurial Outcast Carwin, the Biloquist." *European Journal of American Studies* online. Posted February 9, 2010, available at http://ejas.revues.org/document7791.html, accessed on February 16, 2010.

Waterman, Bryan. "The Bavarian Illuminati, the Early American Novel, and Histories of the Public Sphere." *The William and Mary Quarterly* 62.1 (2005): 9–30.

• White, Ed. "Carwin the Peasant Rebel." *Revising Charles Brockden Brown: Culture, Politics, and Sexuality in the Early Republic.* Ed. Philip Barnard, Mark L. Kamrath, and Stephen Shapiro. Knoxville: University of Tennessee Press, 2004, pp. 41–59.

Williams, Daniel E. "Writing under the Influence: An Examination of *Wieland*'s 'Well Authenticated Facts' and the Depiction of Murderous Fathers in Post-Revolutionary Print Culture." *Eighteenth-Century Fiction* 15. 3–4 (2003): 643–68.

Wolfe, Eric A. "Ventriloquizing Nation: Voice, Identity, and Radical Democracy in Charles Brockden Brown's *Wieland*." *American Literature* 78 (2006): 431–57.

Ziff, Larzer. *Writing in the New Nation: Prose, Print, and Politics in the Early United States.* New Haven, CT: Yale University Press, 1991, ch. 7.

Chapter 4 first voice (letter)
5 second voice (Tevia)
6 Carwin introduced